CONTEMPORARY MANAGEMENT

SECOND EDITION

CONTEMPORARY MANAGEMENT

SECOND EDITION

DAVID D. VAN FLEET

Arizona State University West

in collaboration with
Ricky W. Griffin, Texas A & M University

HOUGHTON MIFFLIN COMPANY   BOSTON

Dallas   Geneva, Illinois   Palo Alto   Princeton, New Jersey

Cover photograph by Gabrielle Keller.
Illustrations: Illustrious, Inc.
Part Opener One: Lou Jones
Part Opener Two: Courtesy Reynolds Metal Company
Part Opener Three: Andrew Sacks/Tony Stone Worldwide
Part Opener Four: © M. L. Thomas 1978
Part Opener Five: Photo by Jim Sims/Southdown, Inc. 1989 Annual Report
Part Opener Six: Courtesy J. P. Morgan/Photo by Tom Hollyman

Printed in the U.S.A.

Library of Congress Catalog Card Number: 90-83057

ISBN: 0-395-47223-7

CDEFGHIJ-D-98765432

For Ella, Marijke, and Dirk
Who enable and empower my work

BRIEF CONTENTS

PART ONE
MANAGEMENT: AN INTRODUCTION   **2**
Chapter 1   The World of Management and Managers   *4*
Chapter 2   Management Theory: Past and Present   *32*
Chapter 3   Managerial Ethics and Social Responsibility   *62*

PART TWO
PLANNING AND DECISION MAKING   **92**
Chapter 4   Organizational Environments and Goals   *94*
Chapter 5   Managerial Planning   *122*
Chapter 6   Strategy and Strategic Planning   *148*
Chapter 7   Decision Making   *176*

PART THREE
ORGANIZING   **204**
Chapter 8   Organizing Concepts   *206*
Chapter 9   Organization Design   *234*
Chapter 10   Staffing and Human Resources   *262*
Chapter 11   Information Systems   *292*

PART FOUR
LEADING   **320**
Chapter 12   Leadership   *322*
Chapter 13   Employee Motivation   *350*
Chapter 14   Interpersonal Processes   *378*
Chapter 15   Interpersonal Communication   *408*

PART FIVE
CONTROLLING   **434**
Chapter 16 *Organizational Control*   *436*
Chapter 17 *Control Techniques and Methods*   *462*
Chapter 18 *Operations Management*   *488*
Chapter 19 *Productivity and Quality*   *514*

PART SIX
SPECIAL CHALLENGES OF MANAGEMENT   **542**
Chapter 20 *Organization Change and Development*   *544*
Chapter 21 *International Management*   *568*
Chapter 22 *Management in the Future*   *594*

APPENDIX
MANAGERIAL CAREERS   **619**
Glossary   *635*
Name and Company Index   *652*
Subject Index   *663*

CONTENTS

Preface   xxi

PART ONE MANAGEMENT: AN INTRODUCTION   2

1
The World of Management and Managers   4

Prelude Case: **Disney Manages for the Future**   6

What Is Management?   8
A Definition of Management   8
The Complexity of Management   9
The Pervasiveness of Management   10

Kinds of Managers   11

Levels of Management   11
Areas of Management   13

Management Today **Small Business and Entrepreneurship: Entrepreneurs Overcontrol**   14

The Manager's Job   15
Planning and Decision Making   15
Organizing   16
Leading   16
Controlling   17

Management Roles and Skills   17
Management Roles   18
Management Skills   20

Successful Management   22
Efficiency   22
Effectiveness   23

How Do Managers Become Successful?   23
Education   23
Experience   24

Management Today **The World of Management: Business Schools in Europe**   25

Plan for the Book   25

Chapter Summary   27

Enhancement Case: **American Airlines Takes Off**   29

2
Management Theory: Past and Present   32

Prelude Case: **Intel Is on Top**   34
The Importance of History and Theory   36

The Origins of Management Theory   37

   Management Today **Management in Practice: Wells Fargo Remembers Its Past   38**

Ancient Management   38
Precursors of Modern Management   40

The Classical School   40
Scientific Management   40
Administrative Management   43
Assessment of the Classical School   45

The Behavioral School   45
The Hawthorne Studies   45
Human Relations   46
Contemporary Behavioral Science   47
Assessment of the Behavioral School   48

The Quantitative School   48
Management Science   48
Operations Management   49
Management Information Systems   49
Assessment of the Quantitative School   49

Contemporary Management Theory   50
Systems Theory   50

   Management Today **The World of Management: Lloyd's Means More than Coffee   51**

Contingency Theory   53
Emerging Perspectives   54

Chapter Summary   56

   Enhancement Case: **Kmart Keeps on Pushing   59**

3

Managerial Ethics and Social Responsibility   62

   Prelude Case: **Exxon Spills   64**

The Nature of Ethics   66
The Meaning of Ethics   66
The Formation of Ethics   67

Managerial Ethics   68
Ethics and Management   68

   Management Today **The World of Management: In Japan Politics Means Money   71**

The Ethical Context of Management   71

Managing Ethics   73
Top-Management Support   73
Codes of Conduct   73

The Nature of Social Responsibility   74
Historical Development   74
Arguments About Social Responsibility   76

Approaches to Social Responsibility   78
Social Obligation   78
Social Reaction   79
Social Involvement   80

   Management Today **Small Business and Entrepreneurship: New Companies Clean Up   81**

Areas of Social Responsibility   83

The Government and Social Responsibility   83
Government Regulation of Business   83
Business Influence on Government   84

Chapter Summary   85

   Enhancement Case: **Ashland Spills   87**

The Entrepreneurial Spirit   90

PART TWO PLANNING AND DECISION MAKING   92

4

Organizational Environments and Goals   94

Prelude Case: **Kellogg Comes Roaring Back   96**

The Nature of Organizational Goals   98
Definition and Purpose of Goals   98
Steps in Goal Setting   98

Organizational Environments and Goal Setting   101

Management Today **Small Business and Entrepreneurship: Incubators Provide Buffer from Environment   101**

The General Environment   101
The Task Environment   104
Environments and Goals   106

Management Today **Ethical Dilemmas of Management: Westinghouse Plans for a Nuclear Future   107**

Managing Multiple Goals   108
Kinds of Goals   108
Goal Optimization   110

Effective Goal Setting   111
Barriers to Effective Goal Setting   111
Overcoming the Barriers to Goal Setting   113

Management by Objectives   115

Management Today **The World of Management: Cypress Cranks with Turbo MBO   115**

The Nature of MBO   115
The Mechanics of MBO   116
The Effectiveness of MBO   116

Chapter Summary   117

Enhancement Case: **American Express Walks a Tightrope   119**

5

Managerial Planning   122

Prelude Case: **Woolworth Changes Course   124**

Planning in Organizations   126

Why Managers Plan   126
Responsibilities for Planning   126

Management Today **Small Business and Entrepreneurship: Baking Success at Mrs. Fields   128**

Kinds of Planning   128
Strategic Planning   129
Tactical Planning   130
Operational Planning   130

Time Frames for Planning   132
Long-Range Planning   132
Intermediate Planning   133
Short-Range Planning   133
Integrating Time Frames   133

Contingency Planning   134
The Nature of Contingency Planning   134

Management Today **The World of Management: Fiat Adjusts its Course   135**

Contingency Events   136

Managing the Planning Process   137
Roadblocks to Effective Planning   137
Avoiding the Roadblocks   139

Tools and Techniques for Planning   140
Forecasting   140
Other Planning Techniques   142
Using Planning Tools and Techniques   142

Chapter Summary   144

Enhancement Case: **Black & Decker Turns Around   145**

6

Strategy and Strategic Planning   148

Prelude Case: **Mars, The Venerable Candy Maker   150**

The Nature of Strategic Planning   152
The Components of Strategy   152
Strategy Formulation and Implementation   153
The Levels of Strategy   153

Environmental Analysis   155
Environmental Forces   155
The Organization-Environment Interface   157

Corporate Strategy   158
Grand Strategies   158
Protfolio Approaches   158

Management Today **Management
in Practice: Hershey Sweetens
Bottom Line   159**

Management Today **The World
of Management: Daimler-Benz,
German Juggernaut   163**

Business Strategy   163
The Adaptation Process   163
Competitive Strategies   165

Functional Strategies   166

Management Today **Small Business
and Entrepreneurship: Liz Claiborne
Targets Success   167**

Strategy Implementation   170

Chapter Summary   171

Enhancement Case: **Borden Switches
Strategies   173**

Decision Making   176

Prelude Case: **General Electric's Bold
Decision Maker   178**

The Nature of Decision Making   180
Decision Making Versus Problem Solving   180
Decision-Making Conditions   181

Approaches to Decision Making   183
The Rational Model   183
The Behavioral Model   184
Other Behavioral Processes   185

Management Today **Management
in Practice: ABC's Miniseries: Too Much
of a Good Thing   186**

The Decision-Making Process   187
Defining the Situation   187
Generating Alternatives   188
Judging Alternatives   189
Choosing the Best Alternative   190
Implementing the Alternative   190

Management Today **Ethical Dilemmas
of Management: Beech-Nut's
Not-So-Natural Apple Juice   191**
Evaluating the Results   191

Innovation and Decision Making   192
Encouraging Innovation   192
The Innovation Process   193

Decision-Making Techniques   194
The Payoff Matrix   195
Decision Trees   196
Other Techniques   197

Chapter Summary   198

Enhancement Case: **Compaq
Computer's Think Tank   200**

**The Entrepreneurial
Spirit   202**

**PART THREE
ORGANIZING   204**

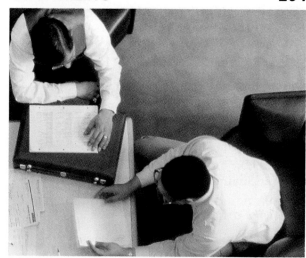

Organizing Concepts   206

Prelude Case: **McDonnell Douglas's
Brave New World   208**

The Nature of Organizing   210
The Organizing Process   210
Key Organizing Components and Concepts   211

Designing Jobs   211
Job Specialization   212
Alternatives to Specialization   213

Grouping Jobs   215
Departmentalization by Function   216
Departmentalization by Product   217
Departmentalization by Location   218
Other Considerations in Departmentalization   218

Authority and Responsibility   219
Delegation   219

   Management Today **Small Business
   and Entrepreneurship: Fantastic Sam's
   Far-Flung Empire   220**

Decentralization   221

   Management Today **The World
   of Management: Samsung's Formula
   for Success   223**

The Span of Management   223
Wide and Narrow Spans   224
Tall and Flat Organizations   224
Factors Influencing Group Effectiveness   224

Line and Staff Positions   227

Chapter Summary   228

   Enhancement Case: **IBM Downsizes
   and Upgrades   231**

9

Organization Design   234

   Prelude Case:
   The Unlimited Limited   236

The Nature of Organization Design   238
The Meaning of Organization Design   238
The Role of Organization Charts   238

**Early Approaches to Organization
Design   240**
The Bureaucratic Design   240
System 4 Design   241

**Contingency Factors Affecting
Organization Design   243**

Size   243
Technology   243
Environment   245

**Contemporary Organization
Design Alternatives   247**
The Organic Design   247
The Matrix Design   247
The Divisional Design   250

   Management Today **The World
   of Management: ICI's
   Divisional Headaches   252**

Other Designs   253

Corporate Culture   253
Determinants of Culture   254
Components of Culture   254
Consequences of Culture   255

   Management Today **Ethical Dilemmas
   of Management: Too Much Innovation
   at Johnson & Johnson?   256**

Chapter Summary   257

   Enhancement Case: **Pepsico's
   High-Performance Design   259**

10

**Staffing and
Human Resources   262**

   Prelude Case: **Toyota Takes
   Its Time   264**

The Nature of Staffing   266
The Staffing Process   266
Legal Constraints   267

Human Resource Planning   268
Job Analysis   268

   Management Today **The World
   of Management: Expansion
   and Contraction Problems   269**

Forecasting Supply and Demand   269
Matching Supply and Demand   270

The Selection of Human Resources   271
Recruiting   271
Selection   273
Orientation   275

Training and Development 276
Assessing Training and Development Needs 276
Popular Training and Development Techniques 276
Evaluating the Effectiveness of Training 276

Performance Appraisal 278
Objective Measures 278
Judgmental Methods 278
Management by Objectives 279
Feedback 280

Compensation and Benefits 280
Wage and Salaries 280
Benefits 282

Labor Relations 283
How Unions Are Formed 283

Management Today **Ethical Dilemmas of Management: Problems in Paradise 285**

Collective Bargaining 285

Chapter Summary 287

Enhancement Case: **AT&T's New People Approach 289**

11

Information Systems 292

Prelude Case: **Benetton's Instant Information System 294**

The Nature of Information Systems 296
Information Systems and the Manager's Job 297
Effective Information 298

Basic Components of Information Systems 298

Developing Information Systems 299
Information System Needs 299
Kinds of Information Systems 301

Management Today **The World of Management: KLM: A Quality System 302**

Matching Needs and Systems 303

Managing Information Systems 305
Integrating Systems 305
Using Systems 306

Information Systems and Organizations 307
Effects 307

Management Today **Management in Practice: Westinghouse Goes Around the World with E-Mail 309**

Limitations 309

New Information Technologies 310
Computer Software 311
Telecommunications 311
Artificial Intelligence 312
Hypertext 313

Chapter Summary 313

Enhancement Case: **Federal Express: Keeping Track of Everything 316**

The Entrepreneurial Spirit 319

PART FOUR LEADING 320

12

Leadership 322

Prelude Case: **Bill Marriott—Leader, Manager, or Both? 324**

The Nature of Leadership 326
Leadership Versus Management 326
The Challenges of Leadership 327

Power and Leadership 328
Types of Power 328
Uses, Limits, and Outcomes of Power 329

Leadership Traits 331

Leadership Behaviors 331
The Michigan Studies 332
The Ohio State Studies 333

Situational Approaches 334
The LPC Model 335
The Path-Goal Model 337

Management Today **The World of Management: Keeping Everyone Happy at Hitachi 339**

The Participation Model 340
An Integrative Framework 342

Other Contemporary Perspectives 343
Charismatic Leadership 343
Entrepreneurial Leadership 344

Management Today **Ethical Dilemmas of Management: Taking Symbols Seriously 345**

Symbolic Leadership 345

Chapter Summary 346

Enhancement Case: **Leadership Changes at Apple 348**

13

Employee Motivation 350

Prelude Case: **Motivation at L.L. Bean 352**

The Nature of Human Motivation 354
Historical Perspectives 354
The Motivational Process 355

Important Human Needs 356
The Need Hierarchy 356
The Two-Factor View 357

Management Today **Small Business and Entrepreneurship: On Their Own Terms 358**

Affiliation and Achievement 359

Complex Models of Employee Motivation 360
The Expectancy Model 361
Performance and Satisfaction 363
Equity in the Workplace 364
Goal-Setting Theory 365
Employee Participation 365

Management Today **The World of Management: Participation Pays Off 366**

Reinforcement Processes 366
Kinds of Reinforcement 367
Schedules of Reinforcement 368

Reward Systems and Motivation 370
Kinds of Rewards 371
Effective Reward Systems 371

Management Today **Management in Practice: Du Pont Experiments with Rewards 372**

New Reward Systems 372

Chapter Summary 373

Enhancement Case: **Avis: When Workers Are Owners 375**

14

Interpersonal Processes 378

Prelude Case: **A. O. Smith Relies on Groups to Survive 380**

The Interpersonal Character of Organizations 382

The Nature of Groups 382
Definition of a Group 383
Kinds of Groups 383

The Psychological Character of Groups 385
Why People Join Groups 385
Stages of Group Development 386
The Informal Organization 388

Important Group Dimensions 388
Role Dynamics 388
Cohesiveness 390
Norms 391

Managing Groups in Organizations   **392**
Managing Functional Groups   392

   Management Today   **Ethical Dilemmas of Management: Peer Pressure at Dean Witter**   **393**
Managing Task Forces and Committees   393
Managing Work Teams   395

   Management Today   **The World of Management: What Makes a Miracle?**   **396**
Managing Quality Circles   396

Group Decision Making   **397**
Advantages of Group Decision Making   397
Disadvantages of Group Decision Making   398
Techniques for Group Decision Making   398

Conflict Between People and Groups   **399**
The Nature of Conflict   400
Managing Conflict   401

Chapter Summary   **403**

   Enhancement Case: **CBS Beset by Conflict**   **405**

15

Interpersonal Communication   408

   Prelude Case: **Communication Works at Wal-Mart**   **410**

The Nature of Interpersonal Communication   **412**
The Definition of Communication   412
The Pervasiveness of Communication   412

The Communication Process   **413**
The Communication Model   414
Important Behavioral Processes   415

Forms of Interpersonal Communication   **417**
Oral Communication   417
Written Communication   418
Nonverbal Communication   419

The Formal Communication Network   **420**
Vertical and Horizontal Communication   420

   Management Today   **Ethical Dilemmas of Management: Reward: A Clear Conscience**   **421**
Information Systems   421

The Chief Information Officer   422

Managing Communication   **422**
Barriers to Effective Communication   422
Improving Communication Effectiveness   424

The Grapevine   **426**
The Nature of Grapevines   426
Advantages and Disadvantages of Grapevines   426

   Management Today   **Management in Practice: Grapevine Troubles at Apple**   **428**

Chapter Summary   **428**

   Enhancement Case: **Open Communication at Herman Miller, Inc.**   **430**

The Entrepreneurial Spirit   **432**

PART FIVE
CONTROLLING   434

16

Organizational Control   436

   Prelude Case: **Reebok's Off and Running**   **438**

The Nature of Control 440
Reasons for Control 440
Areas of Control 441

Management Today **The World of Management: What Quality Really Means 442**

The Planning-Control Link 442

Approaches to Control 443
Steering Control 444
Concurrent Control 444
Postaction Control 445
Multiple Controls 445

Establishing a Control System 446
Setting Standards 446
Assessing Performance 448
Comparing Performance with Standards 448
Evaluating and Adjusting 449

Effective Control 449
Integration 449
Objectivity 450
Accuracy 451
Timeliness 452
Flexibility 452

Managing Control 452
Understanding Resistance to Control 453

Management Today **Small Business and Entrepreneurship: Depending on the Employee 454**

Overcoming Resistance to Control 454

Responsibility for Control 456
Line Managers 456
The Controller 457

Chapter Summary 457

Enhancement Case: **Ryder Tries to Get on the Road Again 459**

17

Control Techniques and Methods 462

Prelude Case: **Blockbuster's Busting Out 464**

The Nature of Control Techniques 466
The Importance of Control Techniques 466

Management Today **Small Business and Entrepreneurship: Entrepreneurs May Not Make Managers 467**

Strengths and Weaknesses 468

Budgets 468
The Budgeting Process 469
Types of Budgets 470
Fixed and Variable Costs in Budgeting 471
Managing the Budgeting Process 472

Financial Analysis 473
Ratio Analysis 473
Audits 476

Other Control Techniques 477
Human Resource Control 477
Marketing Control 478

Management Today **The World of Management: British Airways Flies Right 479**

Computers and Control 482
Kinds of Computers 482
Contributions to Control 482
Advantages and Disadvantages 483

Chapter Summary 483

Enhancement Case: **Making the Orioles Sing 485**

18

Operations Management 488

Prelude Case: **Cummins Grinds Its Wheels Finer 490**

The Nature of Operations Management 492
The Meaning of Operations Management 492
The Importance of Operations Management 492

Management Today **Ethical Dilemmas of Management: Responsible Operations Management 494**

Planning for Operations 494
Operations Decisions 495
Operations Planning 497

Managing Operations 498
Organizing for Operations 499
Change and Operations 500

Operations Control   501
Inventory Control   501
Quality Control   502
Scheduling Control   503

   Management Today **The World of Management: Ford and Mazda Team Up for Profits   505**

Cost Control   505

Operations Control Techniques   506
PERT   507
MRP   508

Trends in Operations Management   509
Chapter Summary   510

   Enhancement Case: **Bethlehem Shapes Up Fast   511**

19

Productivity and Quality   514

   Prelude Case: **Corning Takes Nothing for Granted   516**

The Nature of Productivity   518
The Meaning of Productivity   518
Levels and Forms of Productivity   518
The Importance of Productivity   520

Productivity Trends   520
Trends in the United States   521
International Trends   522

Improving Productivity   523
Operations and Management   524
Motivation and Involvement   525

   Management Today **The World of Management: Harley-Davidson's Long Ride Back   526**

The Productivity-Quality Link   526

The Nature of Quality   527
The Meaning of Quality   527
The Importance of Quality   529

   Management Today **Small Business and Entrepreneurship: Ben and Jerry's Spells Success Q-U-A-L-I-T-Y   530**

Improving Quality   531
Quality Assurance   531
Operational Techniques   532

   Management Today **Management In Practice: Dairy Queen's Struggling Empire   533**

Related Control Issues   534
Speed and Time   534
Flexibility   535

Chapter Summary   536

   Enhancement Case: **Westinghouse Gets Some Respect   537**

The Entrepreneurial Spirit   540

PART SIX
SPECIAL CHALLENGES OF MANAGEMENT   542

20

Organization Change and Development   544

   Prelude Case: **Double Trouble at Unisys   546**

The Nature of Organization Change   548
Reasons for Change   548
Planned Organization Change   550

Steps in Planned Change 551

Managing Organization Change 552

Resistance to Change 553
Overcoming Resistance to Change 553

Management Today **The World of Management: Beecham Changes with the Times** 554

Areas of Organization Change 555

Strategic Change 555
Structural Change 556

Management Today **Management in Practice: Cutting Out Layers at the Franklin Mint** 557

Technological Change 558
People-Focused Change 558

Organization Development 558

The Nature of Organization Development 559
Organization Development Techniques 560

Organization Revitalization 561

Reasons for Revitalization 561
Stages in Revitalization 562

Chapter Summary 563

Enhancement Case: **Caterpillar Sheds Its Cocoon** 565

21

International Management 568

Prelude Case: **Texas Instruments Goes Global** 570

The Nature of International Management 572

The Meaning of International Business 572
The Growth of International Business 573

The International Environment 575

The General Environment 575

Management Today **Ethical Dilemmas of Management: Protest or Profits?** 578

The Task Environment 580

Planning for International Business 580

The Decision to Go International 580
International Strategies 581

Management Today **Small Business And Entrepreneurship: International Niches** 582

Organizing an International Business 584

Organization Design 584
Staffing 587
Information Systems and Communication 587

Leading in an International Business 588
Controlling in International Business 589
Chapter Summary 590

Enhancement Case: **Nestlé Conquers the World** 592

22

Management in the Future 594

Prelude Case: **Biotech: A Whole New Frontier** 596

The Changing Role of Management 598

Forces for Change 598

Management Today **Small Business and Entrepreneurship: Cetus Joins the Fight** 599

Effects of Change 600

General Issues 601

Organizational Governance 601
Global Interdependence 601
Information Technology 603

Management Today **The World of Management: Lasers in Our Lives** 604

Organizational Dynamics 605

Specific Issues 605

Stress 605
Career Issues 607
Changing Demographics at Work 608
Drugs and Drug Testing 609
Alcoholism and Smoking 609

Preparing for the Future 610

Be Aware 610
Continue to Learn 611
Be Adaptable 611
Be Professional 612

Chapter Summary 613

Enhancement Case: **Cypress: A Model Company for the Future   615**

The Entrepreneurial Spirit   618

APPENDIX MANAGERIAL CAREERS   619

What Is a Career?   619
Career Choice   619
Choosing a Career   621
Life Stages and Career Stages   622

Career Development   624

Career Planning   624
Career Management   624

Women and Minorities   627
Managerial Careers for Women   627
Managerial Careers for Minorities   629

Special Career Issues   630
Dual Incomes and Dual Careers   630
Affirmative Action   630

Summary   632

Glossary   635

Name and Company Index   652

Subject Index   663

PREFACE

As I began work on the second edition of *Contemporary Management*, two things were apparent to me. First, contemporary organizations are changing. These changes are due to a number of factors. More and more pressure is being felt by those in organizations to act in socially acceptable ways. Our world is shrinking in terms of communication and organizational interaction. New organizations are constantly being created. For those reasons, coverage of *ethics and social responsibility, international management*, and *small business and entrepreneurship* has been expanded in this edition of *Contemporary Management*.

Second, feedback from students, instructors, and reviewers told me that the four criteria used for the first edition—that the book be *understandable, interesting, up-to-date*, and *accurate*—had been met. My goal in writing both the first and second editions of *Contemporary Management* has been to present the principles and practices of management while conveying its importance and excitement. Meeting those four criteria has brought me closer to my goal. In the second edition, I have continued to use a writing style that is interesting to students, I have updated the material to reflect current theories and recent events, and I have added several new pedagogical elements to make the book even more accessible to students.

This edition, then, is designed to reflect the important changes taking place in today's organizations, as well as to uphold the standards that were set in the first edition of *Contemporary Management*.

Understandable

The material in *Contemporary Management* is organized for smooth and logical flow from topic to topic. The writing style is one that is accessible to students; it is a personal one, intended to involve readers in the material. Straightforward and precise language, careful sequencing of material, and numerous analogies and examples help make ideas clear to the reader. Beyond the accessible writing, clarity is enhanced through the liberal use of drawings, tables, photographs, and other aids to understanding.

Interesting

The text continues to keep readers involved and interested by using examples of real people and organizations from around the world. All of the cases represent real organizations so that students can see the realism and relevance of the concepts presented in the chapters. Because the examples used in the text and the companies highlighted in the cases are recognizable, and because they deal with small and large firms, business and nonbusiness organizations, successes and failures, student interest is enhanced.

Up-to-date

All of the cases in the second edition are new and are based on the most current references available. In addition, the research-based text material has been updated to ensure that students are not being presented with concepts that recent research has negated.

Accurate

This text is firmly grounded in academic research and current theory. However, consistent with the readability criterion, strings of references are not included in the body of the material. To keep students' attention directed at the concepts, rather than at memorizing names and dates for tests, citations are used in the running text only when absolutely necessary. Detailed reference notes are located at the end of each chapter.

ORGANIZATION

To respond to reviewer feedback and improve accessibility, a few changes have been made in the organization of *Contemporary Management*. Users of the first edition felt that the material on careers should be included in an appendix rather than an early chapter in the book. That change has been made. They also felt that the importance of ethics merited an early introduction; that material is now in the first part of the book. Other changes in the contents include the addition of two new chapters—"Information Systems" and "Productivity and Quality." Other slight adjustments have also been made to enhance continuity.

Contemporary Management continues to be organized around the traditional management functions: planning and decision making, organizing, leading, and controlling. These four functions effectively capture the main characteristics of the manager's job, while providing an excellent framework for the presentation of basic principles, current practice, and ongoing research.

Part One defines management, introduces the manager's job including managerial ethics and social responsibility, and provides an historical perspective on management. The four chapters in Part Two deal with environments, goals, planning, strategies, and decision making. Part Three contains chapters on basic organizing concepts, organization design, human resource management, and information systems. Part Four describes current thinking on leadership, motivation, interpersonal processes (including groups), and interpersonal communication. The four chapters in Part Five cover the controlling function, control techniques, operations management, and productivity and quality. Finally, Part Six deals with several special issues: organization change and development, international management, and the future of management.

SPECIAL FEATURES

Management Practice

The concepts discussed in *Contemporary Management* are related to management practice in several ways. Each chapter opens with a *Prelude Case* that describes an actual situation or event, thereby setting the stage for the concepts to be presented in the chapter. *Prelude Case Updates*, which are found throughout each chapter, more clearly link concepts to the Prelude Case material. In addition, numerous examples throughout the text illustrate chapter concepts in terms of well-known organizations. Many chapters also contain boxed inserts entitled *Management Today: Management in Practice*. These boxes present longer, more detailed examples for students. Finally, at the end of each chapter, students are asked to apply the concepts of the chapter to both the Prelude Case (through the *Prelude Case Wrap-Up* and questions) and an *Enhancement Case* (with questions), which is yet another real world example of the material in the chapter.

Ethics

As I have already noted, ethics is important in our increasingly complex society. For that reason, it is given special attention in this edition. About half of the chapters contain boxed inserts entitled *Management Today: Ethical Dilemmas of Management* that present detailed examples of ways in which the chapter concepts have raised ethical issues for managers. In addition, Chapter 3 is completely devoted to the topics of ethics and social responsibility. Finally, some issues that may have ethical implications are noted in the final chapter, "Management in the Future."

International Management

Global economic conditions are also increasingly important. In recognition of this, over two-thirds of the chapters contain boxed inserts entitled *Management Today: The World of Management*, which present detailed examples of the chapter concepts in an international or global setting. In addition, Chapter 21 is completely devoted to the topic of international management. Finally, wherever relevant, international examples are used to illustrate the material being discussed.

Small Business and Entrepreneurship

The role and importance of small businesses and entrepreneurship in our economy are recognized and stressed in several ways. First, over half of the chapters contain boxed inserts entitled *Management Today: Small Business and Entrepreneurship* that present detailed examples of how the chapter concepts apply to small business owners and/or entrepreneurs. Second, each major part of the text concludes with a section entitled, *The Entrepreneurial Spirit*. This section links the concepts of that part of the book to entrepreneurs and their special problems and opportunities.

Pedagogical Aids

Contemporary Management is designed to make learning as effective as possible. Each chapter begins with a *Chapter Outline* and a set of *Learning Objectives* to serve as a "road map" through the chapter and point out its "landmarks." New to this edition are *Learning Checks*, which are located throughout each chapter to call students' attention to major points they should have learned as they progress through the chapter. As noted earlier, *Prelude Case Updates* are placed throughout each chapter to link specific chapter concepts to the introductory case. Each chapter ends with five additional aids. There is a *Chapter Summary*, which covers the major points of the chapter. Next is a list of important terms in *The Manager's Vocabulary*; these terms are defined in the chapter and are included in the *Glossary* at the end of the text. The key terms are followed by a *Prelude Case Wrap-Up* and questions tying the case to the chapter material as a whole. Then come questions—*Review Questions, Analysis Questions,* and *Application Questions and Exercises*—designed to extend the student's understanding and appreciation of the chapter material. Finally, the *Enhancement Case*, with its own questions, concludes the chapter. Additional pedagogical aids include *marginal notes* and the use of *photographs* with informative captions to reinforce the learning process and make it more interesting.

SUPPLEMENTARY MATERIALS

A complete instructional package is available to supplement this text and reinforce the reader's understanding of management concepts. All parts of the package were revised and coordinated by Dr. Fraya W. Andrews so that they form a truly integrated whole. The students' *Study Guide* includes information on how best to use the text. It outlines each chapter in some detail and provides space for the user to add his or her own notes as well. Practice test questions (along with answers) are included to assist users in preparing for examinations, and a series of exercises helps users learn about themselves as managers and about the handling of managerial situations.

ACKNOWLEDGMENTS

Although only one name appears on the cover, the title page indicates that this edition was a collaborative effort between Ricky Griffin and me. As noted in the Preface to the First Edition, Ricky assisted me through that project; in this edition, his assistance was substantial and went from planning the edition all the way through reading galleys and page proofs. I am deeply indebted to Ricky, for, without his generous help, relocating a family and starting a new job at the same time as preparing a new edition might have been simply impossible.

In addition, colleagues over the years have influenced my thinking. The more significant of those are: Bob Albanese, Gary Anders, Bruce Baldwin, Art Bedeian, Don Hellriegel, Tom Howard, Roger Hutt, Hans Jensen, Al Keally, Jack Larsen, John Moore, Greg Moorhead, Tim Peterson, Kyle Reed, Art Thompson, Gary Yukl, and Dick Woodman. In addition, I want to thank Otis Baskin and the other people at Arizona State University, West Campus who created a climate that encouraged personal development and stimulated my writing.

Many colleagues contributed to the final form of this book through their reviews and comments, and I would like to thank each of these reviewers individually, by name:

Dave Aiken
Hocking Technical College

James Baird
Community College of Finger Lakes

Roger K. Baker
Illinois Central College

Becky Tyler Bechtel
Cincinnati Technical College

M. Lou Cisneros
Austin Community College

Benjamin Findley, Jr.
University of Sarasota

Elaine Fry
Nicholls State University

Matthew Gross
Moraine Valley Community College

Lisa Gundry, Ph.D.
DePaul University

Anthony Jurkus
Louisiana Technical University

Sylvia Keyes
Bridgewater State College

Kenneth Lacho
University of New Orleans–Lakefront

David Lang
*City University of New York—
Kingsborough Community College*

Rick A. Lester
University of North Alabama

Dr. Fredric L. Mayerson
Kingsborough Community College

Coenraad L. Mohr, Ph.D.
Illinois State University

Lee H. Neumann
Bucks County Community College

Joseph O'Grady
Champlain College

James W. Peelle
Carl Sandburg College

Donald Pettit
Suffolk County Community College

Gary Poorman
Normandale Community College

Thomas J. Shaughnessy
Illinois Central College

Deborah A. Reed
Community College of Beaver County

Dr. Deborah L. Wells
Creighton University

Mary Reed
Delta Junior College

Douglas Wozniak
Ferris State College

Susanne Schmalz
University of Southwestern Louisiana

Penny Wright
San Diego State University

Gene Schneider
Austin Community College

John Zeiger
Bryant College

As I have noted, the ancillaries for *Contemporary Management* were prepared by Dr. Fraya W. Andrews. Fraya worked closely with me and with the staff of Houghton Mifflin to ensure that each supplement is of the highest quality. She is delightful to work with, and the ancillaries are exceptional teaching and learning aids.

I also want to acknowledge the help of my family. Writing a text is hard on one's family; mine had to put up with the pressures of writing and publishing as much as I, if not more. We learned to share our love for one another in new ways during this time, and that made it all possible.

CONTEMPORARY
MANAGEMENT

SECOND EDITION

Management:
An Introduction

This part of the book introduces you to the world of management and managers. Chapter 1 discusses that world in general and provides you with a basic understanding of various kinds of managers and managerial tasks. Chapter 2 presents a brief overview of management theory and its historical development. Chapter 3 completes this part of the book with a discussion of managerial ethics and the social responsibility of managers.

CHAPTER OUTLINE

I. What Is Management?
  A. A Definition of
     Management
  B. The Complexity of
     Management
  C. The Pervasiveness of
     Management

II. Kinds of Managers
  A. Levels of Management
  B. Areas of Management

III. The Manager's Job
  A. Planning and Decision
     Making
  B. Organizing
  C. Leading
  D. Controlling

**IV. Management Roles and
Skills**
  A. Management Roles
  B. Management Skills

V. Successful Management
  A. Efficiency
  B. Effectiveness

**VI. How Do Managers Become
Successful?**
  A. Education
  B. Experience

VII. Plan for the Book

C
H
A
P
T
E
R

1

After studying this chapter you should be able to

1. Define management and describe its complexity and pervasiveness.

2. Identify several kinds of managers, both in terms of levels and in terms of areas.

3. Describe the manager's job from the standpoint of functions.

4. Describe the manager's job from the standpoint of both roles and skills.

5. Define successful management in terms of efficiency and effectiveness.

6. Discuss how managers become successful through education and experience.

The World of Management and Managers

DISNEY MANAGES FOR THE FUTURE

During the 1970s, the Disney company seemed to have lost the magic touch it had enjoyed under the management of its founder, Walt Disney. Top managers seemed more interested in real estate transactions, especially with the Arvida unit of the company, than with its more creative activities. Disney's theme parks became totally dominant, and pictures seemed to have become a thing of the past. Indeed, the Disney company was being pursued by corporate raiders who appeared intent on taking it over and dismantling it to sell it unit by unit at a profit.

Walt's nephew, Roy Disney, resigned from the company in protest over the direction it was going and then initiated a movement among stockholders to change things. In 1984, he succeeded. The company hired Michael D. Eisner away from his position as president of Paramount Pictures. Eisner became president and chief operating officer of Disney, and Roy became vice chairman. Since that time, the company has returned to pictures with tremendous success, although it

has also continued to expand and modernize its theme parks.

Eisner sold Disney's real estate unit, Arvida, to JMB Realty Trust for around $400 million. This moved the company out of real estate while simultaneously providing it with the cash it needed to expand its entertainment operations through acquisitions and to further develop its parks and hotels. The move also served as a symbol of change to let employees and those outside the Disney company know what direction Eisner intended to take the company in the future.

Eisner began hiring new personnel to rejuvenate the company; however, he worked hard to ensure that the company did not become a battleground of "old Disney" personnel fighting against his "new people." He created an environment in which setting goals and achieving them became dominant and linked compensation to performance for everyone, including himself. By improving communication and motivation, he has tried to ensure that everyone knows and understands the

corporate culture. Working hours may be long, but enthusiasm is high in the invigorated Disney organization.

Disney's film production units, which have been expanded to three—Walt Disney Pictures, Touchstone Pictures, and Hollywood Pictures—are now quite successful. The marketing and distribution division of Buena Vista Pictures handles all marketing and distribution for all three film companies; this not only keeps costs low but also permits multiple markets to be served by only one group of employees.

Disney has also moved to become a major player in the video market. It has over half a century of film material and is releasing it on video in a carefully orchestrated program. Additionally, the company is expanding the number of outlets of its video products, is expanding its Disney Channel on cable television, and has returned to network television as well.

In like manner, the company is increasing its efforts to license and sell products using its many characters. It is expanding its own

One consequence of Disney's enhanced effectiveness has been the need for a variety of new construction projects. Michael Eisner and friends are shown at the groundbreaking ceremonies for Splash Mountain. Seven 19-foot tall dwarfs are used as pillars at Disney's new headquarters building in California.

chain of stores and hopes to have a 100-shop organization operating in shopping malls. The company is also mailing its catalogue to more than eight million households to expand sales of its products. These efforts have been successful: by the late 1980s they had netted the company around $100 million.

Theme park attendance has risen dramatically as new rides and renovation have taken place. A new park is open in Japan near Tokyo, and another is scheduled to open near Paris, France, in 1992. A three-dimensional musical attraction, *Captain EO*, is highly successful, as are Splash Mountain, Typhoon Lagoon, and other

new attractions. New joint ventures, such as the Disney–MGM Studios Hollywood theme area in Florida, are also proving to be successful as the Disney company pursues its entertainment business more fully. All in all, Eisner has turned the Disney company around and seems to be having fun doing it.

SOURCES: "An American in Paris," *Business Week*, March 12, 1990, pp. 60–64; "Walt Disney World and Universal Studios Fight over Film Lands," *The Wall Street Journal*, April 27, 1989, pp. A1 and A12; "Will Mickey Get Caught in an Ad Trap?" *The Wall Street Journal*, March 23, 1989, p. B1; "A Sweet Deal for Disney Is Souring Its Neighbors," *Business Week*, August 8, 1988, pp. 48–49; "Disney Chief Animates Fantasyland," *USA Today*, October 2, 1986, pp. 1B–2B.

T he Disney company illustrates the world of management and managers extremely well. The company was being run by one group of managers, its founders and their colleagues, then a second group took over, and finally a third group. Each group of managers had a different vision of what the company should be doing, and each group tried to accomplish goals based on that vision. Each group had different skills and abilities that impacted performance. Such diversity is common in management.

Debbie Bird owns and operates Reflections, a hair salon in College Station, Texas. George Steinbrenner, former owner of the New York Yankees professional baseball team, was known for his frequent managerial changes and his acquisitions of high-priced players in the annual attempt to win the World Series. The chief executive officer (CEO) of The Ford Motor Company must make decisions every day that affect thousands of people and involve millions of dollars.

Each of these people is a manager. Each leads and directs the activities within his or her organization, and each is accountable for the performance of that organization. Moreover, each of these organizations and the people who manage them illustrate the diversity noted in the Disney case.

This book is about the world of management and managers. Together we will explore the dynamic nature of the management process in all its forms. As you read and study the book, you will come to better appreciate the nature of organizations and the manager's job. And you will develop insights into how you can function effectively as a successful manager.

This preparatory chapter provides you with an overview of management and the manager's job. First it defines management, noting its complexity and pervasiveness. It then identifies and classifies different kinds of managers and describes the manager's job in terms of managerial functions, roles, and skills. The characteristics of successful management are followed by a discussion of where successful managers come from. The chapter concludes with an overview of the entire book.

WHAT IS MANAGEMENT?

A Definition of Management

□ *Management* is a set of activities directed at the efficient and effective utilization of resources in the pursuit of one or more goals.

Management can be defined as a set of activities directed at the efficient and effective utilization of resources in the pursuit of one or more goals. Three distinct elements of this definition, which are illustrated in Exhibit 1.1, warrant special discussion.

First, managerial work involves activity.[1] Managers do not sit around all day and think. Instead, they talk, listen, read, write, meet, observe, and participate. Their days are filled with action. As we will see, most managerial activities can be classified into one of four categories: planning, organizing, leading, and controlling.

Management also involves the efficient and effective use of resources. These may be human resources (assembly-line workers, managers, and dealers for

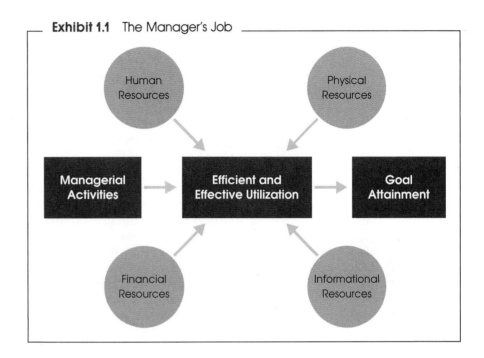

Exhibit 1.1 The Manager's Job

Ford), physical resources (buildings, office furniture, and raw materials for Dow Chemical), financial resources (retained earnings, product sales, and bank loans for Safeway), and informational resources (sales projections and market research for Procter & Gamble).

Third, our definition of management notes the importance of organizational goals. **Goals** are targets organizations aim for. They can be developed for many different areas and levels of an organization. The setting of appropriate goals is a very important part of the manager's job.

The Complexity of Management

As you might have gathered from the preceding points, management is an extremely complex process. Part of this complexity stems from the different activities managers engage in.[2] Another part is due to the fact that managers must change activities frequently. In the United States about half of a manager's activities take less than nine minutes to perform. That is, the typical manager will stop doing one thing and start something else every nine minutes. This pattern contrasts sharply with the duration of activities of managers in other countries, however.[3]

Whatever the reasons for these patterns, there are clear differences in the complexity of the manager's job across national boundaries. Nevertheless, the managerial job always requires enormous energy and has many rewards. Its complexity continually serves as a source of new excitement, and its diversity is a reward for those seeking new challenges.

The Pervasiveness of Management

Another characteristic of managerial work is its pervasiveness—its influence in contemporary society and its applicability in many different situations.[4] Table 1.1 identifies some of the organizations that people might come into contact with in their daily activities. And this is only the tip of the iceberg. For example, the Coca-Cola that someone buys from Safeway is sold to the store by a local distributor, who buys it from a licensed bottler, who purchases the syrup from the Coca-Cola Company.

Management is not limited to businesses. It is also practiced in universities, government agencies, health care organizations, social organizations, and families. Indeed, management can be found in virtually every collection of people who find it necessary to coordinate their activities. Thus, it is well worth developing a better understanding of how these organizations function and of the men and women who lead them.

This book is generally focused on management as it is applied to business firms, although it gives some attention to management in government and in universities and health care situations. You should remember, though, that much of what we discuss is applicable to other organizations as well.

LEARNING CHECK

You should now be able to define management and describe its complexity and pervasiveness.

TABLE 1.1
Organizations That Influence Our Daily Activities

Activity	Organizations Influencing Activity
1. Get up and dress	General Electric alarm clock; Procter & Gamble toiletries; General Foods breakfast items; local newspaper
2. Drive to work	Ford automobile; Texaco gasoline; U.S. highway; parking garage
3. Work	Employing company; interaction with other companies
4. Go to lunch	Locally owned delicatessen
5. More work	Employing company; interaction with other companies
6. Go to doctor's appointment	Group practice clinic; Blue Cross health insurance
7. Buy food	Safeway store; food from Hormel, Coca-Cola, Campbell, Stouffer, local dairy and meat packer; write check on local bank
8. Go home and rest	Mail from Sears and Exxon; Broyhill recliner; Sony stereo
9. Watch TV	TV from RCA; "LA Law" (set in law office)
10. Go to bed	Sealy mattress; Cannon sheets

KINDS OF MANAGERS

Levels of Management

□ Levels of management are vertical differences among managers from the lower part of the organizational structure to the top.

If we take a hypothetical organization and draw two horizontal lines through it, as in Exhibit 1.2, we have a common way of classifying managers: top, middle, and first-line.

TOP MANAGERS   **Top managers** are those at the upper levels of the organization. The dividing lines in Exhibit 1.2 are somewhat arbitrary, but top management is usually considered to include the chief executive officer and the vice presidents of the organization. Roger Smith, the CEO of General Motors, is a top manager. So is John Sculley, president of Apple Computer. Top managers set the overall organizational goals and determine strategy and operating policies. They also represent the organization to the external environment, working with government officials, labor leaders, and executives in other organizations. The job of CEO is demanding, and turnover is common.[5]

MIDDLE MANAGERS   **Middle managers** make up the largest group in most companies. Their ranks extend from top management all the way down to those immediately above first-line management. They include such titles and positions as plant manager, division manager, and operations manager. These people implement the strategies and policies set by top managers, and they also coordinate the work of first-line managers. Middle managers are often responsible for major innovations.[6]

The middle manager's job is changing, and some experts warn that the future for such positions is questionable. Unionization will probably not become widespread among managers, and some jobs may indeed disappear in the wake of new technology.

FIRST-LINE MANAGERS   **First-line managers** are those who supervise operating employees. They are called supervisors, department managers, office managers, and foremen. These are usually individuals' first management positions. In contrast to middle and top managers, first-line managers spend much of their time directly overseeing the work of operating employees. As is the case with middle managers, the job of the first-line manager is changing dramatically.[7]

PRELUDE CASE   UPDATE

The Disney company case indicates how the goals of an organization can change and how important those goals are to the activities of management. Managers at Disney must cope with a complex world of products, films, videos, theme parks, specialty rides, joint ventures, and international business,

Exhibit 1.2   Levels of Management

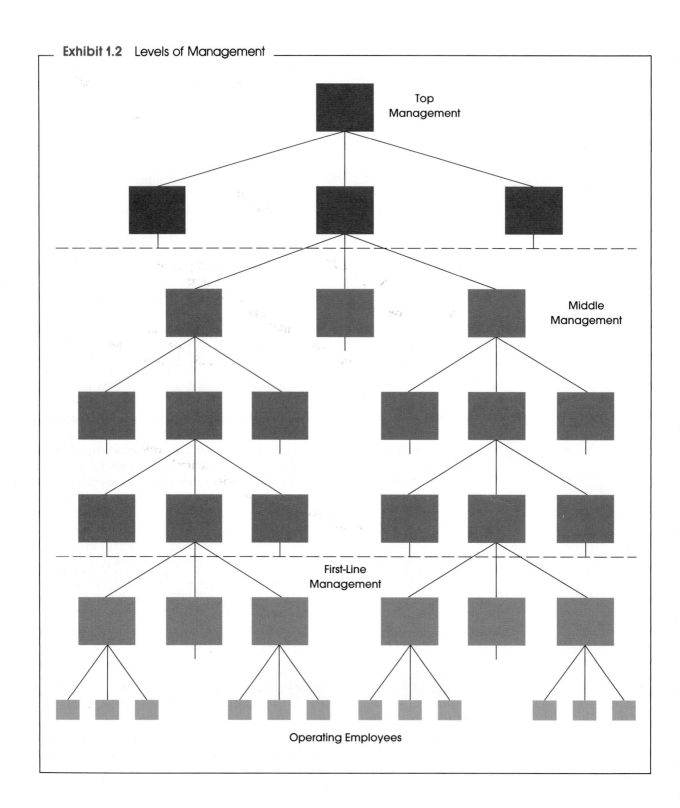

to name some of the major components. The case clearly focuses on top managers, particularly the president, Michael Eisner, but it should be apparent that managers at all levels must be intimately involved with the operations of the company for it to continue to succeed.

Areas of Management

☐ Areas of management are the primary activities in which the manager is engaged.

Another useful way of differentiating among kinds of managers is by area. The most common areas of management are marketing, operations, finance, and human resources.

MARKETING MANAGERS   **Marketing managers** are those who are responsible for pricing, promoting, and distributing the products and services of the firm. They conduct market research, plan advertising campaigns, set prices, and oversee distribution networks. At K mart, the top marketing manager is a vice president. At the middle-management level are regional advertising directors, and store-level advertising managers are at the first-line level. Almost 14 percent of the CEOs of the largest U.S. firms started their careers in marketing.[8]

OPERATIONS MANAGERS   **Operations managers** are those responsible for actually creating the goods and services of the organization. The vice president of manufacturing for Procter & Gamble (top), the regional transportation manager for Safeway (middle), and the quality control manager for the Texas Instruments plant in Lubbock, Texas (first-line), are all operations managers. Other responsibilities of operations managers include production control, inventory control, and plant layout. Over 10 percent of American CEOs come from the ranks of operations managers.[9]

FINANCE MANAGERS   **Finance managers** are responsible for managing the financial assets of the organization. They oversee the firm's accounting systems, manage investments, control disbursements, and are responsible for maintaining and providing relevant information to the CEO about the firm's financial health. Finance managers are clearly important: nearly 20 percent of American CEOs have a background in this area.[10]

HUMAN RESOURCE MANAGERS   Another important area of management is human resources, or HRM. **Human resource managers** are responsible for determining future human resource needs, recruiting and hiring the right kind of people to fill those needs, designing effective compensation and performance appraisal systems, and ensuring that various legal guidelines and regulations are followed. Because HRM is a fairly new area of management, at

SMALL BUSINESS AND ENTREPRENEURSHIP

Entrepreneurs Overcontrol

Most entrepreneurs as they start their businesses are involved in all aspects of the operations of the firm out of sheer necessity—there is no one else to do them. Many of those same entrepreneurs, however, continue to try to keep that much involved even as the firm's activities expand and new personnel are added. The entrepreneur ends up overcontrolling.

These entrepreneurs want to "keep on top of everything" through direct contact rather than through information provided by others. This failure to utilize the knowledge and skills of others is a common cause of many small-business problems. The reason may be that the entrepreneur feels more knowledgeable than anyone else about the firm and its operations. Or the entrepreneur may simply want to maintain careful control over his or her own money.

Failure to involve others can send signals to employees that they are not trusted. That can demoralize them and even cause them to start behaving in untrustworthy ways. Or, more likely, that obsession with control will cause high turnover with resultant high costs of recruiting and training new personnel.

Successful entrepreneurs adapt in one of several ways. Some learn to change their management styles to fit the changing organization. Others sell the business to someone who is a capable manager and move on to start another new venture. Some elect to remain in the more technical side of the firm's operations, hiring others to manage the growing organization. Finally, some elect to keep the organization from growing, preferring a small organization that they can run to a larger one that they cannot run.

SOURCES: "Entrepreneurs Often Fail as Managers," *The Wall Street Journal*, May 15, 1989, p. B1; Albert V. Bruno, Joel K. Leidecker, and Joseph W. Harder, "Why Firms Fail," *Business Horizons*, March-April 1987, pp. 50–58; Joseph G. P. Paolillo, "The Manager's Self Assessments of Managerial Roles: Small vs. Large Firms," *American Journal of Small Business*, January-February 1984, pp. 59–62.

least in terms of its representation at the upper levels in most organizations, few CEOs have an HRM background.

OTHER AREAS OF MANAGEMENT Besides marketing, operations, finance, and human resources, there are other areas that require management. Administrative or general management is perhaps the most common of these. **Administrative managers** are generalists, overseeing a variety of activities in several different areas. Other kinds of managers include public relations, research and development, and international managers.

Most managers tend to perform in only one area of management at any given point in time. However, small-business managers frequently need to be able to perform in several areas. As indicated in *Management Today: Small Business and Entrepreneurship*, many small-business founders fail as the firm grows because they continue to try to perform in all areas of management when they can no longer do so.

LEARNING CHECK

You should now be able to identify several kinds of managers, both in terms of levels and in terms of areas.

THE MANAGER'S JOB

With an understanding of levels and areas of management as a foundation, we can now take a closer look at the manager's job from the standpoint of its basic functions, roles, and skills.

Management functions are the sets of activities inherent in most managerial jobs. Many of these activities can be grouped into one of four general functions: planning and decision making, organizing, leading, and controlling. The relationships among these functions are shown in Exhibit 1.3.

Planning and Decision Making

◻ *Planning* and *decision making* involve determining the organization's goals and deciding how best to achieve them.

As noted in Exhibit 1.3, **planning** and **decision making** involve determining the organization's goals and deciding how best to achieve them. The purpose of planning is to provide managers with a blueprint of what they should be doing in the future. That is, just as a carpenter looks at a blueprint to determine which rooms to put in a new house, how they are to be configured, and so forth, a manager looks at plans to determine what course has been charted for the organization. For example, suppose top managers at Kodak decide that the firm should attempt to increase its market share of 35mm film by 10 percent by the year 2000 and that ten new products should be developed and put on the market within that same time frame. These targets serve as the blueprints for other managers. Marketing managers must launch new advertising campaigns, production managers must figure out how to cut costs (so that prices may be reduced), and finance managers must determine the effects of increased promotional expenditures and product revenues on cash flows. Similarly, market research managers must begin to determine what new products will be successful, and R&D managers must start developing them.

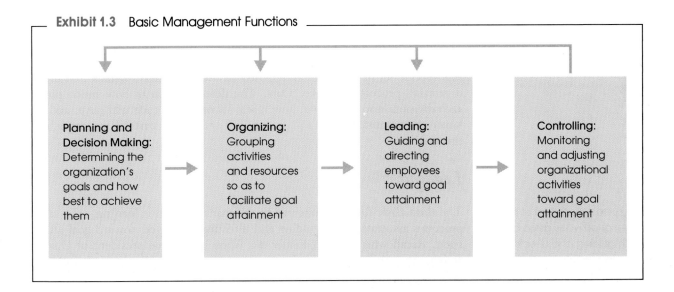

Exhibit 1.3   Basic Management Functions

| Planning and Decision Making: Determining the organization's goals and how best to achieve them | Organizing: Grouping activities and resources so as to facilitate goal attainment | Leading: Guiding and directing employees toward goal attainment | Controlling: Monitoring and adjusting organizational activities toward goal attainment |

Miguel Luis Fairbanks

There are many different kinds of managers and many different areas that require effective management. Joyce Goldstein owns and manages Square One, a restaurant in San Francisco. She concentrates on marketing, and allows her investors to concentrate on managing the firm's finances.

In general, the planning process consists of three steps. First, goals and objectives are established. This is usually done by top management. Next, strategic plans are developed. Strategic plans serve as the broad, general guidelines that chart the organization's future. Strategic planning is also performed by top management. Finally, tactical plans are developed, often by middle managers. Decision making pervades each of these activities.[11]

Organizing

◻ *Organizing* is the process of grouping activities and resources in a logical and appropriate fashion.

The second basic managerial function is organizing. **Organizing** is the process of grouping activities and resources in a logical and appropriate fashion. In a very basic sense, it is creating the organizational chart for a firm. Quaker Oats, for example, has a domestic foods division, an international foods division, and a division for Fisher-Price toys. Decisions that brought about the creation of this specific set of divisions, as opposed to a different mix, were a part of the organizing process at Quaker Oats. The determination of how much power each division head is to have, how many subordinates each will have, and the kinds of committees that will be needed are also a part of the organizing process.[12]

Leading

◻ *Leading* is the set of managerial activities associated with guiding and directing employees toward goal attainment.

The third basic function inherent in the manager's job is **leading**—the set of processes associated with guiding and directing employees toward goal attainment. Recall what Michael Eisner did when he became president of Disney: among other things, he sold the real estate unit to clearly show his intended direction for the company, he convinced old and new employees to work together rather than to battle one another, he improved communication and motivation, and he linked rewards to performance. Each of these activities was part of the leading function. Eisner served as an effective role model and as a prime motivator for people at Disney. Key parts of leading are motivating employees, managing group processes, and dealing with conflict and change.[13] Note that each of these relates to behavioral concepts and processes.

Controlling

☐ *Controlling* is the process of monitoring and adjusting organizational activities toward goal attainment.

The final basic managerial function is controlling. **Controlling** is the process of monitoring and adjusting organizational activities toward goal attainment. Consider Kodak's attempt to increase its market share by 10 percent by the year 2000. Now assume that this goal was set in the year 1990, and that managers at Kodak believe that the market share growth will be evenly distributed across the ten-year period; that is, there should be an increase of about 1 percent each year. In 1991 an increase of 1.2 percent would indicate that things are on target. No increase in 1992, however, would signify a problem; increased advertising may be required. An increase of 3 percent during 1996 may suggest that advertising can be reduced somewhat. This method of monitoring progress and making appropriate adjustments is controlling.[14]

PRELUDE CASE UPDATE

Marketing managers, operations managers, finance managers, and human resource managers are all used by the Disney company, although they have specific job titles rather than these more general labels. Those managers need to plan each new venture for the firm as well as maintain existing facilities and properties. New ventures, such as the Disney–MGM Studios Hollywood theme area, have to be carefully organized and led. Thorough control must be exercised to ensure that plans are followed and goals achieved.

LEARNING CHECK

You should now be able to describe the manager's job from the standpoint of functions.

The sets of activities inherent in most managerial jobs, then, can be grouped into the four general functions of planning and decision making, organizing, leading, and controlling. All managers enact each of these, although the exact mixture varies over time and with the manager's position in the organization.

MANAGEMENT ROLES AND SKILLS

The manager's job can also be described in terms of roles and skills. A manager's role in an organization is similar to an actor's role in a play—it consists of certain things he or she is expected to do and ways in which he or she is expected to behave. Skills are the various talents managers need to perform their roles effectively.

Management Roles

☐ Roles are things a manager is expected to do and ways in which he or she is expected to behave.

Research suggests that managerial roles fall into three general categories. As shown in Exhibit 1.4, roles begin with the formal authority bestowed on managers by their organization. This authority is accompanied by a certain amount of status. Three interpersonal roles, three informational roles, and four decisional roles follow from this status.[15]

INTERPERSONAL ROLES   There are three **interpersonal roles** in the manager's job. The first is that of **figurehead.** When serving as a figurehead, the manager simply puts in an appearance as a representative of the organization. When he takes a visitor to dinner, attends a ribbon-cutting ceremony, or serves as a company representative at a wedding or funeral, he is playing the figurehead role.

The second role is that of **leader.** As a leader, the manager hires employees, motivates them to work hard, and deals with behavioral processes.

The third role is that of **liaison,** which involves dealing with people outside the organization on a regular basis. For example, a designated manager might establish a good working relationship with a particular banker. When she is able to get an emergency loan for the firm at short notice without having to go through all the formal channels, she is successfully filling the liaison role.

INFORMATIONAL ROLES   There are also three basic **informational roles** in the manager's job. The first is the role of **monitor,** in which the manager actively watches the environment for information that might be relevant to the organization. A manager who reads *The Wall Street Journal*, asks employees about work-related problems they are having, and closely scrutinizes television commercials for competitors is a monitor.

The opposite of the monitor role is that of **disseminator.** In this role the manager relays information that he has gleaned through monitoring to the appropriate people in the organization. For instance, an article in *The Wall Street Journal* may be of little direct use to one manager but of considerable value to a colleague. To fill the role of disseminator successfully, the first manager will clip the article and pass it on.

The third informational role is that of **spokesperson.** The spokesperson role is similar to the figurehead role, but the manager in the spokesperson role presents information of meaningful content and/or answers questions on the firm's behalf. During the Union Carbide disaster in India in 1985, for example, when a poison gas leak from a plant killed thousands of people, managers regularly appeared at news conferences to make statements about new events and to answer reporters' questions. The *Exxon Valdez* oil spill in 1989 showed how crucial the spokesperson role can be. In this case, the slowness with which Exxon's CEO responded to the disaster damaged the public's trust in the company. Another use of the role may have had a different result.

DECISIONAL ROLES   The final category of managerial roles is **decisional** in nature; that is, these are the roles that managers take when they make deci-

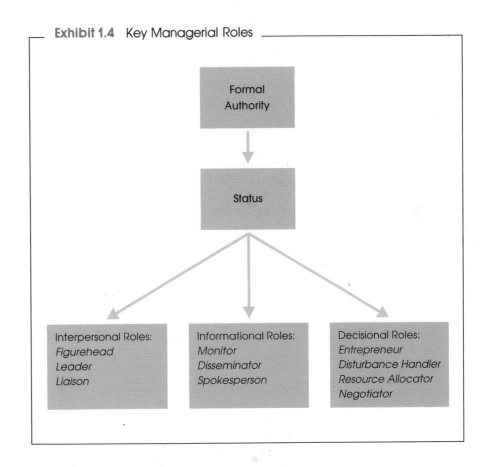

Exhibit 1.4   Key Managerial Roles

Formal Authority

Status

Interpersonal Roles:
Figurehead
Leader
Liaison

Informational Roles:
Monitor
Disseminator
Spokesperson

Decisional Roles:
Entrepreneur
Disturbance Handler
Resource Allocator
Negotiator

sions about a variety of things. First there is the role of **entrepreneur,** in which the manager looks for opportunities that the organization can pursue and takes the lead in doing so. If a manager at Dow Chemical notices that a particular waste by-product can easily be transformed into a new, potentially marketable product and then submits a proposal offering to take charge of the initiative, she is being an entrepreneur.

The role of **disturbance handler** is also important. This role involves the manager in resolving conflicts between, say, two groups of employees, between a sales representative and an important customer, or between another manager and a union representative.

The **resource allocator** role focuses on determining how resources will be divided up among different areas within the organization. If a manager has $275,000 to divide among three departments, each of which has requested $100,000, he will have to decide how to distribute the funds.

Finally, there is the role of **negotiator.** In this role the manager attempts to work out agreements and contracts that operate in the best interests of the organization. Such agreements might be labor contracts, purchasing contracts, or sales contracts.

In summary, there are ten basic managerial roles that fall into three categories. Each role is important and must be properly executed. Whether a manager will perform the roles successfully is determined by the extent to which she or he possesses the necessary management skills.

Management Skills

☐ Skills are the various talents managers need to perform their roles effectively.

Some people can play baseball better than others; some people can play the guitar better than others. The thing that sets good players apart is their skill level. In a similar fashion, good managers tend to possess a certain mix of skills that sets them apart from others. Most people agree that the primary skills needed for effective management are technical, interpersonal, conceptual, and diagnostic.[16] Exhibit 1.5 illustrates the relative importance of these skills by level of management.

TECHNICAL SKILLS **Technical skills** are the skills a manager needs to perform specialized tasks within the organization. In the Mayo Clinic, technical skills are those possessed by physicians, nurses, and lab technicians. At Dean Witter Reynolds, they are the skills associated with understanding investment opportunities, tax regulations, and so forth. The electrical and mechanical engineering skills possessed by the professional engineers at Hewlett-Packard are the relevant technical skills for that organization.

As shown in Exhibit 1.5, technical skills are very important for first-line managers. Because they spend much of their time working with operating employees, they must have a good understanding of the work those employees are doing. Technical skills are slightly less important for middle managers, since a greater proportion of their time is devoted to managerial activity, and even less important (although not unimportant) for top managers.

INTERPERSONAL SKILLS **Interpersonal skills** are the skills a manager needs to work well with other people. They include the ability to understand someone else's position, to present one's own position in a reasonable way, to compromise, and to deal effectively with conflict. As with technical skills, interpersonal skills are most critical at the first-line level (because these managers spend so much time interacting with subordinates), moderately important for middle managers, and of less importance to top managers.

In general, the better any manager's interpersonal skills are, the more effective he or she is likely to be. Some managers, however, such as Harold Geneen, the former CEO of ITT, have been successful in spite of limited interpersonal skills.

CONCEPTUAL SKILLS **Conceptual skills** relate to a manager's ability to think in the abstract. Managers need to be able to see relationships between forces that others cannot see, to understand how a variety of factors are interrelated, and to take a global perspective of the organization and its environment. A manager who recognizes an opportunity that no one has seen and then successfully exploits that opportunity has drawn on conceptual skills.

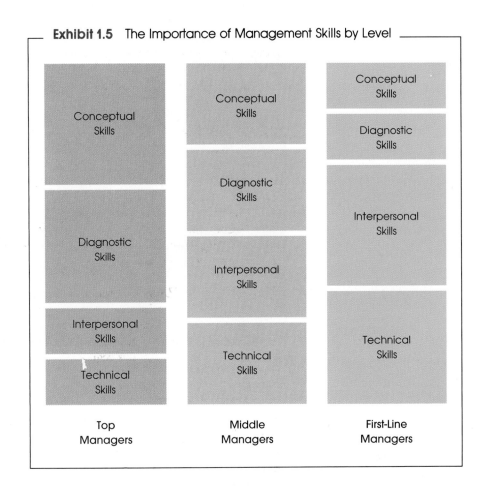

Exhibit 1.5 The Importance of Management Skills by Level

As shown in Exhibit 1.5, conceptual skills are most important for top managers, because their job is to identify and exploit new opportunities. These skills are moderately important for middle managers and of less importance to first-line managers.

DIAGNOSTIC SKILLS **Diagnostic skills**—the skills used to define and understand situations—are equally important. If a plant manager at Alcoa notices that turnover at the plant is increasing, she needs to address the situation in some way. The first step is to define the problem (unacceptable turnover). Next she must determine what is causing the problem and identify one or more ways to reduce it. For example, closer inspection may show that only one department is affected, which suggests a problem specific to that department. Appropriate action might include discussions with the department manager, the entire work group, or both.

As shown in Exhibit 1.5, diagnostic skills follow the same pattern as conceptual skills: they are most important at the top, moderately important in the middle, and least important at the bottom of the managerial hierarchy.

Technical, interpersonal, conceptual, and diagnostic skills are all necessary

Successful managers need to have a variety of skills. George Johnson and David Moore have made their business—Quality Croutons—a big success and list McDonald's, Pizza Hut, and United Airlines among their customers. Johnson uses his technical and diagnostic skills to run the internal operations, while Moore uses his interpersonal and conceptual skills to attract new business.

LEARNING CHECK

You should now be able to describe the manager's job from the standpoint of both roles and skills.

for effective management. As we have seen, top managers need a large measure of conceptual and diagnostic skills and a lesser degree of interpersonal and technical skills, whereas first-line managers need the reverse combination. Middle managers need an equal measure of each kind of skill. In the next two sections we explore the criteria used to evaluate managerial success and how managers acquire the skills necessary to meet those criteria.

SUCCESSFUL MANAGEMENT

At several points in the discussion so far, the notion of successful management has been raised. Exactly what is successful management? Successful management is the achievement of both efficiency and effectiveness.

Efficiency

□ *Efficiency* means operating in such a way that resources are not wasted.

Efficiency means operating in such a way that resources are not wasted. Allowing surplus funds to sit idly in a bank account drawing little interest, having employees do nothing while waiting for new work, generating large amounts of waste by-products from a poorly designed production system, and acquiring but not using valuable information are examples of inefficiency. Note that inefficiency can relate to any category of resources. One key to successful management is to avoid this kind of situation. An efficient manager will invest surplus funds promptly and wisely, devise employee work schedules so that people always have something to do, design production systems so that little is wasted, and use all the relevant information at his or her disposal.

Effectiveness

☐ *Effectiveness* means doing the right things in the right way at the right times.

Successful managers will also be effective. **Effectiveness** means doing the right things in the right way at the right times. A manager who enters a new market just before it starts expanding, gets out of a market before it collapses, and maintains an appropriate competitive posture is more effective than one who enters a market as it starts to decline, gets out of a market just before it starts growing, and does not maintain an appropriate competitive posture. Wal-Mart managers, for instance, started carrying under-the-cabinet kitchen appliances well before most other merchants, dropped home computers just before the market slumped, and always stay in touch with competitors' pricing policies.[17] Consistent actions such as these are a hallmark of effectiveness. Effectiveness combined with efficiency is the hallmark of successful management.

LEARNING CHECK

You should now be able to define successful management in terms of efficiency and effectiveness.

HOW DO MANAGERS BECOME SUCCESSFUL?

Is it just luck when managers combine effectiveness with efficiency? It is true that managers are sometimes just plain lucky, but more often than not they become successful because they are prepared.[18] This preparation usually consists of a combination of education and experience that gives an individual the technical, interpersonal, diagnostic, and conceptual skills necessary to contribute to an organization's efficiency and effectiveness.

Education

A formal education leading to a college degree is the first step in most people's managerial careers. In 1988, 88 percent of the CEOs of *Business Week's* top 1,000 corporations held a college degree.[19] Education does not stop there, however. Many managers return to school and get a graduate degree (usually a Master of Business Administration, or M.B.A.). They also attend advanced training and development programs sponsored by universities, private consulting firms, or their own companies. These activities are apt to continue throughout a manager's career.

For years American managers emphasized formal education more than their foreign counterparts did, but this is changing. *Management Today: The World of Management* describes how European managers in particular are concentrating more on formal education as a way to the top.

Experience

An education alone, of course, does not promise a person an executive position. Most people must still work their way up in an organization, sometimes making mistakes and suffering setbacks along the way.

Experience comes in a variety of forms. People often work while in college, and they may hold full-time jobs before they enter college in the first place. After finishing school they might accept an initial job assignment with a company that offers them a position, in the hope that they will later earn promotions. They may also accept transfers to different departments to broaden their experience.

Company changes are also common, and many people leave the first firm they work for and take a new job with another. Indeed, companies such as Procter & Gamble, General Foods, General Mills, and IBM have such good training programs that other organizations actively recruit people who have worked there for a few years.[20] Over the course of a person's career, she or he is likely to work in a number of different jobs, usually for more than one company.

LEARNING CHECK

You should now be able to discuss how managers become successful through education and experience.

Marc Pokempner

Most managers learn their skills through a combination of experience and education. The Dean of the University of Chicago's Graduate School of Business recently decided to increase the school's emphasis on interpersonal skills. The students shown here—participating in an exercise designed to improve their understanding of others—are enrolled in the school's M.B.A. program.

THE WORLD OF MANAGEMENT

Business Schools in Europe

Management and business education are not new. However, educational programs in management and business outside the United States are relatively new. Managers from all over the world are now able to receive business education in a variety of locations, including the Soviet Union, and the European institutions that have emerged have become highly regarded. In response, business education in the United States has also become more global in nature.

The oldest program in Europe is IMI, the International Management Institute, in Geneva, Switzerland, which was founded in 1946. In 1957, Nestle founded the International Management Development Institute, IMEDE, in Lausanne, Switzerland. Then came IESE, the Instituto de Estudios Superiores de la Empresa, in Barcelona, Spain, and INSEAD, the Institut Européen d'Administration des Affaires, in Fontainebleau, France. The newest is probably the London Business School, which was begun in 1965.

INSEAD is arguably the most prestigious of these institutions, and its graduates are able to secure positions in countries throughout the world. Graduates of most of the other programs tend to work in their native countries. These programs are all designed for those who already have completed a baccalaureate education, and many of them are clearly patterned after the M.B.A. degree that is so dominant in the United States.

These programs sharpen all of the manager's skills. Interpersonal skills are developed through group assignments. Conceptual skills are developed through discussions with fellow students, the faculty, and visiting executives. Technical skills are improved through case and consulting assignments. The typical program takes about one hundred hours per week and anywhere from nine months to two years to complete.

American business schools are also striving to provide a more global perspective for their graduates. New courses in international fields are being offered, and virtually all basic courses now have a section on international, multinational, and/or global business activity. Innovative approaches to develop a better understanding of diverse cultures and even to require that graduates speak a foreign language are being explored at some U.S. institutions.

SOURCES: "Iron Curtain MBA," *Fortune*, September 25, 1989, p. 12; Jeremy Main, "B-Schools Get a Global Vision," *Fortune*, July 17, 1989, pp. 78–86; Shawn Tully, "Europe's Best Business Schools," *Fortune*, May 23, 1988, pp. 106–110; "MBA's Are Hotter Than Ever," *Business Week*, March 9, 1987, pp. 46–48; Jeremy Main, "How 21 Men Got Global in 35 Days," *Fortune*, November 6, 1989, pp. 71–76.

PLAN FOR THE BOOK

Exhibit 1.6 presents the blueprint we will follow as we explore specific aspects of the manager's job. As you can see, the framework for the book follows the management functions described earlier in this chapter. Part One, "Management: An Introduction," provides a foundation for further study. This chapter introduces you to the world of management and the manager's job. Chapter 2 deals with past and contemporary management theory. Then Chapter 3 discusses managerial ethics and the social responsibility of managers.

Exhibit 1.6 Plan for the Book

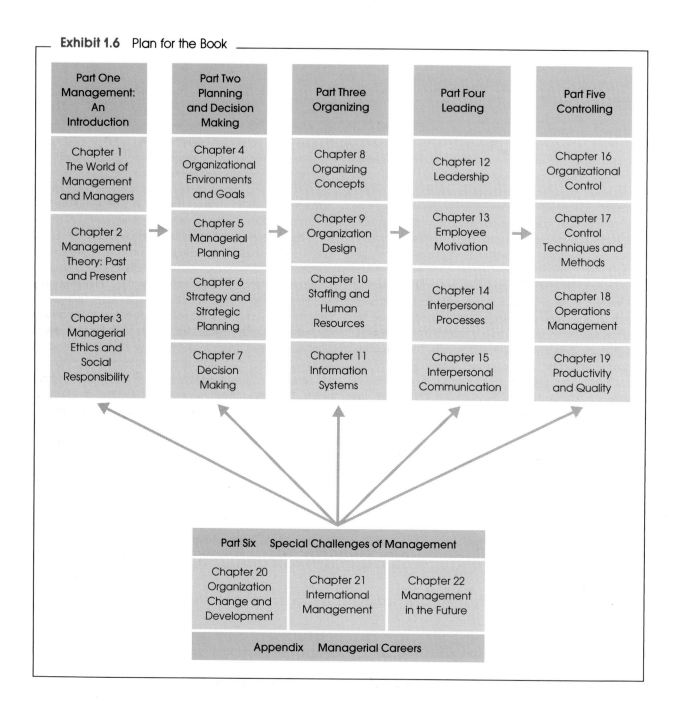

"Planning and Decision Making," which make up the first management function, are discussed in Part Two. The four chapters in this part deal with organizational environments and goals, planning, strategy, and decision making. The third part "Organizing," treats the second basic management function. Its four chapters focus on organizing concepts, organization and job design, staffing and human resources, and information systems.

Part Four, "Leading," also has four chapters, which deal with leadership, motivation, interpersonal processes, and interpersonal communication. The final management function, "Controlling," is the subject of Part Five. The chapters in this part discuss controlling concepts and techniques, operations management, and productivity and quality. Finally, the last part of the book, "Special Challenges of Management," describes the important concepts of organization change and development, international management, and management in the future. The book ends with an appendix on managerial careers.

Chapter Summary

Management can be defined as a set of activities directed at the efficient and effective utilization of resources in the pursuit of one or more goals. Management is complex in part because of the large number of different activities that managers engage in and in part because managers must change activities frequently. Management is pervasive: it occurs in private and public, large and small, and religious and penal organizations.

Managers exist at all organizational levels. Although the actual number of levels varies among organizations, most companies have three: top managers, middle managers, and first-line managers. Additionally, there are different kinds of managers within any given organization. Again, although not all organizations have all of these or only these, some of the more common kinds of managers in terms of areas are marketing managers, operations managers, finance managers, human resource managers, and administrative managers.

All managers perform four general functions to varying degrees: planning and decision making, organizing, leading, and controlling. Likewise, although not to the same extent, all managers perform ten different roles in three broad categories—interpersonal, informational, and decisional. Interpersonal roles include those of figurehead, leader, and liaison. Informational roles include monitor, disseminator, and spokesperson. Decisional roles are entrepreneur, disturbance handler, resource allocator, and negotiator. Finally, managers need four different types of skills: technical skills, interpersonal skills, conceptual skills, and diagnostic skills.

Successful management involves achieving both efficiency and effectiveness. Efficiency means operating in such a way that resources are not wasted. Effectiveness means doing the right things in the right way at the right times. Most managers are not able to achieve equal amounts of each of these, and some organizations might require more of one than the other, but a combination is always the hallmark of success.

Most high-level managers have not only college degrees but graduate education as well. Although a number of majors are studied by managers, business education at either the undergraduate or the graduate level is very common. Education alone, however, does not guarantee success as a manager. Experience in a variety of forms is necessary too. Managers can begin to gain experience on a part-time basis during college or even high school, but they will certainly gain full-time experience with one or more companies in managerial jobs over a considerable period of time.

The Manager's Vocabulary

management	leader
goals	liaison
top managers	informational roles
middle managers	monitor
first-line managers	disseminator
marketing managers	spokesperson
operations managers	decisional roles
finance managers	entrepreneur
human resource	disturbance handler
managers	resource allocator
administrative managers	negotiator
planning	technical skills
decision making	interpersonal skills
organizing	conceptual skills
leading	diagnostic skills
controlling	efficiency
interpersonal roles	effectiveness
figurehead	

Prelude Case Wrap-Up

Our prelude case for this chapter describes how the Disney company changed over time from an organization led by its creative founder to one led by less creative individuals to one that is again being led by a creative executive. Although the case concentrates on events at the highest levels of the organization, the complexities and pervasiveness of management can readily be seen.

The Disney company had become so successful that its creative talents were being taken for granted and executives were focusing on real estate as the major income-producing component of the firm. This "double message" told creative people that they were not highly valued by the company, which in turn had a negative impact on their performance and even caused some to leave to form their own organization.

Michael Eisner has returned the Disney company to its original mission of providing quality entertainment to customers, but he has also broadened its scope far beyond films and a couple of narrow theme parks. Eisner has forged an organization that is pursuing multiple entertainment strategies in films, videos, theme parks, hotels, new types of rides and ventures, and products based on or using Disney characters. This expanded mission has revitalized the company, and its creative talents are now functioning well as more and more box office hits are released and more rave reviews of new rides are published.

Some critics argue that Eisner is making the Disney company too commercial. They feel that using the Disney characters to endorse food products, automobiles, or airlines is inappropriate. Whether those individuals will be persuasive enough to alter current practices remains to be seen. The company is aware of these criticisms, though, and does monitor the use of the characters closely to try to protect their images. Nevertheless, this criticism and increased competition from other theme parks, especially those of Universal Studios, will necessitate diligent managerial control in the years to come.

Prelude Case Questions

1. Describe Michael Eisner's managerial position in terms of the type of organization in which it occurs, the level of the organization, and the area of management.

2. Which managerial functions does Eisner perform most frequently? Why? Which managerial roles and skills does he enact most often? Why?

3. Do you think the Disney company will continue to be successful, or will increased competition or other factors limit it in some way? Why or why not?

Discussion Questions

Review Questions

1. What is management? Does it exist in all organizations? Why or why not?

2. Identify different kinds of managers, both by levels and by areas of management.

3. What are the major functions of management? Briefly describe each.

4. List the ten roles of management. List the skills of management.

5. In what ways does the text indicate that managers become successful? In what other ways might managers become successful?

Analysis Questions

1. Think of someone you know who is a manager. Describe that person's management position in terms of the type of organization in which he or she works, his or her level in the organization, and the area of management in which he or she practices.

2. Which managerial functions and roles does this person perform most frequently? Why? Which skills does this manager seem to be best at using?

3. Did this person rely on education, experience, or a combination of both to become a manager? How?

4. Describe either real or hypothetical managers who differ markedly from one another in terms of the relative amounts of the managerial functions they perform or the roles that they enact. How and why do they differ?

5. Do you think a person can be a manager without being involved with people in some relatively direct way? Why or why not?

Application Questions and Exercises

1. Look in a current issue of a leading business or management magazine such as *Fortune*, *Business*

Week, or *Forbes* to locate a story about a manager. Using that story as your source of information, answer analysis questions 1, 2, and 3 for the person in the article.

2. Interview a local manager to determine what functions she or he does most, what roles she or he enacts most, what skills she or he uses most, and what education and experience she or he has had to become a manager. Share your information with the class and compare your findings with those of other students.

3. Compare and contrast the relative proportions of the different management functions and roles performed by a first-line manager in a very small or-

ganization and by a first-line manager in a very large organization. Now do the same thing for two top-level managers. What do you learn from this experience?

4. What managerial career goals do you have? Which functions and/or roles do you think you would perform best? What are your strongest managerial skills? How do they fit with your thoughts about functions and roles?

5. Do you think efficiency and effectiveness are equally important for churches, manufacturing firms, universities, civic clubs, and the military in time of war? Why or why not?

ENHANCEMENT CASE

AMERICAN AIRLINES TAKES OFF

American Airlines was one of the few airlines that seemed to thrive in the move toward deregulation. Indeed, American had done so well that by 1989 it had become the leading airline in the United States in terms of revenue passenger miles, the standard yardstick of the industry, and in terms of market share, which was almost 18 percent compared with second-place United's 17 percent. Much of that success is attributable to the company's chairman, Robert L. Crandall.

Born in Rhode Island, Crandall attended fourteen schools in twelve years and then went to the University of Rhode Island. After graduation he served in the Army and then sold insurance in Philadelphia, where he won a scholarship to graduate school in business administration. That education proved very important to his later career by providing him with the knowledge base for a variety of managerial jobs.

After earning his graduate degree, Crandall worked for Eastman Kodak, Hallmark Cards, Trans World Airlines, and Bloomingdale's. During that time he went from a supervisor in a credit department to senior financial officer. Then in 1973 he began his career with American Airlines. He joined the company as chief financial officer in the New York home office and quickly demonstrated his technical

skill. In 1980 he became president, and in 1985 he became chairman.

Crandall's work habits have become a legend at American. He generally rises at 5:00 A.M. and does calisthenics or jogs before he arrives at work at 7:00. He is usually the first to arrive and the last to leave. He calls meetings on weekends and early in the morning—one 5:00 A.M. meeting was attended by someone in pajamas, and the spouses of subordinates requested and got a reduction in the number of weekend meetings. Although these work habits have led to such nicknames as Fang, Darth Vader, and Attila the Hun, they have also created a lot of respect.

Crandall's work habits have been a part of his success, but they are only a part—another part is the technical skill that got him where he is, and still another is his understanding of people. He recognizes that there are two sides to every story and is willing to listen to both, and he praises subordinates when it is appropriate. This kind of understanding is behind one of his more innovative labor relations concepts, the two-tier structure.

Crandall noted that other airlines were terminating employees and asking unions to cut wages. Although he too had reduced employment, he did not like to do so. He asked his unions to agree to a two-tier

Courtesy of American Airline Corporation/Photo by Gary Blockley

Under Robert L. Crandall's leadership, American Airlines has become one of the largest and most successful airlines in the world.

business research environment) has become so successful that it may soon become the world's dominant computer reservation system.

SABRE enabled Crandall to introduce Super Saver fares and also made "frequent flier" programs possible. These, in turn, enabled American to attract more customers and made it easier for travel agents to use American flights. When travel agents use the SABRE system, even to book flights for other airlines, American gets a user fee. By the mid-1980s, SABRE was immensely successful—about half of its revenues were profits.

The government has also watched American closely. After American moved its home office from New York to Dallas, a taped offer by Crandall to raise prices in cooperation with Braniff led to a costly settlement. In another incident, the Federal Aviation Administration fined American for not performing proper maintenance. Crandall's response was to praise the government, hire 1,500 more workers, and spend $100 million more on maintenance to avoid any subsequent problems.

In 1989 Crandall began to expand American's fleet. He ordered huge numbers of new aircraft, especially long-range, wide-body MD-11s from McDonnell Douglas Corp. Clearly he plans to use those aircraft to expand his international operations, particularly in Asia and Europe as those parts of the world expand as major business markets. However, Crandall has not neglected his domestic operations. Hubs in Raleigh-Durham, North Carolina, and Nashville, Tennessee, have been improved; new planes for domestic service have been acquired; and the SABRE system has been upgraded. All in all, American Airlines stands ready to face the future from a position of solid strength within the industry.

wage structure whereby existing workers would retain their wages but new workers would be hired at substantially lower wages. This would permit lower overall wage costs without layoffs. After a lot of discussion and negotiation, the unions agreed to the concept.

Such innovation is characteristic of Crandall's success. During the 1960s, American was working with IBM to develop automated ticketing and reservation systems but had not yet implemented them. Crandall simply ordered that the terminals be put into service and made to function right. SABRE (semi-automatic

SOURCES: "American Aims for the Sky," *Business Week*, February 20, 1989, pp. 54–55 and 58; "'Wrong-Way' Crandall Is Looking Like an Ace," *Business Week*, June 6, 1988, pp. 34–35; Howard Banks, "Calmness Itself," *Forbes*, March 21, 1988, pp. 39–40; "American Takes No. 1 from United," *USA Today*, December 9, 1988, p. B1; Kenneth Labich, "How Airlines Will Look in the 1990s," *Fortune*, January 1, 1990, pp. 50–56.

Enhancement Case Questions

1. Describe Crandall's route to managerial success in terms of education and experience. In what ways do you think he might have improved this route (shortened the time or heightened the quality)?

2. Which managerial functions does Crandall perform most frequently? Which roles? Why?

3. In which managerial skills does Crandall seem strongest? Weakest? Cite specific examples to support your views.

4. How has American Airlines benefited from its management?

Chapter Notes

1. Henry Mintzberg, "The Manager's Job: Folklore and Fact," *Harvard Business Review*, July-August 1975, pp. 49–61. See also Brian Dumaine, "What the Leaders of Tomorrow See," *Fortune*, July 3, 1989, pp. 48–62.

2. Ibid. See also Henry Mintzberg, *The Nature of Managerial Work* (New York: Harper & Row, 1973), and William Whitely, "Mangerial Work Behavior: An Integration of Results from Two Major Approaches," *Academy of Management Journal*, June 1985, pp. 344–362.

3. Don Hellriegel, John Slocum, and Richard Woodman, *Organizational Behavior*, 5th ed. (St. Paul, Minn.: West, 1989), p. 13. See also Ford S. Worthy, "How CEOs Manage Their Time," *Fortune*, January 18, 1988, pp. 88–97, Andrew Kupfer, "How to Be a Global Manager," *Fortune*, March 14, 1988, pp. 52–58, and Thomas A. Stewart, "How to Manage in the New Era," *Fortune*, January 15, 1990, pp. 58–72.

4. See Page Smith, *The Rise of Industrial America* (New York: McGraw-Hill, 1984).

5. See Mintzberg, *The Nature of Managerial Work*. See also Carrie Gottlieb, "And You Thought You Had It Tough," *Fortune*, April 25, 1988, pp. 83–84, and "After the Merger, More CEOs Left in Uneasy Spot: Looking for Work," *The Wall Street Journal*, August 27, 1986, p. 15.

6. "Caught in the Middle," *Business Week*, September 12, 1988, pp. 80–88. See also Rosemary Stewart, "Middle Managers: Their Jobs and Behaviors," in Jay W. Lorsch, ed., *Handbook of Organizational Behavior* (Englewood Cliffs, N.J.: Prentice-Hall, 1987), pp. 385–391, and Rosabeth Moss Kanter, "The Middle Manager as Innovator," *Harvard Business Review*, July-August 1982, pp. 95–105.

7. See Steven Kerr, Kenneth D. Hill, and Laurie Broedling, "The First-Line Supervisor: Phasing Out or Here to Stay?" *Academy of Management Review*, January 1986, pp. 103–117.

8. Louis E. Boone and James C. Johnson, "The 801 Men (and 1 Woman) at the Top: A Profile of the CEOs of the Largest U.S. Corporations," *Business Horizons*, February 1980, pp. 47–52. See also David L. Kurtz, Louis E. Boone, and C. Patrick Fleenor, *CEO: Who Gets to the Top in America* (East Lansing, Mich.: Michigan State University Press, 1989).

9. Boone and Johnson.

10. Ibid.

11. See George Steiner, *Top Management Planning* (New York: Macmillan, 1969), for a classic discussion of planning.

12. See Robert C. Ford, Barry R. Armandi, and Cherrill P. Heaton, *Organization Theory* (New York: Harper & Row, 1988), for a recent review of the organizing function.

13. See Mintzberg, *The Nature of Managerial Work*, for additional perspectives on the role of behavioral processes in management.

14. See William H. Newman, *Constructive Control* (Englewood Cliffs, N.J.: Prentice-Hall, 1975), for a general overview of control.

15. Mintzberg, *The Nature of Managerial Work*. For recent examples, see "Leaders of the Most Admired," *Fortune*, January 29, 1990, pp. 40–54.

16. Robert L. Katz, "Skills of an Effective Administrator," *Harvard Business Review*, September-October 1974, pp. 90–102.

17. "Two Wal-Mart Officials Vie for Top Post," *The Wall Street Journal*, July 23, 1986, p. 6. See also Sarah Smith, "America's Most Admired Corporations," *Fortune*, January 29, 1990, pp. 58–63.

18. Fred Luthans, "Successful vs. Effective Real Managers," *Academy of Management Executive*, May 1988, pp. 127–132.

19. "A Portrait of the Boss," *Business Week*, October 21, 1988, pp. 27–32, 71–326.

20. "Desperate to Know Where Grads of Procter & Gamble Are Hiding?" *The Wall Street Journal*, August 20, 1986, p. 15.

CHAPTER OUTLINE

I. **The Importance of History and Theory**

II. **The Origins of Management Theory**
   A. Ancient Management
   B. Precursors of Modern Management

III. **The Classical School**
   A. Scientific Management
   B. Administrative Management
   C. Assessment of the Classical School

IV. **The Behavioral School**
   A. The Hawthorne Studies
   B. Human Relations
   C. Contemporary Behavioral Science
   D. Assessment of the Behavioral School

V. **The Quantitative School**
   A. Management Science
   B. Operations Management
   C. Management Information Systems
   D. Assessment of the Quantitative School

VI. **Contemporary Management Theory**
   A. Systems Theory
   B. Contingency Theory
   C. Emerging Perspectives

CHAPTER

2

After studying this chapter you should be able to

1. Discuss the importance of history and theory to the field of management.

2. Discuss ancient management and trace its development.

3. Describe and assess the classical school of management theory.

4. Describe and assess the behavioral school of management theory.

5. Describe and assess the quantitative school of management theory.

6. Identify major components of contemporary management theory.

Management Theory: Past and Present

INTEL IS ON TOP

In the late 1960s, Intel began operations in a former Santa Clara pear orchard. As its creative engineers introduced one new technological innovation after another, the company rapidly became a major player in the computer chip field. In 1970 it developed the first computer chip with more than 1,000 bytes of memory, the 1K DRAM chip. In 1971 it developed the first microprocessor and moved computing from physically large computers to desk top machines. Every two to four years since then, Intel has unveiled newer and more powerful microprocessors. Since those machines have almost always appeared before competitors could announce their new products, Intel has retained its dominance in a highly competitive market.

Revenues at Intel have risen from $2,672 in 1968 to nearly $3 billion as of 1989. The only rough period occurred in the mid-1980s. Profits fell during that time period, and losses for 1985 and 1986 totaled nearly $200 million. Management closed two factories and reduced employment by about 6,000 to cut costs and regain its losses. Profits quickly rebounded and were around $450 million by 1989. Top management learned to not become complacent simply because of past successes.

Intel's success record is a result of many factors, among them creative, hard-working people, the right timing, and a unique organizational environment. That environment is one in which talented, industrious people thrive; hence it is probably the most important factor in Intel's success. It not only leads to top performance at Intel but is also envied by others. Since young engineers frequently try to obtain jobs with Intel rather than work for its competitors, the company has relatively little trouble maintaining its supply of creative, hard-working personnel. In the Silicon Valley in California, where job hopping among high-tech companies is prevalent, turnover at Intel is exceptionally low.

The Intel environment is complex, but some aspects of it clearly stand out. Rewards are strongly linked to performance; thus, individuals may receive a zero raise or as much as a 20 percent raise depending upon how well they have performed. Plaques and stock are given every six months to those who achieve special results. Further, every seven years, personnel get eight weeks of paid leave, a sabbatical during which time they can rest and rejuvenate so that when they come back to work they will be fired up and ready to go for another seven years.

Intel's chief executive officer (CEO), Andrew Grove, does not have a reserved parking space, has his office in a snap-together cubicle like all other office personnel, and does not even have a door to his cubicle. The absence of a door ensures that anyone can readily come in and talk to him. Just because he is accessible, however, does not mean he is easy-going. Grove is known to be a demanding taskmaster who sets high standards of performance for himself and everyone else in his organization and expects that everyone will live up to those standards.

Intel's corporate headquarters are still located in Santa Clara, California, where the company began in the 1960s.

Grove was among the engineers who first came together to form Intel, and it is his management that has guided the company through much of its recent success. As the 1990s arrive, however, Grove and Intel will face their greatest challenge. Work stations, rather than personal computers (PCs), are becoming the wave of the future for offices. Intel's chips have dominated the PC market, but the company did not enter the chip market for work stations until 1989. Grove's strategy was to continue to dominate the PC market but to also strive to dominate the work station market. Of course, Motorola, which has long dominated the work station market, has other ideas.

SOURCES: Carrie Gottlieb, "Intel's Plan for Staying on Top," *Fortune*, March 27, 1989, pp. 98–100; "Intel Still Rules Silicon Valley," *USA Today*, April 11, 1989, p. 7B; "Intel Introduces Powerful 80486 Chip, But High Price May Limit Initial Sales," *The Wall Street Journal*, April 11, 1989, p. B5; "Intel to Motorola: Race Ya," *Business Week*, March 13, 1989, p. 42; "Can Andy Grove Practice What He Preaches?" *Business Week*, March 16, 1987, pp. 68–69.

The Intel case that opens this chapter suggests several of the theoretical bases of management. Focusing on cutting costs and keeping organizations highly efficient might be one such theoretical base. Another might be to stress the human element and try to ensure that people want to work for your organization. Still another might be to concentrate on performance, on being effective. To understand how Intel arrived at its current approach to management, it is useful to know its origins. So too with any organization, as we see in the following example.

A Polaroid plant in upstate New York began to suffer from problems of low morale and declining productivity a few years back. Company officials tried to solve those problems but were unable to do so because they were at a loss to account for the causes. Then the corporate historian went to work and soon explained what was going on: over a fifteen-year period, management had gradually increased its control over the work, which in turn had resulted in negative reactions from workers. No single manager had seen the problem because each had taken a narrow view of the situation.[1]

What can we learn from this example? Among other things, we can learn to appreciate better the value of history. This chapter is about the historical development of management theory. First we will look at additional justifications for studying history and theory. Then we will investigate management in antiquity and discuss three major schools of thought, the classical, the behavioral, and the quantitative. The chapter concludes with a summary of contemporary management theory.

THE IMPORTANCE OF HISTORY AND THEORY

☐ An understanding of history helps managers to understand current developments better and to avoid repeating mistakes.

There are several reasons why it is useful for managers to be familiar with history and theory. These reasons are summarized in Exhibit 2.1. An understanding of history serves two primary purposes. First, it helps managers understand current developments better. This is what happened at Polaroid. History also helps managers avoid repeating mistakes. If a certain course of action did not work well several years ago, it might not be any more successful today. Of course, if relevant circumstances have changed, it very well might work now.

In similar fashion, an understanding of management theory and an appreciation of the value of theory in general are helpful. Theory helps the manager organize information. Systems theory, for example, allows the manager to categorize a large, complex network of variables into a single framework. This framework in turn helps the manager develop a better understanding of how the variables are related to one another. (Systems theory is covered later in this chapter.) Theory also helps the manager approach problems in a systematic fashion. Using a framework like the one just mentioned, the manager can classify certain variables as causes and others as effects. The manager might then be able to predict certain effects based on certain causes. For example, if ad-

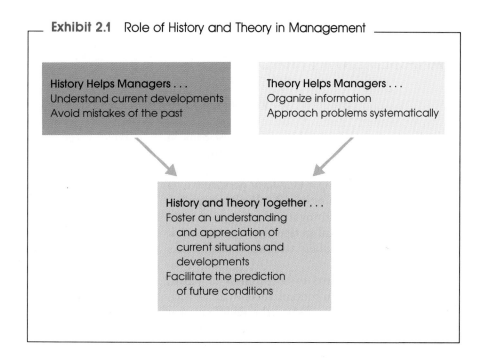

Exhibit 2.1   Role of History and Theory in Management

History Helps Managers . . .
Understand current developments
Avoid mistakes of the past

Theory Helps Managers . . .
Organize information
Approach problems systematically

History and Theory Together . . .
Foster an understanding
    and appreciation of
    current situations and
    developments
Facilitate the prediction
    of future conditions

vertising is a cause and sales increases are effects, the manager can develop a theory (or model) of how various advertising increases or decreases will affect changes in sales.

A knowledge of both history and theory helps the manager understand and appreciate current conditions and developments. This understanding also facilitates his or her ability to predict various future conditions. For example, a plant manager at Chrysler who remembers the bad decisions made by the company in the past and who understands why those decisions were made can avoid repeating them today. Similarly, if he or she understands the interrelationships among critical conditions affecting the plant, the manager can better predict the future effects of changes in those conditions. Thus, history and theory are both valuable parts of the manager's tool kit.[2] As indicated in *Management Today: Management in Practice*, an understanding of its history has helped Wells Fargo.

LEARNING CHECK
You should now be able to discuss the importance of history and theory to the field of management.

THE ORIGINS OF MANAGEMENT THEORY

As a scientific discipline, management is only a few decades old. Examples and illustrations of management in use, however, go back thousands of years. In this section we first consider several of these ancient examples and then trace the conditions that led to the emergence of contemporary management.

MANAGEMENT IN PRACTICE

Wells Fargo Remembers Its Past

Wells Fargo, founded in 1852, is the oldest bank in California. It has benefited from understanding its own history and even employs a corporate historian to help managers develop a long-term perspective on the roots of the organization. As Wells Fargo has grown, and especially during its recent years of rapid expansion, that historical perspective has enabled it to compete more successfully than many other banks in that region.

Although it has started to do business in Japan, Wells Fargo continues to concentrate on what historically has always been its focus—the middle-market firms (those with revenues of $25 to $125 million) in California. By contrast, other California banks have aggressively tried to provide a full range of services to a wide variety of customers across extended geographic regions. Wells Fargo does not ignore other customers or geographic areas, but it does not expend organizational money and managerial effort to aggressively pursue them at this time.

Wells Fargo has stressed cost control and uses a chief information officer to help integrate its approach to operations. This was particularly important when it acquired Crocker National Bank from Britain's Midland Bank in 1986 (Midland, in turn, had acquired Crocker in 1981). The addition of Crocker virtually doubled the size of Wells Fargo and presented enormous problems in meshing the two organizations. Large numbers of employees, including 1,600 managers, were eliminated in the merger, but, now that the integration is complete, morale is high and performance is very good.

Wells Fargo's performance, indeed, has been outstanding. For a bank that concentrates on a California market, its national rankings are impressive. In 1987 it ranked number one in return on assets, number two in return on equity, and tenth in terms of loan quality. That success enables Wells Fargo to consider expanding its operation with even further acquisitions in the near future.

SOURCES: John Heins, "Wells Fargo & Co.," *Forbes,* February 6, 1989, p. 51; "Eastward Ho! A Wells Fargo Team-Up in Tokyo," *Business Week,* August 21, 1989, p. 82; George Palmer, "Best in the West," *The Banker,* February 1988, pp. 53–55; "On the Western Front," *The Economist,* March 26, 1988, pp. 33–37; Carol Haig, "Clinics Fill Training Niche," *Personnel Journal,* September 1987, pp. 134–139; "Profiting from the Past," *Newsweek,* May 10, 1982, pp. 73–74.

Ancient Management

If we look at the accomplishments of many ancient civilizations, we can clearly see that they must have used management concepts and techniques. For example, consider the complexities inherent in building the Egyptian pyramids or managing the vast Roman Empire. It is doubtful that such things could have been done without using effective management.

Exhibit 2.2 presents a time line of ancient management practices. One of the earliest recorded uses of management is the Egyptians' construction of the pyramids, but the Babylonians, the Greeks, the Chinese, the Romans, and the Venetians also practiced management. Management concepts were also discussed by Socrates, Plato, and Alfarabi.[3]

In spite of this widespread practice of management, however, there was little interest in management as a scientific field of study until about a hundred years ago. There are several reasons for this. For one thing, there were few large businesses until the late nineteenth century. Governments and military organizations were not interested in increasing profits and therefore paid little attention to efficiency or effectiveness. For another thing, the first field of commerce to be studied was economics, and economists were initially more concerned with macro economic issues than they were with micro management concerns. This pattern began to change during the nineteenth century.

Exhibit 2.2   Ancient Management Practices

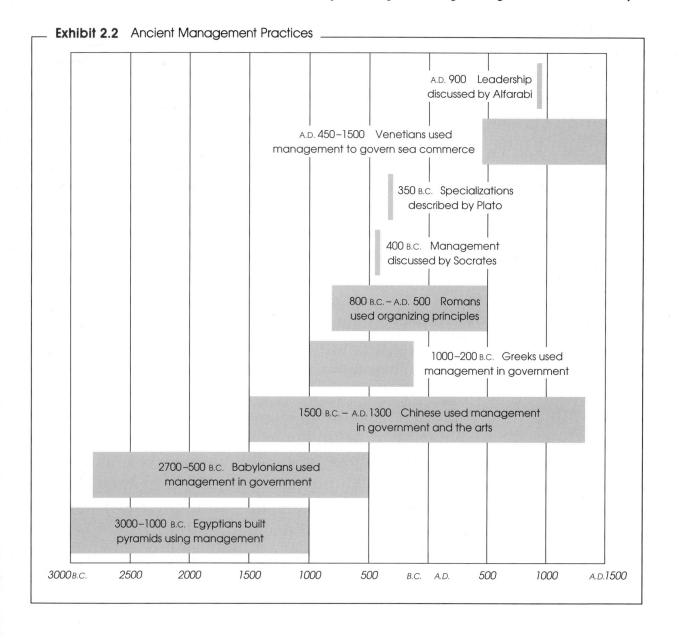

Precursors of Modern Management

During the Industrial Revolution, the **factory system** began to emerge. Factories brought together for the first time large numbers of workers performing a wide variety of different jobs. Managers in charge of these factories had to cope with new kinds of problems—problems related to coordinating and supervising this kind of arrangement. They also had to contend with emerging societal concerns about child labor, working hours and conditions, and minimum wage levels.

One of the first people to confront these issues was the British industrialist Robert Owen, who improved working conditions in his plants, set a higher minimum working age for children, provided meals for his employees, and shortened working hours. Charles Babbage, another Englishman, recognized the importance of efficiency and the human element in the workplace. Andrew Ure was among the first to teach management concepts in a university, and many of his students went on to hold management positions in Great Britain. Charles Dupin studied these British advances and applied them in his native France. In America, Daniel McCallum saw the need for systematic management in the railroad industry and implemented many innovative practices.[4]

Thus, throughout the nineteenth century there was a growing awareness of the need for more systematic approaches to management. As a result of these early efforts, schools of management thought soon began to emerge. Today there are three major schools, each of which has been developed since the changes brought about by the Industrial Revolution. These three management theories are known as the classical school, the behavioral school, and the quantitative school.

THE CLASSICAL SCHOOL

The **classical school** of management emerged around the turn of this century. It is actually composed of two distinct subareas: scientific management and administrative management. Historically, scientific management focused on the work of individuals, whereas administrative management was concerned with how organizations should be put together.

Scientific Management

The goal of **scientific management** in the early days was to determine how jobs should be designed so as to maximize the output of an employee. The pioneers of scientific management were Frederick W. Taylor and Frank and Lillian Gilbreth.

Taylor was an industrial engineer interested in labor efficiency. At his first job, for Midvale Steel Company in Philadelphia, Taylor observed a phenomenon he subsequently labeled "soldiering": laborers working at a reduced pace. When he talked to other managers about the problem, he discovered that they were unaware of its existence. This was because they actually knew very little about the jobs their employees were performing.

Taylor decided that something needed to be done. First he studied each job and determined the most efficient way to perform it. He then installed a piece-rate pay system, which means that a worker is paid according to what he or she has actually produced at the end of the day.

Encouraged by his results at Midvale, Taylor left the company and became an independent consultant. Much of his most significant work was done at Simonds Rolling Machine Company and at Bethlehem Steel Corp. At Simonds he studied and redesigned jobs, introduced rest breaks, and adapted the piece-rate pay system. The results were improved output and morale. At Bethlehem he applied his ideas to the tasks of loading and unloading railcars, with equally impressive results.

Over the years Taylor gradually solidified his thinking about work and developed what came to be called scientific management.[5] The practice of scientific management rests on four distinct steps, which are summarized in Exhibit 2.3. First the manager should develop a science for each element of the job; that is, he should study the job and determine how it should be done. This replaced the "rule-of-thumb" methods that managers had been using. Second, the manager should scientifically select and then train, teach, and develop workers. This replaced the previous system in which each worker trained him- or herself. Third, the manager should cooperate with workers to ensure that they are using the scientific steps already developed, that is, he should monitor their work to be sure they adhere to the one best way. Fourth, the manager assumes all planning and organizing responsibilities while the workers perform their tasks.

Taylor's ideas and methods created quite a stir. There were protests from organized labor and a congressional investigation. In recent years evidence has

Exhibit 2.3 Scientific Management

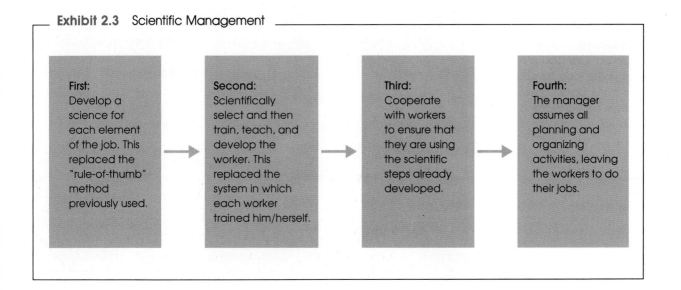

First:	Second:	Third:	Fourth:
Develop a science for each element of the job. This replaced the "rule-of-thumb" method previously used.	Scientifically select and then train, teach, and develop the worker. This replaced the system in which each worker trained him/herself.	Cooperate with workers to ensure that they are using the scientific steps already developed.	The manager assumes all planning and organizing activities, leaving the workers to do their jobs.

been uncovered that suggests that some of Taylor's experiments were not carefully performed and that someone else did part of his writing for him. However, his ideas have had a profound influence on contemporary business in areas ranging from assembly-line technology to compensation systems.[6]

Frank and Lillian Gilbreth were also notable pioneers in the scientific management movement. Their work was popularized first in a book and later in a movie entitled *Cheaper by the Dozen*, a reference to their application of scientific management practices to their family of twelve children.

Frank's work contributed to the craft of bricklaying and to medicine. He observed that even though bricklaying was one of the oldest construction technologies known, there were no generally accepted work guidelines on how to lay bricks efficiently. He applied the principles of scientific management by first studying and then standardizing the steps involved. His methods reduced the total number of steps undertaken by the bricklayer from eighteen to five and more than doubled output. He also made major contributions to the medical field by streamlining operating room procedures, thus greatly reducing the time the average patient spent on the operating table.

Lillian also made a variety of important contributions. She was primarily interested in ensuring that the welfare of the worker was not forgotten. She assisted Frank in the areas of time and motion studies and industrial efficiency and was an early contributor to personnel management.

In addition to Taylor and the Gilbreths, several other people made important contributions to scientific management. Henry Gantt, an associate of

Most people today have some appreciation for the role that robotics play in contemporary organizations. In many ways, the steps an organization uses in deploying robots draws from the early writings of scientific management. Managers and engineers study jobs, select the right kind of robot for each job, and then program the robots to perform the job exactly as planned.

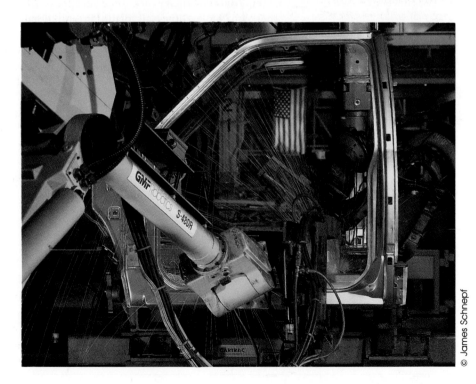

Taylor's, developed the Gantt Chart, which is a device for scheduling work over a span of time. It is still used today. He also worked in the area of pay systems. Harrington Emerson applied scientific management to the railroad industry and was an eloquent spokesperson before government audiences. Morris Cooke did some writing for Taylor and applied scientific management to the public sector.[7]

Administrative Management

□ *Administrative manage-ment,* the second important subarea of the *classical school,* dealt with the structure of organizations.

The second important subarea of classical management theory is called **administrative management.** Whereas scientific management focused on the work of individual employees, administrative management was concerned with how organizations should be structured. The primary contributors to this area were Henri Fayol and Max Weber.

Henri Fayol was the Taylor of administrative management; that is, he was perhaps its greatest contributor and most visible proponent. Drawing on more than fifty years of industrial experience, Fayol developed fourteen general guidelines, or principles, of management.[8] These principles are summarized in Table 2.1. Fayol believed that these principles were universally valid and that if they were applied and followed, they would always enhance managerial effectiveness.

□ Weber defined *bureau-cracy* as a formal organiza-tional structure with rational rules and guidelines and an emphasis on technical competence.

Max Weber was a German sociologist who was the first to describe the concept of **bureaucracy.**[9] The bureaucratic form of organization is one based on a comprehensive set of rational rules and guidelines with an emphasis on technical competence as the basis for determining who would get what jobs. Weber's guidelines were similar in concept to Fayol's fourteen principles and were designed for managers to use in structuring their organizations. Weber assumed that the resulting structure would be the most appropriate one, regardless of the situation.

Other noteworthy contributors to administrative management included Chester Barnard, who added to our understanding of authority and power distributions in organizations; Mary Parker Follett, who worked in the areas of goal setting and conflict resolution; and Lyndall Urwick, who tried to integrate some of the central ideas of scientific management with those of administrative management.

PRELUDE CASE UPDATE

Intel introduced the 8088 chip in 1979; it had 29,000 transistors built into it and operated at a speed of 0.3 million instructions per second. In 1982, Intel introduced the 80286 chip, the 80386 chip in 1985, and the 80486 in 1989. The year 1989 also saw the introduction of the i860 chip, which had the equivalent of 1 million transistors and operated at a speed of 33 million instructions per second. The development of the 80486, or i486, chip involved the work of sixty engineers and numerous designers for over a year. The initial work schedule for that project was planned and controlled so well that the target deadline was missed by only seventeen hours. In order to accomplish this sort of precision, Intel uses many of the concepts of the classical school of management, such as scheduling, determining the exact time for tasks to be performed, and integrating tasks in a project.

TABLE 2.1 Fayol's Management Principles

Principle	Explanation
1. Division of labor	The more people specialize, the more efficiently they can perform their work.
2. Authority	Managers have the right to give orders so that they can get things done.
3. Discipline	Members of an organization need to respect the rules and agreements that govern the organization.
4. Unity of command	Each employee must receive his or her instructions about a particular operation from only one person. Fayol believed that if an employee was responsible to more than one boss, conflicting instructions and confusion would result.
5. Unity of direction	The efforts of employees should be coordinated and directed by only one manager in order to avoid different policies and procedures.
6. Subordination of individual interest to the common good	The interests of employees should not take precedence over the interests of the organization as a whole.
7. Remuneration	Compensation for work done should be fair to both the employee and employer.
8. Centralization	Decreasing the role of subordinates in decision making is centralization; increasing their role is decentralization. Fayol believed that managers should retain final responsibility but that they also need to give their subordinates enough authority to do their jobs properly. The problem is to find the proper amount of centralization in each case.
9. Scalar chain	The line of authority in an organization—often represented by the neat boxes and lines of the organization chart—runs in order by rank from top management to the lowest level of the company.
10. Order	Materials and people should be in the right place at the right time. In particular, people should be in the jobs or positions best suited for them.
11. Equity	Managers should be both friendly and fair to their subordinates.
12. Stability and tenure of staff	A high employee turnover rate is not good for the efficient functioning of an organization.
13. Initiative	Subordinates should be given the freedom to formulate and carry out their plans.
14. Esprit de corps	Promoting team spirit will give the organization a sense of unity.

SOURCE: Henri Fayol, *General and Industrial Management*, trans. C. Storrs, p. 19. Copyright © 1949 Lake Publishing Company. Reprinted by permission.

Assessment of the Classical School

The classical school of management has a number of strengths and weaknesses. On the plus side, managers today are still using many of the insights and developments of these pioneers. The early theorists also helped bring the study of management to the forefront as a valid scientific concern. On the negative side, many of their ideas now seem quite simplistic and relevant only in isolated settings. For example, many people are motivated by a variety of factors beyond economic incentive. Moreover, the classical school tended to underestimate the role of the individual—a flaw that was primarily responsible for the growth of the second school of thought, the behavioral school.[10]

THE BEHAVIORAL SCHOOL

Although many early theorists ignored, or at least neglected, the human element in the workplace, there were a few scattered voices in the wilderness. Mary Parker Follett, for example, recognized the potential importance of the individual. So did Hugo Munsterberg. Munsterberg, a German psychologist, published a pioneering book in 1913 that subsequently became the cornerstone of industrial psychology.[11] The real catalyst for the emergence of the **behavioral school,** however, was a series of research studies conducted at the Hawthorne plant of Western Electric between 1927 and 1932.[12] This research has come to be known as the **Hawthorne studies.**[13]

☐ The *behavioral school* focused on the potential importance of the individual in the workplace.

The Hawthorne Studies

The Hawthorne studies actually consisted of several experiments, but two in particular are noteworthy. In the first, the researchers manipulated the lighting for a group of workers and compared the women's subsequent performance with the performance of a group whose lighting had not been changed. Quite surprisingly, performance improved in both groups. The researchers gradually increased the lighting in the experimental group, and both groups of workers continued to improve their production. In a related study, reducing the lighting had little negative impact on performance until the work area became so dark that the workers couldn't see well.

In the other major experiment, the researchers established a piecework pay system for a group of nine men. If it was true that people are motivated solely by money, each of the workers should have produced as much as possible in order to get as much pay as possible. As in the earlier study, however, the researchers found an unexpected pattern of results. They discovered that the group established a standard level of acceptable output for its members. People who fell below this standard were called chiselers and were pressured to do more. On the other hand, people who produced too much were labeled ratebusters and were pressured to bring their output into alignment with that of the rest of the group.

Because of these and other studies, the researchers at Hawthorne concluded that a variety of social factors previously unknown to managers were of critical importance. For example, the researchers attributed the results in the lighting study to the fact that the workers were receiving special attention for the first time. They also concluded, from the findings of the piecework experiment, that social pressure was a powerful force to be reckoned with.

Human Relations

□ The *human relations* model recognizes that people have their own unique needs and motives that they bring to the workplace.

The Hawthorne studies gave birth to an entirely new way of thinking about workers. This view, illustrated in Exhibit 2.4, focuses on the importance of the individual in the workplace. Whereas previous views ignored the role of the individual, the **human relations** model recognizes that people have their own unique needs and motives that they bring into the workplace with them. While at work, an individual is exposed to the task, a supervisor, and so forth, but she or he also experiences a social context. This context includes membership in the work group and the possible satisfaction of social needs such as the need to be with others and the need to be liked and accepted by them.

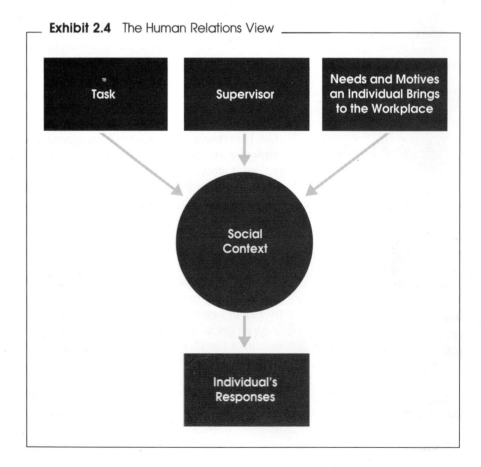

Exhibit 2.4   The Human Relations View

TABLE 2.2
Theory X and Theory Y

Theory X Assumptions	Theory Y Assumptions
1. People do not like work and try to avoid it.	1. People do not naturally dislike work; work is a natural part of their lives.
2. People do not like work, so managers have to control, direct, coerce, and threaten employees to get them to work toward organizational goals.	2. People are internally motivated to reach objectives to which they are committed.
3. People prefer to be directed, to avoid responsibility, to want security; they have little ambition.	3. People are committed to goals to the degree that they receive personal rewards when they reach their objectives.
	4. People will both seek and accept responsibility under favorable conditions.
	5. People have the capacity to be innovative in solving organizational problems.
	6. People are bright, but under most organizational conditions their potentials are underutilized.

SOURCE: Douglas McGregor, *The Human Side of Enterprise* (New York: McGraw-Hill, 1960), pp. 33–34, 47–48.

Understanding the pressures and challenges faced by subordinates is one way to better appreciate behavioral processes in the workplace. At Lincoln Electric, all new managers are required to spend eight weeks on the welding line, as Rob Shepard, a recent M.B.A. graduate from Harvard, is doing before he assumes his new managerial post.

These factors then combine to influence such responses as satisfaction and performance.

Two writers are particularly identified with the human relations movement. Abraham Maslow proposed a well-known hierarchy of human needs, which will be discussed in Chapter 13.[14] The other primary proponent of human relations is Douglas McGregor, who described two quite different opinions of workers that managers might hold. These opinions, called **Theory X** and **Theory Y,** are summarized in Table 2.2. According to McGregor, Theory X typified pessimistic managerial thinking. The more optimistic Theory Y was the view he felt was more appropriate.[15]

Contemporary Behavioral Science

Although the views espoused by early human relations theorists had some validity, they were also somewhat naive and simplistic. For example, these theorists believed that if managers made workers happier, the employees would work harder. Contemporary behavioral science takes a more complex view. It acknowledges and attempts to explain a variety of individual and social processes as both determinants and consequences of human behavior. For example, performance is caused by many things, including motivation and ability. As a consequence of performing at a high level, people may achieve a variety of rewards. These rewards may in turn affect future motivation and, consequently, performance again. Thus, instead of presenting simple, universal principles, contemporary behavioral science presents complex, contingency views, which are discussed in later chapters. Today, an understanding of human behavior is seen as an important tool that managers can use to do a better job of drawing on the important human resources that all organizations have.

PRELUDE CASE UPDATE

Andrew Grove, Intel's CEO, is a Hungarian émigré who has a chemical engineering degree. One of the original team of engineers at Intel, he became the architect of the strategy that has helped Intel dominate its field. Although he shuns executive perquisites and is open to listen to employees, including their criticisms, he has also been known to upbraid employees publicly. Shunning perquisites, being open to communication from below, creating an organizational environment in which creative people can succeed, and linking rewards to performance all are consistent with the behavioral school of management.

Assessment of the Behavioral School

LEARNING CHECK

You should now be able to describe and assess the behavioral school of management theory.

The behavioral school yielded some significant but simplistic insights into the role of the individual in the workplace. Behavioral scientists today continue to work toward a better understanding of human behavior in organizational settings. Like the classical school, the behavioral view is an important but incomplete theory of management. Another important piece of the puzzle is the quantitative school of management thought.[16]

THE QUANTITATIVE SCHOOL

The third school of management thought is the **quantitative school.** As the term implies, this approach focuses on quantitative or measurement techniques and concepts of interest to managers. It has its roots in World War II, when the military sought new and better ways to deal with troop movement, arms production, and similar problems. There are three branches of the quantitative school: management science, operations management, and management information systems.

□ *Management science,* one branch of the *quantitative school,* develops advanced mathematical and statistical tools and techniques for managers.

Management Science

Management science is concerned with the development of sophisticated mathematical and statistical tools and techniques that the manager can use, primarily to enhance efficiency.[17] For example, a manager might use a management science model to help her decide how large a new plant needs to be.

The model would contain a number of equations related to such things as projected production volume at the plant, construction cost per square foot, utility costs for plants of different dimensions, and so forth, and the solutions would give the manager useful guidelines as to how big to make the plant. Companies such as Delta Air Lines and American Airlines use management science models to plan flight schedules, to set rate structures, and to schedule maintenance.

Advancements in the management science area have been greatly helped by breakthroughs in computers and other forms of electronic information processing. Such innovations as the personal computer enhance managers' access to the tools and techniques of management science. On the other hand, in the country most associated with high technology, Japan, some managers still adhere to traditional approaches to problem solving and encourage employees to use an abacus rather than a computer to make rapid calculations.

Operations Management

☐ *Operations management* focuses on the application of mathematical and statistical tools to managing an organization's processes and systems.

Operations management is somewhat like management science but is focused more on application.[18] It concerns the various processes and systems an organization uses to transform resources into finished goods and services. Decisions about where a plant should be located, how it should be arranged, how much inventory it should carry, and how its finished goods should be distributed are all elements of operations management, which is used by General Motors, Black & Decker, and IBM in managing their assembly plants. Since many aspects of operations management are related to control, an entire chapter is devoted to it later in the book.

Management Information Systems

☐ A *management information system* (MIS) is a system created specifically to store and provide information to managers.

Management information systems, or **MISs,** make up the third branch of the quantitative school. An MIS is a system created specifically to store and provide information to managers. For instance, an MIS for a large manufacturer like Westinghouse might contain information about everything from the finished goods inventory of a plant in Seattle to the number of operating employees at a service center in St. Louis. The data are kept as current as possible, so a marketing manager in New York can tap into the system and check the inventory levels in Seattle while a human resource manager in Houston is verifying the number of employees in St. Louis. Of course, most systems of this type make extensive use of computer technology. We will learn more about MIS in Chapter 11, "Information Systems."

Assessment of the Quantitative School

LEARNING CHECK

You should now be able to describe and assess the quantitative school of management theory.

The primary value of the quantitative school lies in the portfolio of tools it provides for management. These tools can greatly enhance a manager's decision making, planning, and control. At the same time, we should remember that tools cannot replace human intuition and insight. A manager needs to choose the right tools for the job, apply them properly, and then understand what the results mean.

CONTEMPORARY MANAGEMENT THEORY

In recent years several new perspectives on management have emerged. These have not yet attained the stature of schools of thought, but they still provide useful techniques and approaches that managers should understand. In this section we will explore systems theory, contingency theory, and other emerging ideas.

Systems Theory

◻ *Systems theory* is an approach to understanding how the different elements of an organization function and operate.

Systems theory is an approach to understanding how organizations function and operate.[19] It is illustrated in Exhibit 2.5. A system is an interrelated set of elements that function as a whole. Note that it has four basic parts. First, the system receives from the environment the four kinds of inputs, or resources, that were included in the definition of management in Chapter 1. For an organization like Texaco, human resources include managers and oil field personnel, physical resources include oil and pipelines, financial resources are derived from product sales and stockholder investment, and informational resources include OPEC proclamations and demand forecasts.

Exhibit 2.5   The Systems Model

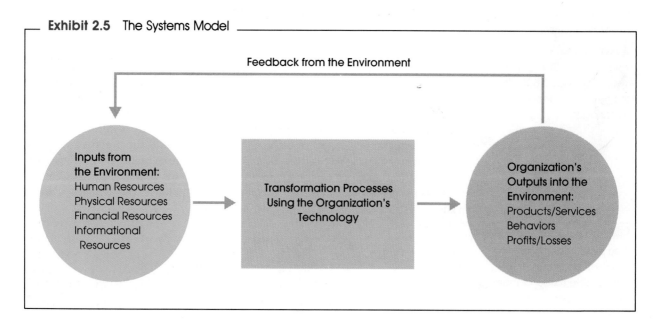

Feedback from the Environment

Inputs from
the Environment:
Human Resources
Physical Resources
Financial Resources
Informational
  Resources

Transformation Processes
Using the Organization's
Technology

Organization's
Outputs into the
Environment:
Products/Services
Behaviors
Profits/Losses

THE WORLD OF MANAGEMENT

Lloyd's Means More than Coffee

Lloyd's of London is one of the world's best-known business organizations. In 1988 it was three hundred years old. Yet it is not a company and has no shareholders—it is a society of underwriters with a unique history. Lloyd's Coffee House opened in 1688 and quickly became a meetinghouse for businessmen engaged in marine insurance. In 1769 those involved in this enterprise became perturbed at all of the other business being conducted at Lloyd's and so moved to a new and larger location. The new location was not a coffee house but strictly a meeting place for those engaged in marine insurance.

After this move, a committee was established to determine who could use the facilities for business. Then in 1871 Lloyd's was incorporated by an act of Parliament. Five other acts have been passed to specify and define the precise nature of Lloyd's. Lloyd's is administered by the Council (much like a board of directors) and the Corporation (like a corporate staff). It has agents located throughout the world. These agents are firms whose job is to send information to the firm in London and to handle claims for damage or losses.

Lloyd's operates as a pooling cooperative: that is, members, or Names as they are called, share resources and risks. If the risk is great, more Names are recruited to absorb that risk. The big disadvantage to this approach is that all members must agree to any changes that might be made in the contract. Clearly this process can be cumbersome and slow.

Lloyd's has other problems as well. The difficulty of getting information quickly, which is often the case with insurance claims, and scandals that have left too many Names in debt have led to efforts to make changes at Lloyd's. Moves to limit liability are under way and other aspects of membership may also be regulated to reduce future scandals.

Coordinating Lloyd's insurance activities, the flow of information (including five publications), the various activities of its over 30,000 members, and its numerous insurance contracts is a gigantic task. Lloyd's could benefit from a systems approach to its management that would recognize the interdependencies among its parts and provide necessary information to the right groups at the right time.

SOURCES: Peter Ohlhausen, "Lloyd's: A Premium on Security," *Security Management,* January 1, 1989, p. 55; "More Bad News for Lloyd's of London Names," *The Economist,* December 3, 1988, p. 88; "Lloyd's Studies Liability Limit for Its Members," *The Wall Street Journal,* September 9, 1988, p. 12; Montieth M. Illingworth, "The Stakes of the Mission," *American Way,* September 15, 1988, pp. 79–80, 114–116, 134.

Second, these various resources are transformed through a variety of processes into outputs. These processes represent the organization's technology. The third part of the model, outputs, includes products or services, behaviors, and profits or losses. For Texaco, products are gasoline and oil, behaviors are the impact of its employees on the environment, and profits or losses are reflected in the level of funds put back into or taken from the environment. Finally, feedback from the environment provides the system with additional information about how well its actions are being accepted. As indicated in *Management Today: The World of Management*, an organization like Lloyd's of London could certainly benefit from a systems approach to its management.

INTERACTION WITH ENVIRONMENT   This point—interaction with the environment—is one of the major contributions systems theory makes to the manager. This notion comes from the concept of open systems. An open system is one that actively interacts with its environment, whereas a closed system does not. All organizations are open systems, so managers need to remember that they must always monitor and be sensitive to their environments. Organizations with managers who forget this are almost invariably left behind. For example, for years American Motors assumed it could just go on producing Ramblers and not worry about what other car manufacturers were doing. As a result of this attitude, the company eventually fell so far behind its competitors that it could never hope to catch up again. The company was subsequently bought by Chrysler and ceased to exist as an independent entity.

◻ *Subsystem interdependencies* are the different ways in which a change in one part of an organization affects other parts.

SUBSYSTEM INTERDEPENDENCIES   Another useful contribution of systems theory is the notion of **subsystem interdependencies.** A subsystem is a system within a system; for example, each Hewlett-Packard assembly plant is a subsystem, as are the marketing and human resource divisions. Virtually all subsystems within a parent system are highly interdependent—that is, a change in one affects the others. When managers make a change, therefore, they must carefully consider the consequences of that change on all related subsystems.

A good example of subsystem interdependencies occurred in 1986, when General Motors Corporation's automobile dealerships were beset by falling sales and bloated inventories. To help alleviate the problem, GM decided to finance cars for consumers at a previously unheard-of 2.9 percent interest rate. However, GM's financing division, General Motors Acceptance Corp., or GMAC, could not handle this level of financing. Such interest rates would have hurt its profit margins and consequently lowered its bond ratings. GM itself had to underwrite the low interest rates, even though this would ordinarily have been the responsibility of GMAC. Thus, the needs of one subsystem, GM dealerships, necessitated a certain course of action, but the environmental circumstances surrounding another subsystem, GMAC, kept it from responding appropriately.[20]

◻ When two or more people or units working together produce more than they could working alone, *synergy* has occurred.

◻ *Entropy* is failure caused by a closed-system approach to management.

◻ *Equifinality* suggests that the same goal may be achieved through different means.

SYNERGY, ENTROPY, AND EQUIFINALITY   Three other concepts of systems theory are also useful. **Synergy** suggests that two people or units can achieve more working together than working individually. When a retail chain like K mart purchases Walden Book Co., it is partially because managers recognize that the two businesses complement one another. **Entropy** is what happens when organizations take a closed-system perspective: they falter and die. Studebaker and W. T. Grant made this mistake. The key is to stay in tune with the environment and work hard at keeping the organization stimulated and vital. Finally, **equifinality** is the idea that two or more paths may lead to the same place. Dow Chemical and Union Carbide can pursue different strategies, for example, and yet be equally effective in the chemical industry.

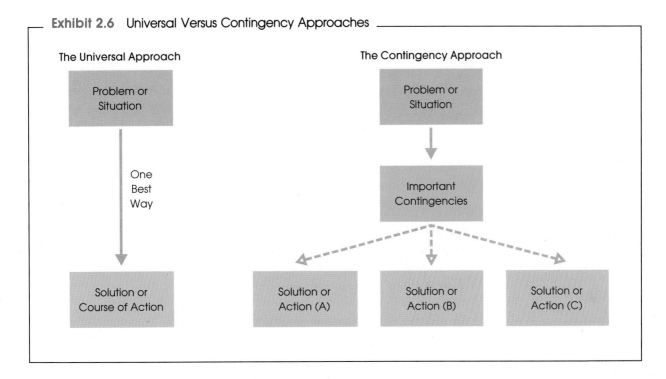

Exhibit 2.6 Universal Versus Contingency Approaches

The Universal Approach

Problem or Situation

One Best Way

Solution or Course of Action

The Contingency Approach

Problem or Situation

Important Contingencies

Solution or Action (A)

Solution or Action (B)

Solution or Action (C)

Contingency Theory

☐ *Contingency theory* argues that appropriate managerial actions depend on certain major elements of situations.

A second important contemporary perspective on management is **contingency theory,** which argues that appropriate managerial actions in a situation depend on, or are contingent on, certain major elements of that situation.[21] Early approaches to management problems sought universal answers. As illustrated in the left portion of Exhibit 2.6, the premise was that a given problem or situation could be solved or acted upon in "one best way." In contrast, the contingency approach recognizes that there are few, if any, "one best ways" in management, because the complexities of human behavior and social systems like organizations make every situation somewhat unique. The right portion of the exhibit acknowledges these complexities. It suggests that when a manager is confronted with a problem or situation, he or she must examine important contingencies. One of several potential solutions or actions may then be seen as appropriate. What will work best in one situation might not be best in another situation.

Contingency theory, however, does not suggest that every single problem is totally unique. Theories are still useful guides to thinking, and although situations may vary, different problems can often be handled quite similarly.

APPLICATIONS OF CONTINGENCY THEORY Almost every aspect of management has embraced the contingency philosophy. For example, there are contingency theories of goal setting, planning, organization design, job design, leadership, motivation, and control. We will look at these theories in later chapters. Before moving on, however, let's examine a real situation in which managers did not take a contingency orientation and paid a high price.

The organization in question is People Express Airlines. In its early, profitable days, the airline used minimal organizational structure, rewarded everyone on the basis of profits, had few controls, and worked hard to equalize power among all levels of employees. This approach worked, and the organization grew rapidly. Eventually it went into a rapid decline, however, and in 1986 it was bought by Texas Air. The most common explanation for People's demise was that its style of management was well suited to a small, rapidly growing company but did not fit the larger, more stable firm the airline became. Thus, important situational contingencies changed, dictating the need for a different approach to problems. The company's failure to respond to these changing circumstances played a major role in its fall from grace.[22]

Emerging Perspectives

In addition to systems and contingency theory, other emerging perspectives are worth noting. These ideas are very new and have not yet withstood the

Takeshi Yuzawa

Managers today have become quite interested in learning from their Japanese counterparts. Kyocera corporation is currently one of the fastest growing firms in Japan. The Kyocera workers shown here are present for roll call and morning exercises. While many American managers resist going this far, most U.S. managers who work for Kyocera's San Diego office wear Japanese workers' jackets to demonstrate their commitment to the basic corporate philosophy.

test of time. Thus, they may continue to evolve into more fully framed theories of management, or they may go the way of fads and be replaced by new ideas yet to come.

□ *Theory Z suggests that a blend of Japanese and American management characteristics is most successful.*

THEORY Z   **Theory Z** was popularized in the early 1980s by William Ouchi.[23] During that period a great deal of attention was being given to the success of Japanese organizations and the differences between American and Japanese management practices. Ouchi studied numerous American firms, such as Hewlett-Packard, Eastman Kodak, and Procter & Gamble, to determine why and how they continued to be so successful when other companies were losing ground.

He found that most American firms followed a set of business practices he called the Type A (for American) model, whereas the typical Japanese company followed a different set, which he called the Type J (for Japanese) approach. Type A business practices included such things as short-term employment, individual responsibility for work, and specialized career paths. Type J business practices were characterized by such things as lifetime employment, collective responsibility, and non-specialized career paths. Highly successful American firms, however, followed neither of these approaches. Instead they used a modified approach that capitalized on various strengths of the Type J model but also used Type A methods when cultural factors dictated. The business practices of these successful firms included long-term employment, individual responsibility with collective decision making, and moderately specialized career paths. Ouchi attributed these companies' success to this approach and suggested that a flexible management position incorporating the strengths of both the American and Japanese models would lead to successful competition. This is known as Theory Z.

□ *Management excellence is practicing the eight attributes of successful firms identified by Peters and Waterman.*

MANAGEMENT EXCELLENCE   The idea of **management excellence** was popularized in the mid-1980s by Thomas Peters and Robert Waterman.[24] They studied numerous successful American businesses, including Digital Equipment, IBM, and Walt Disney Productions. They concluded that managers in these firms were characterized by a set of eight attributes, which are summarized in Table 2.3. One is a bias for action, which means that excellent firms tend to do something rather than sit back and wait for a prompt. They also stick to the knitting—they do only what they know how to do. Walt Disney Productions knows how to entertain, so it operates theme parks and makes movies rather than branching out into the automobile business.

PRELUDE CASE UPDATE

Many of the attributes of well-managed firms noted by Peters and Waterman can be found at Intel. Intel clearly has a bias for action, almost always beating its competitors in the introduction of new chip designs. It uses its pay-for-performance system to ensure productivity through people. It sticks to its knitting, producing chips rather than making PCs or work stations itself. It

TABLE 2.3
Attributes of Excellence

Attribute	Explanation
1. *A bias for action*	A preference for doing something—anything—rather than sending a question through cycles and cycles of analyses and committee reports
2. *Staying close to the customer*	Learning the customer's preferences and catering to them
3. *Autonomy and entrepreneurship*	Breaking the corporation into small companies and encouraging them to think independently and competitively
4. *Productivity through people*	Creating in *all* employees the awareness that their best efforts are essential and that they will share in the rewards of the company's success
5. *Hands-on, value driven*	Insisting that executives keep in touch with the firm's essential business
6. *Stick to the knitting*	Remaining with the business the company knows best
7. *Simple form, lean staff*	Few administrative layers, few people at the upper levels
8. *Simultaneous loose-tight properties*	Fostering a climate where there is dedication to the central values of the company combined with tolerance of all employees who accept those values

SOURCE: "The Basic Attributes of Excellence" from *In Search of Excellence* by Thomas J. Peters and Robert H. Waterman, Jr. Copyright © 1982 by Thomas J. Peters and Robert H. Waterman, Jr. Reprinted by permission of Harper & Row, Publishers, Inc.

learned during the mid-1980s the importance of keeping a simple, lean organization. The existence of other attributes may be inferred from the Prelude Case description and the previous updates in this chapter.

You should now be able to identify major components of contemporary management theory.

It is still too early to assess the validity of either Theory Z or management excellence.[25] Each offers the manager useful suggestions, but neither should be followed too rigidly. There are few "quick fixes" in the managerial world. Managers should consider ideas such as these within their own situational context and use them only as they are appropriate.

Chapter Summary

Knowledge of history will help you better understand current developments and avoid repeating mistakes. An understanding of theory helps you organize and further comprehend information that is available to you as a manager. It also enables you to be more systematic in your approach to problems so that you can reach better solutions.

The study of management is a recent phenomenon. During the nineteenth century the factory system began to emerge, and problems associated with the organization and operation of businesses grew.

The classical school of management emerged around the turn of this century and consists of two major subareas: scientific and administrative management. Scientific management focused on the work of individuals and sought to determine how jobs could be designed to maximize employee output. Administrative management focused on how organizations should be structured for best performance.

The behavioral school actually began at about the same time as the classical school, with the work of Munsterberg, but it did not have a significant impact on the field until later. The Hawthorne studies brought about that change. This movement—in particular the work of Maslow and McGregor—did much to advance the view that more humanistic approaches to the treatment of workers were needed. Contemporary behavioral science takes a more complex view of the worker, acknowledging and attempting to explain a variety of individual and social processes as both determinants and consequences of human behavior.

The quantitative school of management theory emerged during World War II, when the military sought new and better ways to deal with the managerial problems of modern warfare. Management science is concerned with the development of mathematical and statistical tools and techniques for managers. Operations management is similar but tends to focus on the application of techniques to operational aspects of management. Management information systems (MIS) are created to store and provide information for managers.

The major components of contemporary management theory include systems theory, contingency theory, and the emerging perspectives of Theory Z and management excellence. Among the useful contributions of systems theory are the study of an organization's interaction with its environment, subsystem interdependencies, and the concepts of synergy, entropy, and equifinality. Contingency theory suggests that there is no "one best way" to manage; however, it does not hold that every case is unique. Theory Z recommends a combination of Japanese and American management practices that seems to

have worked well in the United States. Management excellence identifies a number of attributes that seem common to a group of companies that were judged "excellent" by researchers.

The Manager's Vocabulary

factory system	operations management
classical school	management information
scientific management	systems (MIS)
administrative	systems theory
management	subsystem
bureaucracy	interdependencies
behavioral school	synergy
Hawthorne studies	entropy
human relations	equifinality
Theory X	contingency theory
Theory Y	Theory Z
quantitative school	management excellence
management science	

Prelude Case Wrap-Up

Our Prelude Case for this chapter describes how Intel went from a brand-new firm in 1968 to the dominant manufacturer of personal computer chips by 1989. The history of Intel suggests that it uses aspects of each of the major schools of management as well as of contemporary management theory in achieving and maintaining that success. It also suggests that Intel's organizational environment is a major key to its effectiveness. That environment is one in which creative, hard-working people are rewarded and enjoy the challenges presented to them.

Despite its success, Intel and its CEO, Andy Grove, face serious challenges in the future. Businesses are shifting away from personal computers toward work stations, and the work station market is dominated by Motorola. In 1988 about 60 percent of the 287,000 technical work stations in existence were based on Motorola's 68000 family of chips. About 17 percent of those work stations were based on RISC chips, 15 percent on other chips, and less than 9 percent on Intel chips. Coming from that far behind is an enormously difficult challenge for any organization.

RISC (reduced instruction set computing) chips cut down on the number of instructions needed by a computer and so increase speed dramatically. Intel had traditionally used a different and competing design. However, in 1989 Intel began to produce RISC chips as well as the family of chips it had been producing for over twenty years. It was moving to remain the dominant firm in the personal computer chip market while at the same time seeking to become a major competitor in the work station and RISC chip market. Intel also has to consider the Japanese, who are working to develop yet another technology that could compete in the personal computer chip market.

Because the risk involved in trying to succeed in both the personal computer and work station markets is so great, Intel also began to expand other parts of its business during 1989. Those other parts include thousands of memory chips and other semiconductors that are used in everything from VCRs to automobiles, special computers used by the Department of Defense, and private-label desk top computers.

Prelude Case Questions

1. What are the major factors that have accounted for Intel's success? Do you think they are likely to continue to be as important in the future? Why or why not?
2. Describe Andrew Grove as a manager. If you were a stockholder of a company, would you like to have him working for you? Would you like to work for him? Why or why not? Why might the same individual respond quite differently to these two questions?
3. Do you think Intel will continue to be successful? Why or why not?
4. Recommend some other directions in which Intel might go to continue to be as effective in the future as it has been in the past.

Discussion Questions

Review Questions

1. Briefly explain why history and theory are important to the field of management.

2. What are the important contributions and weaknesses of the classical school of management?
3. What are the important contributions and weaknesses of the behavioral school of management?
4. What are the important contributions and weaknesses of the quantitative school of management?
5. Describe systems theory and contingency theory.

Analysis Questions

1. Given the importance of history and theory, how can many managers operate successfully without a good understanding of either? Would they do better with such an understanding? Why?
2. Do you think ancient civilizations could have emerged without management? Why or why not?
3. Which school of management theory do you feel most closely matches your present ideas about how management should function? Why?
4. Do you think management theories of the past were relatively simple because the theorists did not know much or because the managerial world they were describing was relatively simple? Defend your view.
5. Take the opposite view to the one you took in question 4 and defend that one instead. What have you learned by this?

Application Questions and Exercises

1. Identify an ancient, primitive, or prehistoric civilization. Consult library sources and describe some of the management practices of that civilization.
2. Identify a practicing manager with whom you are familiar. Which school of management theory seems to best describe that person's managerial practices? Why?
3. Interview a local business manager to see which school of management seems to best describe that manager's practices. Use specific examples to support your view.
4. Interview one or more local business managers to see if any of the emerging perspectives seem to be reflected in their thinking or practices.
5. Illustrate the concepts of synergy, entropy, and equifinality in a system other than a business one. (You may need to look up some articles on systems to answer this question fully.)

ENHANCEMENT CASE

K MART KEEPS ON PUSHING

Sebastian S. Kresge founded a five and dime store in 1897. He rapidly expanded that into a chain of S. S. Kresge's Five and Ten Cent Stores that became simply S. S. Kresge in 1912 and later the Kresge Company. By the 1960s, there were numerous such chains—Woolworth, W. T. Grant Co., and Ben Franklin Stores—but the main competition was between Woolworth and Kresge.

In 1957, Harry Cunningham became vice president of Kresge and toured the country visiting the company's 725 stores. While traveling, he visited the E. J. Korvette discount store in Garden City, New Jersey. By discounting prices, Korvette moved its stock quickly. This rapid turnover in stock reduced carrying costs, thereby enabling the company to more than make up for the reduced prices. Cunningham was impressed.

In 1959, Cunningham became president and had a vice president begin to recruit and train employees for discount operations even though Cunningham had not yet announced that Kresge was going to move in that direction. Cunningham closed Kresge stores in eroding neighborhoods and reopened them as small, limited-line discount stores called Jupiter stores. In these stores, the new personnel were trained and obtained the experience they needed to compete in discounting.

Then in 1961, Cunningham officially announced that Kresge would move into discounting under the name K mart. He had another vice president gather information about running discount stores—salaries of personnel, operating ratios, layouts, and all other pertinent information. The company committed $80 million to obtain leases and merchandise for thirty-three stores.

The first K mart opened in Michigan in 1960. Thirty-three stores had been opened by the end of that year, and twenty more stores were added the next year. This rapid expansion, coupled with low margins and local autonomy for store managers, quickly enabled K mart to beat its competition. Woolworth began to open its discount stores, Woolco, too late and was never able to compete successfully. Woolco went out of business in 1983. However, other competition emerged to keep the pressure on K mart. Target and Wal-Mart as well as specialized discounters, especially in toys, began to take K mart customers by the 1970s. So K mart responded in the mid-1970s by entering shopping malls, expanding into smaller communities with scaled-down stores, and expanding its offerings to include pharmacies, automotive, and home improvement departments.

In 1977 Kresge became the K mart Corporation to reflect its success in discounting. At that time it had become the second largest retailer in the United States behind Sears. The company was operating 1,782 stores (1,367 K marts, 329 Kresges, and 86 Jupiters). It was also growing at a rate of nearly 200 stores per year. Although the rate of new store openings has slowed, K mart continues to grow and has well in excess of 2,200 stores at present. By late 1988, K mart was being touted in some circles as a possible contender to take over the number one spot from Sears.

Nevertheless, the problems of success and growth are never over. In 1980 Bernard Fauber became chairman of K mart and began to develop a new strategy for the firm. Growth through the expansion of new stores has nearly ended, so the company is trying to expand its market and its market image. Instead of being just "the saving place" where lower-income groups can acquire good merchandise at inexpensive prices, K mart is seeking to attract higher-income groups with name brand and designer merchandise. It is remodeling and restocking to change its image. In the early 1980s, it began carrying Izod sports shirts, Puma running shoes, Seiko watches, and designer jeans. By the late 1980s, it had actress Jaclyn Smith endorsing a line of women's clothing and cookbook author Martha Stewart agreeing to a kitchenware line. Its remodeling efforts have meant brighter store colors, modern display racks, more specialty departments, and a rearrangement of departments so that the high-markup counters are at the front of the store.

Recognizing the importance of its distribution system, K mart is also streamlining and modernizing that component of its business. It has opened highly automated distribution centers of over a million square feet each. It has also automated its sales and inventory systems. By responding to store orders rapidly, the distribution centers can lower individual store inventory needs and in this way cut short-term borrowing costs by millions of dollars.

Because K mart is a mature business, it is also seeking to expand by diversifying, primarily through acquisitions and joint ventures. K mart purchased Furr's Cafeterias; invested in Astra, a Mexican discount chain; and helped Daiei, a large Japanese retailer, set up a discounting operation for its businesses. In 1987 Joseph Antonini became chairman and continued to push these forms of expansion. Adding to its already existing acquisition of Waldenbooks, Pay Less Drug Stores, and Builders Square home improvement stores, Antonini acquired Makro Inc., a cut-rate warehouse club chain, and Bruno's Inc., a major grocery and general merchandise chain.

In 1985 K mart began experimenting with banking services. San Francisco's First Nationwide Bank be-gan setting up banking stations in K marts and by 1987 had decided that the experiment was a success and moved to rapidly expand its operations into what might eventually be as many as 1,000 K marts. Other banks, such as United Savings and Standard Federal Bank in Illinois, are also opening up K mart branches or automated teller machines. In addition, Statewide Realty has branches in stores in Michigan and Wisconsin, and InsurUSA operates in over 100 K mart stores.

In 1989 K mart launched its strongest effort yet to change its image. K mart and CBS Inc. announced a joint promotion effort. Each week, 72 million homes were flooded with K mart circulars with game cards, and banners at every K mart store promoted CBS television shows. Numbers shown on commercials during the television shows matched game card numbers for prizes (mostly mugs, although vans, Hollywood vacations, and TV sets were also awarded).

K mart continues to develop and expand. It tries to understand and respond to the needs of its customers. It is trying to expand its customer base as well. Whether or not it will become the number one retailer as a result of these efforts remains to be seen, but clearly recent moves by Sears suggest that K mart is seen as a real threat.

SOURCES: "CBS to Launch Unusual Linkup with K mart to Promote Shows," *The Wall Street Journal*, May 10, 1989, p. B6; "K mart Buffs Image, Builds Earnings," *USA Today*, August 16, 1988, p. 3B; "K mart Woos Customers with Bank," *USA Today*, October 2, 1987, pp. 1B–2B; "How Kresge Became the Top Discounter," *Business Week*, October 24, 1970, p. 62; "Will K mart Ever Be a Silk Purse?" *Business Week*, January 22, 1990, p. 46.

Enhancement Case Questions

1. Why might Kresge have been successful initially? Was that success strategy carried forward in its growth and expansion? Why or why not?
2. Does knowing K mart's history provide you with a better understanding of its current practices? Why or why not?
3. What school or schools of management theory seem best to describe K mart's management? Has this changed over time, and if so, in what ways?
4. Recommend some other directions in which K mart might go or any other things K mart might do to continue to try to become the number one retailer.

Chapter Notes

1. "Profiting from the Past," *Newsweek*, May 10, 1982, pp. 73–74.
2. Alan L. Wilkins and Nigel J. Bristow, "For Successful Organization Culture, Honor Your Past," *Academy of Management Executive*, August 1987, pp. 221–227, and Alan M. Kantrow, "Why History Matters to Managers," *Harvard Business Review*, January-February 1986, pp. 81–88.
3. See Daniel A. Wren, *The Evolution of Management Thought*, 3rd ed. (New York: Wiley, 1987), and Claude S. George, Jr., *The History of Management Thought* (Englewood Cliffs, N.J.: Prentice-Hall,

1968), for general discussions of ancient management practices.

4. See Wren, *The Evolution of Management Thought*, for details about these and other management pioneers.

5. Frederick W. Taylor, *Principles of Scientific Management* (New York: Harper and Brothers, 1911).

6. See Charles D. Wrege and Ann Marie Stotka, "Cooke Creates a Classic: The Story Behind F. W. Taylor's Principles of Scientific Management," *Academy of Management Review*, October 1978, pp. 736–749.

7. See Wren, *The Evolution of Management Thought*.

8. Henri Fayol, *Industrial and General Management*, trans. J. A. Conbrough (Geneva: International Management Institute, 1930).

9. Max Weber, *Theory of Social and Economic Organization*, trans. T. Parsons (New York: Free Press, 1947).

10. Stephen J. Carroll and Dennis J. Gillen, "Are the Classical Management Functions Useful in Describing Managerial Work?" *Academy of Management Review*, January 1987, pp. 38–51.

11. Hugo Munsterberg, *Psychology and Industrial Efficiency* (Boston: Houghton Mifflin, 1913).

12. Paul R. Lawrence, "Historical Development of Organizational Behavior," in Jay W. Lorsch, ed., *Handbook of Organizational Behavior* (Englewood Cliffs, N.J.: Prentice-Hall, 1987), pp. 1–9.

13. R. G. Greenwood, A. A. Bolton, and R. A. Greenwood, "Hawthorne a Half Century Later: Relay Assembly Participants Remember," *Journal of Management*, vol. 9, no. 2 (1983), pp. 217–231. See also Elton Mayo, *The Human Problems of an Industrial Civilization* (New York: Macmillan, 1933), and Fritz Roethlisberger and William Dickson, *Management and the Worker* (Cambridge, Mass.: Harvard University Press, 1939), for details of the actual research. See Wren, *The Evolution of Management Thought*, for a summary.

14. Abraham Maslow, "A Theory of Human Motivation," *Psychological Review*, July 1943, pp. 370–396.

15. Douglas McGregor, *The Human Side of Enterprise* (New York: McGraw-Hill, 1960).

16. See Gregory Moorhead and Ricky W. Griffin, *Organi-zational Behavior*, 2nd ed. (Boston: Houghton Mifflin, 1989), for a review of recent happenings in the field of organizational behavior.

17. See Robert Markland, *Topics in Management Science*, 3rd ed. (New York: Wiley, 1987).

18. See Everett E. Adam, Jr., and Ronald J. Ebert, *Production and Operations Management*, 4th ed. (Englewood Cliffs, N.J.: Prentice-Hall, 1989), for a review. See also Richard B. Chase and Eric L. Prentis, "Operations Management: A Field Rediscovered," *Journal of Management*, Summer 1987, pp. 339–350.

19. See Donde P. Ashmos and George P. Huber, "The Systems Paradigm in Organization Theory: Correcting the Record and Suggesting the Future," *Academy of Management Review*, October 1987, pp. 607–621, and Fremont Kast and James Rosenzweig, "General Systems Theory: Applications for Organization and Management," *Academy of Management Journal*, December 1972, pp. 447–465.

20. "Buyers Respond to New GM Incentives; Questions Remain on Company Strategy," *The Wall Street Journal*, August 29, 1986, p. 2.

21. See Fremont E. Kast and James E. Rosenzweig, *Contingency Views of Organization and Management* (Chicago: Science Research Associates, 1973), for an early summary of contingency theory.

22. "Airline's Ills Point Out Weaknesses of Unorthodox Management Style," *The Wall Street Journal*, August 11, 1986, p. 15.

23. William Ouchi, *Theory Z—How American Business Can Meet the Japanese Challenge* (Reading, Mass.: Addison-Wesley, 1981).

24. Thomas Peters and Robert Waterman, Jr., *In Search of Excellence* (New York: Harper & Row, 1982).

25. Tom Peters, "Restoring American Competitiveness: Looking for New Models of Organizations," *Academy of Management Executive*, May 1988, pp. 103–109, and Michael A. Hitt and R. Duane Ireland, "Peters and Waterman Revisited: The Unended Quest for Excellence," *Academy of Management Executive*, May 1987, pp. 91–98.

CHAPTER OUTLINE

I. The Nature of Ethics
   A. The Meaning of Ethics
   B. The Formation of Ethics

II. Managerial Ethics
   A. Ethics and Management
   B. The Ethical Context of
      Management

III. Managing Ethics
   A. Top-Management Support
   B. Codes of Conduct

IV. The Nature of Social Responsibility
   A. Historical Development
   B. Arguments About Social
      Responsibility

V. Approaches to Social Responsibility
   A. Social Obligation
   B. Social Reaction
   C. Social Involvement

VI. Areas of Social Responsibility

VII. The Government and Social Responsibility
   A. Government Regulation
      of Business
   B. Business Influence on
      Government

CHAPTER

3

LEARNING OBJECTIVES

After studying this chapter you should be able to

1. Define ethics and discuss their nature and how they are formed.

2. Describe the relationship between ethics and management, particularly the ethical context of management.

3. Understand the management of ethics, including the necessity for top-management support and codes of conduct.

4. Define social responsibility and discuss arguments both for and against it.

5. Discuss approaches to social responsibility.

6. Identify the general areas of social responsibility.

7. Discuss the role of government in business's social responsibility.

Managerial Ethics and Social Responsibility

PRELUDE CASE

EXXON SPILLS

An event occurred during the third week in March of 1989 that has plagued Exxon ever since. One of Exxon's supertankers, the *Valdez*, hit a rocky reef off Alaska's Prince William Sound spilling over ten million gallons of oil into the water, where it quickly spread along the coastline. Despite the enormity of the spill and the problems it caused, nearly a week went by before Exxon's CEO, Lawrence G. Rawl, met with reporters to discuss the event.

The captain of the vessel was known to have a drinking problem and had attended a detoxification program. Although he had been drinking earlier in the day of the event, there was no evidence that he was visibly drunk or even seriously impaired at the time the tanker left shore. Further, the course that was to be followed required a sharp right turn at a critical juncture, and his instructions clearly called for that turn. (Some experts feel that a series of earlier turns is the proper way to navigate the channel in question.) The captain did, however, leave the bridge to his third mate, who may

or may not have been qualified to navigate the waters where the accident occurred. The third mate claimed to have issued an order to turn but also claimed that the ship did not seem to respond. That lack of response may have been caused by the ship, the wind and water conditions, or slowness on the part of the helmsman to execute the order.

Although it was unclear who was at fault, nevertheless a major spill had occurred, and the CEO was slow to deal with the publicity surrounding it. That slow action caused the public to believe that Exxon was not accepting its responsibility to clean up the oil. Further, Rawl's initial statements blamed the U.S. Coast Guard and Alaskan officials for the delay in efforts to clean up the spill. Early public relations efforts followed Rawl's lead and were sketchy and not very informative. Then a top executive told a group of consumers that the public would pay for the cleanup in the form of higher prices for gasoline.

Exxon and its executives quickly became the target of jokes, calls for consumers to boy-

cott Exxon spread over radio talk shows, and some people cut up their credit cards and mailed them back to the company. At a stockholders' meeting in May of that year, Rawl fielded hundreds of questions about the company's handling not just of the spill but also of its public relations efforts. Some shareholders suggested write-in candidates like actor Robert Redford for chairman.

As the story unfolded, Exxon's responsibility and its role in the affair became less clear. Calm weather hindered initial chemical efforts to disperse the oil to such an extent that the Coast Guard was reluctant to approve further chemical applications. A conflict between Exxon and the Coast Guard ensued as to who, then, was responsible for the oil reaching beaches, where it is far more difficult to remove and far more damaging to wildlife. Amoco had used that argument successfully after an earlier spill to get most damage claims disallowed in court; hence, it was clearly a good legal stand for Exxon to take.

Exxon finally began to get control over publicity by refusing to

Luc Novovitch/Gamma Liaison

James D. Wilson/Woodfin Camp & Associates

discuss the blame for the spill and instead continually stressing that its attention and efforts needed to be on cleaning up rather than assigning blame. Although that approach seems to have worked in alleviating immediate public concern, and although Rawl had no

trouble being re-elected as chairman, there is a lingering caution in the public mind. Exxon does not appear to have suffered any lasting damage from this spill, but another incident could prove disastrous.

The Exxon oil spill off the coast of Alaska has raised many questions about managerial ethics and corporate responsibility to society. Lawrence Rawl, Exxon CEO, has been forced to defend his actions and those of his company in many different forums, including this 1989 press conference.

SOURCES: "Exxon Tries to Spread the Blame Around Even Before Valdez Claims Go to Trial," *The Wall Street Journal*, June 7, 1989, p. B8; "One Way to End a Career," *Newsweek*, May 29, 1989, p. 52; "Who's That Screaming at Exxon? Not the Environmentalists," *Business Week*, May 1, 1989, p. 31; Peter Nulty, "The Future of Big Oil," *Fortune*, May 8, 1989, pp. 46–49; "Public Angry at Slow Action on Oil Spill," *USA Today*, April 21, 1989, pp. 1B–2B.

The Prelude Case about Exxon clearly shows that ethics and social responsibility are important to business. If a large company does not handle ethical issues well or is not socially responsible, it may receive well-deserved criticism, but even companies that put out their best efforts can quickly become embroiled in an event that captures the public's attention. Response may be slow or fast, extensive or limited, effective or ineffective, and each of these may occur in ways the organization least expects. Some organizations know how to deal with ethical issues; others think they are responding effectively only to find that the public feels they are dragging their feet; still others, perhaps, respond only as far as necessary to stay within the law. Obviously ethics and social responsibility are important issues that every manager today must learn to deal with.

In addition to the Exxon oil spill incident, consider the following events, which have made headlines in recent years:

❑ Numerous charges have been leveled at members of Drexel Burnham Lambert, E. F. Hutton, and Dean Witter Reynolds for improper practices. At Dean Witter those charges even involved criminal action against one broker.
❑ Five key executives at Anheuser-Busch were fired because of alleged kickbacks from suppliers.
❑ General Electric was fined $1.04 million for defrauding the U.S. Air Force of $80,000.[1]

Each of these examples relates to a set of issues that are of considerable importance to managers in today's business world: ethics and social responsibility. Insider trading scandals, blatant disregard for environmental concerns, illegal business practices, and other scandals have brought these issues into the forefront of the American business consciousness. They are explored in detail in this chapter.

The chapter first examines the nature of ethics and then discusses managerial ethics and how organizations can manage their members' ethical behavior. It then looks at the nature of corporate social responsibility and approaches to it. After investigating areas of social responsibility, it concludes by examining the role of government in this field.

THE NATURE OF ETHICS

The Meaning of Ethics

❑ *Ethics* are those standards or morals a person sets for him- or herself regarding what is good and bad or right and wrong.

What are ethics? Ask any four experts and you'll probably get four different answers—you may even get more. For our purposes, let's define **ethics** as those standards or morals a person sets for himself or herself regarding what is good and bad or right and wrong.[2]

It is important to note the distinction between something that is ethical and something that is legal. The law defines various kinds of acts as acceptable or unacceptable. In contrast, ethics often go beyond the law and are based more on prevailing societal norms and expectations. Thus an action can be both legal and ethical, legal but unethical, or both illegal and unethical. There are differences of opinion as to whether an action can be ethical but illegal.

For example, suppose you are a manager for a large manufacturing company. Today you found a $100 bill on the floor and turned it in to the company lost-and-found department. This action is both legal and ethical. You also became aware that another manager is stealing company property for his own use, but you decided not to do anything about it. Although your action here is not illegal, it is probably unethical. The other manager's actions, though, are both unethical and illegal. Suppose you take $20 from petty cash to help a janitor who has no money to feed his family. Some would argue that this action, though illegal, is ethical. Clearly, then, the determination of ethical behavior is complex, and it is clouded by individual values, opinions, and logic.

The Formation of Ethics

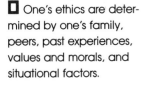 One's ethics are determined by one's family, peers, past experiences, values and morals, and situational factors.

Where do ethics come from? How are they formed? Exhibit 3.1 illustrates the most common factors that determine individual ethics.

FAMILY INFLUENCES   Family influences play a key role in determining an individual's beliefs as to what is and is not right. For example, a person who grows up in a setting where both parents are extremely ethical is likely to develop higher ethical standards than one who is not taught the importance of such behavior.

Exhibit 3.1 The Formation of Individual Ethics

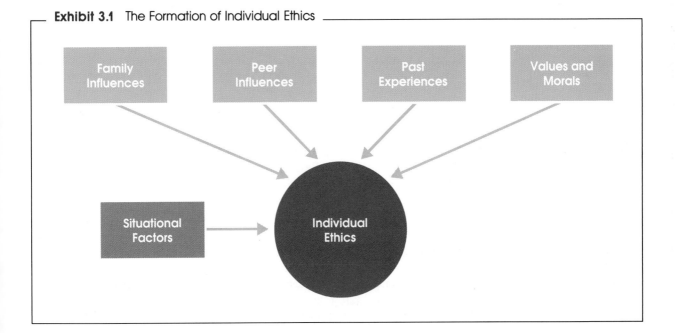

PEER INFLUENCES   Peer influences are also quite important in determining a person's ethics. Classmates and others in a person's social network can shape her ethics. Peer pressure, for instance, can help determine how much a person will engage in such questionable activities as shoplifting, experimenting with drugs, and so forth.

PAST EXPERIENCES   As a person grows, her past experiences can also play a role in determining the evolution of her standards. If she behaves unethically in a given situation and suffers negative consequences (feelings of guilt, getting caught), her behavior will probably be more ethical next time. Conversely, if her unethical behavior does not lead to feelings of guilt but instead leads to rewards, she may choose to behave the same way when she is next confronted with a similar situation.

VALUES AND MORALS   At a more general level, basic values and morals influence ethics. A person who is profoundly religious will almost certainly have strong feelings about what is right and wrong. Such beliefs will probably carry over to help shape his personal ethics as well.

SITUATIONAL FACTORS   Finally, situational factors are important. These are events that occur in an almost random way and that have the potential to determine behavior that may or may not be consistent with a person's ethics. For example, consider an employee who is very honest and hardworking. His wife loses her job, and the family begins to have trouble making ends meet. One day, when things look especially bad, he is offered an opportunity to make some extra money by selling a company secret to a competitor. His financial situation and his despair at seeing his family suffer might cause him to accept the unethical offer. This factor is situational because if his wife had not lost her job or if he had not been offered the opportunity to sell company secrets, he might well have remained a dedicated, honest, and loyal employee throughout his career.

LEARNING CHECK

You should now be able to define ethics and discuss their nature and how they are formed.

MANAGERIAL ETHICS

Managers of organizations are not robots. They are not programmed always to do the same thing, regardless of the circumstances. Indeed, because of the multitude of situations that confront managers and the ethical context of their jobs, ethics are one of the most important factors in their behavior.[3] Managerial ethics, then, refers to ethics applied to management.

Ethics and Management

☐ Many managers face *ethical dilemmas,* or two or more conflicting ethical issues.

Managers face ethical dilemmas almost every day. **Ethical dilemmas** occur when a manager is faced with two or more conflicting ethical issues. Table 3.1 highlights several common situations that require ethical decisions.

TABLE 3.1
The Ethical Dilemmas of
Management

Situations involving the . . .	May lead to ethical dilemmas regarding . . .
Relationship of the firm to the employee	Hiring and firing Wages and working conditions Privacy
Relationship of the employee to the firm	Conflicts of interest Secrecy and espionage Honesty and expense accounts
Relationship of the firm to the environment	Customers Competitors Stockholders Suppliers and dealers Unions Community

SOURCE: Adapted from Thomas M. Garrett and Richard J. Klonoski, *Business Ethics*, 2nd ed. (Englewood Cliffs, N.J.: Prentice-Hall, 1986), pp. viii–x.

RELATIONSHIP OF THE FIRM TO THE EMPLOYEE   The relationship of the firm to the employee involves the ways in which the organization chooses to treat its employees in different situations in which ethics can come into play. In the area of hiring and firing, for instance, managers must make ethical decisions regarding who is the most qualified, how to treat minorities, and so forth.

Wages and working conditions must also be considered. Managers must establish a pay level that will satisfy employees but that is not excessive. Similarly, the employer needs to provide a work environment that is relatively safe and free from hazards. A reasonable degree of job security is also something most people consider to be an ethical concern.

There are also ethical issues regarding the private lives of employees. Employees who have drinking or drug problems may be of concern to the organization, even if they are keeping their problems separate from the workplace. An area of related interest is garnishment of wages, which happens when a creditor forces the organization to pay a portion of an employee's wages toward that employee's debts.

RELATIONSHIP OF THE EMPLOYEE TO THE FIRM   Other issues relate to the relationship of the employee to the firm. The focus here is how the individual behaves vis-à-vis the organization.

Conflicts of interest are one major consideration. **A conflict of interest** exists when an employee is put into a situation in which his decisions may be compromised because of competing loyalties. Suppose a purchasing manager accepts a free vacation from a major equipment supplier. The next time the company needs to buy a new piece of equipment, the manager may feel obligated to give the contract to that supplier. Wal-Mart feels so strongly about

□ In a *conflict of interest*, an employee is put into a situation in which his decisions may be compromised because of competing loyalties.

this that it will not allow a merchandise buyer to accept meals or gifts from sales representatives.[4] Moonlighting is also an issue: when an employee has another job in addition to her primary one, fatigue may hinder her performance in both jobs.

Secrecy and espionage are also valid considerations. For example, an employee of a computer firm might have plenty of opportunities to sell information about new products to other companies.

Finally, basic issues such as stealing and dishonest handling of expense accounts are relevant. When an employee takes home a pad of paper from the office or makes a long-distance call on the company telephone to an old friend or family member, he is technically stealing. Likewise, a manager who has lunch with a friend and writes it off on her expense account is stealing.

RELATIONSHIP OF THE FIRM TO THE ENVIRONMENT   There are also broad ethical considerations in how the organization interacts with various elements of its environment. A critical component of this relationship is the customer. Managers must contend with a number of issues involving customers, answering such questions as What should we say when we advertise? What should our warranty be? How should we price our products? and How concerned should we be with product safety?[5]

Relations with competitors are also important. Price cutting and unfair competition can drive smaller firms out of business. Price fixing is illegal, however, and companies often face considerable pressure to work illegally with competitors to set prices and minimize price competition. A few years ago, for instance, American Airlines was charged with suggesting to Braniff that each airline should raise some of its fares to and from Dallas. At the time, price cutting had lowered fares to the point where both airlines were losing money, but neither was willing to take the initial step to raise fares to a profitable level.[6]

Relations with stockholders are obviously crucial. Managers have the responsibility of working in stockholders' best interests and of reporting appropriate information to them on a timely basis. Similarly, questions about the appropriate levels of executive compensation and benefits affect stockholders.

Large companies with considerable power over their suppliers and dealers are often in situations in which ethical dilemmas arise. For example, if Chrysler does not keep its dealers properly informed about upcoming model changes, price adjustments, and so forth, the dealers can become resentful. However, too much information might leak into competitors' hands.

Relations with unions also involve ethical issues. If a firm divulges too much information about its profitability, the union might increase its wage demands. Too little disclosure, however, is not conducive to ethical bargaining.

A last factor is the community and surrounding environment. In recent years there has been a trend for communities that are hungry for industry to offer concessions on taxes and utilities, free land, and other incentives. When a company plays competing communities against one another, it may be violating ethical norms. Where building business networks is critical, managers may be tempted to grant favors or provide inside information to establish those

THE WORLD OF MANAGEMENT

In Japan Politics Means Money

Japan's political system rests on money. Japanese politicians are invited to about fifty weddings each month and are expected to provide a cash gift at each of them, and the going rate in 1989 was $150 each. Personal service to the voters is also expected; to provide it members of Parliament may spend around $900,000 per year for their staffs. Many other demands involve the expenditure of money. Yet members of Parliament receive only $150,000 a year in salary and expenses. The rest of the money comes from supporters, many of whom are businesses.

This expectation for gifts and service on the part of constituents, coupled with the low salary and expense monies provided, means that businesses provide large sums of money to politicians. This, then, gives those businesses the opportunity to extract favors, including favors that may be against the law, as one recent scandal shows.

In June 1988 a newspaper published a story alleging that the deputy mayor of a major city took bribes from Tokyo's Recruit Company, a rapidly growing conglomerate. In July the paper accused the prime minister, Noboru Takeshita, and the former prime minister of taking bribes. In December the finance minister admitted he profited from Recruit and resigned. In February 1989, the former chairman of Recruit and three other top executives were arrested for violating laws and paying bribes. In March the former chairman of Nippon Telegraph & Telephone was arrested on charges of accepting a bribe. On April 11, Takeshita apologized to Parliament and admitted to having received donations of about $1 million from Recruit, which, although legal, was an unusually large amount. Only days later it was disclosed that Takeshita had failed to mention a loan of about $380,000 from Recruit in explaining his involvement with the firm. Again, it was a legal transaction, but his failure to mention it further eroded his credibility. On April 25, Takeshita resigned.

The prosecutor investigating the Recruit scandal worked throughout 1989, and 1990 saw more arrests and resignations. The Japanese government wrestled with the worst scandal in its history at a time of increasing hostility in international competition.

SOURCES: "Takeshita Resignation Is Likely to Weaken Japan's Government," *The Wall Street Journal*, April 26, 1989, pp. A1, A10; "Sinking in a Sea of Yen," *Newsweek*, April 24, 1989, pp. 49–50; "The Dark Side of Japan Inc.," *Newsweek*, January 9, 1989, p. 41.

connections.[7] As can be seen in *Management Today: The World of Management*, this problem has caused a tremendous scandal recently in Japan. Other issues of particular interest might be pollution and other environmental impacts, participation in United Way activities, and so forth.

The Ethical Context of Management

It is obvious from this discussion so far that management activities occur within an ethical context. The key dimensions of this context are illustrated in Exhibit 3.2.[8]

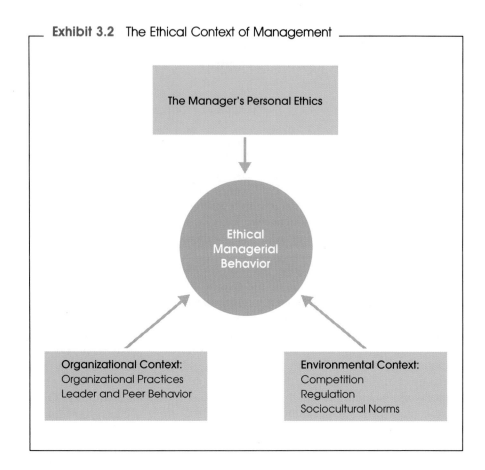

Exhibit 3.2   The Ethical Context of Management

The Manager's Personal Ethics

Ethical Managerial Behavior

Organizational Context:
Organizational Practices
Leader and Peer Behavior

Environmental Context:
Competition
Regulation
Sociocultural Norms

First, the manager's **personal ethics,** as explored earlier in this chapter, are a major ingredient of her ethical context. Her own values, predilections about right and wrong, and sense of justice and fairness all come into play. Her susceptibility to situational factors is also relevant.

Second, the specific **organizational context** is important to the ethical managerial context. Of special interest are organizational practices and the behavior of leaders and peers.

Organizational practices are ways in which the organization deals with the ethical situations it encounters. Some organizations reward people who report improprieties and punish those guilty of committing them. Others tend to punish those who make misdeeds public and do little or nothing to the guilty parties.[9] For instance, a few years ago a manager at Citibank reported to his superiors that one division of the bank was engaging in illegal activities to increase its profits. He was fired.[10]

The behavior of leaders and peers can be a big influence on the individual manager's ethical context. If those surrounding a manager routinely engage in unethical behavior, he is likely either to start such practices himself or to leave the organization.

The **environmental context** is the third vital factor. Competition, as we have seen, is a major force to consider. When competition is keen, there is strong pressure to resort to whatever means are available to get an advantage.

Regulation by the government also determines the ethical context. Too much regulation can handcuff the manager so much that she is forced to bend the rules or the law to compete. By the same token, too little regulation can provide too many opportunities to engage in questionable ethical practices.

LEARNING CHECK

You should now be able to describe the relationship between ethics and management, particularly the ethical context of management.

The norms of the sociocultural environment make up the last major part of the ethical context of management. In some countries bribes, price gouging, and industrial espionage are normal business practices. In other countries managers are expected to follow accepted ethical behavior. Some people believe that ethical standards in the United States have slipped during the past few years.[11]

MANAGING ETHICS

Because managers have become increasingly aware of the importance of ethics, they have also taken a greater interest in how they and their organizations should attempt to manage this area. In fact, a retired executive recently gave $30 million to the Harvard Business School to fund the teaching of ethics.[12] Today the two most common approaches to the management of ethics are through top-management support and formal codes of conduct.

Top-Management Support

For organizations to develop and maintain a culture in which ethical managerial behavior can thrive, top management must support such behavior. There are several things that executives can do to demonstrate such support.

First, they can adhere to ethical standards themselves. This is probably the most important thing that can be done to promote ethical behavior throughout the organization. If middle and lower-level managers see top managers behaving unethically, they are likely to follow suit.

Another important action is to provide and encourage training in ethics. Union Carbide set up training sessions on ethics after the Bhopal tragedy, Boeing has a program to "sensitize" employees to ethical conflicts, the Sun Company supplements a compliance questionnaire with talks by its corporate counsel, and at Hercules managers must sign forms saying that they have abided by policy.[13] In addition, General Dynamics, McDonnell Douglas, Chemical Bank, and American Can Company have initiated ethics training for their employees.[14]

Codes of Conduct

☐ Company *codes of conduct* emphasize the importance of ethical behavior in all activities.

Another important step in the management of ethics is establishing **codes of conduct,** which usually state the importance of following ethical business practices in all areas of the organization's activities. These codes are symbolic but meaningful statements of the company's concern.

Professional groups such as the American Psychological Association and the American Management Association have long had such codes for their members. More and more often, however, individual companies are developing their own codes of ethical conduct. One recent survey found that 75 percent of the United States's twelve hundred largest companies had formal ethics codes such as Johnson & Johnson's shown in Exhibit 3.3. [15]

THE NATURE OF SOCIAL RESPONSIBILITY

☐ Social responsibility refers to the obligations of an organization to protect and/or enhance society.

Whereas ethical behavior is a phenomenon primarily at the individual level, social responsibility applies more to the organizational level. **Social responsibility** refers to the obligations of the organization to protect and/or enhance the society in which it functions. [16] As we will see, however, people hold different opinions as to its real nature.

Historical Development

Over the years there have been many different views of social responsibility. [17] One writer has noted that the historical development of these views has involved three identifiable crises in America. [18]

The first crisis occurred between 1860 and 1890. During this era the so-called captains of industry, such as Andrew Carnegie, John D. Rockefeller, J. P. Morgan, Cornelius Vanderbilt, and others, were creating the giant steel, oil, banking, and railroad corporations that came to dominate American industry. In contrast to earlier organizations, these mammoth entities held enormous power in our emerging industrial society. Abuses of this power—labor lockouts, kickbacks, discriminatory pricing, and predatory business practices—caused both a public outcry and governmental action, and several laws were passed to regulate the way in which business was carried out. These early laws indicated for the first time the interdependence of business, government, and the general public. [19]

The second crisis took place within the narrower time span of the few years following the stock market crash of 1929. Mergers and general business growth had continued, and by the 1920s big business had truly come to dominate the American economy. Because of this, most Americans blamed large corporations for the Great Depression, and President Roosevelt and other supporters of the New Deal succeeded in passing more legislation targeted at them. In particular, laws from this era specifically delineated the social responsibilities of businesses and reinforced the importance of fairness and ethical practices at all levels.

The third crisis took place during the 1960s and early 1970s, a period characterized by a great deal of social unrest and public awareness. Young people

—— **Exhibit 3.3**   Johnson & Johnson's Code of Ethical Conduct ——————

Our Credo

We believe our first responsibility is to the doctors, nurses and patients,
to mothers and fathers and all others who use our products and services.
In meeting their needs everything we do must be of high quality.
We must constantly strive to reduce our costs
in order to maintain reasonable prices.
Customers' orders must be serviced promptly and accurately.
Our suppliers and distributors must have an opportunity
to make a fair profit.

We are responsible to our employees,
the men and women who work with us throughout the world.
Everyone must be considered as an individual.
We must respect their dignity and recognize their merit.
They must have a sense of security in their jobs.
Compensation must be fair and adequate,
and working conditions clean, orderly and safe.
We must be mindful of ways to help our employees fulfill
their family responsibilities.
Employees must feel free to make suggestions and complaints.
There must be equal opportunity for employment, development
and advancement for those qualified.
We must provide competent management,
and their actions must be just and ethical.

We are responsible to the communities in which we live and work
and to the world community as well.
We must be good citizens — support good works and charities
and bear our fair share of taxes.
We must encourage civic improvements and better health and education.
We must maintain in good order
the property we are privileged to use,
protecting the environment and natural resources.

Our final responsibility is to our stockholders.
Business must make a sound profit.
We must experiment with new ideas.
Research must be carried on, innovative programs developed
and mistakes paid for.
New equipment must be purchased, new facilities provided
and new products launched.
Reserves must be created to provide for adverse times.
When we operate according to these principles,
the stockholders should realize a fair return.

Johnson & Johnson

Used with permission of Johnson & Johnson.

lashed out at the government, big business, and other dimensions of what they called the Establishment. There were campus sit-ins, business boycotts and bombings, and protest marches about dozens of social causes. Government began to take a greater role in business, getting involved in everything from regulations for packaging over-the-counter drugs to consumer warnings on cigarettes, and business tried to respond by espousing a greater commitment to benefiting society. The effects of this crisis are still being felt today.

PRELUDE CASE UPDATE

Environmental crises such as the *Valdez* oil spill discussed in the Prelude Case may well lead to yet another crisis that will be seen as a further development in views regarding business's social responsibility. The way management handles such events as they occur will greatly influence society's reaction. If the events are handled promptly with little environmental impact, the public's view of business's social responsibility is likely to be essentially unchanged. However, if delays in response occur and/or the impact is severely negative, then the public view will likely move toward governmental regulation and control.

Arguments About Social Responsibility

As we might infer from this history, the debate about the proper role of business organizations in society is far from over. In fact, today there are several factors that argue against social responsibility and several others that argue for a high level of social responsibility. The most prominent of these are summarized in Table 3.2.[20]

□ Critics argue that social responsibility can lead to decreased profits, increased power, lack of accountability, inexpert handling of social problems, and conflicts of interest.

ARGUMENTS AGAINST SOCIAL RESPONSIBILITY   One major argument against social responsibility is that it decreases corporate profits. When Exxon gives thousands of dollars to support the arts, for instance, the money is actually being taken out of the pockets of stockholders. Economists like Milton Friedman argue that such practices run counter to the basic premises underlying American capitalism.[21] This is an economic view that tends to be narrow, focuses on the short term, and assumes competitive markets with little impact on one another.

Another argument against social responsibility is that it gives big business even more power, destroying the checks and balances among the government, business, and the general public. Increased activities of a socially responsible nature might tip the scales in favor of business.

Accountability is also an issue. Ford can use its money in any way it wants, so the company is not accountable for the results of its activities. The PTL Ministry claimed it was collecting money to help the poor. In reality, however, the money was being used, in a large part, to provide church officials with a lavish lifestyle.

Some people also argue that business organizations have no expertise in the area of social responsibility. Therefore, it would be better to leave such activities in the hands of people more skilled in social programs, such as teachers, social workers, and art administrators, for instance.

Finally, some critics of social responsibility argue that such activities lead to conflicts of interest. Suppose that Du Pont was contemplating a donation of $100,000 to charity. If one of its managers learned that a member of Congress who favored a certain charity was working on legislation affecting the chemical

TABLE 3.2
Arguments For and
Against Social
Responsibility

For	Against
1. Like individuals, corporations are citizens.	1. Social responsibility will decrease profits, thus contradicting the real reason for corporations' existence.
2. Since business creates some problems, it should help solve them.	2. Social responsibility gives corporations too much power.
3. Organizations have ample resources to help society.	3. Corporations are not accountable for the results of their actions.
4. Business, government, and the general public are partners in our society.	4. Corporations may lack the expertise to be socially responsible.
5. Arguments against social responsibility can be logically refuted.	5. Corporations may have conflicts of interest in how they spend their money.

industry, this knowledge, theoretically, could influence the company's decision about where to spend the money.

☐ Proponents counter that business's social responsibility derives from its power and resources and its position as a citizen in partnership with government and the public.

ARGUMENTS FOR SOCIAL RESPONSIBILITY   Several compelling arguments can also be made in favor of social responsibility. These views tend to be broader and have a longer time perspective. One argument here is that corporations are citizens, in the same way that individuals are. As such, they have the same responsibilities as individual citizens to improve society as a whole.

Proponents of social responsibility also argue that the great power enjoyed by business carries with it great responsibility. In particular, business has the power to produce products, set prices, influence consumer preferences, pay employees, and so forth. Further, since business creates some problems (water and air pollution, for example), it can be argued that business should help solve them. Social responsibility can be seen as an important way to limit or constrain the power of business.

It can also be argued that the vast resources available to companies can be used most effectively by being returned to society, at least in part. By and large, the business sector is in at least as good a position as the government to return wealth to its users in some way.

The idea of partnership is also important. If indeed business, government, and the public are partners in our society, each must attempt to protect, maintain, and nourish that society.

Last, simple arguments of logic can be used to defend social responsibility. In particular, logic can be used to refute each of the arguments against social responsibility. For example, it can be argued that existing laws sufficiently constrain corporate power so that socially responsible corporate behavior provides business with no additional power. With all such arguments out of the way, social responsibility seems quite desirable.

All these arguments seem to revolve around numerous complicated questions. Who is the beneficiary and who pays the costs (employees, stockholders,

Proponents of social responsibility often argue that businesses have the same citizenship obligations as individuals and that the enormous power and resources of business should be partially directed at improving society in general. Noted consumer activist Ralph Nader, shown here with members of interest groups he formed or runs, has argued for this position on a number of different occasions.

LEARNING CHECK

You should now be able to define social responsibility and discuss arguments both for and against it.

customers, suppliers, the general public)? Should organizations be proactive, initiating action, or reactive, waiting to be pushed into action? What are a business's rights, and what are its privileges? Should organizations do only what is legally required, or should they also do what is morally obligated?

APPROACHES TO SOCIAL RESPONSIBILITY

Given the persuasive arguments both for and against social responsibility, it comes as no surprise that businesses take dramatically different views of how they should behave. In general, there are three basic approaches that characterize business postures.[22] These are summarized in Exhibit 3.4.

Social Obligation

☐ *Social obligation* refers to meeting economic and legal responsibilities but not going beyond them.

The **social obligation** view is most consistent with the argument that any business activity that is not directly aimed at profits is inadvisable. The company that takes this approach is willing to meet its social obligations as mandated by societal norms and government regulation, but it is not willing to do more. Thus it meets its economic and legal responsibilities but does not go beyond them.

Tobacco companies such as Philip Morris have reduced their advertising in the United States and have put consumer warnings on every package of cigarettes they sell. However, they did not choose to take these measures; they were forced to by government regulation. In other parts of the world where such regulation is not in force, they are still heavily promoting their products. Hence, although they are doing nothing illegal, they are following the letter of the law and not its spirit.[23]

Another recent example involves McDonald's, which in 1987 began a $20 million advertising campaign designed to improve the nutritional image of its products. Critics complained that the ads were deceptive in that they ignored several unpleasant nutritional components while truthfully listing the positive elements of the food. If true, such claims suggest that McDonald's takes a social obligation approach, at least in this instance. (As we will see, McDonald's has taken a different stand in other cases.)[24]

Social Reaction

☐ *Social reaction* goes beyond social obligation by also responding to appropriate societal requests.

The firm using a **social reaction** approach is one that meets its social obligations but is also willing to react to appropriate societal requests and demands. That is, the company will make limited and specific positive contributions to social welfare.

Exhibit 3.4 Approaches to Social Responsibility

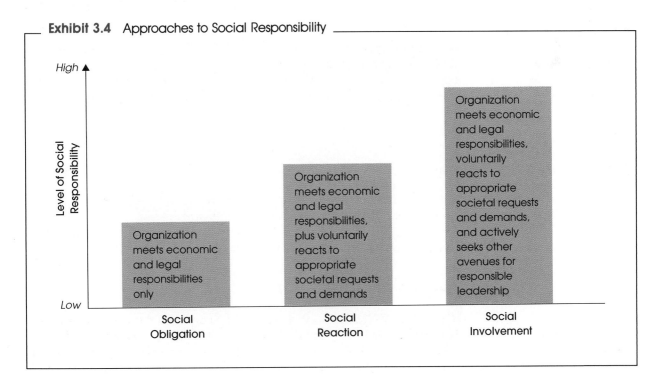

For example, many large corporations such as Exxon and IBM routinely match employee contributions to worthwhile charitable causes with contributions of their own. These actions fall under the heading of social reaction. So do the actions of the company that agrees to help local charities and civic organizations by providing free meeting space or donating funds to support Little League baseball teams. The key point to note is *reaction:* the normal pattern is for the civic group to knock on the company's door and ask for help, which the firm then agrees to give.

PRELUDE CASE UPDATE

Exxon's handling of the *Valdez* oil spill is clearly a further example of the social reaction approach to social responsibility. Exxon reacted to public expressions of indignation and concern rather than taking the initiative on its own. The somewhat lengthy delay between the event and Exxon's CEO's public response is also consistent with the social reaction approach.

◻ *Social involvement* goes beyond obligations and requests and actively seeks ways to benefit society.

Social Involvement

The firm using the **social involvement** approach to social responsibility fulfills its obligations and responds to requests, just as the other two types of

The social involvement approach to social responsibility involves actively seeking ways to make a contribution to society. Many businesses are focusing some of these efforts on enhancing the quality of American schools. For example, Arco Oil & Gas Company sponsors a program sending employees into public school classrooms to tutor minority students.

© 1989, Steve Smith

SMALL BUSINESS AND ENTREPRENEURSHIP

New Companies Clean Up

One result of contemporary business is the creation of wastes that are not easily disposed of. Some of these wastes are toxic. Whereas some companies act very responsibly and take care of their wastes, others do not. Part of the problem is that some of these companies do not know how to handle waste products. To Alan McKim, that represented an entrepreneurial challenge and opportunity.

Noting that American business generates hundreds of tons of toxic waste every year, McKim decided to go into the business of cleaning up after others. In the early 1980s, he borrowed $13,000 from friends, bought a specially equipped truck, and opened a waste-cleanup company called Clean Harbors, Inc.,

located in Massachusetts. Since that time, Clean Harbors has grown rapidly. It now has a fleet of over two hundred trucks and its annual revenues exceed $100 million.

Numbers of similar firms have sprung up across the country. The largest such firms are listed on the New York Stock Exchange and have annual profits as great as Clean Harbors' total sales. The toxic waste disposal industry presents many opportunities for entrepreneurs, whether in large companies or small ones. Those who have recognized and taken advantage of those opportunities have sometimes benefited enormously.

SOURCES: D. A. Zwicker, "The Solution to Pollution," *The Lamp,* Summer 1989, p. 24; "Environment: Hazards Such as Toxic Waste Spark a Potent Grass-Roots Movement," *Business Week,* September 25, 1989, p. 154; "The Big Haul in Toxic Waste," *Newsweek,* October 3, 1988, pp. 38–39; "Dirty Job, Sweet Profits," *U.S. News & World Report,* November 21, 1988, p. 54.

---

companies do. In addition, however, it actively seeks other ways in which to help.

One example of the social involvement view is provided by McDonald's, which has established Ronald McDonald houses to help the families of sick children. This is clearly above and beyond the call of corporate duty. Another example is the recent trend toward corporate support of the arts. Some corporations, such as Sears and General Electric, have taken an active role in supporting artists and cultural performers. Such actions may well lead to higher profits, but this is by no means guaranteed, and the corporate motive appears to be primarily altruistic. Another example would be that of Land's End, a mail-order house that some business analysts might think is responsive to customers to an unnecessary degree.[25] Yet another example would be the Turner Broadcasting System cartoons to make socially responsible points. *Captain Planet* is a science fiction cartoon in which the superhero battles environmental villains.[26] And some firms move in to fill the gap left when other companies do not act in a completely responsible way. *Management Today: Small Business and Entrepreneurship* describes just such a firm.

> **LEARNING CHECK**
>
> You should now be able to discuss approaches to social responsibility.

TABLE 3.3 Areas of Social Responsibility

General Areas	Specific Concerns
Ecology and environmental quality	Cleanup of existing pollution Design of processes to prevent pollution Aesthetic improvements Noise control Dispersion of industry Control of land use Required recycling
Consumerism	Truth in lending, in advertising, and in all business activities Product warranty and service Control of harmful products
Community needs	Use of business expertise in community problems Reduction of business's role in community power activities Aid with health-care facilities Aid with urban renewal
Governmental relations	Restrictions on lobbying Control of business political action Extensive new regulation of business Restrictions on international operations
Business giving	Financial support for artistic activities Gifts to education Financial support for assorted charities
Minorities and disadvantaged persons	Training of hard-core unemployed Equal employment opportunity and quotas for minority employment Operation of programs for alcoholics and drug addicts Employment of persons with prison records Building of plants and offices in minority areas Purchasing from minority businesses Retraining of workers displaced by technology
Labor relations	Improvement of occupational health and safety Prohibition of "export of jobs" through operations in nations with low labor costs Provision of day-care centers for children of working mothers Expansion of employee rights Control of pensions, especially vesting of pension rights Impatience with authoritarian structures; demand for participation
Stockholder relations	Opening of boards of directors to public members representing various interest groups Prohibition of operations in nations with "racist" or "colonial" governments Improvement of financial disclosure Disclosure of activities affecting the environment and social issues
Economic activities	Control of conglomerates Breakup of giant industry Restriction of patent use

SOURCE: From Keith Davis and Robert L. Blomstrom, *Business and Society: Environment and Responsibility*, 3rd ed., (New York: McGraw-Hill, 1975). Reproduced with permission of McGraw-Hill, Inc.

AREAS OF SOCIAL RESPONSIBILITY

Assuming that an organization wants to be at least modestly active in taking social responsibility, where does it turn? How does it spend its efforts and its money? Table 3.3 summarizes some of the more common areas of activity.[27]

As we can see, numerous areas of social responsibility are available. For instance, in the area of business giving, a company can offer financial support to the arts, provide gifts to education, and contribute to charitable causes. Most organizations that want to be socially responsible select a set of activities to pursue; that is, they are probably active in more than one narrow area but not in all areas. There are those, however, who would argue that all organizations should be more socially responsible to their employees, particularly women and racial minorities, to ensure that not only are laws complied with but also that moral obligations are met. Companies like 3M and Golden West Financial are working hard to meet obligations to minorities.[28]

LEARNING CHECK

You should now be able to identify the general areas of social responsibility.

THE GOVERNMENT AND SOCIAL RESPONSIBILITY

A final area of significance is the link between the government and social responsibility. Generally, the government is actively working to regulate and control business while business is attempting to influence the government, as summarized in Table 3.4.

Government Regulation of Business

Since the crisis of the late 1800s, already discussed, the government of the United States has taken an active role in the regulation of business. Much of **government regulation** has been concerned with enhancing the social responsiveness and awareness of business and with protecting the best interests of society from abuse by big business.

□ *Government regulation* is concerned with enhancing business's social responsiveness and awareness and with protecting the best interests of society.

Government regulation has generally focused on four basic areas. First, the government has attempted to ensure **fair labor practices** by passing legislation regarding hiring wages, union relations, and so forth. Second, it has worked for **environmental protection** from pollution by business as well as other organizations. Third, **consumer protection** has theoretically been achieved by numerous laws dealing with truth in advertising, pricing, and warranties. Fourth, a set of regulations has been developed to **guarantee the safety and health** of both employees and consumers.

In general, the enforcement of these regulations has been assigned to several different and sometimes conflicting governmental agencies. Businesses today must contend with the Occupational Safety and Health Administration

TABLE 3.4
The Business-Government
Relationship

Government Regulation of Business	Business Influence on Government
1. Ensures fair labor practices 2. Protects the environment 3. Protects consumers 4. Guarantees safety and health	1. Gains favorable legislation and lessened scrutiny through personal contacts 2. Enchances the company image to government officials and the general public 3. Influences legislation by using lobbyists 4. Aids political candidates through donations

(OSHA), the Environmental Protection Agency, the Fair Labor Standards Board, the Equal Employment Opportunity Commission, the Federal Trade Commission, and the Food and Drug Administration.[29]

Critics argue that this level of regulation is excessive and does more harm than good. For example, Goodyear Tire & Rubber at one time generated 345,000 pages of computer reports to comply with one new OSHA regulation. Moreover, the company reported that it spent over $35 million each year to comply with federal regulations and that it took thirty-four employee-years just to fill out the necessary forms.[30] OSHA seems to be responding to criticisms, however, and advocates of government regulation argue that we would all be subjected to business abuses without it.[31]

Business Influence on Government

Just as the government regulates business, so does business attempt to influence the government. Such efforts, of course, must be relatively subtle and are often quite indirect. In general, there are four common approaches businesses use to influence government.

First, company managers try to develop personal contacts with influential government leaders, because such contacts can lead to favorable legislation and lessened scrutiny from the government. Second, many companies, especially large ones, employ public relations firms to enhance their image with government officials and the general public.

□ A *lobbyist* is a person who works in a seat of government specifically to influence the legislators.

Third, many businesses employ lobbyists. A **lobbyist** is someone based in a seat of government—either Washington or a state capital—for the express purpose of influencing the legislative body. A lobbyist for the oil industry, for example, might work to persuade key congressional leaders to vote for an upcoming bill that would result in increases in oil prices.

□ *Political action committees* solicit funds from organizations and then make contributions to political candidates in order to gain their favor.

Finally, some organizations make direct contributions to political candidates. Such contributions are heavily restricted and can be made only under certain circumstances. In recent years, organizations have started creating **political action committees,** or **PACs,** that solicit money from a variety of organizations and then make contributions to several candidates for office in order to gain their favor. For example, between 1987 and 1988 Federal Express's political action committee Fepac contributed over $200,000 to Democratic campaigns. In 1988, as the congressional session ended, Democratic sponsors pushed a controversial bill through both the House and the Senate that allowed certain tax benefits for Federal Express employees.[32]

These days there is no apparent widespread opposition to business influence on government, but there have been times when things have gone too far. Some financial contributions have been so large that they almost constituted a direct bribe, and some have been made on the condition that the candidate would take a certain position on a specific issue. Clearly, such practices are unethical and violate all premises of social responsibility. In all likelihood business and government will continue to work hard to influence one another legally and publicly, but occasional abuses will probably still surface from time to time.

LEARNING CHECK

You should now be able to discuss the role of government in business's social responsibility.

Chapter Summary

Ethics are the standards or morals a person sets for himself or herself about what is good and bad or right and wrong behavior. Ethics are formed by a variety of factors: family influences, peer influences, past experiences, values and morals, and situational factors.

Managers face ethical dilemmas or conflicts every day. These dilemmas occur in the relationship of the firm to the employee, the relationship of the employee to the firm, and the relationship of the firm to the environment. The key dimensions of the ethical context of management are personal ethics, the organizational context, and the environmental context.

Managers must understand ethics and know how their organizations should attempt to manage them. For organizations to develop and maintain cultures that lead to ethical managerial behavior, it is essential for top management to support such behavior. In addition, the organization can develop a code of conduct, which serves as a guide to managers and a reminder of the importance of ethical behavior to the organization.

Social responsibility is the obligations of the organization to protect and/or enhance the society in which it functions. There are several arguments both for and against social responsibility.

There are three basic approaches to social responsibility: Social obligation, social reaction, and social involvement. Social obligation means doing only what is legal and economical. Social reaction refers to doing what is legal and economical but also voluntarily reacting to some demands. Social involvement means doing both of these plus actively seeking other ways of benefiting society.

Areas of social responsibility include ecology and environmental quality, consumerism, community needs, government relations, business giving, minorities and disadvantaged people, labor relations, stockholder relations, and economic activities.

Government regulates and controls business. Government regulation has generally focused on four areas: ensuring fair labor practices, protecting our environment, protecting consumers, and guaranteeing the health and safety of employees and customers. Critics feel that the burden of regulation is too great; proponents of regulation feel it is the lesser of two evils.

Business also tries to influence government in various ways. Executives and their firms contribute to political campaigns and maintain contacts with influential government leaders. Public relations departments and/or firms are used to enhance the image of companies and lobbyists are used to influence legislation more directly. These attempts to influence government do not appear to be generating widespread negative reaction in the general public, so they are likely to continue in the future, even though abuses occasionally are made public.

The Manager's Vocabulary

ethics	social involvement
ethical dilemmas	government regulation
conflict of interest	fair labor practices
personal ethics	environmental protection
organizational context	consumer protection
environmental context	safety and health
codes of conduct	guarantees
social responsibility	lobbyist
social obligation	political action
social reaction	committees (PACs)

Prelude Case Wrap-Up

Our Prelude Case for this chapter describes a major social responsibility issue for Exxon. In discussing the event and how it was handled some months later, CEO Rawl indicated that the captain of the ship should not have been allowed back on a ship the first time he had a drink after having attended Exxon's detoxification program. Further, Rawl felt that he should have made a public appearance sooner than he did. However, he continued to stress that the effort should be on repair and prevention rather than on assigning blame.

Surprisingly, environmental groups seemed to use the event not so much to criticize Exxon as to try to convince the public to use less oil. Avoiding the issue of who was to blame in the particular situation, the Sierra Club, Greenpeace U.S.A., and the Environmental Defense Fund argued that the problem is not Exxon but rather that our country uses too much oil. This lack of criticism from major environmental groups was clearly appreciated by Exxon executives and helped them diffuse adverse public reaction.

A long-term concern from the *Valdez* incident revolves around the future of oil exploration and development along the shores of the United States. Stiffer legislation and toughening public opinion coupled with continued high usage of oil will mean that the United States will become highly dependent on imported supplies. Such dependence can lead to shortages of supply with resulting lines at gasoline stations and extremely high prices, which would aggravate inflation. Indeed, it was exactly those phenomena

that led to the exploration and development of our oil reserves in Alaska in the first place.

Prelude Case Questions

1. What do you think was the extent of Exxon's responsibility in the oil spill? Why? Defend your response against alternatives.
2. Go to the library and see if you can locate material explaining what has finally transpired in legal actions resulting from the *Valdez* oil spill.
3. What might Exxon have done before and after the incident to have more effectively handled the situation?
4. Discuss the pros and cons of using less oil in this country. Give details to support each argument.

Discussion Questions

Review Questions

1. What are the three general types of situations in which ethics are important to managers? What are the key dimensions of the manager's ethical context?
2. How can ethics be managed by organizations?
3. What is meant by social responsibility? What are the arguments for and against it?
4. What general approaches to social responsibility do organizations take?
5. What is the government's role with regard to business's social responsibility? Why has it assumed that role? How does business influence government?

Analysis Questions

1. Make a list of five ways in which you feel it is ethical for students to behave. Then list five that you feel are unethical. What are the strongest influences on your feelings about what is ethical and unethical student behavior?
2. Identify an action that is both legal and ethical. Legal but unethical. Illegal but ethical. Both illegal and unethical.
3. How useful are codes of conduct or codes of ethics to business firms? Explain your response.
4. The proponents of social responsibility claim that the arguments against responsibility are flawed. Study those arguments and explain how each

might be flawed. Give details to support your claim.

5. Which area of social responsibility do you feel is most in need of action? Which is least in need of action? Why?

Application Questions and Exercises

1. Obtain codes of conduct from several professional associations (for medical practitioners, lawyers, accountants, and so forth) and compare them. What similarities and differences can you note?

2. Go to the library and identify several PACs from the last presidential election. What companies participated in them? What particular influence did they seek? How effective was each of the PACs?

3. Interview a local businessperson to obtain her or his views on social responsibility. What actions, if any, has this person taken? What were her or his motivations?

4. Select one area of social responsibility and try to obtain from published sources or directly from companies examples of companies that are exemplars in that area.

5. Interview a local government official to obtain his or her views on the government regulation of business at the local level. Zoning, sign ordinances, pollution, hours of operation, noise, traffic flows, and other issues might be used to stimulate the conversation. Why might this official feel the way he or she does?

ENHANCEMENT CASE

ASHLAND SPILLS

On Sunday, January 3, 1988, John R. Hall, the CEO of Ashland Oil Inc., the Ashland, Kentucky, oil refiner, received a phone call. A fuel oil tank belonging to an Ashland Oil subsidiary, Ashland Petroleum Company in Floresse, Pennsylvania, had ruptured. Over one million gallons of diesel fuel spilled into the Monongahela River. Hall was told that the reason for the rupture was unknown and that the spill could be relatively easily contained. Acting on the basis of that information, he elected not to visit the site or make a public statement, but he dispatched an emergency management team to handle the situation while he monitored events.

During the course of business on Monday, it became apparent to Hall that he had been given incorrect and incomplete information. The spill was not from a new tank, as he had been led to believe, but rather from a reconstructed tank made of forty-year-old steel and for which Ashland did not have proper permits. Further, the tank had not been tested as completely as it should have been. To make matters worse, the river current was so swift that the spill was not being contained and was threatening the water supply of 750,000 Pennsylvania residents. Local water companies and other public officials down-

stream from the spill were phoning Ashland demanding action. Things seemed to be getting out of hand.

On Tuesday Hall flew to Pittsburgh. First, he visited the spill site at Jefferson Borough, outside Pittsburgh. Then he held a press conference. Bothered by his company's operating procedures, he felt that the only way to gain control of the emotional situation was to be frank and honest. He admitted that Ashland did not have a written permit for the tank but promised to do everything he could to have the spill cleaned up.

Hall remained in the Pittsburgh area for two more days. During that time, he met with government officials, talked with the governors of Ohio and West Virginia, where the spill was headed, and held meetings with numerous local newspaper editors. As the crisis lessened, he returned to Kentucky and began to prepare for the legal battles that follow such an incident.

Although Ashland moved quickly to clean up the spill and was forthright about mistakes, it was still indicted for violating federal environmental laws. Numerous damage claims filed against the firm were not awarded, however, because Ashland was able to successfully demonstrate that it was impaired in its efforts to act promptly and effectively by government agency restrictions.

Ashland, however, had a history of problems with regulatory agencies, which made it harder to convince the public that it was not entirely at fault. Ashland had been found guilty of rigging bids with other contractors in order to charge higher prices for highway work in Tennessee and North Carolina. It had been charged with wrongfully firing two employees because they refused to cover illegal payments made to firms overseas. The former chairman of Ashland had only recently been accused of selling important Ashland documents to Iran in order to manipulate the supply and price of oil for his personal gain. The company had on so many occasions violated either explicit laws or implicit public expectations that its efforts to clean up the spill and the explanations about those efforts were immediately suspect.

SOURCES: Arthur Sharplin and Robert Martin, "At Ashland, More Than Their Oil Is Crude," *Business and Society Review*, Winter 1989, pp. 29–39; "Ashland Just Can't Seem to Leave Its Checkered Past Behind," *Business Week*, October 31, 1988, pp. 122–126; R. E. Mesloh, "Battelle Determines Cause of Ashland Tank Failure," *Oil and Gas Journal*, September 26, 1988, p. 48; "Oil Spill in the Midwest Provides Case Study in Crisis Management," *The Wall Street Journal*, January 8, 1988, p. 19.

Enhancement Case Questions

1. What was the extent of Ashland Oil's responsibility in the oil spill? Why? Compare your response with that from the Prelude Case. Are there any differences? Why or why not?
2. Which approach to social responsibility seems to best describe Ashland in this situation? Cite specific examples to support your view.
3. What might Ashland have done to more effectively handle the situation?
4. What can Ashland do to offset its history of problems in the area of social responsibility? Do you think it is likely to do so? Why or why not?

Chapter Notes

1. "Dean Witter Braces for a Backlash in Boston," *Business Week*, March 6, 1989, p. 86; "Drexel Faces a Stockholder Suit Claiming Injury from Wrongdoing Alleged by SEC," *The Wall Street Journal*, September 9, 1988, p. 10; "Anheuser-Busch Co. Is Shaken by Its Probe of Improper Payments," *The Wall Street Journal*, March 31, 1987, pp. 1, 22; "Companies Get Serious About Ethics," *USA Today*, December 9, 1986, pp. 1B–2B.
2. See F. Neil Brady, "Aesthetic Components of Managerial Ethics," *Academy of Management Review*, April 1986, pp. 337–344.
3. Thomas M. Barrett and Richard J. Kilonski, *Business Ethics*, 2nd ed. (Englewood Cliffs, N.J.: Prentice-Hall, 1986).
4. John Huey, "Wal-Mart—Will It Take Over the World?" *Fortune*, January 30, 1989, pp. 52–61.
5. Patricia Sellers, "Getting Customers to Love You," *Fortune*, March 13, 1989, pp. 38–49.
6. "Antitrust Chief Says CEOs Should Tape All Phone Calls to Each Other," *The Wall Street Journal*, February 3, 1986, p. 23.
7. "The Dark Side of Japan Inc.," *Newsweek*, January 9, 1989, p. 41.
8. For other perspectives, see H. Brice and T. Wegner, "A Quantitative Approach to Corporate Social Responsibility Programme Formulation," *Managerial and Decision Economics*, June 1989, pp. 163–170; Eugene Szwajkowski, "Organizational Illegality: Theoretical Integration and Illustrative Application," *Academy of Management Review*, July 1985, pp. 558–567.
9. Erik Jansen and Mary Ann Von Glinow, "Ethical Ambivalence and Organizational Reward Systems," *Academy of Management Review*, October 1985, pp. 814–822.
10. Roy Rowan, "The Maverick Who Yelled Foul at Citibank," *Fortune*, January 10, 1983, pp. 46–56.
11. Myron Magnet, "The Decline & Fall of Business Ethics," *Fortune*, December 8, 1986, pp. 65–72.
12. "Harvard's $30 Million Windfall for Ethics 101," *Business Week*, April 13, 1987, p. 40.
13. "Ethics Training at Work," *The Wall Street Journal*, September 9, 1986, p. 1.
14. "Ethics on the Job: Companies Alert Employees to Potential Dilemmas," *The Wall Street Journal*, July 14, 1986, p. 17.
15. "Companies Get Serious About Ethics," pp. 1B–2B.

16. See Frederick D. Sturdivant, *Business and Society: A Managerial Approach*, 3rd ed. (Homewood, Ill.: Richard D. Irwin, 1985).

17. See Archie Carroll, *Business and Society: Ethics and Stakeholder Management* (Cincinnati, Ohio: Southwestern, 1989), for a review of the evolution of social responsibility.

18. Stahrl W. Edmunds, "Unifying Concepts in Social Responsibility," *Academy of Management Review*, January, 1977, pp. 38–45.

19. Page Smith, *The Rise of Industrial America* (New York: McGraw-Hill, 1984).

20. Keith Davis, "The Case For and Against Business Assumption of Social Responsibility," *Academy of Management Journal*, June 1973, pp. 312–322.

21. Milton Friedman, *Capitalism and Freedom* (Chicago: University of Chicago Press, 1962).

22. See S. Prakash Sethi, "A Conceptual Framework for Environmental Analysis of Social Issues and Evaluation of Business Response Patterns," *Academy of Management Review*, January 1979, pp. 63–74. See also Steven L. Wartick and Phillip L. Cochran, "The Evolution of the Corporate Social Performance Model," *Academy of Management Review*, October 1985, pp. 758–769.

23. "Smoking Section: Cigarette Companies Develop Third World as a Growth Market," *The Wall Street Journal*, July 5, 1985, p. 1.

24. "Fast-Food Chains Draw Criticism for Marketing Fare as Nutritional," *The Wall Street Journal*, April 6, 1987, p. 23.

25. "A Mail-Order Romance: Land's End Courts Unseen Customers," *Fortune*, March 13, 1989, pp. 44–45.

26. Richard Zoglin, "The Greening of Ted Turner," *Time*, January 22, 1990, pp. 58–60.

27. Keith Davis and Robert L. Blomstrom, *Business and Society: Environment and Responsibility*, 3rd ed. (New York: McGraw-Hill, 1975).

28. Alan Farnham, "Holding Firm on Affirmative Action," *Fortune*, March 13, 1989, pp. 87–88.

29. "Make the Punishment Fit the Corporate Crime," *Business Week*, March 13, 1989, p. 22.

30. "Many Businesses Blame Governmental Policies for Productivity Lag," *The Wall Street Journal*, October 28, 1980, p. 1.

31. Greg Densmore, "Scannell Brings New Look to OSHA," *Occupational Health & Safety*, January 1, 1990, pp. 18–21; William J. Rothwell, "Complying With OSHA," *Training and Development Journal*, May 1, 1989, pp. 52–54; "Time to Reform OSHA," *Industry Week*, January 2, 1989, pp. 46–48; "OSHA Opening Its Ears to Advice, Peel Claims," *Engineering News-Record*, May 4, 1989, p. 11.

32. "How to Win Friends and Influence Lawmakers," *Business Week*, November 7, 1988, p. 36.

THE ENTREPRENEURIAL SPIRIT

This first part of the book has introduced you to the world of management and managers. You were first given an overview of that world and a basic understanding of the variety of managers and managerial tasks. Then you received a brief overview of management theory and its historical development. A discussion of managerial ethics and social responsibility concluded this part. Each of the chapters indicated that the material being presented was applicable to all organizations. Of particular interest, however, is its application to entrepreneurs and small-business managers. This short section extends your awareness of that subject.

An entrepreneur is someone who organizes, operates, and assumes the risk of a business venture. Entrepreneurs, then, are managers and part of the world of management. They plan, make decisions, organize, lead, and control their organizations. They enact all of the management roles and require all of the management skills of other managers, although the extent of each role and the need for each skill vary with the particular circumstances in which the entrepreneur operates. The key distinction, then, between other managers and an entrepreneur is that the entrepreneur personally assumes the risks of the enterprise as well as enacting the management roles.

Injecting the spirit of entrepreneurship into both large and small businesses at all levels has recently become a subject of interest. Managers have learned that they must be creative and willing to take risks if they are to avoid attacks by competitors or takeover experts. Some organizations have expended considerable effort to maintain an entrepreneurial spirit. The issue, then, becomes one of creating an organizational culture that supports and even rewards entrepreneurship.

Toys 'R' Us, even though it has grown into an extremely large organization, maintains each store as an independent small business under its corporate umbrella. The store managers are held responsible for the performance of their stores just as a small-business entrepreneur is responsible for his or her business. By granting authority to go along with that responsibility, Toys 'R' Us tries to create the atmosphere of a small, entrepreneurial business. Pentech International Inc., although smaller than Toys 'R' Us, maintains an entrepreneurial spirit by concentrating on small market niches such as Erasables, erasable marking pens; Gripstix, pencils with special grooves to fit children's fingers better; and Twins, crayons with different colors at each end. By 1989 Pentech's efforts had enabled it to reach almost $20 million in revenues and $2 million in profits.

Entrepreneurial organizations are so diverse that you can find all the schools of management theory represented in them. Intel and K mart, which were discussed in the Prelude and Enhancement Cases in Chapter 2, both have entrepreneurial aspects, and both reflect different mixes of schools of management theory. Other large companies that possess the entrepreneurial spirit and follow several different theories at once include 3M, Walt Disney Productions, Digital Equipment, Eastman Kodak, and Colgate-Palmolive. And, of course, small businesses also display this same range in managerial theory.

The *Management Today: Small Business and Entrepreneurship* example in Chapter 3 clearly indicates that some small, entrepreneurial organizations are arising to fill the social responsibility gap left by other organizations. Criticisms leveled against the "captains of industry" and suggestions that they be called "robber barons" instead show that some members of the public believe that entrepreneurs also must behave in ethical ways and have social responsibilities. The efforts of smaller, entrepreneurial firms such as the Sun Company and Hercules to ensure ethical behavior suggest that some entrepreneurs and entrepreneurial organizations care strongly about social responsibility issues. When Reebok, the maker of fashionable athletic shoes, established an annual prize for young people who strive to promote freedom of expression, it was acting in a socially responsive as well as creative, entrepreneurial way.

As you will see in later chapters, some of the material in this book is more appropriate to larger firms, and other material is appropriate for all firms. Throughout the text, the concepts that most clearly fit smaller, entrepreneurial organizations will be emphasized, as well as their importance in our contemporary economy.

SOURCES: Vijay Sathe, "From Surface to Deep Corporate Entrepreneurship," *Human Resource Management*, Winter 1989, pp. 389–399; D. B. Balkin, "Reward Policies That Support Entrepreneurship," *IEEE Engineering Management Review*, June 1, 1989, p. 73; Stuart Gannes, "America's Fastest-Growing Companies," *Fortune*, May 23, 1988, pp. 28–40; "Hot Growth Companies," *Business Week*, May 22, 1989, pp. 90–91; Bill Saporito, "Companies That Compete Best," *Fortune*, May 22, 1989, pp. 36–44; "Big Vs. Small," *Time*, September 5, 1988, pp. 48–50; "Reebok Foots the Bill for Human Rights," *Business Week*, April 25, 1988, p. 72; "The Obituary That Should Not Have Run," *U.S. News & World Report*, January 4, 1988, pp. 82–83; "Ethics Training at Work," *The Wall Street Journal*, September 6, 1986, p. 1; Howard H. Stevenson and Jose Carlos Jarrillo-Mossi, "Preserving Entrepreneurship as Companies Grow," *Journal of Business Strategy*, vol. 7, 1986, pp. 10–23; Nicholas C. Siropolis, *Small Business Management: A Guide to Entrepreneurship*, 4th ed. (Boston: Houghton Mifflin, 1990).

TWO

Planning and Decision Making

This part of the book introduces you to the first major managerial function, planning and decision making. Chapter 4 discusses organizational environments and goals, two important contextual elements of planning. Chapter 5 then describes the overall planning process. Strategy and strategic planning are discussed next in Chapter 6. Finally, Chapter 7 focuses on managerial decision making, a critically important part of planning.

CHAPTER OUTLINE

I. The Nature of Organizational Goals
   A. Definition and Purpose of Goals
   B. Steps in Goal Setting

II. Organizational Environments and Goal Setting
   A. The General Environment
   B. The Task Environment
   C. Environments and Goals

III. Managing Multiple Goals
   A. Kinds of Goals
   B. Goal Optimization

IV. Effective Goal Setting
   A. Barriers to Effective Goal Setting
   B. Overcoming the Barriers to Goal Setting

V. Management by Objectives
   A. The Nature of MBO
   B. The Mechanics of MBO
   C. The Effectiveness of MBO

C
H
A
P
T
E
R

4

After studying this chapter you should be able to

1. Define goals, note their purpose, and identify the steps in the goal-setting process.

2. Identify and describe both the general environment and the task environment and the relation of each to goal setting.

3. Discuss the meaning of multiple goals to organizations from the standpoint of kinds of goals as well as goal optimization.

4. Discuss effective goal setting, including barriers to such effectiveness and how to overcome those barriers.

5. Describe the nature, purpose, and mechanics of management by objectives.

Organizational Environments and Goals

KELLOGG COMES ROARING BACK

The Kellogg cereal company was founded early in this century on a mistake. It seems that Dr. J. H. Kellogg was experimenting with methods for making health foods more appetizing and nutritious for his patients when he accidentally discovered how to make wheat flakes. His brother, W. K. Kellogg, bought the commercial rights to this process and soon discovered how to make not just wheat but also corn and rice flakes.

Kellogg started selling the cereal to the public in 1906. Through a combination of aggressive advertising and expansion, the company changed the way people around the world thought about breakfast. Other companies like General Mills and General Foods soon entered the market, however, and competition started to grow.

Acknowledging that the competition could not be ignored, managers at Kellogg nevertheless believed that they could remain on top. Indeed, they set a goal of controlling 50 percent of the worldwide market for breakfast cereals. During the decades of the 1950s and 1960s, Kellogg remained comfortably at the head of the pack, and its market share inched ever closer to the magic 50 percent target.

In the 1970s, however, troubles emerged at Kellogg. Among other things, it seems that management had become complacent and had lost touch with consumers. Demand for breakfast cereals had started to decline, and competitors like Quaker Oats and Nabisco were stealing market share from Kellogg. And increasingly health-conscious consumers were turning away from heavily sweetened cereals.

Kellogg's managers, led by CEO William E. LaMothe, quickly realized they had to fight back if they were to turn things around and remain on top. They decided to tackle a number of areas at once in order to re-establish their pre-eminence in the cereal industry. For one thing, Kellogg began a ruthless expansion plan of new products targeted at every conceivable market segment. Raisin Squares, for example, were introduced to compete with Nabisco's shredded-wheat cereals. Crispix was introduced to compete with Ralston Purina's Chex cereals.

Industry experts were also arguing that the adult segment of the cereal market was mature—that it would not grow very much in the future. Kellogg attacked this notion by increasing advertising directed at adults and by introducing several new cereals aimed at health-conscious Americans. Prominent among these are Müeslix and Nutri-Grain Biscuits. The result? Adult Americans are now eating 26 percent more cereal than they did just five years ago.

Kellogg has also invested heavily in research and development and new forms of technology. Building 100 at Battle Creek, Michigan (Kellogg's headquarters),

for example, is the most efficient and heavily automated cereal plant in the world. The building has four floors the size of football fields and churns out cereal twenty-four hours a day, seven days a week. And all this is accomplished without a single human being—it's all done with computer-monitored machines.

Kellogg's executives also get involved with quality control. Every morning, for instance, they gather for breakfast and sample a variety of cereals from a different Kellogg plant. They evaluate each sample as "satisfactory" (the highest rating), "acceptable," or "below stan-dards." The appropriate plant manager then receives a report of their evaluations.

Finally, Kellogg has not forgotten its foreign markets. Aggressive advertising and expansions have led to dramatic sales gains around the world. The Australians, for example, are even more health-conscious than Americans and eat Just Right, a mineral-laden, vitamin-fortified cereal created by Kellogg just for them. And the Japanese, who still eat fish and rice, are starting to buy Genmai Flakes, a whole-grain rice cereal Kellogg has tailored just for their tastes.

Kellogg managers are committed to making the highest quality cereals possible. As part of this commitment, managers and other employees gather for breakfast each morning to sample and evaluate various Kellogg cereals.

SOURCES: Patricia Sellers, "How King Kellogg Beat the Blahs," *Fortune*, August 29, 1988, pp. 54–64; "Cereal King Kellogg Feels Its Oats," *USA Today*, August 31, 1989, p. 3B; "Big G Is Growing Fat on Oat Cuisine," *Business Week*, September 18, 1989, p. 29; "Oat Bran Heartburn," *Newsweek*, January 29, 1990, pp. 50–52.

Kellogg provides an excellent example of a company that has had to respond to various elements of its environment in a number of different ways. It is also a company that uses goals effectively as a way to guide itself toward where it wants to go. Without goals, organizations are like ships without rudders—they wander aimlessly, without direction, and often end up in rough water. And a failure to understand and respond to the organization's environments can be equally devastating.

This chapter, the first of four devoted to planning and decision making, discusses organizational environments and goals. First it looks at the nature of organizational goals. Then it discusses the environment and how that affects goals and the processes associated with setting goals. The chapter explores ways to enhance the effectiveness of goal setting and finishes by discussing management by objectives, one commonly used goal-setting method.

THE NATURE OF ORGANIZATIONAL GOALS

Exactly what are goals? Why are they important? How are they established? Let's answer these basic questions first.

Definition and Purpose of Goals

☐ A *goal* provides direction for an organization and represents a desired state or condition that the organization wants to achieve.

A **goal** can be defined as a desired state or condition that the organization wants to achieve, a target the organization wants to hit. When Kellogg states that it wants to control 50 percent of the cereal market, it is specifying a market share goal it wants to achieve and then maintain.

Like targets, goals are supposed to provide a clear purpose, or direction, for the organization. When Stanley Gault became CEO of Rubbermaid, he decided to make the company much more innovative. He set a goal of increasing sales 15 percent annually. He also pledged increased employee participation and promised greater rewards for innovation. Rubbermaid's employees enthusiastically accepted these ideas and have met the sales goal every year. And the company is now recognized as one of the most innovative in the world.[1] At Rubbermaid, then, goals are clearly serving their intended purpose—they are providing guidance and direction for everyone.

Steps in Goal Setting

☐ *Goal setting* is a six-part process resulting in a set of consistent and logical goals that permeate the entire organization.

Goal setting is a six-part process, as shown in Exhibit 4.1. The end result of this process should be a set of consistent and logical goals that permeate the entire organization.

The managers in the organization first scan the environment for opportunities and threats (step one) and then assess organizational strengths and weak-

Exhibit 4.1   The Goal-Setting Process

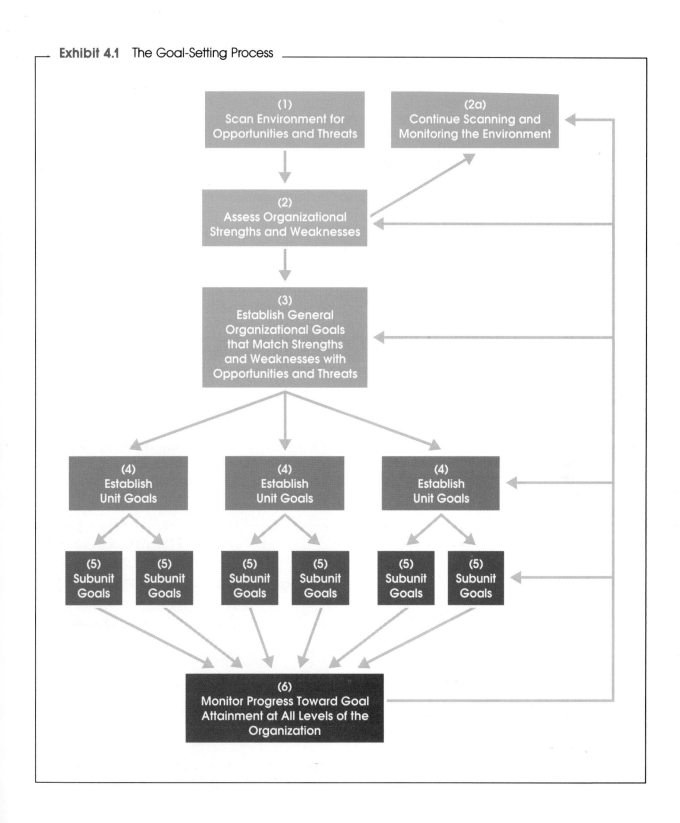

nesses (step two). For a company such as Disney, opportunities might include new foreign markets for its theme parks and new ideas for movie projects, and threats could include other entertainment companies and movie producers. Disney's organizational strengths might involve marketing savvy in the theme park industry, a solid reputation, and surplus capital. Its weaknesses could be the firm's dependence on its theme parks for operating funds and an image that does not appeal to teenagers and young adults.

The next step in goal setting is to establish general organizational goals that match strengths and weaknesses with opportunities and threats (step three). Disney's managers might decide to open three new theme parks in other countries by the year 2020 and make fifteen new movies per year for the next ten years. This leads to steps four and five, setting unit and subunit goals. The theme park unit might decide that one new park every ten years is the best target, and its subunits would then set specific goals for new rides and attractions, attendance levels at existing parks, and so forth. The last step (step six) is for managers to monitor progress toward goal attainment at all levels of the organization. This progress subsequently affects all of the other steps as the cycle repeats itself. For example, a string of bad movies might cause Disney to halt film production until managers can straighten out the problems.[2]

LEARNING CHECK

You should now be able to define goals, note their purpose, and identify the steps in the goal-setting process.

Organizations set a variety of goals dealing with a number of different areas. Outboard Marine Corporation (OMC) has general organizational goals suggesting that the firm wants to be a worldwide, low-cost producer of recreational boating equipment. As a result of these general goals, specific units within OMC have goals related to cost, market share, growth, and so forth.

Photo by Michael Mauney/Courtesy Outboard Marine Corp.

SMALL BUSINESS AND ENTREPRENEURSHIP

Incubators Provide Buffer from Environment

Small businesses in the United States face a bewildering network of threats in their efforts to first survive and then grow and prosper. Such businesses are often undercapitalized, and many would-be entrepreneurs lack experience. Little wonder, then, that many small businesses go under in less than a year.

To combat this high mortality rate and to give small businesses a greater chance of success, a new concept has been born—the incubator. An incubator is a protected environment where small businesses are insulated from some of the threats and costs they might otherwise have to bear. For example, businesses in an incubator usually receive accounting and legal services for a reduced fee and share access to a receptionist, secretarial services, and computer and facsimile equipment. They often get reduced rent and expert consulting information. And the entrepreneurs themselves often serve as a support group

for one another. After the business becomes profitable, it moves out of the incubator into the competitive environment.

There are three basic types of incubators. One type is affiliated with a local university. Another is a not-for-profit arrangement established by state or local governments. The other type is a for-profit arrangement by which investors provide incubator services in return for a share of future profits and/or a percentage of ownership.

To date, the impact of incubators has been generally positive. For example, businesses that start in incubators and then go out on their own have a higher success rate than do businesses that start out on their own. On the other hand, some incubators have started out in bad locations and have suffered from poor management themselves. On balance, however, the future of the incubator concept looks promising.

SOURCES: "Fledgling Firms Learn to Fly in Incubators," *USA Today,* May 8, 1989, p. 3E; "Small Businesses Blossom Near Atlanta," *The Wall Street Journal,* March 28, 1989, p. B1; "Louisiana Strives to Foster Growth of Entrepreneurs," *The Wall Street Journal,* July 7, 1989, p. B2; "Business Incubators Suffer Growing Pains," *The Wall Street Journal,* June 16, 1989, p. B1.

ORGANIZATIONAL ENVIRONMENTS AND GOAL SETTING

We have seen that the environment plays a major role in the goal-setting process. Indeed, the environment often determines whether a company succeeds or fails. *Management Today: Small Business and Entrepreneurship* describes how some small businesses are protected from their environment by being placed in an incubator. In this section we explore the nature of the environment in more detail. First let's look at what is called the general environment. We will then discuss the task environment.[3]

☐ The *general environment* is the overall set of forces that characterize the setting of an organization.

The General Environment

The **general environment** is the overall set of forces that characterize the setting of an organization.[4] These forces are not necessarily associated with other

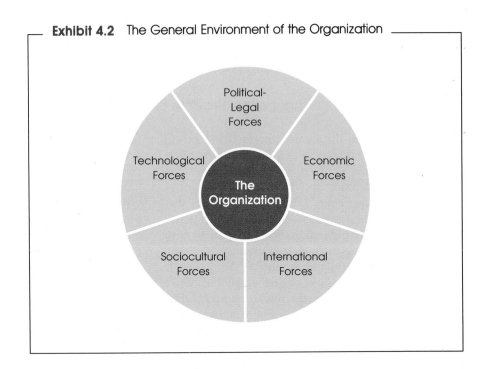

Exhibit 4.2   The General Environment of the Organization

specific organizations but are part of the general context of the organization. As illustrated in Exhibit 4.2, the general environment consists of five unique sets of forces: political-legal, economic, international, sociocultural, and technological.[5] Managers must consider each of these if they are to be effective in establishing goals.

POLITICAL-LEGAL FORCES   **Political-legal forces** are those forces associated with the governmental and legal system within which a firm operates. Regardless of where a company is located, many phases of its operations are regulated by the government. In the United States, hiring, safety, wages, trade practices, and union activities, among other things, are regulated. There is even more control in many foreign countries. India, for instance, requires that a foreign firm doing business inside its boundaries must be partially owned by Indian investors and must employ a specified percentage of local workers. Political-legal forces also work in many subtle ways. In the United States, the extent to which Congress and the president are in favor of business influences corporate tax legislation, foreign trade opportunities, and merger activity, among other things. And governmental stability is also an important factor. Businesses can be fairly confident that the governments of countries such as the United States, France, and Canada are stable, but much less confident of conditions in Iran and Panama.

ECONOMIC FORCES   **Economic forces** are also an important part of the general environment. Critical economic forces include inflation, economic growth, interest rates, and unemployment. During periods of inflation, for ex-

☐ *Political-legal forces* relate to the governmental and legal system in which the organization exists.

☐ *Economic forces* are factors such as inflation, growth rates, interest rates, unemployment, and so forth.

ample, firms must pay more for materials, maintenance services, and utilities. Economic growth rates play a role in determining the extent to which demand for the firm's products and services is increasing, decreasing, or staying the same. Interest rates are important because they determine how much it will cost the organization to borrow money and how readily customers can borrow money to buy products and services. Finally, unemployment influences the supply of available labor. If unemployment is low, the firm may have to pay higher wages to attract capable employees.

□ *International forces* are those associated with increased international business opportunities, competition, and so forth.

INTERNATIONAL FORCES   We have seen the importance of **international forces** several times. Multinational firms such as Union Carbide, IBM, Boeing, Ford, Nestlé, and Unilever are clearly affected by these forces, but so are organizations doing business on a purely domestic level. The local Ford dealer, for instance, must compete with Nissan and Toyota dealers. International forces influence such things as prices, quality expectations, and so forth. Other countries also serve as potentially important markets for many businesses. The Coca-Cola Company sees much of its future growth coming from foreign markets. And many American-made movies that barely break even at home earn substantial profits abroad. Similarly, Nestlé realized years ago that the small country of Switzerland, where it was founded, was not an adequate market, and thus became perhaps the first of the true multinationals.[6]

□ *Sociocultural forces* are the customs and values of the society in which the organization is operating.

SOCIOCULTURAL FORCES   The **sociocultural forces** of the general environment are the customs and values that characterize the society within which the firm is operating. Such forces influence consumer tastes and preferences, employee expectations and attitudes, and the accepted role of business in that society. For example, bribery and under-the-counter payments are accepted practice in some countries, and workers in many places will accept much less pay than American workers will. It is important to recognize, of course, that culture does not always remain the same within national boundaries. The cultures of New York and Los Angeles are quite different, and both are very different from that found in the Midwest. Sociocultural forces are also important to an understanding of the subtle determinants of business. Although many people are aware of the vast differences in Japanese and American business practices, few truly understand why these differences exist.

□ *Technological forces* include the rate of technological change, the state of current technology, and similar factors.

TECHNOLOGICAL FORCES   Finally, **technological forces** also form an important part of the general environment. The rate of technological change in the past few years, especially in the area of computers and their applications in decision making, information management, and production systems, has been very significant. Indeed, such breakthroughs are changing the entire nature of the workplace. Automated production systems can produce higher-quality products of a more diverse nature in a shorter period of time with fewer workers than anyone even dreamed of just a few years ago. Robotics, artificial intelligence, and further advancements in computer technology will probably accelerate at an even faster pace in the years ahead, so technological forces will become even more important in the future.[7]

The Task Environment

□ The *task environment* consists of those specific elements in the environment that influence an organization.

The **task environment** is also of considerable importance to organizations. It consists of those specific elements in the environment that influence the target company. As shown in Exhibit 4.3, the task environment has six dimensions: customers, competitors, unions, regulators, suppliers, and partners.[8]

□ *Customers* are those people or groups that purchase the organization's products and/or services.

CUSTOMERS   **Customers** are those people or groups that buy the goods or services produced by the organization. For some organizations, the customer is the ultimate consumer—the person who actually uses the products or services. This is the case for restaurants like Red Lobster and Pizza Hut and retailers like Banana Republic, Waldenbooks, and Radio Shack. For other organizations, the customer is the distributor. For example, we don't buy a can of soda from PepsiCo. We buy it from a grocery store or a vending machine, which bought it from PepsiCo. Customers can also be other organizations, in the way that schools and hospitals are customers for food distributors. Whoever they are, customers are clearly important to any organization since it is they who exchange money for the products or services provided by the organization.

□ *Competitors* are those organizations that offer alternative products to customers.

COMPETITORS   **Competitors**—those organizations that offer similar or alternative products or services to potential customers—are also important. Some competitive relationships are clear. Exxon competes with Chevron and Mobil, Boeing competes with McDonnell Douglas, and McDonald's competes with Burger King and Wendy's. Other competitive relationships are more subtle, however. When a student's car breaks down, he might consider buying a new one from Subaru, repairing the old one at the Sears automotive center, buying a motorcycle from Yamaha, or buying a bicycle from Raleigh. Thus, Subaru, Sears, Yamaha, and Raleigh are competing for the same dollars.

□ *Unions* are organized groups of operating employees that collectively bargain with the organization over issues such as wages, hours of work, and so forth.

UNIONS   **Unions** are also an important part of the organization's task environment. Witness, for example, the troubles of Texas Air Corporation in its dealings with Eastern's unions. Almost one-fourth of the U.S. labor force is unionized today. Larger firms such as Westinghouse and General Electric must contend with multiple unions, and firms that are not unionized often work to keep unions from organizing their work force. In recent years union activity has spread to such nontraditional professions as university faculties, engineers, and first-line managers. Thus, unions are likely to remain a critical element to consider when setting organizational goals.

□ *Regulators* are organizations or groups that attempt to influence or control a target organization.

REGULATORS   **Regulators** are organizations or groups that actively attempt to influence the target organization. Formal regulatory agencies such as the Equal Employment Opportunity Commission, the Occupational Safety and Health Administration, the Environmental Protection Agency, and the Federal Trade Commission affect what organizations can and cannot do. Less formally, interest groups such as the National Organization for Women, MADD, the Sierra Club, and local consumer groups also work to influence business organizations.

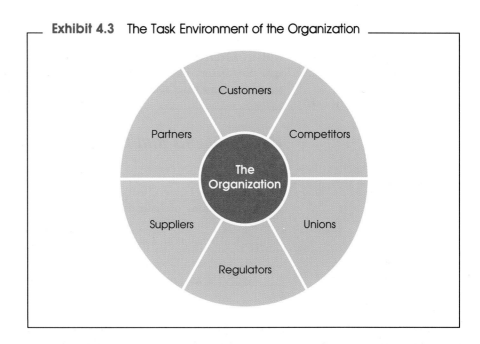

Exhibit 4.3   The Task Environment of the Organization

Customers

Competitors

Partners

The Organization

Suppliers

Unions

Regulators

☐ *Suppliers* are those organizations that provide resources to a target organization.

SUPPLIERS   Suppliers—the fifth part of the task environment—provide resources to the firm. For example, Continental Airlines buys food from Marriott food services, jet fuel from Shell Oil, and airplanes from Boeing, borrows money from First City Bank Corporation, and hires employees recommended by the Texas Employment Commission. Each of these organizations is supplying Continental with needed resources. The prices suppliers charge, their delivery schedules, and the quality of what they provide are important considerations for managers.

☐ *Partners* are other organizations a target firm works with on a particular project.

PARTNERS   Finally, many organizations today are increasingly entering into joint ventures with **partners.** A joint venture is when two or more firms agree to work together—sharing the risks and the rewards—on a particular project.[9] Chevrolet and Toyota jointly operate a plant in California that produces Chevrolet Luminas and Toyota Camrys. IBM has over forty joint ventures with different partners. And American Express frequently cosponsors promotions with various airlines. These and other kinds of partnership arrangements are expected to become increasingly popular in the years ahead. Hence, managers will also need to be increasingly sensitive to them in setting organizational goals.[10]

PRELUDE CASE UPDATE

Kellogg is clearly affected by several elements of its environments. In terms of the general environment, the company is moving increasingly into international markets and is using new forms of technology for producing cereal. And new concerns about health have altered consumer thinking about cereals. Within the task environment, Kellogg has targeted specific customer groups with its advertising and has had to contend with increased activity by competitors. Regulators like the Food and Drug Administration and various agricultural suppliers have also no doubt played big roles at Kellogg in recent years.

Environments and Goals

Clearly, then, an organization's environments play a vital role in the establishment of goals. These effects are felt in two ways, as shown in Exhibit 4.4. First, dimensions of both the general and the task environment affect initial goal-setting processes. Second, they affect ongoing activities aimed at goal attainment. *Management Today: Ethical Dilemmas of Management* describes some of

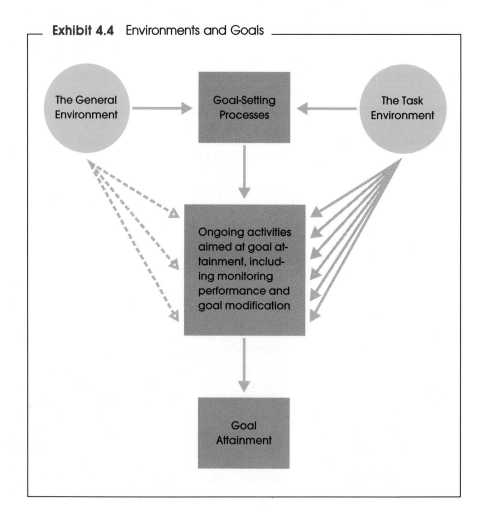

Exhibit 4.4 Environments and Goals

ETHICAL DILEMMAS OF MANAGEMENT

Westinghouse Plans for a Nuclear Future

Whenever a corporation attempts to do business in a controversial market, it must contend with a variety of ethical dilemmas. Toxic waste disposal companies, bioengineering laboratories, and abortion clinics are prime examples. Another is nuclear power.

Nuclear power was once hailed as the energy source of the future. However, depressed oil prices and safety concerns stemming from the Three Mile Island and Chernobyl disasters have curtailed much of the optimism of only a few years ago about nuclear power.

Westinghouse, however, has recently renewed its commitment to the construction and operation of nuclear power–generating facilities. Indeed, even though they have not received an order for a new plant in over ten years, managers at Westinghouse believe that orders will start coming in again around 1992 and they fully expect to have at least one new

nuclear power facility in operation by the end of this century.

Although they admit the controversial nature of such projects, Westinghouse officials believe that they can effectively meet the demands for cheap energy while simultaneously addressing safety and environmental concerns. In particular, they plan to introduce a new, smaller-scale design that will have much better safety systems than do existing facilities.

Westinghouse sees nuclear power plants as an important part of its strategy but is also working hard to address environmental concerns and pressures. Indeed, Westinghouse is moving into the business of toxic and hazardous waste collection and disposal. The company has also planned a new ad campaign to clarify its image to the public and to communicate more clearly its approach to both nuclear power and waste disposal.

SOURCES: "Westinghouse, Expecting a Rebound for Nuclear Power, Plans New Plant," *The Wall Street Journal*, April 21, 1989, p. B4; "Westinghouse Hastens to Nation's Wastes," *The Wall Street Journal*, November 22, 1988, p. A5; "Westinghouse Slates Campaign to Clarify What It Really Does," *The Wall Street Journal*, May 11, 1989, p. B6.

the ethical concerns confronted by Westinghouse as it attempts to balance its goals against environment pressures.

Dimensions of the general environment have occasional effects that might call for modification of goals and/or of strategies for achieving them. Because the parts of this environment are so diffuse, changes tend to be slow and rather subtle. For example, tobacco companies like RJR and alcohol companies like Hiram Walker have gradually expanded into other areas of business as changing sociocultural mores and values have altered people's attitudes and behaviors regarding smoking and drinking. In contrast, the task environment is characterized by frequent effects associated with rapid shifts. Thus, when General Motors announces a new rebate program, Ford and Chrysler are quick to follow suit. Likewise, when a union announces a strike, managers recognize that the labor leaders are serious about their demands.

> **LEARNING CHECK**
>
> You should now be able to identify and describe both the general environment and the task environment and the relation of each to goal setting.

107

MANAGING MULTIPLE GOALS

One fact that should be apparent is that an organization does not have a single goal. Regardless of its size or diversity, any organization must pursue a variety of goals in order to survive. In this section we will explore how managers deal with multiple goals. First let's identify the major types of goals that organizations usually attempt to achieve, and then we'll explore the concept of goal optimization.

Kinds of Goals

□ Organizational goals vary in terms of levels, areas, and time frame and specificity.

Organizations can pursue a variety of different kinds of goals. Exhibit 4.5 shows that goals can be differentiated by level, area, and time frame and specificity.

GOALS BY LEVEL   One useful perspective for describing goals is their level in the organization. For example, we noted in Chapter 1 the various levels of management that characterize most organizations. It follows logically, then, that each such level is likely to have its own goals. At the top are the purpose and mission of the organization, as determined by the board of directors. An organization's **purpose** is its reason for existence. For instance, the purpose of Corning Glass, Reebok, and Compaq Computers is to make a profit, whereas the purpose of the Mayo Clinic is to provide health care. An organization's **mission** is the way it attempts to fulfill its purpose. Honda Motor Company attempts to fulfill its purpose—making a profit—by manufacturing and selling automobiles, motorcycles, and lawn mowers. K mart's mission is to sell large quantities of merchandise at a small markup.

□ An organization's *purpose* is the reason it exists. Its *mission* is the way in which it attempts to fulfill its purpose.

Top-management goals are those that define the strategy (the broad plans that set the overall direction) of the organization. Several years ago, the former CEO of Citicorp, Walter Wriston, set three broad goals for the bank that determined the strategy Citicorp would follow—earnings growth of 15 percent per year, a 20 percent return on stockholders' equity, and becoming the world's first truly international banking system. Even today, Wriston's successor, John Reed, has continued to work toward the same set of goals.[11]

Middle managers also set goals. These goals follow logically from the strategic goals set by top managers. A plant manager for Dow Chemical, for example, might have goals for reducing costs and increasing output for the next year by a certain amount. Likewise, at Citicorp the head of one of the corporation's large banks will have goals designed to contribute to the three general goals noted above.

Of course, first-line managers also have goals. These might relate to specific projects or activities pertinent to the manager's job. For instance, a first-line supervisor in a Dow Chemical Co. plant might have the goal of reducing costs in her unit by 5 percent. And a Citicorp banker sent to open a small branch in a new foreign location will have goals consistent with the corporation's goal of internationalization.

GOALS BY AREA   It is also possible to differentiate goals by areas of management, also discussed in Chapter 1. That is, goals can be established for each functional area within an organization. Managers in the marketing area might develop goals for sales, sales growth, market share, and so forth. Operations managers can establish goals for costs, quality, and inventory levels. Financial goals can relate to return on investment and liquidity. Human resource goals can relate to turnover, absenteeism, and employee development. Research and development goals might include innovations, new breakthroughs, and so forth. Finally, in a slightly different vein, managers might set social goals such as contributions to the community through the United Way and so forth.

As shown in Exhibit 4.5, goals can also be established for each area across different levels. For example, within the marketing area of Lever Brothers there will be goals for top managers (increase total sales by 10 percent), middle managers (increase sales of three different products by 8 percent, 10 percent,

Exhibit 4.5   Kinds of Goals

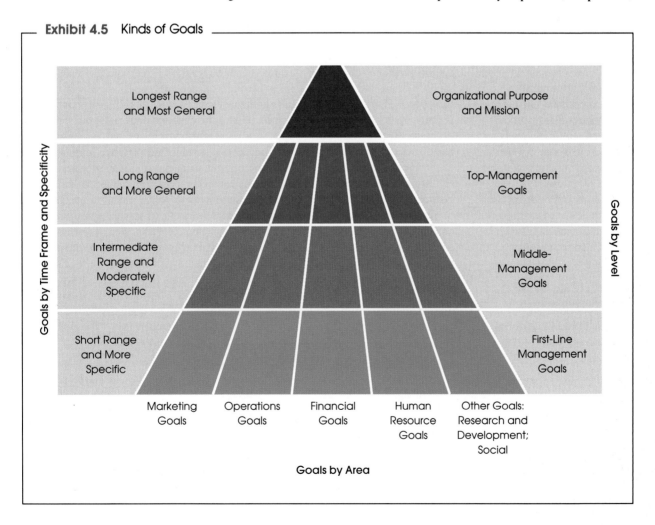

© James Schnepf

Managers must often juggle multiple goals. Harley Davidson recognized a few years ago that it needed to overhaul its entire product line if it was going to survive. However, the firm also needed to maintain its short-term cashflow while the changes were being made. William G. Davidson, a vice president at Harley Davidson, modified paint and trim on the firm's motorcycles for several years, giving them the appearance of new models, while other managers focused on longer-term manufacturing changes.

☐ *Goal optimization* is the process of achieving an effective balance among the different goals of an organization.

and 13 percent, respectively), and first-line managers (increase sales of one product within a certain territory by 6 percent).

GOALS BY TIME FRAME AND SPECIFICITY   The last dimension along which we can classify goals is time frame and specificity. Most organizations establish long-range, intermediate, and short-range goals. At Kodak long-range goals might extend ten years ahead; intermediate goals, for the next five years; and short-range goals, for the next year.

Specificity refers to the extent to which the goal is precise or general. A precise goal for Sears might be to increase sales in a certain store by 14 percent next year. Note that the goal specifies the unit, the target level, and a time frame. As noted above, Citicorp has a goal of providing worldwide banking services. This is a very general goal in that it specifies no time frame and establishes only a broadly stated target.

As we can see in Exhibit 4.5, goals tend to take a longer time and be more general at the top of the organization, and they are usually shorter range and more specific at the lower levels of the organization.

Goal Optimization

Suppose a plant manager in an organization sets a goal of reducing costs by 10 percent. One way to do this might be to buy cheaper materials and put more pressure on workers. Now suppose a marketing manager in that organization has decided to increase sales by 5 percent by promoting product quality, and a human resource manager in the same organization has decided to cut turnover by 20 percent. In all likelihood, the actions of the first manager will hurt the chances of the other two managers achieving their goals.

This is where goal optimization becomes important. **Goal optimization** is the process of balancing and trading off between different goals for the sake of organizational effectiveness. Achieving the balance called for in goal optimization is a difficult task. The manager usually starts with a set of conflicting, disparate, and diverse goals. Using talent, insight, and experience, and with the appropriate level of flexibility and autonomy, she then arranges them into a unified, consistent, and congruent set of organizational goals.

PRELUDE CASE   UPDATE

We can now see how managers at Kellogg have had to balance a variety of goals in their efforts to remain number one in the cereal market. For example, consider various current activities and how goal conflict was possible. Increased advertising expenses have been necessary to fight back against competition. At the same time, however, Kellogg is spending over $1 billion on what will be the world's largest cereal plant in Memphis. When complete, the plant will be the most technologically advanced food processing facility in the world. Yet, someone had to decide how much could be spent on the plant versus how much would go to advertising. And this decision had to be made against still other competing demands, such as the company's international efforts.

The optimization process allows the organization to pursue a unified vision and helps managers maintain consistency in their actions. In the example mentioned earlier, a middle manager might help the marketing, plant, and human resource managers compromise on their respective goals so that each can make progress in his or her area without getting in the way of the others. For the kinds of optimizing necessary at Kellogg, the chief executive officer and his vice presidents were no doubt involved in the decisions that had to be made.

EFFECTIVE GOAL SETTING

Now let's look at some more specific insights into and guidelines for effective organizational goal setting. We should first consider the six major barriers to effective goal setting. Then we will explore several methods for overcoming these barriers.

Barriers to Effective Goal Setting

☐ There are six major barriers to effective goal setting.

The six major barriers to goal setting are illustrated in Table 4.1. Each of these barriers can potentially cause managers to set goals ineffectively.

SETTING INAPPROPRIATE GOALS   One key barrier is setting inappropriate goals—goals that do not fit the organization's purpose, mission, or strategy. For example, a state university goal of earning a 10 percent profit next year would clearly be inappropriate, given the institution's purpose and mission. At a more subtle level, goals that do not fit the strategy of the firm can also be inappropriate. If K mart decided to open an expensive, high-fashion department store in downtown New York, this goal would conflict with the retailer's strategy of operating discount stores in the suburbs. Although new ventures like this might work, they are appropriate only if they are well conceived and reflect conscious decisions to change strategy.[12]

TABLE 4.1
Barriers to Effective
Goal Setting

Barriers
1. Managers set inappropriate or incorrect goals.
2. Managers set unattainable or impossible goals.
3. Managers overemphasize quantitative or easily measured goals.
4. Managers overemphasize qualitative or ambiguous goals.
5. Managers mistakenly reward ineffective goal setting.
6. Managers fail to reward effective goal setting.

SETTING UNATTAINABLE GOALS   Another barrier to effective goal setting is establishing unattainable goals. This means setting goals that are impossible to achieve. Goals should be challenging, but if they are unattainable they will eventually stop working as an effective incentive. To use the target analogy again, a darts player likes to have to try hard to hit the center of the board, but if the bull's eye is so small that she can never hit it, she will eventually stop trying. Similarly, a sales manager at Procter & Gamble who sets a goal of tripling product sales in the territory within one year has probably aimed for an unattainable goal. Instead he should set a challenging but realistic goal for sales growth. This will serve as an incentive and will motivate people to work to achieve it.[13]

OVEREMPHASIZING QUANTITATIVE GOALS   A third barrier is overemphasizing quantitative goals. If everything else is equal, managers will probably find it best to state goals quantitatively so that they can more easily assess the extent to which those goals are achieved. At the same time, it is easy to overemphasize quantitative goals. If we go back to an earlier example, recall that Citicorp set three goals; two of these—earnings growth of 15 percent a year and a 20 percent return on shareholders' equity—were quantitative, and the other—becoming an international bank—was qualitative. The problem becomes clear when managers try to assess Citicorp's performance. Because of the mix of goals, they may tend to focus on the first two because they are easier to measure than the third.

OVEREMPHASIZING QUALITATIVE GOALS   Of course, it is also easy to go too far in the other direction. As the previous paragraph implies, the problem again comes from assessing goal accomplishment. If a plant manager at Alcoa sets a goal of increasing worker morale and cutting costs, how will she determine her performance? How is morale measured? And is a 2 percent cut in costs an indication of success, or is 20 percent needed? Thus, overemphasizing qualitative goals is just as much of a problem as overemphasizing quantitative goals.

REWARDING INEFFECTIVE GOAL SETTING   Another barrier to effective goal setting occurs when an organization rewards ineffective goal setting. For example, suppose a food services manager for American Airlines aims to cut the number of unused meals on American flights and to reduce passenger complaints about the quality of those meals. At the end of the year, a senior manager notes that unused meals have been cut by 10 percent and complaints have dropped 3 percent. At first glance this looks successful. However, it could be that food services has decreased the number of meals that are loaded onto planes to begin with and that flight attendants are giving coupons for free flights to passengers who don't get meals. The small costs savings from fewer meals being served is going to be more than offset by more free flights in the future. If the food services manager is rewarded, such poor goal setting will continue.

NOT REWARDING EFFECTIVE GOAL SETTING   A related problem occurs when managers do set good goals but are not rewarded for their efforts. Consider a human resource manager at Exxon who sets a goal of reducing turnover by 4 percent and increasing employee training by twenty hours a year. At the end of the year, turnover has been trimmed by 3.8 percent and training has been increased by seventeen hours, even though the budget for training has actually been cut by top management. If the manager's boss focuses on the fact that the goals were not fully achieved, he will be failing to reward effective goal setting.

Overcoming the Barriers to Goal Setting

□ There are five major guidelines for facilitating effective goal setting.

Fortunately, a number of useful guidelines for facilitating effective goal setting are available. The five guidelines, summarized in Table 4.2, help to offset or overcome the barriers just discussed.

UNDERSTANDING THE PURPOSE OF GOALS   First and foremost, managers must understand and remember the purpose of goals. As we saw at the beginning of this chapter, a goal is a target, and targets are things to be aimed at but not necessarily hit every time. A manager who sets appropriate goals and then comes close to achieving them is probably doing a good job. A manager who sets ineffective goals is probably not doing such a good job. If managers keep in mind that goals are targets and not absolute levels of performance that must be achieved regardless of the circumstances, they will go a long way toward enhancing the effectiveness of goal setting.[14]

STATING GOALS PROPERLY   Goals should also be stated in proper form if they are to be most effective. As far as possible, goals should have three attributes. First, they should be concise, that is, as brief as possible. Second, they should be specific. They should state clearly what their focus is (sales, costs, or whatever) and what is to be accomplished (increase or decrease, and by what amount). Finally, they should indicate a time frame for accomplishment. Thus, if General Electric wants a certain business to increase its market share by 10 percent within three years, it should state the goal in just that

TABLE 4.2
Overcoming Barriers to Effective Goal Setting

Guidelines for Effective Goal Setting
1. Managers should understand the purpose of goals.
2. Managers should state goals properly.
3. Managers should ensure goal consistency.
4. Managers should communicate goals to others.
5. Managers should reward effective goal setting.

way—the goal is concise, specific, and has a time frame. Of course, not all goals can fit this format. Whenever possible, however, managers should use it as a model for goal setting.

ENSURING GOAL CONSISTENCY   Managers should also strive for goal consistency. This essentially relates back to the notion of optimization discussed earlier. Goals should be consistent both horizontally (between areas) and vertically (between levels of management). Such consistency will play a key role in enhancing the effectiveness of goal setting.

COMMUNICATING GOALS TO OTHERS   In a related vein, communication of goals to others in the organization is also important. As simple as this sounds, managers occasionally make the mistake of setting goals and then not letting other people know about them. Without this information, the organization's employees cannot be working in a unified manner to achieve the firm's goals. Managers can communicate their goals in written form or in meetings. One method for communicating goals, management by objectives, is explored in the final section of this chapter.

LEARNING CHECK

You should now be able to discuss effective goal setting, including barriers to such effectiveness and how to overcome those barriers.

REWARDING EFFECTIVE GOAL SETTING   Finally, goal setting can be made more effective if it is properly rewarded. We have already noted the problems of rewarding ineffective goal setting and not rewarding effective goal setting. If managers can overcome these tendencies and make sure that they reward effective goal setting, effectiveness will certainly increase. Again, management by objectives is a useful method for dealing with this situation.

Motorola has had to undergo major changes in its approach to doing business in order to compete with the Japanese. The firm initially set a goal of improving quality ten-fold, and later raised it to be virtually defect-free. Robert N. Weisshappel, a manager in the firm's cellular-telephone operations, has helped carry the message throughout the organization. The goals have been widely embraced because they were clear, widely communicated, and consistently applied throughout the organization.

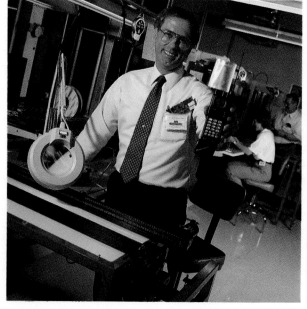

Gwendolen Cates

THE WORLD OF MANAGEMENT

Cypress Cranks with Turbo MBO

Cypress Semiconductor Corporation has grown from a small concern generating $3 million in revenues in 1984 to one of the fastest-growing companies in America, raking up over $80 million in sales in 1988. A key to the success enjoyed by Cypress is an elaborate goal-setting system called "Turbo MBO."

Turbo MBO is a comprehensive computer-driven system planned and designed by Cypress CEO T. J. Rogers. Every Monday morning, project managers map out what needs to be accomplished that week. The data are entered into the computer, which in turn massages it into operational goals and reports. On Tuesday, managers sit at their computers and review goals for each of their subordinates for the week. Goals are adjusted so as to balance the workload while simultaneously achieving the overall goals for the week.

On Wednesday, vice presidents review the goals and provide additional assistance to managers having trouble. On Thursday, more attention is devoted to areas where additional resources are needed, and steps are taken to get every goal on track. On Friday, the work for the week is completed, and performance data are entered to match against the original goals. On Monday, the whole process is repeated.

To outsiders, the system seems cumbersome. However, it only takes an average of a few hours a week for each manager, and it serves to provide guidance and direction to everyone in the company. Rogers says that the Turbo MBO system helps get new products developed and to the marketplace in half the time of his competitors and credits it with being one of the major reasons for Cypress's success.

SOURCES: Brian Dumaine, "What the Leaders of Tomorrow See," *Fortune*, July 3, 1989, pp. 48–62; Steven B. Kaufman, "The Goal System That Drives Cypress," *Business Month*, July 1987, pp. 30–32; "Speed Freaks," *Barron's*, May 23, 1988, pp. 15, 42–43.

MANAGEMENT BY OBJECTIVES

☐ *Management by objectives (MBO) is a procedure for collaborative goal setting between managers and their subordinates throughout the organization.*

Over the years, managers have explored several different approaches to help them do a better job of setting goals. One very popular method is management by objectives. **Management by objectives, or MBO,** is a technique that has been specifically developed to facilitate the goal-setting process in organizations through collaboration between managers and their subordinates. MBO goes by a number of different names, such as *management by goals* and *management by results. Management Today: The World of Management* describes how one company, Cypress Semiconductor, uses a modified form of MBO. Here we will learn about the general framework that is most often used.[15]

The Nature of MBO

In its purest form, MBO is a process of collaborative goal setting between a manager and his or her subordinates. The idea is that the superior and subordinate will jointly determine goals for the subordinate, with the understanding

115

that the subordinate's future rewards will depend on how well he attains the goals.

Two basic assumptions underlie the use of MBO. First, goals should come down the organization from top to bottom. Goals start at the top of the organization, then flow down to each successive level until they reach the bottom ranks of the firm. The second assumption of MBO is that, through the process of collaboration, employees will become more committed to achieving organizational goals. They will take part in setting their own goals and will be rewarded in relation to their success in reaching those goals.

The Mechanics of MBO

Exhibit 4.6 summarizes the steps involved in using MBO. First, organizational goals are established by top management. Through a series of meetings, everyone then agrees on a set of collaborative goals. This collaboration begins with the communication of organizational goals. Each employee then meets individually with his or her immediate superior to discuss the superior's goals and how the employee can help achieve them. The two then agree on goals for the subordinate. These goals should be as verifiable as possible, and they are usually written down. The superior then counsels the employee in how to "attack" the goals. Finally, the two decide on what resources the subordinate needs to achieve the goals.

As employees of the company work toward the goals, they commonly hold periodic reviews to assess their progress. It may be necessary to adjust resources or modify the goals if the subordinate is having unforeseen problems. Ideally, however, few modifications are made. At the end of the stated time period (usually one year), the boss and the employee hold another meeting to evaluate the degree of goal attainment. Employees are rewarded according to how well they have attained the goals, and new goals are set for the next year.

The Effectiveness of MBO

Many organizations have used MBO, including Alcoa, Tenneco, Black & Decker, RCA, Du Pont, and General Foods. Indeed, at one time or another almost half of the Fortune 500 have used MBO. Not surprisingly, some organizations have enjoyed tremendous success with the technique, although other companies have had disappointing results.

In general, when MBO is used properly, it does seem to enhance motivation and communication, facilitate effective goal setting, and provide a useful framework for evaluating performance and allocating rewards. But it also increases paperwork (since goals are written down) and may focus too much attention on the short-term period for which goals have been set rather than on longer-term issues.

On balance, MBO does seem to be a useful technique for enhancing the effectiveness of organizational goal-setting activities. The key is to use the technique appropriately and to match it to the particular characteristics of the organization.[16]

LEARNING CHECK

You should now be able to describe the nature, purpose, and mechanics of management by objectives.

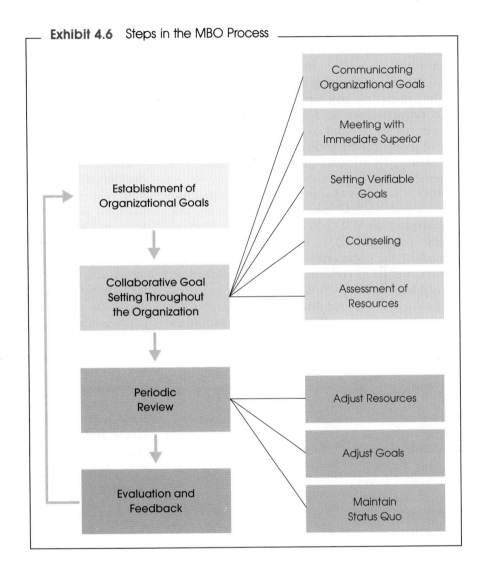

Exhibit 4.6 Steps in the MBO Process

Chapter Summary

A goal is a desired state or condition that an organization wants to achieve. The steps in the goal-setting process are (1) to scan the environment for opportunities and threats; (2) to assess organizational strengths and weaknesses; (3) to establish general organizational goals; (4) to establish unit and (5) subunit goals; and (6) to monitor progress toward goal attainment and provide feedback as the cycle repeats.

The general environment is the set of forces that characterize the setting of the organization. There are five such forces: political-legal, economic, international, sociocultural, and technological. The task en-

vironment consists of those specific elements in the general environment that affect the target organization. There are six of these: customers, competitors, unions, regulators, suppliers, and partners. The environment is important because it affects not only goal setting but also ongoing activities aimed at goal attainment.

Regardless of their characteristics, all organizations must pursue many goals in order to survive. Those goals may be differentiated by level of management, area, and time frame and specificity. Goal optimization is the process of balancing and trading off between different goals for the sake of organizational effectiveness.

There are six major barriers to effective goal setting: (1) setting inappropriate goals, (2) setting un-attainable goals, (3) overemphasizing quantitative goals, (4) overemphasizing qualitative goals, (5) rewarding ineffective goal setting, and (6) not rewarding effective goal setting. In order to overcome these barriers, managers need to (1) understand the purpose of goals, (2) state goals properly, (3) ensure goal consistency, (4) communicate goals to others, and (5) reward effective goal setting.

MBO is a process of collaborative goal setting between a manager and his or her subordinates. The basic steps in the MBO process are (1) to establish organizational goals, (2) to set goals collaboratively throughout the organization, (3) to employ periodic reviews, and (4) to evaluate and provide feedback to the organization. Steps two and three can be elaborated to suggest the finer detail necessary to make the process truly effective. If used properly, MBO can often improve organizational effectiveness.

The Manager's Vocabulary

goal	competitors
goal setting	unions
general environment	regulators
political-legal forces	suppliers
economic forces	partners
international forces	purpose
sociocultural forces	mission
technological forces	goal optimization
task environment	management by
customers	objectives (MBO)

Prelude Case Wrap-Up

The Prelude Case for this chapter details how Kellogg initially took advantage of a new product innovation to establish a dominant position in the new industry it had created. Complacency eventually caused the company to slip a bit, but Kellogg has come roaring back now and is again inching toward its long-standing goal of a 50 percent share of the breakfast cereal market.

However, the dynamic and volatile environment faced by most food-processing companies can still spell trouble. For example, recent findings about the positive benefits of oat bran caught Kellogg in a dis-

advantaged position relative to General Mills, maker of such cereals as Cheerios and Raisin Nut Bran. Since a very high percentage of General Mills's products contain oat bran, those cereals have enjoyed a tremendous surge in popularity. Kellogg, in contrast, was producing only a few cereals with oat bran and had to scramble to stop market share erosion to General Mills.

Indeed, the aggressive efforts of General Mills in the United States have taken away market share from most other cereal makers, including Kellogg. Kellogg has been slow to respond to the General Mills challenge and has only recently started introducing some successful oat cereals.

On the other hand, Kellogg is still considered the top American cereal maker in the international market, whereas General Mills is only a bit player. Indeed, one reason that General Mills caught Kellogg napping was that the cereal giant was concentrating so keenly on international expansion. Overall, then, Kellogg is still well poised to compete successfully in foreign markets. And to add an ironic postscript, new findings that call into question the value of oat bran serve to underscore the volatility of the environment faced by food companies. These findings may renew Kellogg's momentum in the United States, but may also render their huge financial commitment to oat bran unnecessary.

Prelude Case Questions

1. What elements of the general and task environments beyond those discussed in the case might Kellogg have to contend with in the future?
2. How does Kellogg stack up in terms of strengths and weaknesses? Opportunities and threats? Give details.
3. What role have goals played at Kellogg? Identify an apparent example of goal optimization.
4. What goals might Kellogg consider for the future? Do you think it should change its goal of 50 percent market share? Why or why not?

Discussion Questions

Review Questions

1. What are the six steps in the organizational goal-setting process?

2. What are the five forces that constitute the general environment? Think of an organization with which you are familiar and give two examples of how each force has affected or might someday affect the organization.
3. What are the six elements that constitute the task environment? Think of an organization with which you are familiar and give two examples of how each element has affected or might someday affect the organization.
4. List the various kinds of goals that an organization is likely to have, and explain why goal optimization is important.
5. List six barriers to effective goal setting and five ways to overcome those barriers.

Analysis Questions

1. Much of the chapter discussion of the environment focuses on how the environment affects the organization and how the organization has to respond to the environment. Sometimes, though, the organization can affect or change its environment. Identify ways that an organization might at least attempt to change part of both the general and the task environment.
2. Using Kellogg or another organization with which you are familiar, develop a set of hypothetical goals that the organization might develop that relates to each dimension of both the general and the task environments.
3. What kinds of goals would a not-for-profit organization such as your college or university have? What might be the similarities and differences be-

tween those goals and the goals of a business operating for profit?
4. Using the general guidelines for overcoming barriers to goal setting, develop at least two very specific suggestions for overcoming each barrier.
5. Imagine you are a subordinate in an organization that uses MBO. What elements of the MBO process might you object most strongly to? In what ways might you be able to "beat the system"?

Application Questions and Exercises

1. Take a sheet of paper and across the top write "strengths," "weaknesses," "opportunities," and "threats." List as many of each for your college or university as you can think of. Compare your list with those of your classmates.
2. List the major goals you have for yourself (for example, grades, graduation date, career, personal, and so forth) and then classify them into some meaningful framework. Can you see any areas in which you will have to optimize inconsistent or contradictory goals?
3. Interview a local businessperson and ask the individual to identify the goals he or she has for the business. Classify them into the kinds discussed in the chapter.
4. What goals does your instructor have for this class? Have any barriers affected his or her goals? If so, how might those barriers be overcome?
5. Develop a management-by-objectives system that your instructor might conceivably use to teach this class. What major problems would exist with such a system? What beneficial results might occur?

ENHANCEMENT CASE

AMERICAN EXPRESS WALKS A TIGHTROPE

American Express was started in 1845 when Henry Wells formed an express delivery company in Buffalo, New York. His goal was to deliver mail more efficiently than the federal government. He merged with two competitors in 1859 to form American Express. Wells and one of his vice presidents, William Fargo, later pulled out and formed still another com-

pany, which they named Wells Fargo & Company. Meanwhile, American Express, or AmEx, continued to prosper.

AmEx eventually moved into financial services and gradually dropped out of the express delivery business altogether. Today, AmEx is one of the most recognized and respected corporations in the world. But the company is also walking a tightrope as it seeks to respond to competition on a variety of fronts.

A key part of AmEx is its credit card business. Credit card companies earn a commission paid by the merchant on each sale charged to the card. When the card carries with it a line of credit, additional profits are made on interest charges when card holders stretch their payments. Finally, card holders also usually pay an annual fee for the card.

For years, AmEx catered to upper-class and business travelers almost exclusively. Having an American Express card, especially a gold or platinum one, was a status symbol, and the cards were generally accepted only at nicer restaurants, hotels, and shops, as well as by airlines and car rental companies. Many larger corporations also established corporate accounts with AmEx, and American Express was almost synonymous with traveler's checks.

In contrast, bank credit cards like Visa and MasterCard were targeted more to middle-class consumers and were more likely to be accepted at mid-level restaurant, hotel, and retail chains. In recent years, however, things have started to change dramatically.

Much of this change came because the bank cards wanted a bigger piece of the lucrative business market. Visa and MasterCard started attracting upscale merchants that had previously accepted only the AmEx card. The bank cards also started to aggressively seek corporate accounts. They also introduced premium gold cards with higher credit limits and an aura of status. And both also now offer traveler's checks.

American Express management recognized this threat before it could do serious damage and devised a counterattack. Specifically, AmEx set four broad goals for 1997:

- ☐ Double the world card base to sixty million members
- ☐ Triple the merchant base to six million
- ☐ Quadruple annual charges to $300 billion
- ☐ Maintain the card's image of prestige and status

To date, AmEx seems to be moving toward these goals. Some managers have worried that striving to accomplish the first three is contradictory with the

Ella Fitzgerald. Cardmember since 1961.

Membership Has Its Privileges.

Don't leave home without it.
Call 1-800-THE CARD to apply.

American Express works hard to create an upscale and sophisticated image for its products. Ads such as the one shown here of singer Ella Fitzgerald portray celebrities in eye-catching situations.

fourth, but most think it can be done. For example, Exxon now accepts the AmEx card at 14,000 outlets, and talks are under way between AmEx and K mart, Burger King, and Domino's Pizza.

AmEx has also attacked the bank cards on their own turf with the Optima card, a revolving charge card with a floating interest rate. And AmEx has also introduced a myriad of other services tied together with its incredible computerized information system. For example, you can now buy mutual funds and life insurance from American Express. And when you charge a plane ticket to France on your AmEx card, the company will follow up by mailing you a brochure advertising luggage and flight insurance. You can even call a 900-number (and pay for the call) to learn about weather conditions wherever you're going.

Perhaps the biggest challenge faced by AmEx, however, is further market penetration in foreign markets. Complex banking regulations and local competition have made it difficult for AmEx to achieve success in some markets. On the plus side, the company has done well in both West Germany and the Far East. On the other hand, Italian merchants have been reluctant to pay commissions and many refuse to honor the card. And local competition in France has made profits hard to come by in that country.

SOURCES: "American Express Promotes Its Gold Card," *The Wall Street Journal*, June 9, 1989, p. B4; "American Express Chases After the Fast-Food Market," *The Wall Street Journal*, April 15, 1989, pp. B1, B5; "Do You Know Me?" *Business Week*, January 25, 1988, pp. 72–82; "How AmEx Is Revamping Its Big, Beautiful Money Machine," *Business Week*, June 13, 1988, pp. 90–92; "American Express Card Users in Italy Meet Some Resistance from Merchants," *The Wall Street Journal*, August 10, 1989, p. A10; "Owning All of Shearson Could Prove Costly for American Express," *The Wall Street Journal*, March 6, 1990, pp. A1, A14.

Enhancement Case Questions

1. What are the strengths, weaknesses, opportunities, and threats faced by AmEx?
2. What elements of the general and task environments are most relevant to AmEx?
3. Evaluate the goals AmEx has set for 1997.
4. What barriers might exist to reaching the goals? How might those barriers be overcome?

Chapter Notes

1. Carol Davenport, "America's Most Admired Corporations," *Fortune*, January 30, 1989, pp. 68–94.
2. See Max D. Richards, *Setting Strategic Goals and Objectives*, 2nd ed. (St. Paul, Minn.: West, 1986), for more discussion of the goal-setting process.
3. See David Ulrich and Margarethe F. Wiersema, "Gaining Strategic and Organizational Capability in a Turbulent Business Environment," *Academy of Management Executive*, May 1989, pp. 115–122, for a recent discussion of the role of organizational environments.
4. Richard L. Daft, *Organization Theory and Design*, 3rd ed. (St. Paul, Minn.: West, 1989).
5. See John W. Meyer and W. Richard Scott, eds., *Organizational Environments* (Beverly Hills, Calif.: Sage, 1983), for a review.
6. Jeremy Main, "How to Go Global—And Why," *Fortune*, August 28, 1989, pp. 70–75.
7. Brian Dumaine, "What the Leaders of Tomorrow See," *Fortune*, July 3, 1989, pp. 48–62.
8. James D. Thompson, *Organizations in Action* (New York: McGraw-Hill, 1967), and Gregory G. Dess and Donald W. Beard, "Dimensions of Organizational Task Environments," *Administrative Science Quarterly*, March 1984, pp. 52–73.
9. Rosabeth Moss Kanter, "Becoming PALS: Pooling, Allying, and Linking Across Companies," *Academy of Management Executive*, August 1989, pp. 183–193.
10. Jeremy Main, "The Winning Organization," *Fortune*, September 26, 1988, pp. 50–60.
11. Edward Boyer, "Citicorp: What the New Boss Is Up To," *Fortune*, February 17, 1986, p. 40.
12. Max Richards, *Setting Strategic Goals and Objectives* (St. Paul, Minn.: West, 1986).
13. See Edwin W. Locke, "The Ubiquity of the Technique of Goal Setting in Theories of and Approaches to Employee Motivation," *Academy of Management Review*, July 1978, pp. 594–602.
14. See Craig Pinder, *Work Motivation* (Glenview, Ill.: Scott, Foresman, 1984), and Richards, *Setting Strategic Goals and Objectives*.
15. See Stephen J. Carroll and Henry L. Tosi, *Management by Objectives* (New York: Macmillan, 1973), for a general discussion of MBO. See also Locke, "The Ubiquity of the Technique of Goal Setting," and Pinder, *Work Motivation*.
16. Jack N. Kondrasuk, "Studies in MBO Effectiveness," *Academy of Management Review*, July 1981, pp. 419–430. See also Jan P. Muczyk and Bernard C. Reimann, "MBO as a Complement to Effective Leadership," *Academy of Management Executive*, May 1989, pp. 131–138.

CHAPTER OUTLINE

I. Planning in Organizations
   A. Why Managers Plan
   B. Responsibilities for Planning

II. Kinds of Planning
   A. Strategic Planning
   B. Tactical Planning
   C. Operational Planning

III. Time Frames for Planning
   A. Long-Range Planning
   B. Intermediate Planning
   C. Short-Range Planning
   D. Integrating Time Frames

IV. Contingency Planning
   A. The Nature of Contingency Planning
   B. Contingency Events

V. Managing the Planning Process
   A. Roadblocks to Effective Planning
   B. Avoiding the Roadblocks

VI. Tools and Techniques for Planning
   A. Forecasting
   B. Other Planning Techniques
   C. Using Planning Tools and Techniques

C
H
A
P
T
E
R

5

LEARNING OBJECTIVES

After studying this chapter you should be able to

1. Discuss the nature of planning, including its purpose and where the responsibilities for planning lie within the organization.

2. Identify and define three major kinds of plans.

3. Describe three major time frames for planning and how these time frames are integrated within organizations.

4. Define contingency planning and describe contingency events.

5. Discuss how to manage the planning process by avoiding the roadblocks to effective planning.

6. Describe forecasting and other tools and techniques for planning and how to use them.

Managerial Planning

WOOLWORTH CHANGES COURSE

F. W. Woolworth Company was a business going nowhere. For years, Woolworth variety stores (often called "five and dimes") were a fixture all across the country. You could find them everywhere, and the company itself was a major force in American retailing. But then the environment changed and Woolworth failed to change with it. First came the large-scale migration of the American people to the suburbs and the subsequent birth of the shopping mall. Next was the advent of the discounters, led by Woolworth's rival, Kresge company and its K mart stores.

The shifting population base left many Woolworth stores in declining neighborhoods. But the company made little effort to follow the consumer to the suburbs. And K mart, with its expanded merchandise lines and discount prices, changed the way Americans shopped. When managers at Woolworth finally recognized what was happening, they tried to respond. But every step they took seemed to be the wrong one.

Perhaps their biggest blunder was following Kresge into discounting with the Woolco chain. Woolco executives never seemed to get the hang of cost controls or site selection. Even though there were 336 Woolco stores in operation by 1982 and they were generating over $2 billion in annual sales, they were only marginally profitable. And even those meager profits were dropping rapidly.

Company executives finally came to the realization that they were headed in all the wrong directions. Thus, in late 1982 the Woolco operation was shut down altogether. And company officials developed a new set of plans that have steered the venerable retailer back toward the top of the heap.

The new direction that Woolworth managers chose to follow was specialty retailing. (A specialty retailer is one that carries a single or narrow product line, such as shoes or men's clothing, rather than trying to carry a full line of merchandise that appeals to many different people.) The company had purchased Kinney Shoes

in 1963 and the Richman Brothers clothing chain in 1969. Both specialty chains had remained profitable throughout Woolworth's period of decline. Thus, managers reasoned that rather than try to operate a single large variety store in a shopping mall, it made more sense to operate several small specialty shops.

An ambitious set of plans was formulated to make Woolworth the king of the specialty retailers. First, it was decided that the company could not be afraid of failure. Managers argued that it stands to reason that if several new specialty stores are opened, a few are likely to fail. Next, managers decided to develop and maintain a sophisticated information system that allowed them to track customer profiles and purchasing patterns. These data could then be used to identify other potential markets.

For example, a spectacularly successful business for Woolworth has been Foot Locker, a division of Kinney. The first Foot Locker was opened in 1974, stimulated in

Woolworth has been incredibly successful at specialty retailing. For example, Kinney (general shoe lines), Richman (clothes), Lady Foot Locker (women's sports shoes), and Champs (sporting goods) have all been big hits for the retailer. Woolworth owns a number of other specialty chains as well and is expanding aggressively.

Photos by Andy Freeberg

part because Kinney stores were selling more and more athletic shoes. Foot Locker was an immediate success because of the jogging boom. Managers subsequently discovered that almost 80 percent of Foot Locker customers were men. But since women were also exercising more, the company decided to open Lady Foot Locker. That chain, too, has prospered. It should come as no surprise, then, that Kids Locker was born in 1987.

Woolworth has also enjoyed many other successes as well. Herald Square sells stationery and party goods. Afterthoughts sells inexpensive fashion accessories. Champs is well on its way toward becoming a national sporting goods chain. And harkening back to the company's roots, Woolworth Express stores, selling limited product lines, have also proliferated.

SOURCES: Bill Saporito, "Woolworth to Rule the Malls," *Fortune*, June 5, 1989, pp. 145–156; "How They're Knocking the Rust Off Two Old Chains," *Business Week*, September 8, 1986, pp. 44–45; "Specialty Stores Spruce Up Bottom Line," *USA Today*, February 26, 1988, pp. 1B–2B; Bill Saporito, "Retailing's Winners & Losers," *Fortune*, December 18, 1989, pp. 69–80.

W hen most people think of fast-growing retailers, they think of Wal-Mart (145 new stores in 1988), McDonald's (600 new stores in 1988), and Benetton (over 200 stores in 1989). In fact, however, Woolworth opened more new stores in 1988 than these three chains combined—over 1,100 new stores altogether. What accounts for the newfound success being enjoyed by Woolworth? The most fundamental factor is effective planning. Managers at Woolworth took a careful look at their environment and discovered a new path to success. And this new path, specialty retailer, has continued to pay handsome dividends.

This chapter focuses on planning as a basic management function. First it looks at the nature of planning. It then identifies major kinds of plans and discusses time frames for planning. After investigating contingency planning, it discusses ways in which the planning process can be more effectively managed. Finally, it identifies some important planning tools and techniques.

PLANNING IN ORGANIZATIONS

What is planning? To better understand it, we must first define and clarify its purpose and then identify who in the organization is responsible for planning.

Why Managers Plan

□ A *plan* is a blueprint or framework an organization uses to describe how it expects to achieve its goals. *Planning* is the process of developing plans.

A **plan** is a blueprint or framework used to describe how an organization expects to achieve its goals. **Planning**, then, is simply the process of developing plans. In essence, planning is determining which path among several to follow.[1]

For example, when Harry Hoffman became CEO of Waldenbooks in 1979, he developed several plans for achieving his goal of making the bookseller the leader in its industry. His plans called for rapidly increasing the number of stores in the chain, increasing promotional activities to boost the sales of each store, and expanding the product line. Each of these activities was part of a systematic effort to dramatically increase the company's sales. In terms of planning, Hoffman could have chosen to maintain the status quo, branch out into other markets, maintain a pattern of slow growth, or any of several other alternatives. His choice of rapid growth, then, was the creation of his particular blueprint for action.[2]

In other words, any goal might be approached in several ways. Planning is the process of determining which is the best way to approach a particular goal. Waldenbooks chose the path that seemed best for it. The same holds true for Woolworth. Of course, it's also possible to choose a wrong path. And this fact makes planning all the more important.

Responsibilities for Planning

□ All managers need to be involved in the planning process.

Given the obvious importance of planning, it is essential to identify planning responsibilities: that is, who does an organization's planning? The answer is quite simple: all managers are involved in the planning process.

Photo by J. T. Miller/Courtesy PSE&G

While all managers need to be involved in the planning process, some organizations rely on a specialized planning staff for assistance. Glenn Rogers is the manager of strategic planning for Public Service Enterprise Group. His staff provides centralized support services for managers of Enterprise's different subsidiaries engaged in strategic planning.

Exhibit 5.1 identifies several important planning centers within an organization. Planning starts with top management, which, working with the board of directors, establishes the broad goals and strategies of the firm. The usual approach is for the top management team to develop these goals and strategies and then submit them to the board for approval.

Many large organizations, such as Tenneco, General Motors, General Electric, Boeing, and Ford, also make use of a planning staff.[3] As noted in the exhibit, a planning staff is a group of professional planners at the top level of the organization. They assist line managers, providing expertise and various resources necessary to develop appropriate kinds of plans. They also coordinate and integrate the planning activities of other levels of the organization.

Middle managers play several roles in the planning process.[4] They work together to assist with strategic planning, and they undertake tactical planning

Exhibit 5.1   Planning Centers in an Organization

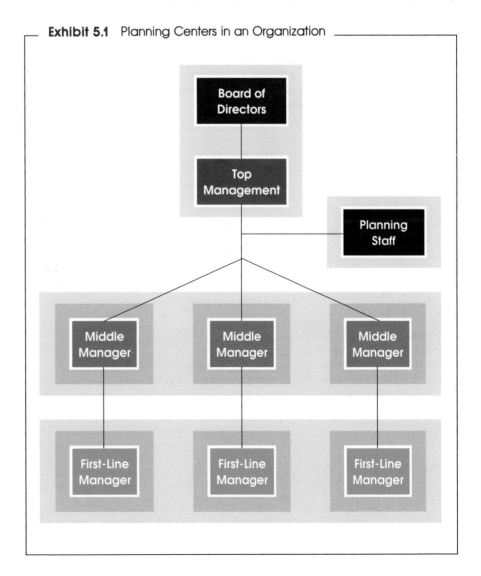

SMALL BUSINESS AND ENTREPRENEURSHIP

Baking Success at Mrs. Fields

One of the biggest entrepreneurial success stories in recent years has been Mrs. Fields' Cookies. The chain of cookie shops started when Debbi Fields decided to go into business for herself. She worried that she had few marketable skills at the time, but everyone who tried her cookies proclaimed them the best in the world. So, what better business to enter than the cookie business?

Using a start-up loan from her husband, Fields opened her first shop in Palo Alto, California, in 1977. After a slow start (she had to give cookies away the first day), the business took off. Today there are several hundred of her stores around the world.

What factors led to the success of Mrs. Fields' Cookies? One element was a good idea to begin with. Another was product quality. Still another critical component, however, has been Fields's ability to maintain control over every aspect of her burgeoning

empire. This control, in turn, has resulted in a well-integrated and consistent approach to doing business.

For example, Mrs. Fields' shops are not franchised; each is owned by the parent corporation. This tight control of ownership allows Fields to keep every aspect of her planning neatly integrated. She knows what she wants to be doing in five years, for example, and then sets forth a series of short-range plans to get there. She gets input from middle-level managers, store managers, and customers. And she subsequently keeps them informed about what's going on.

Fields recently bought La Petite Boulangerie, a 120-store bakery chain. This acquisition was a carefully planned part of her strategy for growth. And the integrated approach to planning that has proven successful in the past has allowed the new chain to be efficiently merged with the old one.

SOURCES: "Tough Cookies?" *Fortune*, February 13, 1989, p. 112; "How the Cookie Crumbled at Mrs. Fields," *The Wall Street Journal*, January 26, 1989, p. B1; Alan Furst, "The Golden Age of Goo," *Esquire*, December 1984, pp. 324–330.

LEARNING CHECK

You should now be able to discuss the nature of planning, including its purpose and where the responsibilities for planning lie within the organization.

(these types of planning are discussed below). They also work individually to develop and implement planning activities within their respective divisions or units.[5]

First-line managers must also be actively involved in planning. Like middle managers, they work together to make plans that affect more than one department or unit and work individually to plan for their own units. Their efforts mostly involve assisting with tactical planning and developing operational plans.[6] As you can see in *Management Today: Small Business and Entrepreneurship*, a well-integrated planning system that links all levels of the organization can be a major ingredient in organizational success.

KINDS OF PLANNING

Given the fact that organizations naturally have a large number of plans at any one time, and given the variety of areas for which plans can be developed, it is not surprising that planning falls into different categories. This section identifies and discusses the three major kinds of planning activities that go on in organizations. As shown in Exhibit 5.2, these can be described in terms of different levels of scope and different time frames.

Strategic Planning

☐ *Strategic planning* involves formulating the broad goals and plans to guide the general directions of the organization.

Strategic planning formulates the broad goals and plans developed by top managers to guide the general directions of the organization.[7] As illustrated in Exhibit 5.2, strategic plans are very broad in scope and have an extended time frame. Strategic planning follows from the major goals of the organization and indicates what businesses the firm is in or intends to be in and what kind of company its top managers want it to be. The key components of a strategy, then, outline how resources will be deployed and how the organization will position itself within its environment.

PepsiCo provides an excellent example of a firm with a well-conceived and well-executed strategic plan. Specifically, managers at PepsiCo have decided that the company will compete in three general areas of the food industry: soft drinks, fast food restaurants, and packaged snack foods. Its soft drink business, led by Pepsi-Cola and Slice, is so well established that many people equate it with PepsiCo. The fast food business is also thriving, however, led by Pizza Hut, Taco Bell, and Kentucky Fried Chicken. And finally, the snack

Exhibit 5.2 Kinds of Planning Activities

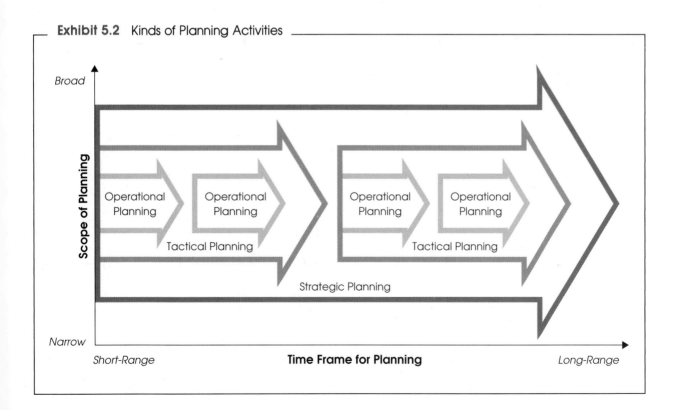

food business, called Frito-Lay, has such successful products as Fritos Corn Chips, Lays Potato Chips, and Doritos.[8]

PRELUDE CASE UPDATE

The effects of strategic planning on Woolworth have been tremendous. Perhaps the biggest turning points in the company's history were the decisions to pull out of discounting and to concentrate on specialty retailing. Each of these decisions involved millions and millions of dollars and the lives of thousands of company employees. The basic question, then, was one of resource deployment. And the answer clearly defined how Woolworth wanted to be positioned in its environment.

Tactical Planning

□ *Tactical planning* has a moderate scope and an intermediate time frame.

Whereas strategic planning has a broad scope and extended time frame, tactical planning has a moderate scope and an intermediate time frame. **Tactical planning** tends to focus on people and action; that is, it is concerned with how to implement the strategic plans that have already been developed. It also deals with specific resources and time constraints. Tactical planning is more closely associated with middle management than with top management.

When PepsiCo first bought Kentucky Fried Chicken, for example, managers developed several tactical plans to implement an aggressive growth strategy. First, managers noted that most of Kentucky Fried Chicken's business was done at night, whereas McDonald's does most of its business at lunch. So tactical plans were developed to increase Kentucky Fried Chicken's lunchtime business while retaining current levels of evening business. Second, PepsiCo managers plan to actively expand Kentucky Fried Chicken's menu offerings to include such things as roasted chicken and salad bars. Finally, PepsiCo also plans to offer home delivery, at least in some markets.

Operational Planning

□ *Operational planning* has a relatively narrow scope and a short time frame. Two basic kinds of operational plans are *standing plans* and *single-use plans.*

The third kind of planning is **operational planning,** which can take a variety of forms. In general, operational planning has the narrowest focus and the shortest time frame. Such plans are usually supervised by middle managers but executed by first-line managers. As illustrated in Table 5.1, there are two basic kinds of operational plans, standing plans and single-use plans.

STANDING PLANS Plans that are developed to handle recurring and relatively routine situations are called **standing plans**. Basic kinds of standing

TABLE 5.1
Operational Planning in
Organizations

Kinds of Operational Planning	
Standing Plans	*Single-Use Plans*
Policies	Programs
Standard Operating Procedures	Projects
Rules and Regulations	

plans include policies (the most general), standard operating procedures, and rules and regulations (the most specific).

☐ *Standing plans* are designed to handle recurring and relatively routine situations. Three forms are *policies, standard operating procedures,* and *rules and regulations.*

Policies are general guidelines that govern relatively important actions within the organization. For example, PepsiCo might establish a policy that no individual owning a stake in a McDonald's franchise will be allowed to acquire a franchise for a Pizza Hut restaurant. Similarly, the company could also establish policies concerning the control of advertising campaigns, restaurant appearance, and sources of cooking supplies.

Standard operating procedures, or **SOPs,** are more specific guidelines for handling a series of recurring activities. The manager of a Taco Bell restaurant, for example, might have a set of SOPs for inventory management. Following the SOPs, the manager could set desired levels of ingredients for each menu item, determine appropriate reorder schedules and amounts, and line up local suppliers. Following a set of SOPs, then, is fairly mechanical.

Finally, **rules and regulations** are statements of how specific activities are to be performed. A rule for a Kentucky Fried Chicken restaurant, for example, might dictate company policy regarding employee tardiness. Such a rule might state that if an employee is late to work three times in a two-month period, she or he is to be warned and told that the next incident may result in termination.

SINGLE-USE PLANS   The second major category of operational plans is **single-use plans**—plans set up to handle events that happen only once. The two types of single-use plans are programs and projects.

☐ *Single-use plans* are developed to handle events that only happen once. Two forms are *programs* and *projects.*

A **program** is a single-use plan for a large set of activities. The integration of Kentucky Fried Chicken into the PepsiCo system is a good example of a program. This integration was a major operation involving thousands of people and hundreds of operating systems. In all likelihood, several task forces were created to handle the transition, and millions of dollars were spent to make Kentucky Fried Chicken an integral part of the PepsiCo organization.

A **project** is similar to a program but usually has a narrower focus. A menu addition at Kentucky Fried Chicken, for example, can be considered a project. Market research determines that a particular new product will sell well, a recipe is developed and tested, relevant information is relayed to restaurant managers, the product is advertised and becomes a part of the regular menu, and managers move on to new things.

LEARNING CHECK

You should now be able to identify and define three major kinds of plans.

TIME FRAMES FOR PLANNING

Regardless of what kind of plan a manager is developing, it is important for him or her to recognize the role of the time factor. Chapter 4 notes that goals are often long range, intermediate, or short range in scope. Similarly, plans also focus on long-range, intermediate, and short-range time frames.

Long-Range Planning

◻ *Long-range planning spans several years to several decades.*

Long-range planning covers a period that can be as short as several years to as long as several decades. Virtually all large companies have long-range plans. Suppose, for example, that Boeing is planning to introduce a new generation of airplanes in ten years. This is a long-range plan. Given this plan, Boeing's managers can begin to develop other pertinent long-range plans. They may need to find a site for a new factory in six years so that the plant can be operational in eight years. They must arrange financing for the purchase of plant materials, construction costs, and raw materials for the new planes. They will need to be ready to take over operations at the plant in eight years, so after four years the managers might want to identify who will be in charge and subsequently train those people.

In general, long-range plans are primarily associated with activities such as major expansions of products or facilities, development of top managers, large

Courtesy of Shell Oil Company

Organizations must often engage in long-range planning, focusing on projects and activities extending many years into the future. Shell Oil Company recently put into operation project Bullwinkle, the world's tallest fixed offshore drilling platform. Shown here being towed into position, Bullwinkle took years to plan and construct. In addition, the project is a critical component in Shell's drilling plans for the next twenty years.

issues of new stocks and bonds, and the installation of new manufacturing systems. Top managers are responsible for long-range planning in most organizations. For example, Michael D. Eisner, CEO of Disney, recently said, "I think in terms of decades. The Nineties are EuroDisneyland. I've already figured out what we can do for 1997, and I've got a thing set for 2005."[9]

Intermediate Planning

☐ *Intermediate planning focuses on a time horizon of from one to five years.*

Intermediate planning generally involves a time perspective of between one and five years. Because of the uncertainties associated with long-range plans, intermediate plans are the primary concern of most organizations. Accordingly, they are usually developed by top managers working in conjunction with middle managers.

Intermediate plans are often seen as building blocks in the pursuit of long-range plans. If Apple Computer has a long-range plan to have ten major computer systems available for sale in ten years, its managers might begin by developing an intermediate plan to get four new systems under way within the next three years. At the end of three years, they would assess the situation and devise a new intermediate plan for the next time period.

Short-Range Planning

☐ *Short-range planning covers a period of less than one year.*

Finally, **short-range planning** covers time periods of one year or less. These plans focus on day-to-day activities and provide a concrete base for evaluating progress toward the achievement of intermediate and long-range plans. To use the Apple example, a short-range plan might be to get two new projects under way within the next year. The managers can thus focus on a specific set of activities (getting two new products under development) that need to be accomplished within the time frame (one year).

Integrating Time Frames

We have seen that intermediate plans should build toward the pursuit of long-range plans, but all three time frames ideally should be integrated, as shown in Exhibit 5.3. In the top part of the diagram, a company develops a long-range plan spanning ten years, an intermediate plan for five years, and a short-range plan for one year. Conceptually, at least, the short-range plan is identical to the first year of the intermediate plan, which in turn corresponds to the first five years of the long-range plan. *Management Today: The World of Management* highlights Fiat's difficulties in achieving the desired integration of plans across different time horizons.

At the end of one year, the short-range plan may or may not have been fulfilled, of course, so managers must develop a new short-range plan and modify the intermediate and long-range plans as appropriate. This is shown in the bottom part of Exhibit 5.3. Suppose, for example, that Dr. Pepper has de-

Exhibit 5.3 Integrated Time Frames for Planning

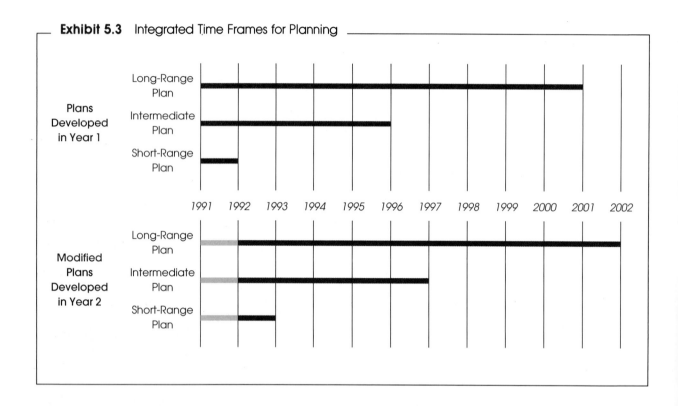

You should now be able to describe three major time frames for planning and how these time frames are integrated within organizations.

veloped a short-range plan to increase total sales by 5 percent and a long-range plan to increase sales by 25 percent. At the end of the first year, however, sales have increased by only 2 percent. Dr. Pepper's managers might then revise the intermediate plan down to 9 percent and the long-range plan down to 22 percent. This process of monitoring and adjusting plans relates to another important part of the process, contingency planning.

CONTINGENCY PLANNING

☐ *Contingency planning* is identifying alternative courses of action that might be followed if various conditions arise.

Contingency planning is the part of the planning process in which managers identify alternative courses of action that the organization might follow if various conditions arise.[10] Again, this is something that most companies do.

The Nature of Contingency Planning

The general nature of contingency planning follows the process shown in Exhibit 5.4. As illustrated, managers develop an initial plan (A) that specifies possible contingency events that might dictate modification of the original plan. The organization then monitors ongoing activities so that it will know

THE WORLD OF MANAGEMENT

Fiat Adjusts its Course

For decades, Fiat was a successful European automobile maker. Then came the oil crisis of the 1970s and tremendous competition from the Japanese. Fiat was caught with an aging product line, high costs, and an image of poor quality. At first, Fiat was devastated. But over time, its managers have developed an effective set of short- and long-range plans to turn things around.

In the short run, Fiat is working hard to build up its nontransportation businesses. For example, the company has operations in financial services, biotechnology, and robotics. These and other new ventures have made Fiat less susceptible to cyclical fluctuations in the automobile industry and less vulnerable to Japanese competition.

Over the longer term, however, Fiat hopes to remain a major player in the world automobile business. To achieve this, the company is initiating several long-term joint ventures with a variety of worldwide partners. For example, Fiat and General Motors have a joint venture in continental Europe, and Fiat and Ford have one in Britain.

When the European trade barriers drop in 1992, Fiat wants to be poised for opportunity but also in a position to deal with surprises. So, the company has outlined several short-term plans, each developed from a more comprehensive set of long-range plans based on different scenarios. A few years ago, many industry observers were writing Fiat off. Now, however, and thanks in large part to its new emphasis on planning, Fiat is clearly on its way back up.

SOURCES: "Its Turnaround Was Brilliant, But Can Fiat Stay the Course?" *Business Week,* August 15, 1988, pp. 66–70; "Fiat Is Setting Ambitious Goals for 1992 and Beyond," *The Wall Street Journal,* June 17, 1988, p. 22; "Agnelli on Cars, Greens, and Japan," *Fortune,* July 31, 1989, pp. 133–136.

if and when the events occur. Depending on the nature of the contingencies, the organization might continue its original plan (A), change to a contingency plan (B), or change to another contingency plan (C).[11]

PRELUDE CASE UPDATE

Woolworth managers use contingency planning as they develop and test ideas for new stores. Whenever a manager comes up with a concept that has some promise, he or she must first prepare a written plan outlining its merits and potential pitfalls. If other managers think the new concept is viable, Woolworth will open two stores in good locations and see how they do. If the results are encouraging, ten additional stores are opened the second year. And if they do well, a major expansion plan is put into place. Thus, a new concept is introduced incrementally and may be abandoned or pushed forward as the initial experiences dictate.

Exhibit 5.4   Contingency Planning

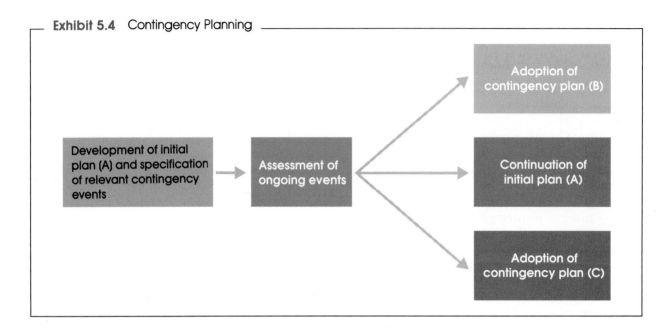

Contingency Events

Obviously, the identification of contingency events is a critical part of contingency planning. If the events are not properly identified, or if their relevant indicators are poorly understood, the entire process of contingency planning can fall apart.[12]

In general, critical contingency events relate either to the extent to which the ongoing plan is being accomplished or to environmental events that might change things in the future. For example, Burger King is in the midst of a major expansion program in the United States and Europe. Its managers might break down their intermediate plan into a series of five short-range plans, each of which calls for one hundred new U.S. restaurants and fifty new European restaurants at the end of each calendar year. One contingency event would then be the extent to which the short-range plans are being realized. If there are ninety-six new U.S. restaurants and fifty-one new European restaurants at the end of the first year, the managers may conclude that things are going well. In contrast, sixty new U.S. and fifteen new European restaurants would indicate a problem. The managers' contingency plans might call for a revision of the original plan or increased efforts to catch up in the second year as well as efforts to determine why the plan was not met.

The other kind of contingency event, as noted above, relates to the environment. Burger King's managers might have based their European expansion plans on the assumption that McDonald's and Wendy's would continue to expand at current rates. If McDonald's unexpectedly begins to double its rate of European expansion, Burger King might be forced to change its own plans.

Clearly, contingency planning is an important part of any organization's overall planning process. It should never be neglected, but should instead be an integral part of ongoing planning activities. In addition, there are other things managers should do to facilitate effective planning. The next section addresses some of these.

MANAGING THE PLANNING PROCESS

As we have seen several times already, planning is a vital part of all managerial jobs. Two additional dimensions of planning, understanding the roadblocks to effective planning and knowing how these roadblocks can be avoided, are critical if planning is to be carried out properly.

Roadblocks to Effective Planning

What can go wrong when managers set out to develop plans? In truth, any number of factors can disrupt effective planning.[13] Let's look at Table 5.2 and consider five of the most common ones.

THE ENVIRONMENT   In Chapter 4 we looked at the importance of the environment in goal setting and planning. Most organizations operate in environments that are both complex and dynamic. That is, managers must contend with a great many environmental forces and dimensions (complexity) and with the fact that these forces and dimensions change rapidly (dynamism). In combination, these factors make it harder to develop effective plans. For example, General Electric recently plunged into factory automation. Demand dropped, other automation systems turned out to be more advanced than GE's, and soaring costs drove prices up. Each of these factors resulted from environmental complexity and dynamism. Consequently, GE's original plans for sales and income from automation were not realized.[14]

RESISTANCE TO CHANGE   Another factor that can impede effective planning is resistance to change. By its very nature, planning involves change.

TABLE 5.2
Roadblocks to Effective Planning

Roadblocks
1. The environment might be so complex and/or changing that managers fail to plan effectively.
2. Managers might resist change for a variety of reasons and avoid planning that might lead to change.
3. Effective planning might be constrained by labor contracts, government regulations, or scarce resources.
4. Managers might not plan effectively because the plans are developed from poor or inappropriate goals.
5. Lack of time and/or money can limit managers' ability to plan effectively.

Fear of the unknown, preferences for the status quo, and economic insecurity can combine to cause managers to resist change and as a result to avoid planning that might begin that change. General Electric has the goal that all of the company's businesses should be number one or two in their respective industries. A GE manager who had little hope that her business would be able to meet this standard might recognize that planning could undermine her role in the company and might therefore avoid planning activities.

SITUATIONAL CONSTRAINTS   Similarly, various situational constraints can hinder effective planning. Suppose that Westinghouse would like to undertake a full-scale expansion program, but its human resource managers learn that the company does not have enough managerial talent to support expansion at the desired rate. As a consequence, the rate of expansion has to be scaled back to fit the availability of managers. Other constraints that can affect planning include labor unions and contracts, government regulations, a scarcity of raw materials, and a shortage of operating funds.

POOR GOAL SETTING   Poor goal setting is a significant roadblock to effective planning. Since goal setting is the first step in the planning process, any of the things that might impede proper goal setting (which are discussed in Chapter 4) by definition also hinder effective planning.

TIME AND EXPENSE   Finally, effective planning can be limited by the time and expense involved. Like most things worth doing, planning takes a considerable amount of time. Because of the pressures that affect them, most managers might occasionally find it difficult to undertake planning activities. Similarly, acquiring the necessary information to develop effective plans can cost money. Managers at Polaroid who want to know about future trends in amateur photography, for instance, might need to conduct extensive market research or buy the information from private market research firms. Faced with such expenses, they may be tempted to take short cuts or evade the issue altogether.

PRELUDE CASE   UPDATE

Woolworth faced several obstacles when it decided to abandon discounting for specialty retailing. For one thing, the decision to shut down a major division and eliminate thousands of jobs was clearly a difficult one. Not surprisingly, several managers at Woolworth argued that it should not be done. And the complex and dynamic environment facing all retailers is always a hurdle—but even more so when a proposed change is a major one. The company also faced financial constraints from the weak discounting operation. The expense involved in shutting down the division limited what else the company could do for a while. And finally, some managers fought the new strategy simply because they were more comfortable with the old one—regardless of the fact that it wasn't working.

Avoiding the Roadblocks

Fortunately for managers, there are some useful guidelines that can help them avoid these roadblocks. Six of the most basic ones are summarized in Table 5.3.

START AT THE TOP   For planning to be effective, it must start at the top. Top managers must set the goals and strategies that lower-level managers will follow. Andrew Grove, CEO of Intel, leads each of his company's planning groups. This leadership conveys a strong and clear message to everyone that planning is important.

RECOGNIZE THE LIMITS   Managers must also recognize that no planning system is perfect. Because of its very nature, planning has limits and cannot be done with absolute precision. Coca-Cola spent years planning to introduce a new formula for its flagship product. Even though the company did everything "by the book," the change was disastrous and had to be dropped within a short time.

COMMUNICATE   Communication, especially vertical communication within the organizational hierarchy, can also facilitate effective planning. If top managers know what middle and first-line managers are doing, they can continue their own planning activities better. At Intel, great efforts are made to make sure that every manager who might potentially be affected by a decision or plan is made aware of it.

PARTICIPATE   In similar fashion, participation aids effective planning because managers who are fully involved in planning are more likely to know what is going on, to understand their own place in the organization, and consequently to be motivated to contribute. One of the keys to the success recently enjoyed by Ford has been increased participation by managers in all aspects of planning.

INTEGRATE   We have already noted that long-range, intermediate, and short-range plans must be properly integrated. The better these plans are inte-

TABLE 5.3
Avoiding the Roadblocks
to Effective Planning

Improving Planning Effectiveness
1. Planning should start at and be led by the top level of an organization.
2. Managers should recognize the limits and uncertainties of planning.
3. Managers should communicate what they are doing to other levels in the organization.
4. Managers should actively participate in planning.
5. Managers should make sure that long-range, intermediate, and short-range plans are well integrated.
6. Managers should develop contingency plans.

grated, the more effective the organization's overall planning system will be. Toyota has always done a good job of integrating the various time frames across which it plans. Short-term model changes, for example, almost always mesh nicely with longer-term new model introductions.

DEVELOP CONTINGENCY PLANS The final technique for enhancing planning is to develop contingency plans. As we have discussed, contingency plans are alternative actions that a company might follow if conditions change. If competitors such as Honda and Nissan change their approach to marketing, for example, Toyota will no doubt have several different contingency plans from which to choose.

TOOLS AND TECHNIQUES FOR PLANNING

In this section we briefly look at a variety of quantitative tools and techniques that can assist managers in their planning activities: forecasting, linear programming, and break-even analysis. The chapter concludes with some observations about the use of these and other tools.[15]

□ *Forecasting* involves developing systematic predictions about the future.

Forecasting

Forecasting is the systematic development of predictions about the future. One of the most critical kinds of forecasting that managers must do is revenue forecasting.

REVENUE FORECASTING All organizations depend on revenues to remain in operation. For businesses, revenues come from the sales of products and services. For banks, revenues come from interest paid by borrowers. The government derives its revenues from taxes, and schools and universities get much of their revenues from the government.

It follows logically that managers need to know what their future revenues will be before they can plan effectively. If Alcoa wants to open a new plant, its managers need to know that they will have enough funds available to pay for it. Similarly, Austin Community College needs to know what its budget will be next year so it can hire instructors, schedule classes, and so forth.

Thus, one of the first pieces of information most managers seek when developing plans is a projection of future revenues. This is developed through revenue forecasting, which involves statistical projections based on past earnings.

One important part of planning is forecasting. In some markets, such as athletic footwear, consumer tastes and preferences change rapidly. Thus, accurate forecasting is critical. As a color forecaster for Reebok, Sara Fredericksen predicts consumers' future color preferences.

OTHER KINDS OF FORECASTING Managers occasionally need to develop forecasts for other areas as well. For example, technological forecasting involves predicting breakthroughs and innovations before they happen.[16] Other forecasts might deal with the availability of raw materials, future tax rates, future changes in consumer tastes, or future space restrictions (such as students at a university or patients in a hospital). Indeed, virtually any aspect of the environment might be fair game for forecasting.

☐ Two useful forecasting techniques are *time-series forecasting* and *Delphi forecasting.*

FORECASTING TECHNIQUES   Managers can use numerous quantitative techniques to assist them in developing forecasts. One technique is **time-series forecasting,** which involves plotting the subject of the forecast (sales, demand, or whatever) against time for a period of several years. A "best-fit" line is then determined and extended into the future. An example is given in Exhibit 5.5, which plots the number of units sold for the years 1985–1991. As the line moves beyond 1991, it can forecast a demand of 2,750 in 1992 and 3,000 in 1993.

Another common technique is **Delphi forecasting.** Delphi forecasting is the systematic refinement of expert opinion. Under the Delphi method, a panel of experts is asked to make various predictions. Each individual then shares his or her response with the rest of the panel, and the process is repeated. After a few repetitions, the experts fine-tune their opinions and a consensus—the forecast—usually emerges.[17]

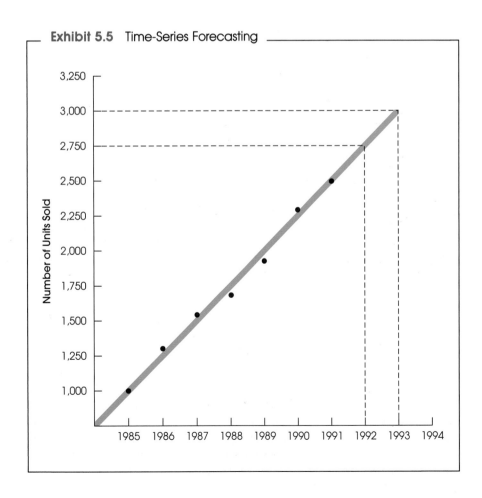

Exhibit 5.5   Time-Series Forecasting

Other Planning Techniques

Several planning techniques in addition to forecasting are used by managers. Two of the more common are linear programming and break-even analysis.

◻ Other popular planning techniques include *linear programming*, and *break-even analysis*.

LINEAR PROGRAMMING   A very useful method for determining the optimal combination of resources and activities is called **linear programming,** or **LP.** Consider a small manufacturer who produces sofas, chairs, and ottomans. Each product is made of wood frames, fabric coverings, and wooden legs. Further, each goes through the same production and inspection system. Employees can only work on one product line at a time. Since it is usually costly to change frequently from one line to another, and since each product has a different profit margin, the question is how to schedule the work—how many sofas, chairs, and ottomans should be produced during a given period in order to optimize the efficient use of resources and simultaneously satisfy demand.

LP quantifies the required raw materials and human resources, profit margins, and demand for each product into an equation. The entire set of equations is then solved, and the resulting solution suggests the best number of units of each product to produce.

BREAK-EVEN ANALYSIS   Another useful planning technique is **break-even analysis.** Break-even analysis helps the manager determine the point at which revenues and costs will be equal. For example, suppose that a manager is trying to decide whether or not to produce a new product. There are two kinds of costs associated with the product, fixed and variable. Fixed costs are costs that are incurred regardless of the level of output: rent or mortgage payments on the plant, taxes, guaranteed wages and salaries, and so forth. Variable costs are costs that result from producing the product: raw materials, direct labor, and shipping. Total costs, then, are the fixed costs plus variable costs. Because fixed costs always exist, the total cost line never begins at zero, but begins at the minimum level of fixed costs if nothing is produced. Total costs rise from there in direct proportion to the volume of output.

To determine the break-even point, the manager plots total costs and total revenues on the same graph, as shown in Exhibit 5.6. Total revenues are simply the projected selling price times the volume of output. The point at which the lines cross is the break-even point. If the company produces and sells less than this, it will have a loss because total costs exceed total revenues for the product at the given selling price. If it produces and sells more, it will make a profit. If the break-even point is too high, the manager might decide to raise the selling price in order to reach it sooner.

Using Planning Tools and Techniques

In using various tools and techniques for planning, the manager needs to remember two things: the relative strengths and weaknesses of these aids and the increasingly important role of the computer.

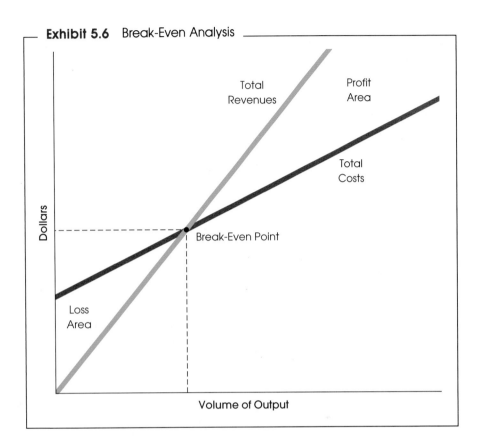

Exhibit 5.6   Break-Even Analysis

Total Revenues

Profit Area

Total Costs

Dollars

Break-Even Point

Loss Area

Volume of Output

Most carpenters know how to use a handsaw, a table saw, a saber saw, and a ripsaw, and good carpenters know when to use each one. In similar fashion, managers should recognize that the various techniques described here are tools and that some are useful in some situations whereas others are useful in other situations.

When choosing a technique, a manager needs to consider several points. On the positive side, these tools offer powerful ways to address certain kinds of problems—they help simplify and organize information, they make planning easier, and they are applicable in a wide variety of situations, to name a few. On the negative side, they may not reflect reality accurately, some factors may not be quantifiable, the tools may be costly to use, and the manager may use a technique too rigidly without giving enough credibility to either intuition or insight.

As virtually everyone knows, the last several years have seen a revolution in information technology. The foundation of this revolution has been the computer, in particular the personal computer. This machine greatly enhances the manager's ability to use quantitative techniques in a meaningful fashion. Today's managers have certainly added another powerful tool to their kit. Tomorrow's managers will be even better equipped to handle the complex and dynamic nature of the planning process.

LEARNING CHECK

You should now be able to describe forecasting and other tools and techniques for planning and how to use them.

Chapter Summary

A plan is a blueprint or framework used to describe how an organization expects to achieve its goals. Planning is the process of developing plans or of determining how best to approach a particular goal. Because it is so important, every manager must be involved in the planning process.

The three major kinds of plans are strategic, tactical, and operational. Strategic plans are the broad, long-term plans developed by top managers to guide the general directions of the organization. Tactical plans are designed to implement strategic plans and hence have a moderate scope and intermediate time frame. Operational plans have the narrowest focus and the shortest time frame and are executed by first-line managers.

The three major time frames for planning are long-range, intermediate, and short-range planning. Long-range planning covers a period that can be as short as several years or as long as several decades. Intermediate planning generally takes a time perspective of about one to five years. Short-range planning covers time periods of one year or less and focuses on day-to-day activities, thus providing a basis for evaluating progress toward the achievement of intermediate and long-range plans. Each of these time frames should be integrated with the others to ensure smooth functioning of the organization.

Contingency planning is the part of the planning process that identifies alternative courses of action that an organization might follow if various different conditions arise. Critical contingency events relate either to the extent to which the ongoing plan is being accomplished or to environmental events that might change things in the future.

Roadblocks to effective planning include the environment, resistance to change, situational constraints, poor goal setting, and the time and expense of planning. Guidelines for avoiding these roadblocks include starting at the top, recognizing the limits to planning, communicating, participating, integrating, and developing contingency plans.

Forecasting is the systematic development of predictions about the future. Revenue forecasting is one of the most critical kinds of forecasting performed by an organization. Time-series and Delphi forecasting are techniques that can be used to make such predictions. Linear programming and break-even analysis are other tools that managers can use in planning.

The Manager's Vocabulary

plan	program
planning	project
strategic planning	long-range planning
tactical planning	intermediate planning
operational planning	short-range planning
standing plans	contingency planning
policies	forecasting
standard operating	time-series forecasting
procedures (SOPs)	Delphi forecasting
rules and regulations	linear programming (LP)
single-use plans	break-even analysis

Prelude Case Wrap-up

Our Prelude Case for this chapter describes the previous problems and current successes of one of this country's oldest retailers, F. W. Woolworth Company. Woolworth had failed to respond to environmental shifts. And when it did try, it often failed. Now, however, an emphasis on specialty retailing has pushed the company back on track.

But managers at Woolworth remember the lessons of complacency. Rather than sitting back and resting on their laurels, they are busy looking for still more specialty markets they can enter. The end of the Prelude Case, for example, mentions the new Woolworth Express stores. These stores carry only the top-selling items from the regular Woolworth variety stores. The results so far are impressive—a typical Express is one-fifth the size of a regular variety store but does three times the sales volume.

Of course, the company has not been without its failures. For example, one concept that didn't pan out was Face Fantasies, a discount cosmetics outlet. Customers simply didn't like the cheap make-up the store was selling. But in keeping with its willingness to tolerate an occasional flop, managers at Woolworth cut their losses by closing the stores that had been opened and immediately began looking for another concept that could occupy the same retail space.

Woolworth has also started planning over an extended time horizon. For example, the company has projected opening one thousand Woolworth Express stores by the year 2000. Thus, managers have already started implementing a series of shorter-range plans for opening about a hundred each year.

Prelude Case Questions

1. What examples of tactical and operational planning might you expect to find at Woolworth?
2. What similarities and differences might exist between the kind of planning Woolworth executives might do and the kind of planning that an individual Woolworth store manager might do?
3. Identify other possible examples of contingency planning that Woolworth might do beyond the illustration given in one of the case updates.
4. What kinds of quantitative planning tools and techniques might Woolworth find useful?

Discussion Questions

Review Questions

1. Identify and describe the three basic kinds of planning done by most organizations.
2. How should organizations integrate plans that span different periods of time?
3. What are contingency plans? How are they developed?
4. Identify several roadblocks to effective planning. Suggest ways around these roadblocks.
5. How should managers view the various quantitative techniques available to help them plan?

Analysis Questions

1. Do you think an organization could function effectively without planning? Why or why not?
2. If all managers are supposed to plan, why should planning start at the top? Could it start at the bottom? How?
3. Describe a contingency plan you once developed. How closely did the steps you followed coincide with those outlined in this chapter?
4. Why might different kinds of organizations have different conceptions of what long-range planning means?
5. Do you think that more accurate forms of forecasting are likely to be developed? Why or why not?

Application Questions and Exercises

1. Interview a local manager or administrator and find out what time horizons are most relevant to his or her planning activities.
2. What kinds of plans and time horizons does your school or university use?
3. Does the concept of planning time frames have any relevance to you personally? If so, list your long-range, intermediate, and short-range plans. Do they correlate with each other well?
4. Interview a local manager and find out if she or he uses contingency plans. If not, why? If so, learn about the process that is used.
5. Interview the registrar of your school or university. Ask what the projected enrollment is for next year and the year after. Find out what technique was used in developing the forecast.

ENHANCEMENT CASE

BLACK & DECKER TURNS AROUND

Nolan Archibald, CEO of Black & Decker Corp., has always worked toward a vision. One of his earlier visions was to play in the National Basketball Association. Although he managed to get a tryout with the Chicago Bulls, he didn't make the team. But he has succeeded in achieving another vision—running and turning around a major American corporation.

Archibald became president of Black & Decker in 1985. To his dismay, he found the company going nowhere. It had just bought General Electric's small appliance business, but at a price he thought was excessive. And the company's bread-and-butter line of power tools was rapidly losing market share to such competitors as Skil and Makita. Worse still, Black & Decker's products were suffering from poor quality and an eroding image.

To turn things around, Archibald developed a three-step system with planning as the cornerstone.

In particular, he decided that he must develop a coherent and logical plan for the company and then communicate that plan to everyone. For example, even with all its problems, the Black & Decker name was still respected. And the company had strong pockets of success around the globe.

Thus, Archibald decided to develop a global strategy to tie everything together. In the past, the company's British division had done what it wanted, as had the French and German divisions. As a result, the company made over one hundred different electric motors, the most expensive part of its products. Under the unified strategy, there are now less than twenty standard motors used around the globe. Eventually, Black & Decker managers hope to use only five motors.

Other initiatives focused on improving product quality, recapturing lost market share, and convincing customers that the company would again be a major force in its industries. Although some were skeptical, Archibald's vision eventually prevailed.

The second part of Archibald's efforts focused on people. He hired a number of successful executives from other companies by selling them on his vision for Black & Decker. These managers have injected new enthusiasm and creativity into the company. For example, the new head of the power tool business in-troduced over sixty products in just two years and took the company to the forefront of the growing cordless tool market.

Finally, the third action developed by Archibald revolved around cutting costs. Although Black & Decker had remained profitable through the years, profit margins had become increasingly small. To bring costs back into line, the company shut down five plants and imposed wage cuts at several others.

As a result of Archibald's three-step approach, Black & Decker once again became a formidable worldwide competitor in both power tools and appliances. But Archibald wasn't finished. He wanted to purchase at least one new major business to integrate with Black & Decker's existing operations. First he pursued American Standard, but was unsuccessful.

Then, in late 1989, he succeeded in buying Emhart Corporation. Emhart makes industrial products, hardware and home improvement products, and outdoor products like lighting systems and rakes. The acquisition doubled the size of Black & Decker but also increased its debt dramatically. Still, those who know Archibald believe in his vision, and they remain confident that the short-term dip in profits brought about by the acquisition will soon give way to dramatic new profits.

SOURCES: John Huey, "The New Power in Black & Decker," *Fortune*, January 2, 1989, pp. 89–94; "Black & Decker Cuts a Neat Dovetail Joint," *Business Week*, July 31, 1989, pp. 52–53; "Black & Decker Goes to Full-Court Press," *The Wall Street Journal*, November 10, 1988, p. A8.

Enhancement Case Questions

1. What kinds of plans are illustrated or implied in this case?
2. What kinds of contingency planning does a company like Black & Decker need to engage in?
3. When Archibald began to formulate his ambitious plans, he no doubt encountered some resistance. What were the most likely major roadblocks? How do you think he handled them?
4. What planning time horizons are most important for a consumer-oriented firm like Black & Decker?

Chapter Notes

1. See Arie P. De Geus, "Planning as Learning," *Harvard Business Review*, March-April 1988, pp. 70–74.

2. "Waldenbooks Peddles Books a Bit like Soap, Transforming Market," *The Wall Street Journal*, October 10, 1988, pp. A1, A4.

3. George A. Steiner, *Top Management Planning* (New York: Macmillan, 1969).

4. Hugo Uyterhoeven, "General Managers in the Middle," *Harvard Business Review*, September-October 1989, pp. 136–145.

5. See Charles W. Hofer and Dan Schendel, *Strategy Formulation: Analytical Concepts* (St. Paul, Minn.: West, 1978); Richard F. Vancil and Peter Lorange, "Strategic Planning in Diversified Companies," *Harvard Business Review*, January-February 1975, pp. 81–90; Rosemary Stewart, "Middle Managers: Their Jobs and Behavior," in Jay W. Lorsch, ed., *Handbook of Organizational Behavior* (Englewood Cliffs, N.J.: Prentice-Hall, 1987), pp. 385–391.

6. See Leonard A. Schlesinger and Janice A. Klein, "The First-Line Supervisor: Past, Present, and Future," in Jay W. Lorsch, ed., *Handbook of Organizational Behavior* (Englewood Cliffs, N.J.: Prentice-Hall, 1987), pp. 370–384.

7. See Michael E. Porter, *Competitive Advantage* (New York: Free Press, 1985), and Charles W. L. Hill and Gareth R. Jones, *Strategic Management: An Analytical Approach* (Boston: Houghton Mifflin, 1989).

8. Carol Davenport, "America's Most Admired Corporations," *Fortune*, January 30, 1989, pp. 68–94.

9. Gary Hector, "Yes, You *Can* Manage Long Term," *Fortune*, November 21, 1988, p. 68.

10. Ricky W. Griffin, *Management*, 3rd ed. (Boston: Houghton Mifflin, 1990).

11. Donald C. Hambrick and David Lei, "Toward an Empirical Prioritization of Contingency Variables for Business Strategy," *Academy of Management Journal*, December 1985, pp. 763–788.

12. Ari Ginsberg and N. Venkatraman, "Contingency Perspectives of Organizational Strategy: A Critical Review of the Empirical Research," *Academy of Management Journal*, July 1985, pp. 421–434.

13. George A. Steiner, *Strategic Planning: What Every Manager Must Know* (New York: Free Press, 1979).

14. Noel Tichy and Ram Charan, "Speed, Simplicity, and Self-Confidence: An Interview with Jack Welch," *Harvard Business Review*, September-October 1989, pp. 112–120.

15. See Robert E. Markland, *Topics in Management Science*, 3rd ed. (New York: Wiley, 1989), for detailed discussions of these and other techniques.

16. R. Balachandra, "Technological Forecasting: Who Does It and How Useful Is It?" *Technological Forecasting and Social Change*, January 1980, pp. 75–85.

17. See Andre L. Delbecq, Andrew H. Van de Ven, and David H. Gustafson, *Group Techniques for Program Planning* (Glenview, Ill.: Scott, Foresman, 1975). See also Ruth S. Raubitschek, "Multiple Scenario Analysis and Business Planning," in Robert Lamb and Paul Shrivastava, eds., *Advances in Strategic Management* (Greenwich, Conn.: JAI Press, 1988), V, 181–205.

CHAPTER OUTLINE

I. The Nature of Strategic Planning
   A. The Components of Strategy
   B. Strategy Formulation and Implementation
   C. The Levels of Strategy

II. Environmental Analysis
   A. Environmental Forces
   B. The Organization-Environment Interface

III. Corporate Strategy
   A. Grand Strategies
   B. Portfolio Approaches

IV. Business Strategy
   A. The Adaptation Process
   B. Competitive Strategies

V. Functional Strategies

VI. Strategy Implementation

CHAPTER

6

LEARNING OBJECTIVES

After studying this chapter you should be able to

1. Describe the nature of strategic planning, including the components and levels of strategy and strategy formulation and implementation.

2. Understand the environmental forces important to strategic planning and how managers position their organizations within those forces.

3. Identify major approaches to corporate strategy.

4. Identify major approaches to business strategy.

5. Identify the major functional strategies developed by most organizations.

6. Describe the process of strategy implementation.

Strategy and Strategic Planning

MARS, THE VENERABLE CANDY MAKER

The Mars company is best known for its popular candy products like Milky Way, M&Ms, and Snickers. But the company competes in a variety of other markets as well, including packaged foods and pet foods. The $12 billion enterprise is family owned and managed, and is thus one of the largest private businesses in the world. Mars is also an international firm, albeit one with a stormy and checkered history.

In 1932, Frank Mars told his son Forest that the family's Chicago-based candy business was not big enough for both of them. He gave his son the foreign rights to Milky Way and sent him to Great Britain. Forest quickly built a large company of his own, including a profitable candy line plus a very successful pet food business.

After a bitter legal battle, Forest regained control of the family business in 1964 and integrated it with his burgeoning foreign operation to form a single Mars organization. In 1973, his sons, Forest, Jr., and John, assumed the positions of copresidents of the business.

One of the unique characteristics of Mars is that it is a tall organization (one with many levels) with few symbols of power or prestige. For example, no one at Mars has an office, not even the copresidents. Desks are arranged in circles in a single huge room with senior managers in the middle and other managers flowing out in spokes. The idea is to promote communication and openness. A tall structure has also afforded ample opportunity for promotion. One strange company quirk is that everyone at the company—including each copresident—punches a time clock.

Mars has always put a premium on people. It hires the best managers available and pays top salaries to keep them. On the negative side, though, the large number of family members in the business is still an occasional barrier because other talented managers realize that the top spots are unlikely to be open to them.

The money saved on fancy offices goes into a state-of-the-art plant and the best equipment. All Mars factories use the newest production methods, and quality is a top priority. One observer went so far as to note that the company's dog food plants are as clean as some hospitals.

The Mars of today is centered around three large businesses and one smaller one. As already noted, the candy business is the one most associated with the Mars name. Other popular mainstays in the Mars candy business include Twix and Three Musketeers. Mars is also a major player in the pet food industry. Its leading brands here are Kal Kan, Pedigree, and Whiskas. In addition, Mars has a profitable packaged foods business centered around the Uncle Ben's brand name. Its leading products are rice and prepared dinners. Finally, Mars operates a small electronics business. Its primary products are various kinds of coin changers.

After a period of rapid growth and market leadership in the

The Mars Company is perhaps best known for its popular candies, such as M&M's, Snickers, and Milky Way. However, as part of the company's strategy, other units within the firm make packaged foods (rice, prepared dinners, etc.), pet food (Pedigree, Whiskas, etc.), and coin changers.

1970s, Mars has floundered a bit of late. For example, it refused to grant the makers of *E.T.* the rights to use M&M candy in the movie, so they instead chose Reese's Pieces—a move that dramatically boosted sales of that product. The maker of Reese's Pieces, Hershey, has also made

other inroads, most noticeably with its recent acquisition of Cadbury. That move leapfrogged Hershey over Mars to the number one spot in the candy business.

Mars has also had trouble with new forays into salted snacks and frozen confectionery products. Several large international firms

have entered not only the candy business but also the pet food and packaged foods industries. Mars has responded with a barrage of new products and advertising campaigns, but it is too early to tell whether the venerable firm will regain its footing or tumble by the wayside.

SOURCES: "Mars Struggles to Reclaim Candy Crown," *The Wall Street Journal*, March 29, 1989, p. B1; Bill Saporito, "Uncovering Mars' Unknown Empire," *Fortune*, September 26, 1988, pp. 98–104; Jane Myers, "Mars Shuffles Shops, but Maintains Strategy," *Advertising Age*, February 1, 1988, p. 73.

B y most objective indicators, Mars has been a very effective organization. And even though the company is struggling a bit now, Mars executives are convinced they can still turn things around. One reason for Mars's current downturn is that environmental circumstances constantly change for most businesses. Thus, it becomes very difficult to always make exactly the right decisions and do exactly the right things. But managers must still make a concerted effort to understand their environment and take appropriate action. The activities involved in doing these things are a part of strategy and strategic planning.

This chapter is about the various elements of strategy and strategic planning. First it describes the nature of strategic planning. It then focuses on environmental analysis and discusses corporate, business, and functional strategies. The chapter ends with a description of strategy implementation.

THE NATURE OF STRATEGIC PLANNING

In Chapter 5 we learned that **strategic plans** are the broad plans developed by top management to guide the general directions of the organization. To expand on that definition and to describe the nature of strategic planning better, we need to identify the components of strategic planning, draw a distinction between strategy formulation and strategy implementation, and note the levels of strategy.

The Components of Strategy

□ Strategy has four basic components: *scope, resource deployment, competitive advantage,* and *synergy.*

In general, strategy can be thought of as having four basic components: scope, resource deployment, competitive advantages, and synergy.[1]

The **scope** of strategy specifies the position the firm wants to have in relation to its environment. More specifically, it details the markets in which the firm wants to compete. For example, the scope of Ford's strategy specifies that the company wants to produce and sell automobiles around the world, whereas Timex's specifies that it wants to produce and market low-priced watches.

Resource deployment indicates how the organization intends to allocate resources. General Electric wants each of its businesses to be either number one or number two in its industry. This suggests that GE might sell a business that is number five and losing ground, allocate enough resources to a business firmly entrenched as number one for it to stay there, and provide new resources to a business that is number three and gaining ground on number two.

Competitive advantage is the specification of what advantage or advantages the firm holds relative to its competitors. IBM's competitive advantages include its well-known name and dominance of the computer market. Likewise, Kodak used its strengths in name recognition and distribution channels to introduce a new line of batteries.

© Ethan Hoffman

Many firms attempt to achieve synergy as a part of their strategies. Sony recently bought Columbia Pictures for this very reason. Sony's founder, Akio Morita, thinks movies and video technology are natural complements to one another. That is, Sony video equipment can be paired with Columbia movies in a variety of different formats.

Synergy is the extent to which various businesses within the firm can expect to draw from one another. Disney, for example, realizes considerable synergy from its theme parks, movies, and merchandising businesses. Families familiar with Disney characters from movies and books are motivated to visit the theme parks. After an enjoyable experience, they are subsequently motivated to buy merchandise and see future movies.

Strategy Formulation and Implementation

Another important element of strategic planning is the distinction between **strategy formulation** and **strategy implementation.**[2] Actually, the words themselves convey the meaning of the two terms: formulation is the set of processes involved in creating or developing strategic plans, and implementation is the set of processes involved in executing them, or putting them into effect. Most of our attention in this chapter is directed to formulation issues, although the end of the chapter touches on implementation.

The Levels of Strategy

☐ The three general levels of strategy are *corporate, business,* and *functional.*

A final important perspective to understanding the nature of strategic planning is the levels of strategy. As indicated in Exhibit 6.1, there are three such levels: corporate, business, and functional.

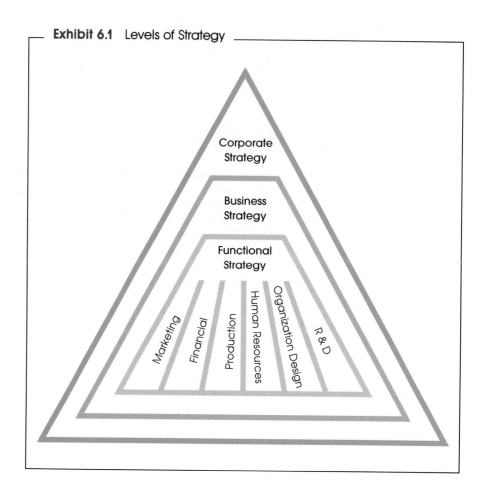

Exhibit 6.1 Levels of Strategy

(Pyramid diagram: Corporate Strategy, Business Strategy, Functional Strategy — Marketing, Financial, Production, Human Resources, Organization Design, R & D)

The **corporate strategy** charts the course for the entire organization and attempts to answer the question "What businesses should we be in?" K mart has developed a corporate strategy that calls for continued growth and emphasis on volume retailing.

A **business strategy** is charted for each individual business within a company. Managers at K mart have set strategies for its discount store division, its bookstore division, and its home improvement store division. Although there may be some similarities in business strategies across divisions, there are also clear differences.

Similarly, **functional strategies** are developed to correspond to each of the basic functional areas within the organization. As indicated in Exhibit 6.1, common functional strategies include marketing, financial, production, human resource, organization design, and research and development. K mart has a marketing strategy of low-cost, volume retailing, a financial strategy that calls for low debt, and a human resource strategy that emphasizes hiring college graduates as management trainees.

Clearly, each level of strategy is important. If any level is neglected, the entire organization can and will suffer. We shall therefore consider each one in more detail, but first we'll look at another important dimension of strategic planning, environmental analysis.

P R E L U D E   C A S E   U P D A T E

Many of the concepts described here are illustrated at Mars. For example, Mars allocates relatively few resources to its electronics business (resource deployment) but is able to transfer production technologies among each of its other three businesses (synergy). It also pursues quality as a competitive advantage. Mars has a corporate strategy that dictates four basic businesses and subsequently develops a business strategy for each of them. Finally, top executives at Mars are responsible for formulating strategy, and middle managers are responsible for implementation.

ENVIRONMENTAL ANALYSIS

The starting point in strategic planning is developing a thorough understanding of the organization's environment. Many of the key issues involved here are discussed in Chapter 4. However, from a strategic management perspective, managers need to think in terms of basic environmental forces and how to balance them against the organization's strengths and weaknesses.

Environmental Forces

□ The five critical *environmental forces* are the *threat of new entrants*, the *power of suppliers*, *jockeying among contestants*, the *threat of substitute products*, and the *power of buyers*.

There are five critical **environmental forces** that must be considered in strategic planning.[3] In general, these forces relate to the competitor dimension of the firm's task environment discussed in Chapter 4. They are illustrated in Exhibit 6.2.

THREAT OF NEW ENTRANTS   The **threat of new entrants** refers to the ease with which new competitors can enter a market. For example, it takes very little in the way of resources to enter the restaurant business, the dry-cleaning business, or the home video rental business, so in these environments the threat of new entrants is high. On the other hand, it takes a tremendous investment to enter the automobile business or the petroleum-refining business, so in these instances the threat of new entrants is fairly low.

POWER OF SUPPLIERS   The **power of suppliers** refers to the extent to which suppliers can influence the organization. If Delta Air Lines wants to

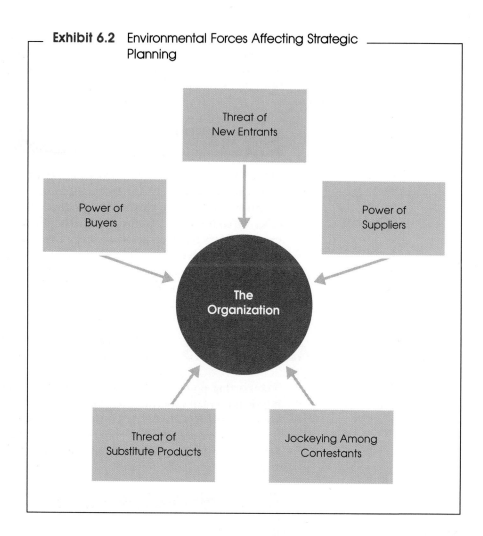

Exhibit 6.2 Environmental Forces Affecting Strategic Planning

buy fifty jumbo jets, it can deal with only three suppliers—Boeing, McDonnell Douglas, and Airbus. Thus, each of these suppliers has considerable power over Delta and can take a hard line on price, delivery, and so forth.

JOCKEYING AMONG CONTESTANTS **Jockeying among contestants** refers to the extent to which major competitors in a market are constantly trying to outmaneuver one another. In the fast food industry, for example, McDonald's, Burger King, and Wendy's are almost always running promotions aimed at one another. Burger King may be touting its method of cooking hamburgers while Wendy's is pushing its newest sandwich and McDonald's is running price specials. Each contestant is trying to get the upper hand.

THREAT OF SUBSTITUTE PRODUCTS The **threat of substitute products** is the extent to which a new product might supplant demand for an existing product. For instance, calculators eliminated the need for slide rules, and personal computers are reducing the market for typewriters. Some products seem to have indefinite staying power, whereas others come and go quickly, so businesses aim to maintain a line of stable products and services while taking advantage of new market opportunities presented by fluctuating consumer tastes and preferences.

POWER OF BUYERS   The fifth environmental force is the **power of buyers.** Organizations that rely on only one or just a few major customers for most of their sales are susceptible to this threat. For example, Lockheed sells virtually all of the airplanes it makes to the U.S. military. Thus, the military and its various branches have considerable power over Lockheed and can negotiate on everything from price to delivery date to the color of the planes.

The Organization-Environment Interface

After managers have developed a clear understanding of relevant environmental forces, they must come to grips with how they want to interact with those forces. Indeed, the purpose of strategy is to determine what position in the environment the firm wishes to take. As shown graphically in Exhibit 6.3, the key to developing effective strategy is to understand environmental opportunities and threats and organizational strengths and weaknesses.

For example, in 1989 Ford found itself with several billion dollars in surplus funds (an organizational strength). Managers at Ford also believed, however, that the company lacked a strong enough presence in the luxury car market (an

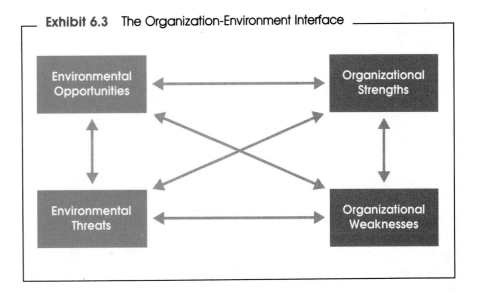

Exhibit 6.3   The Organization-Environment Interface

organizational weakness). Meanwhile, Toyota and Nissan were introducing new luxury car divisions (both environmental threats). Managers at Ford learned that Jaguar was for sale (an environmental opportunity) but that General Motors was already negotiating a purchase (still another threat). So Ford jumped in and paid a premium price to acquire Jaguar first. The result was a successful organization-environment interface achieved by matching environmental opportunities and threats with Ford's organizational strengths and weaknesses.

CORPORATE STRATEGY

As defined earlier, corporate strategy involves the determination of what businesses the firm expects to compete in. The two most common approaches to corporate strategy are the development of a grand strategy and the use of a portfolio approach.

Grand Strategies

☐ Three alternative *grand strategies* are *growth, retrenchment,* and *stability.*

A **grand strategy** is an overall framework for action developed at the corporate level. It is generally used when the corporation competes in a single market or in a few highly related markets. There are three basic grand strategies that organizations adopt—growth, retrenchment, or stability.

A **growth strategy** is adopted when the corporation wants to generate high levels of growth in one or more areas of operations. For example, Wal-mart is pursuing a growth strategy by opening over one hundred new stores each year and moving rapidly into markets all across the United States. And *Management Today: Management in Practice* describes how Hershey has used a growth strategy to regain the number one spot in the candy business from Mars.

A **retrenchment strategy** is employed when managers want to shrink operations, cut back in some areas, or eliminate unprofitable operations altogether. Firestone pursued a retrenchment strategy when it recently cut its work force from 107,000 to 55,000, closed eight of its plants, and sold off several unrelated businesses.

Finally, a **stability strategy** is used when the organization wants to maintain its status quo. Such an approach is often adopted immediately after a period of sharp growth or retrenchment. For example, following its recent shift in pricing strategy, Sears is attempting to maintain stability.

Portfolio Approaches

☐ The *portfolio approach* involves identifying *strategic business units (SBUs)* and then classifying them in some meaningful framework.

When the firm competes in several different markets simultaneously, it often uses one of several different portfolio approaches. A **portfolio approach** to corporate strategy views the corporation as a collection of different businesses. The foundation of portfolio approaches is the concept of the strategic business unit, or SBU.

MANAGEMENT IN PRACTICE

Hershey Sweetens Bottom Line

Hershey Foods Corporation was founded early in the twentieth century by Milton Hershey. The company grew to become the dominant firm in the candy industry with a simple formula: it produced high-quality products, incurred low costs, and used virtually no advertising. Much of Hershey's stock is held by a board of trustees, making the company almost invulnerable to takeover. A share of the company's profits also goes to support a Pennsylvania home for orphaned children.

In the 1970s, Hershey managers decided they needed to branch out beyond the candy businesses. Accordingly, they embarked on a diversification strategy that included hotels, a theme park, a chain of ice cream parlors, and several other unrelated businesses. Unfortunately, this strategy did not work and Hershey eventually surrendered its number one position in the candy industry to its rival, Mars Company.

Richard Zimmerman was named CEO of Hershey in 1985 and decided to refocus the company on its roots while simultaneously seeking avenues for new growth. First of all, he bought several other candy companies—those led by Dietrich Corporation (5th Avenue, Luden's Cough Drops, and other products) and Cadbury's (Almond Joy, Mounds, and other brands). He also sold several of Hershey's unrelated businesses, including the ice cream chain. Finally, he increased advertising dramatically.

The results have been quite impressive. For one thing, Hershey now owns half of the twenty top-selling candy products in the United States. Its top product, Reese's Peanut Butter Cups, is pressing Snickers, made by Mars, for the number one spot. Hershey also increased its market share from 15.3 percent in 1980 to 20.5 percent in 1988. And sales are expected to continue to increase strongly throughout the 1990s.

SOURCES: "Why Hershey Is Smacking Its Lips," *Business Week,* October 30, 1989, p. 140; "A Trimmer Hershey Craves More Brands for Its Food Business," *Philadelphia Inquirer,* January 8, 1989, pp. 1G–2G; "The Sweet Smell of Success," *Fortune,* April 24, 1989, pp. 30–32.

STRATEGIC BUSINESS UNITS   A **strategic business unit,** or **SBU,** is an autonomous division or business operating within the context of another corporation. The SBU concept was born in the early 1970s at General Electric. Managers at GE felt that they needed some sort of framework to help them manage the diverse businesses under the corporate umbrella. Close scrutiny suggested that GE was actually engaged in forty-three distinct businesses, so each of these businesses was clearly defined as an SBU for purposes of corporate strategy. In short order, several other large firms, including Union Carbide and General Foods, began to realize that they too comprised a set of SBUs.

In general, an SBU has the following characteristics:

1. It has its own set of competitors.
2. It is a single division or set of closely related divisions within the corporation.

3. It has its own distinct mission.
4. It has its own strategy that sets it apart from other SBUs within the organization.

The strategic business units of Mars, which are illustrated in Exhibit 6.4, all have these four characteristics.

THE PORTFOLIO MATRIX   Of course, the notion of SBUs by itself is of only marginal value to managers. It is only when managers can logically group the SBUs into meaningful categories that this approach becomes truly significant. The best known of several different portfolio approaches is the **portfolio matrix** method. The portfolio matrix method classifies SBUs along two dimensions: market growth rate and relative market share. Market growth rate is the extent to which demand for the product in question is growing rapidly, at a modest pace, or not at all. Relative market share is the proportion of that market controlled by the product.

If we classify market growth rate as high or low and relative market share as high or low, we get the two-by-two matrix shown in Exhibit 6.5. Note that this creates four different categories of products. Classifying SBUs into the appropriate cells helps managers figure out how to manage them better.

Stars are businesses whose products have a high share of a fast-growing market. When IBM personal computers were first introduced, they were clearly stars. The market was expanding dramatically, and the IBM PC controlled a large portion of it. Of course, since market growth rates must even-

□ In the *portfolio matrix*, SBUs are classified as *stars, cash cows, question marks,* or *dogs.*

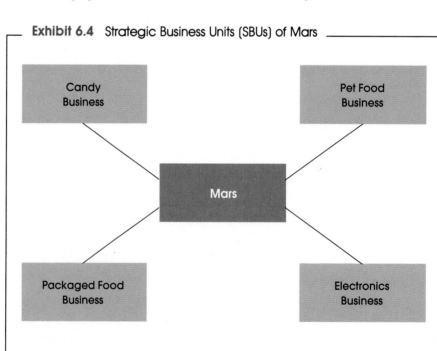

Exhibit 6.4 Strategic Business Units (SBUs) of Mars

Exhibit 6.5 The Portfolio Matrix

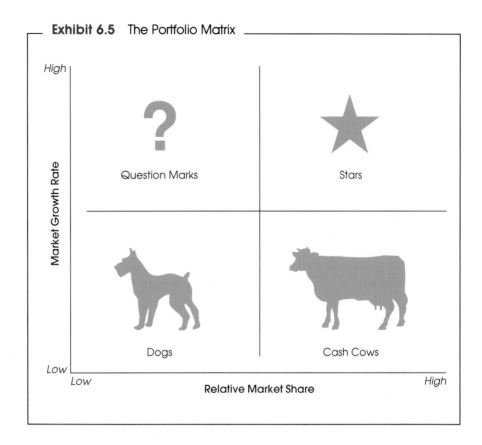

tually stabilize, stars tend to be fairly short-lived.[4] Other recent stars have included Chrysler's minivans, compact disc players, and Diet Coke. Obviously, managers like stars. Stars need little investment to be sustained and generate large amounts of revenue.

Cash cows are products that control a large share of a low-growth market. If market growth stabilizes and the product can still control a large portion of it, it has become a cash cow. Since the market is stable, there is little need to promote products aggressively, so they generate large amounts of cash with relatively little support. Current cash cows include Crest toothpaste, Right Guard deodorant, and Coca-Cola Classic.

Question marks are products with a small share of a growing market. When confronted with a question mark, a manager must decide whether to invest more resources in the hope of transforming it into a star, simply maintain the status quo, or drop the product or business from the portfolio. For example, Bausch & Lomb controls the lion's share of the market in the contact lens industry. Divisions of Revlon and Johnson & Johnson have been trying to gain a larger share of the market for the past few years but have made little headway. For them, the contact lens business is a question mark, whereas it is a star for Bausch & Lomb.

Dogs are products or businesses with a small share of a stable market. Trying to salvage dogs is very difficult because growth has to come at the expense of competing products. Given their unappealing nature, dogs tend not to stay around long. An example might be a small division of an electronics division that still produces black-and-white televisions. Similarly, because of the growing popularity of compact discs and disc players, businesses that produce vinyl records and turntables might turn into dogs in the future.

The key to using the portfolio matrix is to manage the portfolio effectively. For instance, cash cows can be used to generate the resources needed to support stars and maintain question marks. Dogs are usually sold or dropped, although occasionally they are turned into viable products again.

On balance, the portfolio matrix is the dominant view of corporate strategy today. Managers are comfortable with it, and research generally supports its validity.[5] *Management Today: The World of Management* describes how Daimler-Benz has adopted a portfolio approach to managing its various businesses. Nonetheless, it should be seen for what it is—a guiding framework to be used with caution and judgment.

LEARNING CHECK

You should now be able to identify major approaches to corporate strategy.

One common approach to corporate strategy is the portfolio approach. The Howard Savings Bank recently established a new division called The College Store®. Its target market is high school students planning their financial needs for college. The College Store® represents an SBU under the corporate umbrella.

Used by permission The Howard Savings Bank

THE WORLD OF MANAGEMENT

Daimler-Benz, German Juggernaut

Germany's Daimler-Benz is one of the largest and strongest automobile manufacturers in the world. Led by its flagship Mercedes-Benz line, the company has been synonymous with quality and prestige. However, like other automobile makers, Daimler has also been susceptible to market fluctuations and increased competition from the Japanese.

In an effort to offset cyclical variations and further insulate itself from competition, in 1985 managers at Daimler outlined a new strategy calling for diversification and growth. The first acquisition was MTU, a large German engine manufacturer. AEG, an electronics and appliance manufacturer, was the next acquisition.

Managers at Daimler quickly amassed a conglomeration of enterprises that make everything from toasters to airplanes and from coffeepots to combat tanks. Recognizing that they were in danger of creating an organization that is too complex to compete

effectively, managers reorganized the firm into three major businesses: one for automobiles; one for aerospace operations; and one for electronics, automation, and communications products and operations. They also classified anywhere from five to fifteen units within each of the three major business groups as individual units (similar to SBUs).

Such an arrangement allows the company to keep its overall vision relatively simple, focusing on the three major business groups. It also allows each business, however, to buy, sell, and/or transform a variety of different operations without changing its overall complexion.

When the final changes are implemented, set to follow the government's approval of the acquisition of MBB, a major aircraft manufacturer, Daimler-Benz will account for over 4 percent of West Germany's gross national product and will be one of the largest and most powerful corporations in the world.

SOURCES: "The Even-Bigger Shadow Daimler Could Cast," *Business Week,* May 22, 1989, pp. 54–55; "Putsch and Shove at Daimler-Benz," *Fortune,* August 17, 1987, p. 92; "Daimler-Benz Resists Bonn's New Lures to Take Over State-Run Aerospace Firm," *The Wall Street Journal,* June 20, 1988, p. 8.

BUSINESS STRATEGY

As we saw earlier, business strategy is the strategy managers develop for a single business. A business strategy is developed for each SBU within a portfolio matrix and for single-product firms that are not broken down into SBUs. The following sections explore a useful conceptual framework for understanding business strategy and identify and discuss the major kinds of business strategy that firms adopt.

The Adaptation Process

☐ According to the *adaptation model,* managers must solve *entrepreneurial, engineering,* and *administrative* problems.

One popular approach to business strategy is the **adaptation model,** which suggests that managers should focus on solving three basic managerial problems by adopting one of three forms of strategy.[6] The model is illustrated in Exhibit 6.6.

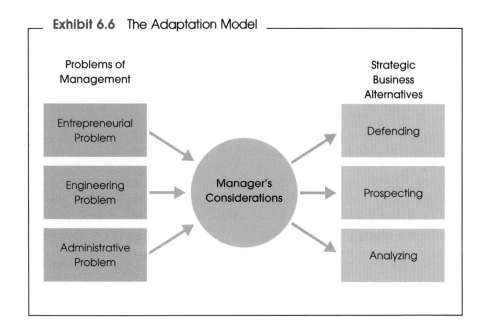

Exhibit 6.6   The Adaptation Model

Problems of Management

Entrepreneurial Problem

Engineering Problem

Administrative Problem

Manager's Considerations

Strategic Business Alternatives

Defending

Prospecting

Analyzing

PROBLEMS OF MANAGEMENT   The first of the three managerial hurdles is the **entrepreneurial problem.** This problem involves determining which business opportunities to undertake, which to ignore, and so forth. Decisions regarding the introduction of a new product or the purchase of another business relate to the entrepreneurial problem.

The **engineering problem** involves the production and distribution of goods and services. For example, Canon might elect to manufacture its own facsimile machines, to have them manufactured by someone else, or to combine the two methods in some way. Similarly, the plant that produces the facsimile machines might use traditional assembly lines staffed by employees, total automation, or some combination. Finally, the company might do its own distribution or subcontract distribution to a wholesaler. Each of these decisions relates to the engineering problem.

The **administrative problem** involves structuring the organization. Top managers at Canon might choose to give operating managers considerable power and autonomy to make important decisions, or to retain most of that power at the top. They might also choose to have a large number of different divisions or to maintain only a handful of divisions. These are aspects of the administrative problem.

☐ Three common strategic business alternatives are *defending, prospecting,* and *analyzing.*

STRATEGIC BUSINESS ALTERNATIVES   According to the model, firms can use a variety of strategies to address these problems. In general, managers usually choose one of three basic alternatives, as shown in Exhibit 6.6: defending, prospecting, and analyzing.

Defending is the most conservative approach to business strategy. Defenders attempt to carve out a clearly defined market niche for themselves and then work hard to protect that niche from competitors. They tend to ignore trends and remain within their chosen domain. They concentrate on efficiency and attempt to create and maintain a loyal group of customers. Mobil, Levi Strauss, many regional universities, and most local community hospitals use the defending mode of strategy.

Prospecting is the exact opposite of defending. Prospectors attempt to discover and exploit new market opportunities. They prefer to avoid dependence on a narrow product or product group. Indeed, they attempt to shift frequently from one market to another. 3M is a good example of a prospector; one of its goals is to have 25 percent of its sales coming from products that did not exist five years ago.[7] Other well-known prospectors include Westinghouse, Bendix, and Litton Industries.

Analyzing is a midrange approach that falls between defending and prospecting. Analyzers attempt to move into new market areas, but at a deliberate and carefully planned pace. The analyzer keeps a core set of products that provide predictable revenues but at the same time systematically looks for new opportunities. Examples of analyzers are Procter & Gamble, Unilever, and Nestlé.

Overall, the adaptation model is a useful framework for helping managers understand business strategy. It has been supported by research and is well known among practicing managers.[8]

Competitive Strategies

⬛ Three competitive strategies are *differentiation, overall cost leadership,* and *targeting.*

In addition to the adaptation model, there are three competitive strategies that are pursued by some businesses: differentiation, overall cost leadership, and targeting. **Differentiation** is the process of setting the firm's products apart

One common competitive strategy that businesses can adopt is differentiation. Frieda Caplan is chair and founder of Freida's Finest, a grocery supply firm that specializes in exotic fruits and vegetables such as taro root, passion fruit, and kiwano. By searching for unusual products and creating a market for them, Caplan differentiates her operation from more traditional suppliers.

© Robert Holmgren

from those of other companies. Such differentiation might be in terms of quality (Volvo, IBM, Rolex), style (Ralph Lauren, Calvin Klein), or service (Maytag, Federal Express, American Express).

Overall cost leadership involves trying to keep costs as low as possible so that the firm is able to charge low prices and thus increase sales volume and/or market share. Examples of companies that use the cost leadership strategy are discount retailers like K mart and Wal-Mart, manufacturers like Bic and Black & Decker, Southwest Airlines, and Motel 6.

Finally, **targeting** occurs when a firm attempts to identify and focus on a clearly defined and often highly specialized market. Some companies produce cosmetics just for blacks, for instance, or food for regional markets (chili in the Southwest, clam chowder in the Northeast). Others attempt to focus on special categories of consumers (the young, the upper class, and so forth). *Management Today: Small Business and Entrepreneurship* demonstrates how one entrepreneur became enormously successful by focusing on a special target market—professional working women.

LEARNING CHECK

You should now be able to identify major approaches to business strategy.

FUNCTIONAL STRATEGIES

We saw earlier that the lowest level of strategy in the organization includes functional strategies. The six basic types of functional strategy are listed in Table 6.1, along with their major areas of concern.

□ Functional strategies are often developed for *marketing, finance, production, research and development, human resources,* and *organization design.*

MARKETING STRATEGY The **marketing strategy** is the functional strategy that relates to the promotion, pricing, and distribution of products and services by the organization. For example, Reebok has determined that it will sell only to fashionable retailers and will avoid discount chains. The firm also limits the amount of apparel it produces, even though it could sell more.[9] These decisions are a part of the firm's marketing strategy. Similarly, decisions about how many variations of each product to market (six versus nine sizes of Crest toothpaste dispensers), desired market position (Sears versus K mart for the number one position in retailing), pricing policies (high prices with an emphasis on quality versus lower prices with an emphasis on quantity), and distribution channels (Timex's early decision to sell only through drugstores) are all a part of the development of the marketing strategy.

FINANCIAL STRATEGY The **financial strategy** of a firm is also important. Companies need to decide whether to pay out most of their profits to stockholders as dividends, retain most of the earnings for growth, or take some position between these extremes. They must also make decisions about the proper mix of common stock, preferred stock, and bonds and establish policies regarding how surplus funds will be invested and how much debt the organization can and is willing to support. For example, Disney's financial strategy calls for low debt, and it managed to spend almost $1 billion from operating

SMALL BUSINESS AND ENTREPRENEURSHIP

Liz Claiborne Targets Success

In the early 1970s, Liz Claiborne saw a golden opportunity. More and more women were entering the workplace, but Claiborne reasoned that clothing makers were not meeting their needs. In particular, she believed that most clothing makers were making the same kinds of outfits they had made for years, outfits not necessarily appropriate for professional business settings. And the few clothing companies that were selling to professional women were focusing on the upscale consumers who could pay hefty price tags.

In 1976, Claiborne, her husband, and two of their friends launched Liz Claiborne Inc. Their target market was working women, and their strategy was to provide these women with professional apparel at reasonable prices. After a few years of struggling, the business took off in the late 1970s, and by the 1980s, Liz Claiborne was one of the fastest-growing companies in the United States.

Along the way, managers at Claiborne were careful to not tamper with their formula. They were often tempted, for example, to expand too quickly, to turn their products upscale to achieve larger profit margins, or to turn downscale and tap the discount markets. They kept their original goal in mind, however, and achieved sales of over $1 billion per year by the end of the 1980s. At that time, Claiborne retired from active involvement in the corporation and turned things over to Jerome Chazen, the last of the original four partners still working full-time with the company.

Chazen had already been in charge of marketing and merchandising. He outlined plans to continue using reasonably priced clothing for professional working women as the core of Liz Claiborne's operations. He also indicated, however, that the company would continue to branch out into other areas.

The two areas holding the most promise for the company are men's fashions and direct retailing. The firm's retail outlets, called First Issue, are generally used for test-marketing purposes and for getting fast responses from consumers regarding trends and preferences. The door remains open, however, for more aggressive expansion in this area. The men's fashion business is also doing quite well. However, in keeping with Claiborne's history, managers are still proceeding cautiously on all fronts.

SOURCES: Bill Saporito, "Retailing's Winners & Losers," *Fortune,* December 18, 1989, pp. 69–80; "Liz Claiborne's New Chief Stays Inquisitive," *The Wall Street Journal,* May 30, 1989, p. B13; Stuart Gannes, "America's Fastest-Growing Companies," *Fortune,* May 23, 1988, pp. 28–40.

funds on Epcot Center without incurring any debt.[10] At the other extreme, Texas Air, the parent company of Continental and Eastern, is hundreds of millions of dollars in debt.

PRODUCTION STRATEGY In many ways, **production strategy** follows from marketing strategy. For example, if a company emphasizes quality, production costs may be of secondary importance. On the other hand, if price is to be emphasized, low-cost production techniques may become critical. Several areas of concern are usually addressed in this strategy. The location of

TABLE 6.1
Basic Functional Strategies

Functional area	Major concerns
Marketing	Product mix
	Market position
	Distribution channels
	Sales promotions
	Pricing issues
	Public policy
Finance	Debt policies
	Dividend policies
	Assets management
	Capitalization structure
Production	Productivity improvement
	Production planning
	Plant location
	Government regulation
Research and development	Product development
	Technological forecasting
	Patents and licenses
Human resource	Personnel policies
	Labor relations
	Executive development
	Governmental regulation
Organization design	Degree of decentralization
	Methods of coordination
	Bases of departmentalization

SOURCE: Ricky W. Griffin, *Management,* 3rd ed. (Boston: Houghton Mifflin, 1990), p. 209. Copyright © 1990 Houghton Mifflin Company. Adapted by permission.

plant sites is a production issue. So too are production planning and productivity improvement efforts. Production managers must also deal with governmental agencies such as the Environmental Protection Agency. In recent years, the production strategy has become even more complex because more and more companies subcontract the manufacture and assembly of their products to other firms. For example, Kodak's new line of 35mm cameras is made by various Japanese manufacturers.

RESEARCH AND DEVELOPMENT STRATEGY   The **research and development strategy** relates to the invention and development of new products and services as well as the exploration of new and better ways to produce and distribute existing ones.[11] Some firms, such as IBM, Rubbermaid, and Texas Instruments, spend large sums of money on R&D, whereas others spend less. Long-term gains from R&D investment can be impressive, as in the case of

Bridgestone Tire Company, where a strong R&D program has increased worker productivity by 10 percent each year for over a decade.[12]

HUMAN RESOURCE STRATEGY   Most organizations also develop a **human resource strategy.** This might deal with issues such as whether the firm plans to pay premium wages to get better-qualified workers, whether it will welcome unions, how it will attempt to develop executives more effectively, and how it will comply with federal regulations such as the equal employment opportunity guidelines.

ORGANIZATION DESIGN STRATEGY   Finally, companies often develop an **organization design strategy,** which is concerned with how the various positions and divisions within the organization will be arranged. For example, some organizations allow field managers to make fairly important decisions without consulting the home office, whereas others require home office personnel to approve nearly all field decisions. The determination of which policy

One important functional strategy for consumer products firms is the marketing strategy. Polaroid, the world's largest maker of instant cameras, has turned its marketing attention toward younger consumers. The firm even seeks input from younger consumers in designing and marketing new products. For example, the Polaroid Cool Cam was introduced in 1988. Partially because the camera had been designed and advertised with input from the target market—teens—first year sales were 30 percent higher than projected.

to follow is a part of the organization design strategy. (Organization design is discussed more fully in Part Three.)

Integration as well as development of the six major functional strategies is crucial. Specifically, managers must make sure that all functional strategies follow logically from a unified corporate and business strategy and that they fit logically together. For example, if the marketing strategy calls for a sales increase of 50 percent, the production strategy might be to build a new plant to come on line in five years. This strategy in turn means that the human resource strategy will include a provision for developing the necessary managerial talent to run the plant and that a financial strategy must be developed to pay for the plant. The organization design strategy needs to specify how the new plant will fit into the existing organizational structure.

LEARNING CHECK

You should now be able to identify the major functional strategies developed by most organizations.

PRELUDE CASE UPDATE

We can now see more clearly the various functional strategies pursued by Mars. In particular, the company advertises heavily (part of its marketing strategy), avoids debt (part of its financial strategy), emphasizes quality (part of its production strategy), seeks new product innovations (part of its research and development strategy), hires high-quality people (part of its human resource strategy), and uses a tall (many-layered) organization structure (part of its organization design strategy).

STRATEGY IMPLEMENTATION

◻ Strategy implementation is achieved through tactical planning, contingency planning, and integration with organization design.

The final part of strategic planning, and one we will only briefly review, is the implementation of strategic plans by managers of the organization.[13] Exhibit 6.7 summarizes the process of strategy implementation. First, it must follow logically from strategy formulation: that is, managers first must formulate and then systematically implement strategies. Implementation itself consists of three elements. Tactical planning, as detailed in Chapter 5, is the real way in which strategy is implemented. Contingency planning, also described in Chapter 5, is also important for the proper implementation of strategic plans. Finally, strategy and organization design must be properly integrated. A mismatch can result in numerous problems for organizations and can serve as a major barrier to the effective accomplishment of strategic plans.

In reality, of course, strategy implementation is far more comprehensive and complex than this simple overview implies. Each strategy and its corresponding organizational context is unique, making each effort to implement a strategy unique as well. In many ways, then, much of the material in other chapters of this book is in some way an attempt to show how all or part of a strategic plan developed by top management is implemented.

LEARNING CHECK

You should now be able to describe the process of strategy implementation.

Exhibit 6.7 Strategy Implementation

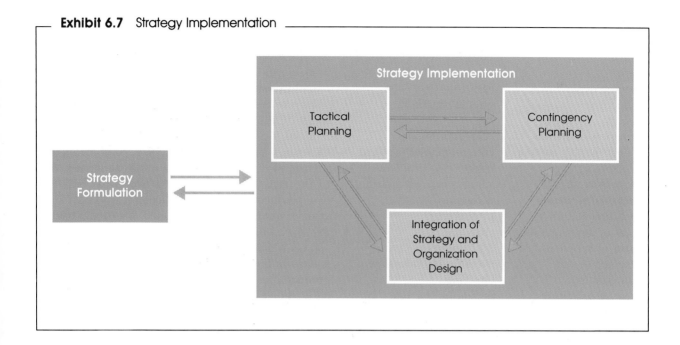

Chapter Summary

Strategic planning is the broad planning of top management to guide the general direction of an organization. There are four basic components of strategy: scope, resource deployment, competitive advantage, and synergy. Strategy formulation is the set of processes involved in creating or developing strategic plans, and strategy implementation is the set of processes involved with executing those plans. Finally, there are three levels of strategy: corporate strategy, business strategy, and various functional strategies.

Environmental analysis is the specific study of the company's environment and how it affects the company. Five critical environmental forces must be considered: the threat of new entrants, the power of suppliers, jockeying among contestants, the threat of substitute products, and the power of buyers. Managers must understand these forces and use them as a framework to match environmental threats and opportunities with organizational strengths and weaknesses.

Corporate strategy means determining what businesses the firm expects to compete in. Three grand strategies are growth, retrenchment, and stability. Some organizations also use a portfolio approach involving strategic business units, or SBUs. The portfolio matrix is a system for analyzing SBUs in terms of relative market share and the growth rate of the market.

A business strategy is the strategy developed for a single business within an organization. The adaptation model is the most popular view of business strategy and suggests that managers should focus on solving three basic managerial problems—entrepreneurial, engineering, and administrative—by adopting one of three forms of strategy—defending, prospecting, or analyzing. Other competitive alternatives include differentation, overall cost leadership, and targeting.

Functional strategies constitute the lowest level of strategy in an organization. There are six basic types: marketing, financial, production, research and development, human resource, and organization design.

Following strategy formulation, implementation involves three elements: tactical planning, contingency planning, and integration of the strategy with the organization's design.

The Manager's Vocabulary

strategic plans	portfolio matrix
scope	stars
resource deployment	cash cows
competitive advantage	question marks
synergy	dogs
strategy formulation	adaptation model
strategy implementation	entrepreneurial problem
corporate strategy	engineering problem
business strategy	administrative problem
functional strategies	defending
environmental forces	prospecting
threat of new entrants	analyzing
power of suppliers	differentiation
jockeying among	overall cost leadership
contestants	targeting
threat of substitute	marketing strategy
products	financial strategy
power of buyers	production strategy
grand strategy	research and
growth strategy	development strategy
retrenchment strategy	human resource strategy
stability strategy	organization design
portfolio approach	strategy
strategic business unit	
(SBU)	

Prelude Case Wrap-Up

The Prelude Case for this chapter focuses on the Mars company. As we see, Mars operates four different businesses. One makes candy, one makes packaged food products, one makes pet food, and one makes electronic moneychangers. The case also describes the history of the company and its general approach to managing its operations.

As noted in two case updates within the chapter, Mars allocates resources across the four businesses according to different formulas, has an overall corporate strategy, four different business strategies, and clearly identifiable functional strategies.

We can also view the four businesses as SBUs within a portfolio matrix framework. The candy and pet food businesses are clearly cash cows, reaping huge profits in stable markets. The packaged foods business is close to being a star, gaining market share in a growing market. Finally, the electronics business is a question mark, maintaining low sales and profits in an expanding market.

Unfortunately, as noted at the end of the case, Mars has lately fallen on hard times. When Hershey bought Cadbury, it acquired such popular brands as Almond Joy, Mounds, and York Peppermint Patties. Other new products from Hershey, combined with a barrage of new entries from Nestlé, awakened Mars to the fact that it desperately needed to introduce new products of its own. Although it has taken a few years to get going, Mars has indeed started introducing several new candy products.

This is a profound switch for the venerable candy maker. In the old days, it wanted to have only a few products, each of which commanded huge sales bases. For example, Snickers Bars alone brought in $440 million in 1988. But since candy buyers seldom buy the same product twice in a row, manufacturers actually need to have as many products as possible in stores. The proliferation of products through both innovation and acquisition is what led Hershey past Mars. But Mars has finally started playing the game itself and should regain lost ground now.

Prelude Case Questions

1. Which of the five critical environmental forces seem most relevant for Mars? Why?
2. In your opinion, how should Mars position its organizational strengths and weaknesses against environmental opportunities and threats?
3. What are the entrepreneurial, engineering, and administrative problems faced by Mars?
4. Is Mars a defender, a prospector, or an analyzer? Does Mars use differentiation? Overall cost leadership? Targeting? Use details to support each answer.

Discussion Questions

Review Questions

1. What are the three levels of strategy? Do all firms have all three levels? Why or why not?
2. What are the five critical environmental forces that

organizations must consider when developing strategies? How do organizations go about positioning themselves relative to those forces?

3. Identify three grand strategies that organizations might choose to pursue.
4. What are the three problems of management and the three strategic business alternatives described in the adaptation model?
5. What are the six basic functional strategies most organizations develop?

Analysis Questions

1. Apply the concepts of corporate, business, and functional strategies to your university or college.
2. Which of the five environmental forces are more likely to exist together than others? Identify other examples of organizations likely to be affected by each of the five forces.
3. What are the risks involved in selling dogs quickly? Why would anyone want to buy a dog?
4. Identify examples beyond those noted in the chapter to illustrate defenders, prospectors, and analyzers.
5. What are the critical issues in implementing a new strategy within an organization?

Application Questions and Exercises

1. Select any large business with which you are familiar. Characterize the five environmental forces that affect that organization and outline organizational strengths and weaknesses and environmental threats and opportunities.
2. Research an organization that has at various times pursued growth, retrenchment, and stability strategies. Identify the factors that led to various shifts from one to another.
3. Identify a large multibusiness corporation (your instructor may have suggestions). Characterize each of the businesses within the portfolio matrix.
4. Interview a manager at a local company and try to identify as many strategic approaches or concepts as possible that her or his organization might be pursuing.
5. Outline a strategic plan for a not-for-profit organization such as a church or hospital. What are the similarities and differences in planning between these kinds of organizations and profit-seeking firms?

ENHANCEMENT CASE

BORDEN SWITCHES STRATEGIES

Borden, generally thought of as a milk producer with a cow for a mascot, has gone through three significant transformations in recent years. First of all, several years ago managers decided to undertake a dramatic diversification strategy. Using profits from the company's highly successful dairy business, Borden bought dozens and dozens of businesses, including everything from a women's apparel business to a fertilizer company.

A few years ago, however, managers began to realize that their disparate businesses were not performing as well as they might and decided to develop a new strategy. The idea was that they would sell many of the unrelated businesses and use the proceeds to buy new businesses that fit within a narrower range of markets. Beginning in the early 1980s, this second phase of strategic planning was put into place.

During much of the 1980s, Borden sold many of the businesses it had previously owned and bought many others. In 1986 the company appointed a new CEO, Romeo Ventres, to finish implementing the new strategy. Ventres immediately set a new goal of increasing sales by 15 percent each year and announced that the company would seek to build itself around six major businesses.

One of the businesses within the Borden corporation is its dairy company. Borden dairies produce various milk, ice cream, and cheese products. A second business is pasta. Buying several regional pasta companies has enabled Borden to become the first national pasta enterprise. The third business is "niche" grocery products. Well-known brand names for this business are ReaLemon juice and Eagle sweetened condensed milk.

The fourth business Borden is concentrating on is salty snacks. Its potato chips and other products put Borden behind PepsiCo's Frito-Lay business in this market. Fifth is consumer do-it-yourself products like Elmer's glues and Krylon spray paint. Finally, the sixth business within Borden is a variety of firms that make specialty industrial chemicals like resins and polyvinyl chloride films.

Borden has developed an innovative strategy for each of its businesses that involves linking regional businesses into an international organization. This allows the firm to capitalize on the economies of scale associated with large-scale operations while simultaneously targeting regional markets.

For example, Borden bought such well-known regional pasta concerns as Gioia in Buffalo, Viviano in Pittsburgh, Anthony's in Los Angeles, and Prince in Boston. Borden uses the factories of those companies to continue to produce their original products plus Borden's own national brand name, Creamette. It then markets both brands within each region, using the distribution channels already in place. The same approach is being used in salty snack foods and dairy products.

These approaches led to enormous growth for Borden. For example, total company sales grew from $4.3 billion in 1979 to $7.2 billion in 1988. Profits also increased substantially.

In 1989, however, Borden embarked on a third strategic path involving a series of cutbacks. In particular, Ventres decided that operating costs had become excessive and that steps were needed to streamline various operations. The basic framework of the cutbacks involved selling or closing 65 of Borden's 265 plants worldwide and reducing its 46,000-member work force by 7,000. Most of the cutbacks were associated with the company's dairy business, where cutthroat competition has hurt sales and profits.

Another potential problem on the horizon for Borden is the health boom in the United States. Most of the products Borden makes (such as chips and milk) are in the various categories many people are concerned about. At this point, at least, Ventres says he isn't worried, however, and that everything will work out fine.

SOURCES: Bill Saporito, "How Borden Milks Packaged Goods," *Fortune*, December 21, 1987, pp. 139–144; "Borden Feasts on Acquisitions," *USA Today*, April 29, 1988, pp. 1B–2B; Walter Guzzardi, "Big Can Still Be Beautiful," *Fortune*, April 25, 1988, pp. 50–61; "Borden Plans to Shrink Dairy Business, Streamline Food, Consumer Operations," *The Wall Street Journal*, September 29, 1989, p. A2.

Enhancement Case Questions

1. What are the strengths, weaknesses, opportunities, and threats faced by Borden?
2. What approach(es) to corporate strategy is Borden pursuing?
3. What approach(es) to business strategy is Borden pursuing?
4. Is Borden achieving synergy? Why or why not?

Chapter Notes

1. See Charles W. L. Hill and Gareth R. Jones, *Strategic Management: An Analytical Approach* (Boston: Houghton Mifflin, 1989), for a review.

2. Arthur A. Thompson and A. J. Strickland III, *Strategy Formulation and Implementation*, 3rd ed. (Dallas: Business Publications, 1986).

3. Michael E. Porter, *Competitive Strategy: Techniques for Analyzing Industries and Competitors* (New York: Free Press, 1980). See also Walter Kiechel III, "Corporate Strategy for the 1990s," *Fortune*, February 29, 1988, pp. 34–42.

4. See "Personal Computers: And the Winner Is IBM," *Business Week*, October 3, 1983, pp. 76–79. See also "Mike Armstrong Is Improving IBM's Game in Europe," *Business Week*, June 20, 1988, pp. 96–101.

5. See, for example, Ian C. MacMillan, Donald C. Hambrick, and Diana L. Day, "The Product Portfolio and Profitability—A PMS-based Analysis of Industrial

Product Businesses," *Academy of Management Journal*, December 1982, pp. 733–755.

6. Raymond E. Miles and Charles C. Snow, *Organizational Strategy, Structure, and Process* (New York: McGraw-Hill, 1978).

7. "Masters of Innovation," *Business Week*, April 10, 1989, pp. 58–63.

8. Donald C. Hambrick, "Some Tests of the Effectiveness and Functional Attributes of Miles's and Snow's Strategic Types," *Academy of Management Journal*, March 1983, pp. 5–26.

9. Stuart Gannes, "America's Fastest-Growing Companies," *Fortune*, May 23, 1988, pp. 28–40.

10. "Disney's Epcot Center, Big $1 Billion Gamble, Opens in Florida," *The Wall Street Journal*, September 16, 1982, pp. 1, 19.

11. Donald C. Hambrick and Ian C. MacMillan, "Efficiency of Product R&D in Business Units: The Role of Strategic Context," *Academy of Management Journal*, September 1985, pp. 527–547.

12. Bernard Krisher, "A Different Kind of Tiremaker Rolls into Nashville," *Fortune*, March 22, 1982, pp. 136–146.

13. Thompson and Strickland, *Strategy Formulation and Implementation*.

CHAPTER OUTLINE

I. The Nature of Decision Making
  A. Decision Making Versus Problem Solving
  B. Decision-Making Conditions

II. Approaches to Decision Making
  A. The Rational Model
  B. The Behavioral Model
  C. Other Behavioral Processes

III. The Decision-Making Process
  A. Defining the Situation
  B. Generating Alternatives
  C. Judging Alternatives
  D. Choosing the Best Alternative
  E. Implementing the Alternative
  F. Evaluating the Results

IV. Innovation and Decision Making
  A. Encouraging Innovation
  B. The Innovation Process

V. Decision-Making Techniques
  A. The Payoff Matrix
  B. Decision Trees
  C. Other Techniques

C
H
A
P
T
E
R

7

After studying this chapter you should be able to

1. Describe the nature of decision making, differentiate it from problem solving, and identify decision-making conditions.

2. Describe the rational model of decision making, the behavioral model, and other behavioral processes.

3. Describe the decision-making process.

4. Discuss the nature of innovation and its relation to decision making.

5. Describe decision-making techniques, including payoff matrices and decision trees.

Decision Making

GENERAL ELECTRIC'S BOLD DECISION MAKER

During the 1980s, General Electric went through as radical a transformation as any large company has in the history of American business. Much of this transformation was the product of major executive decisions made by Jack Welch.

When Welch was named CEO of GE in the early 1980s, the company consisted of over one hundred businesses, many of them small and/or only marginally profitable. The GE name was known for light bulbs, toasters, irons, and other consumer products. Welch believed, however, that such a company was ill-suited to the competitive world his company would confront as the twentieth century drew to a close. In particular, he believed that a few global powerhouses like Philips, Siemens, and Toshiba would dominate the industries in which GE was competing. Accordingly, Welch starting taking steps to put GE in the same league as these firms.

During the remainder of the 1980s, Welch sold operations worth $9 billion, bought other companies worth $16 billion, reduced the company's work force by 100,000 people, and narrowed the set of businesses down from over one hundred to fourteen. He also established the goal that each of the fourteen businesses within the GE umbrella would be either number one or number two in its respective market.

Among the bigger acquisitions made by Welch were RCA, which itself owned NBC television, and investment banker Kidder Peabody. Among the set that were sold were GE's small-appliance business (to Black & Decker), a coal mining operation, and a computer chip manufacturer.

Among his industry peers, Welch is known as a ruthless manager who will make any decision that needs to be made. Insiders, however, report that Welch agonizes over the decisions that will bring hardship to others. Especially traumatic, for example, was the series of decisions Welch felt he had to make in reducing the company's work force.

When Welch talks about GE, one of the things he points to proudly is how he eliminated much of the bureaucracy. His predecessor at GE, Reginald Jones, had a finance background. Jones did marvelous things for the company. But along the way, he also created so many checks and balances for decision makers that even the simplest and most routine decision had to have several approvals before it could be implemented. Jones believed, for example, that a manager could never have too much information. Welch overcame many of these bureaucratic hurdles by eliminating the need for so many approvals, by insisting that managers make more of their decisions individually, and by dramatically cutting back on paperwork.

Illustrative of Welch's approach was a decision made late in the last decade involving billions of dollars. With its acquisition of RCA, GE controlled 23 percent of the U.S. color television market and 17 percent of its VCR market. Moreover, the business was

Gregory Heisler

John Madere

One recent innovation Jack Welch has supported at General Electric has involved processing waste plastic into new construction materials. The demonstration plastic house shown here being built is a possible replacement for traditional wood construction.

quite profitable. One day, however, a large French firm called Thomson S.A. indicated an interest in acquiring the business from GE. Thomson itself had a very profitable global medical equipment business—exactly the type that Welch coveted.

So Welch offered to trade businesses, much the way that kids trade baseball cards. He says that he made the decision in thirty minutes, spent only two hours with Thomson officials working out the basic deal, and signed a letter of intent only five days later. Although it took several months for complicated legal contracts to be prepared, the basic decision itself was made very quickly. And Welch sees this as the model for how he wants things done at GE.

SOURCES: Stratford P. Sherman, "Inside the Mind of Jack Welch," *Fortune*, March 27, 1989, pp. 38–50; Noel Tichy and Ram Charan, "Speed, Simplicity, Self-Confidence: An Interview with Jack Welch," *Harvard Business Review*, September-October 1989, pp. 112–120; Peter Petre, "What Welch Has Wrought at GE," *Fortune*, July 7, 1986, pp. 43–47; "Jack Welch: How Good a Manager?" *Business Week*, December 14, 1987, pp. 92-103.

Jack Welch has had to make many decisions during his career at GE. The Prelude Case covers only a few of the more significant ones. Decision making is a critical part of virtually every manager's job and almost all organizational activities. It is covered here because it is perhaps most closely linked to planning. However, the organizing, leading, and control functions also involve decision making.

This chapter first explores the nature of decision making more fully. Then it identifies major approaches to decision making and outlines the decision-making process itself in detail. It relates decision making to innovation and concludes with a brief discussion of some useful decision-making techniques.

THE NATURE OF DECISION MAKING

As noted earlier, decision making is a pervasive part of all managerial activities. Virtually every action managers take involves making one or more decisions. For example, a simple decision to raise prices must be made within the context of its probable effects on consumer and competitive behavior; one must also consider how much to raise prices, when to initiate the new prices, and a variety of other issues. Decision making is most closely linked to planning, since all planning involves making decisions.[1]

Decision Making Versus Problem Solving

□ *Decision making* is the process of choosing one alternative from among a set of potentially feasible alternatives.

We can define **decision making** as the process of choosing one alternative from among a set of alternatives. It is important at this point to draw a distinction between decision making and problem solving, a related managerial activity. A decision-making situation exists when there is not an obvious and clear course of action. When managers make decisions, therefore, they identify a number of potentially feasible alternatives and choose what they believe to be the single best alternative for their situation. For example, before Harry Cunningham made the decision to open the first K mart stores, he had several options: to open only one or two on a trial basis, to stay in variety retailing with the Kresge stores, to move into another branch of retailing (such as food or specialty retailing), or to open several K mart stores. Cunningham chose the fourth alternative, and the rest, as they say, is history. The point is that he actually had several alternatives.

□ *Problem solving* is the process of determining the one and only course of action that fits the situation.

Problem solving, in contrast, occurs when the manager discovers that there is one and only one course of action that fits the situation. Suppose that a plant manager for a small electronics firm realizes that turnover in the plant has increased substantially over the past year. Investigation uncovers the cause: wage rates in the plant have not kept up with the prevailing wage rate in the area, so employees are leaving to take higher-paying jobs in other companies. If the manager's assessment is correct, there is only one alternative—

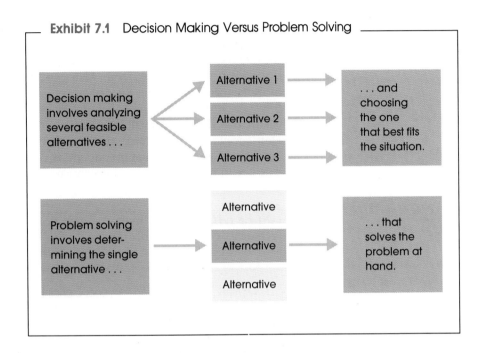

Exhibit 7.1 Decision Making Versus Problem Solving

Decision making involves analyzing several feasible alternatives . . .

Alternative 1
Alternative 2
Alternative 3

. . . and choosing the one that best fits the situation.

Problem solving involves determining the single alternative . . .

Alternative
Alternative
Alternative

. . . that solves the problem at hand.

address the wage issue somehow. Of course, that solution now subsequently requires a decision: should the manager raise wages, keep them where they are and live with higher turnover, or offer incentives other than higher wages? Thus, decision making and problem solving are distinct processes, as illustrated in Exhibit 7.1, but they may also be interrelated.[2]

Decision-Making Conditions

□ There are three possible decision-making conditions managers may face: *certainty, risk,* and *uncertainty.*

It is also instructive to note that virtually all decisions are made under conditions of certainty, risk, or uncertainty.[3] These three situations are illustrated in Exhibit 7.2.

CERTAINTY Decision making under a condition of **certainty** occurs when the manager knows exactly what the alternatives are and that the probabilities associated with each are guaranteed. In reality, of course, managers encounter few situations of this nature. One example that approximates this condition occurs when American Airlines decides to buy a new jumbo jet. The company has exactly three alternative suppliers—Boeing, McDonnell Douglas, or Airbus—and knows the probable reliability, cost, delivery time, and so forth for each alternative.

RISK Under a condition of **risk,** the manager has a basic understanding of the available options, but the probabilities associated with each are uncertain; that is, some element of risk is associated with each outcome. For example, suppose Dow Chemical is considering two possible sites for a new plant. Except for taxes, the two sites are equal. Site 1 has a relatively high tax rate, but the rate is not likely to be increased for several years. Site 2 has a low tax rate that will be increased next year. Managers at Dow might conclude that there is a 40 percent chance that the new tax rate at Site 2 will be higher than that at Site 1, a 30 percent chance that it will be slightly lower, and a 30 percent chance that the tax rate will be increased only a little beyond its current level. Dow's managers must consequently deal with a large element of risk in making their decision. Decision making under conditions of risk occurs frequently. The key to making effective decisions in these circumstances is correctly estimating the probabilities.[4]

UNCERTAINTY The most common decision-making condition that managers must confront is **uncertainty.** In this case, not only are the probabilities hard to assess, but the list of available alternatives is as well. That is, the man-

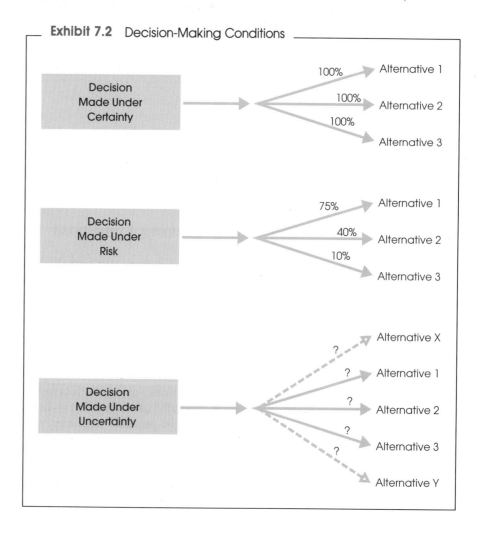

Exhibit 7.2 Decision-Making Conditions

ager might not even be able to identify all the feasible alternatives that he should be considering. This is the situation managers face in today's changing scene in Eastern Europe and the Soviet Union. Strong trends in those areas toward a free market economy appear to hold considerable promise for businesses and managers who are able and willing to supply the right goods and services at the right price. Still, considerable uncertainty persists regarding a possible reversion to a command economy, competition from other countries, the spending power of consumers in those countries, and so forth. Managers contemplating a decision to enter one or more of those markets, then, face considerable uncertainty.

PRELUDE CASE UPDATE

Jack Welch at General Electric has clearly had to make most of his decisions in a state of uncertainty. For example, one major question he faced was whether the company could continue to be effective with fewer and fewer consumer products bearing the General Electric name. Every business he bought and every business he sold was accompanied by a big question mark. And although most of his decisions appear to have been correct ones, not all have turned out so well. For example, Kidder Peabody continues to struggle. Further, most experts agree that it will be at least ten more years before anyone will know if Welch's decision to trade businesses with Thomson was a good idea.

APPROACHES TO DECISION MAKING

Are there any consistent ways in which managers make decisions? The answer to this question is clearly no—the complexities and variations in human behavior make the identification of consistent patterns of decision making virtually impossible.[5] There is a general consensus, however, that most managerial decision making follows one of two models: the rational model or the behavioral model.[6]

The Rational Model

☐ The *rational model* of decision making assumes that managers have perfect information and that they are rational.

The **rational model** of decision making is the one that many managers claim to follow. In fact, as we shall see, this is often not really the case. The basic premises of the rational model are summarized in Table 7.1.[7]

First, this model assumes that managers have perfect information—they have all the information that is relevant to the situation and it is completely accurate. Second, the model assumes that the decision maker has an exhaustive list of alternatives from which to choose. If there are eight potential decisions,

TABLE 7.1

Rational and Behavioral Models of Decision Making

Rational Model	Behavioral Model
1. The decision maker has perfect information (relevant and accurate).	1. The decision maker has imperfect information (incomplete and possibly inaccurate).
2. The decision maker has an exhaustive list of alternatives from which to choose.	2. The decision maker does not have a complete set of alternatives or does not completely understand those he or she does have.
3. The decision maker is rational.	3. The decision maker has bounded rationality and is constrained by values, experiences, habits, etc.
4. The decision maker always has the best interests of the organization at heart.	4. The decision maker will select the first minimally acceptable alternative (satisficing).

the rational model assumes that the manager has complete knowledge and understanding of all of them.

Next, as the model's name implies, it holds that the manager will always be rational. It assumes that the manager is capable of systematically and logically assessing each alternative and its associated probabilities and making the decision that is best for the situation. Finally, the rational model assumes that the manager will always work in the best interests of the organization. Even if her decision makes her suffer, the manager will still be motivated to make the decision that any other manager in the same organization would make in that situation. Thus, if the clearest course of action will result in budget cuts for a manager's own department, she is expected to choose that alternative anyway.

Clearly, the rational model is not always realistic in its depiction of managerial behavior. A variety of forces, including emotions, fatigue, individual preferences, and personal motives, are likely to intervene in most decision-making situations. The behavioral model represents an attempt to incorporate these individual processes into managerial decision making.

The Behavioral Model

☐ The *behavioral model* of decision making assumes that information is not perfect and that managers are not always rational.

The **behavioral model** of decision making was first explained by Herbert Simon, who was subsequently awarded a Nobel prize for his contributions.[8] The basic premises of the behavioral model are also summarized in Table 7.1.

First, this view assumes that the manager has imperfect information—it might be incomplete and/or parts of it might be inaccurate. Second, the behavioral model assumes that the manager also has an incomplete list of alternatives. There may be alternatives that the manager simply does not know about, he may not completely understand some of the alternatives, and the probabilities associated with various alternatives may be difficult to predict.

□ *Bounded rationality* suggests that rationality is constrained by values and experiences and by unconscious reflexes, skills, and habits.

□ *Satisficing* occurs when a manager selects the first minimally acceptable alternative without conducting a thorough search.

The manager is also assumed to be characterized by **bounded rationality.** This means that he may attempt to be rational but his rationality is constrained by his own values and experiences and by unconscious reflexes, skills, and habits. For example, if a manager has a history of making decisions in a certain fashion, he will probably continue to follow that same pattern, even when an objective observer might see the need for a new approach. Finally, the behavioral model assumes that decision makers engage in what is called satisficing. **Satisficing** is selecting the first minimally acceptable alternative even though a more thorough search could uncover better ones. For example, suppose a college student wants a job in marketing, preferably in marketing research, with a minimum salary of $25,000 and within one hundred miles of his hometown. When he is offered a job in marketing (although it is in sales) for $25,500 at a company eighty miles from home, he may be inclined to take it. A more comprehensive search, however, could have revealed a job in marketing research for $30,000 only twenty-five miles from home.

Other Behavioral Processes

Beyond the concepts of bounded rationality and satisficing, there are also other important behavioral processes that affect how decisions are made. One such process is called **escalation of commitment.** The idea behind escalation of commitment is that people sometimes make a decision and then become so committed to it that they fail to see that it was incorrect. For example, suppose an investor buys stock in a company for $50 a share. As the price starts to drop, the investor may doggedly hold on to the stock—not wanting to take a loss—when others see that it is a lost cause. Thus, instead of selling the stock

Even the most successful managers can become so committed to a decision that they ignore evidence that it may be a poor one. An Wang, founder of Wang Labs, spent fourteen years grooming his son Fred to succeed him as CEO of the firm. When the time came, most observers felt Fred was not qualified to be given the job. Wang persisted, however, because of his commitment to his son and to the Chinese custom of fathers passing wealth on to their sons. Unfortunately, three years later the company was experiencing severe problems and Fred Wang resigned from his position.

Richard Howard

MANAGEMENT IN PRACTICE

ABC's Miniseries: Too Much of a Good Thing

In 1983, the ABC television network aired a miniseries called "The Winds of War." Based on a novel about World War II by Herman Wouk, the miniseries was a ratings success and earned considerable profits for the network.

At the time, there was considerable discussion about the possibility of a sequel to the miniseries. Wouk had already written a sequel to the novel entitled "War and Remembrance." The problem, ABC executives argued, was that the sequel was considerably longer and more complex. Therefore, profits would be much more elusive.

Even though most industry observers never expected the follow-up to be made, ABC executives announced that they would indeed film the next story. They reached this decision despite projections that the project would only break even, at best.

Shortly after filming had started, ABC was bought by Capital Communications. Capital's managers were known for tight financial control and logical and rational decision making. When they looked closely at the "War and Remembrance" project, they foresaw a probable loss of around $20 million. In retrospect, they should probably have pulled the plug immediately. Inexplicably, however, they gave the go-ahead to continue filming.

The first eighteen hours of the miniseries were aired in November 1988, and the remaining fourteen hours were shown in May 1989. Ratings for the sequel were lower than expected, and most observers believe ABC lost far more than $20 million. Final figures have never been released, and the network may recoup some of its investment from foreign sales. Overall, however, it seems that managers had several opportunities to stop the project and cut losses, but they continued on toward ever-escalating losses without serious reservation.

SOURCES: "ABC's 'War and Remembrance' Fails to Deliver Audience, Big Losses Loom," *The Wall Street Journal*, November 28, 1988, p. B4; "'War' Miniseries Starts Strong, But Loss is Expected," *The Wall Street Journal*, November 22, 1988, p. A6; "NBC Again Triumphs in Ratings Sweeps; CBS Slips by ABC to Take Second Place," *The Wall Street Journal*, November 30, 1988, p. A12.

for $40 and taking a 20 percent loss, the investor may continue to hold on to it until the total investment is lost. *Management Today: Management in Practice* describes how managers at ABC were guilty of this error in their production of a costly miniseries.

Other behavioral forces that affect decision making include power, political behavior, and coalitions. Power, discussed more fully in Chapter 12, is the ability to affect the behavior of others. Political behaviors are activities carried out for the specific purpose of acquiring, developing, and using power to obtain a preferred course of action. Finally, coalitions are informal alliances of people or groups formed to achieve a common goal.[9] For example, suppose a ten-person board of directors is deciding on a new CEO for a corporation. If the board is split into factions of three, three, and four members, no single faction can get its way. However, by forming a coalition, any two factions that can compromise on a candidate will control a majority vote.

LEARNING CHECK

You should now be able to describe the rational model of decision making, the behavioral model, and other behavioral processes.

186

THE DECISION-MAKING PROCESS

The preceding section raises the question of how decisions are made. Let's explore that issue from another perspective: the ideal decision-making process. "Ideal" means that this is the process managers should use to make decisions most effectively. The steps in the ideal decision-making process, summarized in Exhibit 7.3, include defining the situation, generating alternatives, judging each alternative, choosing the best alternative, implementing the chosen alternative, and evaluating the results. Of course, many situations dictate changes in this process, but if managers follow these steps with some reasonable degree of commitment, they are more likely to make the best decision.[10]

Defining the Situation

The first step is for the manager to recognize the need for a decision and to define its parameters. Sometimes the catalyst for a decision is the recognition that a problem exists. For example, if company turnover increases by 10 percent, profits unexpectedly drop by 15 percent, or a customer files a lawsuit against the company, a problem clearly exists, and the manager needs to respond by making appropriate decisions.

Positive developments can also prompt the need to make a decision. For example, the manager of an organization with surplus profits needs to decide how those profits should be used. Likewise, a manager who makes offers to five outstanding engineers and then has all of them accept must decide about their initial job assignments.

Exhibit 7.3   The Ideal Decision-Making Process

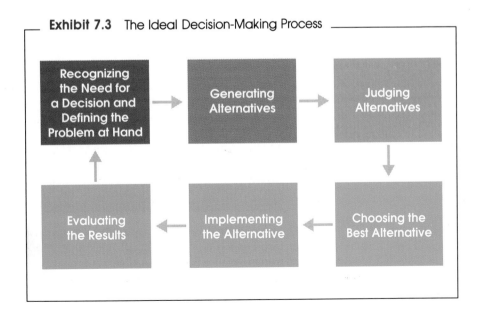

A new business opportunity can also act as a catalyst. For example, managers at Kodak reacted to such an opportunity when they entered the battery market. Increased demand and cost-cutting technological breakthroughs combined to provide a perfect opportunity—Kodak had high name visibility and resources to back the venture, and it was looking for new markets to enter.

Clearly, this is a stage at which some of the individual processes included in the behavioral model come into play. An individual's predispositions and motives might influence how she or he sees the decision situation. For example, if a manager has a negative attitude about labor unions, she might define a situation prompted by a union-organizing campaign strictly in terms of how to avoid unionization. Similarly, bounded rationality can affect how the manager defines and approaches the decision.

Generating Alternatives

The second step of the decision-making process is to generate alternatives. Since one of the characteristics of a decision-making situation is that the manager must choose from several alternatives, the identification of those alternatives must be a very important part of the process. After all, if the "best" alternative is never considered, the "right" decision can never be made.

It is usually best to try to identify standard and obvious alternatives as well as innovative and unusual ones. Standard solutions are those that simply come to mind with little thought, such as things that the organization or the manager has done in the past. Innovative approaches may be developed through such strategies as **brainstorming**—bringing people together and asking them to suggest alternatives to the problem.[11] They are encouraged to let their imaginations run wild and not to mock or ridicule the suggestions of others. Although many of the ideas suggested in such sessions are of little practical value, a surprisingly large number may have potential.

Of course, one consideration in choosing how much time to devote to generating alternatives is the costliness and significance of the decision. If the decision is extremely important, the organization is likely to conduct a lengthy and thorough search for alternatives. If it is fairly minor, the search may be brief. When Union Carbide decided to build a new corporate headquarters, the firm spent more than two years looking for sites, but when a high school gets ready to buy its softball team new uniforms, it will no doubt spend much less time and energy searching for alternatives.[12]

□ *Brainstorming* is the process of bringing people together and asking them to think of alternatives.

P R E L U D E   C A S E   U P D A T E

Jack Welch at General Electric has clearly had to practice both of these activities. For example, his original assessment that GE had to remake itself in order to remain an effective global competitor was a clear instance of defining a decision making situation. Moreover, each business he sold and each business he bought was no doubt decided upon only after a careful generation of alternatives. For example, RCA was only one of several different acquisitions he was contemplating at the time.

Judging Alternatives

After an acceptable list of alternatives has been generated, the manager must evaluate each alternative on that list. Exhibit 7.4 provides a useful framework for assessing alternatives.[13]

This assessment format involves subjecting each alternative to three questions. First, the manager asks if the alternative is feasible. Can it even be done? For instance, if one alternative calls for a general layoff of operating employees but the firm has a labor contract that prohibits such layoffs, that alternative is not feasible. Similarly, if a company has limited capital, alternatives that require capital outlays are not feasible and might be eliminated.

Second, the manager addresses the extent to which the alternative is satisfactory—the extent to which it actually addresses the problem. Suppose the company is trying to raise $1 million. One alternative is to sell some land the company owns. An appraisal suggests that the land will bring in $500,000, so the manager must either combine this alternative with another to raise the desired funds or drop the alternative from consideration.

Third, the manager needs to consider the possible related consequences of the alternative. In some cases such consequences might render the alternative unacceptable. A plan to boost sales of a particular product by increasing advertising might work well within that narrow context. However, the boost in advertising might cut profits to an unacceptable level, the firm might not have the production capacity to meet the new level of demand, and managers in

Exhibit 7.4 Evaluating Alternatives

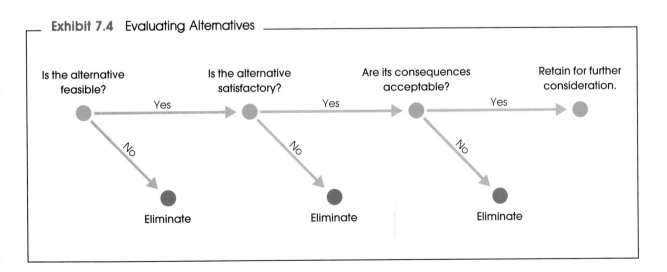

charge of other products might resent funds being diverted to another manager's product. Thus the alternative might be both feasible and satisfactory but have such objectionable side effects that it is unacceptable.

Choosing the Best Alternative

After the manager has evaluated the alternatives, she must choose one of them. The evaluation phase can probably eliminate some of the alternatives, but in most cases a few will remain. How does a manager decide which alternative is the best? One approach is to select the one that has the highest overall levels of feasibility and satisfactoriness and the fewest undesirable consequences. Of course, comparing these considerations may be difficult.

The manager should also consider the way in which the decision was originally defined. This may provide clues as to which alternative is truly best. For example, assume that the original goal was to reduce turnover as much as possible, regardless of the costs. If that is still the goal, the manager might choose an alternative that promises to reduce turnover substantially but that carries a high cost rather than an alternative that would reduce turnover by a moderate level and cost only a moderate amount. If the original goal was to reduce turnover by a reasonable amount, or if that goal is more desirable now, the second alternative might be better.

Finally, the manager may be able to choose several alternatives simultaneously. Suppose he is hiring an assistant and has two strong candidates for the position. One strategy is to offer the position to one candidate and keep the other candidate on hold. If the first offer is refused, the manager still has a very acceptable alternative.

Choosing alternatives is frequently an extremely difficult process. Consider the problem faced by IBM in deciding whether to leave South Africa, where the corporation had a long history and 1,500 employees. Only after months of internal agonizing as to the best course of action did IBM's managers decide that the deteriorating political situation warranted a change in the company's policy. A related issue that occasionally arises pertains to the ethics of the various alternatives available. *Management Today: Ethical Dilemmas of Management* recounts how managers at Beech-Nut recently handled just such a situation.

Implementing the Alternative

After choosing the preferred alternative, the manager must still put it into effect. In some instances, this is fairly easy—the manager calls the chosen job applicant and offers her the job, or buys the plot of land chosen for a new plant. In other situations, however, implementation can be quite complicated. Members of the organization might resist changes brought about by the decision to hire someone for a new position. Similarly, even though it might be easy to buy the land for a new plant, it might be nearly impossible to convince townspeople that the plant should be built.

ETHICAL DILEMMAS OF MANAGEMENT

Beech-Nut's Not-So-Natural Apple Juice

In the late 1980s Beech-Nut, a subsidiary of the Swiss giant Nestlé, was fighting a furious battle for market share in the highly competitive baby food and juice market. The company's chief competitors were Heinz and Gerber. Beech-Nut had a reputation for quality and purity and was using that image as one of its weapons. In particular, the company was promoting the fact that its apple juice was made from 100 percent pure juice and contained no additives or substitutes.

One day, however, Jerome LiCari, director of research and development at Beech-Nut, made a startling discovery. For several years, Beech-Nut had been buying apple juice concentrate from Interjuice Trading Company. For a variety of reasons, LiCari began to question the purity of the juice his company was purchasing from them. His in-depth analysis led him to believe that Interjuice was actually selling Beech-Nut apple juice that had been extended with chemical additives.

LiCari informed his superiors, assuming they would act quickly to correct the error. However, because Beech-Nut was being pressured by Nestlé to boost profits, top managers decided that it would cost too much money, and perhaps their jobs as well, if they admitted their mistake. Accordingly, they decided to continue to sell the stock they had and only then look for a new supplier.

When news of this incident reached the press, however, reactions were swift and dramatic. Among other penalties, Beech-Nut has had to pay around $25 million in fines, penalties, and legal fees. And its share of the juice market has plunged dramatically. Finally, top managers at Beech-Nut have been charged with criminal offenses and may face jail terms.

SOURCES: "What Led Beech-Nut Down the Road to Disgrace," *Business Week*, February 22, 1988, pp. 124–128; "Beech-Nut: The Case of the Ersatz Apple Juice," *Newsweek*, November 17, 1986, p. 66; "Unit of Nestlé Settles Dispute on Infant Ads," *The Wall Street Journal*, July 7, 1989, p. B3.

The key to effective implementation is proper planning. Changes take time, are subject to unexpected pitfalls, and don't always work as expected. Managers need to exercise patience and understanding during this phase. (These and related issues are covered in more detail in Chapter 20.)

Evaluating the Results

One big mistake managers occasionally make is to implement an alternative and then assume that the problem has been corrected. Things seldom go this smoothly. It is necessary to follow up and evaluate the results of the alternative in light of the original situation. One general way to handle this stage is shown in Table 7.2. First, state the desired consequences of the decision and estimate how long it will take to realize those consequences. For example, suppose the catalyst for the decision was an unusually high absenteeism level.

TABLE 7.2
Evaluating the Results of a Decision

Basic Steps in Evaluating a Decision	
Step 1	State the desired consequences of the decision and estimate how long it will take to realize those consequences.
Step 2	Implement the alternative chosen as part of the decision-making process.
Step 3	Assess the actual consequences of the decision in light of the desired consequences.

The manager might conclude that the desired consequence of the chosen alternative is to reduce absenteeism by 10 percent within one year. The chosen alternative is to pay a bonus to workers with a low absenteeism rate, so this alternative is implemented (step two) as a part of normal organizational procedures. After a year, the manager measures absenteeism again (step three). If it has declined to the appropriate level, the problem has been solved. If not, more time, a new solution, or both might be needed to solve it.

One of the reasons why so many managers neglect the last step is that they fear what might happen if their idea has been unsuccessful. In some organizations this kind of "failure" is considered a major black mark against the manager responsible for making the decision. For example, Richard J. Mahoney, CEO of Monsanto, has a reputation for being very unforgiving of subordinates who make bad decisions.[14]

<hr/>

LEARNING CHECK

You should now be able to describe the decision-making process.

INNOVATION AND DECISION MAKING

☐ *Innovation* is the process of identifying and utilizing new, unusual, and/or creative solutions and alternatives to problems.

One key element of effective decision making we have not yet fully addressed is innovation. **Innovation** involves the identification and utilization of new, unusual, and/or creative solutions and alternatives to problems.[15] In this section we explore the nature of innovation and its role in decision making.

Encouraging Innovation

In a sense, innovation requires harnessing and channeling the creative talents of people in organizational settings. Generally, for innovation to occur in organizations, it must be managed properly. This means that it should be encouraged by such actions as trying to hire creative people, soliciting new ideas, providing an open forum for opinions, and so forth. Brainstorming is also a useful technique for generating creative ideas.

Creativity must also be rewarded. People who come up with new ideas should be recognized for their contributions, and those contributions should be reflected in salary increases, promotion decisions, and other meaningful

James Miller/Miller Photo

Making decisions often involves innovation. At this paper company, waste products as well as conventional fuels are used to generate electricity. Excess power is sold to other firms, cutting utility costs for the firm and also increasing its flexibility. Such innovative approaches to doing business can enhance organizational effectiveness in a variety of ways.

ways. Such actions, which are easy to describe but harder to perform, will foster and maintain a corporate culture that enhances innovative decisions and breakthroughs.

The Innovation Process

To manage innovation within a decision-making context, organizations are advised to follow a number of practices. One general approach that can promote innovation is illustrated in Exhibit 7.5.[16]

First, as already stated, the organization should foster a culture that facilitates the generation of new ideas and suggestions. Innovative firms often set aside a fund earmarked for new proposals and ideas, and they usually recognize and reward the developers of new ideas. After an idea has been suggested, managers must conduct a preliminary analysis of the merits of the proposal. The analysis is usually a feasibility study that examines the potential costs and benefits of the idea.

A third step is to commit resources to the project (assuming, of course, that it is feasible). Such a commitment might take the form of a specific line item in the budget or perhaps the development of a single-use plan, such as a project or program, as described in Chapter 5. Whatever the form, the goal is to provide the resources necessary to make the idea a reality.

Exhibit 7.5   The Innovation Process in Organizations

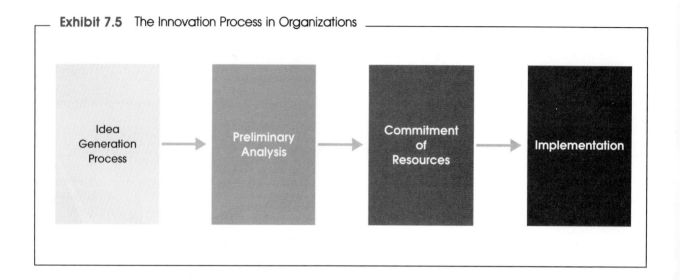

Finally, the project or idea is actually implemented. This phase is the actual translation of the idea into a tangible product or course of action. Some organizations starve a project by not supporting it properly, and others devote too many resources to an idea and expect too great a return. Innovative firms seem to be able to strike an effective balance at this stage. The key is to maintain a realistic perspective on what the organization can and cannot expect.

PRELUDE CASE UPDATE

Jack Welch tries hard to foster a climate of creativity and innovation at General Electric. He believes such forces are vitally important to the success of an organization such as GE. First of all, he tries to hire people who have basic creative skills. He also tries to develop creativity among those who already work for him. In addition, Welch rewards people who come up with innovative ideas. He also tries to let people know that they will not get punished if a new idea doesn't work out. And he demonstrated his own creativity when he structured the deal to trade businesses with Thomson.

DECISION-MAKING TECHNIQUES

As with planning, there are several useful techniques that managers can utilize to enhance their decision-making skills. Two of the more popular techniques are the payoff matrix and decision trees. Let's discuss each of these, then briefly note a few others.

The Payoff Matrix

☐ A *payoff matrix* determines the expected values for two or more alternatives, each of which is associated with a *probability* estimate.

☐ The *expected value* of an alternative is the sum of all its possible outcomes multiplied by their respective probabilities.

The **payoff matrix** involves the calculation of expected values for two or more alternatives, each of which is associated with a probability estimate.[17] **Probability** is the likelihood, expressed as a percentage, that an event will or will not occur. If something is certain to happen, its probability is 1.00. If it is certain not to happen, its probability is 0. If there is a fifty-fifty chance, its probability is .50.

The **expected value** of an alternative is the sum of all its possible outcomes multiplied by their respective probabilities. Thus, if there is a 50 percent chance that an investment will earn $100,000, a 25 percent chance that it will earn $10,000, and a 25 percent chance that it will lose $50,000, the expected value (EV) of the investment is

$$EV = .50(100,000) + .25(10,000) + .25(-50,000)$$
$$= 50,000 + 2,500 - 12,500$$
$$= \$40,000.$$

To illustrate how this concept relates to the payoff matrix, let's look at an extended version of an investment decision. Suppose that we are considering buying either a computer business or a sailboat business. We have determined that the success of each business is dependent on inflation. If inflation increases, we make $5 million from the computer business or $3 million from the sailboat business. If inflation decreases, however, we lose $4 million in the computer business but only $2 million in the sailboat business. We have also worked out that there is a 70 percent chance that inflation will increase and a 30 percent chance that it will decrease.

The resultant payoff matrix is shown in Exhibit 7.6. The expected values are calculated as described above. For the computer business, the expected value is

$$EV = .70(5 \text{ million}) + .30(-4 \text{ million})$$
$$= 3.5 \text{ million} - 1.2 \text{ million}$$
$$= \$2.3 \text{ million}.$$

For the sailboat business, the expected value is

$$EV = .70(3 \text{ million}) + .30(-2 \text{ million})$$
$$= 2.1 \text{ million} - .6 \text{ million}$$
$$= \$1.5 \text{ million}.$$

Thus, investing in the computer business is likely to result in a higher profit than investing in the sailboat business.

Payoff matrices have a number of applications in organizational settings, and the popularity of personal computers promises to make them even more pervasive. Of course, the manager always needs to remember that the estimates of expected value are only as good as the quality of the estimates for potential payoffs and their associated probabilities.

Exhibit 7.6 The Payoff Matrix

	Inflation Increases (.70)	Inflation Decreases (.30)
Buy Computer Business	+ $5,000,000	– $4,000,000
Buy Sailboat Business	+ $3,000,000	– $2,000,000

Decision Trees

□ *Decision trees are extensions of payoff matrices through second- and third-level outcomes.*

Decision trees are basically an extension of payoff matrices.[18] They include second- and third-level outcomes that can result from the first outcome. Consider a medium-sized manufacturing company that is thinking about building a new plant. It needs the plant because demand for the company's products is projected to increase. There is some chance that the increase will be large, or high, and some chance that it will be small, or low, so the manager is trying to decide whether to build a large or a small plant. This decision scenario is illustrated in decision tree format in Exhibit 7.7.

First, the manager must decide on the size of the new plant. Regardless of the size of the plant that she chooses, demand will either be high or low. If there is high demand and she built a small plant, another decision will be necessary. Probable alternatives include building another small plant, selling the new small plant and building a bigger one, and leaving the demand unsatisfied. Of course, if the manager built a small plant and demand is low, no further action is needed.

If the manager built a large plant and demand is high, again no action is needed. On the other hand, if she built a large plant and demand is low, there are again new alternatives to consider: should the plant produce at partial capacity, with the rest of the plant sitting idle; should the plant produce at capacity and create an excess inventory in hopes of future increases in demand; or should the manager again wait for more information?

To use the decision tree, the manager needs to estimate probabilities for each alternative on all branches of the tree. Then, working backward from the right to the left, she would be able to estimate the expected values of building a large and a small plant.

As with payoff matrices, the key to the effective use of decision trees is to estimate the probabilities of each potential outcome accurately. Again, computers make decision trees much easier for managers to use.

Other Techniques

☐ Other decision-making techniques include *inventory, queuing,* and *distribution models.*

Other fairly common quantitative techniques for decision making are inventory models, queuing models, and distribution models.

An **inventory model** helps the manager plan the optimal level of inventory to carry. For example, ordering large quantities of raw materials decreases the chances that the organization will run out but increases storage costs. Ordering smaller quantities reduces the storage costs but increases the chances of running out. An inventory model can help estimate how much material should be ordered, how often, when, and so forth.

Queuing models help plan waiting lines—in a Kroger store, for instance. Having one check-out operator will reduce costs but increase waiting lines and

Exhibit 7.7 The Decision Tree

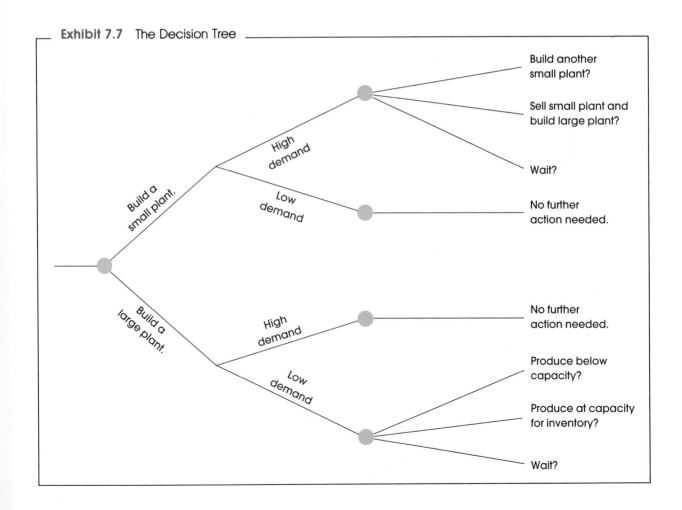

therefore customer dissatisfaction. Having twenty check-out operators on duty at all times will keep customers happy but will dramatically increase personnel costs. Queuing models help determine the best number of operators to have on duty at various times of the day.

Finally, **distribution models** help managers plan routes for distributing products. Suppose a company needs to drop off shipments of products at twenty different points around the city. Left to their own devices, drivers might not proceed from one stop to another in the best sequence. A distribution model helps develop that sequence so as to minimize travel time, fuel expenses, and so forth.

LEARNING CHECK

You should now be able to describe decision-making techniques, including payoff matrices and decision trees.

Chapter Summary

Decision making is most closely linked with the managerial function of planning. Decision making is the process of choosing one alternative from among a set of alternatives. Problem solving occurs when a manager must determine the one and only alternative that fits a particular situation. Decisions are made under three conditions: certainty, risk, and uncertainty.

There are two general approaches to decision making, the rational model and the behavioral model. The rational model assumes perfect information, an exhaustive list of alternatives, managers who are capable of systematically and logically assessing those alternatives, and managers who will always work in the best interests of the organization. The behavioral model is a modification of this approach and assumes imperfect information, an incomplete list of alternatives, bounded rationality, and satisficing behavior. Escalation of commitment, power, political behaviors, and coalitions also influence decision making.

The decision-making process involves six steps. Defining the situation, the first step, involves recognizing the need for a decision and defining its parameters. The second step calls for generating alternatives from which to choose. Next the manager must evaluate, or judge, the alternatives. The fourth step in the decision-making process is selecting the best alternative from those available. Implementing the alternative, or putting it into effect, is the fifth step, and involves careful planning. The final step is to evaluate the results of the decision and of the decision-making process.

Innovation involves the identification and utilization of new, unusual, and/or creative solutions and alternatives to problems. Innovation should be encouraged and rewarded so that the creative talents of an organization's members are used. The company should foster a culture that facilitates the generation of new ideas and suggestions.

Numerous techniques have been developed to aid managers in making decisions. Two general techniques are the payoff matrix and decision trees. Other techniques include inventory, queuing, and distribution models.

The Manager's Vocabulary

decision making	innovation
problem solving	payoff matrix
certainty	probability
risk	expected value
uncertainty	decision trees
rational model	inventory model
behavioral model	queuing model
bounded rationality	distribution model
satisficing	
escalation of commitment	
brainstorming	

Prelude Case Wrap-Up

General Electric is the subject of this chapter's Prelude Case. After assuming the position of CEO for General Electric, Jack Welch made a number of major decisions that transformed it into a very different kind of firm—one that Welch believes is capable of remaining a global competitor.

Decision making has been a central theme to many of Welch's activities and changes. From a purely managerial viewpoint, Welch's efforts to streamline decision-making processes by making GE less bureaucratic were aimed at improving decision making within the organization. In recent years, many other firms have followed this path—eliminating levels of red tape so that the managers closest to decision-making situations can more effectively make those decisions.

Welch himself exemplifies a number of different decision-making processes. For example, he faces few conditions of certainty. Instead, many of his decisions are made under circumstances of either risk or uncertainty.

In many cases, he also seems to work hard to follow a strictly rational model. For example, his initial strategic decision to reshape the entire corporation came only after a detailed and careful analysis of the various alternatives available to him. In other instances, he follows more of a behavioral process. For example, his decision to trade businesses with Thomson was probably made before he could thoroughly explore all of his options.

Prelude Case Questions

1. Take a single decision made by Welch and walk through the steps in the decision-making process to see how the final decision might have been reached.
2. How important is innovation to a company like General Electric? Why?
3. Explain how one of the quantitative decision-making techniques might be used at General Electric.
4. Discuss circumstances in which bounded rationality, satisficing, escalation of commitment, power, political behaviors, and/or coalitions might have affected decisions at General Electric.

Discussion Questions

Review Questions

1. What is the difference between decision making and problem solving?
2. Describe the three basic conditions under which managers make decisions.

3. Compare and contrast the rational and behavioral models of decision making.
4. List and describe the steps in the decision making process.
5. What is the role of innovation in decision making?

Analysis Questions

1. Try to identify a decision-making circumstance that has elements of both certainty and uncertainty.
2. It might be argued that decision making and problem solving are almost the same but only different in the number of alternatives that are considered. Do you agree or disagree with this assertion? Why?
3. Which model of decision making do you think is most common? Is a given manager most likely to follow one of the models almost exclusively, or will the same manager go back and forth between models? Why?
4. Identifying all the potential alternatives to a decision situation may be too costly, if not impossible. Yet satisficing is a problem if too few alternatives are explored. How might a manager guard against these extremes?
5. Can innovation be practiced apart from decision making, or are the two always linked? Why?

Application Questions and Exercises

1. Identify a decision you recently made. Characterize it in terms of the conditions that existed at the time.
2. Interview a local manager. Explain the differences between the rational and behavioral decision-making models and then ask him or her which model best describes his or her approach to making decisions. Ask for details and examples.
3. Identify a routine decision you have to make in the near future (such as which classes to take next term). Make the decision following the steps outlined in the text for the decision-making process.
4. Research a company like Rubbermaid or 3M and learn more about how it tries to foster innovation and creativity.
5. Apply one of the quantitative decision-making techniques, such as the payoff matrix, to a decision you need to make.

ENHANCEMENT CASE

COMPAQ COMPUTER'S THINK TANK

Rod Canion's name is not exactly a household word. But that may change during the coming years, especially if he is able to continue his remarkable performance as the president of one of this country's fastest-growing businesses, Compaq Computer.

Canion graduated from the University of Houston in 1968 and went to work as an engineer for Texas Instruments. He stayed there until 1982, working his way up through the ranks and dreaming of starting his own company one day.

That day came in 1982. Canion took two of his friends and coworkers to lunch and sketched out his plans for a new computer system on the back of a paper place mat. He convinced them that they should leave Texas Instruments and start their own enterprise. The three of them acquired the necessary financial backing and established Compaq later that same year.

Whereas most companies start small and then grow (hopefully), Compaq seemed like a big business almost from day one. The company set a U.S. record for first-year sales by a start-up company in 1983 ($111 million), was listed on the New York Stock Exchange in 1985, made the Fortune 500 listing in 1986 (the fastest a new company ever made that list), and reached sales of $1.22 billion in 1987 (another record).

Several critical factors have contributed to Compaq's success. For one thing, the company has always been careful to introduce only high-quality and technologically advanced equipment. Managers also go out of their way to maintain good relations with distributors, retailers, and customers. And Compaq has also successfully beat IBM to the marketplace with many of its recent innovations.

Another factor contributing to the company's success has been its institutionalized approach and commitment to rational and logical decision making. Canion realized early on that in a volatile industry like computers, rash and emotional decision making frequently leads to disaster. Accordingly, he and his top-management team deliberately set out to avoid such errors.

At Compaq, they call their approach to decision making "the process." It is essentially an ongoing, introspective consensus-management system. At the top of the organization, it is practiced by a product strategy team headed by Canion. Its other members are the top dozen or so engineers and executives in the firm.

The team meets eight to twelve hours a week. To make sure all issues are adequately processed, Canion assigns two members of the team to defend opposing points of view. This prevents the team from reaching a consensus too quickly and helps ensure that all sides are given a fair hearing.

To see how the approach works, back in 1986, before its growth really took off, Compaq was exploring the possibility of a merger with Tandy Corporation. Tandy, parent company of Radio Shack, is known for its low-cost production methods. Canion wanted the merger, and everything seemed in line to pull it off. At the last minute, however, opposing viewpoints from other members of the product strategy team convinced the majority of the members that

As Compaq Computer's impressive booth at a trade show indicates, the company has become a major player in its industry in just a few years.

Courtesy Compaq Computer Corporation

the merger might hurt Compaq's high-class engineering image. The idea was subsequently dropped.

Sometimes ideas are debated for months. Team members use this time to question other key people outside the group for their opinions and to acquire additional information. The overall goal is that every decision will be made as rationally and as logically as possible.

A possible problem in such a system is conflict and resentment over the final outcomes. However, Compaq executives have two norms that help offset these problems. First, everyone understands "the process" and feels free to discuss and debate issues without

getting too personally involved. Two executives can shout at each other for an hour over a disagreement over how to do something and then put that issue aside and go to lunch together. Second, after a decision is made, each manager is expected to accept it and support it, regardless of how he or she felt beforehand.

To date, "the process" seems to be working just fine. Many experts today believe that Compaq is the company with the best chance of unseating IBM as kingpin of the PC industry. Of course, there is always the chance that Compaq will make a misstep or that "the process" will one day fail.

SOURCES: "How Compaq Gets There Firstest With the Mostest," *Business Week*, June 26, 1989, pp. 146–150; "Compaq Vs. IBM: Peace Comes to Shove," *Business Week*, March 13, 1989, p. 132; "Quiet Power Behind the PC Rebellion," *USA Today*, November 15, 1988, pp. 1B–2B; Stuart Gannes, "America's Fastest-Growing Companies," *Fortune*, May 23, 1988, pp. 28–40.

Enhancement Case Questions

1. Should other companies adopt Compaq's approach to decision making? Why or why not?
2. Do you think it is possible to be too rational and objective in making decisions? Why or why not?
3. What factors do you think have accounted for Compaq's success?
4. Visit the library and determine how Compaq is doing today.

Chapter Notes

1. George P. Huber and Reuben R. McDaniel, "The Decision-Making Paradigm of Organizational Design," *Management Science*, May 1986, pp. 572–589.
2. G. Donaldson and J. Lorsch, *Decision Making at the Top* (New York: Basic Books, 1983).
3. Kenneth MacCrimmon and Ronald Taylor, "Decision Making and Problem Solving," in Marvin Dunnette, ed., *Handbook of Industrial and Organizational Psychology* (Chicago: Rand McNally, 1976), pp. 1397–1454.
4. L. S. Baird and H. Thomas, "Toward a Contingency Model of Strategic Risk Taking," *Academy of Management Review*, April 1985, pp. 230–243.
5. David W. Miller and Martin K. Starr, *The Structure of Human Decisions* (Englewood Cliffs, N.J.: Prentice-Hall, 1976).
6. Amitai Etzioni, "Humble Decision Making," *Harvard Business Review*, July-August 1989, pp. 122–126.
7. Alvar Elbing, *Behavioral Decisions in Organizations*, 2nd ed. (Glenview, Ill.: Scott, Foresman, 1978).
8. Herbert A. Simon, *Administrative Behavior* (New York: Free Press, 1945).
9. Thomas A. Stewart, "New Ways to Exercise Power," *Fortune*, November 6, 1989, pp. 52–64.
10. M. W. McCall and R. E. Kaplan, *Whatever It Takes: Decision-Makers at Work* (Englewood Cliffs, N.J.: Prentice-Hall, 1985).
11. A. F. Osborn, *Applied Imagination* (New York: Charles Scribner & Sons, 1963).
12. Walter McQuade, "Union Carbide Takes to the Woods," *Fortune*, December 13, 1982, pp. 164–174.
13. This section draws heavily from Ricky W. Griffin, *Management*, 3rd ed. (Boston: Houghton Mifflin, 1990).
14. Peter Nulty, "America's Toughest Bosses," *Fortune*, February 27, 1989, pp. 40–54.
15. I. Summers and D. E. White, "Creativity Techniques: Toward Improvement of the Decision Process," *Academy of Management Review*, April 1977, pp. 99–107.
16. Andre Delbecq and Peter Mills, "Managerial Practices That Enhance Innovation," *Organizational Dynamics*, Summer 1985, pp. 24–34.
17. Robert Markland, *Topics in Management Science*, 3rd ed. (New York: Wiley, 1989).
18. Everett Adam and Ronald Ebert, *Production and Operations Management*, 4th ed. (Englewood Cliffs, N.J.: Prentice-Hall, 1989).

THE ENTREPRENEURIAL SPIRIT

This section of the text has focused on the important managerial functions of planning and decision making. First it introduced you to the nature of organizational environments and goals, and then it discussed managerial planning. Following this discussion, it dealt with the topic of strategy and strategic planning. Finally, it concluded with a discussion of decision making.

All of these functions and issues are just as important to small businesses and to rapidly growing entrepreneurial firms as they are to large corporations. There are also likely to be some important differences, however. One critical difference is that the owner-manager of a new business must clearly understand what she or he wants to accomplish, even more than the manager in a large, stable company. If a person starts a new business and really intends to keep it small, he or she can adopt certain kinds of procedures and follow a certain path to fulfill that goal. On the other hand, if the goal is rapid growth, a different course of action altogether will be dictated. For example, he or she will need more extensive financing, a more sophisticated business plan, and so forth.

The environment and goals for a small business are likely to be much simpler and clearer than those for a large corporation. Consider the case of Sunset Gardens, a locally owned nursery in College Station, Texas. The owner's goals are quite modest—he wants to earn enough profits to support his lifestyle and to provide him with the independence he could never have working for someone else. Likewise, although his environment is by no means simple or stable, it is nevertheless easier to assess and understand than the environment of a larger business. His customers all come from the local community, he has three major competitors (all of whom he knows), he has no unions, he must meet the requirements of a set of regulators, and he buys all his products from a stable set of suppliers.

Circumstances are quite different, however, for a rapidly growing firm like Golden Valley Microwave or TCBY Enterprises. These firms are growing at an average rate of 70 percent or more per year and are on their way to becoming large businesses. Indeed, most entrepreneurial firms like these have growth as their major goal. A top executive of Toys 'R' Us, another fast-growing business, recently said, "The only thing I know how to manage is growth. We're in the growth business. What we sell is toys." The environment of such businesses is also perhaps *more* complex and dynamic than that faced by some large but more stable businesses. That is, complexity is induced by both the number of elements in the environment plus the rate at which that number is growing. Almost by definition, the bigger a firm gets, the more customers, competitors, unions, regulators, and suppliers it gets. And partnership agreements also become more common.

All types of planning activities are also unique for both small and entrepreneurial businesses. For most small businesses, for example, planning horizons tend to be fairly short. Thus, the owner of a small ice cream parlor who is considering an expansion next year might be engaged in long-range planning. Contingency planning is also likely to be much simpler and easier to define. But the owner-manager might also inadvertently serve as a roadblock for planning if she becomes overly resistant to change. And the owner-manager might want so much to do everything that she or he also makes poorer decisions. Constraints and the time and expense of planning are also likely to be important. At the strategic level, few truly small businesses have to worry about corporate strategy. However, concepts of business strategy are highly relevant. Likewise, the various functional strategies are also important. For example, as a part of their financial strategy, many small-business owners borrow money to open their business, whereas others use personal savings.

A rapidly growing entrepreneurial firm faces different challenges in each of these areas, most of them affected by the rapid change that accompanies rapid growth. Some grow so fast, for example, that long-range planning is impossible. Contingency planning is also very hard to do, and forecasting is difficult. For example, at one point in its early stages, conventional forecasting measures projected that in five years Sun Microsystems would be half the size of the entire U.S. economy!

From the standpoint of strategy, rapidly growing firms are likely to reach a point where they need to acquire new businesses to continue their growth, and they are likely to have the cash to pursue those acquisitions. For example, Reebok bought both Avia and Rockport in recent years as a way of propelling continued growth.

Finally, decision making also has some unique characteristics in these types of firms. In a typical small business, for example, the accuracy of the decisions its owner-manager makes is critical. A big company like Exxon can easily stand to lose tens or hundreds of thousands of dollars if an incorrect decision is made. A smaller company, however, might be forced to close its doors if a much smaller error is made. For example, underestimating sales by 3 or 4 percent won't destroy Exxon. But a small oil drilling operation with a shoestring budget might well go under if it makes the same error.

Entrepreneurial firms often make decisions in unique ways. For example, the Enhancement Case at the end of Chapter 7 details how Compaq strives for rationality and objectivity in the decisions it makes. In contrast, another rapidly growing business, Sun, works just as hard to make its work settings emotional and fun. Many decisions the company makes are based more on intuition and gut feelings than on objective facts and figures.

Regardless of the approach they take, however, both small businesses and rapidly growing ones bring to the planning and decision-making process the true entrepreneurial spirit that fuels our economy and that gives many daring people a chance to succeed.

SOURCES: "Hot Growth Companies," *Business Week*, May 22, 1989, pp. 90–93; Stuart Gannes, "America's Fastest-Growing Companies" *Fortune*, May 23, 1988, p. 36.

Organizing

This part of the book introduces you to the subject of organizing. Chapter 8 discusses organizing in general and gives you a basic understanding of many of the concepts used in organizing. Chapter 9 provides an overview of how those concepts are used in creating different organization designs. In Chapter 10 the issues surrounding staffing and human resource management are discussed. Chapter 11 completes this part of the book with a discussion of information systems and how they are used by organizations.

CHAPTER OUTLINE

I. The Nature of Organizing
A. The Organizing Process
B. Key Organizing Components and Concepts

III. Designing Jobs
A. Job Specialization
B. Alternatives to Specialization

III. Grouping Jobs
A. Departmentalization by Function
B. Departmentalization by Product
C. Departmentalization by Location
D. Other Considerations in Departmentalization

IV. Authority and Responsibility
A. Delegation
B. Decentralization

V. The Span of Management
A. Wide and Narrow Spans
B. Tall and Flat Organizations
C. Factors Influencing Group Effectiveness

VI. Line and Staff Positions

C
H
A
P
T
E
R

After studying this chapter you should be able to

1. Discuss the nature of organizing, describe the organizing process, and identify key components and concepts involved in organizing.

2. Discuss job design in organizations, including job specialization and alternatives to it.

3. Indicate how jobs are grouped, giving particular attention to grouping by function, product, and location.

4. Define and discuss authority and responsibility and the related concepts of delegation and decentralization.

5. Discuss the concept of the span of management, its impact on the shape of organizations, and how a manager might determine the span that will make a group effective.

6. Define line and staff positions and indicate their role in organizational analysis.

Organizing Concepts

MCDONNELL DOUGLAS'S BRAVE NEW WORLD

Family-owned and -operated Mc-Donnell Douglas, one of the top aerospace companies in the world, found itself in trouble during the late 1980s. Although it was doing well over $15 billion a year in business, two fatal accidents involving its DC-10 aircraft had tossed cold water on its commercial aviation business. The impact of these accidents was probably made worse by the three other well-publicized DC-10 crashes that had occurred during the previous fifteen years and by the company's involvement in controversy and scandal during the 1970s and 1980s.

To correct the situation, Mc-Donnell Douglas made aggressive sales efforts for commercial aircraft and began using mission planners (integrated hardware and software systems for planning routes and maneuvers). By early 1989, orders were booming. Indeed, in February 1989 McDonnell Douglas took over $10 billion in orders in a single day. The popular MD-80 model used in commercial aviation was in such

demand that McDonnell Douglas was having trouble keeping up with orders for it. Then, in mid-1989, the company found that its outside suppliers could not keep up with the demand and its inexperienced workers could not keep the assembly operations moving on schedule. Its very success was spelling losses for the firm. So severe were its difficulties that its Douglas Aircraft division had losses of over $200 million in the first half of 1989 and the overall organization had about $60 million in losses for that same period, although they were offset by a one-time accounting charge of nearly $180 million.

In an effort to alleviate these difficulties, McDonnell Douglas made several changes. Among the more significant changes was the beginning of a massive reorganization of the organization focusing on quality. To spearhead the reorganization, McDonnell Douglas moved Robert H. Hood from the presidency of the highly profitable missile systems division to the presidency of the Douglas Aircraft

division. It replaced the entire top-management structure and also hired Joel D. Smith, a former United Auto Workers staff member, to assist in bringing organizing concepts from the Nummi venture between General Motors and Toyota into McDonnell Douglas. The success of Nummi, which uses Japanese concepts with American workers, was thought to be transferable, and it was felt that Smith could enact such a transfer, especially since he had once been a rank-and-file worker and union member.

The basic plan, as it now stands, is to simplify the organizational structure by reducing the number of levels of management and by creating worker teams with authority to act on the many problems they face in day-to-day operations. The focus of the reorganization is on quality; hence its name, the Total Quality Management System. Previously, engineers worked at certain functions—design, production, quality control, and so forth—on a variety of classes of airplanes. Now,

Alan Levenson

McDonnell Douglas, one of the largest aerospace firms in the world, has recently made a number of changes in its organization structure in order to enhance its competitiveness. One of McDonnell Douglas's most popular planes is the MD-11, shown here during construction.

engineers work at a variety of functions for a single aircraft. This product focus broadens the experience of the personnel and sharpens their focus on market forces, especially the impact of quality on sales.

The use of worker teams that have authority to act on day-to-day issues means that fewer supervisory personnel are needed. In like manner, fewer supervisors means fewer midlevel managers and, in turn, fewer top managers. McDonnell Douglas has implemented these changes in a rather drastic manner. It has eliminated all managerial and supervisory positions (over 5,000 in all) and has replaced those positions with newly designed ones (only 2,800 of them). The former holders of

those positions have applied for the new positions; most of those who do not succeed will be employed as technicians who will advise and assist the worker teams. Total employment is therefore not substantially reduced, although nearly everyone has a different task than he or she had before.

This reorganization is designed to accomplish several things. For one thing, it will focus the company's personnel, both managerial and nonmanagerial, on quality. For another, it should improve communication among members of the organization, again both managerial and nonmanagerial. Employees now work in small teams, and there are fewer levels of management in the organiza-

tion. However, the abrupt manner of implementation itself has caused confusion and controversy. In the first year of implementation, this confusion increased communication problems.

Other results have also been mixed. More quality problems are being caught when they occur in the workplace, but that also means that the production lines do not move as quickly as they were initially scheduled. Some workers are also confused about the reporting hierarchy; with no immediate superior, they wonder if they are supposed to report to the vice president in charge of their specific product or someone else. Finally, obtaining a consensus within each work team, an approach used by the Japanese, is not always easy or even possible, although McDonnell Douglas feels that employees will, in time, learn to use such systems.

SOURCES: Ronald Henkoff, "Bumpy Flight at McDonnell Douglas," *Fortune*, August 28, 1989, pp. 79–80; "McDonnell Tries New Tack on Quality," *The Wall Street Journal*, April 24, 1989, p. B8; "Orders Cap Jetmaker's Turnaround," *USA Today*, February 8, 1989, pp. 1B–2B; "Planemakers Have It So Good, It's Bad," *Business Week*, May 8, 1989, pp. 34–36.

M cDonnell Douglas is attempting to improve its internal operations through a substantial reorganization of the company. It found that the pattern of organization that had evolved over the years was no longer appropriate. It needed to change its organization to more nearly fit a newer, more complex environment. In Chapter 1 we noted that **organizing** was the second basic managerial function, following planning and decision making. Organizing was defined as the process of grouping activities and resources in a logical and appropriate fashion. At McDonnell Douglas, the former organization might have been eminently logical, but it was deemed no longer appropriate. This chapter is the first of four devoted to the organizing function and to helping you understand when different organizations are and are not logical and appropriate.

This chapter defines and describes five basic concepts of organizing: designing jobs, grouping jobs, dealing with authority and responsibility, establishing the span of management, and managing line and staff positions. The next chapter focuses on how these components are put together to form organization designs. Chapter 10 addresses approaches to staffing, and Chapter 11 explores organizational information systems.

THE NATURE OF ORGANIZING

We have already defined organizing. However, to develop a more comprehensive understanding of this critical function, we need to elaborate on this definition by addressing the nature of organizing and identifying its key components.

The Organizing Process

□ The *organizing* process involves shaping the organization as it grows, shrinks, or changes.

Giant, complex organizations such as AT&T, Exxon, and General Motors were not created in a day. Nor were your neighborhood dry-cleaning establishment and favorite pizza parlor. Instead, most organizations start out in one form and then evolve into other forms as they grow, shrink, or otherwise change.[1]

Consider the case of a programmer who develops a new applications software package for personal computers. She starts out writing code and preparing copies of the materials on her home computer in the morning hours. She then tries to sell them in the afternoons. On Saturday she updates her records, and on Sunday she works on new developments.

Suppose, however, that her new software is a real breakthrough and she has trouble performing all of these activities. Eventually she looks for help. First she hires a part-time salesperson and a part-time bookkeeper, which allows her to devote more time to production and invention. Sales continue to expand, and soon she moves her business out of her home into a small workshop. The salesperson and the bookkeeper become full-time employees, and she must also hire a production assistant.

In a few years the programmer may be in charge of two sales managers, each of whom oversees eight sales representatives. She may also have larger facilities and several dozen production workers, in addition to a production manager, a full-time accountant, and a personnel manager. At this point the programmer's scope of operation has expanded from a true one-person effort to a full-fledged organization.

Each of the steps the programmer takes along the way, such as creating new jobs, grouping those jobs under new management positions, and delegating authority to those managers, is a part of the organizing process. Moreover, she can never truly be finished organizing. New circumstances, opportunities, and threats will always cause her to modify and adjust her organization to more efficiently and effectively meet competition.[2]

Key Organizing Components and Concepts

The above example touches on three of the basic concepts of organizing: creating, or designing, jobs; grouping jobs; and delegating authority. The five components that make a complete picture of organizing are described below.[3]

Designing jobs is one basic component. As we will see, this process involves determining the best level of job specialization to use. It also involves grouping jobs into meaningful categories, the second major component of organizing. This grouping, called departmentalization, is necessary for facilitating supervision and coordination.

Authority and responsibility must also be properly defined. Between a manager and his subordinates, this is accomplished through delegation. Across the entire organization, it is called decentralization.

The span of management is the fourth critical component of organizing. This refers to the number of subordinates who report to a given manager. For example, a manager may coordinate the efforts of three people or as many as thirty people.

Finally, attention needs to be directed to the management of line and staff positions. Line positions are usually considered to be those in the direct chain of command that hold the responsibility for accomplishing organizational goals. Staff positions, in contrast, are generally thought to be advisory positions primarily used to facilitate the work of line managers.[4]

LEARNING CHECK

You should now be able to discuss the nature of organizing, describe the organizing process, and identify key components and concepts involved in organizing.

DESIGNING JOBS

☐ The basis of *job design* is *job specialization*, defining the tasks that set one job apart from others.

Job design is the process of determining what procedures and operations are to be performed by the employee in each position. For example, a new employee at a Honeywell assembly plant or even a local travel agency doesn't simply sit down and start working. Instead the manager shows him how to do the job. Moreover, this manager is not making the job up as she goes along. Other operating managers and managers from the human resource department at some time carefully decided how it should be performed, basing their decisions on what was the best design for the job.

The basis for all job design activities is job specialization. Let's investigate the nature of job specialization and then identify several alternative approaches to designing jobs.

Job Specialization

We first considered the topic of **job specialization** back in Chapter 2, during our discussion of scientific management. Frederick W. Taylor, the chief proponent of scientific management, advocated extremely high levels of specialization and standardization as ways to increase the efficiency of organizations.[5]

The nature of job specialization at an abstract level is illustrated in Exhibit 8.1. Let's use the Goodyear Tire & Rubber Company as an example. Essentially, Goodyear has one "job": making and selling tires. In order to execute this job, however, it must break it down into smaller jobs. One job is buying the raw materials, another is transforming these materials into tires, and still another is distributing the tires to dealers. And, of course, there are hundreds more. Further, several people are needed to perform most of these specialized jobs.

We can note from the exhibit that the smaller jobs that are created through specialization add up to the total. That is, if it were possible to add up the contributions of each of the individual jobs, the total would equal the original overall job of the organization, including managerial coordination.

Specialization has a number of advantages and disadvantages. On the plus side, it allows each employee to become an expert. If the job is simple and straightforward, the people trained to do it should become very proficient.

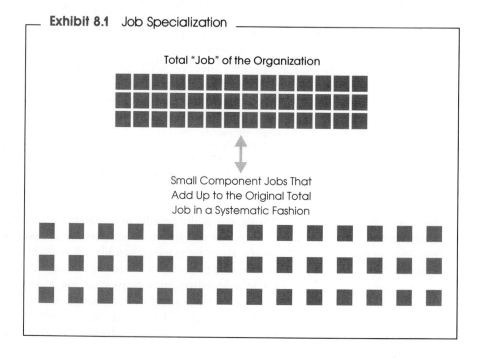

Exhibit 8.1 Job Specialization

Total "Job" of the Organization

Small Component Jobs That
Add Up to the Original Total
Job in a Systematic Fashion

Specialization also allows managers to exercise greater control over workers, since they can easily observe and monitor employees doing simple jobs. Specialization is also presumed to facilitate the development of equipment and tools that can increase the efficiency of the job holder.[6]

On the other hand, it is possible to overspecialize. If the job is simplified too much, employees may spend so much time passing the work from person to person that efficiency is actually decreased. Even more significant is the problem of boredom and job dissatisfaction. If jobs are too simple and specialized, workers quickly get bored performing them; they become dissatisfied and lower their performance, or they might consider looking for more exciting work elsewhere.[7] To counter these problems, managers have begun to search for alternatives that will still maintain the positive benefits that specialization can provide.

Alternatives to Specialization

□ Overspecialization can lead to boredom and dissatisfaction. Managers often use such alternatives as *job rotation, job enlargement,* and *job enrichment.*

The three most common alternatives to job specialization are shown in Exhibit 8.2, which uses a single square to represent job specialization at the top. Such jobs can be thought of as narrowly defined and standardized. The three alternatives are job rotation, job enlargement, and job enrichment.

JOB ROTATION   **Job rotation** involves systematically moving employees from one job to another. As noted in the exhibit, the jobs themselves are still narrowly defined and standardized. For instance, suppose an employee works in a Sunbeam toaster-assembly plant. The assembly operation involves four sets of jobs. During the first week of the month, the employee plugs preassembled heating units into a base. The next week she connects four wires that make the heating unit operational. The third week is spent installing the chrome cover over the toaster unit, and the next week is devoted to testing each toaster and packing it in its box. In the fifth week the employee rotates back to the first job again.

Ford, Prudential Insurance, and Bethlehem Steel have all experimented with job rotation, and many companies use this system in one form or another. Unfortunately, however, job rotation by itself isn't very successful at decreasing the boredom associated with highly specialized jobs. Each of the jobs our toaster assembler performs is still fairly monotonous. In general, job rotation is used as a way to train employees in a variety of skills and as a part of a more comprehensive job design strategy.[8]

JOB ENLARGEMENT   In contrast to job rotation, **job enlargement** actually changes the nature of the job itself. As shown in Exhibit 8.2, this system involves adding more activities to the job. Job enlargement might be used in the toaster factory to decrease the total number of jobs from four to two. One set of workers might now plug in the heating element and attach the wires, and the other set could then attach the covers and pack the toasters into boxes.

IBM, Maytag, AT&T, and Chrysler have all tried job enlargement. In general, the results have been somewhat more positive than for job rotation, and workers report slightly less boredom with enlarged jobs. Still, adding more and more simple activities to a job that is already simple doesn't really change the nature of the work that much.[9]

☐ *Job enrichment* gives the worker more discretion in deciding how to perform various activities.

JOB ENRICHMENT   The final alternative to job specialization to be considered here is **job enrichment.** Exhibit 8.2 points out the critical difference between job enlargement and job enrichment: under job enrichment, workers are given more activities to perform *and* more discretion in how to perform them.[10]

Suppose, for example, that workers at the Sunbeam toaster plant are told that they have to insert the heating element first and then attach the wires in a specified order using standard equipment. After enrichment they are given various options: they can attach the wires before inserting the element, use a different kind of tool to attach the wires, and so on. Similarly, the inspection operation might dictate that defective toasters should be turned over to a supervisor, who then decides what to do. Enrichment can give the inspector more discretion: she might repair small problems herself, take the defective toaster back to the worker who caused the defect, or give it to a supervisor.

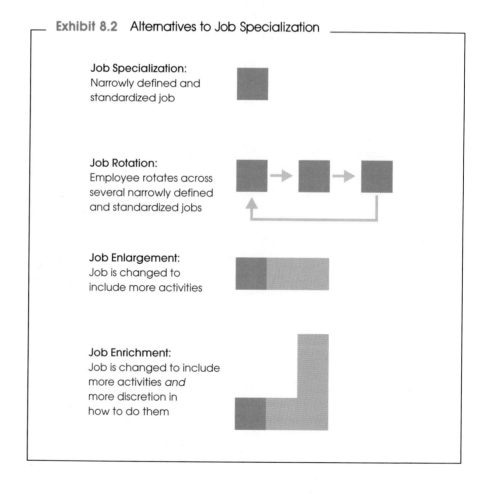

Exhibit 8.2   Alternatives to Job Specialization

Job Specialization:
Narrowly defined and standardized job

Job Rotation:
Employee rotates across several narrowly defined and standardized jobs

Job Enlargement:
Job is changed to include more activities

Job Enrichment:
Job is changed to include more activities *and* more discretion in how to do them

Many firms are searching for effective ways to design jobs. The three Lockheed engineers shown here have each rotated through a number of different assignments during their careers. And they are also being given more and more autonomy to pursue their tasks in ways they think are most effective.

Photo by Paul Fusco/Magnum/Courtesy of Lockheed

You should now be able to discuss job design in organizations, including job specialization and alternatives to it.

AT&T, Texas Instruments, General Foods, Texaco, and John Hancock have all used job enrichment. Although this approach is far from being universally successful, it does frequently decrease employee boredom and dissatisfaction. Many organizations are continuing to experiment with new, innovative ways to design employee jobs.[11]

P R E L U D E   C A S E   U P D A T E

In the McDonnell Douglas case, high turnover among bored and dissatisfied workers, with its resultant increase in new and inexperienced workers, and coordination problems between specialized jobs, were preventing the company from meeting its delivery dates. Clearly, McDonnell Douglas needed to reassess the level of job specialization in its production system.

GROUPING JOBS

☐ *Departmentalization* frequently groups jobs according to one of three bases: function, product, and location.

After jobs have been designed, the next part of the organizing process is grouping those jobs into logical sets. This step is important because properly grouped jobs make it easier to coordinate and integrate activities and in this way achieve the goals of the organization. The process of grouping jobs is called **departmentalization** or departmentation.

The key word here is, of course, *logical*. Managers do not just randomly pull together whatever jobs are at hand and call them a department. Instead, they must use a plan or a set of guidelines. These guidelines are the basis for departmentalization. The most common groupings are by function, by product, and by location. First let's discuss each of these bases for departmentalization, and then we can briefly note others that are occasionally used.

Departmentalization by Function

When organizations departmentalize by function, they group together employees who are involved in the same or similar functions or broad activities. An illustration of how a company that uses **functional departmentalization** is organized appears in Table 8.1. Note that this organization has a marketing department, a finance department, and a production department. Thus, marketing researchers, product managers, advertising managers, sales managers, and sales representatives are all included in the marketing department, and operations managers, distribution managers, plant managers, and quality control managers are all in the production department.

The key advantages of this approach are that, since each department is staffed by experts in that particular function or activity, the managers in charge of each function can easily coordinate and control the activities within the department; moreover, areas of responsibility are clearly defined.

On the other hand, functional departmentalization also has certain disadvantages. Decision making tends to be slow. Employees might concentrate so much on their functional specialties that they lose sight of the total organization, and communication between departments is difficult.[12]

☐ Many small companies use *functional departmentalization*, which leads to easy coordination of activities, expert staffs, and clear definitions of responsibilities.

One popular method of grouping jobs—or departmentalization—is by function. The General Foods group shown here represents such an approach. They all work in marketing and, at this meeting, are discussing advertising strategy.

Jeffrey Henson Scales

TABLE 8.1
Departmentalization by
Function, Product, and
Location

Structure	Departments	Positions
Functional Organization	Marketing	Marketing researchers, product managers, sales managers, etc.
	Finance	Budget analysts, accountants, financial planners, etc.
	Production	Operations managers, plant managers, quality control specialists, etc.
Product Organization	Product Group A	Financial, marketing, and production managers for packaged foods
	Product Group B	Financial, marketing, and production managers for small retail chains
	Product Group C	Financial, marketing, and production managers for a third product
Locational Organization	North American Operations	Production, distribution, financial, marketing, and human resource managers for the U.S.A., Canada, and Mexico
	European Operations	Production, distribution, financial, marketing, and, human resource managers for Europe
	Southeast Asian Operations	Production, distribution, financial, marketing, and human resource managers for Southeast Asia

Smaller organizations tend to use the functional approach to departmentalization, but as they grow, they often change bases. Frequently they go on to adopt departmentalization by product.

Departmentalization by Product

▢ *Product departmentalization* is common among midsized organizations and enables them to keep activities together, speed up decision making, and monitor the performance of product groups.

When organizations use **product departmentalization,** they group together all the activities associated with individual products or closely related product groups. A simple example of this approach is also shown in Table 8.1. Product Group A might be a line of packaged foods, such as cereals, instant breakfast mixes, and so forth. All of the financial, marketing, and production activities associated with this line of products are grouped together in this department. Product Group B could consist of several different small retail chains. As in Group A, all the marketing, financial, and operations functions for these chains are grouped together.

There are several advantages to product departmentalization. For one thing, all of the activities associated with unique products are kept together. Marketing cereal might be quite different in nature from marketing a retail chain. For another, decision making is faster because the managers responsible for individual products are closer to those products. Finally, it is easier to monitor the performance of individual product groups under this arrangement.

As you might expect, of course, product departmentalization also has several disadvantages. First, administrative costs are higher because each department has its own marketing research team, its own financial analysis team, and so forth. Second, conflict or resentment occasionally arises between departments because each thinks the other is getting more than its fair share of attention or resources.[13]

Departmentalization by Location

□ *Locational departmentalization is especially appropriate for multinational organizations because it keeps expert managers close to their organizations.*

The third major form of departmentalization is **locational.** In this situation, jobs that are in the same or nearby locations are grouped together in a single department. Table 8.1 presents a simplified view of a company that uses this approach. All of the activities of the organization that pertain to North America—production facilities, distribution systems, financial considerations, marketing activities, and human resource management activities—are grouped together in one department. Likewise, similar activities that relate to European operations are grouped together, as are those that relate to Southeast Asian operations.

This approach to departmentalization gives managers the basic advantage of being close to the location of their decision-making responsibilities. Managers in North America might not be fully in tune with cultural and social norms in Europe, understand the nature of European marketing, or appreciate the financial difficulties involved in foreign exchange rates. By putting a manager with the requisite insights and authority directly on the scene, the company might achieve more effective operations.

On the other hand, this approach results in a duplication of staff, just as product departmentalization does. For instance, the company would need a marketing manager in North America, one in Europe, and one in Southeast Asia. Nonetheless, this approach is becoming more widely used, especially by firms that decide to go multinational.[14]

Other Considerations in Departmentalization

Some companies use other bases of departmentalization, and it is very common to mix bases of departmentalization within the same organization.

One approach occasionally used by organizations is to departmentalize by customer. Using this approach, the company groups together activities associated with individual customers or customer groups. A midwestern bank, for example, might have departments for consumer loans, business loans, and agricultural loans.

Time also serves as a base for departmentalization. For instance, a plant might operate on three shifts, and the company might view each shift as a department.

Departmentalization by sequence occurs when a sequence of numbers or other identifying characteristics defines the separation of activities. When going through registration, students frequently get into different lines on the basis of their last names, their student numbers, or their class standing.

This discussion of departmentalization has considered each base in its pure form, but in reality most organizations use multiple bases or combine bases. One way to mix approaches is by level. For example, a firm might use product departmentalization at the top but departmentalize each product group by function. Each marketing department could then be broken down by location or customer.

Similarly, bases of departmentalization might be mixed at the same level to suit individual circumstances. A firm doing business in Europe on a moderately small scale might decide to establish a marketing group in Paris but keep all production in the United States, at least until sales grow. Thus the marketing activities are broken down by location, but the production activities are not. Consider what form of departmentalization is used by Fantastic Sam's in *Management Today: Small Business and Entrepreneurship.*

LEARNING CHECK

You should now be able to indicate how jobs are grouped, giving particular attention to grouping by function, product, and location.

AUTHORITY AND RESPONSIBILITY

Another important part of the organizing process is determining how authority and responsibility will be managed.[15] At the level of an individual manager and his or her subordinates, this is the delegation process. At the total organizational level, it is related to decentralization.

Delegation

☐ *Delegation*—assigning tasks to subordinates—involves giving the employee the *responsibility* for a job, the *authority* to perform it, and *accountability* for seeing that it gets done.

Delegation is the process through which the manager assigns a portion of his task to subordinates. In discussing delegation, let's first identify the steps in the process and then address barriers to effective delegation.

STEPS IN DELEGATION   Delegation essentially involves three steps, as shown in Exhibit 8.3.

First, the manager assigns **responsibility.** For example, when a manager tells a subordinate to prepare a sales projection, order additional raw materials, or hire a new assistant, he is assigning responsibility.

Second, the manager must also grant the **authority,** or power, necessary to carry out the task. Preparing a sales projection may call for the acquisition of sensitive sales reports, ordering raw materials may require negotiations on

SMALL BUSINESS AND ENTREPRENEURSHIP

Fantastic Sam's Far-Flung Empire

Sam M. Ross founded his hair-cutting organization, Fantastic Sam's, in Memphis, Tennessee, in 1974. Almost immediately, Fantastic Sam's began selling hair-cutting and hair salon franchises and subfranchises, and during the mid-1980s it became one of the fastest-growing chains in the United States. In 1987 its parent organization, SMR Enterprises, began to expand into cosmetology schools because the franchises were having so much trouble finding qualified, licensed cosmetologists to run them. SMR Enterprises plans to be operating over one hundred cosmetology schools nationwide by the mid-1990s.

By 1988, Fantastic Sam's had around 1,300 individual salons or units and was continuing to expand at a rate of several hundred units per year. Sam Ross felt that around 4,000 units would be an optimum size for his chain, and he hopes to achieve that level by the early 1990s. The units are located throughout the United States as well as in several other countries. Within the United States, they are located primarily in the Midwest and the Sunbelt region. Other countries that have units include Australia, Bahrain, Canada, Europe, and Japan.

Within the Fantastic Sam's structure there are numerous regional franchisees who can sell local franchises. Thus, a local franchise may be purchased from a regional franchisee or from the national Fantastic Sam's organization. The Philadelphia region, for instance, includes all of Pennsylvania, southern New Jersey, all of Delaware, and part of Maryland. The regional office, in addition to selling franchises, provides a central warehouse for the hair care products that are to be distributed to the individual, local salons.

SOURCES: "Coupon Clipped," *Marketing News,* October 9, 1989, p. 2; "Not So Fantastic Sam," *Venture,* December 1988, p. 40; "Fantastic Sam's Sees 50 More Stores in N.E.," *Capital District Business Review* (Albany, New York), May 4, 1987, p. 6; Paula Wade, "Fantastic Sam's Sets Training Goal," *Commercial Appeal* (Memphis, Tennessee), February 14, 1987, p. B12.

price and delivery dates, and hiring a new assistant may mean submitting a hiring notice to the human resource department. If these activities are not a formal part of the subordinate's job, the manager must give him the authority to do them anyway.

Finally, the manager needs to create **accountability.** This suggests that the subordinate incurs an obligation to carry out the job. If the sales report is never prepared, if the raw materials are not ordered, or if the assistant is never hired, the subordinate is accountable to his boss for failing to perform the task.

Of course, these steps are not carried out in rigid, one-two-three fashion. Indeed, in most cases they are implied by past work behavior. When the manager assigns a project to a subordinate, for instance, the subordinate probably knows without asking that he has the authority necessary to do the job and that he is accountable for seeing to it that it does, indeed, get done.

BARRIERS TO DELEGATION Unfortunately, the ideal delegation process seldom materializes. Several factors can contribute to this failure. For one thing, the manager might be too disorganized to delegate systematically. For

Exhibit 8.3 The Delegation Process

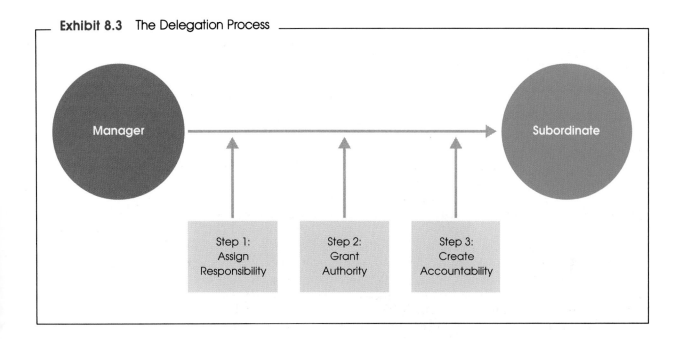

another, she may be afraid that her subordinate will do such a good job that she will look bad in comparison. Alternatively, she may be afraid that the subordinate is incapable of doing the job properly. Finally, the subordinate may be unwilling or unable to accept the job anyway.[16]

Decentralization

◻ *Decentralized* organizations delegate power and control to lower levels, whereas *centralized* organizations keep power and control at the top level.

A closely related issue is **decentralization**—the result of maximum delegation throughout the organization. General Electric, Sears, and Xerox are extremely decentralized; McDonald's, K mart, and Boeing are just the opposite. IBM has recently moved from being centralized to becoming much more decentralized in an effort to speed decision making and respond more quickly to its customers.[17]

Under conditions of decentralization, power and control are systematically delegated to lower levels in the organization. Under conditions of **centralization,** however, power and control are systematically kept at the top of the organization.

Some organizations choose to practice decentralization in order to keep managers who are close to problems responsible for making decisions about them. That is, managers who come into contact with customers, supplies, and competitors on a daily basis may be in a better position to make certain decisions than managers who are isolated back at headquarters.

In general, decentralization is usually pursued when the environment is complex and uncertain, when lower-level managers are talented and want more say in decision making, and when the decisions are relatively minor. In

Brian Smith

Effective delegation and decentralization can enhance the contributions that people make to an organization and often lead to creative solutions to problems. For example, management at Florida Power and Light decided to let meter readers have more say in their jobs. The meter readers formed a team and created a system to alert themselves whenever they were approaching a house with a fierce dog.

contrast, centralization is often practiced when the environment is more stable, when the home office wants to maintain control, when lower-level managers are either not talented enough or do not want a stronger voice in decision making, and when decisions are more significant.[18]

Management Today: The World of Management describes how Samsung, a major Korean conglomerate, uses decentralization in its operations. Part of the reason behind its decentralization is to speed up decision making, and another is to ensure that the individual companies can respond quickly to customer wants and needs.

LEARNING CHECK

You should now be able to define and discuss authority and responsibility and the related concepts of delegation and decentralization.

PRELUDE CASE UPDATE

An interesting form of delegation is taking place at McDonnell Douglas as it decentralizes. It is assigning responsibility to groups or teams of workers rather than to individuals. This means, of course, that authority and accountability also reside within the group instead of with a single individual.

MANAGEMENT TODAY

THE WORLD OF MANAGEMENT

Samsung's Formula for Success

A *chaebol* is a Korean family-owned and -operated conglomerate. Chaebols are "financial cliques." These cliques are formed to acquire economies of scale, particularly in financing but also in marketing and distribution. Patterned from a Japanese organizational arrangement, the *zaibatsu*, the chaebols have become very powerful in Korea and very successful worldwide. Companies such as Daewoo, Hyundai, Lucky-Goldstar, and Samsung are among the more well known of the chaebols.

Samsung was formed in 1938 as a trading store to export fruit and dried fish to Manchuria. Its founder, Lee Byung-Chull, was from a wealthy family and had studied at Tokyo's Waseda University. Lee kept his Japanese connections and incorporated many Japanese practices in the Samsung Group. Samsung has an open system of examinations and recruitment to bring the best personnel to the organization. It offers high wages, good benefits, and good working conditions. Training is important at Samsung. Every employee must complete a twenty-four-day indoctri-

nation and education program that emphasizes teamwork and Samsung business beliefs.

The Samsung Group consists of numerous separate companies. Among the product lines covered by those companies are consumer electronics, semiconductors, hotels, shipbuilding, textiles, refined sugar, food processing, genetic engineering, insurance, aerospace, robots, and paper. Each company has been delegated the authority to run itself, but the central administrative group sets extremely tight standards for performance. To ensure that those standards are achieved, careful planning is strongly emphasized.

As labor costs have risen and international competition has increased, Samsung has had to go public to raise capital for thirteen of its companies. This has weakened, although certainly not eliminated, the family control over the group. To keep control within the family, a family member, Lee Kun-Hee (the founder's youngest son), recently was chosen to run the company.

SOURCES: Ira Magaziner and Mark Patinkin, "They're Hungrier," *Report on Business Magazine*, October 1, 1989, pp. 110–118; Andrew Tanzer, "Samsung South Korea Marches to Its Own Drummer," *Forbes*, May 16, 1988, pp. 84–89; John McBeth and Mark Clifford, "Rivals—and Partners, the Participants in Seouls' Aerospace Venture," *Far Eastern Economic Review*, June 9, 1988, pp. 104–105; S. Yoo and S. M. Lee, "Management Style and Practice of Korean Chaebols," *California Management Review*, Summer 1987, pp. 95–110.

THE SPAN OF MANAGEMENT

Another important concept in organizing is the **span of management**—the number of subordinates who directly report to a given manager. Companies must consider the relation of this number to group effectiveness and to overall organizational effectiveness. Let's look at the notions of wide and narrow spans, the effects of span of management on the "height" of the organization, and factors that influence effectiveness.

Wide and Narrow Spans

If a manager has a large number of subordinates, he is said to have a wide span of management. Similarly, having relatively few subordinates defines a narrow span of management.

What difference does it make? At the request of an early management pioneer, a French mathematician, A. V. Graicunas, attempted to illustrate the impact of wide and narrow spans.[19] Graicunas noted that groups contain three basic kinds of relationships: direct (the manager's one-on-one relationship with each subordinate), cross (relationships among subordinates), and group (relationships between groups of subordinates). Using a mathematical formula for these relationships, Graicunas showed that as the number in a group increases linearly, the number of total relationships increases exponentially. That is, the number of interactions or relationships increases rapidly as more people are added to the group.

Although Graicunas's work is not based on business organizations, it does carry an important message: that groups involve a complex network of interrelationships, and the complexity of that network increases greatly as the group grows larger.

Other early writers, such as Ralph Davis and Lyndall Urwick, sought to identify the ideal span for all managers, but they quickly realized that an ideal number did not exist. Indeed, the appropriate span varies considerably from one setting to another.[20] This fact relates to both the effects of the span of management on organizations and the factors that influence a particular group's effectiveness.

Tall and Flat Organizations

One key effect of span of management on organizational structure concerns the "height" of the organization. As illustrated in Exhibit 8.4, a wide span of management results in an organization that has relatively few levels of management—a **flat organization.** On the other hand, a narrow span of management adds more layers of management and therefore leads to a **tall organization.**

In general, flat organizations tend to be characterized by greater communication between upper- and lower-level management, an increased capacity to respond to the environment, and lower total managerial costs than tall organizations. In recent years many corporations, including Sears, CBS, Avon, General Motors, and IBM, have taken steps to eliminate layers of management in an effort to create a more streamlined and efficient organization.[21]

Factors Influencing Group Effectiveness

A group's effectiveness and the impact of the span of management depend on the circumstances of the situation, but what exactly are those circumstances? Several of the more important ones are noted in Exhibit 8.5.

The competence of both the manager and his subordinates is one significant factor. If both are competent, a wide span is possible, but if either is less competent, a narrower span may be dictated.

Physical dispersion is another important variable. In general, if the manager and the subordinates are scattered throughout a building or territory, a narrow span is indicated. If, on the other hand, everyone works in close proximity, a wider span can be used.

Exhibit 8.4 Tall Versus Flat Organizations

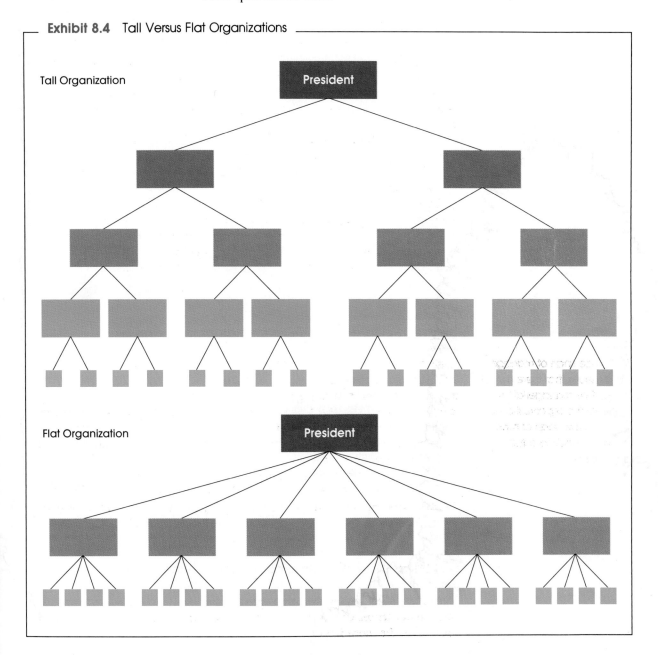

Exhibit 8.5   Factors Influencing the Span of Management and Group Effectiveness

A wide span of management may be more effective when:	A narrow span of management may be more effective when:
1. Managers and subordinates are highly competent.	1. Managers and/or subordinates are not highly competent.
2. Managers and subordinates work in close proximity.	2. Managers and subordinates are widely dispersed.
3. People prefer low supervision.	3. Managers want close control over their subordinates.
4. Subordinates perform similar tasks.	4. Each subordinate performs a different task.
5. A manager's sole task is supervising subordinates.	5. Managers have nonsupervisory tasks to perform.
6. Little interaction between managers and subordinates is necessary.	6. Managers and subordinates must interact with each other on a regular basis.
7. Work is highly standardized.	7. Work is not highly standardized.
8. New problems seldom arise.	8. New problems arise frequently.

Preferences are also an important factor in some situations. If everyone wants a wider span, then that is what should be used. A narrow span may be desirable, though, if the manager wants one.

Task similarity is significant, too. The manager will probably want a narrower span if each subordinate is doing a different job, whereas a wider span can be adopted when everyone is performing similar tasks.

The degree to which the manager has nonsupervisory work to do is also an important consideration. If all the manager has to do is supervise her subordinates, she can use a wider span. On the other hand, if the manager has many other tasks to perform, she may not be able to supervise several people, and a narrower span may be indicated.

A related factor is the required interaction between the manager and the subordinates. Since interaction takes time, it follows that the more interacting a manager needs to do, the narrower the span will need to be. Similarly, less required interaction between manager and subordinates will allow for a wider span of management.

You should now be able to discuss the concept of the span of management, its impact on the shape of organizations, and how a manager might determine the span that will make a group effective.

Standardization is another important variable influencing the span of management. Highly standardized work, like task similarity, can accommodate a wider span than lack of standardization can.

Finally, the frequency of new problems should be considered. If new problems arise often, a narrow span may be necessary, whereas few new problems will allow for a wider span.

In summary, the company must consider several factors when organizing a group and establishing the span of management.[22] Each of these factors, along with others that might be relevant, must be properly assessed and considered by the manager if he is to achieve effective group performance.[23]

PRELUDE CASE U P D A T E

McDonnell Douglas's creation of work groups or teams that have the authority and accountability to perform tasks complicates the concept of the span of management. Since there is no direct manager in charge of each of these groups, in one sense they are autonomous. Thus, there is no span of management. However, since their activities are coordinated at the next-higher level of management, one could argue that those managers have had a tremendous increase in the sizes of their spans.

LINE AND STAFF POSITIONS

☐ The traditional distinction between *line positions* (in the direct chain of command) and *staff positions* (advisory or supportive roles) is fading as managers become better educated and more experienced.

The last element of the organizing process is the idea of line and staff positions. **Line positions** are traditionally defined as those in the direct chain of command with specific responsibility for accomplishing the goals of the organization. **Staff positions** are positions outside the direct chain of command that are primarily advisory or supportive in nature. These differences are shown in Exhibit 8.6.

The roles of president and division head are line positions. Each has goals that derive from and contribute to those of the overall organization. The positions of special assistant and legal adviser are staff positions. These people perform specialized functions that are primarily intended to help line managers. For example, the legal adviser is not expected to contribute to corporate profits. Instead, she answers questions from and provides advice to the president about legal issues that confront the firm.

Historically, staff managers tended to be better educated, younger, and more ambitious than their line counterparts. They were frequently hired directly out of school, whereas line managers usually worked up the corporate ladder. Moreover, there tended to be considerable conflict between line and staff managers, especially when staff managers were given the responsibility of finding shortcomings in the efforts of line managers.[24]

In recent years, however, this state of affairs has begun to change. The results of one survey show that top managers have started redirecting the efforts

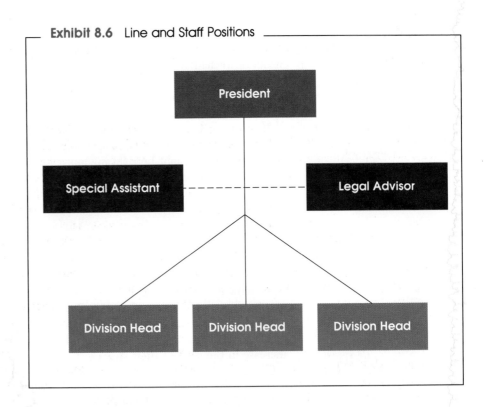

Exhibit 8.6   Line and Staff Positions

of their staff managers in more cooperative and constructive directions.[25] Staff positions are also beginning to lose part of their glamour. Recent corporate cutbacks have often reduced the number of staff positions, and line managers have been given greater decision-making power and discretion. These jobs have therefore become more attractive to people graduating from college as well as to those managers already in staff positions.[26]

In the future, the distinction between line and staff managers is likely to become vaguer. Effective managers are starting to see that everyone within the company is really on the same team and that the best approach is to promote cooperation among all members of the organization.

Chapter Summary

Organizing is the process of grouping activities and resources in a logical and appropriate fashion. Key components and concepts in organizing include designing jobs, grouping jobs, managing authority and responsibility, the span of management, and line and staff positions.

Designing jobs is the process of determining based on job specialization what procedures and operations are to be performed by an employee in a position. Specialization has advantages and disadvantages.

The three most common alternatives to specialization are job rotation, job enlargement, and job enrichment.

The process of grouping jobs into logical sets in order to make it easier to coordinate and integrate activities is known as departmentalization. The most common bases are by function, product, and location. Function refers to what the jobs involve, so functional departmentalization refers to grouping together those jobs that call for similar work. Product departmentalization refers to grouping together all activities associated with one product (project, process, program, etc.). Departmentalization by location involves recognizing the advantages of physical or geographical proximity as a basis for grouping jobs.

Another part of organizing is delegating authority and responsibility. Authority is the power to get things done; responsibility refers to who is supposed to get them done. Delegation involves both. Delegation is the process by which a manager assigns a portion of his or her task to subordinates. Decentralization is the result of delegation. In decentralization, power and control are systematically delegated to lower levels of the organization. Decentralization enables organizations to respond more rapidly to their environments by keeping in close touch with customers, suppliers, and competitors.

Another concept of organizing, the span of management, refers to the number of subordinates who directly report to a given manager. In wide spans managers maintain loose supervision; narrow spans permit closer supervision. Wide spans result in fewer levels of management, or flat organizations; narrow spans result in more levels, or tall organizations. Flat organizations tend to have better communication, an increased capacity to respond to the environment, and lower total managerial costs.

The last part of organizing is the concept of line and staff positions. Traditionally, line positions are in the direct chain of command and carry specific responsibility for accomplishing the goals of the organization. Staff positions are out of the direct chain and are primarily advisory or supportive in nature.

The Manager's Vocabulary

organizing
job design
job specialization
job rotation
job enlargement
job enrichment
departmentalization
functional
  departmentalization

product
  departmentalization
locational
  departmentalization
delegation
responsibility
authority
accountability
decentralization

centralization
span of management
flat organization

tall organization
line positions
staff positions

Prelude Case Wrap-Up

Our Prelude Case for this chapter describes McDonnell Douglas's attempt to respond to problems through reorganization. The company was having trouble with outside suppliers who could not keep up with their demand as well as with inexperienced workers who could not keep the assembly operations moving on schedule.

A massive reorganization of the organization focusing on quality was therefore initiated. The entire top-management structure of a major division was replaced, and the overall organizational structure was simplified by reducing the number of levels of management and creating worker teams with authority to act on many day-to-day problems. The delegation of responsibility to groups or teams of workers means, of course, that authority and accountability also reside within the group instead of within a single individual.

In addition, product departmentalization has replaced functional departmentalization for engineers. The reorganization is designed to focus the company's personnel, both managerial and nonmanagerial, on quality and to improve communication among members of the organization.

Many workers, although initially suspicious, have begun to take McDonnell Douglas seriously and to try to adapt to the new organizational arrangements. Divisions are starting to cooperate with one another, and work that was normally done in only one division may now be done in more than one. This enables the company to meet customer expectations regarding delivery times. In addition, new products and major modifications of existing ones are being designed to ease the financial problems of the firm. Its most exciting new product has been a revolutionary alteration in the design of helicopters that tested successfully early in 1990. Reworking its mission-planning software is an example of a major modification of an existing product. McDonnell Douglas hopes that these moves, taken together, will enable the company to become highly profitable.

Prelude Case Questions

1. Which concepts presented in this chapter are illustrated in the McDonnell Douglas case? Cite specific examples.
2. What were the major aspects of the reorganization at McDonnell Douglas?
3. What are the strengths and weaknesses of each of the major aspects identified above?
4. Do you feel that McDonnell Douglas's reorganization will enable it to become a highly profitable firm in the future? Why or why not?

Discussion Questions

Review Questions

1. What is job specialization? What are its benefits and limitations?
2. What is departmentalization? What are the common bases for departmentalization?
3. Identify and describe the major parts of the delegation process. What are centralization and decentralization?
4. What are the major differences between tall and flat organizations? Why are these important?
5. What are the major factors influencing group effectiveness?

Analysis Questions

1. Specialization has dominated organizations for centuries. Do you think it is likely to continue, or will companies move toward less specialization in the future? Why or why not?
2. How can organizations deal with the boredom and dissatisfaction created by specialization? Suggest some ways other than those mentioned in the chapter.
3. Comment on this statement: "You can delegate authority, but you can't get rid of your obligation."
4. Do companies that are heavily centralized have managerial processes similar to or different from those of companies that are heavily decentralized? Why?
5. Which kind of position is more important to an organizaion, line or staff? Why? Could an organization function with only one of these kinds of positions? Why or why not?

Application Questions and Exercises

1. Interview a local businessperson in your community to find out what the structure of his or her organization is like. How many levels of management are there? Do both line and staff positions exist? How are jobs grouped? Are the spans of management the same for every manager? Draw a chart for the organization and share it with your class.
2. Go to the library and try to determine the form of departmentalization used at the executive level by companies ranked near the very top of the Fortune 500 list (the top 50, say). Now try to obtain the same information for smaller firms (those ranked in *Fortune's* second 500—perhaps those between 900 and 1,000). Repeat this process for very small firms, such as local businesses. Are there differences? If so, why? If not, why not?
3. Assume that you are starting a new business. A marketing consultant says you can sell 100,000 units at $50 each. An engineering consultant says that the only way in which you can manufacture these units for substantially less than $50 each is to use 1,024 production workers. If the span of management is fixed (constant) at two people per manager, how many levels of management and how many managers will you need? If the span is fixed at four people per manager, what changes will occur? What if the span increases from four at the very top of the organization to thirty-two foremen to supervise the 1,024 production workers? If the salary for each manager is the same in each of these cases, which one will cost the least?
4. Find examples of organization charts to share with the class. Try to find several that are very different from one another. Using concepts in this chapter, try to explain them.
5. A former president of the American Management Association is reported to have argued that we should get rid of the terms *line* and *staff*. Why might he have made that argument?

ENHANCEMENT CASE

IBM DOWNSIZES AND UPGRADES

Many organizations evolved with tall structures involving many levels of management and narrow spans of management. Increasingly, however, competition is forcing changes in those structures. Most notably, many organizations are downsizing: that is, they are eliminating levels of management to reduce the size of the overall organization and to flatten the structure. These flatter organizations tend to have better communication between upper- and lower-level management, an increased capacity to respond to the environment, and lower total managerial costs.

IBM is a case in point. IBM used geographic departmentalization in forming IBM-Europe and IBM-United States to recognize the distinct differences in those two markets. In 1986 it reorganized its fast-growing European operations. The first part of that reorganization involved delegation to local subsidiaries in Europe. Marketing activities constituted most of that delegation, since the intent was to make the firm more responsive to customers. The second part of the reorganization was to split IBM-Europe into two groups, each reporting to the Paris headquarters. France, Italy, and West Germany, which were the fastest-growing countries for IBM, made up one group, and all of the other countries made up the other. The presidents of each country's local subsidiary report to a group executive. These group executives are part of an executive operating committee that is responsible for IBM-Europe's overall operating performance.

In 1987 C. Michael Armstrong took over operations in Paris and continued the reorganization through decentralization. Headquarters staff was reduced by about 40 percent, which led to a significant drop in administrative costs. Groups of European customers have been brought to the United States to meet with top development executives, who assure them that European customers' views are being taken seriously. The sales force has been increased to ensure excellent customer service, and each country is being encouraged to decentralize its operations.

IBM's reorganization has also involved its domestic operations, IBM-United States. It has begun a five-year program designed to reduce its overall size by around 20,000 people through a gradual process. Rather than fill vacancies with new personnel, IBM retrains and transfers existing personnel if they so desire. If employees are not interested in this option, they are provided with liberal severance benefits to encourage their resignation and make it easier. By early 1988 about 15,000 personnel had chosen early retirement. Normal attrition and transfers are just about equal to new hires, so the goal could be accomplished without having to resort to the outright termination of personnel.

However, some movement has been necessary. As of early 1988, over 21,000 employees have had to relocate. In one of its first moves in this reorganization, nearly 5,000 of the 7,000 persons in IBM's corporate staff were transferred to IBM-United States. Along with the transfer went a delegation from the corporate staff to IBM-United States. One interesting aspect of this movement has been that most personnel have not seen their reassignments in negative terms. About one-fourth view the reassignments as lateral moves, and the remainder view them as promotions. Clearly those perceptions make the reorganization much smoother to implement than if the reassignments were seen as demotions by those people involved.

The purpose of all this delegation is to get domestic marketing and worldwide product development closer to the customers. IBM's education personnel have also been transferred so that they are closer to the people they are supposed to train. In fact, nearly 2,000 of the 5,000 transferred personnel have been in education. By moving them just this one step closer to those who use the educational services, IBM has improved communications and reduced travel time. Further, the education group is now in a position to develop training programs to better fit the needs of its clientele.

This tremendously increased attention to its customers has led to the demise of the "not invented here" attitude that was characteristic of IBM prior to the 1980s. From 1986 to 1988 alone, IBM's sales force increased over 20 percent, which made it about three times larger than its nearest competitor. Design meetings with literally thousands of customers take place at seminars around the country to secure their inputs into new hardware and software. A whole new division has been created to do nothing but develop software packages and services for customers. Usability labs have been established in which customers and hired researchers try out software while programmers watch them through one-way mirrors. Video cameras tape the sessions, focusing on finger movements on keyboards and screens and also facial expressions.

Five autonomous product groups have also been created, and the general managers of those groups have been delegated a great deal of decision-making authority. Four of the five groups—personal computer systems, midrange systems, mainframes, and communications—develop products for their particular markets. The fifth group is charged with developing state-of-the-art technology such as memory chips for the other groups and for outside customers. In a further effort to accomplish its long-term objectives, IBM has acquired Rolm and 16 percent of MCI Communications, which will provide the company with expertise in voice and data networks.

SOURCES: T. L. Lautenbach, "MIS at IBM: Improving the Business Through Better Communications," *Academy of Management Executive*, February 1989, pp. 26–28; "A Bold Move in Mainframes," *Business Week*, May 29, 1989, pp. 72–78; "Big Changes at Big Blue," *Business Week*, February 15, 1988, pp. 92–98; "Mike Armstrong Is Improving IBM's Game in Europe," *Business Week*, June 20, 1988, pp. 96–97, 100–101; "Vaunted IBM Culture Yields to New Values: Openness, Efficiency," *The Wall Street Journal*, November 11, 1988, pp. A1–A4.

Enhancement Case Questions

1. Which concepts presented in this chapter are illustrated in the IBM case? Cite specific examples.
2. What were the major aspects of the reorganization at IBM?
3. What are the strengths and weaknesses of each of the major aspects identified above?
4. Do you feel that IBM's reorganization will enable it to continue to dominate the computer field in the future? Why or why not?

Chapter Notes

1. Robert H. Miles, *Macro-Organizational Behavior* (Santa Monica, Calif.: Goodyear, 1980).
2. Henry Mintzberg, *The Structuring of Organizations* (Englewood Cliffs, N.J.: Prentice-Hall, 1979).
3. See Robert C. Ford, Barry R. Armandi, and Cherrill P. Heaton, *Organization Theory: An Integrative Approach* (New York: Harper & Row, 1988), for a more complete listing of the components of organizing.
4. For an alternative view of organization design, see Michael W. Stebbins, "Organization Design: Beyond the Mafia Model," *Organizational Dynamics*, Winter 1989, pp. 18–30.
5. Frederick W. Taylor, *Principles of Scientific Management* (New York: Harper & Brothers, 1911).
6. See Adam Smith, *Wealth of Nations* (New York: Modern Library, 1937, originally published 1776), for a classic treatment of the advantages of job specialization.
7. Ricky Griffin, *Task Design—An Integrative Approach* (Glenview, Ill.: Scott, Foresman, 1982).
8. Ibid.
9. Ibid.
10. Frederick Herzberg, *Work and the Nature of Man* (Cleveland: World Press, 1966), and Robert Ford, "Job Enrichment Lessons from AT&T," *Harvard Business Review*, January-February 1973, pp. 96–106.
11. Recent analyses of job design issues may be found in Roger L. Anderson and James R. Terborg, "Employee Beliefs and Support for a Work Redesign Intervention," *Journal of Management*, September 1988, pp. 493–500, Donald J. Campbell, "Task Complexity: A Review and Analysis," *Academy of Management Review*, January 1988, pp. 40–52, and R. W. Griffin and D. D. Van Fleet, "Task Characteristics, Performance,

and Satisfaction," *International Journal of Management*, September 1986, pp. 89–96.

12. Ford, Armandi, and Heaton, *Organization Theory*.

13. Miles, *Macro-Organizational Behavior*.

14. Richard L. Daft, *Organization Theory and Design*, 3rd ed. (St. Paul, Minn.: West, 1989).

15. Henry Mintzberg, *Power In and Around Organizations* (Englewood Cliffs, N.J.: Prentice-Hall, 1983).

16. Dale McConkey, *No Nonsense Delegation* (New York: AMACOM, 1974).

17. "IBM Unveils a Sweeping Restructuring in Bid to Decentralized Decision-Making," *The Wall Street Journal*, January 29, 1988, p. 3.

18. Mintzberg, *Power In and Around Organizations*.

19. A. V. Graicunas, "Relationships in Organizations," *Bulletin of the International Management Institute*, March 7, 1933, pp. 39–42.

20. David D. Van Fleet and Arthur G. Bedeian, "A History of the Span of Management," *Academy of Management Review*, October 1977, pp. 356–372.

21. For an example, see "CBS Inc. Is Said to Be Planning More Dismissals," *The Wall Street Journal*, September 26, 1986, p. 4.

22. For additional information on the span of management, see David D. Van Fleet, "Span of Management Research and Issues," *Academy of Management Journal*, September 1983, pp. 546–552.

23. For a recent discussion of such factors, see Edward E. Lawler III, "Substitutes for Hierarchy," *Organizational Dynamics*, Summer 1988, pp. 4–15.

24. See Vivian Nossiter,"A New Approach Toward Resolving the Line and Staff Dilemma," *Academy of Management Review*, January 1979, pp. 103–106.

25. "Lean But Not Mean," *The Wall Street Journal*, October 28, 1986, p. 1.

26. "Where the Action Is: Executives in Staff Jobs Seek Line Positions," *The Wall Street Journal*, August 12, 1986, p. 29.

I. **The Nature of Organization Design**
   A. The Meaning of Organization Design
   B. The Role of Organization Charts

II. **Early Approaches to Organization Design**
   A. The Bureaucratic Design
   B. System 4 Design

III. **Contingency Factors Affecting Organization Design**
   A. Size
   B. Technology
   C. Environment

IV. **Contemporary Organization Design Alternatives**
   A. The Organic Design
   B. The Matrix Design
   C. The Divisional Design
   D. Other Designs

V. **Corporate Culture**
   A. Determinants of Culture
   B. Components of Culture
   C. Consequences of Culture

CHAPTER

9

After studying this chapter you should be able to

1. Discuss the meaning of organization design and the role of organization charts.

2. Describe early approaches to organization design, including the bureaucratic design and System 4 design.

3. Name and discuss several major contingencies that affect organization design.

4. Name and discuss several major contemporary organization design alternatives.

5. Define and discuss corporate culture, including its determinants, components, and consequences.

Organization Design

THE UNLIMITED LIMITED

Limited was founded in 1963 by Leslie H. Wexner in Columbus, Ohio, with only a $5,000 initial investment. By the late 1980s, it was the number one women's apparel merchandising firm in the United States. Wexner's original concept was to sell high-fashion, moderately priced merchandise to young women. By keeping in touch with consumer tastes and trends, manufacturing new products quickly, and maintaining tight inventory controls, Wexner became very successful. His success led to tremendous expansion and to strategies such as the opening of Limited Express, which began in 1980 to target even younger customers. Limited Inc., has never been in the red, and profits have fallen only a few times in the history of the firm.

Limited's organizational arrangements are not easily identified because of the amazing complexity and rapid change that characterizes both the industry and the firm. Limited uses thousands of suppliers and factories and has formed over a dozen joint ventures to ensure its supply. For instance, it joined with Daewoo, the South Korean conglomerate,

to open a wool sweater factory in Costa Rica. Suppliers are critical because the strategy involves overseas manufacturing and rapid-response distribution. In this way Limited can resupply its stores in weeks, whereas the usual industry pattern takes months.

The clothes themselves are knockoffs (look-alike copies) and originals patterned after successful designs introduced elsewhere. This means that the products have fancy, if phoney, Italian labels (Limited's Forenza line and Lerner's Venezia label) or Australian labels (Limited's Outback Red line and Lerner's Hunters Run) and have been produced in Hong Kong or Taiwan. Although everyone is aware of this, the goods sell.

Limited Inc.'s holdings are diverse. The divisions are all separate store chains catering to different clientele, with the exception of Mast Industries, a merchandise procurement unit that serves mostly The Limited and Limited Express. The four largest divisions are The Limited, Lerner, Lane Bryant (which sells fashionable clothing to women size 14 and larger), and Brylane

(a mail-order option). The smaller divisions include Limited Express, Victoria's Secret (which sells sexy lingerie), Sizes Unlimited (which specializes in larger sizes under the Lerner label), and Henri Bendel (an expensive New York City style-setting clothier).

Although they target different markets, many of these divisions overlap one another because they operate autonomously. A nightgown selling for over $100 at Bendel's, for instance, might also be available for about $80 at Victoria's Secret. The success of Limited Inc.'s strategy, then, depends upon the customer not shopping in both stores or at least trading down so that the parent company makes money no matter where the customer shops.

In 1988 Limited Inc. acquired the Abercrombie & Fitch chain as its newest division to expand its markets to include men (it also has Express Men as a menswear section in some Express shops). In 1989 Limited began discussions with executives of R.H. Macy & Co. that could lead to a joint venture, an acquisition, or some sort of shared ownership arrangement between the two firms.

Verna Gibson, president of The Limited Inc.'s stores division, has presided over the firm's efforts to shake off the slump it entered in the late 1980s. New attention to both product line and store layout seems to have gotten the specialty retailer moving forward one again.

Limited Inc. is known for its rapid growth. At one point, Lane Bryant had about 580 stores and over 7,500 employees, and was planning to add 200 stores, which would mean adding two regional managers, thirty-two district managers, two hundred store managers, four hundred supervisors, and thousands of sales clerks in just one year. Limited's growth slowed markedly, however, in the late 1980s with a general fashion retailing slump and vigorous competition from such specialty retailers as The Gap.

In response to that competition, Limited began to expand its stores in terms of size and product lines. Victoria's Secret began to carry bedroom and bathroom furnishings. Limited stores quadrupled their size, were given completely fresh looks, and added many new clothing collections, such as Limited Two children's wear and Cacique lingerie. The strategy was to shift from younger customers to the thirty-something customer, who had more purchasing power. Twenty-three such stores were opened in 1988 and about that same number in 1989.

What this means, of course, is that Limited is beginning to compete more directly with major department stores and specialty shops. It has clearly demonstrated its ability to totally dominate the specialty and women's apparel market. Whether or not it can effectively move into markets long associated with department stores remains to be seen, but the indicators in 1989 suggested that it can. That may well be why Limited and Macy's are discussing their futures together.

SOURCES: "Visual Merchandiser of the Year," *Stores*, January 1990, pp. 159–166; "Macy May Seek an Investment from Limited," *The Wall Street Journal*, May 18, 1989, pp. A3, A6; "Limited Inc., on New Tack, Pulls Ahead of Retail Gang," *The Wall Street Journal*, February 24, 1989, pp. B1, B4; "It's Turnaround Time for Verna Gibson," *Business Week*, February 20, 1989, pp. 117–118; "Limited Inc. Struggles to Improve Its Growth in Sales," *The Wall Street Journal*, October 13, 1988, p. B6; Steven R. Weiner, "The Unlimited?" *Forbes*, April 6, 1987, pp. 70–74.

O ne of the keys to understanding Limited Inc. is to understand its organization. It has numerous divisions, all but one of which are retail chains. Its central headquarters and distribution center are in Columbus, Ohio, but it has regional offices all over the country. Under the regional offices are district offices, and under them are the stores themselves. In the stores, the top-down hierarchy includes managers, supervisors, sales clerks, and custodial personnel. Limited has joint ventures with other organizations to ensure that supplies of its products will be uninterrupted. It is a large, complex organization, and understanding it involves not only the concepts introduced in Chapter 8 but others as well.

Chapter 8 identified and discussed a number of basic organizing concepts. This chapter considers how these concepts are integrated into one overall organization design. First it discusses the nature of organization design and summarizes some early approaches to it. Then it describes three important contingency factors that can affect organization design and several contemporary approaches to this design. To conclude, it considers the nature of organizational culture. Each of these subjects will help us better understand companies like Limited Inc.

THE NATURE OF ORGANIZATION DESIGN

What do we mean by organization design? We must answer this question before we discuss the idea of the organization chart.

The Meaning of Organization Design

□ *Organization design refers to the overall arrangement of positions and the interrelationships among positions within an organization.*

We can define **organization design** as the overall configuration of positions and interrelationships among positions within an organization. More specifically, let's think of the design of an organization as being like a jigsaw puzzle: it consists of a number of pieces put together in a certain way.

All organizations have certain things in common: they use one or more bases of departmentalization, they have line and staff positions, and so forth. At the same time, however, no two organizations are exactly the same. Some use functional departmentalization and others use product departmentalization; some have wide spans of management and others have narrow spans of management; some are decentralized and others are centralized. Thus, determining exactly how the various pieces of a specific organization are to be put together results in its organization design.

□ *Organization charts— pictures or maps of organizations—may be useful to small companies for clarifying relationships.*

The Role of Organization Charts

To many people, organization design is best represented by the **organization chart**. Throughout this book organization charts have been used to present ex-

Exhibit 9.1   The Organization Chart

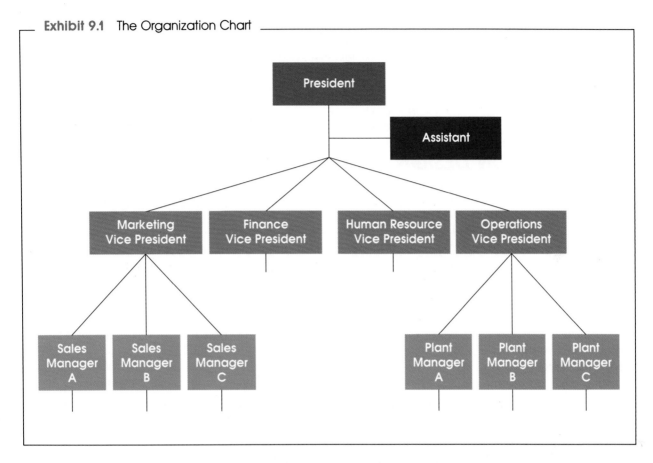

amples and to illustrate important points. Now let's examine the chart itself, using the simplified chart for a small manufacturing company shown in Exhibit 9.1. Note that the chart is composed of a series of boxes, each of which is connected to others with one or more lines. Each box represents a management position within the firm, and each line represents the nature of the relationship between that position and other positions.

Several things about the company can be gleaned from the organization chart in the exhibit. For one thing, we can see that the firm is departmentalized by function. Each function is headed by a vice president; the four vice presidents report to a president. We can also see that the marketing vice president has three sales managers under his control and the operations vice president has three plant managers under her control. Finally, we can see that the president has a staff assistant.

The organization chart can be thought of, then, as a picture or map of the organization. Such charts are especially useful to small businesses. They help newcomers better understand their place in the overall scheme of things, and they clarify reporting relationships between positions.

However, as an organization grows in size, it becomes more difficult to use organization charts because of the large number of positions and the complex relationships that can exist among those positions. For example, in large, complex firms such as AT&T, Du Pont, and Union Carbide, some managers report to more than one higher-level manager. In such cases, organization charts may not be used at all, and if they are, they usually show only the major positions in the organization.

EARLY APPROACHES TO ORGANIZATION DESIGN

Back in Chapter 2 you were introduced to administrative management, the area of classical management theory concerned with organizational structure. The chapter briefly noted the contributions of the German sociologist Max Weber. Weber was one of the first to describe how organizations should be designed to promote effectiveness.

The Bureaucratic Design

□ According to Weber, the formal system of authority of a bureaucracy should lead to rational and efficient organizational activities.

Weber coined the term *bureaucracy* to describe what he saw as the ideal kind of organization design.[1] His goal was to identify and prescribe a set of guidelines that, if followed, would result in the most efficient method of managing the organization. The foundation of his bureaucratic guidelines was the creation of a formal and legitimate system of authority. This system, he argued, would serve to guide rational and efficient organizational activities.

The guidelines Weber developed to create this system are summarized in Table 9.1. First, managers should strive for a strict division of labor. Each position should be clearly defined and filled by an expert in that particular area. Second, there should be a consistent set of rules that all employees must follow in performing their jobs. These rules are supposed to be impersonal and rigidly enforced. Third, there should be a clear chain of command—everyone should report to one, and only one, direct superior. Moreover, communication should always follow this chain and never by-pass individuals. Fourth, business should be conducted in an impersonal manner. In particular, managers should maintain an appropriate social distance from their subordinates and not play favorites. Finally, advancement within the organization should be based

TABLE 9.1
The Ideal Bureaucracy

Weber's Organizational Guidelines
1. The division of labor should be clearly defined.
2. One consistent set of rules should apply to all employees.
3. A clear chain of command and communication should exist.
4. Business should be conducted in an impersonal manner.
5. Advancement should be based solely on expertise and performance.

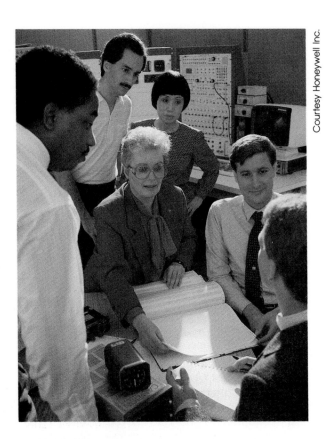

Courtesy Honeywell Inc.

System 4 organization design emphasizes openness, flexibility, communication, and participation. Honeywell has most of these basic characteristics. For example, the firm recently established a leadership development program designed to help people further their careers. The Honeywell managers shown here are working together in an open and collaborative fashion.

on technical expertise and performance, rather than on seniority or favoritism. Weber expected this to enhance employee loyalty to the organization.

Over the years, however, the term *bureaucracy* has come to connote red tape and slow, hassle-ridden decision making. Many universities, hospitals, and governmental agencies have a bureaucratic flavor to them. In fact, the bureaucratic approach to organization design may be appropriate when the organization's environment is stable and simple. However, since few organizations today have such environments, this approach should be used only with the greatest care.[2]

System 4 Design

☐ The flexibility of *System 4* often leads to increased effectiveness, but it is not appropriate for every organization.

As the human relations school of thought emerged, new perspectives on organization design naturally also emerged.[3] One of the more popular views has come to be known as the **System 4** approach.[4] This view holds that the bureaucratic model has numerous drawbacks and deficiencies and advocates an entirely different way of designing organizations. Its basic premises are summarized in Table 9.2.

The proponents of System 4 design argue that organization design can be described as a continuum. At one end of the continuum is the bureaucratic de-

TABLE 9.2 System 1 and System 4 Organization Designs

System 1 Organization	System 4 Organization
1. **Leadership process** includes no perceived confidence and trust. Subordinates do not feel free to discuss job problems with their superiors, who in turn do not solicit their ideas.	1. **Leadership process** includes perceived confidence and trust between superiors and subordinates. Subordinates discuss job problems with their superiors, who solicit ideas.
2. **Motivational process** taps only physical, security, and economic motives through the use of fear and sanctions. Unfavorable attitudes prevail among employees.	2. **Motivational process** taps a full range of motives through participatory methods. Attitudes are favorable toward the organization and its goals.
3. **Communication process** is such that information flows downward and tends to be distorted, inaccurate, and viewed with suspicion by subordinates.	3. **Communication process** is such that information flows freely—upward, downward, and laterally. The information is accurate and undistorted.
4. **Interaction process** is closed and restricted; subordinates have little effect on goals, methods, and activities.	4. **Interaction process** is open and extensive; superiors and subordinates affect goals, methods, and activities.
5. **Decision process** occurs only at the top of the organization; it is relatively centralized.	5. **Decision process** occurs at all levels through group processes; it is relatively decentralized.
6. **Goal-setting process** is located at the top of the organization; discourages group participation.	6. **Goal-setting process** encourages group participation in setting high, realistic objectives.
7. **Control process** is centralized and emphasizes fixing of blame for mistakes.	7. **Control process** is dispersed and emphasizes self-control and problem solving.
8. **Performance goals** are low and passively sought by managers, who make no commitment to developing the human resources.	8. **Performance goals** are high and actively sought by superiors, who make a commitment to developing, through training, human resources.

SOURCE: Adapted from Rensis Likert, *The Human Organization* (New York: McGraw-Hill, 1967), pp. 197–211. © 1967. Reprinted by permission.

sign, called System 1 in the table; at the other is System 4, a design that has more openness, flexibility, communication, and participation. In between are other organization designs that show characteristics relatively similar to System 1, called System 2, or relatively similar to System 4, called System 3.

The premise is that most organizations start out as bureaucracies like System 1 organizations. Theoretically, through a series of prescribed steps, managers can transform the organization first to a System 2, then to a System 3, and ultimately to a System 4 design.

Those who designed this approach helped demonstrate that the bureaucratic model is not the only way in which organizations can be designed, and one early study at General Motors found that a System 4 design was indeed more effective.[5] On the other hand, the System 4 model, like the bureaucratic model before it, was presented as a universal guideline that all managers should follow. As we see in the next section, research has shown that there are no universal guidelines; instead, the appropriate form of organization design for any given company is contingent on a variety of critical factors.

LEARNING CHECK

You should now be able to describe early approaches to organization design, including the bureaucratic design and System 4 design.

CONTINGENCY FACTORS AFFECTING ORGANIZATION DESIGN

☐ Size, technology, and the environment are contingency elements that affect the appropriate design for an organization.

In Chapter 2 we saw that the contingency approach to management suggests that no single method of management will always be successful. Three major situational elements that have been found to affect the appropriate design for an organization are size, technology, and the environment.[6]

Size

Obviously, the size of an organization can be assessed in any number of ways—by number of employees, assets, sales, and so forth. In most cases, however, these characteristics are closely related. Regardless of what criteria are used, General Motors, Exxon, and Tenneco are large companies, and a neighborhood dry cleaner, a locally owned pizza parlor, and a small-town automobile garage are small organizations.

The effects of size on organization design are summarized in Exhibit 9.2. In particular, research has found that large and small organizations differ from one another in three important ways.[7] First, smaller organizations tend to be less specialized than large organizations. It is not uncommon for every employee in a small company to have to be able to perform a number of different jobs, but as the company grows, each employee tends to stick to one well-defined job.

Second, smaller organizations tend to be somewhat less standardized than large ones. This means that they have fewer rules for how things should be done and more flexibility in how employees can confront problems. Again, as the organization grows, it has a tendency to create more rules and to eliminate some of the individual flexibility in problem solving.

Finally, organizations tend to be more centralized when they are small. This relates to the fact that the original owner or founder is probably still in charge and is accustomed to having the final say in decision making, whereas in larger organizations, decision making tends to become more and more decentralized. Managers of growing organizations should recognize that alterations in the design of the company may be necessary as it becomes larger and larger.

Technology

Technology is the set of conversion processes used by an organization to transform inputs into outputs. Obviously, the job of transforming crude oil into refined petroleum at Shell is quite different from the job of repairing a fuel pump in the garage at a local Chrysler dealership. It follows, then, that the Shell refinery and the Chrysler dealership will have quite different management needs, one manifestation of which is the kind of organization design that is appropriate.

The most common approach to describing technology is to classify it as unit or small-batch, large-batch or mass-production, or continuous-process.[8]

Exhibit 9.2 The Effect of Size on Organization Design

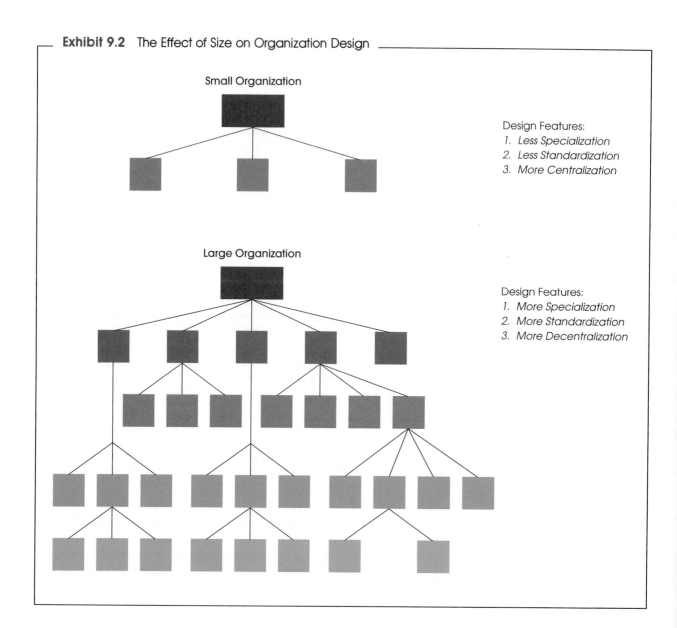

Small Organization

Design Features:
1. *Less Specialization*
2. *Less Standardization*
3. *More Centralization*

Large Organization

Design Features:
1. *More Specialization*
2. *More Standardization*
3. *More Decentralization*

Unit or **small-batch technology** is used when the product is made in small quantities, usually in response to customer orders. For example, Boeing doesn't keep an inventory of 747s on hand; instead, it makes them to customer specifications after they have been ordered. Tailor shops and printing shops use a similar approach to production.

Large-batch or **mass-production technology** occurs when the product is manufactured in assembly-line fashion by combining component parts into a finished product. Products are made for inventory instead of according to customer specifications. Examples include a Nissan assembly plant for manufacturing cars and a Maytag plant that makes washing machines.

☐ System 4 design works best in *unit* or *small-batch technology* and *continuous-process technology*. A System 1 design may be more appropriate for companies that use *large-batch* or *mass-production technology*.

Finally, **continuous-process technology** means that the composition of the raw materials is changed through a series of mechanical or chemical processes. A Pennzoil refinery, a Miller brewery, and a Union Carbide chemical plant all use continuous-process technology.

In general, the appropriate form of organization design used by a company depends at least in part on its dominant technology. Organizations that rely on unit or small-batch technology are often more effective if they use a System 4 design, which allows them the flexibility to react quickly to customer needs and expectations. Large-batch or mass-production organizations, on the other hand, may be more effective if they use a System 1 type of design. Such organizations are more amenable to rules, regulations, and other formal practices. Continuous-process firms, like unit or small-batch companies, may be most effective if they adopt a System 4 organization design because they need its flexibility to oversee their complete technology as well as to enhance the introduction of automated production processes into the system.[9]

Within the System 4 framework, some new organizational arrangements have emerged. Most involve the use of employee groups working as teams rather than as isolated individuals. **Quality circles** are groups of employees that focus on how to improve the quality of products. **Semi-autonomous work groups** are groups of workers who operate with no direct supervision to perform some specific task, such as assembling an automobile or producing a circuit board for an electronic product.

Environment

A third factor that has been found to directly affect the appropriate design of an organization is the environment. Chapter 4 discussed the environment extensively. Now we need to relate it more directly to organization design.

Several different perspectives on the impact of the environment have been developed, and a synthesized view that captures the essential points of each is

Technology is one important contingency factor that can affect organization design. Varian Associates makes high-technology systems and components using a unit or small batch technology. The firm strives to remain flexible and responsive to customer needs.

Varian Associates, Inc.

☐ *Environmental uncertainty is affected by* complexity *and* change. *High complexity and frequent change create a high level of uncertainty.*

shown in Exhibit 9.3.[10] The basic idea is that **environmental uncertainty** can be captured by two dimensions, **environmental change** and **environmental complexity**. The exhibit places these two dimensions in a graph.

When the environment changes frequently, is dynamic, and is difficult to predict, it has a high rate of change. In contrast, if the environment seldom changes, is fairly static, and is relatively easy to predict, it has a low rate of change. Similarly, if the environment contains many different elements, it can be considered to have a high level of complexity. When the number of elements is low, however, the complexity of the environment is also low.

When change and complexity are both high, uncertainty is also high. In this instance, a System 4 type of organization design will probably be most effective. However, when both change and complexity are low, so too is uncertainty. For this condition, a System 1 or bureaucratic design might work best.

For example, let's consider Intel Corporation and a small liberal arts college. Intel competes in a complex and rapidly changing environment—the electronics industry. Faced with uncertainty, it uses a System 4 design, which allows it to respond quickly and relatively easily to shifts, threats, and opportunities in the environment. In contrast, the college functions in a relatively stable and simple environment—higher education. Confronted with little uncertainty, it uses a System 1 design, akin to a bureaucracy.

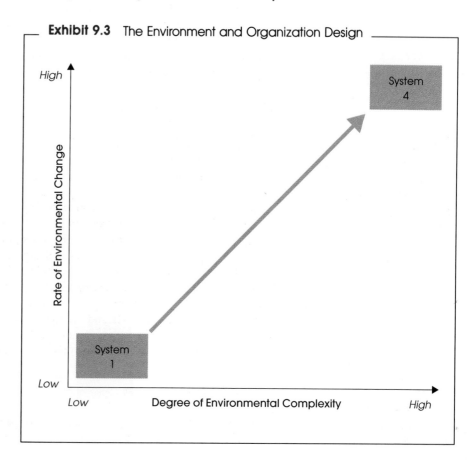

Exhibit 9.3   The Environment and Organization Design

It is up to the manager to analyze the three factors of size, technology, and environment effectively and then properly match the design of the organization to them. Now let's explore some of the more common design alternatives that many companies currently adopt.

PRELUDE CASE UPDATE

In the Limited case, the impact of the environment seems clear. There is constant change and a high degree of uncertainty in the retail apparel industry. Such an environment necessitates a design that is flexible and adaptive, as is Limited's. Limited's decentralized, autonomous divisions are largely responsible for that flexibility.

CONTEMPORARY ORGANIZATION DESIGN ALTERNATIVES

As we have repeatedly seen, there is no one best method for organization design, managers must carefully consider their circumstances and choose the one that is most appropriate for those circumstances. Three options that are being chosen with increasing regularity are the organic design, the matrix design, and the divisional design.[11]

The Organic Design

☐ An *organic design,* in contrast to a *mechanistic design,* is based on open communication systems, a low level of specialization and standardization, and cooperation.

The **organic design** was developed in the early 1960s by two British researchers and is similar in some ways to the System 4 design.[12] Its designers' goal was to help managers better align their organizations with their environments. They found that some firms could effectively use what they called a **mechanistic design**—a design similar to System 1 that was found to work best in stable conditions. For example, the Singer Sewing Machine Company operates in an environment that is fairly stable, has few domestic competitors, and so forth, so Singer might be best designed along mechanistic lines. In contrast, firms such as Limited in the Prelude Case and others like Hewlett-Packard and Levi Strauss use an organic design, which is presumed to be most effective when the environment is fluid and when constant adjustments are necessary to respond to shifts and changes. The organic organization is based on open communication systems, a low level of specialization and standardization, and cooperation. These characteristics are summarized in Table 9.3.

The Matrix Design

☐ An organization can retain the efficiency of functional departments and gain the advantages of product departmentalization through the use of the *matrix design.*

Another important contemporary form of organization design is the **matrix design**, which is created by superimposing a product-based form of depart-

TABLE 9.3 Mechanistic and Organic Designs

Mechanistic	Organic
1. Tasks are fractionated and specialized; low emphasis on clarifying relation between tasks and organizational objectives.	1. Tasks are more interdependent; emphasis on relevance of tasks and organizational objectives.
2. Tasks tend to remain rigidly defined unless altered formally by top management.	2. Tasks are adjusted and redefined through interaction of organizational members.
3. Specific role definition (rights, obligations, and technical methods prescribed for each member).	3. Generalized role definition (members accept general responsibility for task accomplishment beyond individual role definition.)
4. Hierarchic structure of control, authority and communication. Sanctions derive from employment contract between employee and organization.	4. Network structure of control, authority, and communication. Sanctions derive more from community of interest than from contractual relationship.
5. Information relevant to situation and operations of the organization is formally assumed to rest with CEO.	5. Leader not assumed to be omniscient; knowledge centers identified where located throughout organization.
6. Communication is primarily vertical between superior and subordinate.	6. Communication is vertical and horizontal, depending on where information resides.
7. Communications primarily take the form of instructions from superiors and of information and requests for decisions from inferiors.	7. Communications primarily take form of information and advice.
8. Insistence on loyalty to organization and obedience to superiors.	8. Commitment to organization's tasks and goals valued over loyalty or obedience.
9. Importance and prestige attached to identification with organization and its active members.	9. Importance and prestige attached to affiliations and expertise in external environment.

SOURCE: Adapted from Tom Burns and G. M. Stalker, *The Management of Innovation* (London: Tavistock Publications, 1961), pp. 119–122. Used with permission.

mentalization on an existing functional departmentalization.[13] An example is shown in Exhibit 9.4.

Note that in the exhibit four functional departments are arrayed across the top of the organization, and each is headed by a vice president. Down the side of the organization are listed three project managers. Each of these managers is similar to the head of a product-based department (as shown by the dashed lines). In the matrix, each manager heads up a project that cuts across functional areas (shown by the shaded areas). Thus the employees within the matrix are a part of two (or more) departments and report to two (or more) bosses at the same time.

The rationale for a matrix is really quite simple: the functional departments allow the firm to develop and retain unified and competent functional specialists, and the product design directs special and focused attention to individual products or product groups. The matrix allows the firm to use the advantages of both forms simultaneously.

For example, suppose a firm using the matrix design wants to create and produce a new product. Specialists from each of the functional departments are brought together and formed into a team under the direction of the project manager. The new product gets the specialized attention it needs from each functional area, but each specialist can work on many projects at the same time and still have a functional "home."

In recent years, many companies, including Monsanto, NCR, the Chase Manhattan Bank, and Prudential Insurance, have adopted the matrix form of organization design. There are generally clear indications of when a matrix should be used, although the design has disadvantages as well as advantages.

WHEN TO USE A MATRIX   In general, a matrix design is most likely to be effective in one of three situations.[14] First, it may be useful when the firm has a diverse set of products and a complex environment. Although the diverse set of products suggests product departmentalization, the strength provided by the functional approach might be necessary to retain the requisite number of specialists.

Exhibit 9.4 The Matrix Design

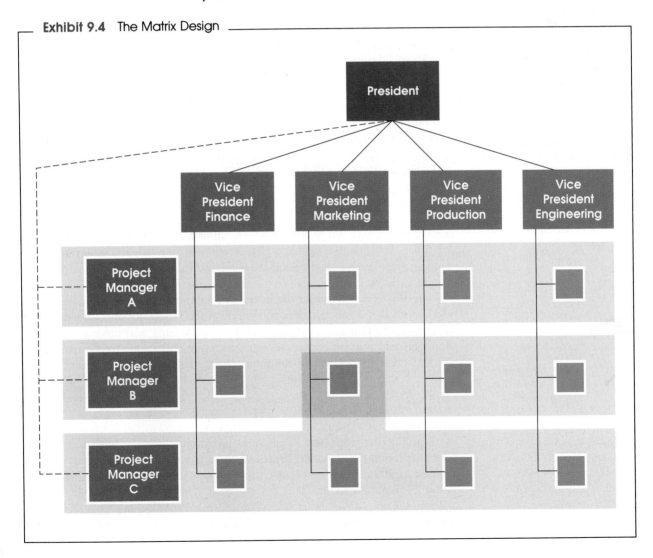

The matrix might also be called for when there is a great deal of information to be processed. In highly uncertain environments accentuated by broad product lines, for example, the organization is confronted with a mountain of information. The matrix allows managers to categorize this information systematically and direct it to a pocket of key individuals.

Finally, the matrix organization design might be appropriate when there is pressure for shared resources. A company may need eight product groups yet have the resources to hire only four marketing specialists. The matrix provides a way for the eight groups to share the talents of the four specialists.

ADVANTAGES OF THE MATRIX   Clearly, the matrix design has certain advantages.[15] For one thing, it is very flexible: teams can be created, changed, and dissolved without major disruption. For another, it often improves motivation: since the team has so much responsibility, its members are likely to be committed to its success and will feel a great sense of accomplishment.

Another significant advantage of the matrix is that it promotes the development of human resources. Managers get a wide range of experiences and as a result can take increasingly important roles in the firm. The matrix can also enhance cooperation. Since there is so much interdependence among team members, it is important that they work well together. A final advantage is that managerial planning is facilitated: because so much of the day-to-day operation of the organization is delegated to the teams, top managers have considerably more time to concentrate on planning.

DISADVANTAGES OF THE MATRIX   There are also major disadvantages to the matrix approach to organization design. Paramount among these is the potential conflict created by having a number of bosses. If a marketing specialist is a part of three project groups and still has work to do within his functional role, he may not be able to satisfy all of his bosses when he is pressured for time. Another disadvantage is that coordination is difficult in a matrix. Two or more groups might need the same information and each could end up paying a market research firm to get the information without realizing that the other group or groups could use it too. A final drawback is the fact that group work tends to take longer than individual work. Each manager in a matrix is likely to spend considerable amounts of time meeting and talking with other managers and putting one set of activities aside and picking up others. Thus she may have less individual time to devote to task accomplishment.[16]

The Divisional Design

□ Under the *divisional design,* an organization establishes fairly autonomous product departments that operate as strategic business units.

A third popular approach to organization design is the **divisional design,** which combines a product approach to departmentalization with strategic business unit strategy, as discussed in Chapter 6. An example of this kind of design is shown in Exhibit 9.5.

Each division of the organization is responsible for all aspects of the management of a given product or product family. A company such as General

Exhibit 9.5 The Divisional Design

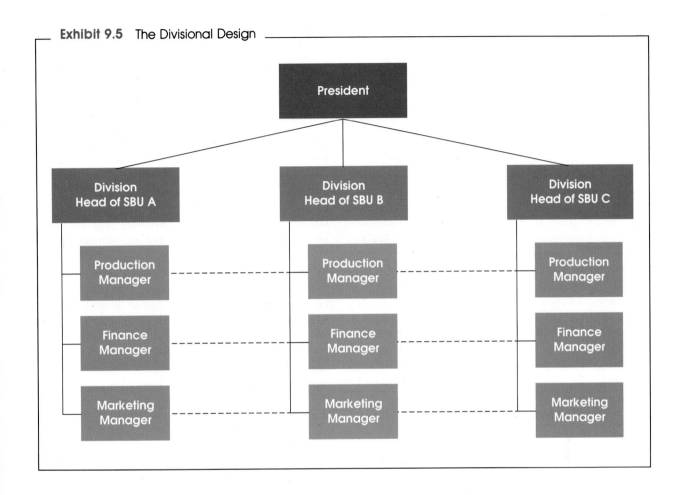

Foods, for example, establishes a division for each of its major types of food products; each division then takes care of its own suppliers and handles its own advertising campaigns, and the head of the division is usually given the title of vice president (although titles such as *division head* and *division manager* are also common).

Each division is also thought of as a strategic business unit, or SBU. That is, each has its own market and competitors. Moreover, a division might be a star, a cash cow, a question mark, or a dog, so it might be sold, used to generate cash for other divisions, given extra cash, or put on a "wait and see" basis.

Note that positions in the different divisions in the exhibit are linked by dashed lines. These indicate that cooperation between divisions is encouraged, although usually not required. For instance, two divisions of General Motors might link up to negotiate a better contract with a supplier, or two divisions of General Foods might use the same advertising agency. Each division, however, is free to undertake and terminate such arrangements as it chooses.

Finally, we should note that even though the divisions are given considerable autonomy, certain functions are probably retained at a centralized level.

THE WORLD OF MANAGEMENT

ICI's Divisional Headaches

ICI, Imperial Chemical Industries, was formed through a four-company merger in Great Britain in 1926. Since the year of its founding, ICI had never had a losing year until 1980. At that time, however, it was in trouble. To deal with its problems, a massive reorganization effort was made. That effort seems to have enabled it to again become profitable, although its earnings continue to be more erratic than management and owners would like.

ICI had grown into a strong divisional structure with many of the dysfunctional characteristics of bureaucracies. The focus of its divisions was on internal efficiency rather than on long-term market growth, and there were no coordinating mechanisms accross divisions. Each division was headed by a board, which in turn was represented on the main board. Each member of the main board oversaw the activities of a staff function, a geographical area, and a business sector. This arrangement frequently pitted directors against one another as they tried to get support for their own areas.

After the reorganization, ICI decentralized and made each divisional head responsible for his or her own group's performance. Directors now no longer represent particular interests but rather take a global view of overall operations, although they do continue to oversee particular areas. Levels of staff have been eliminated to bring top management closer to business operations. Those in charge of geographic areas work with the heads of businesses, which serve or are located in those areas to develop plans and to resolve problems. As a direct result of this reorganization, ICI also began to move to sell units that were unprofitable and to acquire subsidiaries, especially in the United States, where it plans to earn about 25 percent of its revenues by the end of the 1990s.

SOURCES: "No More OTC Drugs Output for ICI," *Chemical Week,* October 18, 1989, p. 10; "ICI Nears Completion of Canadian Revamp," *Chemical Week,* October 4, 1989, p. 12; "The Legacy of Harvey-Jones," *Management Today,* January 1987, pp. 35–88; Richard I. Kirkland, Jr., "A Busy Body Bent on Doing Better," *Fortune,* August 3, 1987, p. 60.

At General Motors, for instance, all labor negotiations for all divisions are handled at the corporate level.[17] Although the divisional design generally works well, it can have problems, as indicated in *Management Today: The World of Management*, which describes events at Imperial Chemical Industries.

PRELUDE CASE UPDATE

Limited uses the divisional design. Its divisions are headed by presidents and operate with considerable autonomy, although some coordination is also used. Marketing research and purchasing are centralized whereas selling is decentralized. This enables Limited to purchase the same product line for use by different chains selling to different markets.

Other Designs

The view that seems to be emerging in organization design is that there is no "one best way" to organize and that companies should use whatever design seems most appropriate for them to accomplish their objectives. As a result, numerous hybrid designs have appeared in ongoing organizations. "Hybrid" means that different parts of the same organization are designed along different lines—one part may be divisional, another may use a matrix, and still others may be more or less bureaucratic in design. Some of those designs that merit noting include new venture units and alternative ownership patterns.

New venture units or "skunkworks," as they are informally called, are small, semi-autonomous, voluntary work units. They are protected from many normal day-to-day corporate activities and pressures so that they can concentrate on the generation of new ideas or the development of new products or ventures. Companies that have used this design include Boeing, Genentech, Inc., Hewlett-Packard, IBM, Monsanto Company, NCR Corp., Westinghouse, and 3M.[18]

Alternate ownership patterns have also emerged as a variety of designs are increasingly being used in an attempt to bring new ideas or new monies into the organization. For instance, **employee stock ownership plans (ESOPs)** transfer stock ownership to employees in an effort to increase their commitment, involvement, and motivation. This also means, however, that executives cannot set corporate policy and strategy without involving the employees. **Research and development limited partnerships (RDLPs)** are consortia, usually among high technology firms, that are designed to do basic research. The resources come from participating firms' contributions, and those firms then share in the results of the research. **Joint ventures,** whereby two firms jointly form a third one to produce a new product, are also becoming more common. Ford and Nissan recently entered into a joint venture to make minivans together. Finally, many firms are buying into other companies to establish **equity positions** through the purchase of significant portions of stock. This financial interdependency tends to lead to endeavors that have benefits for both firms.[19]

☐ *New venture units are small, semi-autonomous, voluntary work units that develop new products or ventures for companies.*

LEARNING CHECK

You should now be able to name and discuss several major contemporary organization design alternatives.

CORPORATE CULTURE

☐ The shared experiences, stories, beliefs, norms, and actions of an organization are called its *corporate culture.*

A final element of organizations we should consider here is **corporate culture**—the shared experiences, stories, beliefs, norms, and actions that characterize an organization.[20] Although the concept has been around for centuries, it has only recently become widely regarded as an important issue for managers. The catalyst for this interest was a popular book by Terrence Deal and Allen Kennedy, *Corporate Cultures: The Rites and Rituals of Corporate Life*, published in 1982.[21] Since that time, much attention has been focused on the concept. The basic nature of corporate culture is illustrated in Exhibit 9.6.[22]

Determinants of Culture

As noted in the exhibit, three basic factors determine the culture of an organization. One key determinant is the values held by top management. If top executives are antagonistic toward the government, if they want to stamp out all competition, or if they just want to earn fat profits, they set a certain tone for the firm. On the other hand, if they want to cooperate with the government, if they want to coexist peacefully with competitors, or if they want to treat customers honestly and fairly, a different atmosphere is prevalent.

The history of the organization also helps determine its culture. A company founded by a strong personality, one that leaves a mark on the firm, will follow the original model. For example, Steve Jobs left an indelible imprint on Apple Computer, and Sam Walton is doing the same for Wal-Mart. Similarly, Les Wexner has imbued Limited Inc. with a self-confidence that is overwhelming—those in the organization seem to believe that Limited can do no wrong. Even relatively old companies such as Ford continue to carry vestiges of their founders.

Finally, top management's vision for the firm also helps shape its culture. If the CEO decides that the company needs to undertake significant new ventures and aim for rapid growth and expansion, this vision will permeate the entire organization. On the other hand, if the CEO is content to maintain the status quo and take a defensive posture, this, too, will shape the culture. At Hewlett-Packard, a story about the founders declining a project because it involved bank financing has made the slogan "HP avoids bank debt" part of the company's culture.[23]

Components of Culture

How are these effects translated into culture? In general, they shape five basic components or dimensions that we can use to characterize corporate culture.

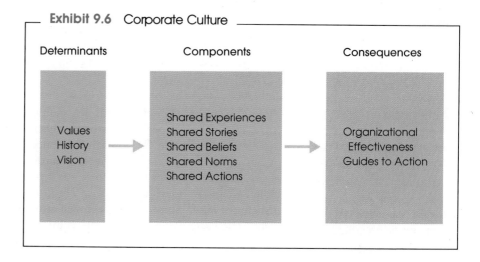

Exhibit 9.6   Corporate Culture

Determinants	Components	Consequences
Values History Vision	Shared Experiences Shared Stories Shared Beliefs Shared Norms Shared Actions	Organizational Effectiveness Guides to Action

Hewlett-Packard is often cited as an example of a firm with a strong and well-defined corporate culture. One Saturday several years ago, co-founder William Hewlett wanted to get into a lab that was locked. He broke the lock and instructed that labs should be open to the firm's engineers 24 hours a day so that they could come and go as they liked. The freedom associated with this practice has become part of the HP culture.

© Robert Holmgren

Shared experiences are the common events that people participate in that become a part of their thinking. For instance, if a group of employees work closely together for an extended period, putting in twelve-hour days and seven-day weeks to create a new product on schedule, this experience becomes a part of the culture. Even after the group breaks up, its members will always have this experience in common.

Shared stories also become a part of the culture. "Do you remember...," "That was the time...," and "This company has always..." are common beginnings to stories that have entered an organization's mythology.

Shared beliefs are those things that all members of the organization accept as fact about the company. Employees at IBM, for example, believe that the company will win any battle it chooses to undertake. Likewise, employees at Wal-Mart believe that they can sell more in any given month than they sold in the previous month.

Similarly, shared norms are generally accepted ways of doing business. A norm at Delta Air Lines is that all employees are expected to help get the job done, so if there is a back-up in passenger luggage at an airport, managers are expected to jump in and help clear the logjam.

Finally, shared actions are day-to-day behaviors that most people will perform. At Texas Instruments the "shirt-sleeve" culture suggests that men will not wear ties to work; in contrast, at IBM, the more formal culture dictates that all the men will wear ties. Other common actions involve work hours, social interactions, and so forth.

☐ Two factors influencing a company's effectiveness are the creation and transmission of a strong corporate culture and the consistency of that culture with the organization's strategy.

Consequences of Culture

Where does this leave us? Although relevant research is scant, there does appear to be a link between corporate culture and organizational effectiveness.[24]

ETHICAL DILEMMAS OF MANAGEMENT

Too Much Innovation at Johnson & Johnson?

Johnson & Johnson uses a highly decentralized and divisionalized organization design. It consists of about 166 individual companies making such diverse products as baby oil, bandages, contraceptives, diapers, headache remedies, shampoos, and sophisticated medical products like Orthoclone OKT3, which is used to reduce the risk of kidney transplant rejection. Johnson & Johnson has also developed a corporate culture that fosters innovation, and innovation involves risk taking and making mistakes. At Johnson & Johnson, making a mistake has almost become a badge of honor because it is a clear indicator that people have been innovative.

This organizational culture has costs, however—costs that go beyond small mistakes. Ethical dilemmas can constantly occur when the products involve the health and safety of others. Disposable diapers, long a highly successful product for Johnson & Johnson, are being challenged by environmentalists because of the disposal problems that result. Yet many working mothers feel that the disposable diaper is a major factor enabling them to be able to work outside of the home and, hence, to realize their career aspirations as well as to make a significant contribution to the economic well-being of their families and communities. Should Johnson & Johnson discontinue the manufacture of the product or not?

Or one could take the example of Retin-A. Retin-A was developed as an acne medication during the 1960s. Then research indicated that it could be used to rejuvenate wrinkled, sun-dried skin. Johnson & Johnson could have used that research to promote and sell large quantities of Retin-A as an age cream, but some people developed severe reactions to Retin-A. Regardless of final Food and Drug Administration action, Johnson & Johnson might have pursued a variety of actions—all the way from taking it off the market because of the reactions of some to pushing it as a "fountain of youth." Again, Johnson & Johnson's organization design and corporate culture presented it with an ethical dilemma.

SOURCES: Stratford P. Sherman, "You're Invited to the CEOs' Ball," *Fortune*, January 15, 1990, pp. 140–144; Benjamin Mindell, "Interest in Retin-A Brings Healthy Sales Figures," *American Medical News*, April 8, 1988, p. 13; Patricia Sellers, "How To Handle Customers' Gripes," *Fortune*, October 24, 1988, pp. 88–92; "At Johnson & Johnson, A Mistake Can Be a Badge of Honor," *Business Week*, September 26, 1988, pp. 126–128; "Johnson & Johnson's Larsen Named Chief," *The Wall Street Journal*, October 25, 1988, p. A5.

LEARNING CHECK

You should now be able to define and discuss corporate culture, including its determinants, components, and consequences.

In particular, two dimensions of culture can affect a company's success. First, it seems to be important for top management to create and transmit a clear and strong culture. There may not be a single best culture, but it does seem that everyone in the company needs to understand what the culture is. Common reasons cited for the success of firms such as IBM, Digital Equipment, Disney, and Delta are that everyone in the organization understands the culture.

The second link between culture and effectiveness is strategy. Effectiveness tends to be enhanced if the corporate culture is consistent with the organization's strategy. When the culture and strategy do not seem to be in tune, effectiveness often suffers. However, even when they are, problems may arise. *Management Today: Ethical Dilemmas of Management* discusses, for instance, problems confronting Johnson & Johnson as a result of its culture.

The second consequence of culture, which is actually a corollary of the first, is that it provides a guide to action for newcomers. A new employee at Texas Instruments can look around the plant, see everyone working in shirt sleeves, and know immediately how he or she should dress the next day. Newcomers also quickly learn whether high performance is expected or not.

Chapter Summary

Organization design refers to the overall configuration of positions and interrelationships among positions within an organization. One early approach to organization design described by Weber was the ideal bureaucracy. Bureaucratic organizations possess some very desirable features, but they are most appropriate in relatively simple and stable environments. Another early approach to organization design was the System 4 view, which uses eight characteristics to describe organizations along a continuum.

Three major contingencies affect organization design: size, technology, and the environment. Technology refers to the set of conversion processes used by an organization to transform inputs into outputs. Environmental uncertainty seems to be accounted for by two components, rate of change and degree of complexity; when these are high, uncertainty is high, and when they are low, uncertainty is low.

There is no one best organization design. Three major contemporary approaches to organization design are the organic design, the matrix design, and the divisional design. The organic design is based on open communications, a low level of specialization and standardization, and cooperation. The matrix design is a combination of product and functional departmentalization. The divisional design combines a product approach with a strategic business unit (SBU) strategy. Each division is responsible for all aspects of the management of a given product or product family.

New hybrid designs are emerging to strive to be effective in differing environments. New venture units, ESOPs, RDLPs, joint ventures, and equity positions are among the more widespread of such other designs.

The major determinants of corporate culture are the values held by the top management of the organi-zation, the history of the firm, and the top managers' vision of the firm. These translate into culture through actions that employees have done together (shared experiences), shared memories or stories, shared beliefs, shared norms (generally accepted ways of doing business), and shared actions. There is a link between corporate culture and organizational effectiveness. Effective organizations have strong, clear cultures that are consistent with their strategies. Further, the corporate culture provides a guide to action for newcomers and for new situations.

The Manager's Vocabulary

organization design
organization chart
System 4
technology
unit technology
small-batch technology
large-batch technology
mass-production
  technology
continuous-process
  technology
quality circles
semi-autonomous work
  groups
environmental
  uncertainty
environmental change

environmental
  complexity
organic design
mechanistic design
matrix design
divisional design
new venture units
employee stock
  ownership plans
  (ESOPs)
research and
  development limited
  partnerships (RDLPs)
joint ventures
equity positions
corporate culture

Prelude Case Wrap-Up

Our Prelude Case for this chapter describes Limited Inc., the number one women's apparel store chain in the United States. The dominance and self-confidence of its founder permeate the organization and have become a significant part of its culture. A divisional structure is in place using predominantly a product line form of departmentalization. However, the environment is so turbulent, with high degrees of both change and uncertainty, that an extremely flexible organization is required. For these reasons, then, Limited Inc. has many aspects of an organic design, especially the high levels of cooperation and communication.

When Limited found itself in a slump in 1987, it decentralized to give its divisional presidents even more authority to react quickly to changes in tastes and fashions. Verna Gibson, president of The Limited stores division, moved to quickly differentiate her stores from those of competitors by increasing their size. She also increased the quality of the merchandise and expanded the product lines. Then, once a month she and her executive staff descend on a Limited store near the company's headquarters and rearrange it. They move shelves and use new lights to experiment with new and different looks. When they are satisfied with the result, it becomes the standard for all other stores to follow. Although this approach is clearly disruptive, Gibson insists that it also helps to keep the store managers and personnel fresh and motivated. The idea seems to work, since Limited stores, after a few months to get used to the new sizes and selections, are earning greater profits per square foot than the industry average.

Some analysts feel that consolidation is likely to increase in the future. Limited is large enough to deal with this trend, which may also account for its talks with Macy's. Limited's experience with its new superstores will also serve it well as it begins to form joint ventures with and compete in the department store market.

Prelude Case Questions

1. Which concepts presented in this chapter are illustrated in the Limited case? Cite specific examples.
2. What are the major characteristics of the organization design at Limited Inc.?
3. What are the strengths and weaknesses of the organization design of Limited? How might the weaknesses be offset by reorganization?
4. What is the organization culture at Limited? Do you feel that its culture will enable it to continue to be highly profitable in the future? Why or why not?

Discussion Questions

Review Questions

1. What is meant by organization design?
2. Describe two major early approaches to organization design.
3. What are three major contingency factors that affect organization design? How do they do so?
4. Briefly describe the major contemporary organization design alternatives.
5. What is corporate culture? Why is it important?

Analysis Questions

1. Comment on these sentences: "The only real value of an organization chart is in doing the analysis necessary to draw it. Once it is drawn, the only value it has is covering cracks in the plaster."
2. Can bureaucratic organizations avoid red tape and other problems usually associated with them? If so, how? If not, why not?
3. Rensis Likert, who developed the System 1–4 approach, said that when he asked managers to describe the best organization with which they had ever been associated, they invariably described a System 4 design; when asked to describe the worst, they described System 1. Yet when he asked, "What would you do if you took over a company in trouble?" they all described actions that characterize System 1 more than System 4! What reasons can you give for this? How could you prevent it?
4. Would you rather work in an organic or a mechanistic organization? Why? Which form of organization would be more likely to appeal to someone who believes "there is a place for everything and everything should be in its place"? Why?
5. What factors could influence corporate culture besides the ones mentioned in the book?

Application Questions and Exercises

1. "Organization charts do more harm than good." Outline arguments both supporting and refuting this statement.
2. Being careful not to use the term *bureaucracy*, interview a local, small businessperson to see which guidelines of the ideal bureaucracy he or she uses

or endorses. Afterwards, ask that person to describe a bureaucracy for you. What might account for your results?
3. What forms of technology can you locate in organizations within your local community? Share your results with the rest of your class.
4. What forms of organization design can you locate

in organizations within your local community? Share your results with the rest of your class.
5. Think of organizations with which you are familiar (family, religious, governmental, educational, etc.). Then identify examples of the components of corporate culture in those organizations. Go to the library and see if you can add to your list.

ENHANCEMENT CASE

PEPSICO'S HIGH-PERFORMANCE DESIGN

After a rather successful beginning in 1896, Pepsi-Cola had to be reorganized under bankruptcy statutes after World War I. It then was able to achieve success by effectively advertising its soft drink as an inexpensive alternative to others. However, the Pepsi-Cola company only began to emerge as a major corporation after World War II, when a top executive left Coca-Cola to join Pepsi. He brought several other top managers with him, and together they remade the Pepsi organization. The image of the beverage was changed from an inexpensive one to a chic one, and the organization was changed into a multidivisional corporation, PepsiCo.

PepsiCo quickly became a large conglomerate. It acquired other firms and was soon in soft drinks, snack foods, restaurants, transportation, and sporting goods. However, the unrelated acquisitions (North American Van Lines, Lee Way Motor Freight, and Wilson Sporting Goods) were not good fits for PepsiCo and so were divested during the 1980s. At that time, PepsiCo developed an organization built around closely related and interdependent operations—restaurants, salty snacks, and beverages.

PepsiCo's restaurant business includes three major chains—Pizza Hut, acquired in 1977; Taco Bell, acquired in 1979; and Kentucky Fried Chicken (KFC), acquired in 1986. These restaurants all use cola syrup, which accounts for the largest part of cola sales. With long-term contracts between these restaurants and the soft drink part of the company, PepsiCo benefits tremendously. In the case of KFC, PepsiCo received a double benefit since KFC had been one of the two largest customers for Coca-Cola

syrup prior to its takeover by PepsiCo. PepsiCo has not entered the hamburger part of the fast food market because of the already established dominance of McDonald's.

Its snack food business, Frito-Lay, was acquired in 1965 and soon dominated the salty snack field. Although its market share has dropped to just under 40 percent, it still commands more than 2.5 times its next-largest rival (Borden) and over four times the third-largest competitor (Proctor & Gamble). Cool Ranch Doritos proved tremendously successful, as did low-fat versions of some established products. In 1989, Frito-Lay acquired Smartfoods Inc. to expand into cheddar cheese popcorn in the Northeast and to use that expertise throughout the country. International operations are also being increased; the company was operating in twenty countries in 1989 and hopes to expand into forty-five countries by the mid-1990s. The international experience can also serve as a source for new products, since those that are successful in one country can be tested in others relatively easily.

The soft drink business has also flourished. New products such as Slice and new flavored versions of Pepsi and Slice coupled with spectacular advertising campaigns featuring such stars as Michael Jackson and Madonna have enabled Pepsi to essentially tie Coca-Cola in supermarket sales. The importance of shelf space and rapid distribution has led both Pepsi and Coca-Cola to develop strong bottling networks of which they own or control substantial portions, Pepsi through MEI Corporation and Coca-Cola through Coca-Cola Enterprises. A "cola war" for

PepsiCo managers are a unique breed. To perpetuate the highly competitive culture the firm has created, it puts new employees through some unusual training experiences. Brian Vent, a recent M.B.A. graduate, was assigned as an assistant manager for a Washington, D.C. Pizza Hut. Within a year or two, however, Vent will likely be promoted to the position of regional manager, responsible for up to 40 restaurants.

market share erupted in 1988, with both companies cutting prices in certain cities and regions as well as internationally. In some of these situations, increases in market share were not enough to make up for the price reductions, which reached as low as ten cents a can. The idea that they might recoup the losses by holding the market share later on, however, kept the battle going.

PepsiCo executives have developed a culture to make their multidivisional design work. That culture is founded on the three P's, "people, people, people." High-performing, entrepreneurial managers are consciously developed throughout the organization. Teamwork without meetings and memos is stressed. Sixty-hour workweeks, including Saturdays and Sundays, are common. The stress is high, but so are the rewards. Top managers get first-class air travel, luxury hotels when traveling, a company car every two years or $11,000 a year, and an annual bonus that could virtually double their salary.

To keep individual managers from becoming too tyrannical in the pursuit of performance, however, all are evaluated, confidentially, by their subordinates. These evaluations are felt to be important to the long-term, continued success of PepsiCo because they bring about more participation and openness. In addition, human resource planning (HRP) is used every year to assess the long-term career potential of each upper-level manager. This helps to keep an emphasis on short-term performance from driving out long-term success.

PepsiCo managers also are very autonomous. When the head of the beverage unit was signing on Michael Jackson to do commercials, he did not even think about notifying the CEO until just before the contract was actually signed. The former head of Japanese operations introduced Diet Pepsi into that market despite his boss's objections. When it failed, his boss praised his risk taking but suggested that a more careful analysis be used next time. Mistakes such as this are reported by virtually all top executives to assure lower-level managers that the organization supports risk taking and innovation.

SOURCES: "Products to Watch," *Fortune*, January 15, 1990, p. 133; Brian Dumaine, "Those Highflying PepsiCo Managers," *Fortune*, April 10, 1989, pp. 78–86; "Frito-Lay's Cooking Again, and Profits Are Starting to Pop," *Business Week*, May 22, 1989, pp. 66, 70; "Pepsi Offers Stock Options to All, Not Just Honchos," *The Wall Street Journal*, June 28, 1989, p. B1; Stephen Kindel and Robert Teitelman, "The Best Companies of the Eighties," *Financial World*, December 27, 1988, pp. 22–30.

Enhancement Case Questions

1. What similarities and differences can you note between PepsiCo and Limited Inc. in the Prelude Case?
2. Describe the PepsiCo organization. What components of design that were discussed in the chapter

can you identify? Cite specific examples of each of them.
3. What are the strengths and weaknesses of the organization design used by PepsiCo? How might it reduce the weaknesses?
4. Do you feel that PepsiCo will continue to be suc-

cessful in each of its three main businesses? Why or why not?

Chapter Notes

1. Max Weber, *Theory of Social and Economic Organization*, trans. T. Parsons (New York: Free Press, 1947).

2. Richard L. Daft, *Organization Theory and Design*, 3rd ed. (St. Paul, Minn.: West, 1989).

3. Daniel Wren, *The Evolution of Management Thought*, 3rd ed. (New York: Wiley, 1986).

4. See Rensis Likert, *New Patterns of Management* (New York: McGraw-Hill, 1961), and *The Human Organization* (New York: McGraw-Hill, 1967).

5. William F. Dowling, "At General Motors: System 4 Builds Performance and Profits," *Organizational Dynamics*, Winter 1975, pp. 23–28.

6. Robert C. Ford, Barry R. Armandi, and Cherrill P. Heaton, *Organization Theory: An Integrative Approach* (New York: Harper & Row, 1988).

7. Derek S. Pugh and David J. Hickson, *Organization Structure in Its Context: The Aston Programme* (Lexington, Mass.: D. C. Heath, 1976); see also "Is Your Organization Too Big?" *Business Week*, March 27, 1989, pp. 84–94.

8. Joan Woodward, *Industrial Organization: Theory and Practice* (London: Oxford University Press, 1965).

9. Patricia L. Nemetz and Louis W. Fry, "Flexible Manufacturing Organizations: Implications for Strategy Formulation and Organization Design," *Academy of Management Review*, October 1988, pp. 627–638.

10. For example, see Tom Burns and G. M. Stalker, *The Management of Innovation* (London: Tavistock, 1961), and Paul R. Lawrence and Jay W. Lorsch, *Organization and Environment* (Homewood, Ill.: Richard D. Irwin, 1967). For a review, see Daft, *Organization Theory and Design*.

11. Henry Mintzberg, *The Structuring of Organizations: A Synthesis of the Research* (Englewood Cliffs, N.J.: Prentice-Hall, 1979).

12. Burns and Stalker, *The Management of Innovation*.

13. Stanley M. Davis and Paul R. Lawrence, *Matrix* (Reading, Mass.: Addison-Wesley, 1977).

14. Harvey F. Koloday, "Managing in a Matrix," *Business Horizons*, March-April 1981, pp. 17–24.

15. See, for example, Jeffrey Barker, Dean Tjosvold, and I. Robert Andrews, "Conflict Approaches of Effective and Ineffective Project Managers: A Field Study in a Matrix Organization," *Journal of Management Studies*, March 1988, pp. 167–178.

16. James Owens, "Matrix Organization Structure," *Journal of Education for Business*, November 1988, pp. 61–65, and Kenneth Knight, "Matrix Organization: A Review," *Journal of Management Studies*, May 1976, pp. 111–130.

17. Mintzberg, *The Structuring of Organizations*.

18. "Westinghouse Gets Respect at Last," *Fortune*, July 3, 1989, p. 92, and Christopher K. Bart, "New Venture Units: Use Them Wisely to Manage Innovation," *Sloan Management Review*, Summer 1988, pp. 35–43.

19. D. Bruce Shine and Donald F. Mason, Jr., "ESOP: The American Workers' Leveraged Buy Out," *Case and Comment*, January 1, 1990, p. 24; "More Competitors Turn to Cooperation," *The Wall Street Journal*, June 6, 1989, p. B1; Tyzoon T. Tyebjee, "A Typology of Joint Ventures," *California Management Review*, Fall 1988, pp. 75–86; and Howard Grindle, Charles W. Caldwell, and Caroline D. Strobel, "RDLP: A Tax Shelter That Provides Benefits for Everyone," *Management Accounting*, July 1985, pp.44–47.

20. Gregory Moorhead and Ricky W. Griffin, *Organizational Behavior*, 2nd ed. (Boston: Houghton Mifflin, 1989), Chapter 16, and W. Jack Duncan, "Organization Culture: 'Getting a Fix' on an Elusive Concept," *Academy of Management Executive*, August 1989, pp. 229–235.

21. Terrence Deal and Allen Kennedy, *Corporate Cultures: The Rites and Rituals of Corporate Life* (Reading, Mass.: Addison-Wesley, 1982).

22. See Deal and Kennedy, *Corporate Cultures*, and Vijay Sathe, "Implications of Corporate Culture: A Manager's Guide to Action," *Organizational Dynamics*, Autumn 1983, pp. 5–23.

23. "Hewlett-Packard's Whip-Crackers," *Fortune*, February 13, 1989, pp. 58–59.

24. See Sathe, "Implications of Corporate Culture," and Ralph H. Kilman, Mary Jane Saxton, and Ray Serpa, eds., *Gaining Control of Corporate Culture* (San Francisco: Jossey-Bass, 1985).

CHAPTER OUTLINE

I. The Nature of Staffing
   A. The Staffing Process
   B. Legal Constraints

II. Human Resource Planning
   A. Job Analysis
   B. Forecasting Supply and Demand
   C. Matching Supply and Demand

III. The Selection of Human Resources
   A. Recruiting
   B. Selection
   C. Orientation

IV. Training and Development
   A. Assessing Training and Development Needs
   B. Popular Training and Development Techniques
   C. Evaluating the Effectiveness of Training

V. Performance Appraisal
   A. Objective Measures
   B. Judgmental Methods
   C. Management by Objectives
   D. Feedback

VI. Compensation and Benefits
   A. Wages and Salaries
   B. Benefits

VII. Labor Relations
   A. How Unions Are Formed
   B. Collective Bargaining

CHAPTER

10

LEARNING OBJECTIVES

After studying this chapter you should be able to

1. Discuss the nature of staffing, including the staffing process and legal constraints.

2. Describe human resource planning and indicate how to use job analysis and forecasts to match supply and demand.

3. Discuss the selection of human resources, including recruiting, selection, and orientation.

4. Describe the assessment of training and development needs, various training and development techniques, and the importance of evaluating those techniques.

5. Define performance appraisal and discuss both objective and judgmental methods, management by objectives, and feedback.

6. Discuss compensation decisions regarding wages and salaries, as well as various kinds of benefits.

7. Discuss labor relations, including how unions are formed and the nature of collective bargaining.

Staffing and Human Resources

TOYOTA TAKES ITS TIME

Toyota is choosy when hiring people to work for it. Its top management believes that careful hiring decisions will result in long-term benefits for the organization. That belief has arisen as Toyota has grown and developed over the past half-century. In 1937, Kiichiro Toyoda founded the Toyota Motor Corporation, and he ran the company until his death in 1952. His son, Shoichiro Toyoda, wanted to be a scientist or an entrepreneur but out of respect for his father's wishes began training as an engineer. When the father died suddenly, Shoichiro was only in his twenties and was hardly ready to take over an international organization. In addition, the company was struggling to recover from a bitter labor dispute, and no one expected the son to be named as president. Nevertheless, in a surprise move, Shoichiro Toyoda was asked to run the company.

Working with the board of directors, Shoichiro quickly established an organizational structure developed around consensus decision making—getting virtually all parties to a decision to agree to it before it is finally chosen. Consensus decision making is slow. However, because of the deep involvement of all participants in the decision process, once a decision is made, it can be implemented rapidly. Deliberate decisions, quickly implemented, then, have become a hallmark of Toyota and are considered a key component to its success. Thus, hiring people to work for the company is also a slow, deliberate, and very detailed process.

Building upon consensus decision making, Toyota's organizational culture emphasizes teamwork, organizational loyalty, and versatility. Everyone in the organization must be able to work cooperatively to achieve its objectives. Deliberate hiring decisions enable Toyota to preserve that culture and to offer long-term employment and loyalty to its workers in return for the performance and loyalty it expects from those workers.

An applicant for a quality control manager's position, for example, takes a battery of tests lasting at least fourteen hours. The test battery is thorough. Reading is tested because instructions and communications tend to be in writing and because all employees are expected to read to develop and expand their skills. Technical knowledge and skills are another part of the testing. Certificates, diplomas, or even years of experience are not considered dependable indicators of what applicants really know about jobs. Applicants must also have interpersonal skills, since everyone must get along with everyone else in order to maintain the organizational culture valued by Toyota. Mathematics, manual dexterity, and job fitness are also tested. Job fitness deals with attitudes and is measured by a questionnaire with one hundred items to which applicants must either agree or disagree.

After being tested, the applicant takes part in workplace simulations. The simulations take place in groups and, like the tests, are thorough. Groups of applicants discuss various problems, such as which automobile features have the greatest potential for market acceptance. Several different people observe these groups, take notes on who says what, and

Toyota goes to great lengths to select the right employees. Equally important is how those employees interact. To promote positive interaction at the firm's Kentucky plant, Toyota picks up the tab when Japanese and American workers such as these bowl together.

evaluate the applicants. Finally, one or more interviews complete the process.

For one applicant at a Kentucky plant, this whole process of tests, simulations, and interviews took over twenty-five hours. Those twenty-five hours were spread over the same number of days, so the applicant had to work somewhere else while trying to get the job at Toyota. After getting the job, however, he indicated that the process was worthwhile; he also felt that his willingness to

submit to this long, difficult process showed that he was the kind of person Toyota was seeking to hire.

Toyota's careful hiring and its organizational culture have earned it a reputation as a highly desirable place to work. As a result, it has numerous applicants for every opening. At the Kentucky plant, for instance, there were over 90,000 applicants for the 2,700 production jobs, and 40,000 of those survived the first rounds of screening. There were also thou-

sands of applicants for only 300 office positions. Of course, the Kentucky economy, which was not in very good condition at the time, also provided a large pool of available and interested workers either out of jobs or seeking better ones than they had. And there were no labor agreements to restrict the number of applicants. In any event, Toyota was able to be highly selective in choosing the very best for its new plant.

SOURCES: "Tech Training at Toyota," *Motor*, January 1, 1990, pp. 43–50; "Toyota Spurns British Aid for Auto Plant," *The Wall Street Journal*, April 18, 1989, p. A18; "Zen and the Art of Auto Sales," *The Wall Street Journal*, March 13, 1984, p. B1; "The Coming Traffic Jam in the Luxury Lane," *Business Week*, January 30, 1989, p. 78; "Toyota's Plan to Build Cars in Europe Adds to Pressures in Competitive Market," *The Wall Street Journal*, January 30, 1989, p. A11; "Toyota Takes Pains, and Time, Filling Jobs at Its Kentucky Plant," *The Wall Street Journal*, December 1, 1987, pp. 1, 29.

T oyota's corporate culture stresses, among other things, teamwork. This means that the process of bringing people into the organization is extremely important because those people must be able to fit in and function with existing teams. Toyota's hiring process, then, is an important part of the organizing function that follows the design of the overall structure of the organization.

Staffing is the process of procuring and managing the human resources an organization needs to accomplish its goals. Staffing, however, is more than hiring. When Toyota hired hundreds of new workers, it was engaged in staffing, but if General Motors gives one hundred managers early retirement, it is also engaging in the staffing process. When UPS sends 450 employees to a training seminar, it is also engaging in staffing. Xerox is involved in staffing when its employees get a new health insurance option. And if Kaiser Aluminum has to close a plant because of safety hazards, it is also exercising part of the staffing process.

This chapter explores the staffing process in detail. First, it provides more background information about the nature of staffing. Then it looks at the selection process and training and development. Performance appraisal and compensation are covered next, and labor relations are explored in the last section.

THE NATURE OF STAFFING

We have already defined staffing, so now let's develop a more complete framework for understanding staffing and for organizing our discussion. Then we can discuss the legal environment of the staffing process.[1]

The Staffing Process

Exhibit 10.1 presents the basic staffing process in detail. First, as indicated along the left side of the framework, the staffing process must take place within a series of legal constraints that restrict what a firm can and cannot do. Within this legal environment, the first actual step is human resource planning, which involves developing a complete understanding of the various tasks within the organization, forecasting how many people are needed and will be available to perform those tasks, and taking steps to match supply with demand.

Several steps follow the initial planning. If Honeywell needs more employees, it must recruit qualified applicants and then choose the ones best suited for the jobs at hand. After joining the company, the new employees need to be trained and developed, and as they work their performance must be evaluated. Of course, they must also be compensated from the time they begin work, and they must have the opportunity to participate in benefit programs. Their compensation may be adjusted as a result of the performance appraisal. Finally, as the exhibit indicates, labor unions may affect and be affected by these various activities.

Who performs these functions? In small firms, one person, usually called the personnel manager, handles them. As an organization grows, a department

Exhibit 10.1   The Staffing Process

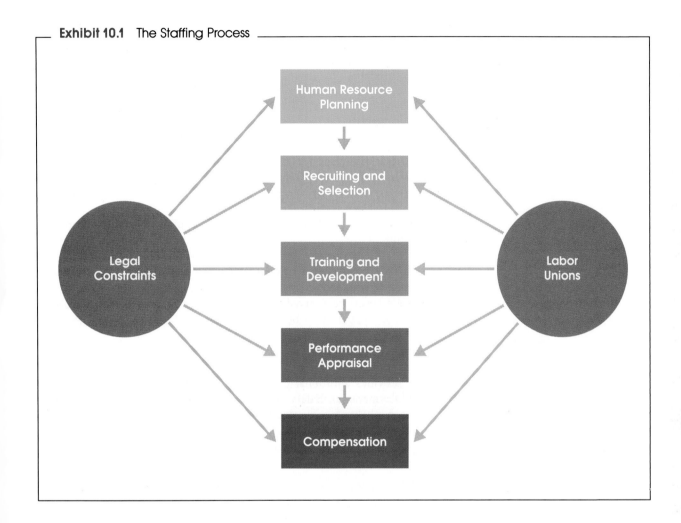

of personnel or human resources is created (*personnel* is the traditional name; the term *human resources* is increasingly used instead). Line managers also assist in performing many of the functions. In the past line managers and human resource managers did not always work well together, but this is changing. Increasingly, line managers and the human resource department jointly try to act in the best interests of the organization.

Legal Constraints

One factor that has contributed to the increased importance of human resource managers is the number and complexity of legal constraints any organization faces. The most significant of these are listed in Table 10.1.

Among constraints on the selection of employees is Title VII of the 1964 Civil Rights Act, which prohibits discrimination on the basis of sex, race, color, religion, or national origin in all areas of employment, including hiring,

TABLE 10.1
Legal Constraints That
Affect Staffing

Staffing Considerations	Legislation
Employee Selection	Title VII of the 1964 Civil Rights Act; Age Discrimination Act; Executive Orders
Compensation and Benefits	Fair Labor Standards Act; Equal Pay Act
Labor Relations	National Labor Relations Act; Labor-Management Relations Act
Other	Occupational Safety and Health Act

layoff, compensation, access to promotion, and training. The Age Discrimination Act prohibits discrimination against people between the ages of forty and seventy. In addition, various executive orders prohibit discrimination in organizations that do business with the government, provide extra protection for Vietnam era veterans, and so forth.[2]

Wages and salaries are affected by the Fair Labor Standards Act, which sets minimum wages that have to be paid to employees, and the Equal Pay Act, which prohibits wage discrimination on the basis of sex.

The National Labor Relations Act governs the collective bargaining process between companies and organized labor unions. The Labor-Management Relations Act provides additional guidelines for dealing with labor unions. Finally, the Occupational Safety and Health Act requires organizations to provide safe, nonhazardous working conditions for employees.

Because of these and other laws, the staffing process is perhaps more affected by the legal environment than any other area of management. It is little wonder, then, that human resource managers have come to be vital members of organizations. *Management Today: The World of Management* illustrates some of the staffing problems companies can face as they expand and contract.

LEARNING CHECK

You should now be able to discuss the nature of staffing, including the staffing process and legal constraints.

HUMAN RESOURCE PLANNING

As we have seen, the first phase of the staffing process is human resource planning. This consists of three steps: job analysis, forecasting human resource supply and demand, and matching supply and demand. These steps are illustrated in Exhibit 10.2.

☐ *Job analysis* refers to the systematic investigation of the nature of the job, which results in a *job description* and an identification of the skills and credentials needed to perform the job, known as a *job specification.*

Job Analysis

Job analysis is the systematic collection and recording of information about jobs in the organization.[3] It actually consists of two different activities. One of these is the development of a **job description**, which summarizes the duties encompassed by the job, the working conditions where the job is performed,

THE WORLD OF MANAGEMENT

Expansion and Contraction Problems

Japanese companies are expanding all over the world (see Prelude Case to this chapter), yet this expansion is not uniform. It is not uniform in two ways—within any given company and across companies. Thus, one division of a Japanese company may be expanding and hiring while another is having to cut back, and one company may be expanding while another is contracting. This means that these companies have at least two kinds of staffing problems: hiring new workers and letting existing workers go.

In their efforts to recruit American workers, Japanese conglomerates formed Recruit USA and Interplace/Transworld Recruit as subsidiaries of Recruit Company in Japan. However, it was discovered in 1989 that these organizations were violating U.S. antidiscrimination laws. Code phrases were being used—"see Adam" when an American was being sought and "talk to Haruo" when a Japanese was wanted. These allegations were not the first. Sumitomo lost a sex discrimination case and settled for nearly $3 million in 1987. Similar cases have been filed against C. Itoh and Nikko Securities. Honda lost a sex and race discrimination case and settled for nearly $6 million in 1988. Charges have also been leveled at NGK SparkPlugs and IBM Japan. The Japanese may be only scapegoats, as some have claimed, but Japanese organizations are having to learn that when they do business in the United States, they must follow U.S. laws.

In order to handle cutbacks, professional outplacement organizations are being used within Japan to find new jobs for employees, especially managers who are no longer needed. Outplacement firms specialize in placing people in new jobs outside the organization for which they currently work. Drake Beam Morin Inc. opened a Tokyo branch in 1982 and has worked with about 150 companies since that time. C. Itoh owns 90 percent of Career Planning Center Company and uses it to help its own managers find new positions. Marubeni and Mitsubishi also have majority interests in outplacement companies. What used to be a rare practice is becoming more commonplace as Japanese companies strengthen their staffing processes to assist employees even in bad times.

SOURCES: "'White People, Black People' Not Wanted Here?" *Business Week*, July 10, 1989, p. 31; "Japanese HR Management Practices: Separating Fact from Fiction," *Personnel*, April 1, 1989, pp. 42–47; Bruce Stokes, "Defusing a Time Bomb," *National Journal*, May 6, 1989, pp. 1125–1126; "Saying Sayonara in a Way That Saves Face," *Business Week*, April 6, 1987, p. 54.

and the tools, materials, and equipment used on the job. The other part of job analysis is the development of the **job specification**, which lists the skills, abilities, and other credentials necessary to perform the job. Taken together, the job description and the job specification provide the human resource manager with the information he or she needs to forecast the supply and demand of labor within the organization.

Forecasting Supply and Demand

Forecasting the supply and demand for various kinds of employees involves using any number of sophisticated statistical procedures.[4] Such techniques are beyond the scope of our discussion, so let's focus on the forecasting process at a general level.

Forecasting demand involves determining the numbers and kinds of employees that the organization will need at some point in the future. If Unisys plans to open three new plants in five years, its human resource managers must begin planning now to staff those plants. Likewise, if the company intends to close a plant, there will be less demand. Demand, then, is based partly on the projected overall growth of the organization and partly on the location of that projected growth.

Forecasting supply involves determining what human resources will be available, both inside and outside the organization. Many upper-level management positions, for example, will be filled by employees currently working for the firm, whereas technical employees like engineers and programmers are usually brought in from the outside.

Matching Supply and Demand

After the appropriate forecasts have been prepared, the results must be compared and actions must be planned. As shown in Exhibit 10.2, three alternatives will exist. If supply is projected to exceed demand, management must plan for normal attrition, layoffs, terminations, and early retirement. If de-

Exhibit 10.2 Human Resource Planning

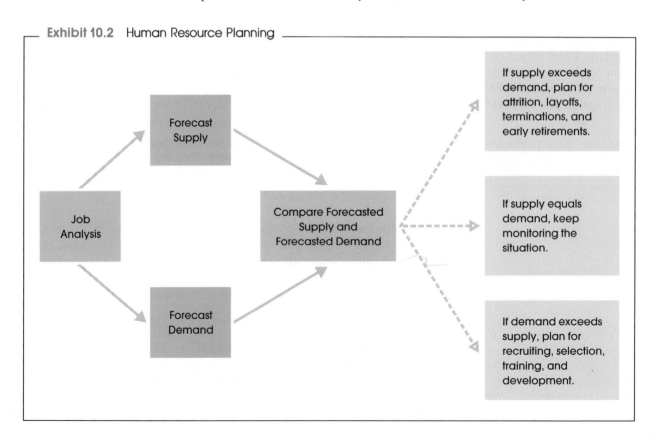

Arlene Gottfried

When an organization forecasts a need for additional employees, there are no assurances it will be able to find them. Ira Cohen, an owner of Shapiro & Cohen Inc., a Bronx produce wholesaler, faced just such a problem. To solve it, he came up with a creative solution. He set up a training program for under-qualified blacks and Hispanics. Those that finish his training program are eligible for union jobs starting at $10 an hour.

LEARNING CHECK

You should now be able to describe human resource planning and indicate how to use job analysis and forecasts to match supply and demand.

mand exceeds supply, management must plan to recruit, select, train, and develop new employees. Finally, if supply and demand are roughly the same, no immediate action is necessary, although the situation should be monitored in case either supply or demand changes. This process can be especially difficult in international business.[5]

THE SELECTION OF HUMAN RESOURCES

If an organization needs to hire more employees, either because of growth or just to replace current employees who leave, it must begin the selection phase of human resource management. This phase consists of three steps: recruiting, the actual selection, and orientation.

Recruiting

☐ Internal *recruiting* is finding current employees who would like to change jobs, whereas external recruiting is finding qualified applicants outside the company.

Recruiting is the process of attracting a pool of qualified applicants who are interested in working for the company. Suppose, for example, that Du Pont wants to add an extra shift of one hundred employees at one of its chemical plants. The company would like to recruit more than one hundred qualified applicants to select from. Less than one hundred does not give the company ample choice, but several thousand applicants would pose a big logistical problem. Therefore, the key is to attract enough recruits, but not too many.

One type of recruiting is internal recruiting—attempting to identify existing employees who want to be transferred and/or promoted. Often called *job posting*, this method may increase worker morale but also may lead to numerous job changes as each internal recruit vacates his or her position.[6] External recruiting is advertising for and soliciting applicants from outside the company, often through want ads (see Exhibit 10.3).

Many organizations frequently use external placement firms and private employment agencies, especially to find applicants for managerial positions. As

___ **Exhibit 10.3** Examples of "Help Wanted" Ads ___

STORE MANAGER. A national window coverings retail chain is looking for a store manager for our Hillsborough Ave. store. Window coverings experience helpful & mgment exp. necessary. Call 813-886-4680

MANAGER TRAINEES. National theater circuit seeks qualified individuals for training positions in multiplex theater operations. College degree preferred. Competitive starting salary, incentive and excellent benefits. Tribune Co. Box Y-352

PERSONNEL MANAGER

Leadership Role...

Nationally recognized non-profit organization seeks experienced, take charge human resource professional who enjoys autonomy to oversee HRIS computerization process, supervise recruiters/ support staff, monitor benefits, and implement recruitment & retention program. Min 4 yrs human resource mgmt exp, incl systems development, computer, benefits and employee relations.

EXCELLENT BENEFITS
(incl 4 Weeks Vacation!)
Send resume with
salary requirements to:
Director of Personnel

YOUNG ADULT INSTITUTE
460 W. 34th St
NYC 10001
Equal Opportunity Employer

VICE PRESIDENT INVESTMENT BANKING

Ferris, Baker Watts, Inc. is looking for an experienced middle market, investment banking professional with a minimum of four years experience in IPO's, M&A or private placements. Experience in public underwriting a plus. Deal execution skills (i.e. strong writing and analytical abilities) and capability to produce quality work under pressure a must. Please forward resume including salary requirements and a listing of transactions worked on to:

Todd L. Parchman
Senior Vice President
Ferris, Baker Watts, Inc.
100 Light Street
Baltimore, Maryland 21202

PLANT MANAGER

Enzymatics, Inc., a rapidly growing medical diagnostics company located in suburban Philadelphia, is looking for a well qualified manufacturing executive to direct manufacturing in the existing semiworks, plan for factory expansion, and hire, train, and motivate the employees in the resulting new factory. The successful candidate will have experience at high volume, precision manufacturing and a thorough knowledge of all the manufacturing disciplines. Green field experience is highly desirable.

Enzymatics offers equity participation, competitive salary, and benefits. Please send resume with salary requirements to:

Enzymatics, Inc.
355 Business Center Drive
Horsham, PA 19044

CUSTOMER SERVICE SUPERVISOR

We are a growth-oriented mfr. seeking an experd. customer service supervisor. Cand. should possess 3-5 yrs. order entry/cust. service exper., strong commun. skills, be detail-oriented and computer literate. We offer a compet. wage and benefit pkg. along with a friendly work env. For immed. consideration send resume with salary history to:

JAMES HARDIE BUILDING PRODUCTS, INC.

26300 La Alameda, #400
Mission Viejo, CA 92691

SOURCE: Top row courtesy of *The Tampa Tribune* and Ferris, Baker Watts, Inc. Bottom row courtesy of Young Adult Institute, Enzymatics, Inc., and James Hardie Building Products, Inc.

technology develops, computerized data bases will increasingly be used to assist human resource professionals in the recruitment task.[7]

Selection

❑ *Application blanks, tests, interviews,* and *assessment centers* help managers decide which applicants to *select* for employment.

Once applicants have been recruited, the organization must select the right ones; **selection** is choosing the best people for the job. A number of techniques are used to facilitate selection, but they must all be job related and have no discriminatory effects.

APPLICATION BLANKS   The typical first step in selection is to have prospective employees complete **application blanks**, which ask for information about background, education, experience, and so forth. An example of an application blank is presented in Exhibit 10.4. Items in application blanks are usually weighted (some twice as important as others, for instance) and then combined to provide an overall predictor of performance.[8]

TESTS   **Tests** are also frequently used to select employees. Common types used in the selection process include ability, skill, aptitude, and knowledge tests.[9] A typing test would be given to applicants for a typist's job, and swimming tests to a potential lifeguard.

INTERVIEWS   **Interviews**—talking with applicants—are perhaps the most common selection technique. Besides evaluating the applicant, the interviewer can use this occasion to promote the company. Unfortunately, despite their widespread use, interviews are rather poor predictors of job success.[10] Judgments of interviewers tend to have low or zero correlation with the later job performance of employees.

ASSESSMENT CENTERS   Finally, **assessment centers** are specially designed techniques used to select managerial employees. They attempt to simulate various parts of the managerial job, such as decision making, time management, giving feedback to subordinates, and so forth, and the potential manager performs these tasks under the observation of skilled human resource managers. The idea is that such simulations provide a good indication of how well the individual will do on the job.

Regardless of which techniques an organization uses, it must be able to demonstrate that it is not discriminating. For example, if a person who scores 100 on a selection test turns out to be a high performer, a person who scores 75 turns out to be an average performer, and a person who scores 50 turns out to be a poor performer, the organization has evidence that the test is a valid predictor of performance. If the test is unrelated to subsequent performance, however, its use is discriminatory and could result in problems for the organization.

Such discriminatory practices were the catalyst for much of the legislation that so tightly controls the human resource area today.[11] Most organizations now work hard not to discriminate in their employment practices.

Exhibit 10.4 A Job Application Blank

Application for Employment

Houghton Mifflin Company

PLEASE PRINT OR TYPE

DATE _____

POSITION FOR WHICH
YOU ARE APPLYING _____

SALARY
EXPECTATION _____

PERSONAL INFORMATION

NAME _____

PRESENT
ADDRESS _____

PERMANENT
ADDRESS _____

SOCIAL
SECURITY NO. _____   HOME PHONE NUMBER _____   WORK PHONE NUMBER _____

HOW WERE YOU REFERRED TO US? _____

SPECIAL SKILLS, ABILITIES, KNOWLEDGE, FOREIGN LANGUAGES, ETC.
(In addition to paid experience, you may also list skills gained as a volunteer.)

PROFESSIONAL REFERENCES (PLEASE INCLUDE TITLE, BUSINESS, AND TELEPHONE NUMBER)

SOURCE: Courtesy of Houghton Mifflin Company.

PRELUDE CASE UPDATE

In the Kentucky Toyota case, a new plant was to open and employees at all levels had to be recruited and selected. Recruitment was obviously external since there were no current employees, and it was relatively easy since the local economy was weak. Selection, on the other hand, was done very deliberately. Application blanks, tests, assessments in the form of simulations, and interviews were all involved.

___ **Exhibit 10.4** A Job Application Blank (cont'd) _____

NAME				

EXPERIENCE   LIST MOST CURRENT POSITION FIRST

COMPANY, ADDRESS, SUPERVISOR	DATES OF SERVICE	TITLE AND DUTIES		REASON FOR LEAVING

EDUCATION

	NAME AND ADDRESS OF SCHOOL ATTENDED	DATES ATTENDED FROM	TO	MAJOR/MINOR	DEGREE + DATE
HIGH SCHOOL					
COLLEGE OR UNIVERSITY					
POST GRADUATE					

Orientation

LEARNING CHECK

You should now be able to discuss the selection of human resources, including recruiting, selection, and orientation.

After a new employee accepts an offer to join the company, such as Bethlehem Steel or Turner Construction, he or she must go through an **orientation** procedure. Such procedures vary widely from company to company. Orientation for operating employees might simply be telling them when to come to work, when they get paid, and who to see if they have a problem. Orientation for managerial and professional employees tends to be more involved. It may take several weeks or months of work with other employees for the newcomer to become totally acquainted with all phases of the organization.

TRAINING AND DEVELOPMENT

☐ Training generally means teaching job skills, whereas development involves more general abilities.

After new employees have been recruited, selected, and oriented, the next logical step is to train and develop them. Training typically involves job skills and applies more to operating employees, whereas most developmental activities are more general in nature and are targeted to managerial employees.[12]

Assessing Training and Development Needs

Of course, before a manager can properly plan training and development activities, she or he must ascertain the training and development needs of both the employees and the organization. For example, if labor-market conditions mean that a university has to hire librarians who are not totally qualified for the job, training needs will be great.[13] If qualified employees are readily available, training needs are considerably less.

Regardless of how much formal training is necessary, employees will need at least some basic work to learn exactly how the organization requires them to perform their tasks. Managerial development, as we learned back in Chapter 1, is a long-term, ongoing process that never really stops.

Popular Training and Development Techniques

Several common techniques used for training and development are noted in Table 10.2. The key, of course, is to match the technique with the goals of the training and development effort. For example, if the goal is for employees to learn about new company procedures, assigned reading might be an effective approach. If Motorola has a goal to teach people how to relate better to others or how to make decisions more effectively, it might use role playing or case discussion groups. Training supervisors in conducting performance reviews might involve behavior modeling.[14] If the idea is to teach a physical skill such as operating a new kind of machine, vestibule or on-the-job training could be the most appropriate option. Whichever technique is used, however, it is important to get the trainees to accept the training.[15]

Rick Ridgeway/Adventure Photo

Organizations often adopt unusual approaches to training employees. This Xerox sales representative is participating in an Outward Bound Professional Development Program. She subsequently used the lessons from her experience to energize her sales team.

Evaluating the Effectiveness of Training

The final dimension of a well-managed training and development program is evaluation. Considering how much time and money companies invest in training and development, they should make sure that the goals of the program are met.[16]

TABLE 10.2 Common Training and Development Techniques

Method	Comments
Assigned Readings	Readings may or may not be specially prepared for training purposes.
Behavior Modeling Training	Use of a videotaped model displaying the correct behavior, then trainee role playing and discussion of the correct behavior. Used extensively for supervisor training in human relations.
Business Simulation	Both paper simulations (such as in-basket exercises) and computer-based business "games" are used to teach management skills.
Case Discussion	Real or fictitious cases or incidents are discussed in small groups.
Conference	Small-group discussion of selected topics, usually with the trainer as leader.
Lecture	Oral presentation of material by the trainer, with limited or no audience participation.
On the Job	Ranges from no instruction, to casual coaching by more experienced employees, to carefully structured explanation, demonstration, and supervised practice by a qualified trainer.
Programmed Instruction	Self-paced method using text or computer followed by questions and answers. Expensive to develop.
Role Playing	Trainees act out roles with other trainees, such as "boss giving performance appraisal" and "subordinate reacting to appraisal" to gain experience in human relations.
Sensitivity Training	Also called T-group and laboratory training, this is an intensive experience in a small group, wherein individuals give each other feedback and try out new behaviors. It is said to promote trust, open communication, and understanding of group dynamics.
Vestibule Training	Supervised practice on manual tasks in a separate work area where the emphasis is on safety, learning, and feedback rather than productivity.
Interactive Video	Newly emerging technique using computers and video technology.

SOURCE: Ricky W. Griffin, *Management*, 3rd ed. (Boston: Houghton Mifflin, 1990), p. 363. Copyright © Houghton Mifflin Company. Adapted by permission.

LEARNING CHECK

You should now be able to describe the assessment of training and development needs, various training and development techniques, and the importance of evaluating those techniques.

For instance, if a training program is designed to increase the proficiency of word-processing operators, the operators' performance should be measured both before and after the training program. If the program is effective, their performance should improve. Lack of improvement might suggest that the training should be revised.

Evaluation is more difficult in the case of managers, but it is not impossible. Managers who participate in many development activities and get high marks in those activities should have a good record of promotions, performance, and so forth. If this is indeed the case, then the organization's development activities appear to be on target.

PERFORMANCE APPRAISAL

☐ *Performance appraisal* is important for verifying the validity of selection methods, providing rewards fairly, and helping employees improve.

After employees have been trained and have settled into their jobs, managers usually begin to evaluate their performance. There are several purposes behind this evaluation, or **performance appraisal.** First, the organization needs evidence to justify the selection techniques it used to hire the person in the first place. Second, since performance is frequently a basis for rewards, it is important to evaluate performance so that those rewards can be provided fairly. Finally, the individual needs to know how well he or she is performing in order to improve.[17] Managers can use several different kinds of techniques for performance appraisal.

Objective Measures

Objective measures of performance appraisal are quantifiable indicators of how well the employee is doing. For instance, it may be possible to count how many units of a product an employee assembles, adjust this number for quality, and arrive at an objective index of performance. Similarly, the number of sales dollars generated by a sales representative reflects performance objectively.

Unfortunately, objective measures are often unavailable or misleading. Assembly-line workers have little control over how many units they produce, and a sales representative with a lot of major customers in his territory should have more sales than one with only a few large customers. For these reasons, managers may need to adjust objective indicators of performance in order to have a valid representation of actual performance.

Judgmental Methods

☐ A *ranking* system measures employees against one another, whereas a *rating* system compares each employee with a standard of performance.

Another common approach to performance appraisal is through **judgmental methods**—having someone, usually the employee's immediate supervisor, subjectively evaluate that person's performance via ranking or rating.

Ranking, as the term implies, means that the supervisor ranks her subordinates in a continuum from high to low performance. Such a procedure forces the manager to differentiate among high, moderate, and low performers, but it also makes feedback more difficult to deliver as each rank must be dependent, and the last person on the list may still be a solid performer.

Rating is comparing each employee with one or more absolute standards and then placing him somewhere in relation to that standard. Two rating scales are shown in Exhibit 10.5. The scales rate the individual's level of conscientiousness and degree of initiative. The manager considers the questions, judges how well the person stacks up, and then circles the appropriate numbers along the scales. Usually managers sum or average the various ratings to arrive at an overall index of performance.

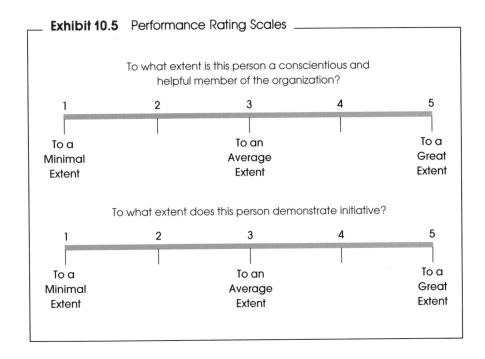

Exhibit 10.5 Performance Rating Scales

To what extent is this person a conscientious and
helpful member of the organization?

| 1 | 2 | 3 | 4 | 5 |

To a
Minimal
Extent

To an
Average
Extent

To a
Great
Extent

To what extent does this person demonstrate initiative?

| 1 | 2 | 3 | 4 | 5 |

To a
Minimal
Extent

To an
Average
Extent

To a
Great
Extent

Rating scales such as these are probably the most common kinds of performance appraisal devices currently in use, but they suffer from a number of problems. For one thing, managers are sometimes inclined to give everyone high, average, or low marks, thus failing to differentiate among them. For another thing, people tend to be influenced by an employee's recent behavior rather than by her overall level of performance over longer periods of time. Guidelines have been developed to improve the process used in rating systems,[18] and Behaviorally Anchored Rating Scales (BARS) and Behavior Observation Scales (BOS) have been developed to vastly improve the instruments used in rating systems.[19]

Management by Objectives

Management by objectives, introduced in Chapter 4 as a vehicle for managing the goal-setting process, also serves as a useful method for evaluating the performance of those managers who set the goals to begin with. For example, suppose a sales manager for Colgate-Palmolive sets a goal of increasing sales in his territory next year by 15 percent. At the end of the year, this goal provides an effective framework for performance appraisal. If sales have indeed increased by 15 percent or more, a positive performance appraisal may be in order. But if sales have increased by only 4 percent, and if the manager is directly responsible for the disappointing results, a more negative evaluation may be forthcoming.

Feedback

The final part of performance appraisal, and often the most difficult, is providing **feedback** to the employee—telling him or her the results of the appraisal.[20] Because it is often so difficult, a computer program has even been developed to assist managers with the feedback task.[21] Feedback is usually given in a private meeting between the superior and the subordinate, and typically the superior summarizes the results of the appraisal, answers any questions, suggests ways to improve, and explains the immediate consequences of the appraisal. A poor evaluation might result in no salary increase, a cutback in authority, or even a warning that the employee will be fired if things aren't turned around. In contrast, a good evaluation can lead to a raise, a bonus, a promotion, or increased responsibilities.

LEARNING CHECK

You should now be able to define performance appraisal and discuss both objective and judgmental methods, management by objectives, and feedback.

COMPENSATION AND BENEFITS

The management of compensation and benefits is another important part of the human resource process. Employees must be paid **compensation**—wages and salaries—and they usually expect to receive various kinds of benefits. The organization also often uses financial incentives to increase motivation and reward past performance.[22]

☐ *A company's wages relative to others in the local economy are known as the wage level. Wage structure is the comparison of wages for different jobs within the company.*

Wages and Salaries

The central part of compensation management involves determining wages and salaries for employees. This determination in turn consists of three parts: wage level decisions, wage structure decisions, and individual wage decisions.

TABLE 10.3
Sample Point System for Wage Determination

Compensable Factors	Points Associated with Degrees of the Factors				
	Very Little	Low	Moderate	High	Very High*
Education	20	40	60	80	100
Responsibility	20	40	70	110	160
Skill	20	40	60	80	100
Physical Demand	10	20	30	45	60

* The job evaluation committee that constructed the system believed that responsibility should be the most heavily weighted factor and physical demand the least. That is why the maximum points for these factors are different.

SOURCE: Ricky W. Griffin, *Management*, 3rd ed. (Boston: Houghton Mifflin, 1990), p. 370. Copyright © 1990 Houghton Mifflin Company. Adapted by permission.

WAGE LEVEL DECISIONS   Management's **wage level** decision is the decision about whether the organization wants to pay higher wages, the same wages, or lower wages than the prevailing rate in the industry or geographic area. If IBM decided that it wants to attract the best possible electrical engineers, it would set a policy of paying recent college graduates starting salaries that are several percentage points higher than those of other companies hiring electrical engineers. Similarly, a small manufacturer might decide to pay the same rates as other local companies and not to attract people on the basis of a high starting wage but to keep wages from being a factor that could force current employees to seek other jobs.[23]

WAGE STRUCTURE DECISIONS   Another important decision pertains to the **wage structure** within the organization. The issue here is whether Job A is worth a higher salary than Job B, or vice versa. The wage structure is usually determined through a **job evaluation**—the process of determining the relative value of jobs within the organization.[24]

Probably the most popular kind of job evaluation is the **point system**. First a committee of workers and managers determines what factors will be used to differentiate and characterize jobs. As shown in Table 10.3, they might include such factors as education, responsibility, skill, and physical demand. Then each factor is assigned points, depending on its perceived importance. For example, points awarded for education required to perform the job might range from 20 to 100.

Table 10.4 shows how these points might then be allocated for three jobs: secretary, office manager, and janitor. In the table the job of office manager warrants 80 points for education needed, 70 for responsibility, 60 for skill, and only 20 for physical demand. Its total, then, is 230 points. This job should therefore be worth more than the secretarial job, which totals 200 points. It in turn is worth more than the janitorial job, with 145 points.

TABLE 10.4
An Application of the Point System

Compensable Factors	Job		
	Secretary II	*Office Manager*	*Janitor*
Education	Moderate = 60	High = 80	Very low = 20
Responsibility	Low = 40	Moderate = 70	Low = 40
Skill	High = 80	Moderate = 60	Low = 40
Physical Demand	Low = 20	Low = 20	High = 45
Total points	200	230	145

The job analysis committee carefully reviews the content of each job and decides what degree of each factor best describes the job.

SOURCE: Ricky W. Griffin, *Management*, 3rd ed. (Boston: Houghton Mifflin, 1990), p. 370. Copyright © 1990 Houghton Mifflin Company. Used by permission.

INDIVIDUAL WAGE DECISIONS   Finally, the manager must address individual wage decisions—deciding how much each person within a job classification is to be paid. Most organizations set wage ranges for jobs within certain point ranges; for instance, a company might decide to pay people $6 to $7 an hour for jobs worth 350 and 375 points. Initial wages are then set according to the employee's experience. A person who is just starting his career might be paid $6, whereas a more experienced person receives, say, $6.30. Later, wages are adjusted according to seniority and/or performance: the new employee might get a fifteen-cents-an-hour raise after six months and another thirty-cent raise for very good performance, bringing his total to $6.45 an hour, whereas the other employee might be given the fifteen-cent raise after six months but no additional increase for performance.

Benefits

☐ Payments to employees other than wages or salaries are known as *benefits*.

Another important part of compensation is the benefit package to be provided. **Benefits,** which are payments other than wages or salaries, add substantial costs to the total compensation received by employees, averaging 36.6 percent or more above the cost of wages and salaries.[25] Common benefits include health, dental disability, and life insurance coverage for the employee (and sometimes her family), and costs for these may be borne entirely by the organization or shared with the employee. Employees also usually receive some pay for time when they don't work, such as vacations, sick days, and holidays. Retirement programs are also common benefits. Not as prevalent but still provided by some organizations are benefits such as counseling programs, physi-

© James Schnepf/Courtesy Quad/Graphics

Organizations provide their employees with many different kinds of benefits. One fairly new benefit is on-site recreational or fitness facilities. Quad/Graphics Inc., a Wisconsin-based printer, provides nonsalary benefits for its employees totaling 40 percent of direct compensation. Founder Harry V. Quadracci is shown here in the company gym.

cal fitness programs, credit unions, and tuition reimbursement for educational expenses related to the job.

Clearly, the benefit package is significant, for several reasons. In addition to representing a major cost to the organization, it is an important factor in attracting and retaining employees. Some organizations have experimented with what is called a "cafeteria benefits package"; under such an arrangement, each benefit is priced and employees can choose those they want within a total price. Therefore a married worker with several children can concentrate her benefits on insurance programs, a single employee can choose more vacation time, and an older worker can put more into retirement. Such programs are expensive to administer but are an attractive feature to many employees.[26]

LABOR RELATIONS

The final aspect of human resource management to be discussed here is **labor relations**, a term that generally refers to dealing with employees when they are organized in a labor union.[27] This section first describes how unions are formed and then addresses collective bargaining.

How Unions Are Formed

☐ The process of forming a union is carefully defined by the government, which created the National Labor Relations Board (NLRB) to oversee union creation.

Given the turbulent history of union-management relations, it should come as no surprise that government regulation closely defines the processes involved in forming a union.[28] The National Labor Relations Board (NLRB) was created to oversee these processes.

The actual steps in forming a union are summarized in Exhibit 10.6. First, someone must generate interest among employees; either disgruntled employees or representatives of large national unions might initiate this action. Next, employees must collect signatures on what are called authorization cards, which indicate that the individuals who sign them believe that an election should be held to determine whether employees are interested in unionization. If fewer than 30 percent of the employees sign the cards, the process ends. If 30 percent or more sign, however, the NLRB conducts an election. It takes only a simple majority of those who vote, not of all eligible employees, to certify the union. If the vote fails, the process ends, but if the vote succeeds, the union is officially certified by the NLRB. It then recruits members and elects officers. Members pay dues (to cover administrative costs) and expect to gain improved employment conditions as a result. After the membership is signed up, the union sets out to negotiate a labor contract with management. Either a contract is agreed on or the union takes various job actions, such as strikes, work slowdowns, and so forth. The contract also specifies a grievance procedure that will be used to settle disputes during the term of the contract.[29]

Obviously, management prefers employees not to belong to unions. In general, the best way to avoid unionization is to treat employees fairly and to give them a voice in how the workplace is governed. Establishing clear guidelines

Exhibit 10.6   How Unions Are Created

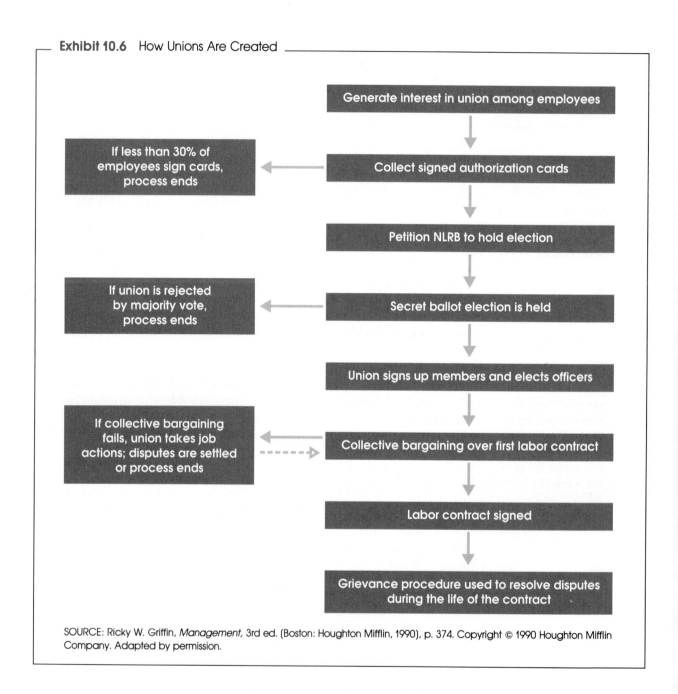

SOURCE: Ricky W. Griffin, *Management,* 3rd ed. (Boston: Houghton Mifflin, 1990), p. 374. Copyright © 1990 Houghton Mifflin Company. Adapted by permission.

for performance appraisals, reward allocations, and promotions, avoiding favoritism, and creating a mechanism for handling disputes are frequently cited ways to help make employees feel that they don't need unions.[30] As *Management Today: Ethical Dilemmas of Management* shows, however, even the best efforts to involve employees can sometimes cause problems. But unions can help management and employees resolve their differences through the formal collective bargaining process, which is our next topic.

ETHICAL DILEMMAS OF MANAGEMENT

Problems in Paradise

One aspect of the staffing process that continues to receive attention is employee involvement or participation. Although not a new idea, it has been having some interesting impacts on both managers and workers because of the clash in value systems that can result.

One of the growing uses of employee involvement is semi-autonomous work teams. Although such teams vary from company to company, most involve small groups of workers who are cross-trained so that they can rotate among jobs to produce a product or service with virtually no supervision. The need for first-level supervisors is then reduced, with corresponding reductions in managers at all levels. Moreover, organizations using such teams generally outperform those doing similar work using more conventional organizational arrangements.

Managers, however, lose some control, especially personal control over the activities of the work group. Managers who value this personal control are very much opposed to employment involvement; those who are not so concerned about personal control support it. Workers have similar value differences. Some feel that the cross-training and rotation are merely used by management to get more for its money than it is paying for. Others feel that it makes their jobs more interesting and challenging.

Where trust is low and alienation high, these differences in value systems can lead to behavior that might otherwise not occur. Managers may try to make involvement activities fail by burdening them with documentation requirements or nuisance reporting to destroy their spread in an organization. Workers may try to erode the effectiveness of such efforts by spreading rumors about how management is using employee involvement to eradicate unions or the like. Clearly, unethical practices can arise when such conflicts in values exist.

SOURCES: Eric Sundstrom, Kenneth P. De Meuse, and David Futrell, "Work Teams: Applications and Effectiveness," *American Psychologist*, February 1, 1990, pp. 120–133; "The Payoff from Teamwork," *Business Week*, July 10, 1989, pp. 56–62; Bernard Portis and Neil Hill, "Improving Organization Effectiveness Through Employee Involvement," *Business Quarterly*, Winter 1989, pp. 58–63; Susan G. Clark, "Employee Involvement Programs: Will "Win/Win" Work?" *National Civic Review*, March 1, 1989, pp. 94–102.

PRELUDE CASE UPDATE

Toyota's culture, with its stress on teamwork and versatility, helps the company keep satisfied employees. The high standards make them feel proud to be accepted, and the cooperative work environment helps them feel that they are important. All of this, in turn, creates an environment in which unions are not very likely to form.

◻ Management and union officials reach agreement on wages, layoff policies, and the like through *collective bargaining*, which results in a mutually binding contract.

Collective Bargaining

Collective bargaining is a discussion process between union and management that focuses on agreeing to a written contract that will cover all relevant aspects of the relationship between the organization and members of the union.[31] In particular, it defines wages, work hours, promotion and layoff policies, benefits, and decision rules for allocating overtime, vacation time, and rest breaks. The union also frequently pushes for a security clause, which is designed to protect the union by requiring that all new employees join the union and that all current employees remain members. In turn, management pushes for a stipulation that it has total control over any and all areas not specifically covered in the contract.

In most cases, strikes are prohibited during the term of the contract, and any strikes that do occur are called wildcat strikes and do not have the official endorsement of the union. Of course, the union can call strikes after the existing contract has expired and when the union and management representatives cannot agree on a new one.

DISCIPLINE Labor contracts frequently devote considerable attention to discipline. Everyone seems to agree that management can discipline employees for just cause, but disputes frequently arise over the meaning of "just cause." In general, representatives make an effort to define work rules very clearly and to set penalties for violating those rules. For example, the first time an employee is late he might receive a reminder about work hours; the second time a note might go in his file; a third offense could lead to a short suspension without pay. If everyone knows the rules and the penalties for breaking them, there will be few legitimate complaints.[32]

Labor relations are an important consideration for all organizations. After a bitter, 9-month strike, the United Mine Workers recently signed a new labor contract with the Pittston Co., a large coal mining company. Shown here are Pittston CEO Paul Douglas, Labor Secretary Elizabeth Dole, UMW President Richard Trumpka, and special mediator W. J. Usery.

GRIEVANCE PROCEDURE Of course, no contract is perfect, and differences of opinion are inevitable. Thus the contract also specifies procedures that everyone will follow to resolve disputes. An employee who feels mistreated often files a written **grievance** with the union and discusses it with her supervisor. If the problem cannot be resolved, union officials and higher-level managers become involved. Ultimately, it may be necessary to make use of an **arbitrator**—a labor law specialist jointly paid by the union and the organization. The arbitrator listens to both sides of the argument, studies the contract, and makes a decision as to how the dispute is to be settled, and both the union and management agree to abide by his or her ruling.

Chapter Summary

Staffing is the process of procuring and managing the human resources an organization needs to accomplish its goals.

Human resource planning is the first phase of the staffing process and involves job analysis, forecasting human resource supply and demand, and matching supply with demand. Job analysis is the systematic collection and recording of information about jobs in the organization resulting in descriptions of jobs and specifications that explain what kind of person is needed for them. With this information forecasts of the demand for and supply of human resources are made. If supply exceeds demand, she or he must make plans to reduce employment through attrition, layoffs, terminations, and early retirements. If demand exceeds supply, the manager must engage in the next process, selection.

The selection phase of human resource management consists of recruiting, selecting, and orienting employees. Recruiting is the process of attracting a pool of qualified applicants interested in working for the organization. Selection is choosing which applicants to hire, using techniques such as application blanks, tests, interviews, and assessment centers. Orientation is the procedure whereby new employees are brought into and informed about the company, its purpose, and their job.

Training is usually job specific, whereas development is more general. Before engaging in such activities, the organization should determine how much and what kinds of training are needed. Training and development involve a wide range of techniques, including role playing, reading, and on-the-job training, and all training and development activities should be evaluated in terms of effectiveness (Do they satisfy the need?) and efficiency (Are they worth the cost?).

Performance appraisal—the evaluation of each employee's performance—is used to justify the selection techniques used, to provide a basis for reward distribution, and to give feedback to the employee. Where employees exert considerable control over their work, the best measures are objective, quantifiable indicators such as units assembled or dollars sold. In other cases judgmental methods such as ranking or rating tend to be used. One approach that has some value when individuals have a fair amount of control over their jobs is management by objectives (MBO), whereby performance is appraised by how well the objectives have been accomplished.

The determination of compensation—wages and salaries—for employees is central to management and involves three types of decisions: wage level, wage structure, and individual wage decisions. Wage level decisions are external; wage structure decisions are internal. Job evaluation is the process used to determine the relative value of jobs within an organization. Benefits are yet another part of compensation management. Health care, dental care, disability and/or life insurance, vacations, sick leave, and holidays are all part of benefits that must be managed.

Labor relations refers to dealing with employees when they are organized into a labor union. The best way to avoid unions is by making them unnecessary. This means treating employees fairly, having them participate in setting clear guidelines for performance appraisal, reward allocation, and personnel decisions, and creating a mechanism for handling disputes. Negotiating a contract—collective bargaining—may be a complex process, since all relevant aspects of the relationship between the organization and members of the union are covered in such contracts.

The Manager's Vocabulary

staffing	ranking
job analysis	rating
job description	management by
job specification	objectives
recruiting	feedback
selection	compensation
application blanks	wage level
tests	wage structure
interviews	job evaluation
assessment centers	point system
orientation	benefits
performance appraisal	labor relations
objective measures of	collective bargaining
performance appraisal	grievance
judgmental methods of	arbitrator
performance appraisal	

Prelude Case Wrap-up

Our Prelude Case for this chapter describes Toyota's staffing process using its Kentucky plant as an example. Even for production workers, a long, careful process was followed. Hours and hours of tests were used to examine general intelligence, literacy, technical knowledge and skills, mathematical skills, and the like. Following these tests, groups used simulation exercises in which they discussed real problems facing Toyota and the automobile industry. During these exercises, evaluators assessed each applicant in terms of interpersonal skills and job knowledge. Finally, interviews were held to select the final applicants.

The reason Toyota is so careful in its staffing process is that it wants to preserve its organizational culture. That culture is built around deliberate decisions quickly implemented, and it emphasizes teamwork, organizational loyalty, and versatility. The careful staffing process ensures that each of these major components of the culture are assessed for each applicant. Hence, those finally hired are those most likely to be able to be strong team players, loyal to the organization, and versatile in their knowledge and skills.

Toyota's test batteries are also designed to assess applicants' willingness to continue learning on the job. Toyota expects its personnel to continue to keep up to date with the latest developments in technology that affect how they do their tasks. The company sponsors technical training to ensure that such continued learning does indeed take place.

Whether or not Toyota will continue to follow such deliberate decision making as it opens its European plants remains to be seen. The pressure of "Europe 1992"—a unified market with greater barriers to entry—has rushed plant location and expansion decisions for many companies, including Toyota. Toyota went from seeking possible sites around December of 1988 to selecting a particular site in April 1989. Further, the move to expand its line into the luxury car market may demand more rapid responsiveness to market forces than it would normally follow.

Prelude Case Questions

1. Which concepts presented in this chapter are illustrated in the Toyota case? Cite specific examples.
2. What are the major characteristics of the staffing process at Toyota?
3. What are the strengths and weaknesses of the staffing process at Toyota? How might the weaknesses be offset?
4. What is the organizational culture at Toyota? Do you feel that this culture will enable Toyota to continue to be successful in the future? Why or why not?

Discussion Questions

Review Questions

1. What are the major components to human resource planning? How are they related?
2. What is selection? What are some of the techniques used in it?
3. What are popular training and development techniques? Where might each be appropriate to use?
4. What are some methods used in performance appraisal? What are the advantages and disadvantages of each?
5. How are unions formed?

Analysis Questions

1. What are the advantages and disadvantages of internal and external recruiting? Which do you feel is best in the long term? Why?
2. How can you determine whether or not a particular technique is valid for selection? What are the costs and benefits of using invalid techniques?
3. An objective measure of performance for a research chemist might be "number of patents obtained." Why might this be a poor method for evaluating the chemist's performance? What might be a better approach?
4. Do you think wages or salaries are more important than benefits? Why or why not?
5. Defend this statement: "Unions would not exist if it weren't for poor management."

Application Questions and Exercises

1. Think of a job with which you are familiar (stock clerk in a grocery store, delivery person for a newspaper, office worker, check-out clerk, etc.) and write a job description and specifications for that job. Now try to get an actual description and specification for that job from the appropriate organization. Compare the two.
2. How are courses evaluated at your institution? What are the advantages and disadvantages of the methods used? (Be sure to consider the standpoints of the institution, instructors, and students.)
3. Locate wage and salary data for managers in well-known organizations, such as a top labor union, a major university, a big business firm, a major state government agency, and so on. What might account for the kinds of differences you observe?
4. Interview a local business manager to determine what forms of performance appraisal he or she has used. Which does he or she prefer? Why?
5. Locate someone (it could be yourself) who has belonged to a union. Why did that person (or you) join the union? If you haven't joined a union, do you think that you would? Why or why not?

ENHANCEMENT CASE

AT&T'S NEW PEOPLE APPROACH

In 1989 the U.S. government awarded the business for its new telecommunications system—Federal Telecommunications System 2000. That business totaled over $25 billion, the largest nonmilitary contract in U.S. history. During the bidding process and the subsequent lobbying, AT&T was accused of predatory pricing, that is, pricing below its direct costs in an effort to drive others out of the market. Despite those charges, AT&T won 60 percent of the business.

In this bidding process, AT&T formed a partnership with the Boeing Corporation. The combination of contacts with government and knowledge about communications as well as extensive production and distribution systems made it a logical partnership. This sort of partnership is just one aspect of what makes AT&T a complex organization, one that is generally regarded as the largest diversified service company in America.

AT&T consists of nineteen business units that are organized along major product lines: switching systems, computers, network computing systems, business communications, and the like. In terms of revenues it is huge. AT&T has over seven times the revenues of MCI, its nearest competitor, and ten times those of US Sprint, the third-place firm. Relative to the "Baby Bells," or regional companies, AT&T is also large. Its revenues are three times those of Bell South, Nynex, or Bell Atlantic and about four times those of American Information Technologies, Pacific Telesis Group, US West, or Southwestern Bell.

AT&T continues to grow more complex. In addition to its partnership with Boeing, it signed an accord with Italy's Italtel that will make Italtel more competitive internationally and will give AT&T a toehold in the expanding European market. AT&T also purchased Paradyne Corporation, a Florida company that is a leading manufacturer of modems (devices that let computers communicate over non-digital telephone lines).

To accomplish all of this, the corporate culture is being radically changed. First, decision making is being decentralized so that the managers responsible for the product line units now have the authority to make major decisions regarding those units. Second, the "not invented here" syndrome is being replaced so that ideas are no longer rejected just because they come from outside the firm. Each of these changes necessitates having a strong staffing process. Managers must be developed, promoted, or hired who can handle the increased uncertainty associated with a more decentralized organization. Likewise, personnel must be developed, transferred, or hired to staff new organizational arrangements.

A strong staffing process becomes even more important when one considers that AT&T has made some of the most significant Equal Employment Opportunity Commission (EEOC) settlements of all times. It had to pay nearly $75 million to settle two EEOC cases during the late 1970s. In addition, it had to hire and promote more women and minorities, especially into managerial positions, during the late 1970s and early 1980s. The number of women and minorities in second-level or higher managerial positions was increased dramatically, as was the number of men in jobs previously held mostly by women (clerical workers and telephone operators). This meant that AT&T was employing newer groups in key positions as it began to develop a new organizational culture and expand its operations.

SOURCES: Peter T. Rux, "T1 Testing and the Standard Answer," *Telephone Engineer and Management*, January 1990, pp. 50–58; "Contract War Dragged On for Months," *USA Today*, December 8, 1989, pp. 1B–2B; Andrew Kupfer, "Bob Allen Rattles the Cages at AT&T," *Fortune*, June 19, 1989, pp. 58–61, 64–65; Kenneth Labich, "Was Breaking Up AT&T a Good Idea?" *Fortune*, January 2, 1989, pp. 82–87; "AT&T and Italy's Italtel Sign Accord, Giving U.S. Giant a Toehold in Europe," *The Wall Street Journal*, June 6, 1989, p. B12; Sharon R. King, "At the Crossroads," *Black Enterprise*, August 1988, pp. 45–48ff; Carol J. Loomis, "AT&T in the Throes of 'Equal Employment,'" *Fortune*, January 15, 1979, pp. 44–48ff.

Enhancement Case Questions

1. Do you think the combination of newer groups in management and striving to evolve a new culture will be beneficial to AT&T? Why or why not?
2. Describe the AT&T organization. What components of design can you identify? How might staffing be involved with each of them?
3. What are the strengths and weaknesses of staffing at AT&T? How might it reduce the weaknesses?
4. Do you feel that AT&T will continue to be successful in each of its main businesses? Why or why not?

Chapter Notes

1. See Wendell L. French, *Managing Human Resources* (Boston: Houghton Mifflin, 1986), for a more detailed treatment of the staffing process.
2. David P. Twomey, *A Concise Guide to Employment Law* (Dallas: Southwestern, 1986).
3. Benjamin Schneider, "Strategic Job Analysis," *Human Resource Management*, Spring 1989, pp. 51–60.
4. Norman Scarborough and Thomas W. Zimmerer, "Human Resource Forecasting: Why and Where to Begin," *Personnel Administrator*, May 1982, pp. 55–61. See also Randall S. Schuler, "Scanning the Environment: Planning for Human Resource Management and Organizational Change," *Human Resource Planning*, October 1989, pp. 257–276.
5. Ruth G. Shaeffer, "Matching International Business Growth and International Management Development," *Human Resource Planning*, January 1989, pp. 29–36.
6. Michael R. Carrell and Frank E. Kuzmits, *Personnel: Human Resource Management*, 3rd ed. (New York: Merrill, 1989).
7. Laura M. Herren, "The Right Technology for Recruiting in the '90," *Personnel Administrator*, April 1989, pp. 48–53.
8. James J. Asher, "The Biographical Item: Can It Be Improved?" *Personnel Psychology*, Summer 1972, pp. 251–269.
9. Frank L. Schmidt and John E. Hunter, "Employment Testing: Old Theories and New Research Findings," *American Psychologist*, October 1981, pp. 1128–1137.

10. Neal Schmidt, "Social and Situational Determinants of Interview Decisions: Implications for the Employment Interview," *Personnel Psychology*, Spring 1976, pp. 79–102.

11. For an interesting look at some of the legal cases regarding selection, see Kathryn E. Buckner, Hubert S. Feild, and William Holley, Jr., "The Relationship of Legal Case Characteristics with the Outcomes of Personnel Selection Court Cases," *Labor Law Journal*, January 1990, pp. 31–40. For a review of recent research on selection, see Edwin A. Fleishman, "Some New Frontiers in Personnel Selection Research," *Personnel Psychology*, Winter 1988, pp. 679–702.

12. Kenneth N. Wexley and Gary P. Latham, *Developing and Training Human Resources in Organizations* (Glenview, Ill.: Scott, Foresman, 1981).

13. Scott B. Mandernack, "An Assessment of Education and Training Needs for Bibliographic Instruction Librarians," *Journal of Education for Library and Information*, Winter 1990, pp. 193–205. See also Michael Gent and Gregory Del'Omo, "The Needs Assessment Solution: Analyzing Your Environment to Find Out How Much, If Any, New Training Is Needed," *Personnel Administrator*, July 1989, pp. 82–85.

14. William M. Fox, "Getting the Most from Behavior Modeling Training," *National Productivity Review*, Summer 1988, pp. 238–245.

15. "Training 101: How to Win Closure and Influence People," *Training and Development Journal*, January 1990, pp. 31–35.

16. Charles D. Pringle and Peter Wright, "An Empirical Examination of the Relative Effectiveness of Supervisory Training Programs," *American Business Review*, January 1990, pp. 1–7, and Stewart J. Black and Mark Mehdenhall, "Cross-Cultural Training Effectiveness: A Review and a Theoretical Framework for Future Research," *Academy of Management Review*, January 1990, pp. 113–136.

17. Jeanette N. Cleveland, Kevin R. Murphy, and Richard E. Williams, "Multiple Uses of Performance Appraisal: Prevalence and Correlates," *Journal of Applied Psychology*, February 1989, pp. 130–135, and Richard I. Henderson, *Performance Appraisal* (Reston, Va.: Reston Publishing, 1984).

18. William M. Fox, "Improving Performance Appraisal Systems," *National Productivity Review*, Winter 1987–1988, pp. 20–27.

19. Gary P. Latham and Kenneth N. Wexley, *Increasing Productivity Through Performance Appraisal* (Reading, Mass.: Addison-Wesley, 1981.

20. Timothy M. Downs, "Predictors of Communication Satisfaction During Performance Appraisal Interviews," *Management Communication Quarterly*, February 1990, pp. 334–354, and James R. Larson, Jr., "The Dynamic Interplay Between Employees' Feedback-Seeking Strategies and Supervisors' Delivery of Performance Feedback," *Academy of Management Review*, July 1989, pp. 408–422.

21. Peter H. Lewis, "I'm Sorry; My Machine Doesn't Like Your Work," *New York Times*, February 4, 1990, p. F27.

22. Charles M. Cumming, "Total Compensation: An Approach to Pay Structure Design," *Compensation and Benefits Review*, January 1989, pp. 37–42, and Allan N. Nash and Stephen J. Carroll, *The Management of Compensation* (Monterey, Calif.: Brooks Cole, 1975).

23. Nash and Carroll, *The Management of Compensation*.

24. "Executive Pay," *Business Week*, May 1, 1989, pp. 46–47, and Thomas H. Patten, Jr., *Employee Compensation and Incentive Plans* (New York: Free Press, 1977).

25. U.S. Chamber of Commerce, *Employee Benefits 1979* (Washington, D.C.: U.S. Government Printing Office, 1980).

26. National Technical Services Unit, *Flexible Compensation: Giving Employees a Choice* (Washington, D.C.: Coopers & Lybrand, 1983).

27. For a general treatment, see Benjamin J. Taylor and Fred Witney, *Labor Relations Law*, 3rd ed. (Englewood Cliffs, N.J.: Prentice-Hall, 1979). For a view of what may be expected in the future, see "Peter Drucker Looks at Unions' Future," *Industry Week*, March 23, 1989, pp. 16–20.

28. See Casey Ichniowski and Jeffrey S. Zax, "Today's Associations, Tomorrow's Unions," *Industrial and Labor Relations Review*, January 1990, pp. 191–208, and French, *Managing Human Resources*.

29. See Taylor and Witney, *Labor Relations Law*.

30. James Rand, "Preventive Maintenance Techniques for Staying Union Free," *Personnel Journal*, June 1980, pp. 497–508.

31. Taylor and Witney, *Labor Relations Law*.

32. Ibid.

CHAPTER OUTLINE

I. **The Nature of Information Systems**
   A. Information Systems and the Manager's Job
   B. Effective Information

II. **Basic Components of Information Systems**

III. **Developing Information Systems**
   A. Information System Needs
   B. Kinds of Information Systems
   C. Matching Needs and Systems

IV. **Managing Information Systems**
   A. Integrating Systems
   B. Using Systems

V. **Information Systems and Organizations**
   A. Effects
   B. Limitations

VI. **New Information Technologies**
   A. Computer Software
   B. Telecommunications
   C. Artificial Intelligence
   D. Hypertext

CHAPTER

11

After studying this chapter you should be able to

1. Describe the nature of information systems, including their effect on the manager's job and the characteristics of effective information.

2. Identify the basic components of information systems.

3. Discuss how to determine information system needs, the kinds of information systems available, and how to match needs with systems.

4. Discuss the importance of integrating and using effective information systems.

5. Describe the impact of information systems on organizations.

6. Describe new information technologies.

Information Systems

BENETTON'S INSTANT INFORMATION SYSTEM

Italy's Benetton Group began in 1955 in Treviso (near Venice) when Luciano Benetton talked his sister into letting him sell the sweaters she was knitting to stores. In the early 1960s, Luciano decided to focus distribution through specialized knitwear outlets. Then, in 1965, the company was formally organized and opened its first factory. In 1967 the first Benetton store opened, and its reputation as a trendy fashion house began.

Benetton's strategy is oriented toward the customer rather than the product, and the organization is designed with that same focus. But it could not maintain this focus without its information system. Benetton's information flows are computerized to ensure a rapid response to changes in markets. For example, a certain proportion of Benetton's products are kept uncolored so that as reports arrive from retail stores identifying which colors are selling best, those products can quickly be colored at production centers and sold to meet the demand. In addi-

tion, the company's manufacturing operation is highly automated and flexible so that it can switch with minimal inefficiency between garment types, styles, and colors. This approach not only makes Benetton more responsive to customers but also enables store managers to have lower inventory-carrying costs.

In its major markets, Benetton is organized into numerous regions, each of which is managed by an agent. The agents show new products to store owners, take orders, select shopkeepers and store managers, and transmit information back to Benetton headquarters for analysis. The headquarters provides standards encompassing everything from window displays to merchandising right down to how to fold sweaters for display.

Benetton's system of information, then, gathers almost instant feedback about what is selling in its stores throughout the world; assists in providing flexibility in manufacturing through direct factory linkages that, in some in-

stances, can be immediately translated into production plans; and facilitates rapid order turnaround. These three characteristics enable Benetton to get a wide variety and a range of styles and colors for products whose life cycles may be less than a full season long.

Under this system, sales forecasting is replaced by virtually "real time" sales information. Speed, however, cannot supersede accuracy at Benetton. If the data are incorrect, errors cannot simply be reworked or shipped to some other area—the data must be both fast and accurate at all times. In the information systems used by many other firms, the flow of information proceeds step by step; although an error has more chances of being detected, it also runs the risk of being compounded. At Benetton, the flow is direct so that errors will not grow unnecessarily, but there is also a smaller chance of detection. New developments in remote computer systems and telecommunications that improve data transmission over long distances are obviously

G. Giansanti/SYGMA

Benetton has become one of the largest specialty retailers in the world. The Benetton family, shown here at their headquarters in Italy, is actively involved in all phases of the firm's operations. A key ingredient to the success of Benetton is the company's elaborate information system. Data from individual stores, like the Florida store pictured here, is transmitted to manufacturing facilities regularly and used in making decisions about new product lines, restocking popular items, and identifying the best colors and sizes.

John S. Abbott

of great value to organizations such as Benetton.

In mid-1989, Benetton began selling its stock directly on Wall Street. The initial offering, which was valued at around $150 million on the New York Stock Exchange, did reasonably well considering the image problem Benetton was having at that time. Its margins had flattened as a result of a gen-eral turndown in retail sales, several store managers had brought lawsuits against the company claiming that franchise laws had been violated, and the U.S. Federal Trade Commission was also looking into those charges. Nevertheless, Benetton seemed to do well with its offering and moved to enter the Tokyo market as well.

Benetton is now branching out into financial services through an affiliate. However, the hard-sell corporate culture behind the tightly-controlled family firm remains unchanged. Since this culture has met with some opposition in retailing, the success of Benetton in financial services is not ensured, despite its magnificent information system.

SOURCES: "Fashionable Tech: How Benetton Keeps Costs Down," *Information Week*, February 12, 1990, pp. 24–25; "Benetton Targets a New Customer—Wall Street," *Business Week*, May 29, 1989, pp. 32–33; Stella Shamoon, "From Fabrics to Finance," *The Banker*, February 1989, pp. 20–26; Janette Martin, "Benetton's IS Instinct," *Datamation*, July 1, 1989, pp. 68/15–68/16; "Why Some Benetton Shopkeepers Are Losing Their Shirts," *Business Week*, March 14, 1988, pp. 78–79; Alan Zakon and Richard W. Winger, "Consumer Draw: From Mass Markets to Variety," *Management Review*, April 1987, pp. 20–27.

Benetton has obtained tremendous success by improving its flow of information about customers' tastes and preferences. It found that rapid, accurate information transmitted directly from retail centers to production centers enabled it to respond to its customers even in a highly volatile market. The importance of information systems, then, would seem apparent. Information systems much like those at Benetton could obviously be used by many other organizations. Consider the following:

❑ Any retail organization could use such systems to monitor sales and move merchandise accordingly.

❑ The systems could be used in service industries to more nearly match the needs of customers with the availability of personnel and supplies.

❑ They could be used in transportation firms to better schedule aircraft, trucks, and other vehicles.

❑ Banks and other financial organizations could use such information to better monitor extensive holdings and transfers of funds.

This chapter discusses another aspect of organization design—information and information systems that are useful to managers. The nature and basic components of information systems are described first. Then the chapter examines how various information systems are designed to match managers' needs. Managing information systems is discussed next, along with the impact of these systems on organizations. Finally, technological developments that are changing the nature of information systems are briefly described.

THE NATURE OF INFORMATION SYSTEMS

❑ *Data* are unorganized facts and figures, whereas *information* consists of data organized in a meaningful way.

Information consists of data organized in a meaningful way. **Data** are merely facts and figures—unorganized pieces of information.[1] As indicated in Exhibit 11.1, they are useless until they are processed and organized in some way. If the Dial Corporation, for example, has a list of figures that show the monthly sales for a product, those data are made more useful—changed into information—when they are analyzed and organized to show seasonal fluctuations and annual trends.

Remember from Chapter 2 that a **system** is an interrelated set of elements that function as a whole. A system, then, consists of a set of components so arranged as to accomplish some purpose. If Dial built a system to produce marketing reports from its sales data, it would have built an information system. If it further arranged for those reports to automatically go to managers who needed the information, it would have a management information system such as those introduced in Chapter 2. The keys to systems, then, are interrelatedness and purpose. An information system must accomplish a purpose through the interaction of its component parts.

Exhibit 11.1 Data and Information

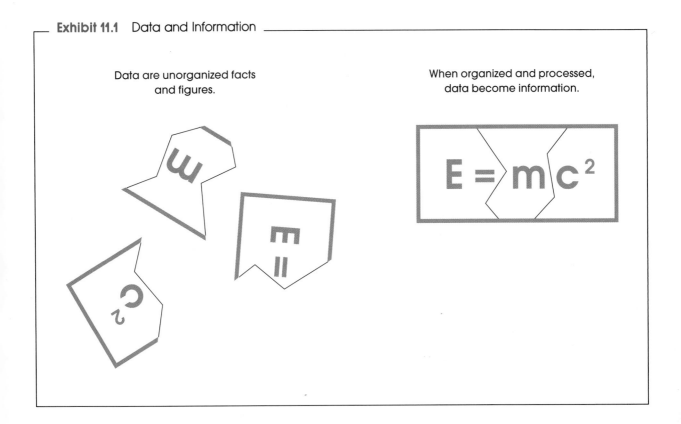

Data are unorganized facts
and figures.

When organized and processed,
data become information.

$$E = mc^2$$

Information Systems and the Manager's Job

The manager's job was discussed in Chapter 1 as consisting of functions, roles, and skills. Managers have always had to be skilled in using information. The nature and importance of information, however, has changed dramatically in recent years because the amount and variety of data coming to managers have grown tremendously. Managers, therefore, have had to become information processors. They have to decide which information to combine to form new information, which information to discard, which to pass along to others, which to put to immediate use, and which to retain for possible use later.

Susan Kidder, an accounting manager for a medium-sized manufacturing firm, could serve as an example. During the course of her normal day, Susan participates in formal and informal meetings on both job- and non-job-related topics. In addition, she receives letters, memos, notes, and other forms of written communication, she gets and makes telephone calls, and she may send or receive a FAX (electronic facsimile) message or use her company's electronic mail (EMail) system. All of the data and information she receives from all of these different sources must be processed in some way.

Effective Information

All managers use information, and the information they get should be effective; that is, it should provide them with what they need to carry out their tasks successfully. To be effective, information must be accurate, timely, complete, and relevant.[2]

These characteristics seem obvious. Yet time after time managers make decisions based on information that is inaccurate. For example, the Japanese overbid for a piece of land in Great Britain and then found that they could not use it because a building on it had been declared historic. The information they had used was inaccurate.[3] Benetton's computerized information system clearly gives timely and complete information that paper systems or centralized systems could not provide. Knowing only the profit per item, for instance, is not enough for deciding how many multiple items to stock, since a product that is less profitable per unit may sell far more units and hence earn more total profit for the firm. Finally, information must be relevant. Data or information on sales in one region may not be highly relevant to sales managers in other regions, and yet many small-business managers try to function with just such irrelevant information on the mistaken assumption that it is better than no information at all.

BASIC COMPONENTS OF INFORMATION SYSTEMS

Every information system has five basic interrelated components. There must be some way to get the data into the system, to analyze or process the data, to store the data and information, and to make the information available to users, as well as some overall control of the system itself. In a simple, noncomputerized system, the data are recorded on paper forms or memoranda that are stored somewhere (boxes, drawers, file cabinets). The analysis is done by people, who then prepare reports that are sent to those who need them. Control is basically by exception; that is, once the system is in place it continues as is unless a problem is detected.

A computerized information system, on the other hand, would look like that shown in Exhibit 11.2. Getting the data into the system involves one or more **input devices.** Analysis and processing are done by a **central processor.** Storage is also accomplished through one or more of several media; in many cases more than one medium is used in case something should happen to one storage device. The information is made available to users through a variety of **output devices.** The central processor and these devices are known as the computer *hardware. Software* refers to the instructions (programs) that enable the hardware to function. Finally, the control system usually involves some form of computer software as well as human monitoring to ensure that the software and the system are functioning as planned.

Exhibit 11.2   Basic Components of Computerized Information Systems

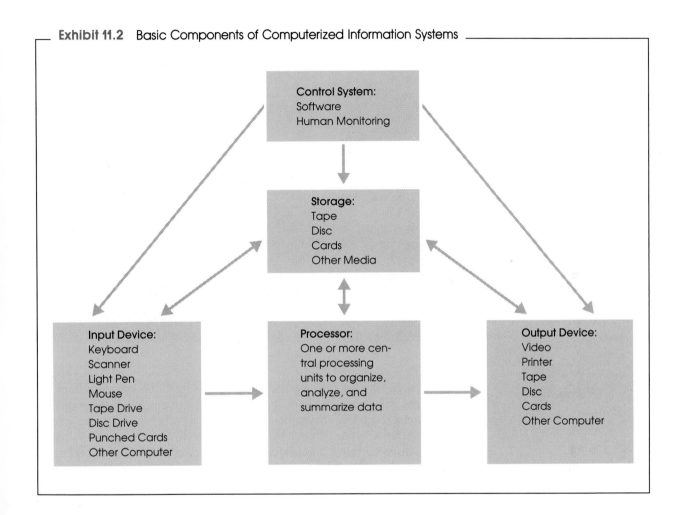

DEVELOPING INFORMATION SYSTEMS

The purpose of an information system is to ensure that proper information is available when needed so that managers do not have to rely on chance or guesswork.[4] Developing a good information system involves knowing the information system needs as well as the kinds of systems that exist or might be developed in the future.

☐ The needs of an organization for information are termed its *information system needs*.

Information System Needs

The **information system needs** of an organization are determined by the kind of organization, its environment, and its size. A high-technology organization,

Compaq Computer Corporation

Information systems are useful in a variety of settings. Frank Herzog, play-by-play announcer for the Washington Redskins NFL football team, uses a system developed by Compaq to retrieve player statistics, schedule his personal activities, budget, write memos, and prepare expense reports.

for instance, has greater information system needs than does a low-technology organization. The more uncertain and complex the environment, the greater is the need for a formal information system. And, all other things being equal, larger organizations have greater information systems needs than do smaller ones; thus Procter and Gamble's information needs would be greater than those of a local retailer.

Within an organization, information needs are influenced by the area and level of management involved. The information systems needs of a production department are different from those of a human resources department, although each usually needs a formal system. Likewise, executive-level managers have different information needs than do supervisors. Each manager has unique information needs, and a well-designed system will tend to be tailored to each of its users rather than merely provide general information to all users.

The process of determining what information each individual needs to perform his or her job is called **information requirements analysis.**[5] This process should be conducted before the information system is developed and then be periodically repeated as part of the updating and maintenance of the system. Normally it involves interviewing individuals to obtain their views on what information they need, in what form, and when. These views must then be verified through the use of some other technique, such as a paper simulation of the individuals' activity or direct observation of them at work. If many people in similar situations are involved, surveys could also be used. In any event, once the information requirements analysis has been completed, it should be integrated into the system and periodically examined to ensure that it is accurate.

Kinds of Information Systems

Information systems can be formal or informal. Informal, unstructured information systems are a major factor in every manager's life.[6] Managers gather impressions through their interactions with others and through their travels in the organization. And there are always emotional reactions to that information. Although this kind of information system is important, it is so situationally specific that few generalizations can be developed about it.

> Information systems may be informal and unstructured or formal and structured, and may be either paper or computer based.

More formal, structured information systems involve record keeping of one sort or another. Formal information systems are very ancient managerial devices.[7] The Sumerians had a complicated tax and governance system whose records were maintained on clay tablets. The Egyptians used papyri for record keeping. Today, virtually all formal systems are computerized. Three common kinds are transaction-processing systems, basic management information systems, and decision support systems, and these systems can further be classified as centralized or distributed. Table 11.1 summarizes the different kinds of information systems, and *Management Today: The World of Management* suggests how one international organization uses formal information systems.

TRANSACTION-PROCESSING SYSTEMS   A system designed to handle routine and recurring transactions within an organization is known as a **transaction-processing system, or TPS.** These were the first formal, structured information systems and were the first to be computerized. A TPS is most useful for tasks that involve a large number of highly similar transactions—filing employee or customer records, handling charge cards, dues notices, subscriptions, and so on. When your local grocery store—ABCO, Kroger, Smitty's, or whatever—uses automated scanners to record each unit sold and its selling price, the information is part of a TPS. Discover, MasterCard, and

TABLE 11.1
Kinds of Information
Systems

System	Description
1. Informal	Unstructured. Information is obtained from day-to-day interactions and impressions, notes, and/or diaries.
2. Formal	Structured. Information is gathered and communicated either on paper or by computer. Information can be either centralized or distributed.
a. Transaction-Processing	Handles routine and recurring transactions.
b. Management Information	Gathers, organizes, summarizes, and reports data for use by managers.
c. Decision Support	Searches for, analyzes, summarizes, and reports information needed by a manager for a particular decision.

THE WORLD OF MANAGEMENT

KLM: A Quality System

KLM Royal Dutch Airlines is not flashy or even all that well known, but it is a solid, profitable international carrier. One reason for KLM's success is that it is flexible; in response to Europe 1992, for instance, KLM has been forging joint ventures, taking equity positions, and proposing mergers all over the world to strengthen its competitive position. It now owns a piece of every Dutch carrier and has an equity position in Air UK (British) as well as in SWA (Italian), NWA (the parent of Northwest Airlines in the U.S.), Sabena (Belgium), and Singapore Airlines. KLM ranked 8th in international passenger traffic during the late 1980s and 25th (out of 178 total) in terms of all traffic moved. The airline has also been highly profitable, posting an annual net income of around $150 million per year during that same time period.

Another factor in KLM's success is that it uses information systems to its advantage. KLM helped found Galileo, a new European computer reservations system, and recently merged its booking system with that of Galileo. It then obtained an equity position in Covia Corporation, which is the computer reservation division of United Airlines and a supplier of software to Galileo. Those moves increased its strength in the sales distribution market in Europe, ensuring it a dominant position. KLM also has a distribution logistics program that enables it to expand its cargo operations to better serve customers throughout the world. Scheduling passengers and cargo through 140 destinations in about eighty countries takes well-designed, well-managed, and highly effective information systems. KLM has developed just such systems.

SOURCES: Arthur Reed, "At 70, Still Looking Ahead," *Air Transport World*, January 1, 1990, pp. 24–28; Henry Lefer, "KLM Cargo: A Changed Structure for a Changing Market; Customer Needs Become Priority," *Air Transport*, March 1, 1989, pp. 72–76; "Quiet KLM: Agile, Aggressive, Profitable," *The Wall Street Journal*, July 14, 1989, p. A8; KLM's Distribution Logistics Program," *Global Trade*, July 1, 1988, pp. 27–30.

Visa all use TPSs to handle the huge volume of transactions with which they must deal.

☐ An *MIS* is a management information system that gathers, organizes, summarizes, and reports information for use by managers.

MANAGEMENT INFORMATION SYSTEMS A **management information system,** or **MIS,** is a system that gathers, organizes, summarizes, and reports data for use by managers. Sometimes called information reporting systems, MISs serve to help link the several parts of an organization together. For a manufacturing firm like the Kingsport Press, for example, a computerized inventory system might track finished goods, work in process, and beginning materials to ensure that customer commitments are met. A marketing representative working with a customer could access the system to determine fairly precisely when an order would be shipped to that customer.

DECISION SUPPORT SYSTEMS A newer, very powerful form of information system is known as a **decision support system,** or **DSS.** A DSS automatically searches for, analyzes, summarizes, and reports information needed by a manager for a particular decision. In a sense, a DSS combines a TPS and an MIS with features that make the system even more automatically responsive to the needs of its users. A finance officer of a company like PepsiCo, for example, might need to know the capital recovery periods and tax consequences of several alternative investment opportunities. The DSS would have the relevant information and be able to present it in a useful way quickly so that the financial officer's decision process could be both fast and accurate.

CENTRALIZED VERSUS DISTRIBUTED SYSTEMS Just as decision making in an organization can be centralized or decentralized, so information systems can be centralized or distributed. In the early days of computer technology, virtually all information systems were centralized. They consisted of data-processing or computer services departments built around large, expensive, mainframe computers. As computer technology changed, it became more and more possible to have the information system components scattered or distributed throughout the organization. Prudential Insurance tends to use a centralized approach, for instance, whereas Travelers Corporation uses a distributed system.[8] Centralized information systems are better coordinated but slower; distributed ones are faster but may result in more duplication of effort. As the power of smaller computers increases and as networking software improves, information systems of the future may be able to obtain the best of both worlds.

Matching Needs and Systems

Since there are a variety of needs for and uses of information and numerous different kinds of information systems, organizations must be careful to match systems with needs. Matching involves working through a series of questions like the following. For what goals is information needed, and what information is needed? In what way can that information be readily obtained, stored, analyzed, and reported? (In a computer system this involves determining the hardware and software to use.) What are the costs and benefits of the various ways of meeting those needs? How might the information and the technology for dealing with it be integrated? After obtaining answers to these questions, the system itself must be actually designed, tested, implemented, and then monitored, maintained, and perhaps improved. As shown in Exhibit 11.3, matching can be thought of as a process itself.

P R E L U D E   C A S E   U P D A T E

In the Benetton case, the need for accurate information about sales at production facilities determined a great deal about the information system to be used. Had the market been one in which customer tastes changed more slowly or lasted longer once changed, the speed of the system could have been slower. The information system had to match management's information needs.

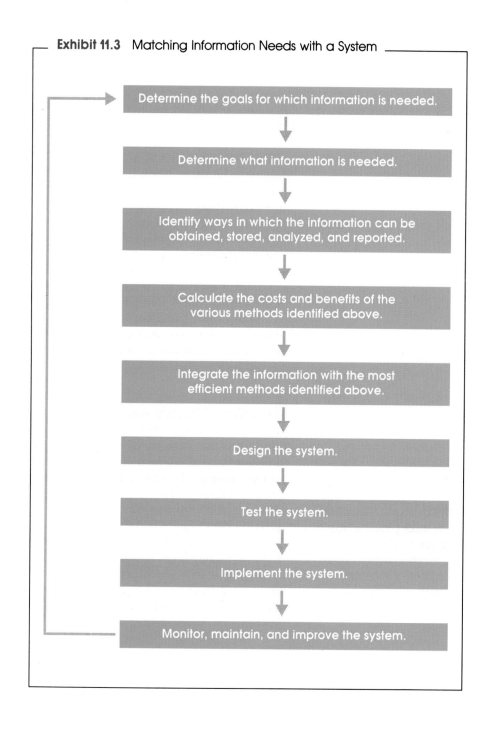

Exhibit 11.3   Matching Information Needs with a System

MANAGING INFORMATION SYSTEMS

Like all other aspects of organizations, once developed, information systems must be managed. In this section of the chapter, we look at that issue.

Integrating Systems

Throughout this chapter, the plural *information systems* has been used because most organizations actually use more than one system. Most middle to large organizations, for instance, would have a marketing system, a production system, and a human resources system.[9] As indicated in Exhibit 11.4, these different information systems must be integrated or linked so that the different kinds of information can merge to form even more useful information.

Integrating systems is not easy. The production system might have been installed on an IBM computer. The marketing system, on the other hand, may use special-purpose computers developed by Intel. Wang computers may be used by the human resources department. Linking these different systems developed and run on different hardware and with different software may be very difficult or even impossible.[10]

Had all the systems been developed at one time, this problem would have been avoided. But developing all of them at once is expensive, and information needs rarely occur at the same intensity. Therefore, most such systems are developed piecemeal. Again, if a common standard for hardware and software were adopted, integration would be much easier, but both hardware and software change and improve so rapidly that agreeing on a standard for even a few years at a time can be very difficult. Luckily, some more recent developments

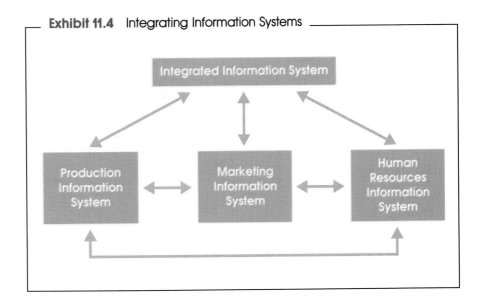

Exhibit 11.4   Integrating Information Systems

in hardware and software are making it easier to develop the necessary links across information systems. Linked systems, which could be used by virtually any company, enable managers to use electronic mail, access information needed to make decisions, and handle virtually all routine business using only a single, integrated information system.[11] Some of these systems are discussed later in the chapter.

Using Systems

Information systems must be used to be of value. You might think that information should somehow be just where you want it when you want it. The reality, of course, is that information must be sought, and learning to use the system to obtain information is critical to the success of the system. For that reason, then, organizations need to spend considerable time and effort to ensure that information systems are easy to use, or user friendly. Well-designed, user-friendly systems can quickly be used, even by those who have had no prior experience with computers, such as very senior workers.[12]

User-friendly information systems are typically designed so that users can examine and easily modify information to maximize its usefulness. The Travelers Corporation uses a team of trained nurses to review health insurance claims. They can access the system and review the medical diagnoses provided with each claim. Using this information, then, they can determine whether or

© 1989 Vickers & Beechler

The effective management of information systems is always an important consideration. Brokerage services like Merrill Lynch and Shearson Lehman Hutton rely on information systems created by Automatic Data Processing, Inc. to help keep track of the stock market. ADP handles all the maintenance and programming work, leaving its customers with less to worry about.

not a second medical opinion is warranted before a surgical procedure is approved. The nurses then add their decision to the data on the claim form for other users of the information.[13]

The use of an information system is one measure of its effectiveness. Many such systems are not, in fact, used because they require considerable computer fluency. However, recent developments are changing that situation.

Robert Kidder, CEO of Duracell, can do more in an hour using his current information system than he previously could in several. That system lets him begin at one level and progress into more and more detail as he desires. He can examine performance across divisions and then probe one division that is out of line with others to try to determine why. The system makes it possible to do all this quickly and easily without upsetting the people in the division he is investigating.[14]

The use of a remote control, a touch screen, or a mouse seems particularly appropriate where the user is not a touch typist.[15] Such devices, however, may not be needed in the future since many schools are training virtually all students to operate keyboards, and keyboard mastery is becoming a symbol of high status rather than low status, as it has been to many managers. More importantly, though, software that enables users to browse through information in almost any direction based on their experience or even hunches makes the system more friendly and powerful. Such software, known as *hypertext*, is just beginning to be used for information systems and promises to be a powerful aid in the future.

LEARNING CHECK

You should now be able to discuss the importance of integrating and using effective information systems.

INFORMATION SYSTEMS AND ORGANIZATIONS

Whether informal or formal, information systems are clearly an important part of organizations. They are not, however, panaceas. They are only tools of management, and, although they can have very beneficial effects, they are also limited. Table 11.2 outlines some of those effects and limitations, which we will now explore.

Effects

☐ Information systems affect performance, organizational structure, and behavior.

Information systems have effects at several different levels. They affect the performance of the organization, the organization's structure and design, and the people within the organization.

PERFORMANCE   There seems to be a growing consensus that information systems do enhance performance. The U.S. Forest Service recently installed an information system to assist it in evaluating how to respond to forest fires. In the past every fire was attacked the morning after it was reported. The

TABLE 11.2
Effects and Limitations of
Information Systems

Effects	Limitations

1. On Performance
  a. They tend to save money.
  b. They generally improve
    performance.
 	
2. On Organizational Structure
  a. A separate unit is created
    to oversee the information
    system.
  b. The organization becomes
    flatter because fewer managers
    are needed.
 	
3. On Behavior
  a. Some employees feel isolated.
  b. Others experience job enrichment.
  c. Some can work at home more.
  d. Some new work groups may be
    formed.
	1. They are costly to develop.
	2. They may be difficult to learn.
	3. Their information can be overly
	   valued.
	4. They cannot handle all complex
	   problems.
	5. Operators may misuse them.
	6. Operators may become
	   discouraged and reject them.
	7. They are dependent on electric
	   power sources.

costs of such efforts would run to $10 million for a major fire. The new information system, however, automatically figures in such natural fire breaks as rivers, enabling some fires to be contained at far lower costs. General Electric, K mart, and American Airlines also are among companies reporting high levels of satisfaction with the performance of their information systems.[16] *Management Today: Management in Practice* describes how information systems have benefited Westinghouse.

ORGANIZATIONAL STRUCTURE Since most organizations create a separate unit to oversee their information system, its first impact on organizational structure is the creation of that unit. In some cases, the head of that unit or the person overseeing all information needs of the firm is a newly created position, the chief information officer, or CIO (discussed more in Chapter 15).[17] The more profound effect of information systems on organizational structures is, however, that with more and better information available throughout the organization, fewer managers, particularly those at middle levels, are needed. IBM, for instance, has eliminated a layer of management in this way, and its span of management may be greatly enlarged through the impact of information systems.[18]

BEHAVIOR The behavioral effects of information systems are not yet well understood. Some individuals feel isolated because they spend their time interacting with computers instead of people. Others enjoy the new technology and are excited about having their jobs enriched in this way. Some people will be able to work at home rather than at a central office and be able to spend more

MANAGEMENT IN PRACTICE

Westinghouse Goes Around the World with E-Mail

Westinghouse uses a variety of information systems and new technologies in its various organizational units and feels that those systems have accounted for about one-third of its white-collar productivity gains. The Westinghouse Electrical Systems Division, for instance, has a finished goods inventory system to assist in the management and control of inventory. Its Electronic Assembly Plant uses computerized robotics to assist in the production of circuit boards for customers in the U.S. Department of Defense. The Westinghouse Productivity and Quality Center uses information systems to develop cost- and time-saving procedures for use within the many different divisions of the company. And teleconferencing has greatly reduced travel time and expenses.

Electronic mail, or E-Mail, as it is usually called, is particularly prevalent at Westinghouse. E-mail, which is the transmission of letters, notes, and documents electronically to another location, began in 1980, and by the end of that decade, over 6,000 personal computers were being used to connect about 11,000 managers and employees as well as about 1,000 customers. All domestic offices and thirty-seven foreign offices are also linked through the system. Overseas usage is particularly important since E-mail costs 90 percent less than overseas calls and letters and 75 percent less than telegraphic approaches such as telegrams or telex.

Westinghouse's president spends about fifteen of his eighty hours each week using E-mail. He uses it at work, at home, and even on trips. He can send memos to managers throughout the organization worldwide, read progress reports on contract negotiations, and send suggestions on a timely basis to managers involved in those negotiations. The process is nearly as fast as a telephone call but does not have the disruptive aspects and produces permanent copy that can be checked later for accuracy. Although using E-mail may mean spending longer hours in front of a computer screen, the speed and cost advantages have made it a permanent part of Westinghouse's information systems.

SOURCES: Roger L. Pacos and John W. Sinn, "An Evaluation of the Finished-Goods Inventory System at Westinghouse Electrical Systems Division," *Production and Inventory Management Journal,* vol. 30, no. 14 (1989), pp. 45–66; "Quality Assurance and What It Means," *Electrical Engineer,* August 1, 1989, pp. 60ff; "Artificial Intelligence and Expert Systems," *Power Engineering,* January 1, 1989, pp. 26–31; "At Westinghouse, 'E-Mail' Makes the World Go Round," *Business Week,* October 10, 1988, p. 110.

time with their families with no detrimental performance effects. New groupings of personnel may form around electronic bulletin board systems. But since there appear to be considerable learning experiences with such systems, the long-lasting behavioral effects will not be fully evaluated or understood for several years to come.

Limitations

The most obvious limitation of information systems is cost. They are expensive to develop, largely because each one must be tailored to fit particular organizational needs. This limitation is closely followed by learning difficulties.

Since most information systems involve doing things differently, and hopefully better, everyone involved must learn the new and different way. Although these two limitations are relatively obvious, they are by no means the only ones.

For one thing, the information derived from an information system may be overly valued. There are those who assign great credibility to information from computers even when the information is actually very rough. Moreover, some tasks or problems simply cannot be handled by information systems. Highly complex tasks or problems may necessitate human intervention, and if people depend upon a system too much, its information can become dysfunctional.

Another problem is that some managers improperly use information systems. Many electronic mail systems when first installed become cluttered with graffiti, messages, and notes left from unknown parties saying all manner of things. This initial period of using the system as much for sport as for business may last weeks or even months. Then, if the system is not user friendly, some managers cease using it. The manager who gives up too soon may fail to eventually realize the power of the new communication system which may be substantial. And, of course, any organization that does not provide for electrical power failures is asking for trouble.

LEARNING CHECK

You should now be able to describe the impact of information systems on organizations.

NEW INFORMATION TECHNOLOGIES

The computer is at the heart of most information systems today. As indicated in Exhibit 11.5, several new information technologies are currently being developed for organizations. We briefly examine those developments in this last section of the chapter.

Exhibit 11.5 New Information Technologies

Computer Software:	Telecommunications:	Artificial Intelligence:	Hypertext:
Data Bases	Teleconferencing	Decision Support	Help Systems
Spreadsheets	Telecommuting	Systems	On-line
Word Processing	Networking	Knowledge-Based	Encyclopedias
Electronic Mail		Systems	Programs Requiring
		Expert Systems	Extensive User
			Interaction

More Basic ← → *More Complex*

Computer Software

Whether the computer is a lap top, desk model, or mainframe unit, data can be stored and manipulated by computers through software. Software that can be used in information systems comes in a variety of types: data bases, spreadsheets, word processors, and electronic mail, to name the most common ones. Data bases permit the user to organize and manipulate primarily numerical data in interconnected ways. Spreadsheets arrange numerical data in a matrix of rows and columns. Word processors and electronic mail deal primarily with text data.

Each of these systems can, to some degree, interrelate with others. Word-Star (a word-processing program), for instance, can work directly with Lotus 1-2-3 (a spreadsheet program). dBase (a data base program) files and handles graphics from almost all graphics programs, such as Harvard Graphics, and it is also well designed for networking and electronic mail functions. As discussed earlier, integrating across software and hardware is difficult but must be done to enable information systems to become as effective as they can be.

Telecommunications

□ *Telecommunications includes teleconferencing, telecommuting, and networking.*

Great strides have also been made in **telecommunications,** which is communication over some distance. Teleconferencing, telecommuting, and networking are three forms already in use by some firms.

Teleconferencing, or videoconferencing, permits individuals in different locations to see and talk with one another. This visual capability clearly overcomes one limitation of other electronic communication systems. The CEO of Wal-Mart, Sam Walton, uses teleconferences to talk directly with employees during their normal Saturday morning meetings.[19] Boeing has also used videoconferencing to communicate more quickly and completely across its sprawling Seattle facilities.[20]

Telecommuting refers to having employees perform their work at home through the use of computers connected to the organization's computer. This is an electronic version of cottage industries, where the product is produced in people's houses and collected at a central location for distribution. Companies such as IBM, American Express, Johnson & Johnson, J.C. Penney, and Blue-Cross Blue-Shield find that this approach saves them office space and enables them to obtain the productivity of good people who otherwise might resist commuting to a central workplace.[21]

Networking involves connecting independent computers directly together so that they can function in interrelated ways. In this way one gains direct access to common software and data bases more easily than through the use of telephone connections between computers. Electronic communication can also be made quicker and more responsive to individuals through the use of a network. Networks at one organizational level can then be linked to others to establish a true information system for the organization. In this way, Local Area Networks (LANs) can be linked. Still to come are Integrated Services Digital Networks (ISDNs), which will link computers and other machines through

Compaq Computer Corporation

New advances in information technology are coming on-line constantly. Houston Lighting & Power uses an AI-based system to keep its generators operating at peak efficiency while minimizing downtime. The system saves the giant utility thousands of dollars in maintenance costs.

the use of digital cabling with wall jacks much like telephones, and Electronic Data Interchanges (EDIs), which enable exact copies of a company's forms to be transmitted from one unit to another.[22]

Artificial Intelligence

□ *Artificial intelligence (AI) refers to attempts to have computers simulate human decision processes.*

Artificial intelligence (AI) refers to attempts to have computers simulate human decision processes. Although many exciting projects are going on in this area, applications are still rather scarce.[23] However, some systems are coming into use, such as the maintenance system at Bechtel and Westinghouse's on-line diagnostics for turbines.[24] The most common ones are decision support systems, knowledge-based systems, and expert systems. As discussed earlier in this chapter, decision support systems are advanced management information systems designed to provide the information needed by managers for particular decisions. Knowledge-based systems are somewhat broader systems that can provide support for more general activities. Expert systems attempt, as much as possible, to capture the expertise of a human in software.[25]

□ *Expert systems build on series of rules to move from a set of data to a decision recommendation.*

The last-mentioned systems, **expert systems,** build on series of rules, frequently if-then rules, to move from a set of data to a decision recommendation. Boeing has been developing expert systems for various uses for some time. One is known as CASE (connector assembly specification expert). CASE produces assembly procedure instructions for each of the 5,000 electrical connectors on an airplane. What used to take over forty minutes of searching through 20,000 pages of printed material now takes only a few minutes to get a computer printout for a specific connector.[26] Working with Texas Instruments, Campbell developed an expert system to capture the expertise of a manager in one of its soup kettle operations.[27] Martin Marietta has developed an expert system to assist in air traffic control.[28] Expert systems are being developed to aid managers in a variety of tasks, including more interpersonal tasks such as providing performance feedback to subordinates.[29]

Hypertext

In most information systems, the user may progress from one level to another in linear fashion. In a hypertext system, the user is able to move in any direction through the information to acquire what is necessary for the particular task at hand. Although the technology behind hypertext possesses many elements associated with artificial intelligence, it should be considered a separate information technology. Hypertext systems have been used in advanced help systems, on-line encyclopedias, and some programs that require a lot of user interaction. Hypertext systems tend to be complicated to develop; however, because they are extremely easy to learn and use, they hold tremendous promise for the future.

LEARNING CHECK

You should now be able to describe new information technologies.

PRELUDE CASE UPDATE

The information system used at Benetton is one in which most, if not all, of these new information technologies could be utilized, especially as Benetton moves into the financial services market, where speed and accuracy of information are even more critical than they are in the clothing market. The use of artificial intelligence could also benefit Benetton. A knowledge-based system could be used to help managers keep up with the company's complex information, and an expert system could be of tremendous use to managers in sharpening their skills at meeting changes in their markets.

Chapter Summary

Information is data organized in a meaningful way. Data are merely facts and figures—unorganized pieces of information. A system is an interrelated set of elements that function as a whole to accomplish some purpose. Because the amount of data has grown in recent years, managers at all levels and in every area have had to become information processors. The information they receive must therefore be accurate, timely, complete, and relevant.

There are five basic interrelated components of any information system. In a computerized system, getting the data into the system involves input devices. Analysis and processing are done by a central processor. Storage is accomplished through one or more media, and in many cases more than one medium is used for backup purposes. Making the information available to users is also accomplished through a variety of output devices. Finally, the control system usually involves some form of computer software as well as human monitoring.

Information systems should eliminate guesswork by ensuring that proper information is available when needed. Developing information systems involves knowing one's information system needs as well as the kinds of systems that exist or might be developed. Information system needs are determined by the kind of organization, its environment, and its size.

Most managers maintain informal, unstructured systems of information, but formal, structured systems predominate in large organizations. Systems designed to handle routine and recurring transactions within an organization are known as transaction-processing systems. A management information system, or MIS, is a system that gathers, organizes, summarizes, and reports data for use by managers. A decision support system, or DSS, is a system that automatically searches for, analyzes, summarizes, and reports information needed by a manager for a particular decision. All these systems can further be classified as centralized or distributed. Organizations must be careful to match their various needs with the many systems available.

Although integrating systems is not easy, it must be done if the total information system is to be effective. Effectiveness is also increased when the systems are user friendly. Many new systems are becoming easier to learn and use.

Information systems affect the performance of the organization, the organization's structure and design, and the people within the organization. There seems to be a growing consensus that information systems do enhance performance. Information systems also have some limitations. They are expensive and can be difficult to learn to use. In addition, the information derived from them may be overvalued, and they may be improperly used or not used at all. And, of course, computerized information systems depend upon electricity to operate and so are vulnerable during power outages.

New information technologies include computer software such as data bases, spreadsheets, word processors, and electronic mail. Telecommunications applications such as teleconferencing, telecommuting, and networking are also extending the application of information systems. Artificial intelligence applications such as decision support, knowledge-based, and

expert systems attempt to simulate human decision processes and are finding some uses today. Hypertext, in which the user may move about informational databases in any direction he or she wishes, is also becoming useful as a managerial tool.

The Manager's Vocabulary

information	management information
data	system (MIS)
system	decision support system
input devices	(DSS)
central processor	telecommunications
output devices	teleconferencing
information system	telecommuting
needs	networking
information	artificial intelligence (AI)
requirements analysis	expert systems
transaction-processing	
system (TPS)	

Prelude Case Wrap-Up

Our Prelude Case for this chapter describes Benetton, a highly successful apparel company. Benetton has always relied on being able to almost instantly meet customer demands for styles and colors. This strategy requires that accurate information about what is selling at each Benetton store can be made quickly available to its production facilities. Benetton's worldwide information system has become a model for the competitive use of information, and many other firms are attempting to design similar systems.

Building on the strength of its information system and its international communications and distribution network, Benetton has recently begun to diversify into the area of financial services. This new, private, family-controlled organization is known as "IN Holding." However, the hard-sell corporate culture behind the family-controlled firm remains unchanged, and since it has met with at least some opposition in retailing, particularly in the United States, where a softer, more consumer-oriented approach is frequently used, the success of Benetton in financial services is not ensured. Nevertheless, its magnificent information system seems so powerful that, to the extent that success in financial services requires such a system, Benetton is ready for such success.

After all, Benetton developed from a small firm in 1955 in which a brother sold his sister's sweaters to local companies to an international organization consisting of nearly 5,000 stores in about eighty countries by 1990. Although it did hire consultants to help it strengthen its operations, especially in the United States, it has always been a strong and successful company.

Prelude Case Questions

1. Which concepts presented in this chapter are illustrated in the Benetton case? Cite specific examples.
2. What are the major characteristics of the information system at Benetton?
3. What are the strengths and weaknesses of that information system? How might the weaknesses be offset?
4. Do you feel that Benetton will continue to be highly profitable in the future? Why or why not? Was the move to financial services sound? Why or why not?

Discussion Questions

Review Questions

1. What is the difference between information and data?
2. What are the different kinds of information systems?
3. What are the key considerations in managing information systems?
4. What are the effects and limitations of information systems?
5. What are new information technologies? What companies are already using some of them?

Analysis Questions

1. Should computerized information systems be duplicates of paper information systems? Why or why not?
2. Would the information needs across organizational levels differ so much that different information

systems would have to be developed, or could an organization really get by with one system?
3. Many people refer to the current period of economic development as the Information Revolution (like the Industrial Revolution). Do you think we are really in the midst of a revolution? Why or why not?
4. Do you think the chief information officer of an organization could become too powerful? If so, how could that be prevented or corrected? If not, why not?
5. Comment on this quotation: "The Turing Test of a computer system is designed to evaluate whether or not a user can tell that it is a computer system rather than a human being providing advice. A system that passes is then a computer system that is indistinguishable from a human. But who would want such a system? Humans are cheaper. What I want is a computer that is readily distinguishable from a human because it is better—it has no emotional problems, does not complain about hard work or overtime, wants no bonuses or retirement, makes no errors in judgment, and won't talk back."

Application Questions and Exercises

1. Interview a local business manager about the use of information systems in his or her organization. What kind(s) of system(s) is (are) being used?
2. Interview a manager in a local organization that is not a business firm (church, voluntary association, service club, college, etc.) about information needs. What needs are expressed? Are any of those needs being met by a formal information system? A computerized system? Explain with details.
3. Interview users of an information system. (They could be users of a library system, but try to talk to others as well.) How effective is the system in meeting their needs? Explain.
4. Go to the library and find a reference to the use of a new information technology by an organization. Share your findings with the class. Which new technologies seem most prevalent among those found by your class?
5. Are any local organizations in your area using expert systems? If so, for what purposes are they using them?

ENHANCEMENT CASE

FEDERAL EXPRESS: KEEPING TRACK OF EVERYTHING

Federal Express began over twenty years ago. In 1965 Frederick W. Smith presented his idea for a package delivery system to compete with the U.S. Postal Service in a paper in an economics class at Yale and received a C on it. Investors were equally skeptical, and Smith had to use his own funds before they would help. However, the idea gradually began to attract them.

In 1973, the company actually began. In the first thirty days of operation, it had fourteen small planes serving twenty-five cities, and it delivered only twenty packages during that time. Federal Express struggled until 1977, when deregulation of the airline industry enabled it to use larger planes and airports in major cities. Routes for its smaller planes became flexible, and it was soon able to get packages to and from almost anywhere in the United States. It went public in 1978 with revenues of around $150 million; its stock sold for $24 a share. Ten years later, its revenues were over $4 billion and the price had risen to over $40 a share.

There are now over 250 planes, 24,000 delivery vehicles, and a work force of over 57,000 handling over one million items (packages and letters) each night. Federal Express operates throughout the United States and in over one hundred foreign countries. In 1988 it added eleven African nations and expanded its Japanese and other Asian operations. In 1989 it bought Tiger International Inc., the parent company for Flying Tigers, the world's largest bulk air cargo company. That move opened up still other routes and also expanded its operations into large packages and bulk cargo. Federal Express's international volume increased about 50 percent from 1987 to 1988 and continues to grow.

Federal Express offers both next morning service and next afternoon service to its customers, as well as the capability to move letters, small packages, and bulk cargo. A description of a typical night at its Memphis, Tennessee, shipping location suggests how it carries out its operations. Packages are picked up by small vans and taken to local airports, from

which the packages are delivered to Memphis. About ninety-five planes arrive in Memphis each night, and about 5,000 employees work there to unload, sort, and reload the million packages and letters. Most of that activity takes place in about four hours. Three systems are used for sorting three kinds of items: documents, small packages, and hazardous, restricted, or odd-shaped packages. The packages are scanned by the computerized information system for tracking purposes while they ride over eighty miles of conveyor belts to other planes. The newly loaded planes then leave Memphis for destinations around the country, and 23,000 couriers collect the packages from airports and deliver them the next day.

Federal Express was one of the first nonfood companies to use bar-code scanning, which tracks the movement of packages throughout its system. Each driver has a hand-held computer, each truck has an electronic messaging system, and each airport and loading location has scanning equipment. This enables Federal Express to scan each package when it arrives and as it moves through every step of its journey. Since all those data are sent back to Memphis, the company knows where every item is at all times. That information not only lets Federal Express reassure customers and meet its tight delivery deadlines but also enables it to schedule its operations more efficiently.

Federal Express has also moved to make tracking information directly available to its major customers. It has installed large terminals in the offices of 7,000 of its larger customers so that they can monitor the location of their shipments. Recently, it also began to sell desk top computers called "Hello Federal" to smaller customers so that they too can monitor shipments. When the customers enter the order number for their shipment, the screen displays its location. Customers who ship as few as only three or so items per day can have a "Hello Federal" terminal.

One major problem Federal Express has been wrestling with has been exacerbated by the Flying Tiger purchase—system integration. The foreign systems have frequently proven so different and difficult to integrate with U.S. systems that expenses have exceeded revenues on some international routes. The Flying Tiger systems were designed for slower-moving large freight rather than the faster-moving letters and packages with which Federal Express normally deals. Integrating these different systems will take some time.

Federal Express still has to figure out a way to deal with facsimile (FAX) transmission machines, too. (Facsimile machines send exact copies of documents electronically.) Its ZapMail facsimile system was a failure and was dropped in 1987, but something will need to be done. The price of reliable facsimile equipment is dropping, more and more FAXs are being used, and acceptance of them is growing. It is now possible to transmit legal documents via FAX for many purposes (although a verifying telephone call is sometimes necessary).

Federal Express is striving to become even more responsive to customer needs to expand and maintain its markets. Its Customer Distribution Services division manages inventories and warehouses for companies that are not in a position to run their own. It is testing the use of kiosks and drop boxes to make it easier for customers to access the system. These, too, are integrated into its information system for tracking and control.

SOURCES: "Rockwell Unit to Reengine 14 Boeing 727 Transports," *Aviation Week and Space Technology*, January 15, 1990, p. 29; "Mr. Smith Goes Global," *Business Week*, February 13, 1989, pp. 66–67; "Federal Express Wasn't an Overnight Success," *The Wall Street Journal*, June 6, 1989, p. B2; "Federal Express to Offer Cheaper Overnight Deliveries," *The Wall Street Journal*, March 8, 1989, p. B1; "Christmas Rush: How Firm Delivers," *USA Today*, December 14, 1989, pp. 1B–2B.

Enhancement Case Questions

1. What similarities and differences can you note between the information systems of Federal Express and Benetton from the Prelude Case?
2. Describe Federal Express's information system. What components that were discussed in the chapter can you identify? Cite specific examples of each of them.
3. What are the strengths and weaknesses of the information system used by Federal Express? How might it reduce the weaknesses?
4. What do you feel Federal Express could do to make its information systems function even better in the future? How or in what way would your suggestions improve its systems?

Chapter Notes

1. See the discussion in N. Ahitov and S. Neumann, *Principles of Information Systems for Management*, 2nd ed. (Dubuque, Iowa: Wm. C. Brown, 1986), or T. H. Athey and R. W. Zmud, *Introduction to Computers and Information Systems* (Glenview, Ill.: Scott, Foresman, 1986).
2. Charles A. O'Reilly, "Variations in Decision Makers' Use of Information Sources: The Impact of Quality and Accessibility of Information," *Academy of Management Journal*, December 1982, pp. 756–771.
3. Carla Rapoport, "Great Japanese Mistakes," *Fortune*, February 13, 1989, pp. 108–111.
4. Robert G. Murdick and Joel E. Ross, *Introduction to Management Information Systems* (Englewood Cliffs, N.J.: Prentice-Hall, 1977).
5. Albert L. Lederer, "Information Requirements Analysis," *Journal of Systems Management*, December 1981, pp. 15–19.
6. J. F. Rockart, "Chief Executives Define Their Own Data Needs," *Harvard Business Review*, March-April 1979, pp. 81–93.
7. See Daniel A. Wren, *The Evolution of Management Thought*, 3rd ed. (New York: Wiley, 1987), and Claude S. George, Jr., *The History of Management Thought* (Englewood Cliffs, N.J.: Prentice-Hall, 1968).
8. "Managing Information: Two Insurance Giants Forge Divergent Paths," *Business Week*, October 8, 1984, p. 121.
9. Cornelius H. Sullivan, Jr., and John R. Smart, "Planning for Information Networks," *Sloan Management Review*, Winter 1987, pp. 39–44.
10. "Linking All the Company Data: We're Not There Yet," *Business Week*, May 11, 1987, p. 151.
11. Malcolm Cole, "Network Your Way to the Automated Office," *Accountancy*, October 1, 1988,

pp. 92–94, and Malcolm Cole, "Less Paper—The First Step to No Paper," *Accountancy*, October 1, 1988, pp. 88–91.

12. Wendell Hahm and Tora Bikson, "Retirees Using EMail and Networked Computers," *International Journal of Technology and Aging*, Fall 1989, pp. 113–124.

13. "Office Automation: Making It Pay Off," *Business Week*, October 12, 1987, pp. 134–146.

14. Jeremy Main, "At Last, Software CEOs Can Use," *Fortune*, March 13, 1989, pp. 77–83.

15. Ibid.

16. "Office Automation: Making It Pay Off."

17. John J. Donovan, "Beyond Chief Information Officer to Network Managers," *Harvard Business Review*, September-October 1988, pp. 134–140.

18. Jeremy Main, "The Winning Organization," *Fortune*, September 26, 1988, pp. 50–60.

19. John Huey, "Wal-Mart—Will It Take Over the World?" *Fortune*, January 30, 1989, pp. 52–61.

20. "Videoconferencing: No Longer Just a Sideshow," *Business Week*, November 12, 1984, p. 117.

21. Janice Castro, "Staying Home Is Paying Off," *Time*, October 26, 1987, pp. 112–113.

22. Susan Kerr, "The Application Wave Behind ISDN," *Datamation*, February 1, 1990, pp. 64–68; Carl Edgar Law, "Update on ISDN's Progress in Europe," *Business Communications Review*, January 1, 1989, pp. 54–56;

Frank Derfler, "Building Network Solutions: Is ISDN Tomorrow's Interoffice Network?" *PC Magazine*, February 13, 1990, pp. 229ff; Kate Evans-Correia, "Hot Technologies in Tomorrow's Offices," *Purchasing*, February 25, 1988, pp. 50–57; and Catherine L. Harris and Dean Foust, "An Electronic Pipeline That's Changing the Way America Does Business," *Business Week*, August 3, 1987, p. 80.

23. Mark S. Fox, "AI and Expert System Myths, Legends, and Facts," *IEEE Expert*, February 1, 1990, pp. 8–22.

24. "Artificial Intelligence and Expert Systems," *Power Engineering*, January 1, 1989, pp. 26–31.

25. "Computer Applications: Software—A Risky Business," *Fairplay International Shipping Weekly*, January 4, 1990, pp. 23–34.

26. Andrew Kupfer, "Now, Live Experts on a Floppy Disk," *Fortune*, October 12, 1987, p. 117.

27. "Turning an Expert's Skills into Computer Software," *Business Week*, October 7, 1985, pp. 104–108.

28. "Martin Marietta: Computers Lead the Way to Inbound Control," *Traffic Management*, January 1, 1990, pp. 50–68.

29. See, for example, Peter H. Lewis, "I'm Sorry; My Machine Doesn't Like Your Work," *New York Times*, February 4, 1990, p. F27.

THE ENTREPRENEURIAL SPIRIT

This third part of the book introduced you to the managerial function of organizing. Organizing concepts and designs were discussed, as well as how to staff organizations and implement information systems.

Organizational design and entrepreneurial style impact upon each other. For example, smaller organizations can sometimes be more bureaucratic than larger ones, but in general entrepreneurial organizations, regardless of size, tend to be more flexible and less bureaucratic than nonentrepreneurial forms. Of course, larger organizations do tend to have more written procedures and policies than do smaller ones. Finally, smaller organizations are far more likely to be organized around functional lines, whereas larger organizations and entrepreneurial organizations frequently are organized around products, projects, or services.

Differences in staffing can be seen as well. Staffing in smaller organizations tends to be more by exception; personnel are sought when an opening occurs or when a new position is dictated by growth. In larger organizations, staffing is more routine; people are being constantly recruited, and, when good individuals are located, they are hired and a place is made for them until openings occur for one reason or another. Any differences in staffing that might exist between more or less entrepreneurial organizations are not really known at the present time, but it seems reasonable to assume that individuals who are entrepreneurial in nature (risk-taking, innovative, creative) would fit better in organizations that are also entrepreneurial. Hence, staffing would involve a search for such matches between individual and organizational characteristics.

The match between organization design and people in the organization might be recognizable across organizations by size as well. Owner-managers of smaller organizations are likely to staff with people they feel will be most productive. This will probably result in a relatively homogeneous work force, whether the individuals are entrepreneurial or not. As the organization grows, it may become more difficult to structure and staff the company using such relatively narrow approaches, and hence more diversity will tend to occur. However, the presence of a strong organizational culture will tend to keep even larger organizations relatively homogeneous.

Information systems in smaller firms are more likely to be paper based, although the constantly changing computer field is making it ever easier for even very small firms to use computer-based information systems. Of course, these will generally be packaged systems rather than ones custom-developed for the firm. Larger firms are far more likely to use computer systems, and many have them developed precisely for their own unique needs and personnel. Likewise, larger organizations are more likely to use new information technologies than are smaller ones. On the other hand, small, highly entrepreneurial organizations may be quick to adopt new technologies and, indeed, may become leaders in the development and use of information systems. Nevertheless, the capital costs required usually preclude any major investment in such technologies by small organizations, even if they are innovative ones.

SOURCES: Jeffrey G. Covin and Dennis P. Bleven, "The Influence of Organization Structure on the Utility of an Entrepreneurial Top Management Style," *Journal of Management Studies,* May 1988, pp. 217–234; Robert C. Ford, Barry R. Armandi, and Cherrill P. Heaton, *Organization Theory: An Integrative Approach* (New York: Harper & Row, 1988); Y. Gasse, "The Utilization of Various Management Techniques and Practices in Small and Medium-Sized Firms," Working Paper Series No. NC88-07 (London, Canada: University of Western Ontario, National Centre for Management Research and Development, 1988); M. Tushman and D. Nadler, "Organizing for Innovation," *California Management Review,* Spring 1986, pp. 74–92; N. R. Smith, *The Entrepreneur and His Firm: The Relationship Between Type of Man and Type of Company* (East Lansing, Mich.: Michigan State University, 1967).

FOUR

Leading

The third basic managerial function is leading, which involves guiding and dealing with the people who work in the organization. Chapter 12 discusses the process of leadership itself, and Chapter 13 describes employee motivation. Interpersonal processes are discussed in Chapter 14, and interpersonal communication in Chapter 15.

CHAPTER OUTLINE

I. The Nature of Leadership
   A. Leadership Versus Management
   B. The Challenges of Leadership

II. Power and Leadership
   A. Types of Power
   B. Uses, Limits, and Outcomes of Power

III. Leadership Traits

IV. Leadership Behaviors
   A. The Michigan Studies
   B. The Ohio State Studies

V. Situational Approaches
   A. The LPC Model
   B. The Path-Goal Model
   C. The Participation Model
   D. An Integrative Framework

VI. Other Contemporary Perspectives
   A. Charismatic Leadership
   B. Entrepreneurial Leadership
   C. Symbolic Leadership

CHAPTER

12

After studying this chapter you should be able to

1. Define leadership, indicate the difference between leadership and management, and identify the challenges of leadership.

2. Name and describe several types of power, including their uses, limits, and outcomes.

3. Briefly discuss the trait approach to the study of leadership.

4. Discuss leadership behaviors and compare and contrast the Michigan and Ohio State studies.

5. Describe several situational approaches to leadership, including the LPC model, the path-goal model, the participation model, and an integrative framework for these models.

6. Discuss such contemporary perspectives on leadership as charismatic, entrepreneurial, and symbolic leadership.

Leadership

BILL MARRIOTT—LEADER, MANAGER, OR BOTH?

The Marriott Corporation can trace its roots back to 1927. In that year, J. Willard Marriott, Jr., opened a nine-seat root beer stand in Washington, D.C. When the weather turned cool and business fell off, Marriott started serving chili con carne and tamales. The business took off, and several new locations were soon opened.

By 1937, Marriott was flourishing to the point that Willard decided to seek new opportunities for growth. His first new venture was obtaining a catering contract with Eastern Airlines. Soon thereafter, Marriott entered the hotel business. And it is that business that today gives Marriott its strongest public identity.

In 1964, Willard Marriott passed the baton to his son, Bill Marriott. At the time, the company had a payroll of 9,600 employees and annual revenues of $84 million. Bill saw a number of attractive business opportunities, however, and soon announced a series of major new initiatives and expansions.

How successful has Marriott become? By 1990, its payroll was over 230,000 employees and it had annual revenues of over $8 billion. There are more than five hundred Marriott hotels around the world. In 1989, Marriott hotels were rated the number one choice for business travelers for the fourth year in a row. And new chains started by the Marriott Corporation—Courtyard, Fairfield Inns, Residence Inns, and Brighton Gardens—were also doing very well. In addition, the food services business, which runs food operations in airports, hospitals, schools, and companies, is growing at a rapid clip.

What accounts for Marriott Corporation's remarkable growth and success? Many observers give much of the credit to Bill Marriott himself. In particular, Marriott plays two roles very well—the role of manager and the role of leader.

From a management perspective, Marriott has a canny knack of making the right decisions. He has used the company's enormous purchasing power to keep costs low, has managed debt wisely, and has avoided many of the financial traps that have hindered other hotel and food services operations. He has also expanded astutely and seems well poised for a new spurt of international growth during the 1990s.

Many people point to Marriott's leadership abilities, however, as the real key to his success. One of his major strengths is his genuine and deeply rooted concern for both his guests and his employees. He believes that the best way to lead people is through example. Therefore, he seldom criticizes others in public, holds his temper in check, always tries to be fair and honest, and behaves with charm and grace. This combination of managerial acumen and interpersonal style has won him many accolades from his em-

ployees. Many of them have worked for Marriott for decades. Indeed, the company has one of the lowest turnover rates in the industry.

Two recent events promise to alter the shape of Marriott Corporation and Bill Marriott's role within it. First, Marriott suffered a heart attack in late 1989. Recovered and back on the job today, Marriott has nevertheless had to change his work habits. For example, he has cut his workday from fourteen hours to ten or twelve. He has also greatly reduced his travel schedule. In addition, he says that from now on he will rely more heavily on his top-management team to help carry the load.

The other event was a decision announced in early 1990 to sell some of the firm's restaurant

operations, including the airline catering business, Roy Rogers restaurants, and several smaller regional chains. The purpose of the divestitures was to allow the corporation to concentrate on its remaining core businesses—lodging and contract services. Indeed, when the planned sales were announced, Marriott also announced that it would almost double its number of hotels to one thousand by the mid-1990s.

Bill Marriott is a hands-on manager who believes in learning about his organization from every angle. For example, he routinely checks under the beds in his hotels to make sure the rooms are being properly cleaned. He also displays charisma and earns his employees' respect by showing his interest and concern for their well-being.

SOURCES: "How Master Lodger Bill Marriott Prophesied Profit and Prospered," *Fortune*, June 5, 1989, pp. 56–57; "Heart Attack Forces Exec to Downshift," *USA Today*, December 11, 1989, pp. 1B–2B; "Marriott Puts Restaurants on Block," *USA Today*, December 19, 1989, p. 3B; "Marriott Unit Is Sold; Others Go on Block," *The Wall Street Journal*, December 19, 1989, p. A3.

B

ill Marriott reflects a valuable but relatively uncommon mix of two key ingredients that are often needed to run a major corporation—managerial ability and leadership ability. Whereas managerial ability relies heavily on objective talents and skills, leadership is much more intangible. Thus, most observers agree that it is very difficult to understand, much less practice, effective leadership.

This chapter first explains the nature of leadership and then defines power and its relationship to leadership. After looking briefly at early trait models of leadership, it examines in more detail two behavioral approaches. Much of its attention, however, is focused on situational approaches. The chapter concludes by discussing other contemporary perspectives on leadership.

THE NATURE OF LEADERSHIP

☐ *Leadership* is an influence process that is directed at shaping the behavior of others.

We can define **leadership** as an influence process directed at shaping the behavior of others.[1] When Don Shula exhorts the members of the Miami Dolphins to play harder, he is leading. When Jack Welch, CEO of General Electric, encourages his managers to work harder, he is leading. And when your friend convinces you to try a new restaurant you have been avoiding, he is also leading. Leadership occurs in a variety of settings and in a variety of ways. Before discussing the various forms of leadership, however, let's first make a clearer distinction between leadership and management and then explore some of the challenges of leadership.

Leadership Versus Management

Leadership and management are in some ways similar but in more ways different. The relationship between the two roles is represented in Exhibit 12.1. Note in particular that people can be leaders without being managers, managers without being leaders, or both managers and leaders at the same time.

Managers can direct the efforts of others because of their formal organizational power. If a boss tells her subordinate to do three things and the person does exactly what she dictated but nothing else, the boss is probably being a manager but not a leader. When Bill Marriott instructs a hotel manager to increase the size of the hotel's catering staff, he is acting as a manager.

On the other hand, a leader doesn't have to rely on her formal position to influence someone. If a secretary organizes a group effort to help a coworker who has personal problems, she is acting as a leader but not as a manager. People at Marriott Corporation often go far beyond the normal duties of their job because of their respect and admiration for Bill Marriott himself.

From the standpoint of organizational effectiveness, people who are both leaders and managers are a valuable resource. Such individuals are able to carry out their managerial responsibilities effectively while also commanding the loyalty and respect of those they lead. But they are also quite scarce. Consequently, they usually are quite successful at doing almost anything they set out to do.

Exhibit 12.1 The Relationship Between Leadership and Management

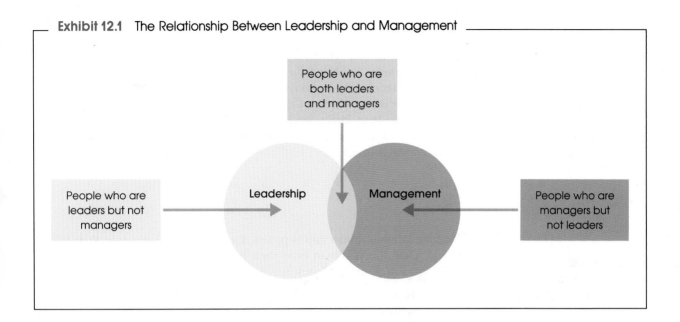

The Challenges of Leadership

In order to fulfill others' expectations of them, leaders must confront numerous challenges. In large measure, the success of any given leader will depend on her or his ability to address these challenges in a way that people will accept. Although any number of challenges are inherent in a given situation, two are relatively constant—multiple constituencies and unpopular decisions.

☐ One leadership challenge is having to satisfy *multiple constituencies*—different groups that may want different things from the organization.

MULTIPLE CONSTITUENCIES **Multiple constituencies** means that the leader must attempt to deal with several different people and groups at the same time in a way that is relatively acceptable to every party. This concern is compounded by the fact that the different constituencies often desire conflicting things from the organization. Employees may demand higher wages, while stockholders desire bigger dividends. Consider the case of Lee Iacocca. While at Chrysler, Iacocca has had dealings with the government, union officials, suppliers, creditors, competitors, and employees. One of his major challenges has been to see that each is in basic agreement with what he feels needs to be done to rebuild the company's health. Bill Marriott must also deal with unions, customers, suppliers, competitors, and stockholders.

☐ Another leadership challenge is having to make decisions that are unpopular with others.

UNPOPULAR DECISIONS Hand in hand with the notion of multiple constituencies is the simple fact that leaders occasionally have to make decisions that are unpopular, at least among some of their constituents. When Iacocca closed plants, employees at those plants clearly were unhappy. Marriott encountered considerable resistance when he announced the decision to sell some of the company's restaurant operations. The mark of a good leader is the ability to recognize when such decisions must be made and the perseverance to see them through.[2]

In addition to these two critical challenges, leaders have others. They must set good examples for their followers, they must continually monitor situations so that new actions can be taken as needed, and they must develop the potential of employees in the organization. Finally, leaders need to use their power wisely and without infringing on the rights and privileges of others. In the next section we turn our attention to a more detailed consideration of power in organizational settings.

POWER AND LEADERSHIP

The foundation of leadership is power. Leaders have power over their followers and wield this power to exert their influence. The various kinds of power can be used in several different ways.

Types of Power

☐ *Legitimate, reward,* and *coercive* power derive from a person's formal position in an organization; *expert* and *referent* power involve personal abilities and traits.

Most people agree that there are five basic types of power: legitimate, reward, coercive, expert, and referent power.[3]

Legitimate power is power created and conveyed by the organization. It is the same as authority. A boss can generally tell subordinates how they should be doing their jobs, how they should allocate their time at work, and so forth. Of course, legitimate power alone does not make someone a leader; all managers have legitimate power, but only some of them are leaders. As we have seen, orders and requests from someone with legitimate power may be carried out by subordinates but only to the minimum extent needed to satisfy the boss.[4]

A second type of power is **reward power**—the power to grant and withhold various kinds of rewards. Typical rewards in organizations include pay increases, promotions, praise, recognition, and interesting job assignments. The greater the number of rewards a manager controls and the more important they are to subordinates, the more reward power the manager has.

Coercive power is the power to force compliance through psychological, emotional, or physical threat. In some settings, such as the military and prisons, coercion may take the form of physical force. In most settings today, though, coercion is practiced more subtly, through verbal reprimands, disciplinary layoffs, fines, demotions, the loss of privileges, and excessive public criticism. As with reward power, the more punitive elements a manager can bring to bear and the more important they are to subordinates, the more coercive power he or she has. However, the use of coercion also tends to increase hostility and resentment.

Expert power is power based on knowledge and expertise. A manager who knows the best way to deal with a difficult customer or a secretary who knows the ins and outs of the organization's bureaucracy has expert power. The more

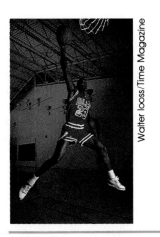

Leadership comes in all shapes and sizes. Michael Jordan, star of the NBA's Chicago Bulls, is a true leader among his teammates. He also has referent power over many of his young fans who wear Air Jordan shoes and who try to imitate his incredible moves on the basketball court.

important the knowledge is and the fewer people who are aware of it, the more expert power the person has.

The fifth type of power is **referent power.** It is referent power that generally sets leaders apart from nonleaders. This type of power is based on personal identification, imitation, and charisma. If a child dresses and talks like his favorite rock singer, the rock singer has referent power over the child. If an ambitious middle manager starts to emulate a successful top manager (dressing like her, going to the same restaurants for lunch, playing the same sports, and so on), the top manager has referent power. This aspect of leadership is covered again later, when we look at charisma.

Of course, most leaders use several different bases of power at the same time. For example, no matter how effective an individual is as a leader, she will sometimes find it necessary to rely on legitimate power. Indeed, many managers who lack leadership characteristics are still somewhat effective by using legitimate and reward power together. Likewise, leaders are often successful by combining expert and referent power.

PRELUDE CASE UPDATE

Bill Marriott clearly possesses all five bases of power. His formal position as CEO, for example, gives him both legitimate and reward power. His demonstrated ability to effectively manage hotel and food service operations also underscores his expert power. Although he seldom, if ever, has to use it, he also has coercive power by virtue of his dominant position in the firm. Finally, Marriott also possesses referent power. His personal integrity and strength of character make those around him want to follow his example as much as they possibly can.

Uses, Limits, and Outcomes of Power

USES OF POWER   There are numerous ways in which power may be used.[5] For one, the manager can make a legitimate request—that is, simply ask a subordinate to do something that falls within the normal scope of his job. The manager may also try to gain instrumental compliance—that is, use reward power by letting the subordinate know that if he does what is needed a reward will be forthcoming.

Coercion is the use of coercive power to get one's way. In the business context, it involves threatening a subordinate. For example, a manager might tell his subordinate that he will be fired if he doesn't perform a specific action. A more reasonable approach might be rational persuasion—convincing the subordinate that compliance is in everyone's best interest. Suppose a manager is trying to initiate a wage reduction. Clearly, most employees will not be enthusiastic, but if the manager can convince everyone that the cuts are necessary and that they will be temporary, people may be more receptive.

Personal identification and inspirational appeals are also used sometimes. These approaches derive from referent power. The idea is that the leader will strive to set a good example and attempt to inspire others to follow it. For example, Sam Walton, founder of Wal-Mart, is one of the richest men in America. Yet he lives a very unpretentious life and treats all Wal-Mart employees as his equal.

Finally, managers occasionally distort information to get their way. Of course, this misuse of expert power can be dangerous and frequently backfires. Consequently, it should seldom, if ever, be used.

LIMITS AND OUTCOMES OF POWER   Regardless of the manager's skill, power always has its limits. As a general rule, people can only be influenced up to a point. Moreover, their willingness to follow someone may be quite short-lived. Few leaders can maintain long-term support for their ideas and programs, especially when mistakes are made and faulty decisions are implemented.

TABLE 12.1   Outcomes of the Uses of Power

Source of Leader Influence	Type of Outcome		
	Commitment	*Compliance*	*Resistance*
Legitimate Power	Possible If request is polite and very appropriate.	Likely If request or order is seen as legitimate.	Possible If arrogant demands are made or request does not appear proper
Reward Power	Possible If used in a subtle, very personal way	Likely If used in a mechanical, impersonal way	Possible If used in a manipulative, arrogant way
Coercive Power	Very unlikely	Possible If used in a helpful, non-punitive way	Likely If used in a hostile or manipulative way
Expert Power	Likely If request is persuasive and subordinates share leader's task goals	Possible If request is persuasive but subordinates are apathetic about task goals	Possible If leader is arrogant and insulting or subordinates oppose task goals
Referent Power	Likely If request is believed to be important to leader	Possible if request is perceived to be unimportant to leader	Possible If request is for something that will bring harm to leader

SOURCE: Table adapted by Gary A. Yukl from information in John R. P. French, Jr., and Bertram Raven, "The Bases of Social Power," in *Studies in Social Power*, Dorwin P. Cartwright, Ed. (Ann Arbor: Institute for Social Research, the University of Michigan, 1959), pp. 150–167. © 1955. Data used by permission of the Institute for Social Research.

□ When managers attempt to use power, they may encounter *commitment, compliance,* or *resistance.*

When people are confronted with an attempt by their boss or leader to influence them, they usually have one of three basic responses: commitment, compliance, and resistance. **Commitment** is the outcome when the manager is also a leader. People are committed to the person and therefore respond favorably to her attempt to influence them. **Compliance** occurs when the boss is strictly a manager but has little leadership quality; employees go along with the request but do not have any stake in the result. Finally, **resistance** occurs when the manager's power base is weak or inconsistent with the situation. In this case employees actively resist the attempt to influence them.

Table 12.1 summarizes the outcomes of different kinds of power uses. In particular, it shows when commitment, compliance, and resistance are likely or possible in different power bases and situations.

In sum, then, various kinds, uses, and outcomes of power are relevant in organizational settings. We are now ready to look more closely at leadership itself. Through the years, writers have focused on three distinct approaches to studying and describing leadership, called the trait, behavioral, and contingency approaches.[6]

LEADERSHIP TRAITS

□ *Leadership traits* were thought to be stable and enduring characteristics that set leaders apart from nonleaders.

One early systematic approach to the study of leadership was the trait approach, whose adherents assumed that great leaders such as Napoleon, Lincoln, and Gandhi possessed a set of stable and enduring **leadership traits** or characteristics that set them apart from followers. Their goal was to identify these traits so that they could be used as a basis for selecting managers.

A great deal of attention was focused on the search for traits, and researchers studied common traits such as intelligence, height, self-confidence, attractiveness, and vocabulary.[7] But, unfortunately, traits proved to be ineffective predictors of leadership. For one thing, the list of characteristics soon grew to such lengths that it became unmanageable. For another, the list of exceptions was almost as long as the list of leaders who possessed each trait. For instance, it has been suggested that leaders are taller than nonleaders, but many historical leaders (such as Napoleon and Hitler) and contemporary leaders (like H. Ross Perot) are of slight build.

People soon realized that the search for leadership traits was interesting but of little scientific merit; consequently, they started focusing attention on other areas instead. The next major approach to the study of leadership was what we now call the behavioral approach.

LEADERSHIP BEHAVIORS

□ The *leadership behavior* approach attempted to differentiate leaders from nonleaders on the basis of their behaviors.

Whereas the trait approach attempted to identify characteristics that differentiated leaders from nonleaders, the behavioral approach sought to define behaviors that set effective leaders apart from ineffective leaders. Although many **leadership behaviors** have been found, those identified by two major sets of studies have received special attention.[8]

Gwendolyn Cates

Ardis Krainik is a strong practitioner of employee-centered leadership. She is the general director of the Lyric Opera of Chicago. Krainik works hard to make the performers feel wanted, to ensure their happiness and contentment, and to create an environment in which their creativity can blossom.

The Michigan Studies

☐ The Michigan studies identified two forms of leadership behavior: job centered and employee centered.

Researchers at the University of Michigan identified two critical leadership behaviors, called job-centered behavior and employee-centered behavior.[9] A leader who practices job-centered behavior closely supervises subordinates so that their performance can be monitored and controlled. His interests are primarily in getting the job done, and he takes an active role in explaining this task.

In contrast, employee-centered behavior focuses on reaching high levels of performance by building a sense of team spirit through the human element of the workplace. An employee-centered leader is concerned with her subordinates' job satisfaction and group cohesion. She is also willing to let employees have a voice in how they do their jobs.

The Michigan researchers felt that job-centered and employee-centered behaviors represent a single dimension, with one of the two basic behaviors at each end. That is, they believed that if leaders become more job centered, they simultaneously become less employee centered, and vice versa. They also felt that leaders who were employee centered would generally be more effective as managers than leaders who were primarily job centered. That is, their employees would perform at a higher level and also be more satisfied.

The Ohio State Studies

□ The Ohio State studies suggested that leaders could choose initiating structure and/or consideration behaviors.

Researchers at Ohio State University identified many of the same concepts as those developed in Michigan but also extended and refined them.[10] They agreed that there were two critical leadership behaviors, which they called initiating structure behavior and consideration behavior. Initiating structure behavior, similar to job-centered behavior, focuses on getting the job done, whereas consideration behavior is like that part of employee-centered behavior that involves employee satisfaction.

The basic difference between the Ohio State and Michigan findings is shown in Exhibit 12.2. As we have noted, the Michigan researchers argued that leaders could be job centered or employee centered, but not both. The Ohio State researchers, however, found that the two forms of behavior were independent. Therefore, as the exhibit shows, a leader can use initiating structure behavior and consideration at the same time.

Much of the early research of Ohio State was conducted with managers from International Harvester (now known as Navistar). In general, the researchers found that high initiating structure behavior resulted in higher performance but also led to lower levels of job satisfaction. High levels of consideration behavior caused higher levels of job satisfaction but lower levels of performance. Clearly, then, the dynamics of leader behavior are complex and anything but straightforward.

Indeed, the notion that one type of leadership will always be appropriate has been unacceptable for many years. Researchers have shifted their efforts to

Exhibit 12.2   Leadership Behaviors

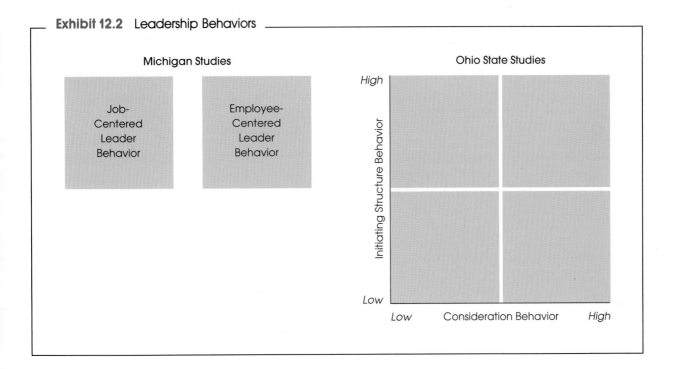

the development of contingency models of leadership, which attempt to define those circumstances in which one form of leadership is best and those in which an alternative style will be more appropriate. The next section introduces several interesting contingency models of leadership.

PRELUDE CASE UPDATE

Bill Marriott actively practices both general forms of leadership identified in the Michigan and Ohio State studies. From the standpoint of job-centered or initiating structure behaviors, he plays a major role in setting goals for the corporation, establishing the standards against which performance will be assessed, and defining what others are supposed to do. On the other hand, from the perspective of employee-centered or consideration behaviors, Marriott also frequently exhibits genuine concern for the welfare and satisfaction of his guests and employees.

SITUATIONAL APPROACHES

☐ *Contingency,* or *situational, approaches* to leadership attempt to specify circumstances under which different kinds of leadership behavior are appropriate.

Earlier in the book we investigated the nature of **contingency**, or **situational, approaches** to management. Leadership was one of the very first areas in which situational theories were developed. Exhibit 12.3 illustrates the differ-

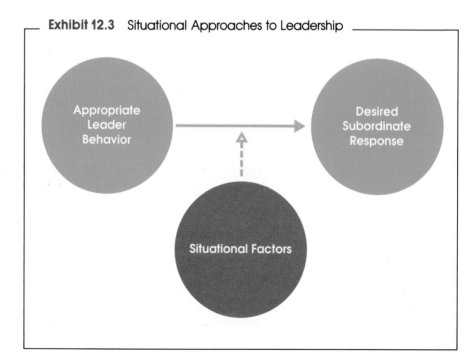

Exhibit 12.3   Situational Approaches to Leadership

ences between behavioral approaches and situational approaches. The behavioral approach is represented by the two circles linked with the solid arrow. The basic premise is that appropriate leadership behaviors lead to desired subordinate responses. For instance, the Michigan researchers assumed that employee-centered behavior would always lead to employee performance and satisfaction.

Situational approaches, in contrast, introduce the third circle into the exhibit. They suggest that situational, or contingency, factors must be considered. Whereas one kind of behavior will work in one setting, a different setting may well dictate a different form of behavior. The goal of situational approaches is to define the situational variables that managers need to consider in assessing how different forms of leadership will be received.

Although a few early researchers noted the potential importance of situational factors, these factors did not receive widespread attention until the 1960s. Since then, however, virtually all approaches to leadership have adopted a situational view. The three most popular widely known situational theories—the LPC Model, the path-goal model, and the participation model—are described next.[11]

The LPC Model

☐ The *LPC model* suggested that appropriate leadership behavior is a function of the favorableness of the situation.

The first of these contingency models of leadership, called the **LPC** (for least preferred coworker) **model**, was developed by Fred E. Fiedler.[12] Fiedler suggested that appropriate forms of leadership style varied as a function of the favorableness of the situation.

LEADERSHIP STYLES   The LPC model includes two basic forms of leadership style, task oriented and relationship oriented. The task-oriented style is similar to the earlier job-centered and initiating structure behaviors, and the relationship-oriented style is like employee-centered and consideration behaviors. The name of the model is derived from a questionnaire developed to measure task-oriented and relationship-oriented style. People who complete the questionnaire do so in reference to the employee with whom they least prefer to work—their least preferred coworker.

One interesting aspect of the LPC model is that leadership style is assumed to be a stable personality trait of the leader. That is, some leaders use one style and others use a different style, and these styles are basically constant. Any given leader is unable to change her or his behavior.

☐ In the LPC model, the favorableness of the situation is determined by *leader-member relations, task structure,* and *position power.*

FAVORABLENESS OF THE SITUATION   As we noted, the LPC model sees appropriate leadership behavior as a function of the favorableness of the situation. Favorableness is defined by three elements—leader-member relations, task structure, and position power.

Leader-member relations defines the nature of the relationship between the leader and the members of the group. If the relationship is characterized by confidence, trust, liking, and respect, it is defined as good and is favorable for the leader. In contrast, if the relationship lacks confidence, trust, and respect, and if the leader and the followers do not like each other, the relationship is bad and unfavorable for the leader.

Task structure is the degree to which the group's task is well defined and understood by everyone. If the task is highly structured, the situation is probably more favorable.

Finally, **position power** is the power vested in the leader's position. Strong power is favorable for the leader, and weak power is unfavorable. Thus the best possible situation is good leader-member relations, a structured task, and strong position power, and the worst situation is poor relations, an unstructured task, and weak power.

STYLES AND SITUATIONS Exhibit 12.4 illustrates how leadership styles combine with the situation to determine group effectiveness. Note that the situation can be defined in eight unique ways. The left side of the chart repre-

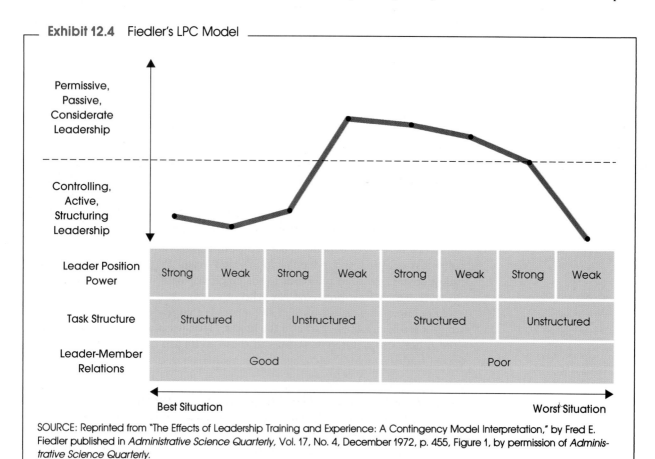

Exhibit 12.4 Fiedler's LPC Model

SOURCE: Reprinted from "The Effects of Leadership Training and Experience: A Contingency Model Interpretation," by Fred E. Fiedler published in *Administrative Science Quarterly*, Vol. 17, No. 4, December 1972, p. 455, Figure 1, by permission of *Administrative Science Quarterly*.

sents the best situation. As the situation progresses to the right, however, it gets gradually worse.

The line above the situations predicts which style of leadership will be most effective in each situation. A task-oriented leader (using "controlling, active, structuring leadership") will be most effective in the best and the worst situations, whereas a relationship-oriented leader ("permissive, passive, considerate") will have better chances in situations of intermediate favorableness.

For example, suppose John has just been appointed the chairman of a task force to develop a new grievance procedure. The task force contains several of John's peers, so his position power is low. The company has no grievance procedure at present and John has been given no guidelines to follow, so the task is unstructured. Finally, John has had some interpersonal problems—poor relations—with a few of the other committee members in the past. If John is by nature a task-oriented leader, the contingency model predicts he will have greater success with the group than if he is a relationship-oriented leader.

On balance, the LPC model has received mixed research support. For example, people have questioned its assumptions about the flexibility of leadership style and how it defines situations. There are also major questions about the questionnaire that is used to measure leadership behavior. At the same time, it was the first major approach to attract our attention to the situation as an important part of leadership.[13]

The Path-Goal Model

□ The *path-goal model* of leadership suggests that leaders should attempt to determine their subordinates' goals and then clarify the paths to achieving them.

The **path-goal model** also provides interesting insights into the situational nature of leadership. This model essentially suggests that the purpose of leadership in organizational settings is to clarify for subordinates the paths to desired goals. That is, leaders should determine what subordinates want from their jobs and then show them how to acquire those things through their work.[14] The basic framework of the path-goal model is shown in Exhibit 12.5.

LEADERSHIP STYLES   Like the other models discussed so far, the path-goal model includes one task-oriented style and one employee-oriented style, called directive and supportive leadership. It also includes an additional one, however, called participative leadership. Participative leadership is the extent to which the leader allows subordinates to participate in decisions that affect them.

SITUATIONAL ELEMENTS   As shown in the exhibit, there are two sets of situational factors that intervene between the leader's behavior and the subordinate's motivation: the subordinate's personal characteristics and environmental characteristics.

The personal characteristics of the subordinate include such things as her perceptions of her own ability, her desire to participate in organizational activ-

Exhibit 12.5 The Path-Goal Model

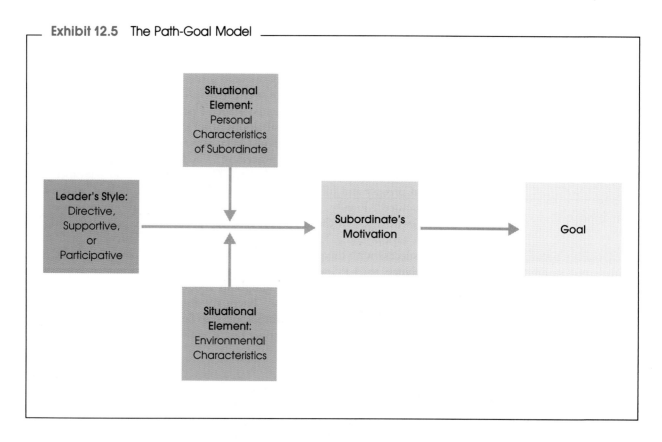

ities, and her willingness to accept direction and control. Environmental characteristics include the extent to which the task is highly structured, the nature of the work group, and the authority system within the organization.

STYLES AND SITUATIONS The LPC model is very precise. In contrast, the path-goal model is very general and suggests that the leader needs to use a lot of common sense. The path-goal model also assumes that a leader's style is flexible and that he can change his style as needed.

In using the model, then, a manager should assess the relevant dimensions of the situation and choose an appropriate combination of behaviors that will complement that situation. For instance, suppose that a subordinate lacks confidence in her abilities and is assigned to a new task that is highly unstructured. It may be appropriate in this situation for the supervisor to be highly directive in order to clarify the subordinate's task demands and reduce her anxiety about being able to get the job done. Similarly, if subordinates want to participate, the leader needs to consider allowing them to do so, whereas if they have no desire to participate, the leader may not even have to think about it. *Management Today: The World of Management* describes how Kazumitsu Minami, president of Hitachi Consumer Products of America, uses the path-goal theory of leadership.

THE WORLD OF MANAGEMENT

Keeping Everyone Happy at Hitachi

Kazumitsu Minami is president of Hitachi Consumer Products of America. He sees a major part of his job as keeping his workers happy and satisfied. So he tries to figure out what they want and then show them how to achieve it.

One of his methods for accomplishing this is maintaining an open-door policy. When workers want to talk with him about something, they find that he is easily accessible and will listen to what they have to say. And he takes action whenever he can. For example, a group of workers recently approached him about the possibility of converting to a four-day workweek. He listened to what they said and then allowed all his employees to vote on the proposal. The shortened workweek lost by a narrow vote.

Most managers would have allowed the matter to end there, knowing that they had listened to the minority and then followed the voice of the majority. Minami, however, felt bad that he still had a group of unhappy workers. So when the company installed a new assembly line to produce videocassette recorders, he put that line on a four-day workweek and allowed those disgruntled workers who wanted to transfer to do so.

Minami also believes that good performance should be followed with big rewards. Consequently, Hitachi has an innovative incentive system that ties pay to performance much more closely than is typical in Japanese firms. On balance, then, Minami is a good practitioner of the path-goal theory of leadership. He listens to employees to figure out what they want and then does everything he reasonably can to help them achieve it.

SOURCES: Henry Eason, "The Corporate Immigrants," *Nation's Business,* April 1987, pp. 12–19; "The Mountain Priest," *Fortune,* August 3, 1987, p. 42; "Hitachi, GM Unit Team Up to Buy National Semiconductor Subsidiary," *The Wall Street Journal,* February 28, 1989, p. B4.

The path-goal model is still in the early stages of development, and several variations exist. It has received generally favorable support from research, however, and will probably continue to be developed and used in the future.[15]

PRELUDE CASE UPDATE

Bill Marriott's behavior clearly follows the path-goal model. When he is making a presentation before the top-management team or the board of directors, for example, he is extremely task oriented—directive—in his demeanor and approach. On the other hand, when he is talking with a cook, a desk clerk, or a porter, he is much more considerate and supportive. He has also become more participative in how he makes decisions. Finally, following the basic premise of the path-goal model, Marriott also works hard to make sure employees understand what they must do to succeed in the company.

The Participation Model

❏ The *participation model* helps managers determine how much participation employees should be allowed in making various kinds of decisions.

The final situational model to be discussed here is the **participation model**, which involves a much more narrow aspect of leadership than do the preceding models. In particular, it addresses the specific question of how much subordinates should be allowed to participate in decision making.[16] As with the other models, the participation model includes alternative styles and situational factors to consider.

LEADERSHIP STYLES   The model includes five degrees of participation:

❏ AI—The manager makes the decision alone, with no input from subordinates (the *A* stands for *autocratic*).
❏ AII—The manager asks subordinates for information that he or she needs to make the decision, but still makes the decision alone. Subordinates may or may not be informed of the decision.
❏ CI—The manager shares the situation with selected subordinates and asks for information and advice. The manager still makes the decision, but keeps subordinates actively informed (the *C* stands for *consultative*).
❏ CII—The manager meets with subordinates as a group to discuss the situation. Information is freely shared, although the manager still makes the decision.
❏ GII—The manager and the subordinates meet as a group and freely share information, and the entire group makes the decision (the *G* stands for *group*).*

SITUATIONAL ELEMENTS   The participation model suggests that a manager needs to ask several questions before choosing a degree of participation. Moreover, different questions are used for different circumstances. In some cases, the manager will have a group-related problem to address, whereas in other cases the problem will relate more to an individual. Moreover, in some cases the goal will be to make a decision as quickly as possible, whereas in other situations the manager will be striving to help an individual or group improve its decision-making skills.

STYLES AND SITUATIONS   Styles and situations are combined in a very structured and precise fashion in the participation model, as illustrated in the decision tree presented in Exhibit 12.6. This particular tree is suggested for a group problem when time is important. The questions involved in the situation are listed above the diagram. The manager asks each in order and answers yes or no. Depending on his answer to any given question, he follows the appropriate path on the tree to the next question. Ultimately, each path ends with a suggested decision-making style. This style is the one that optimizes

*SOURCE: Reprinted from *Leadership and Decision-Making*, by Victor H. Vroom and Philip W. Yetton, by permission of the University of Pittsburgh Press. © 1973 by University of Pittsburgh Press.

Exhibit 12.6   Time-Driven Group Problem Decision Tree for the Participation Model

QR   Quality Requirement: *How important is the technical quality of this decision?*

CR   Commitment Requirement: *How important is subordinate commitment to the decision?*

LI   Leader's Information: *Do you have sufficient information to make a high-quality decision?*

ST   Problem Structure: *Is the problem well structured?*

CP   Commitment Probability: *If you were to make the decision by yourself, is it reasonably certain that your subordinate(s) would be committed to the decision?*

GC   Goal Congruence: *Do subordinates share the organizational goals to be attained in solving this problem?*

CO   Subordinate Conflict: *Is conflict among subordinates over preferred solutions likely?*

SI   Subordinate Information: *Do subordinates have sufficient information to make a high-quality decision?*

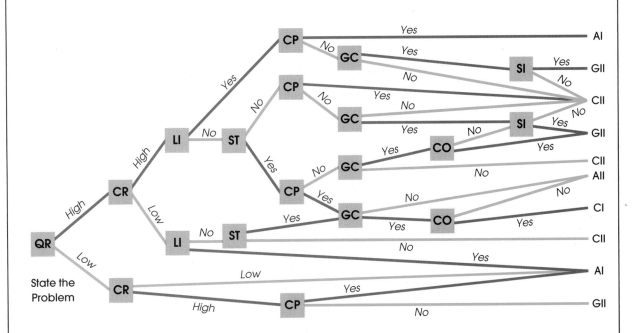

SOURCE: Reprinted from *The New Leadership: Managing Participation in Organizations* by Victor H. Vroom and Arthur G. Jago, 1988, Englewood Cliffs, NJ: Prentice-Hall. Copyright 1987 by V. H. Vroom and A. G. Jago. Used with permission of the authors.

Ed Kashi

Many managers are increasingly recognizing the importance of practicing participative leadership. The group shown here is one of thirty worker teams at Lake Superior Paper Industries. Company managers give each team a great deal of power over hiring, promoting, and firing team members. The teams also manage almost every aspect of how they do their jobs on a day-to-day basis.

subordinates' acceptance of the decision, the quality of the decision (from the organization's standpoint), and the demands on the manager's time.

In general, the participation model has been supported by research and accepted by managers. Of course, it should not be followed too rigidly. Managers should recognize that it provides a set of guidelines rather than a set of rules that should always be followed.

An Integrative Framework

◻ An integrative framework suggests that different elements of the various approaches to leadership can be combined to produce effective leadership in different situations.

Recently, a framework to integrate these diverse results has been devised.[17] As shown in Exhibit 12.7, the framework includes all of the major factors discussed so far—power, traits, behavior, and situations.

This framework essentially suggests that leadership is a complex phenomenon rather than a simple one. It also suggests that all the approaches to leadership have merit and that they should be seen as complementary rather than contradictory. All other things being equal, traits do make a difference in leadership, although given the careful selection process in many organizations, managers will have such similar traits that power or behavior will essentially make the difference in terms of performance.

The situation is shown as surrounding the other components of the framework in order to convey the idea that its impact is general rather than particular. That is, it affects everything, not just one or a few aspects. The situation

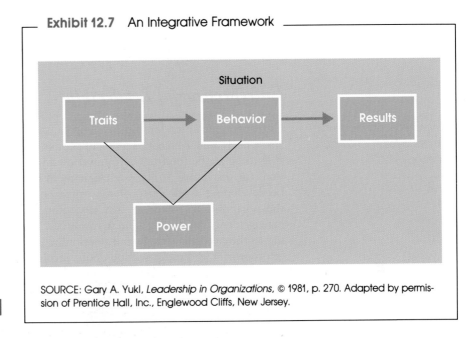

Exhibit 12.7   An Integrative Framework

SOURCE: Gary A. Yukl, *Leadership in Organizations*, © 1981, p. 270. Adapted by permission of Prentice Hall, Inc., Englewood Cliffs, New Jersey.

can influence which behavior is appropriate for leaders, as in the situational models, and it can influence which forms of power are available to the leader. Also, of course, it can directly influence results beyond the leader's impact. For example, a shortage of materials may hinder performance in ways the leader cannot control. Understanding the situation, then, is the key to being an effective managerial leader.[18]

OTHER CONTEMPORARY PERSPECTIVES

Given the obvious importance of leadership, we should not be surprised that researchers are always devoting a lot of attention to identifying new and even more insightful perspectives. Three other contemporary perspectives that it is important to note are charismatic leadership, entrepreneurial leadership, and symbolic leadership.

Charismatic Leadership

☐ *Charismatic leadership relies on attributes of the leader that inspire loyalty and enthusiasm.*

Charisma is an intangible attribute in the leader's personality that inspires loyalty and enthusiasm. Certain leaders, such as Ronald Reagan, Mike Ditka, Jesse Jackson, and Mary Kay Ashe, have charisma. Others, such as Dan Quayle, Jimmy Carter, IBM's John Akers, and Tom Landry, tend to have less charisma. Recently, researchers have tried to link charisma with leadership. In general, it has been suggested that when a leader has charisma, followers trust his or her beliefs, adopt those beliefs themselves, feel affection for the leader, obey the leader unquestioningly, and develop an emotional involvement with the mission of the organization. Although the study of charismatic leadership is still in its infancy, it will probably become more popular in the future.

Entrepreneurial Leadership

☐ *Entrepreneurial leadership attempts to foster innovation and vision.*

Entrepreneurial leadership, sometimes called transformational leadership, is also a fairly new concept. The focus here is on how some managers are always able to be at the forefront of innovation and vision in shaping their organizations for the future.[19] The key elements of entrepreneurial leadership seem to be developing a full grasp of the organization's environment, understanding the organization's place in that environment, attending to proper strategic management, developing human resources, and anticipating rather than reacting to the need for change and development. Like charismatic leadership, entrepreneurial leadership will no doubt receive greater attention in the future.

Nelson Mandela is a charismatic leader. Although imprisoned for twenty-seven years because of his political beliefs, he always retained a position of prominence in South Africa's antiapartheid movement. Mandela was released in early 1990, becoming the main spokesperson for the movement. His ability to gain the confidence of his followers and inspire them to act makes him a highly successful leader.

AP/Wide World Photos

ETHICAL DILEMMAS OF MANAGEMENT

Taking Symbols Seriously

Ethics and social responsibility are popular topics of discussion in corporate America today. One of the clear messages being communicated is that the behaviors of top managers are critical in setting the ethical climate that will permeate the entire organization.

Nowhere has this been more dramatically demonstrated than at Toshiba. In mid-1987, it was learned that Toshiba was selling high-technology equipment to the Soviet Union. The equipment would allow Soviet submarines to run much more quietly than they had in the past. The U.S. government estimated that it would have to spend $40 billion upgrading its submarine detection networks. The sale of the equipment by Toshiba violated a treaty signed by the Japanese government that limits what can be sold to the Soviets.

There was a tremendous outcry in the United States, as well as various threats about boycotts and new trade restrictions. In the end, however, little action was taken because it might have damaged broader relationships with the Japanese.

Back in Japan, however, something happened that few Americans could understand—the top two officials at Toshiba resigned as a public symbol of their sorrow for bringing such embarrassment to the company. Few, if any, American executives would have responded in the same way. In Japan, however, such practices are commonplace. The Japanese feel that the top managers of a firm are its clear and public symbols to the rest of the world. And as symbols, they must sometimes pay a high price for an error in judgment.

SOURCES: "The Battle over Toshiba," *Newsweek,* July 13, 1987, p. 40; "Toshiba Deal with Soviets Angers USA," *USA Today,* July 2, 1987, pp. 1B–2B; "Why Congress Is Letting Toshiba off the Hook," *Business Week,* April 4, 1988, pp. 34–35; "Matter of Honor: Japanese Top Managers Quick to Resign When Trouble Hits Firm," *The Wall Street Journal,* July 7, 1987, p. 19.

Symbolic Leadership

☐ *Symbolic leadership* involves creating and maintaining a strong organizational culture.

LEARNING CHECK

You should now be able to discuss such contemporary perspectives on leadership as charismatic, entrepreneurial, and symbolic leadership.

A third contemporary concept is **symbolic leadership**—leadership associated with establishing and maintaining a strong organizational culture, as discussed in Chapter 9. In fact, leadership is usually seen as the primary determinant of culture. For example, in a company like Levi Strauss, top management takes a very casual approach to leadership, emphasizing informality, open communication networks, and individualism. This is translated into a unique culture that members of the organization recognize and adopt. In contrast, top management at IBM sets a different tone, emphasizing formality, conformity, and managed communication flows. *Management Today: Ethical Dilemmas of Management* describes how the wrong symbols can lead others into unethical behavior. Once again, the notion of symbolic leadership is a new one. Hence, managers are just becoming aware of the importance of symbolism in their work.

345

Chapter Summary

Leadership is an influence process directed at shaping the behavior of others. People can be managers but not leaders, leaders but not managers, or both. The most valuable are those who combine the two qualities, but they are scarce. To fulfill others' expectations of them, leaders must confront numerous challenges, notably multiple constituencies and unpopular decisions.

There are five basic types of power: legitimate, reward, coercive, expert, and referent. Leaders may use each of these forms to influence people to pursue certain goals. When people are confronted with someone's attempt to influence them, their response can be commitment, compliance, or resistance.

Leadership traits are those characteristics of leaders that set them apart from followers. Unfortunately, no one has ever established that any single set of traits can reliably distinguish leaders from nonleaders in a wide variety of situations.

The behavioral approach attempted to differentiate successful or effective leaders from unsuccessful or ineffective ones on the basis of their behaviors. The Michigan studies identified two major leadership behaviors termed job-centered and employee-centered behaviors. They regarded these behaviors as mutually exclusive and felt that employee-centeredness was more effective. The Ohio State researchers also tended to emphasize two major forms of behavior, which they called initiating structure and consideration behaviors. Unlike the Michigan group, the Ohio State researchers felt that these two forms of behavior could and should be combined for most effective leadership.

Situational approaches to leadership attempt to define the circumstances in which one form of leadership is best and those in which an alternative form is more appropriate. The LPC model assumes that the behavior of managers is not changeable and is either task oriented or relationship oriented. Three elements of the situation—leader-member relations, task structure, and position power—are assumed to define appropriate leadership behavior. The path-goal model suggests that the purpose of leadership is to clarify for followers the paths to desired goals. This model assumes that the leadership process involves both subordinates' characteristics and environmental characteristics. The participation model focuses on a narrow but important aspect of leadership: determining how much subordinates should be allowed to participate in decision making. A framework to integrate these diverse models has recently been developed. It suggests that leadership is a complex phenomenon rather than a simple one and that all approaches to leadership have merit and should be seen as complementary rather than contradictory.

Three new and insightful perspectives on leadership focus on charismatic, entrepreneurial, and symbolic leadership.

The Manager's Vocabulary

leadership	contingency (situational)
multiple constituencies	approaches
legitimate power	LPC model
reward power	leader-member relations
coercive power	task structure
expert power	position power
referent power	path-goal model
commitment	participation model
compliance	charisma
resistance	entrepreneurial
leadership traits	leadership
leadership behaviors	symbolic leadership

Prelude Case Wrap-Up

Bill Marriott and the corporation that bears his name are the subjects of our Prelude Case for this chapter. Through his unique blend of managerial ability and leadership, Marriott the man has taken Marriott the hotel and food services company to the top of its industry.

Marriott reflects virtually every aspect of leadership discussed in this chapter. For example, as noted already, he does an exceptional job of playing the roles of both leader and manager. Moreover, he possesses each of the five major types of power and knows exactly when and how to best use each of them.

In terms of traits, Marriott can be characterized as honest, straightforward, of high moral conviction, and genuinely interested in the welfare of others. In addition, he also clearly illustrates the major forms of leadership behavior.

Marriott also recognizes the dangers of using the same approach to leadership in every situation. He has the ability to assess the situation and his audience and then tailor his behavior and demeanor accordingly. Depending on what the various situational context suggests, he can be task oriented, people oriented, and/or participative.

Marriott is also a charismatic individual. He inspires confidence, if not downright awe, from his subordinates. He also practices entrepreneurial leadership on occasion. For example, Marriott has been an industry leader in targeting specific market niches and then starting new lodging chains to address them. And Marriott also recognizes the symbolic nature of his job and goes out of his way to present the sort of image he wants the company to have. For example, he takes great care in his appearance and behavior in all of his business activities and dealings.

Prelude Case Questions

1. Do you think someone could run a corporation such as Marriott if he or she were an outstanding manager but had few leadership qualities? Why or why not?
2. What other traits do you think Marriott possesses besides those noted in the case? Why do you think so?
3. Identify some circumstances that Marriott could encounter in his business in which he could use the participation model.
4. Research the CEOs of other major lodging chains, like Hyatt, Hilton, and Sheraton. Compare and contrast them with Bill Marriott.

Discussion Questions

Review Questions

1. Explain how someone could be a manager but not a leader, a leader but not a manager, or both a leader and a manager.
2. List and define the five types of power.
3. What are the major forms of leadership behavior identified in the Michigan and Ohio State studies?

4. Summarize the LPC, path-goal, and participation models.
5. Describe three contemporary perspectives on leadership.

Analysis Questions

1. Many people have heard the saying "Power corrupts, but absolute power corrupts absolutely." What does this mean? What implications does it have for organizations and for managers?
2. Compare and contrast the three situational approaches to leadership.
3. What leadership traits do you think are most important?
4. What forms of leadership behavior can you identify beyond those discussed in the chapter?
5. Who do you think are today's charismatic leaders?

Application Questions and Exercises

1. Identify a leader whom you respect. List the traits that you think contribute to her or his effectiveness.
2. Interview a local manager or community leader. Find out what he or she thinks contributes most to effective leadership.
3. Think of a situation in which you were forced to play the role of leader. What factors contributed to your success (or lack of success)?
4. Many colleges and universities have a training or development center that offers courses or seminars on leadership. Find out if your school has such a center. If so, interview its director and find out what approaches are used to teach leadership.
5. Write a brief case that describes a situation that could be addressed by using the participation model of leadership. In the case, provide "answers" to the questions asked by the model without specifying them in the words used in the model. Exchange cases with a classmate. Working alone, each of you should ask the questions in the model, determine the answers from the case, and work through the decision tree to a recommended approach. Now compare solutions and see if each of you followed the path through the decision tree as intended by the one who wrote the case.

ENHANCEMENT CASE

LEADERSHIP CHANGES AT APPLE

Steven Jobs and Steven Wozniak reshaped every facet of information processing technology when in the late 1970s they constructed the first personal computer. Working out of a garage, they began to manufacture and market their invention under the name of Apple Computer. The firm exploded and became a multimillion-dollar corporation. When IBM entered the personal computer market, however, the giant business equipment and computer manufacturer used its muscle and reputation to seize control of the market, and Apple was left in the dust.

Wozniak had little interest in being a manager. He stayed away from the day-to-day operations at Apple and played only a technical role in developing new products. Wozniak eventually left the company in early 1985. Jobs, however, had grander ambitions. In particular, he wanted to lead his fledgling company back to the top and overcome what he saw as the all-powerful corporate entity of IBM.

Jobs is a very charismatic person, and his followers at Apple rallied behind him. And Apple did indeed regain some of its lost market share. It became the choice of individualists—people who saw themselves as not wanting to conform to the norms of corporate America.

Problems continued to plague the company, however. For one thing, new products were late and few of them were successful. For another, Jobs doggedly refused to allow Apple's computers to be compatible with IBM equipment, thus essentially keeping Apple out of the business market. Most of Apple's successes came in the education market and, because of its image as the individual's machine, among people who work alone or at home.

Jobs eventually recognized that although he was perhaps an effective leader, he lacked some of the basic managerial skills necessary to run a major corporation. Accordingly, he recruited John Sculley from the presidency of Pepsi-Cola USA. The plan was that Jobs would remain chairman of the board of directors and would run one of the technical groups. He also still owned a large block of Apple stock.

Sculley would be president and would handle all of the day-to-day managerial activities.

Sculley reorganized Apple's nine decentralized divisions into three larger, somewhat more centralized ones. At first, Apple insiders resented Sculley. They saw him as a threat to Jobs and as an outsider who was not really part of the Apple family. He threw himself into the company, however, and became an expert on personal computers and the industry in general. Eventually, and perhaps grudgingly, others in the company began to admire and respect him.

Conflict between the two men was inevitable, however. The board of directors started pressuring Sculley to remove Jobs from the head of the Macintosh division because it was having the same problems that Apple had always had. At first Sculley resisted. Eventually, though, he saw that something had to be done and did indeed ask Jobs to step down.

Jobs maneuvered to remove Sculley from his position, but the board of directors backed the president. Jobs resigned from the board and went on extended leave. He soon realized that he could never return to Apple in any kind of meaningful role and subsequently resigned.

Sculley, meanwhile, developed a bold new strategy to go after a bigger share of the business market. New products were developed that could communicate with IBM equipment. Networking capabilities were also enhanced. Apple subsequently went on a significant growth surge that took the company back to the forefront of the personal computer market. Although it never regained the top spot from IBM, Apple nevertheless again became a prominent player in the personal computer industry.

Sculley replaced Jobs as a sort of corporate hero, both at Apple and in the business world in general. He wrote a well-received book—*Odyssey*—about his own transitions during his managerial career. He took an extended sabbatical that gained headlines in the business press. And during the rest of the 1980s, he quadrupled revenues (to $4 billion) and quintupled profits (to $420 million).

But in the early 1990s, trouble reared its ugly head again. Sculley announced another major reorganization, one that insiders thought was one too many. Profits also started to decline, as did sales. And people at Apple began to grumble that Sculley had become too inaccessible. They had always looked to first Jobs and then Sculley as indicators of what direction they were to take, but many believed that Sculley had stopped sending them the signals.

SOURCES: Bro Uttal, "Behind the Fall of Steve Jobs," *Fortune*, August 5, 1985, pp. 20–24; Brian O'Reilly, "Apple Computer's Risky Revolution," *Fortune*, May 8, 1989, pp. 75–83; "With Its Profits Souring, Apple Plans Cutbacks," *The Wall Street Journal*, January 19, 1990, pp. B1, B3; "Computer Firm's Chief Faces Slowing Growth, Discord in the Ranks," *The Wall Street Journal*, February 15, 1990, pp. A1, A4.

Enhancement Case Questions

1. Who do you think was the better manager—Jobs or Sculley? The better leader? Explain.
2. Can a leader overstay his or her welcome? Can a manager? Explain.
3. What predictions might you make about the future of John Sculley and Apple?
4. Identify as many examples as you can in this case that reflect ideas covered in the chapter.

Chapter Notes

1. See Bernard M. Bass, *Stogdill's Handbook of Leadership*, rev. ed. (Riverside, N.J.: Free Press, 1981), for a thorough review of various definitions of leadership.
2. See Kenneth Labich, "The Seven Keys to Business Leadership," *Fortune*, October 24, 1988, pp. 58–66.
3. John R.P. French and Bertram Raven, "The Bases of Social Power," in Dorwin Cartwright, ed., *Studies in Social Power* (Ann Arbor: University of Michigan Press, 1959), pp. 150–167.
4. Henry Mintzberg, *Power In and Around Organizations* (Englewood Cliffs, N.J.: Prentice-Hall, 1983). See also Thomas A. Stewart, "New Ways to Exercise Power," *Fortune*, November 6, 1989, pp. 52–64.
5. Gary A. Yukl, *Leadership in Organizations*, 2nd ed. (Englewood Cliffs, N.J.: Prentice-Hall, 1989).
6. Bass, *Stogdill's Handbook of Leadership*, and Yukl, *Leadership in Organizations*. See also John W. Gardner, *On Leadership* (New York: Free Press, 1989).
7. Bass, *Stogdill's Handbook of Leadership*.
8. Bass, *Stogdill's Handbook of Leadership*, and Yukl, *Leadership in Organizations*.
9. Rensis Likert, *New Patterns of Management* (New York: McGraw-Hill, 1961), and *The Human Organization* (New York: McGraw-Hill, 1967).
10. Ralph M. Stogdill and A. E. Coons, eds., *Leader Behavior: Its Description and Measurement* (Columbus Bureau of Business Research, Ohio State University, 1957). See also Bass, *Stogdill's Handbook of Leadership*
11. See Bass, *Stogdill's Handbook of Leadership*, for a description of other situational approaches.
12. Fred E. Fiedler, *A Theory of Leadership Effectiveness* (New York: McGraw-Hill, 1967).
13. See Yukl, *Leadership in Organizations*, for a review.
14. Robert J. House and Terrence R. Mitchell, "Path-Goal Theory and Leadership," *Journal of Contemporary Business*, Autumn 1974, pp. 81–98.
15. Bass, *Stogdill's Handbook of Leadership*.
16. Victor H. Vroom and Philip W. Yetton, *Leadership and Decision-Making* (Pittsburgh: University of Pittsburgh Press, 1973), and Victor H. Vroom and Arthur G. Jago, *The New Leadership* (Englewood Cliffs, N.J.: Prentice-Hall, 1988).
17. Yukl, *Leadership in Organizations*.
18. See Abraham Zaleznik, "The Leadership Gap," *The Executive*, February 1990, pp. 7–22.
19. James M. Burns, *Leadership* (New York: Harper & Row, 1978).

CHAPTER OUTLINE

I. The Nature of Human Motivation
  A. Historical Perspectives
  B. The Motivational Process

II. Important Human Needs
  A. The Need Hierarchy
  B. The Two-Factor View
  C. Affiliation and Achievement

III. Complex Models of Employee Motivation
  A. The Expectancy Model
  B. Performance and Satisfaction
  C. Equity in the Workplace
  D. Goal-Setting Theory
  E. Employee Participation

IV. Reinforcement Processes
  A. Kinds of Reinforcement
  B. Schedules of Reinforcement

V. Reward Systems and Motivation
  A. Kinds of Rewards
  B. Effective Reward Systems
  C. New Reward Systems

CHAPTER

13

After studying this chapter you should be able to

1. Discuss the nature of human motivation and explain the basic motivational process.

2. Identify important human needs and discuss two theories that attempt to outline the way in which those needs motivate people.

3. Describe employee motivation from the perspectives of expectancy, satisfaction, equity, goal setting, and participation.

4. Discuss reinforcement processes, including kinds of reinforcement and schedules of reinforcement.

5. Identify several kinds of rewards, indicate how reward systems can be effective in motivation, and describe several new reward systems.

Employee Motivation

MOTIVATION AT L.L. BEAN

Leon Leonwood Bean was an avid, yet frustrated lover of the outdoors. After suffering through several hunting seasons with cold, wet feet, Bean had a brainstorm— a rugged, all-weather boot with leather uppers and a tough rubber sole. In 1912, Bean enlisted the aid of a friend to help him build the "perfect" boot, and the rest, as they say, is history.

Bean advertised the first one hundred pairs of the boots by distributing fliers around town. The boots sold quickly, but his customers soon returned most of them when the leather tops separated from the rubber bottoms. In the spirit that is still felt in the organization's culture today, Bean borrowed enough money to refund every penny to each of his customers.

He then turned his attention to improving on his original design. Bean eventually developed a better boot that could truly withstand the rigors of outdoor life. He used the new boot as the foundation of a mail-order outdoor sporting good business called L.L. Bean. His first catalogues were three-page leaflets mailed to his friends and existing customers. As the company grew, Bean's original philosophy of standing behind everything it sells continued to hold fast.

Over the years, Bean's has grown into a major corporation with two major branches—mail order and retail. The retail store, located in Freeport, Maine, is open twenty-four hours a day. Spanning over 120,000 square feet, the Bean retail store attracts customers and visitors from throughout North America and is one of Maine's biggest tourist attractions.

Mail order, however, is still Bean's biggest business. The company sends out over 116 million catalogues every year. Mail orders are taken in a converted department store in Portland. Telephone operators sitting in long rows in front of computer screens receive more than 10.5 million catalogue order and customer service calls each year. Over eleven million packages are sent out each year. And Bean's does almost half a billion dollars in annual sales.

What holds everything together? Most observers believe the real secret to L.L. Bean's success is the people who work for the company. In many ways imbued with the honest virtues of its founder, the company today still gives refunds when customers complain. It still stresses customer service and an honest, straightforward approach to dealing with everyone.

Such service would never take place, however, if Bean's own people weren't treated well. Employees are paid reasonable wages, are treated with dignity, and have ample opportunity for advancement. They are also given considerable freedom in how they do their job—as long as they do it well. Employees know that they can always put the needs and opinions of the customer first, without fear of reprisal or rebuke from a supervisor who worries too

L.L. Bean is a strong believer in customer satisfaction. One key means of achieving customer satisfaction, Bean managers believe, is making sure employees are well-treated.

much about the cost of something.

The people who answer the telephones in Portland enjoy their work. Although they work fast, speed isn't a goal. Whenever they take a call, they are willing and able to talk as long as the customer wishes, regardless of what they are discussing. For example, a few years ago an operator took a call from a man who was trying to decide what to name his new puppy. Although it was clear that he would not order anything, the customer-service department discussed the question and called the man back with suggestions.

When asked to explain why they enjoy their work so much, Bean's employees cite a variety of different things—pay, working conditions, the quality of their supervision, and so forth. One thing they all agree on, however, is that the way they are treated plays a major role in how they treat others. Since they are treated like mature, honest individuals, they feel inclined to treat their customers exactly the same way.

SOURCES: Dennis Holder, "Lair of the Magic Bean," *American Way*, April 15, 1989, pp. 20–26; Patricia Sellers, "How to Handle Customers' Gripes," *Fortune*, October 24, 1988, pp. 88–100; Beverly Gaber, "Training at L.L. Bean," *Training*, October 1988, pp. 5–9. John Skow, "Using the Old Bean," *Sports Illustrated*, December 2, 1985, pp. 84–88+.

L.L. Bean has prospered because it provides high quality products at reasonable prices and maintains exceptional service quality. Leon Bean recognized almost a century ago what many contemporary managers are just beginning to learn: the success of any business is largely dependent on the willingness of its employees to work together in the best interests of the organization. For employees to do this, three conditions must be met: (1) they must know how to do their jobs, (2) they must have the proper tools, materials, and equipment to do their jobs, and (3) they must want to do their jobs well. This third factor is motivation.

This chapter explores the topic of employee motivation in detail. First it examines the nature of motivation. Then it identifies important human needs that are relevant to the workplace and investigates various complexities of human motivation. It continues by discussing reinforcement processes and concludes with a summary of how reward systems affect motivation.

THE NATURE OF HUMAN MOTIVATION

□ *Motivation* is the set of processes that determine the choices people make about their behaviors.

Let's define **motivation** as the set of processes that determine behavioral choices.[1] Note the word *choices*. You can choose whether to study a lot, study a little, or not study at all. Most employees at L.L. Bean choose to do their best. Our concern here is how managers can help create conditions under which employees will make this same choice.

Historical Perspectives

Managers have been aware of the importance of employee motivation for decades. In general, their thinking about motivation has progressed through three distinct stages.[2]

The traditional view, popular during the era of Frederick Taylor and scientific management, was very simplistic. The dominant opinion in those days was that employees worked only for economic reasons. Presumably, people found work unpleasant and did it only for money, so the more people were paid, the harder they would work. Although the importance of money should not be underestimated, managers soon recognized that money was only one of several factors that led to motivation.

The human relations view, which was part of the human relations school of thought, held that social forces were the primary determinants of motivation. In particular, the adherents of this view believed that the more satisfied people were with their jobs, the harder they would work. As we see later in this chapter, this assumption is also extremely simplistic and not often true.

The human resources view is reflective of most contemporary thinking and takes the most positive attitude toward employee motivation. This philosophy argues that people are actually resources that can benefit the organization that they want to help, and that managers should look on them as assets. These notions relate to current interests in employee participation, workplace democracy, and so forth.

The Motivational Process

Exactly how does motivation occur? Although the complete set of processes is quite complex and not totally understood, we can devise a general framework for the motivational process, which is illustrated in Exhibit 13.1.

☐ *Needs* are drives or forces that initiate behavior.

The starting point in the process is **needs**—drives or forces that initiate behavior. People need recognition, feelings of accomplishment, food, affection, and so forth. When our needs become strong enough, we engage in efforts to fulfill them. For instance, suppose you began to experience pangs of hunger at ten o'clock this morning. By noon the pangs became too great to ignore, so you went looking for a restaurant.

As a result of such efforts, people experience various levels of need satisfaction. If you had a good meal, you are no longer hungry. The extent to which people find their needs satisfied will then influence their future efforts to satisfy the same needs. If the meal was filling but not particularly tasty, you may look for a different restaurant the next time you get hungry.

Exhibit 13.1   The Motivational Process

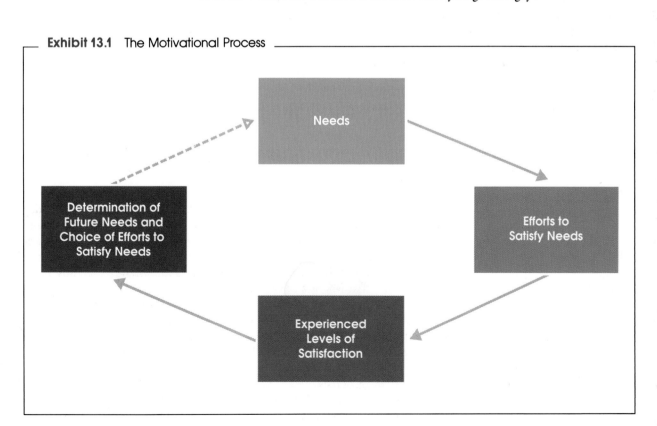

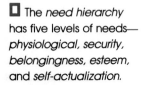
Obviously, then, the motivational process is a dynamic one. We always have a number of needs to satisfy, and we are always at different places in the process of satisfying them. Likewise, different time frames are involved; satisfying your hunger might take only a couple of hours, but satisfying the need to accomplish meaningful work can take months or years.

At any rate, the starting point is always the same—needs. Now let's explore this concept in more detail.

IMPORTANT HUMAN NEEDS

Needs are the starting point in all motivated behavior. Our biological craving for food and water and our emotional longing for companionship are both needs. All people have many needs, even in the workplace, and for many people work itself is an important need.[3] Several different theories that describe human needs in the workplace have been developed. Let's examine two of the more popular ones.

The Need Hierarchy

☐ The *need hierarchy* has five levels of needs—*physiological, security, belongingness, esteem,* and *self-actualization.*

Although several different theories about needs have been advanced, the one most familiar to managers is Maslow's **need hierarchy.**[4] Maslow argued that humans have a variety of different needs that can be classified into five specific groups and then arranged in a hierarchy of importance. Exhibit 13.2 illustrates the basic framework of the hierarchy.

At the bottom are the **physiological needs**—the things we need to survive, such as food, air, and sufficient warmth. In the workplace, adequate wages for

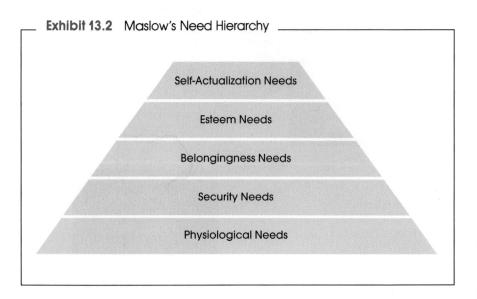

Exhibit 13.2 Maslow's Need Hierarchy

Self-Actualization Needs

Esteem Needs

Belongingness Needs

Security Needs

Physiological Needs

food and clothing, reasonable working conditions, and so forth are generally thought to satisfy these needs.

Next are **security needs,** which reflect the desire to have a safe physical and emotional environment. Job security, grievance procedures, and health insurance and retirement plans are used to satisfy security needs.

Third in the hierarchy are the needs for **belongingness.** These include the desire for love and affection and the need to be accepted by our peers. Making friends at work and being a part of the team are common ways in which people satisfy these needs.

Esteem needs come next. These actually comprise two different sets: the needs for recognition and respect from others and the needs for self-respect and a positive self-image. Job titles, spacious offices, awards, and other symbols of success help satisfy the externally focused needs, and accomplishing goals and doing a good job help satisfy the internally focused ones.

Finally, at the top of the hierarchy are the **self-actualization needs**—the needs to continue to grow, develop, and expand our capabilities. Opportunities to participate, to take on increasingly important tasks, and to learn new skills may all lead to satisfaction of these needs. As described more fully in *Management Today: Small Business and Entrepreneurship*, many people who break away from jobs in large corporations to start their own business may be looking for a way to satisfy their self-actualization needs.

The manner in which the hierarchy is presumed to work is really quite simple. Maslow suggests that we start out by trying to satisfy the lower-level needs. As they are satisfied, they no longer serve as catalysts for motivation. If you eat a big meal to satisfy your physiological hunger, for instance, you will stop looking for restaurants. Similarly, if an employee has satisfied his security needs, he will begin to look for new friendships and other opportunities to satisfy his belongingness needs.

In general, this view provides a convenient framework for managers. It illustrates the ideas that we have various needs, that satisfaction of those needs decreases our motivation to get more satisfaction, and that we can become frustrated trying to satisfy needs that are unattainable. On the other hand, it is difficult to use in a clear-cut and straightforward fashion. For example, managers would have a difficult time assessing the need level for each of their employees and then figuring out how to satisfy them.

The Two-Factor View

□ The *two-factor view* of motivation suggests that employee satisfaction and dissatisfaction are two distinct dimensions affected by different sets of factors.

Another popular way to describe employee needs is by using the **two-factor view,** which was developed by Frederick Herzberg.[5] This model grew from a study of two hundred accountants and engineers in Pittsburgh. Prior to the study, it was commonly believed that employee satisfaction and dissatisfaction, and thus motivation and lack of motivation, were at opposite ends of the same dimension. That is, people were satisfied, dissatisfied, or something in between. However, the Pittsburgh study uncovered evidence that satisfaction and dissatisfaction are considerably more complex than this. The researchers

SMALL BUSINESS AND ENTREPRENEURSHIP

On Their Own Terms

Why would a successful manager with job security, a good income, and a stable career path chuck it all one day and invest his life savings in a Florida marina? Why would a business owner sell her business for a small fortune and retire, only to decide a few years later to start all over again with a new business venture? And why would an entrepreneur turn down an offer to buy his business for more money than he can conceivably make during the next twenty years?

Although there are many possible explanations for these and the hundreds of other parallel stories that are being told, one common thread runs through them all—some people have such an overriding need to be independent, to succeed or fail on their own, to create something from nothing that they will risk everything they have to gamble on taking part in a small business.

Take Dan Gray, for example. Dan started a T-shirt business from scratch, grew it into a thriving operation, and then sold it for $4 million—at the age of twenty-three. Although he planned to rest and travel, he soon grew bored and impatient. So he started another T-shirt business, which has also grown rapidly. But Dan says he will never sell it.

In general, Dan Gray and the thousands of Americans like him have some set of higher-order needs, perhaps something akin to self-actualization, that pushes them to remain independent, to show what they can do, and to succeed in a business environment that takes few prisoners.

SOURCES: "Pursuing a Dream," *The Wall Street Journal,* February 24, 1989, p. R38; "Entrepreneurs of the '90s May Have Older Role Models," *The Wall Street Journal,* June 19, 1989, p. B2; "Entrepreneurs and Second Acts," *The Wall Street Journal,* May 17, 1989, p. B1.

found that one set of factors influenced satisfaction and an entirely different set of factors influenced dissatisfaction—hence the term *two-factor*.

The model is shown in Exhibit 13.3. At the top is the dissatisfaction dimension and some of the factors found to affect it. For example, when pay and security, supervision, working conditions, and so forth are deficient, employees tend to be dissatisfied. When these factors are adequate, however, employees are not necessarily satisfied. Instead, they are simply not dissatisfied.

The bottom of the exhibit shows the other dimension, satisfaction. Factors such as achievement, recognition, and responsibility influence this dimension. When these factors are present, employees should be satisfied. When they are deficient, though, employees are not dissatisfied but merely not satisfied.

The two-factor theory carries some very clear messages for managers. The first step in motivation is to eliminate dissatisfaction, so managers are advised to make sure that pay, working conditions, company policies, and so forth are appropriate and reasonable. Then they can address motivation itself. But additional pay, improvements in working conditions, and so forth will not accomplish this; instead, managers should strive to provide opportunities for growth,

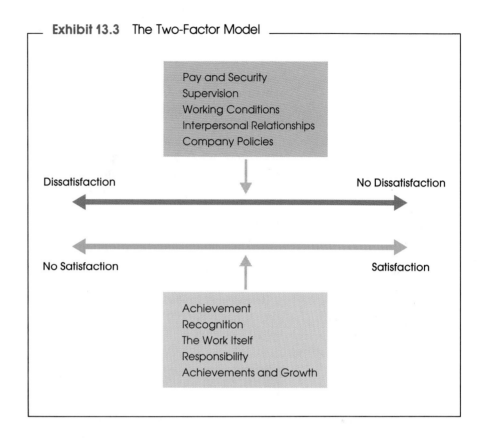

Exhibit 13.3   The Two-Factor Model

Pay and Security
Supervision
Working Conditions
Interpersonal Relationships
Company Policies

Dissatisfaction   No Dissatisfaction

No Satisfaction   Satisfaction

Achievement
Recognition
The Work Itself
Responsibility
Achievements and Growth

achievement, and responsibility. The theory predicts that these things in turn will enhance employee motivation.

The two-factor model has been the source of considerable debate. On the one hand, it has not always been supported by research and is somewhat arbitrary in its classification of factors. On the other hand, it does provide a useful and applicable framework for managers to use.[6]

Affiliation and Achievement

☐ The need for *affiliation* is the need to work with others, to interact, and to have friends.

☐ The need for *achievement* is the desire to excel or to accomplish some goal more effectively than in the past.

Two specific needs incorporated in the need perspective warrant additional discussion. One of these is the need for **affiliation**—the need that most people have to work with others, to make friends in the workplace, and to socialize. Work settings that deprive people of social interaction may lead to dissatisfaction and low morale. The need for affiliation is similar to Maslow's belongingness needs and Herzberg's interpersonal relationships.

Another important employee need is the need for **achievement**.[7] This is the desire that some people have to excel or to accomplish some goal or task more effectively than they did in the past. This need parallels Maslow's need for self-actualization and Herzberg's achievement factor. Research has indicated that people with a high need for achievement tend to have four common characteristics.

First, they set moderately difficult goals. A computer software sales representative, for instance, might set a sales goal of 115 percent of last year's sales. The goal is moderately difficult to reach but can be accomplished through hard work.

Second, they want immediate feedback. A new department manager at a Sears store who calls the store manager every morning to learn how her department did the day before might well have a strong need to achieve.

Third, people with high needs to achieve tend to assume personal responsibility. Suppose a number of plant managers at General Motors are formed into a task force to study ways to improve productivity. If one of them continually volunteers to do the work for the entire group, he might be a high achiever.

Fourth, such people are often preoccupied with their task. An engineer who thinks about her job at Hewlett-Packard while taking a shower, eating breakfast, and driving to work every day might also have a high need to achieve.

Researchers have estimated that only about 10 percent of the American population has this need, but there is evidence that the desire to achieve can be taught to people.[8]

LEARNING CHECK

You should now be able to identify important human needs and discuss two theories that attempt to outline the way in which those needs motivate people.

PRELUDE CASE UPDATE

Employees at L.L. Bean clearly have ample opportunities to satisfy their most important needs. Their physiological needs are satisfied by the wages they earn. Those same wages, combined with reasonable job security, help satisfy their security needs as well. Their belongingness needs and their need for affiliation are satisfied by the myriad opportunities they have for interacting with customers and each other. Esteem needs are most likely taken care of as a result of the high regard in which L.L. Bean as an organization is held by the general public. That is, there is clear reason for people to be proud of the fact that they work for L.L. Bean. And finally, the tremendous autonomy they have concerning how they do their jobs no doubt helps satisfy their self-actualization needs.

COMPLEX MODELS OF EMPLOYEE MOTIVATION

Although an understanding of basic human needs is a necessary starting point for enhancing motivation, managers also need to have a more complete perspective on the complexities of employee motivation. They must understand why different people have different needs, why individuals' needs change, and how employees choose to try to satisfy needs in different ways. There are several useful theories for understanding these complexities.

The Expectancy Model

◻ The *expectancy model* suggests that motivation is determined by how much we want something and how likely we think we are to get it.

The **expectancy model** is perhaps the most comprehensive model of employee motivation, but its basic notion is simple: motivation is a function of how much we want something and how likely we think we are to get it.[9]

As an example, consider the case of Miguel, a new college graduate looking for his first job in business. First he hears about an executive position with Weyerhaeuser with a starting salary of $200,000 per year. He wants the job, but he doesn't apply because he knows he has no chance of getting it. He then hears about a job with a local Safeway store, carrying bags of groceries for customers. He thinks he could get the job, but again he doesn't apply, this time because he doesn't want it. Finally he hears about a management trainee position with Xerox. He will probably choose to apply for this job because it is similar to what he wants and he thinks he stands a good chance of getting it.

The problem, of course, is that in many situations we have various outcomes—some bad and some good—to consider. Suppose Miguel ends up with two reasonable job offers. One pays a little more but is in a less desirable location than the other. Miguel's choice is thus more difficult.

Exhibit 13.4 illustrates the basic expectancy model. As you can see, the theory holds that motivation leads to effort, which, in conjunction with ability

Exhibit 13.4   The Expectancy Model

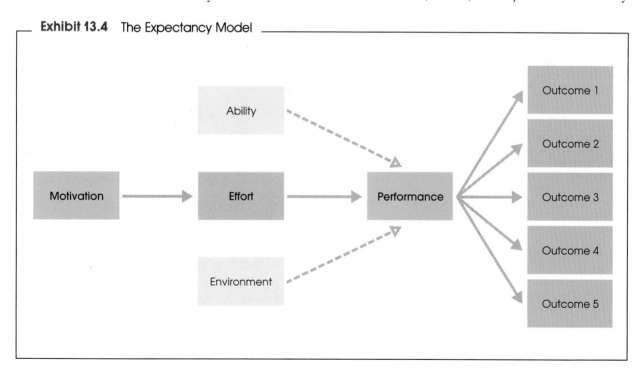

and environmental forces such as the availability of materials and equipment, leads to performance. Performance in turn has multiple outcomes. For example, high employee performance can result in several outcomes: a pay increase, a promotion, and better job assignments. However, it can also lead to stress and to the resentment of less successful colleagues. Therefore, the employee must choose how much effort to exert. She may weigh the potential outcomes and decide that the raise, promotion, and better assignments are more important to her than putting up with the stress and resentment, so she then exerts maximum effort to achieve those things. Another employee in the same situation, though, might put a higher premium on reducing stress and avoiding resentment, and he would consequently exert less effort.

A real example of how the expectancy model works can be drawn from the Chaparral Steel Company, where pay is tied directly to output, promotions are based on merit rather than seniority, all employees participate in a lucrative profit-sharing plan, and all employees have a voice in decision making. Thus, Chaparral is making it easy for workers to figure out what outcomes are available to them and how best to achieve those outcomes.[10]

In summary, the expectancy model implies that managers should (1) recognize that employees have different needs and preferences, (2) try to understand each employee's key needs, and (3) help employees determine how to satisfy each of their needs through performance.

Understanding individuals' needs and trying to satisfy them is important if managers are to be successful in motivating employees. At Wamsutta, a division of Springs Industries, Inc., motivation is achieved, in part, through ensuring employees' well-being and recognizing their accomplishments.

Photo courtesy of Springs Industries, Inc.

Performance and Satisfaction

□ In many cases, performance, followed by rewards, leads to higher levels of employee satisfaction.

Managers must also recognize the complexity of the relationship between performance and satisfaction. In Chapter 2 we noted the belief of the human relationists that employee attitudes, such as satisfaction, would lead to changes in employee behaviors, such as performance. We also noted that this thinking is now considered inaccurate and overly simplistic.

Exhibit 13.5 illustrates the way that researchers now believe the relationship looks. Note in particular that performance is presumed to occur before satisfaction.[11] At first this seems unbelievable, but consider how you evaluate your classes each semester. When someone asks you how you feel about a certain class after the first week, you usually have a fairly neutral reaction. After you have taken the first exam, though, your attitude is somewhat more intense. If you get an A on the exam, you are likely to say the class is great. Under other circumstances, you may come up with a less favorable evaluation.

The same process occurs in work settings. During the early stages of employment, people tend to have fairly neutral attitudes toward the organization and their jobs. After they have worked a while and received various rewards (both extrinsic, like salary increases, and intrinsic, like a feeling of accomplishment), however, their attitudes become more extreme. For example, if Lionel has worked hard and subsequently gets praise and a pay raise, he is likely to express favorable attitudes toward the organization. But if Gayle feels she

Exhibit 13.5   The Relationship Between Performance and Satisfaction

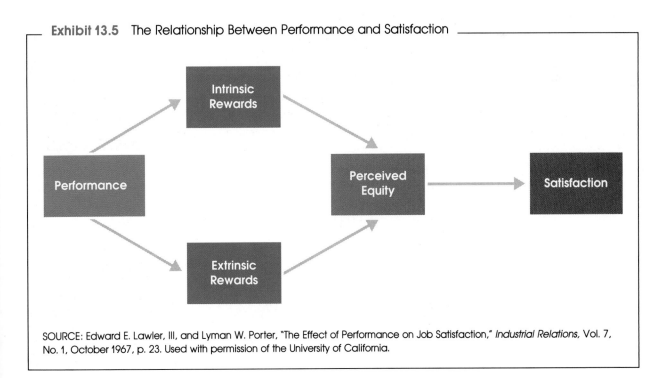

SOURCE: Edward E. Lawler, III, and Lyman W. Porter, "The Effect of Performance on Job Satisfaction," *Industrial Relations*, Vol. 7, No. 1, October 1967, p. 23. Used with permission of the University of California.

worked just as hard but received little recognition and a small raise, she will be inclined to have less favorable attitudes.

Thus, it may be more accurate to argue that performance leads to satisfaction than the reverse. This raises the notion of equity, which, as you will note, is also part of the process shown in Exhibit 13.5. Much of how Lionel and Gayle feel has to do with equity. This subject is discussed next.

Equity in the Workplace

◻ *Equity* is an individual's perception that he or she is being treated fairly relative to others in the organization.

Another complex perspective on employee motivation is the role of **equity,** or fairness, in the workplace. Equity has been found to be a major factor in determining employee motivation.[12] Its power is demonstrated visibly in the sports arena. For example, until 1989, there were no baseball players being paid $3 million a year. However, when Will Clark, one of the game's top players, negotiated a new contract calling for such a salary, others followed suit almost immediately. As a result, by the end of that year, there were ten players earning a salary of over $3 million. Likewise, after an NFL team signs its first-round draft choice each year, almost invariably several veteran players start demanding that their contracts be renegotiated.

Although equity in the workplace is perhaps less visible, it is also important. Exhibit 13.6 illustrates how this works. First, each employee contributes to and gets things from the workplace. We contribute our education, experi-

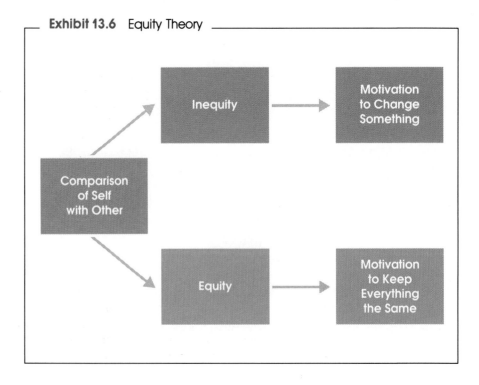

Exhibit 13.6 Equity Theory

ence, expertise, and time and effort, and in return we get pay, security, recognition, and so forth. Given the social nature of human beings, it should come as no surprise that we compare our contributions and rewards to those of others. As a result of this comparison, we may feel equity or inequity.

We should note, of course, that everyone's contributions and rewards don't have to be the same for equity to exist. If Liz has a college degree and ten years on the job and Tom has only a high school degree and no experience, Tom should expect to be paid less. For equity to exist, people must perceive that the relative proportion of rewards and contributions is equal. And if equity is present, people are generally motivated to keep everything as it is.

In contrast, if people experience inequity, they are generally motivated to change something. For example, if someone believes that he is underpaid relative to a colleague, he has several options. He can decrease his efforts, he can ask for a raise, he can ask that his colleague's pay be cut, he can try to convince the colleague that she should work harder to justify her pay, he can quit, or he can rationalize the problem away. Regardless of which option he chooses, he will be uncomfortable with inequity and will try to do something about it.

This viewpoint also conveys several clear messages to managers. First, people should be rewarded according to their contributions. Second, managers should try to ensure that employees feel equity. Finally, managers should be aware that feelings of inequity are almost bound to arise, and when they do, managers must be patient and either correct the problem, if it is real, or help people recognize that things are not as inequitable as they seem.[13]

Goal-Setting Theory

□ According to the *goal-setting theory*, specific and moderately difficult goals may increase motivation.

Still another useful perspective on employee motivation is **goal-setting theory.** Goal setting from a planning perspective was discussed in Part Two. Recent evidence also suggests that goal setting can be applied on an individual level as a way to increase employee motivation. The starting point is for managers and their subordinates to meet regularly. As a part of these meetings, they should jointly set goals for the subordinate. These goals should be very specific and moderately difficult. Assuming they are also goals that the subordinate will accept and be committed to, she is likely to work very hard to accomplish them. The evidence thus far suggests that goal setting will become an increasingly important part of the motivational process in the future.[14]

Employee Participation

□ Employee *participation* can also increase motivation.

Finally, employee **participation** is also being used more and more as a way to enhance motivation in the workplace. Managers are finding that when employees are given a greater voice in how things are done, they become more committed to the goals of the organization and are willing to make ever-greater contributions to the success of the business. Quality circles, discussed later in

THE WORLD OF MANAGEMENT

Participation Pays Off

Its no secret that Japanese car makers have snatched market share from almost every other automobile company around the globe. And none has been more successful than Honda.

Most people also seem to know one of the key ingredients to the Japanese success—employee participation in the workplace. By establishing high levels of cooperation and trust among workers and management, the Japanese companies are able to produce higher-quality cars for lower prices than American firms can.

But is the high level of participation that characterizes Japanese plants transferable to other cultures? Although the final verdict isn't in, the preliminary evidence suggest yes. Honda, for example, has been extremely successful with its new U.S. manufacturing facilities in the Midwest. The company was careful to locate in an area far from entrenched union strongholds.

The people who work for Honda are happy to have a job. And they have also embraced the notion of full-scale participation. Indeed, many of them exclaim that they would never want to work anyplace else. Honda is also getting a payoff. The cars it makes in the United States are just as high quality as those it makes back home in Japan. In fact, it occasionally ships some U.S.-made cars to Japan to be sold there.

SOURCES: Louis Kraar, "Japan's Gung-Ho U.S. Car Plants," *Fortune*, January 30, 1989, pp. 98–108; "The Americanization of Honda," *Business Week*, April 25, 1988, pp. 90–96; "Honda Wins USA's Heartland," *USA Today*, December 2, 1987, pp. 1B–2B.

LEARNING CHECK

You should now be able to describe employee motivation from the perspectives of expectancy, satisfaction, equity, goal setting, and participation.

the book, are one popular method of increasing employee participation. This approach solicits employee volunteers who meet regularly in an attempt to first identify and then recommend solutions for quality-related problems in the workplace.

Many businesses are attempting to encourage participation as a means of enhancing competitiveness.[15] *Management Today: The World of Management* describes how Honda has already used participation to gain a competitive edge.

REINFORCEMENT PROCESSES

☐ *Reinforcement* processes suggest that future behavior is shaped by the consequences of current behavior.

A final question about motivation concerns how and why behaviors stay the same or change. Consider the case of two new workers. One starts out as an average performer and continually gets better, the other starts out as a top performer but becomes a poor performer. What has happened? The answer probably involves reinforcement processes.

The idea of **reinforcement** suggests that future behavior is shaped by the consequences of current behavior. If people's current behavior leads to a reward, they are likely to engage in that same behavior again. But if current behavior does not lead to a reward, or if it leads to unpleasant outcomes, they are more likely to follow a different behavior pattern in the future.

Much of what we know about reinforcement can be traced to psychologists who have studied human learning processes,[16] but more and more people have come to see how clearly the concept relates to organizational settings.[17] The following sections describe kinds of reinforcement and schedules that managers can use to provide them.

Kinds of Reinforcement

☐ Four kinds of reinforcement are *positive reinforcement, avoidance, extinction,* and *punishment.*

As shown in Exhibit 13.7, there are four basic kinds of reinforcement: positive reinforcement, avoidance, extinction, and punishment.[18]

Positive reinforcement is a reward, or desirable outcome, that is given after a particular behavior. For instance, suppose that a supervisor notices a worker doing an extra good job. He stops and tells the worker what a good job he is doing, and then he recommends to his boss that the worker should get a small pay raise. The praise and the pay raise are positive reinforcements, and as a consequence the worker is likely to continue to work hard.

PRELUDE CASE   U P D A T E

Workers at L.L. Bean derive a great deal of positive reinforcement from performing their jobs well. For example, because they give such good customer service, they usually get grateful comments and encouragement from people calling to place orders. Likewise, their supervisors notice when they do an exceptionally good job and also compliment them.

Avoidance also increases the likelihood that someone will repeat a desirable behavior, although it uses a different perspective. In this case, the employee is allowed to avoid an unpleasant situation because of good performance. If a company has a policy that employees who are late for work get penalized and if all employees come to work on time, no penalties are imposed. As long as the threat continues, employees will be motivated to be on time every day.

Extinction is used to weaken behavior, especially behavior that has previously been reinforced. Take a manager of a small office who once allowed employees to come by whenever they wanted to "shoot the breeze." Now the office staff has grown so large that she must curtail this practice. The manager might remain cordial but will continue working at her desk until employees get the message; that is, she just ignores the undesired behavior. Of course, she must also work to guard against resentment and a loss in communication.

Punishment is also used to change behavior, of course. Common forms of punishment in organizations include reprimands, discipline, and fines. Since

Exhibit 13.7 Kinds of Reinforcement

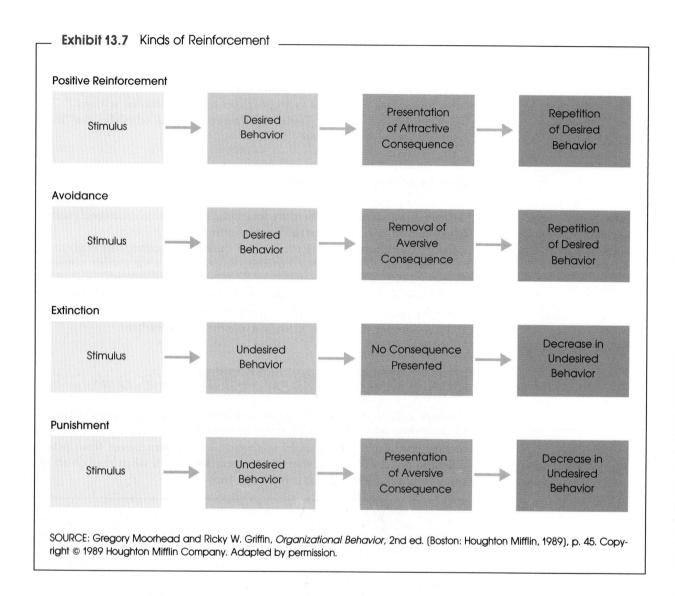

SOURCE: Gregory Moorhead and Ricky W. Griffin, *Organizational Behavior*, 2nd ed. (Boston: Houghton Mifflin, 1989), p. 45. Copyright © 1989 Houghton Mifflin Company. Adapted by permission.

punishment usually engenders resentment and hostility, managers should usually use it only as a last resort. Suppose that an employee has been late for work three times in the last week with no valid excuse. His boss might choose to reprimand him, explaining that another occurrence within the next six months will lead to a suspension.

Schedules of Reinforcement

☐ Schedules of reinforcement include *continuous, fixed* and *variable interval,* and *fixed* and *variable ratio schedules.*

For managers to use reinforcement effectively to enhance motivation, they must know when to provide it. Five basic schedules of reinforcement are available.[19]

Under the **continuous reinforcement schedule,** the manager provides reinforcement after every occurrence of the behavior—the supervisor praises her subordinate every time she sees him doing a good job. Obviously, the power of the praise as reinforcement will rapidly diminish, since it is so common and easy to get.

Under a **fixed interval schedule,** the manager provides reinforcement on a periodic basis, regardless of performance. An example is the Friday paycheck many employees get. The check is obviously important to them, but it really doesn't affect their performance, since they receive it regardless of how hard they work. This schedule is therefore also of limited value as a way to enhance motivation.

The **variable interval schedule** also uses time as a basis for reinforcement, but the time intervals between reinforcement vary. If praise follows this schedule or is tied to random office visits by the manager, it will tend to be more powerful.

Under the **fixed ratio schedule,** the manager provides reinforcement on the basis of number of behaviors rather than on the basis of time. However, the number of behaviors an employee must display to get the reinforcement is constant. For example, suppose Montgomery Ward decides to get more credit card customers. Each sales clerk is asked to solicit new applicants, and the

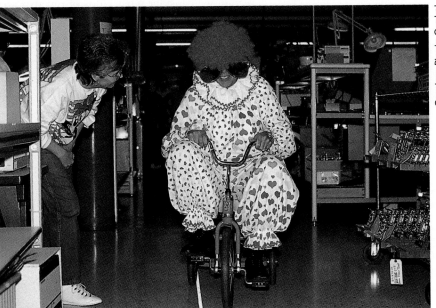

Why would a manager dress up like a clown and ride a trike through the plant? To provide reinforcement, that's why! Managers at Physio-Control, Inc., a subsidiary of Eli Lilly Corp., believe a little levity and disruption is a welcome respite from work. Thus, one of them will periodically dress up in a zany costume and parade around each time a production goal is met.

Courtesy Physio-Control

clerks are given fifty cents for every five applications that are completed. The idea is that each clerk will be highly motivated to get new applicants because each one brings him or her closer to the fifth application needed for another reward.

Finally, there is the **variable ratio schedule,** which is generally the most powerful one for enhancing motivation. Under this arrangement, the manager again gives reinforcement on the basis of behaviors, but the number of behaviors an employee needs to display to get the reinforcement varies. A supervisor might praise a subordinate after the second and fourth indications of good performance, then after the third, fourth, and fifth indications, then after the second one. Thus the subordinate is motivated to continue to work hard, because each incident raises the probability (though not the certainty) that the next will bring praise. (This schedule is the one used in slot machines in casinos in Las Vegas.)

LEARNING CHECK

You should now be able to discuss reinforcement processes, including kinds of reinforcement and schedules of reinforcement.

REWARD SYSTEMS AND MOTIVATION

Regardless of what motivational model or perspective a manager uses, it is typically made operational through the organization's reward system.[20] In this section we consider what kinds of rewards are usually available, the character-

One important part of motivation is providing employees with rewards. Chesapeake Corporation, an integrated paper and forest products company, recently awarded employees 10 shares of company stock as a reward for their service throughout a record earnings year.

Chesapeake Corp.—an integrated paper and forest products company

TABLE 13.1
Characteristics of Effective
Reward Systems

Characteristic	Examples
1. Rewards satisfy the basic needs of employees.	Adequate pay, reasonable benefits, appropriate holidays.
2. Rewards are comparable to those offered by similar organizations in the area.	Pay rates of nearby companies are equal; employees receive the same holiday time as employees in comparable positions in other organizations.
3. Rewards are distributed fairly and equitably.	Employees who work overtime for a special project receive extra pay or compensatory time off; employees in comparable positions receive equal rewards for similar work.
4. The reward system is multifaceted.	A range of rewards are given: pay, benefits, promotion, privileges, etc.; rewards may be obtained in different ways.

istics of effective reward systems, and some interesting reward systems that are just being developed.

Kinds of Rewards

■ A *reward* is anything the organization provides to employees in exchange for their services.

From the standpoint of the employee, a **reward** is anything the organization provides in exchange for services. Clearly, however, outcomes vary in terms of their potency as rewards. One category of reward includes base pay, benefits, holidays, and so forth; these rewards are not tied to performance. A second category includes pay increases, incentives, bonuses, promotions, status symbols (bigger offices, reserved parking spaces), and attractive job assignments. These are rewards in the truest sense; they represent significant forms of positive reinforcement and satisfy many of the basic needs of most employees.

Effective Reward Systems

Obviously, if reward systems are to serve their intended purpose, they must be effective. Effective reward systems tend to have four basic characteristics, as summarized in Table 13.1. First, they must satisfy the basic needs of the employees. Pay must be adequate, benefits reasonable, holidays appropriate, and so forth. Second, the rewards must be comparable to those offered by other organizations in the immediate area. If a Dow Chemical plant is paying its workers $8 an hour and a Union Carbide plant down the road is paying $9, employees at the Dow plant will always be looking for openings at the Carbide facility.

MANAGEMENT IN PRACTICE

Du Pont Experiments with Rewards

Du Pont's fiber division recently developed and implemented one of the most comprehensive and innovative incentive programs in the history of American business. The basic elements of the system are actually quite simple, but their impact may be enormous. All told, around 20,000 workers are participating in the plan.

During the next five years, division workers will get smaller pay increases than their counterparts in other parts of Du Pont. At the end of five years, they will be earning 6 percent less than their peers. If profits at that time fall below 80 percent what is projected, workers get nothing extra. However, if they exceed 80 percent, they get a 3 percent bonus. And 100 percent gets them the 6 percent they gave up.

Finally, if they hit or exceed 150 percent of projections, they get the 6 percent plus a bonus of another 12 percent.

Many Du Pont workers are enthusiastic about the program. They feel it gives them a real opportunity to have an impact and to benefit from their contributions to the firm. Others, however, aren't so sure. For example, some argue that they can really do very little to affect profits. Others worry that the profit projections were set higher than might otherwise be the case in order to reduce bonuses. Regardless of how workers feel, however, experts believe that if the Du Pont experiment is successful, many other businesses are likely to follow suit.

SOURCES: "All Eyes on Du Pont's Incentive Pay Plan," *The Wall Street Journal*, December 15, 1988, p. B1; "Du Pont Transforms a Division's Culture," *Management Review*, March 1989, pp. 37–42; Brian Dumaine, "Creating a New Company Culture," *Fortune*, January 15, 1990, pp. 127–131.

Rewards must also be distributed in a fair and equitable fashion. As we have discussed, people have a need to be treated fairly. If rewards are not distributed in an equitable fashion, employees will be resentful. Finally, the reward system must be multifaceted, which means that it must acknowledge that different people have different needs. A range of rewards must be provided, and people need to be able to attain rewards in different ways. For example, a marketing manager and a financial manager must each have an opportunity for promotion into the ranks of middle management.

New Reward Systems

In an effort to compete with other firms for good employees, many organizations have begun to experiment with new kinds of rewards and new ways to achieve them.[21] *Management Today: Management in Practice* describes how Du Pont Company has worked at developing a new reward system as a way to boost productivity.

One kind of contemporary system ties pay directly to performance, at least more than was done in the past. Another innovation is the all-salaried work

LEARNING CHECK

You should now be able to identify several kinds of rewards, indicate how reward systems can be effective in motivation, and describe several new reward systems.

force. Under this arrangement, all workers are paid by the month rather than by the hour, time clocks are eliminated, and people monitor their own work hours. Both Gillette and Dow Chemical have used this plan.

Skill-based job evaluation systems are also becoming increasingly popular. In this case people are paid according to their level of proficiency, or skill. Teachers with master's degrees, for instance, are paid more than teachers with undergraduate degrees, even though they do the same job. General Foods and Texas Instruments have used this approach, increasing an employee's pay whenever he or she masters a new job or skill.

Chapter Summary

Motivation is the set of processes that determine behavioral choices. The traditional view of motivation was that people worked only for economic reasons. The human relations view argued that if people were satisfied with their work, they would produce more. The human resources view suggests that people are actually resources that can benefit organizations and that managers should maintain and develop them, like other assets, for maximum productivity.

The process of motivation begins with needs—drives or forces that initiate behavior. The existence of needs leads to efforts to try to satisfy those needs. The extent to which needs are satisfied leads in turn to the levels of satisfaction that people experience, which influence their choices of future efforts to satisfy needs. Hence the process begins again.

One early theory was the need hierarchy of Maslow, which established five groups of needs—physiological, security, belongingness, esteem, and self-actualization—arranged in a hierarchy. Another popular theory is the two-factor view, which suggests that one set of factors influences satisfaction and a different set influences dissatisfaction. The needs for affiliation and achievement are also important in their own right apart from their roles in the theories.

The expectancy model is the most comprehensive model of employee motivation. Simply stated, it holds that motivation is a function of how much we want something and how likely we think we are of getting it. Many early writers felt that if managers could satisfy the needs of employees, those employees would perform better. However, research has shown that satisfaction does not cause performance. It is more accurate to say that performance

leads to satisfaction, a key element of which is equity. Whenever people perceive an inequity in their situation, they will try to do something about it; that is, they will be motivated to reduce the perceived inequity. Goal setting and participation are also important ingredients in motivation.

Reinforcement processes are very similar to the process described by the expectancy model. The theory suggests that future behavior is shaped by the consequences of current behavior. There are four basic kinds of reinforcement: positive reinforcement, avoidance, extinction, and punishment. Positive reinforcement is a reward that follows desired behavior; increasing the chances it will be repeated. Avoidance behavior is aimed at avoiding negative consequences. In extinction, nothing happens following a behavior; the behavior is ignored. Punishment, on the other hand, means that the behavior results in an undesirable consequence. The impact of these kinds of reinforcements on behavior is complicated, however, by their schedule, or the frequency with which the reinforcement occurs.

There are numerous kinds of rewards, both extrinsic and intrinsic. These include base pay, benefits, holidays, pay increases, incentives, bonuses, promotions, status symbols, praise, recognition, work assignments, and so on. Effective reward systems tend to have four characteristics: they must satisfy basic needs, be comparable to those used elsewhere, be distributed equitably, and be multifaceted.

The Manager's Vocabulary

motivation
needs
need hierarchy

physiological needs
security needs
belongingness needs

esteem needs	avoidance
self-actualization needs	extinction
two-factor view	punishment
affiliation	continuous
achievement	reinforcement schedule
expectancy model	fixed interval schedule
equity	variable interval
goal-setting theory	schedule
participation	fixed ratio schedule
reinforcement	variable ratio schedule
positive reinforcement	reward

Prelude Case Wrap-Up

The Prelude Case for this chapter details the history of L.L. Bean, a retailer and mail-order firm in Maine that specializes in outdoor equipment. The firm backs up everything it sells and provides exemplary service to all its customers. One major key to Bean's success is its highly motivated and dedicated work force.

For example, as noted in one of the Prelude Case Updates in the chapter, Bean's employees are able to have their basic needs satisfied during the performance of their jobs. Further, using expectancy theory as a framework, employees at Bean's have a clear perspective on what they want and how they might best get it. That is, each person can feel good about his or her work and its value to the organization.

Employees at Bean's are given ample opportunity to perform at a high level, with the result being higher levels of satisfaction. Rewards are also distributed in a fair and equitable manner. In addition, every employee at Bean's has a voice in how his or her job is done. Thus, virtually every aspect of complex employee motivation is represented at L.L. Bean.

Another Prelude Case Update within the chapter notes that positive reinforcement is present within the workplace at Bean's. When employees do their jobs well, they feel good and get positive responses from both customers and supervisors. Thus, they are motivated to continue to do their jobs well.

Finally, employees of L.L. Bean are provided with a variety of both intrinsic and extrinsic rewards. For example, they are paid reasonable wages and have ample opportunity for promotion. And managers combine these various rewards in such an astute fash-

ion that the motivational level of employees seems to always be on the rise.

Prelude Case Questions

1. Identify any aspects of motivation discussed in the chapter that are *not* reflected at L.L. Bean.
2. In your opinion, why don't more firms treat their employees and customers like L.L. Bean?
3. Think of organizations you have done business with that had exceptionally good and exceptionally poor service. Draw some inferences from motivational theory to explain your observations.
4. What effects does the founder of a business have on that business as it grows to a large organization? How are those effects translated into employee motivation?

Discussion Questions

Review Questions

1. What are the three basic historical perspectives through which motivational theory has passed?
2. What are the five basic need levels in Maslow's hierarchy of needs?
3. Summarize the basic premises of expectancy theory.
4. What is the relationship between performance and satisfaction?
5. What are the four basic types of reinforcement? What are the five schedules of reinforcement?

Analysis Questions

1. How important do you think money is in motivation? Explain.
2. Do you agree or disagree with the basic premises of the two-factor theory? Why or why not?
3. How do you think performance and satisfaction are related?
4. Explain how you personally might form equity perceptions in your role as a student.
5. Which new reward system do you think holds the most potential? Why? Why might workers oppose it?

Application Questions and Exercises

1. Interview a local manager or business owner. Ask him or her what motivates people.

2. Interview an operating employee (for example, a blue-collar worker, technician, or secretary) and a professional employee (for example, an administrator or manager). Ask what motivates them and then compare and contrast your findings.

3. Working alone, set some specific and moderately difficult goals for your performance in this class. Then discuss your goals with two or three of your classmates. Are these goals likely to motivate you? Why or why not?

4. What kinds of reinforcement do you think are most effective?

5. Assume you have a company that employs 100 operating employees and 5 managers. For the sake of simplicity, assume you can spend up to $20,000 in total annual compensation (wages, benefits, and so forth) for each operating employee and $40,000 in total annual compensation for each manager. Design a reward system that captures some of the complex motivational perspectives and reinforcement processes.

ENHANCEMENT CASE

AVIS: WHEN WORKERS ARE OWNERS

Although Avis was always a respectable performer in the rental car business, it never really seemed to be able to gain any ground on number one Hertz. One reason some market analysts cite was what seemed like a never-ending succession of owners. During one five-year stretch in the 1980s, for example, Avis was owned at various times by Norton Simon, Esmark, Beatrice, KKR, and Wesray.

While attending a meeting with Wesray investors, Avis managers became concerned that the company was again going to be sold. Instead, they suggested that the company explore the possibility of a new ownership arrangement that might offer benefits to everyone.

The arrangement they were talking about was an ESOP—employee stock ownership plan. The initial attractiveness of an ESOP is attributed to tax advantages. When a company decides to establish an ESOP, it generally borrows money. As the money is repaid, it gets to deduct the interest payments and much of the principal for tax purposes. Lenders only pay taxes on half the interest they receive from ESOP payments, so they charge a lower interest rate. Further, dividend payments on stock held by an ESOP are deductible.

The ESOP fund is used to buy company stock on the open market. A trustee controls the stock and is obligated to vote its shares in the best interests of the employees. As the debt is repaid, shares of stock are

THAT'S WHY I CAN GET YOUR TRAVELERS OUT OF HERE IN NEXT TO NO TIME.

When you hear us say, "We're trying harder than ever," what does that mean to you? It means when your travelers are on the go, we're going to get them going as fast as we can. Because every employee-owner of Avis, Inc. understands that our success depends on keeping you satisfied.

Whether your travelers are renting with our Avis Express® service or dropping off their car with Roving Rapid Return,™ we're making our fast service even faster. Matter of fact, we now offer over 50 Roving Rapid Return locations across the country for your convenience.

Combine all that service with our competitive rates and professionally-maintained GM and other fine cars, and you've got a lot of good reasons to rent from the employee-owners of Avis. Just call your travel consultant today or an owner at 1-800-331-1212. Find out how our company can make your job a little easier.

It's Not Just My Job... It's My Company.

AVIS

We're trying harder than ever.™

Avis Inc.

Avis is one of the most well-known examples of companies that use an ESOP-approach to motivation and rewards. The firm capitalizes on this approach, through ads such as this one, by letting potential customers know that Avis provides quality service because employees are highly motivated.

allocated to employees in proportion to their pay. Even after the shares are allocated to the employee, however, they still reside with the trustee. When the employee leaves the firm, through resignation, retirement, or other means, he or she receives the current market value for the stock.

And how is Avis doing? Much better than at any time in the past three decades. Its market share is 27 percent, an all-time high. And it has scored significant gains at airport locations, where 70 percent of all rental car business is transacted. Customer complaints have dropped dramatically, and profitability has increased sharply.

Of course, ownership alone isn't the entire answer. Hand in hand with ownership at Avis goes employee participation. Since the buyout was completed, the company has formed dozens of employee participation groups. Each group meets on a regular basis and addresses whatever areas to which it thinks it can contribute. For example, such groups have improved everything from the company's public

restrooms to baby seats in rental cars to customer billing arrangements.

The new ownership structure is starting to pay other dividends as well. A new advertising campaign, for example, suggests that many consumers believe that employee ownership improves service. Consequently, many large corporate customers, such as Unisys and Westinghouse, are using Avis more and more.

Attracted by the obvious benefits accruing to Avis and other ESOP-based companies, more and more organizations are studying this concept. One very important way ESOPs may be used in the future is to fund employee retirement programs. Experts are quick to point out, however, that ESOPs work only when they are clearly and strongly linked with increased employee participation. As one person put it, ownership increases an employee's desire to contribute, but this pays off only when the individual has some channel through which to make that contribution.

SOURCES: David Kirkpatrick, "How the Workers Run Avis Better," *Fortune*, December 5, 1988, pp. 103–114; "Stuffing Nest Eggs with ESOPs," *Business Week*, April 24, 1989, pp. 124–125; Katherine J. Klein and Rosalie J. Hall, "Correlates of Employee Satisfaction with Stock Ownership: Who Likes an ESOP Most?" *Journal of Applied Psychology*, November 1988, pp. 630–638.

Enhancement Case Questions

1. What theory or theories of motivation explain why ESOPs appear to work so well?
2. In which organizational situations might ESOPs not be effective? Explain.
3. Explain some possible dangers of ESOPs.
4. What motivational strategies might be linked to ESOPs to make them even more powerful?

Chapter Notes

1. See Richard M. Steers and Lyman W. Porter, eds., *Motivation and Work Behavior*, 4th ed. (New York: McGraw-Hill, 1987), pp. 3–4.
2. Craig Pinder, *Work Motivation* (Glenview, Ill.: Scott, Foresman, 1984).
3. See Walter Kiechel III, "The Workaholic Generation," *Fortune*, April 10, 1989, pp. 50–62.
4. Abraham H. Maslow, "A Theory of Human Motivation," *Psychological Review*, vol. 50, 1943, pp. 370–396.
5. Frederick Herzberg, "One More Time: How Do You Motivate Employees?" *Harvard Business Review*, January-February 1968, pp. 53–62.
6. Pinder, *Work Motivation*.
7. David McClelland, "That Urge to Achieve," *Think*, November-December 1966, p. 22.
8. David McClelland, *The Achieving Society* (Princeton, N.J.: Van Nostrand, 1961).
9. Victor Vroom, *Work and Motivation* (New York: Wiley, 1964). See also Pinder, *Work Motivation*, and Lynn E. Miller and Joseph E. Grush, "Improving Predictions in Expectancy Theory Research: Effects of Personality, Expectancies, and Norms," *Academy of Management Journal*, March 1988, pp. 107–122.
10. Kurt Eichenwald, "America's Successful Steel Industry," *Washington Monthly*, February 1985, p.42.
11. Lyman W. Porter and Edward E. Lawler III, *Managerial Attitudes and Performance* (Homewood, Ill.: Dorsey, 1968).
12. Richard T. Mowday, "Equity Theory Predictions of Behavior in Organizations," in Steers and Porter,

eds., *Motivation and Work Behavior*, pp. 91–113. See also J. Stacey Adams, "Toward an Understanding of Inequity," *Journal of Abnormal and Social Psychology*, November 1963, pp. 422–436.

13. Jerald Greenberg, "Equity and Workplace Status: A Field Experiment," *Journal of Applied Psychology*, November 1989, pp. 606–613; Edward W. Miles, John D. Hatfield, and Richard C. Huseman, "The Equity Sensitivity Construct: Potential Implications for Work Performance," *Journal of Management*, December 1989, pp. 581–588.

14. Gary P. Latham and Edwin Locke, "Goal Setting—A Motivational Technique That Works," *Organizational Dynamics*, Autumn 1979, pp. 68–80.

15. Dean Tjosvold, "Participation: A Close Look at Its Dynamics," *Journal of Management*, Autumn 1987, pp. 739–750.

16. B. F. Skinner, *Beyond Freedom and Dignity* (New York: Knopf, 1971).

17. Fred Luthans and Robert Kreitner, *Organizational Behavior Modification and Beyond: An Operant and Social Learning Approach* (Glenview, Ill.: Scott, Foresman, 1985).

18. Luthans and Kreitner, *Organizational Behavior Modification*.

19. C. B. Ferster and B. F. Skinner, *Schedules of Reinforcement* (New York: Appleton-Century-Crofts, 1957).

20. Edward E. Lawler III, *Pay and Organizational Development* (Reading, Mass.: Addison-Wesley, 1981).

21. "Pay Raise Demands Appear to Be Modest," *The Wall Street Journal*, February 28, 1989, p. A2.

CHAPTER OUTLINE

I. **The Interpersonal Character of Organizations**

II. **The Nature of Groups**
   A. Definition of a Group
   B. Kinds of Groups

III. **The Psychological Character of Groups**
   A. Why People Join Groups
   B. Stages of Group Development
   C. The Informal Organization

IV. **Important Group Dimensions**
   A. Role Dynamics
   B. Cohesiveness
   C. Norms

V. **Managing Groups in Organizations**
   A. Managing Functional Groups
   B. Managing Task Forces and Committees
   C. Managing Work Teams
   D. Managing Quality Circles

VI. **Group Decision Making**
   A. Advantages of Group Decision Making
   B. Disadvantages of Group Decision Making
   C. Techniques for Group Decision Making

VII. **Conflict Between People and Groups**
   A. The Nature of Conflict
   B. Managing Conflict

C
H
A
P
T
E
R

14

After studying this chapter you should be able to

1. Characterize organizations in terms of interpersonal processes.

2. Define a group and elaborate on different kinds of groups.

3. Discuss the psychological character of groups, including why people join groups, the stages of development through which groups tend to move, and the nature of the informal organization.

4. Identify important group dimensions—role dynamics, cohesiveness, and norms—and the relationships among them.

5. Discuss the management of functional groups, task forces and committees, work teams, and quality circles.

6. Describe the advantages, disadvantages, and techniques of group decision making.

7. Discuss the nature of conflict between people and groups and how it can be managed.

Interpersonal Processes

A. O. SMITH RELIES ON GROUPS TO SURVIVE

A. O. Smith Corporation is an old-line manufacturing firm in Milwaukee that manufactures car and truck frames for General Motors, Ford, and Chrysler. During the late 1970s and early 1980s, Smith, like many other American manufacturing firms, was in pretty bad shape. For example, defects at the plant were running in excess of 20 percent. An entire group of workers had to be stationed at the end of the assembly line just to correct mistakes and redo jobs that hadn't been done right to start with.

There was also considerable tension between management and the unions that represented the firm's employees. Long-standing work rules (terms of a labor contract that specify exactly what each job holder is and is not required and/or allowed to do) and open hostility between union leaders and first-line supervisors greatly limited Smith's options.

Another problem was the firm's reward system. Because workers were paid on a piece-rate basis (that is, a specified amount of money for each unit of work completed), there was a strong incentive to produce large quantities, regardless of quality.

In the early 1980s, the seeds for change were planted. Detroit's Big Three, suffering from competition with Japanese automakers, started pressuring Smith and their other suppliers for higher-quality products. Orders also started to drop as more and more automobile production was shifted to foreign plants and to different makes of cars.

Smith's first response in 1981 was to unilaterally install a quality circle program. Quality circles are groups of volunteer employees who meet on a regular basis to help identify and suggest solutions to quality-related problems. Unfortunately, Smith's management did not enlist the assistance and support of the unions or their leaders. As a consequence, although there were modest improvements in quality, the program faded away in 1984 without having accomplished very much.

In same year, things took another big downturn. GM, Smith's biggest customer, cut its orders sharply, and the other U.S. automakers seemed destined to follow suit. Management then turned to the unions and sought a formal collaboration on solving the problems faced by the company. With the assistance of a consulting firm, Smith and the unions formed problem-solving committees on the plant floor, advisory committees of management and union members at the plant level, and a long-range planning committee with union and management representatives.

These actions also brought about only modest improvements in quality. More importantly, however, they resulted in a noticeable change in attitudes. Even though management and union representatives accomplished little of substance, they nonetheless saw

A. O. Smith has been a pioneer of using teamwork as a basis for structuring jobs. Teamwork has led to higher quality and productivity and may well have saved the company.

for perhaps the first time that they could cooperate and work together for the betterment of everyone.

Another major drop in orders forced the layoff of 1,300 workers in late 1987. The unions then had to confront the fact that the company might be forced to shut down if major changes weren't made. New labor contracts were being negotiated at the time, and the two sides agreed to eliminate the piece-rate incentive system in return for a pledge from the company to not cut wages for four years.

Management and labor also agreed to establish work teams throughout the plant that could function with little or no supervision. The ratio of workers to first-line supervisors was cut from 10:1 to 34:1. Each work team also assigns work schedules to its own members, allocates overtime, and orders maintenance when necessary. Although Smith has much more to do, things are improving dramatically. For example, defects have dropped from 20 percent to 3 percent. Absenteeism rates have also improved considerably.

SOURCES: "The Cultural Revolution at A. O. Smith," *Business Week*, May 29, 1989, pp. 66–68; "The Payoff from Teamwork," *Business Week*, July 10, 1989, pp. 56–62; "Is Teamwork a Management Plot? Mostly Not," *Business Week*, February 20, 1989, p. 70; "What Makes Teamwork Work?" *Psychology Today*, December 1989, pp. 16–17.

M

anagers at A. O. Smith Corporation have started improving the organization's performance and effectiveness by capitalizing on the energy and strength provided by one of the most underutilized resources in organizations today: groups. One of the oldest maxims known to mankind is that "two heads are better than one." By applying two heads (or more) to a problem, organizations can often achieve more than if they maintain the old habit of assigning single tasks to individual employees.

Interpersonal relations and groups are a ubiquitous part of organizational life. By definition, they involve networks of interactions among virtually everyone in an organization. Therefore, a manager clearly needs to understand the dynamics of group activities within the organization. This chapter first describes the interpersonal character of organizations. It then explores the nature of groups, establishing their psychological character and examining three critical group dimensions. Next, it investigates some guidelines for using groups in organizations. After discussing group decision making, it concludes by discussing conflict between people and groups.

THE INTERPERSONAL CHARACTER OF ORGANIZATIONS

By their very nature, organizations are composed of people working together. Bosses discuss work assignments and performance issues with their subordinates; peers at all levels conduct regular meetings to develop plans and solve problems; subordinates go to their bosses with problems and questions; sales representatives talk to customers; secretaries take telephone calls. Indeed, research has suggested that the average manager spends around three-quarters of his or her time interacting with others.[1]

□ Much of the work accomplished by an organization is a result of people working together.

In addition, as we will see in later sections of this chapter, much of the work an organization accomplishes is through people working together. Of course, the nature of any given interaction can vary considerably. Two managers talking at the water cooler may be reaching agreement on how to solve a problem, setting up a meeting for later in the day, discussing the latest football polls, deciding whether or not to fire a subordinate, or arguing about how to resolve a point of disagreement.

And a variety of things result from these interactions. People may partially satisfy their belongingness or affiliation needs, they may derive pleasure or enjoyment from the interactions, they may go away feeling angry or frustrated, or they may solve a significant problem or improve the quality of a decision that has to be made. Regardless of the purpose or the consequences, much of the interpersonal nature of organizations occurs within the context of groups.

THE NATURE OF GROUPS

What is a group? First let's examine the concept of a group, and then we can identify the major kinds of groups found in organizational settings.

Definition of a Group

□ A *group* is two or more people who interact regularly to accomplish a common goal.

A **group** can be defined as two or more people who interact regularly to accomplish a common goal.[2] There are three basic elements that are necessary for a group to exist.

First, at least two people must be involved. Although there is no precise upper limit, a group that gets too large usually ceases to function as a group.

Second, the members must interact regularly. This is the reason for setting an upper limit on group size; once a group reaches a certain size—say, twenty people—it becomes so difficult for everyone to interact that smaller groups tend to emerge from within the larger one.

Finally, group members must have a common purpose. Managers at Mobil may create a group to develop a new plan or product; a group of workers might band together to try to change a company policy; a group of friends might go out together for dinner and a movie. In each case members of the group are working toward a common goal.

Kinds of Groups

□ Three common types of groups are *functional groups, task groups,* and *informal groups.*

There are many, many different kinds of groups, but we are most concerned about groups that exist in organizations. In general, most of these can be classified as functional, task, or informal, as shown in Exhibit 14.1.[3]

A **functional group** is created by the organization to accomplish a range of goals with an indefinite time horizon. The operations division at Allen-Bradley, the marketing division of Nissan, the management department at the University of Notre Dame, and the nursing staff at Ben Taub hospital in Houston are all functional groups. Each of these was formed by the organization, has a number of goals, and has an indefinite time horizon—that is, it is not slated to disappear at a certain time in the future. As the exhibit illustrates, functional groups generally conform to departmental boundaries on an organization chart.

A **task group** is created by the organization to accomplish a limited number of goals within a stated or implied time. Hallmark Cards, for example, might appoint a design team to develop a new line of greeting cards. The group is created by the organization, has only one goal, and has an implied time horizon; after the line has been developed and approved, the group will dissolve.

There are actually several different forms of task groups in most organizations. As shown in the exhibit, a matrix design, as discussed in Chapter 9, places task groups under the direction of a project manager. Task forces, most committees, and many decision-making groups are also task groups.

An **informal group**, also called an interest group, is created by the members of the group itself for purposes that may or may not be related to the organization, and it has an unspecified time horizon. Five coworkers who go to lunch together frequently, twelve employees who form a softball team, and three secretaries who take their afternoon coffee break together are examples of informal groups. Each person chooses to participate and can stop whenever he or she wants.

Exhibit 14.1 Kinds of Groups in Organizations

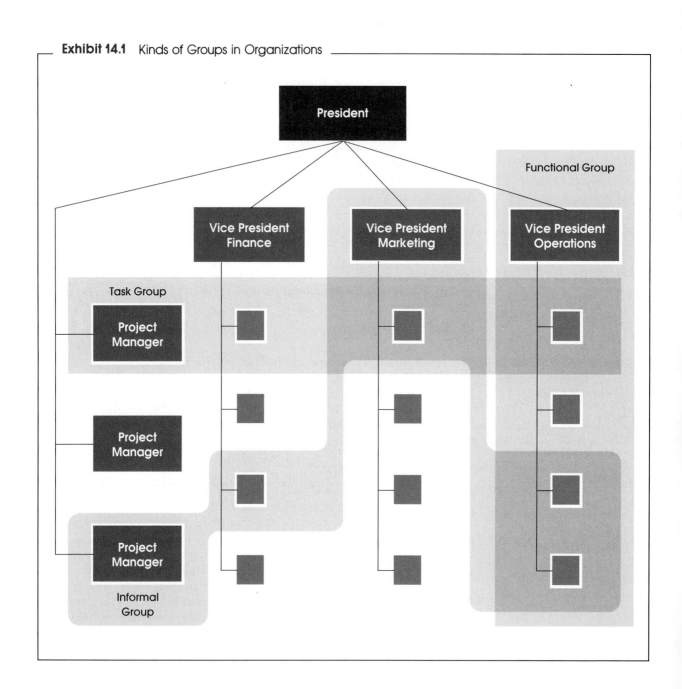

When at lunch, the first group of workers might discuss how to solve an organizational problem (relevant to and in the best interests of the organization), how to steal a machine (relevant to but not in the best interests of the organization), or local politics and sports (not relevant to the organization). As you might guess, informal groups are extremely important to managers and can be a powerful force in determining organizational effectiveness. It is therefore important to understand the psychological character of groups.[4]

Groups have obviously played an important role at A. O. Smith. The various management groups that have always existed in the organization are functional groups. More recently, however, the quality circles and various committees that have been tried are similar to task groups. The new work team arrangements have elements of both functional and task groups. Moreover, informal groups of disgruntled workers have no doubt been common over the years.

THE PSYCHOLOGICAL CHARACTER OF GROUPS

Much of what is known about group processes comes from research in the field of psychology.[5] A substantial portion of this work relates to why people join groups, stages of group development, and the informal organization.

Why People Join Groups

☐ People join groups for a variety of reasons, including interpersonal attraction, activities, goals, and instrumental benefits.

Sometimes people have no choice as to whether to join a group. Students may have to take a certain class, or employees might have to accept a specific job assignment that involves working with a designated group of other people. In many instances, though, people can choose whether to join a particular group. The four most common reasons for doing so are set forth in Table 14.1.[6]

One powerful reason for joining a group is interpersonal attraction. For instance, a new employee might find three other people who work in his department to be especially pleasant and to have interests and attitudes similar to his

TABLE 14.1
Why People Join Groups

Reason	Example
1. Interpersonal Attraction	An employee joins three colleagues for lunch because they share his interest in local politics.
2. Group Activities	An employee joins the company bowling team because she loves to bowl.
3. Group Goals	An employee joins a union because she believes employees should negotiate for higher wages.
4. Instrumental Benefits	A manager joins a golf club because most of his business associates are members and he will make useful contacts.

own, so he might start joining them for lunch most days. He thus joins the group because he is attracted to the members of that group.

Another reason for joining a group is the group's activities. Suppose that another new employee is an avid bowler. She might inquire about and subsequently be invited to join the company bowling team. Of course, she will probably not remain on the team if she dislikes all the other members, but it is not her attraction to them that prompts her to join to begin with. Rather, it is a specific activity that she wants to pursue and that is facilitated by group membership.

A third reason people choose to join groups is that they identify with and want to pursue the goals of the group. This is a common reason for joining unions. Interpersonal attraction is irrelevant, and few people enjoy tedious contract negotiations or strikes. But employees may subscribe to the goals the union has set for its members, such as high wages, better working conditions, and so forth. Similar motives cause people to join the Sierra Club and charitable groups like the United Way and the American Cancer Society.

A final reason for joining groups is the instrumental benefits that may accompany group membership. For example, it is fairly common for college students entering their senior year to join one or more professional associations in order to be able to list it on their résumé. Similarly, a manager might join a certain golf club not because he likes the other members (although he might) or because he likes to play golf (although, again, he might) but in order to make some useful business contacts.

Stages of Group Development

Regardless of the reasons that people join groups, the groups themselves typically go through a period of evolution or development. Although there is no

Exhibit 14.2   Stages of Group Development

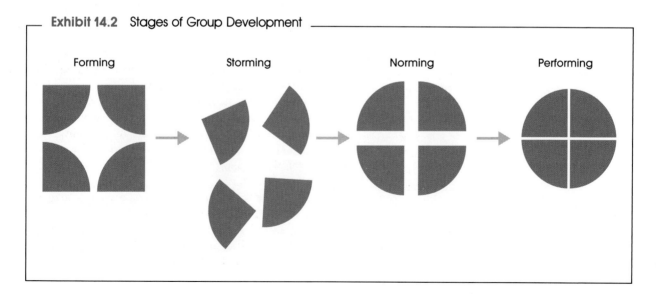

| Forming | Storming | Norming | Performing |

The fourth stage of group development is performing. The workers shown here, a group working on the tunnel underneath the English Channel, have clearly reached this level. They know what's expected of them and work hard to accomplish it.

☐ Groups usually progress through four stages as they develop: *forming, storming, norming,* and *performing.*

rigid pattern that all groups follow, they usually go through the four stages portrayed in Exhibit 14.2.[7]

The first stage is **forming**. As shown by the image on the left side of the exhibit, and as suggested by the term itself, forming involves the members of the group actually coming together to create it. During this stage the members get acquainted and begin to test which behaviors are acceptable and which are unacceptable to other members of the group.

In the **storming** stage, the members begin to pull apart again as they disagree over what needs to be done and how best to do it. Conflict and hostility characterize this stage. Patterns of interaction may be uneven, as suggested by the exhibit, and an informal leader often begins to emerge at this point.

Norming, a common third phase, is characterized by the resolution of conflict and the development of roles (discussed later). People have either left the group, because the conflict is too great, or accepted the group for what it is. Each member takes on certain responsibilities, and everyone develops a common vision of how the group will function.

Finally, the group begins **performing**—moving toward accomplishing its goals, whether those are deciding which movie to see or developing a major planning document for the organization. Of course, as noted earlier, groups may not follow these exact stages in a discrete and observable sequence. They do, however, generally deal with the kinds of issues associated with each of the stages.

The Informal Organization

It is also critical for managers to recognize the existence and importance of the **informal organization**—the overall pattern of influence and interaction defined by the total set of informal groups within the organization.[8] As suggested earlier in Exhibit 14.1, the formal organizational structure is overlaid with informal groups. These groups actually get much of the organization's work done: that is, informal telephone calls, chance meetings at the coffee machine, and impromptu lunch gatherings go a long way toward defining the organization's goals and helping achieve them. Thus, managers should not ignore the power of the informal organization as they go about their business.

IMPORTANT GROUP DIMENSIONS

Groups in and of themselves are of considerable importance and interest. However, managers can gain even greater insights into groups by considering their role dynamics, their level of cohesiveness, and their norms.

Role Dynamics

☐ A *role* is a part a person plays in a group.

What is a **role?** In a movie or play, a role is a part played by an actor. People in groups also play roles.[9] Some people playing the role of "task specialists" might help the group accomplish its goals. Others, called "social specialists," might work to keep everyone happy. A few serve as leaders. Still others, called "free riders," might do very little.

As we have seen, everyone belongs to several different groups. Many people are part of a formal work group, one or more task groups, several informal groups, and a family. Thus each person has various roles to play. A given individual might be a task specialist in one group, the leader in another, and a free rider in a third.

☐ *Role dynamics* are defined by *expected, sent, perceived,* and *enacted* roles.

Exhibit 14.3 illustrates the way in which **role dynamics** occur in a group. Role dynamics are the process whereby a person's expected role is transformed to his or her enacted role. First there is the **expected role,** the role others in the group expect a person to play. The members transmit these expectations in the form of the **sent role.** As we will see in the next chapter, however, communication breakdowns frequently occur, so there may be differences between the expected and sent roles.

Perceptual factors can affect the role process, too. Therefore, still more differences may creep in as the sent role is translated into the **perceived role**—how the individual comes to think he or she should behave in the group. Finally, the **enacted role** is how the person actually behaves, and here too differences can arise. For example, the person might not be capable of executing

Exhibit 14.3   Role Dynamics

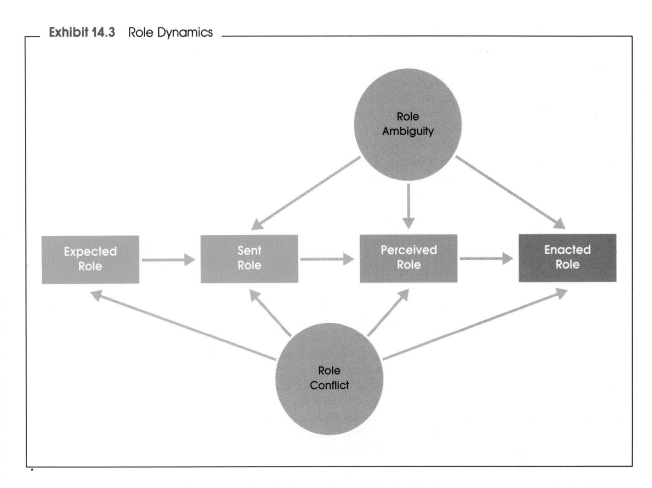

the perceived role, or she might simply choose not to execute it in the way that others expect.

The exhibit also introduces the concepts of role ambiguity and role conflict, two facets of group dynamics that warrant additional explanation.

□ *Role ambiguity* occurs when the sent role is not clear.

Role ambiguity occurs when the sent role is unclear.[10] For instance, suppose a supervisor tells a new employee to prepare a sales forecast for the next period. It is quite possible that the employee does not know where to get the data, how many products to include in the forecast, what form to use for the report, or even what time period is involved. Thus she will probably suffer from role ambiguity.

□ *Role conflict* occurs when there is some degree of inconsistency or contradiction about the role.

Of perhaps even greater concern is **role conflict,** which occurs when the messages about the role are clear but involve some degree of inconsistency or contradiction. There are several forms of role conflict.[11]

Interrole conflict occurs when there is conflict between two or more roles. For example, suppose Bill's boss tells him he has to work more overtime. But Bill was already feeling guilty about working so much and has just resolved to spend more time with his family. Consequently, he will now experience interrole conflict. In contrast, intrarole conflict occurs when two or more people send conflicting messages to a person in the same role. If a marketing vice president tells a sales manager to have the sales force travel more just when the controller is telling the sales manager to cut travel costs, the sales manager will experience intrarole conflict.

Intrasender role conflict arises if the same person transmits conflicting expectations. Suppose that on Monday the boss tells her assistant that it's okay to dress more casually, but on Thursday she reprimands her for not looking professional. The obvious contradiction will result in intrasender role conflict for the assistant.

Finally, person-role conflict arises when the demands of the role are incongruent with the person's preferences or values. An employee experiences this conflict if his job demands a great deal of travel, for instance, but he prefers to remain at home. Similarly, an employee who has strong feelings against military buildups and the arms race may feel uncomfortable when her company gets several defense contracts.

Cohesiveness

□ *Cohesiveness* is the extent to which members of the group are motivated to remain together.

Another important dimension of groups is **cohesiveness,** or the extent to which the members of the group are motivated to remain together.[12] A highly cohesive group is one in which the members pull together, enjoy being together, perform well together, and aren't looking for opportunities to get out of the group. In contrast, a group with a low level of cohesiveness is one in which the members do not like to be together, do not work well together, and would casually leave the group if an opportunity arose.

Exhibit 14.4 shows the determinants and consequences of cohesiveness. As shown, small size, frequent interaction, clear goals, and success tend to foster cohesiveness. For example, if five people (small size) are assigned to a crash project for developing a new product by the end of the year (clear goals), if they must spend virtually all of their working hours together (frequent interaction), and if they achieve a breakthrough sooner than expected (success), they are likely to emerge as a very cohesive group.

In contrast, a large group whose members are physically dispersed and that has ambiguous goals and suffers failures will be less cohesive. Suppose a firm designates eighty-five engineers (large size) located in three different plants (physically dispersed) as a task force to "explore new product ideas" (ambiguous goals). The group fails to come up with any useful ideas (failure). It will probably not be very cohesive.

The exhibit also illustrates various results of cohesiveness. If cohesiveness is high, the group tends to be more effective in attaining future goals, its members are more personally satisfied with the group, and the group will probably continue to exist. On the other hand, if cohesiveness is low, the group is less likely to attain its future goals, members will express more dissatisfaction with the group, and the group is more likely to dissolve or fall apart.

Exhibit 14.4   Determinants and Consequences of Group Cohesiveness

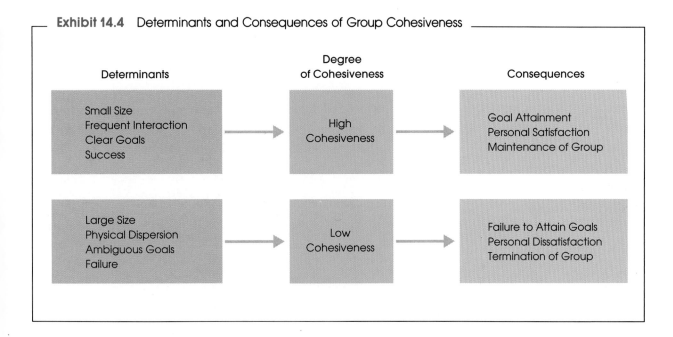

Norms

The importance of cohesiveness is accentuated when we consider it in the context of group norms. A **norm** is a standard of behavior that the group develops for its members.[13] For instance, a group might have a norm against talking to the boss too much. People who violate this norm may be "punished" with unpleasant looks, snide remarks, and the like. The norms themselves are, of course, socially defined and exist only in the minds of the group members.

Norms can arise for any number of work-related behaviors. In a typical work group, there may be norms that define how people dress, the upper and lower limits on acceptable productivity, things that can be told to the boss and things that need to remain secret, and so forth.[14] *Management Today: Ethical Dilemmas of Management* shows how certain norms can also lead to dishonest or illegal behaviors.

When confronted with a set of norms in an established group, an individual might do several different things. One common reaction is to accept and conform to the group norm. A less frequent reaction is total rebellion, in which case the person completely rejects the norm. (Of course, if the norm is important to the rest of the group, the newcomer will probably be ostracized.) There is also creative individuality. In this situation, the person accepts some of the norms, especially the most important ones, but follows his or her own preferences within their limits. For example, if the norm is that employees will not wear jeans to work, a newcomer who prefers to dress casually might be able to get away with wearing jeans once every few weeks, as opposed to never wearing them (conformity) or wearing them every day (rebellion).

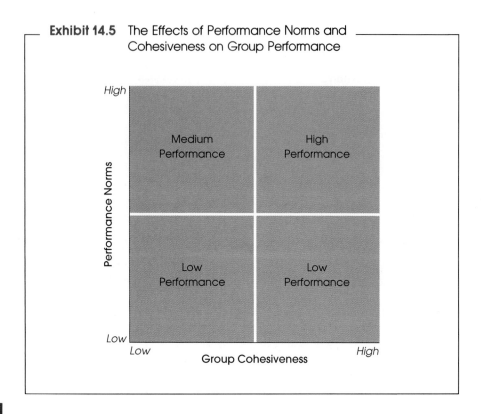

Exhibit 14.5 The Effects of Performance Norms and Cohesiveness on Group Performance

One important norm, that which governs the acceptable level of performance in the group, becomes especially critical when linked with cohesiveness. This pattern is shown in Exhibit 14.5. When performance norms and cohesiveness are both high, the manager has a powerful vehicle for achieving high levels of performance. When performance norms are low and cohesiveness is high, however, the manager has a major obstacle to overcome.

MANAGING GROUPS IN ORGANIZATIONS

☐ Managers can follow certain guidelines in managing *functional groups, task forces* and *committees, work teams,* and *quality circles.*

Since all organizations contain groups, it is obviously important for managers to understand how they should be managed. This section discusses some guidelines for managing various kinds of groups. A special case of managing groups, group decision making, is considered in the next section.

Managing Functional Groups

Virtually all aspects of interaction between a formal leader and his or her work group are related to the management of functional groups, so all of the areas of management covered in the other chapters in this book are pertinent. How-

MANAGEMENT TODAY

ETHICAL DILEMMAS OF MANAGEMENT

Peer Pressure at Dean Witter

Dean Witter Reynolds, Inc., a subsidiary of Sears, is one of the world's largest brokerage houses. Stockbrokers at such houses receive a commission every time a customer buys or sells stock. Therefore, it is in their best interests to entice customers to buy and sell as often as possible.

A group of brokers at Dean Witter's Boston office were recently found to have been taking advantage of their positions to pad their commissions. Specifically, since they had access to their clients' resources, they were selling and rebuying the same securities without the customers' knowledge or con-

sent. Such practices, called "churning," are both illegal and unethical.

Why did it start? One reason was the norms that had emerged among the group of brokers in Boston. A few key brokers had started churning regularly. As others found out what was going on, the group pressured them to join in. After doing it a few times themselves, the newcomers saw that churning was seductively easy. When pressed later for an explanation for their participation, some said they were afraid of being fired; others said they just wanted to be accepted into the brokerage community.

SOURCES: "Dean Witter Braces for a Backlash in Boston," *Business Week,* March 6, 1989, p. 86; Brian Duhaime, "Beating Bolder Corporate Crooks," *Fortune,* April 25, 1988, pp. 193–202; "Merrill Scrambles for the Top of the Junk Heap," *Business Week,* March 5, 1990, p. 76.

ever, several specific implications can be drawn from earlier discussions of group dimensions.[15]

For one thing, the manager should be cognizant of the importance of role dynamics. In particular, she should recognize the potential problems associated with role ambiguity and role conflict and strive to avoid these problems whenever possible. For another thing, the manager needs to realize the importance of group cohesiveness. As we have noted, cohesiveness can be a powerful force in organizations, especially when combined with different levels of performance norms. The manager should therefore work to enhance cohesiveness when it is in the best interests of the organization. Finally, the manager should work to establish high performance norms, by adding hard workers to the group, consistently rewarding high performance, and so forth. Such actions should reinforce current levels of performance norms and simultaneously push them higher.

Managing Task Forces and Committees

Organizations often use task forces and committees to get various kinds of tasks performed. Since both of these are task groups, they can generally be managed in similar ways. There are, however, a few subtle differences.

MANAGING TASK FORCES   Several guidelines that relate specifically to task forces have been developed.[16] A **task force** is a temporary group within an organization created to accomplish a specific purpose (task) by integrating existing functional areas. First, the majority of the group should be line managers. Since they are ultimately responsible for implementing the group's ideas, they should be well represented in the group. Second, the group needs to be provided with all relevant information. It will be more effective if it has access to information that affects its work.

Group members also need the legitimate power necessary to translate group needs back to their respective functional groups. Within the group, though, the emphasis should be on expert power; that is, group members with expertise in specialized areas should be placed in charge of those areas. The task force should also be properly integrated with relevant functional groups. Ideally this follows from the composition of the group, as suggested in the first guideline, but special attention may be required to maintain this integration over time. A last point is to establish group membership with the goal of optimizing technical and interpersonal skills. Members need to know how to do their respective jobs, but they also need to be able to get along with one another.

MANAGING COMMITTEES   Another important part of almost every manager's job at one time or another is managing a committee. A **committee** is a special kind of task group. Committees may have only a few members, or they

Work teams have become very important in many organizations. These workers are part of a "work center" group at Stanley Electronics in Detroit. They meet weekly to manage production and set work schedules. Because of these self-governing teams, there are no inspectors or coordinators in the plant.

The Stanley Works/Photo by Al Ferreira

may have many. Their purpose may be broad and short term or narrow and long term. They are often given names, such as the Grievance Committee, the Steering Committee, or the President's Advisory Committee. They may appear at the bottom of the organization, or they may occur at the highest levels of the firm and have primary responsibility for its management.

Like other kinds of groups, committees can be made more effective if managers follow specific guidelines. For one thing, the goals and limits of the committee's authority need to be clearly specified. This clarity will help keep the committee's activities focused and directed toward its intended purpose. For another, the committee should usually have a specific agenda. Care should also be taken to see that the committee does not interfere too much with its members' normal responsibilities; that is, people should not devote so much time to their committee duties that they neglect their regular jobs.

Finally, it is useful to specify what the output of the committee is to be. For example, suppose a manager creates a committee to locate a site for a new factory. He may want the committee to submit a list of three acceptable sites, either rank-ordered or unranked. He may need a lot of supporting materials for each site, or he may want only the recommendations. Obviously, he should clearly communicate each of these expectations to the committee before it begins to work.[17]

Managing Work Teams

A fairly recent innovation in the use of groups in organizations is the establishment of work teams. A **work team** is a small group of employees that is responsible for a set of tasks previously performed by its individual members and that takes primary responsibility for managing itself. As noted in the Prelude Case, A. O. Smith has adopted the work team concept.

There are several reasons for the use of work teams. Perhaps the most important is that work teams provide a natural vehicle for giving employees more say in their jobs—that is, for increasing participation. Given the general trend toward more participation, work teams are likely to be used more and more often. Moreover, they often result in increased productivity, higher quality, and better employee attitudes.

Organizations that want to use work teams need to consider several guidelines. First of all, it is often necessary to provide some initial training. People who previously did one simple task on their own may need to learn how to perform other tasks and work with others. Perhaps most importantly, organizations that use work teams must be willing to give work team members more responsibility and control over their tasks. If a first-line supervisor is always watching over their shoulders, the work team may actually be a detriment. Only if the team members have some of the responsibility previously held by their managers will they succeed. Finally, selecting new employees may need to be approached differently. They may need heightened interpersonal skills and the ability to work with existing group members. *Management Today: The World of Management* describes the care with which Mazda recruits and trains its work teams.[18]

MANAGEMENT TODAY

THE WORLD OF MANAGEMENT

What Makes a Miracle?

Everyone seems to know about the Japanese miracles—how Japanese companies make top-quality products, how they have such loyal and dedicated work forces, and so forth. What fewer people understand, however, is the care and hard work that go into creating such an organization.

Take Mazda, for example. When the Japanese automaker was getting ready to open its first U.S. assembly plant in Flat Rock, Michigan, it went to unprecedented lengths to find just the right kinds of people.

Like most Japanese companies, Mazda uses work teams in its assembly plants. Not everyone is suited for such a work environment, however. And even

those that are are often unprepared for it. Consequently, Mazda spent $40 million ($13,000 per employee) in hiring and training a highly select group of workers.

Every applicant was thoroughly assessed in terms of interpersonal skills, motivation, aptitude for learning, and an interest in teamwork and participation. After they were hired, the employees completed three weeks of training with other new employees that focused on helping them understand how to function better as part of a group. After that, they received another ten weeks of technical training before they were put to work and became a part of the Mazda team.

SOURCES: "How Does Japan, Inc. Pick Its American Workers?" *Business Week,* October 3, 1988, pp. 84–88; Louis Kraar, "Japan's Gung-Ho U.S. Car Plants," *Fortune,* January 30, 1989, pp. 98–108; "Help Wanted, Room to Advance—Out the Door," *Business Week,* October 30, 1989, p. 42.

Managing Quality Circles

A final type of group with which many managers are beginning to have to contend is the **quality circle,** or **QC.** As briefly noted in Chapter 13, QCs are groups of operating employees formed for the express purpose of helping the organization identify and solve quality-related problems.[19] They are made up of volunteers from the same or related work areas who meet regularly, usually for an hour or so each week, to talk about quality issues faced by the company. Each member is free to suggest problems the group might tackle. Theoretically, the employees are so close to their tasks that they can suggest ideas and opportunities for improvement that might escape the attention of managers.

QCs are quite controversial. Many firms, such as Polaroid, Procter & Gamble, General Foods, and General Motors, have successfully adopted QCs. But others firms have had disappointing experiences with them. If an organization does decide to try QCs, it can at least increase the potential for success. Among hints given by successful companies is, first, to rely totally on volunteers. People who feel coerced to join will be of little value. Second, provide enough time and resources to allow the QC to do its intended job. Third, provide feedback and recognition to the QC regarding its suggestions. For instance, suppose a QC recommends a new way of doing something that results

LEARNING CHECK

You should now be able to discuss the management of functional groups, task forces and committees, work teams, and quality circles.

in substantial cost savings for the company. Managers should, of course, tell the QC of the success of its idea, but they should also communicate that fact to others through the company newsletter, special announcements, and other means. This allows the group members to develop feelings of pride and accomplishment. If an idea is not acceptable or doesn't really do any good, managers should communicate this fact to the group, albeit more subtly.

PRELUDE CASE UPDATE

As noted in the Prelude Case, A. O. Smith had a disappointing experience with quality circles in the early 1980s. A few modest quality gains were made, but the program eventually failed. A major reason for this failure was the way the program was initiated. The company simply decided that it was going to do it and then proceeded without ever consulting or involving the unions. Eventually, then, without the support of the unions, the program fell apart due to lack of enthusiasm by group members and subtle opposition from the rank-and-file union members.

GROUP DECISION MAKING

☐ Group decision making has several advantages and disadvantages relative to individual decision making.

As we have already seen, a great deal of decision making in organizations is done by groups. Executive committees make critical decisions about the company's future, project teams make decisions about which new products to introduce, and grievance committees make decisions about who is right and wrong in organizational disputes. This section outlines the advantages and disadvantages of allowing groups to make decisions and then summarizes three techniques that can be used to promote better group decisions.[20]

Advantages of Group Decision Making

Obviously, there must be certain advantages to group decision making. Why else would it ever be done? Table 14.2 summarizes the four most general advantages.[21] These factors tend to lead to a higher-quality decision than a single individual working alone might have obtained.

One advantage is the fact that more information is available to the group than is available to an individual. Each member is able to draw on his or her unique education, experience, insights, and other resources and (it is hoped) contribute these to the group. Similarly, a group is likely to generate more alternatives to consider than an individual can. That is, some individuals have ideas that escape others, so the total set of alternatives should be greater in the group than for any single individual.

A third advantage is that acceptance of the decision will probably be greater than it would be if an individual made the decision alone. Since more people participated in making the decision, more people will understand its origins.

TABLE 14.2
Advantages and
Disadvantages of Group
Decision Making

Advantages	Disadvantages
Availability of more information	Longer decision-making process
Generation of more ideas	Too much emphasis on compromise
Easier acceptance of decisions	Dominance by an individual
Better decisions often made	Possibility of groupthink

Those who did not participate might well feel that the decision was reached in a democratic fashion. Finally, groups just tend to make better decisions than individuals do. The extra information and additional alternatives, when properly considered and processed, promote a better outcome.

Disadvantages of Group Decision Making

Unfortunately, there are also four disadvantages to group decision making. If these disadvantages did not exist, all decisions would automatically be assigned to groups. These factors, also listed in Table 14.2, serve as barriers to high-quality decisions.

One major disadvantage is that groups tend to take longer to reach a decision, because all members may want to discuss every aspect of the decision. Although this may be a plus, it adds a lot of time to the process. The group may also try too hard to compromise. Some degree of compromise may be necessary and perhaps even desirable, but compromise might be sought to the exclusion of a better decision that the group could have reached with more effort.

It is also possible that a single individual will dominate the process. If this happens, the decision may be too widely accepted because it has the appearance of having been made by the group. Besides, allowing one member to make the decision sets aside all of the potential advantages of group decision making.

Groups involved in making decisions may also succumb to a phenomenon known as **groupthink**.[22] This happens when group members become so interested in maintaining cohesiveness and good feelings toward one another that the group's original goals become lost. In this case the group makes decisions that protect its members as individuals and the group as a whole rather than decisions that are in the best interests of the overall organization.

Techniques for Group Decision Making

Managers have come up with several techniques for capitalizing on the advantages of group decision making while simultaneously minimizing the potential

Alen MacWeeney

Group decision making is a common approach used in many circumstances. Team Viper, shown here, is a group of Chrysler workers who are planning a new sports car the automaker plans to introduce in the next few years. The group meets regularly to make decisions about design, technical specifications, and so forth.

harm from the disadvantages.[23] As we saw in Chapter 5, the **Delphi technique** uses experts to make predictions about future events. These predictions are systematically refined through feedback until a consensus emerges.

The **nominal group technique** is a structured process whereby members individually suggest alternatives, which are then listed on a chart for all to see. All the alternatives are discussed, and each member is asked to rank-order them. The average rankings are listed and the process is repeated until everyone agrees.

The **devil's advocate strategy** is to assign one member the role of devil's advocate; this person is expected to challenge and take issue with the actions of the rest of the group. This is especially valuable in preventing groupthink.

LEARNING CHECK

You should now be able to describe the advantages, disadvantages, and techniques of group decision making.

CONFLICT BETWEEN PEOPLE AND GROUPS

☐ Organizational *conflict* occurs within the context of an organizational setting and can be between individual employees, groups, or whole departments.

One last element of interpersonal relations to be discussed is **conflict.** Conflict may occur between two or more individuals, between two or more groups, and/or between individuals and groups. Most of us are generally familiar with the meaning of conflict. We read in the papers about conflict between countries, we ourselves experience conflict when we argue with friends or relatives, and we observe disagreements between others fairly often. Organizational conflict, then, is conflict that occurs within an organizational setting and can be between individual employees, groups, or whole departments.

The Nature of Conflict

Conflict may be either good or bad. Therefore, it is important to understand not only the relationship between these two aspects of conflict but also the causes and consequences of conflict.[24]

POSITIVE AND NEGATIVE ASPECTS OF CONFLICT   Most people tend to think of organizational conflict as bad and dysfunctional. And sometimes it can be. In many other cases, however, conflict can be a positive force in organizations. The general relationship between conflict and performance is illustrated in Exhibit 14.6.

When there is absolutely no conflict, performance often tends to be very low as well. The reason is that people are often motivated by competition and spurred to action because they think their way of doing something is better than someone else's. Therefore, as conflict increases, so too may performance. At some point, however, represented in the exhibit by the apex of the curve, conflict reaches its highest effective point. Beyond that point, additional conflict begins to cause a deterioration in performance. Ultimately, the conflict may become so great that performance comes to a standstill.

CAUSES AND CONSEQUENCES OF CONFLICT   Depending on the situation, any number of things can lead to organizational conflict. One very

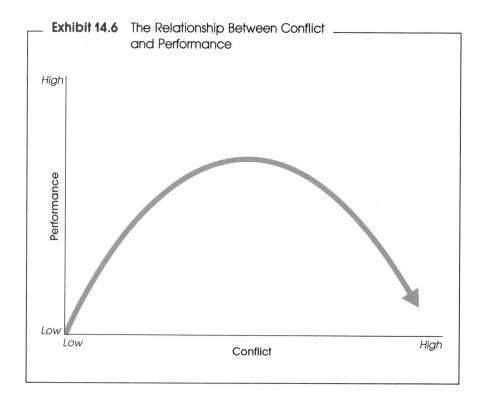

Exhibit 14.6   The Relationship Between Conflict and Performance

common reason for conflict is the interdependencies that may exist between people or groups within the organization.[25] For example, consider the case of an assembly line in a Volvo automobile plant. Work is performed in large blocks by teams of workers and then is passed from one team to another. If one team doesn't do its jobs properly or gets too far ahead or behind in its work, it causes problems for the next group.

Competition between people or groups can also cause conflict, especially when the stakes are high and the competition is a win-lose proposition. For example, if a company establishes a sales contest among sales groups and plans to award a two-week vacation in Hawaii to the winning group, conflict is likely—the stakes are high, and when one group wins the others all lose.

Differences in goals and activities can also lead to conflict. The marketing department, for example, may have a goal of increasing sales by 20 percent and may decide that the best strategies to use in reaching this goal include increasing the number of product options and promising faster delivery times. At the same time, the production department might set a goal of cutting costs by 15 percent and might plan to decrease product options and use slower transportation methods to achieve this goal. The two goals are likely to conflict. Finally, personalities might also come into play. Two people may be unable to work together or simply may not be able to get along.

Just as there are several causes of conflict, there are also several consequences, again both good and bad. One major consequence is hostility. People become hostile toward one another, refuse to cooperate, and generally take an antagonistic posture when forced to deal with others involved in the situation. Withdrawal is also a distinct possibility. The withdrawal may be confined to such things as refusing to socialize with others, or it might extend to actually leaving the organization.

On a more positive note, conflict may also serve to increase motivation. For example, a person who has a mild disagreement with another person may become more motivated to prove that the other is wrong. Assuming that the disagreement is mild, that the competition that results is constructive, and that the "winner" and "loser" will both learn from the experience, this process can be positive. Finally, in a somewhat related vein, performance can also be increased through conflict. For example, consider the case of two plant managers within the same company who disagree over the best way to improve productivity. Each may be allowed to pursue his own ideas, and each may develop new techniques that do actually improve productivity. Thus, the overall performance of the company increases, and each manager can feel like a "winner."

Managing Conflict

Since conflict is so important to managers and has so many consequences, it follows that managers need to know how to manage it. In some settings, it is useful to stimulate or encourage conflict. In others, the manager may want to reduce or prevent it. Finally, in situations where conflict has already arisen and the manager wants to resolve it, still other approaches are called for.

ENCOURAGING CONFLICT   There are several things managers can do to encourage conflict. One obvious approach is to encourage competition. Holding events such as contests, posting individual or group performance data for all to see, and publicizing performance levels can all encourage competition. Of course, as noted earlier, the manager needs to be careful to not let things get out of hand.

Changing procedures can also stimulate a certain degree of conflict. For example, a manager may start requiring extra documentation before new projects are approved. People might then be more careful when they prepare their proposals. They may not like the extra work, but the cost savings may be worth the extra headaches.

Finally, bringing in outsiders to key positions can also stimulate conflict. For example, Beecham, a large British firm, recently hired an American CEO. The company expressed the hope that he would shake things up and infuse new American management techniques into the staid old company.

PREVENTING CONFLICT   Of course, it may also be desirable to prevent the occurrence of conflict in the first place. One strategy is to increase resources. For example, if two departments are likely to argue over access to a new computer network, it may be wise to establish a bigger network so that each department can have full access.

Interdependencies can also be managed so as to avoid conflict. For example, often rules and standard operating procedures can be established that will govern how various situations are to be resolved.

The setting of overall goals can also help prevent conflict. Recall the potential conflict between the marketing department's goal to increase sales and the production department's goal to cut costs. An astute manager might get the two departments to agree that an overall goal of increasing sales and cutting cost is best.

Finally, interpersonal dynamics may also be amenable to a certain degree of management. For example, if a manager knows that one employee is a chain smoker and another is an aggressive nonsmoker, she might make sure that their offices are as far apart as possible to minimize their interactions.

RESOLVING CONFLICT   Of course, regardless of the manager's best intentions, conflict is still likely to occur. Fortunately, there are several things that can be done to resolve conflict. One technique is avoidance, simply ignoring the problem and hoping it will go away. If the conflict is minimal, avoidance may work. However, it should not be used simply because the manager doesn't want to deal with the problem.

Smoothing is somewhat similar to avoidance. Here, though, the manager acknowledges the existence of the conflict but also downplays its importance. Like avoidance, smoothing may be effective if used wisely, but sometimes the conflict is simply too great to go away on its own.

Compromise involves reaching a point of agreement between what each of the conflicting parties initially wanted. For example, suppose a manager and a subordinate have a major disagreement over the subordinate's rude behavior.

The manager might want the employee fired, but the subordinate doesn't want to do anything. A possible compromise might have the subordinate formally apologize for the incident but keep his job. Of course, like other strategies, compromise must be used with care—it is possible that both parties will end up feeling that they have lost.

Finally, the conflict might be resolved through confrontation. Confrontation is the direct approach of addressing the conflict and working together to resolve it. And, indeed, the process itself is often characterized by more conflict as the parties wrestle with issues and debate the best course of action. For example, Control Data Corporation recently established a peer review committee to deal with grievances. Two randomly chosen peers of the aggrieved employee and one "disinterested" executive hear the complaints and help determine the best course of action.

In summary, then, conflict is a major force in organizational settings. The manager needs to be sensitive to the dynamics of conflict and take appropriate steps to encourage, prevent, or resolve conflict in the best interests of all parties concerned.

LEARNING CHECK

You should now be able to discuss the nature of conflict between people and groups and how it can be managed.

PRELUDE CASE UPDATE

A. O. Smith was clearly a victim of extreme forms of conflict between management and unions for several years. The basic reason for this conflict was perceived differences in goals. Unions always thought management wanted to maximize profits at their expense, and management always thought the unions wanted to squeeze every penny out of the company that was possible. More recently, however, both sides have been forced to confront each other and try to resolve their differences. They now have a common goal—survival of the firm as a way to continue making profits for owners and ensuring job security for union members.

Chapter Summary

Organizations are by their very nature highly interpersonal. Virtually all of the work of most organizations is accomplished by two or more people working together. Much of this interaction takes place in the context of groups. A group is two or more people who interact regularly to accomplish a common goal. Groups in organizations can be classified as functional, task, or informal.

People usually choose to join a group because of interpersonal attraction, group activities, group goals, and instrumental benefits. Regardless of why a group is formed, it normally goes through a four-stage developmental process consisting of forming, norming, storming, and performing. The informal organization is the overall pattern of influence and interaction defined by the total set of informal groups within the organization.

In all groups, people play certain parts, or roles. Role ambiguity occurs when the sent role is unclear and the person is not sure what she or he is supposed to do. Role conflict occurs when role messages are clear but inconsistent or contradictory. Another group dimension is cohesiveness, the extent to which the members of the group are motivated to stay together. This is connected to norms, which are the standards of behavior developed by the group.

Norms may relate to performance (such as the quantity and quality of goods produced) or to nonperformance (such as how people should dress or what should be kept secret).

Managing groups is not easy. Fortunately, several guidelines exist that can facilitate the management of functional groups, task forces and committees, work teams, and quality circles.

Group decision making, which is common to American corporations, has four basic advantages and four disadvantages. Managers can use several techniques to enhance the quality of group decision making.

Conflict can be a consequence of many interpersonal processes in organizations. It has both positive and negative attributes and can be stimulated, reduced, or resolved through a variety of techniques.

The Manager's Vocabulary

group	enacted role
functional group	role ambiguity
task group	role conflict
informal group	cohesiveness
forming	norm
storming	task force
norming	committee
performing	work team
informal organization	quality circle (QC)
role	groupthink
role dynamics	Delphi technique
expected role	nominal group technique
sent role	devil's advocate strategy
perceived role	conflict

Prelude Case Wrap-Up

Our Prelude Case for this chapter explores how A. O. Smith, a troubled manufacturing firm, has increasingly started relying on groups to turn itself around. Although the company still has a ways to go, it is definitely on the right track.

American firms looking to regain their competitive edge are often adopting the work team concept. For example, during the last ten years Boeing, Caterpillar, Cummins Engine, Digital Equipment, Ford, General Electric, General Motors, LTV Steel, Proc-

ter & Gamble, and Tektronix have adopted the work team concept in at least some of their locations. Nor is their use confined to businesses—the U.S. Postal Service, the New York City Sanitation Department, and the Philadelphia Zoo have all adopted work teams for their employees.

In many cases, the results of work teams have also been very impressive. At one General Electric plant, for example, productivity increased by 250 percent after work teams were adopted. About 20 percent of the company's 120,000 employees now participate in work teams, and the company is expanding it to as many areas as possible.

At the same time, of course, the work team concept is not a panacea. General Electric has high turnover, for example, because many workers don't want the additional responsibility they must accept and/or don't like switching jobs frequently. Many national and local union officials are also strongly opposed to the work team concept.

Still, most experts agree on two things. First, when properly planned and implemented, work teams do increase productivity and quality and/or lower costs. Second, work teams are almost certain to become more and more pervasive across the American industry scene during the remaining years in this century.

Prelude Case Questions

1. Why do you think union leaders are often opposed to the work team concept?
2. How would you advise a manager who wanted to install work teams in her or his organization? Draw on the topics discussed in this chapter.
3. What mistakes has A. O. Smith made? What potential problems should the company be planning for?
4. What changes might you foresee in the work team concept in the future?

Discussion Questions

Review Questions

1. Identify and define the three basic types of groups.
2. What are the four stages of group development?
3. Describe the various kinds of role conflict.

4. How do performance norms interact with cohesiveness to determine performance?
5. What are the advantages and disadvantages of group decision making?

Analysis Questions

1. Why is there an upper limit on the number of people that can reasonably constitute a group?
2. Have you ever experienced any of the forms of role conflict described in the chapter? Describe as many as possible.
3. If you were a manager in charge of a group that had high cohesiveness but very low performance norms, what would you do?
4. What are the common elements inherent in managing the different types of groups? What are the differences?
5. Have you ever been involved in conflict that had positive payoffs? If so, describe your experience.

Application Questions and Exercises

1. Take a sheet of paper and list several different groups you belong to. List the reason or reasons you joined each group.
2. Interview the manager of a local business. Ask what groups are present in the organization.
3. Describe how your instructor might use quality circles to improve this class.
4. Identify a hypothetical decision that an organization needs to make. Role-play a manager making the decision alone, and then make the decision again in conjunction with a group of classmates. Describe both processes in terms of the advantages and disadvantages of group decision making.
5. Select your favorite athletic team. Analyze it in terms of the various dimensions of groups and conflict discussed in the chapter.

ENHANCEMENT CASE

CBS BESET BY CONFLICT

For years, CBS was the dominant television network in the United States. The broadcasting giant controlled the ratings in daytime programming, evening programming, weekend programming, sports programming, and news. NBC and ABC were always competing for number two. CBS also owned a music-publishing business, a magazine business, and a record business.

In recent years, however, things have changed dramatically. Riding on the strength of programs like "Cheers" and "Cosby," NBC has become the dominant network. ABC has taken over the top spot in news ratings and the number two spot in evening programming, and it is always strong in sports.

There were many theories but few real answers about CBS's fall. Whatever the explanation, the company was ripe for a change. Enter Laurence Tisch. Tisch had amassed a fortune from his ownership of Loews. In the mid-1980s, however, he left control of that company in the hands of his family and started buying stock in CBS. People feared him because of

his enormous wealth, but he insisted he was just after a good investment. He quickly built up a sufficient stake to gain membership on the board of directors.

At the time, CBS was being run by Thomas Wyman. Under Wyman's leadership, unfortunately, the slide for CBS had already started. Ratings had started to fall, and profits were dropping. In addition, first Jesse Helms and then Ted Turner had made overtures about taking over CBS. Backed by the company's board of directors, Wyman had fought off those challenges. But trouble still loomed for the company, and some directors started to lose confidence in Wyman's ability to stay on top.

Tisch had formed an alliance with William Paley, founder of CBS and still the company's largest stockholder. Both men had been critical of several of Wyman's actions, but their discontent was generally limited to some occasional grumbling. The other directors knew that a confrontation was imminent, but no one knew when it would come. Tisch wasn't trusted by the other directors because he was from outside the broadcasting industry. Paley had also become unpredictable.

In 1987, rumors started circulating that Wyman was looking for someone to buy the company. Given the board's earlier fights to remain independent, such actions seemed to make little sense. Wyman denied the allegations, however, and seemed to regain his stature with the board. Then one day at a board meeting, he dropped a bombshell: he announced that he had entered into negotiations with Coca-Cola for that firm to take over ownership of CBS.

The directors were stunned. The credibility Wyman had regained with them vanished instantly. After several hours of heated debate, Wyman was asked to leave the room. The board then voted to replace him, and Tisch and Paley were appointed to find a replacement. To no one's surprise, Paley was named chairman and Tisch was appointed chief executive officer. Paley eventually stepped aside, leaving total control in the hands of Laurence Tisch.

At first, everyone at the company was ecstatic. Tisch had a reputation for turning around companies headed in the wrong direction. He also seemed to take great interest in being actively involved. Soon, however, doubts about him also began to arise.

First of all, he ordered massive cutbacks in the number of employees in the company. All told, several thousand employees were terminated, including several key people in the news division. Over the course of the next few years, he also sold the music-publishing, record, and magazine businesses. He seemed to get a fair price for each, but critics later argued that he could have gotten much more.

As the decade of the 1990s began, CBS's position in the world still had not changed much. The network was constantly number three in the ratings, was only marginally profitable, and still suffered from sagging morale. In a bold move to regain its competitive edge, CBS has bid record sums of money to acquire broadcasting rights for most major sporting events, including the Olympics and professional baseball. The hope is that such events will showcase commercials for CBS's regular programs and therefore improve their ratings.

Observers are divided in their assessment of the future of CBS. Some believe that Tisch has lost his magic and that the company is doomed to mediocrity. Others think he is just biding his time, however, and that he will bring the network back stronger than ever.

SOURCES: "How the CBS Board Decided Chief Wyman Should Leave His Job," *The Wall Street Journal*, September 12, 1986, pp. 1, 15; "The Showdown at CBS," *Newsweek*, September 22, 1986, pp. 54–59; "Seeking Ratings Gains, CBS Pays Huge Sums for Sports Contracts," *The Wall Street Journal*, October 10, 1989, pp. A1, A6; Kenneth Labich, "Has Larry Tisch Lost His Touch?" *Fortune*, February 26, 1990, pp. 99–104.

Enhancement Case Questions

1. What sources of conflict are evident at CBS?
2. The board of directors of any corporation is a group. How might group processes have affected events at CBS?
3. Was the conflict at CBS positive or negative? What criteria might be appropriate in making this judgment?
4. Do you think the group decision-making process at CBS was effective? Why or why not? How could it have been improved?

Chapter Notes

1. Henry Mintzberg, *The Nature of Managerial Work* (New York: Harper & Row, 1973).

2. Linda M. Jewell and M. Joseph Reitz, *Group Effectiveness in Organizations* (Glenview, Ill.: Scott, Foresman, 1981).
3. Marvin E. Shaw, *Group Dynamics—The Psychology of Small Group Behavior*, 4th ed. (New York: McGraw-Hill, 1985).
4. Shaw, *Group Dynamics*.
5. Dorwin Cartwright and Alvin Zander, eds., *Group Dynamics: Research and Theory*, 3rd ed. (New York: Harper & Row, 1968).
6. Shaw, *Group Dynamics*.
7. B. W. Tuckman, "Developmental Sequence in Small Groups," *Psychological Bulletin*, vol. 63, 1965, pp. 383–399. For a more recent treatment of group development stages, see Connie J. G. Gersick, "Marking Time: Predictable Transitions in Task

Groups," *Academy of Management Journal*, June 1989, pp. 274–309.

8. George Homans, *The Human Group* (New York: Harcourt, 1950).

9. David Katz and Robert L. Kahn, *The Social Psychology of Organizations*, 2nd ed. (New York: Wiley, 1978).

10. Katz and Kahn, *The Social Psychology of Organizations*.

11. Ibid.

12. Shaw, *Group Dynamics*.

13. Shaw, *Group Dynamics*. See also Monika Henderson and Michael Argyle, "The Informal Rules of Working Relationships," *Journal of Occupational Behavior*, vol. 7, 1986, pp. 259–275.

14. Daniel C. Feldman, "The Development and Enforcement of Group Norms," *Academy of Management Review*, January 1984, pp. 47–53.

15. James H. Davis, *Group Performance* (Reading, Mass.: Addison-Wesley, 1969).

16. Jay Galbraith, *Organization Design* (Reading, Mass.: Addison-Wesley, 1977).

17. Cyril O'Donnell, "Ground Rules for Using Committees," *Management Review*, October 1961, pp. 63–67.

18. "The Payoff from Teamwork," *Business Week*, July 10, 1989, pp. 56–62.

19. George Munchus, "Employer-Employee Based Quality Circles in Japan: Human Resource Implications for American Firms," *Academy of Management Review*, April 1983, pp. 255–261. See also Ricky W. Griffin, "Consequences of Quality Circles in an Industrial Setting: A Long-Term Field Experiment," *Academy of Management Journal*, June 1988, pp. 280–304.

20. Shaw, *Group Dynamics*.

21. Davis, *Group Performance*. See also John P. Wanous and Margaret A. Youtz, "Solution Diversity and the Quality of Group Decisions," *Academy of Management Journal*, March 1986, pp. 149–159.

22. Irving L. Janis, *Groupthink*, 2nd ed. (Boston: Houghton Mifflin, 1982).

23. Andre L. Delbecq, Andrew H. Van de Ven, and David H. Gustafson, *Group Techniques for Program Planning* (Glenview, Ill.: Scott, Foresman, 1975). See also David M. Schweiger, William Sandberg, and James W. Ragan, "Group Approaches for Improving Strategic Decision Making: A Comparative Analysis of Dialectical Inequity, Devil's Advocacy and Consensus," *Academy of Management Journal*, March 1986, pp. 51–71.

24. Stephen P. Robbins, *Managing Organizational Conflict* (Englewood Cliffs, N.J.: Prentice-Hall, 1974).

25. James Thompson, *Organizations in Action* (New York: McGraw-Hill, 1967).

CHAPTER OUTLINE

I. The Nature of Interpersonal Communication
   A. The Definition of Communication
   B. The Pervasiveness of Communication

II. The Communication Process
   A. The Communication Model
   B. Important Behavioral Processes

III. Forms of Interpersonal Communication
   A. Oral Communication
   B. Written Communication
   C. Nonverbal Communication

IV. The Formal Communication Network
   A. Vertical and Horizontal Communication
   B. Information Systems
   C. The Chief Information Officer

V. Managing Communication
   A. Barriers to Effective Communication
   B. Improving Communication Effectiveness

VI. The Grapevine
   A. The Nature of Grapevines
   B. Advantages and Disadvantages of Grapevines

CHAPTER

15

After studying this chapter you should be able to

1. Define interpersonal communication and discuss its importance and its pervasiveness.

2. Describe the communication process and relevant behavioral processes.

3. Discuss verbal (oral and written) and nonverbal communication.

4. Describe the formal communication network, including vertical and horizontal communication, information systems, and the chief information officer.

5. Discuss barriers to effective communication and how to improve communication effectiveness.

6. Describe the grapevine and discuss its nature, its advantages, and its disadvantages.

Interpersonal Communication

COMMUNICATION WORKS AT WAL-MART

Most people have heard of Wal-Mart, although a surprisingly large number of them have never shopped in a Wal-Mart store. All that will change soon, however. Wal-Mart is on a clear trajectory to become the largest retailer in the world by the mid-1990s. And by the time it gets there, it may also have stores in more than half of the United States!

Wal-Mart was founded by Sam Walton, now recognized as one of the greatest entrepreneurs in American history. After graduating from the University of Missouri, Walton opened a small Ben Franklin five and dime store in Arkansas. He soon became convinced, however, that discounting was the real future of retailing.

Walton's view of discounting defied the conventional wisdom. Most experts at the time believed that a discount operation could only succeed if it was located in an area of at least 50,000 people. Walton thought discounting would also succeed in much smaller markets. Unable to get a big retailer to back him, he bor-

rowed money and opened the first Wal-Mart store in 1962 in the tiny town of Rogers, Arkansas. Shortly thereafter he opened his second store in Harrison, Arkansas. And he hasn't looked back since.

The company has grown by over 30 percent a year for more than twenty years and now has over 1,400 Wal-Mart stores in a twenty-five-state region. It continues to open around 150 new stores every year and plans to be in all fifty states by the end of this decade. Wal-Mart has generated an average annual return to its stockholders of over 40 percent a year for the past ten years. Indeed, a $1,000 investment in Wal-Mart stock back in 1970 would be worth over half a million dollars today.

Although Sam himself is no longer actively involved in the day-to-day management of the company, the culture and spirit he bred into the organization are still a driving force behind the company's ongoing success. One of the richest men in America, Wal-

ton still drives a ten-year old pickup truck with dog cages in the back. He insists that everyone call him Sam and retains his original folksy charm and humor.

One factor that has no doubt contributed to Wal-Mart's success is the premium the company has always put on communication. Each of the company's thousands of employees, called associates, is encouraged to make suggestions, voice complaints, and do everything possible to get good ideas on the table. For example, one associate suggested that Wal-Mart hire retired persons to serve as greeters—standing inside the front door, welcoming shoppers, and offering them the newest advertising circular. The idea was taken to Sam, who thought it was outstanding. Today, every Wal-Mart has a greeter.

The company also allows every associate access to details about the company that most other firms keep restricted to top managers. Indeed, a myriad of figures related to costs and profits are published and circulated to all interested

Wal-Mart associates on a regular basis.

Wal-Mart also keeps in touch with all its stores and distribution centers through an elaborate system that would make the militaries of many countries envious. Every Saturday morning, the top one hundred or so of the company's managers meet at headquarters in Bentonville, Arkansas, to discuss merchandising. They pore over detailed inventory and sales figures to figure out what minute adjustments they need to make. For example, if they are selling children's pants for $3 and K-mart is promoting them at two pair for $5, the price at Wal-Mart is lowered immediately.

The company has its own six-channel satellite television system that enables company officials to broadcast messages live to every store whenever necessary. Sam often uses such opportunities to make his own personal pitch to his associates. He has the uncanny ability to make each member of his audience think he is speaking directly to him or her.

How far can Wal-Mart go? Most observers see no limits to the growth the company can achieve. After all, it's the third largest retailer in the world now and yet serves only one half of the U.S. market. And managers are committed to maintaining the same open culture and dialogue with their associates, no matter how large the company gets.

Communication is an important ingredient in Wal-Mart's success. After an hourly associate suggested the concept of the "people greeter," the idea was presented to Sam Walton, who liked it. Consequently, each Wal-Mart now has someone, such as the elderly gentleman shown here, who greets customers as they come into the store.

SOURCES: John Huey, "Wal-Mart—Will it Take Over the World?" *Fortune*, January 30, 1989, pp. 52–64; "Leaders of the Most Admired," *Fortune*, January 29, 1990, pp. 40–54; "Marketing with Emotion: Wal-Mart Shows the Way," *The Wall Street Journal*, November 13, 1989, p. B1; "Little Touches Spur Wal-Mart's Rapid Growth," *The Wall Street Journal*, September 22, 1989, p. B1.

B

y any measure you care to apply, Wal-Mart is an exemplary business. In its first year of eligibility, the company ranked ninth among over three hundred corporations vying for a spot on *Fortune*'s list of the most admired companies in America. The next year it jumped to the number five spot. As noted throughout the Prelude Case, one key to Wal-Mart's success has always been the open and candid communication that occurs among everyone in the company.

This chapter explores interpersonal communication in detail. First it looks at the importance of communication and investigates the communication process more fully. The chapter then discusses interpersonal communication and the formal communication network in organizations, as well as how communication can be more effectively managed. It concludes by considering the informal communication network in organizations, usually called the grapevine.

THE NATURE OF INTERPERSONAL COMMUNICATION

Let's first define communication and then look at its pervasiveness in managerial work.

The Definition of Communication

☐ *Communication* is the process of transmitting information; *interpersonal communication* occurs between one person and another. For it to be effective, the message received must be essentially the same as the message that was sent.

Communication is the process of transmitting information; if it occurs between people, it is **interpersonal communication.**[1] When two people are talking on the telephone, when a speaker is addressing a large group, and when someone is reading a letter, communication is taking place.

Of course, the message being received might be quite different from the one that was transmitted. A person might not understand what someone else is saying, static on the telephone might interrupt a conversation, and a letter can get lost in the mail. So it is useful to differentiate between simple communication and effective communication.

Simple communication is merely the transmission of information from one person to another. Effective communication, in contrast, occurs when the message that is received has essentially the same meaning as the message that was sent. Clearly, then, it is important for managers to pursue effective communication in the workplace.

The Pervasiveness of Communication

Communication is one of the major ingredients of the manager's job.[2] This is perhaps illustrated best by Table 15.1, which outlines a day in the life of a typical, if hypothetical, manager. Virtually all of the activities listed involve communication in one form or another. The manager writes something that others will read, reads what others have written, talks, and listens.

412

TABLE 15.1
The Pervasiveness of
Communication in the
Manager's Job

Time of Day	Activity
8:00–8:30	Read *The Wall Street Journal*
8:30–8:45	Receive telephone call from headquarters
8:45–9:30	Meet with executive committee
9:30–10:00	Read report from marketing vice president
10:00–11:00	Meet with labor committee
11:00–11:30	Review the day's mail
11:30–12:00	Meet with operations manager
12:00–1:00	Lunch with friends
1:00–2:00	Draft report for board of directors
2:00–2:30	Return three telephone calls
2:30–3:00	Interview prospective assistant
3:00–4:00	Meet with R&D task force
4:00–4:30	Dictate four letters
4:30–5:00	Read report from legal adviser

LEARNING CHECK

You should now be able to
define interpersonal communication and discuss its
importance and its
pervasiveness.

Indeed, research has clearly documented the pervasiveness of communication in management. In one study, for example, it was found that the average manager spends 59 percent of his or her time in scheduled meetings, 22 percent on desk work (such as writing and reading), 10 percent in unscheduled meetings, 6 percent on the telephone, and 3 percent walking around the company premises.[3] All of these activities involve communication.

PRELUDE CASE UPDATE

Although communication is important in any organization, it is especially critical in retailing for a company like Wal-Mart. Managers must communicate with salespersons, other managers, customers, and buyers. Advertising directors write ad copy and communicate with artists, copywriters, agency executives, and so forth. Associates themselves spend most of their time interacting with customers, each other, their supervisors, stockroom personnel, and so forth. Executives like Sam Walton also spend a great deal of their time interacting with others from both inside and outside the organization.

THE COMMUNICATION PROCESS

Now we can explore the communication process itself in more detail. First let's look at a complete model that explains all of the dynamics of communication. We can then note important behavioral processes that influence how communication occurs.

Photo courtesy of Schering-Plough Corporation

Communication is a very important part of effective management. The two managers shown here are from different functional departments of Schering-Plough Research. They meet regularly to discuss and coordinate the activities going on in their respective departments.

The Communication Model

□ The communication process involves a *sender* transmitting a message to a *receiver* through various channels. *Noise* is anything that disrupts the process.

As we have seen, communication involves at least two people. These are represented in Exhibit 15.1 as the **sender**—the person who transmits the message—and the **receiver**—the person who receives the message.

The starting point in the communication process is an idea. This idea may be a fact, an opinion, an observation, or anything else the sender feels a need to transmit. The idea is then translated into a message. This translation process means that the sender must choose the exact mix of words, phrases, and/or sentences that best reflect the content of his idea.

The message is then transmitted through one or more channels—a face-to-face meeting, a letter, a telephone call, a facial expression, or any combination of these. The message is received and retranslated back into an idea.

It is here that the difference between simple communication and effective communication manifests itself. If the idea formed by the receiver is similar to the one originally formulated by the sender, effective communication has occurred. On the other hand, if the ideas are different in one or more important ways, the communication was clearly not effective.

As shown in the exhibit, the process may continue under conditions of two-way communication. That is, the receiver may well respond to the original message with a message of her own. Thus the receiver becomes the sender, transmitting a new message to the original sender, who is now playing the role of the receiver.

The final part of the process is **noise**. Noise is anything that disrupts the communication process. It might be true noise, such as someone in another

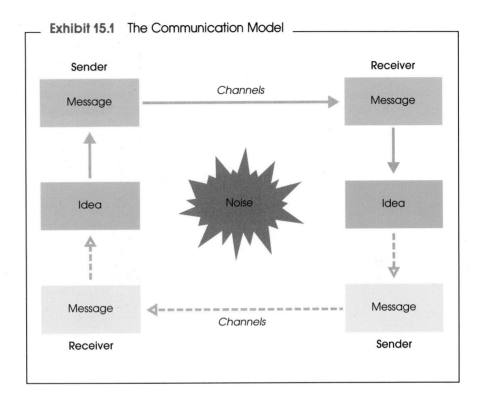

Exhibit 15.1   The Communication Model

room talking so loudly that two people cannot hear each other speak or a radio playing so loudly that the receiver can't hear the sender's voice over the telephone. It can also be other things, however; a letter getting lost in the mail, a telephone call being disconnected, or a typographical error in a report can all reduce communication effectiveness.

Important Behavioral Processes

□ *Attitudes* and *perception* are important behavioral processes that can affect the communication process.

The communication process can also be influenced by a number of important behavioral processes. Two of these, illustrated in Exhibit 15.2, are attitudes and perception.

ATTITUDES   **Attitudes** are our predispositions to respond favorably or unfavorably to something.[4] Each of us has attitudes toward school, jobs, other people, movies, politicians, sports teams, and almost everything else that might be a part of our lives.

Attitudes can affect how we communicate with others in a variety of ways. For example, suppose you have two subordinates. You like one subordinate a great deal and have a high regard for her capabilities and dedication to the organization. In short, you have a positive attitude toward her. You strongly dislike the other subordinate, however, and question his capabilities and dedication—a negative attitude. If the first subordinate asks for extra time off to

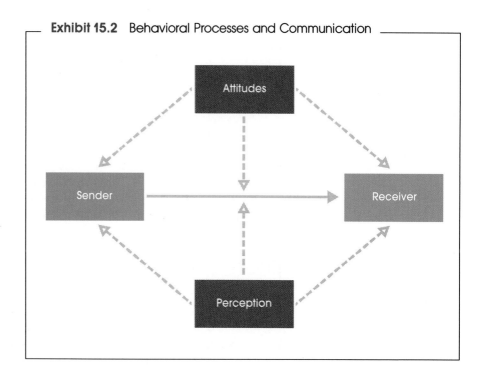

Exhibit 15.2 Behavioral Processes and Communication

visit a sick friend, you are likely to respond in a favorable way and to convey feelings of concern. But if the second subordinate asks for time off for the same reason, you are more apt to deny the request and may even question his truthfulness. Clearly, then, attitudes affect how we communicate with others.

PERCEPTION   The other behavioral process that strongly affects communication is **perception.**[5] Perception refers to the processes by which we receive and interpret information from our environment.

Most people are familiar with real incidents or stories in which two or more witnesses observe the same accident but report different events. Such differences are attributable to perception, which, in general, affects communication through familiarity. People tend to perceive things from a frame of reference with which they are comfortable. In one classic study, for instance, executives were asked to read a case about problems at a steel mill and then to describe the nature of those problems. Five out of six sales managers said the problems were related to sales, but four out of five production managers saw the problems as being related primarily to production.[6]

It follows that perception often affects communication, because if managers see things from a biased perspective, they will respond accordingly. A manager who sees a problem as falling into a certain area will communicate in a certain way with other managers in that area. If the manager perceives the problem in a different way, the communication will be different.[7]

LEARNING CHECK

You should now be able to describe the communication process and relevant behavioral processes.

FORMS OF INTERPERSONAL COMMUNICATION

☐ There are three basic forms of interpersonal communication—oral, written, and nonverbal.

There are three basic forms of interpersonal communication we will consider—oral, written, and nonverbal.

Oral Communication

Oral communication involves the spoken word. Hall conversations, formal meetings, telephone calls, and presentations are examples. The importance of oral communication is underscored by the work of Mintzberg, whose research found that managers often spend between 50 and 90 percent of their time talking to people.[8]

☐ *Oral communication* is easy and facilitates *feedback;* it may also be inaccurate and provides no record.

As noted in Table 15.2, there are advantages and disadvantages to oral communication. One major advantage is that it is relatively easy and comfortable—all a person has to do is open his mouth and let words come out. (Of course, many of us can recall times when we wished we hadn't opened our mouths, but that issue is addressed below. There are also some people who, out of shyness or other reasons, do have trouble with verbal communication.) Picking up the telephone or walking into a colleague's office to schedule a meeting are relatively simple operations, especially when compared to doing the same thing in writing. It has been suggested that more than half of all managers do not have confidence in their own ability to write, so they feel more comfortable with the spoken word. Accordingly, they use oral communication whenever they can.[9]

The second major advantage of oral communication is that it facilitates **feedback**. If the sender wants an answer to a question or a verification that the listener understands what she is saying, all she has to do is ask. Similarly, the listener can interrupt to respond to the message or to seek clarification. An astute speaker can even tell how well the message is being received by looking at the facial expression of the listener.

Of course, there are major disadvantages to oral communication as well. For one thing, it can be quite inaccurate. As we simply talk "off the top of our heads," we can confuse the facts, omit important points, distort things, and so

TABLE 15.2
Advantages and Disadvantages of Oral and Written Communication

Oral Communication		Written Communication	
Advantages	*Disadvantages*	*Advantages*	*Disadvantages*
1. Is easy to use	1. Causes inaccuracies	1. Is fairly accurate	1. Hinders feedback
2. Facilitates feedback	2. Provides no record	2. Provides a record	2. Is more time-consuming

forth. We might also say some things that shouldn't have been said or divulge information inappropriately. Similarly, the listener may not hear everything accurately, or he may misunderstand or forget important details.

Finally, oral communication provides no permanent record of what has been communicated. After a conversation has taken place, the parties may have to recall details of what they said. Since memory can be quite faulty, the lack of a permanent record of the conversation can cause major problems.

Written Communication

☐ *Written communication is accurate and provides a record, but it is slow and limits feedback.*

Written Communication includes memos, letters, reports, and notes. The advantages and disadvantages of this kind of communication are essentially the opposite of those of oral communication, as Table 15.2 points out.

One key advantage is improved accuracy. If a manager needs to write to someone, she can dictate the letter, proofread it, revise it, check the facts, and have the letter retyped before it is mailed.

Likewise, written communication provides a relatively permanent record of the communication. The sender and the receiver can talk about the details of their exchange over the phone several months later and still agree about the contents of the letter.

A major disadvantage of written communication is that it hinders feedback. After the manager decides to write a letter, several days can go by before it is

Written communication is an important part of many organizational activities. These managers are standing in front of an application proposal being sent to the FDA for a new drug SmithKline Beecham wants to develop and market. Such extensive written documentation is often necessary to convey the minute scientific details, prospects, and risks for complex products like drugs.

SmithKline Beecham

dictated, typed, mailed, delivered, and read. If timing is critical, major problems can result from such delays. Of course, overnight delivery services and facsimile machines have reduced this factor to a great extent. However, such methods are expensive for routine correspondence, and legal documents still require original signatures.

Written communication is also more time consuming than oral communication. It takes only a few seconds to pick up the phone and call someone, but it takes days or weeks to correspond. And most managers generally do not prefer to use written communication. We have already noted their lack of confidence in their writing skills; the same study found that most managers regard only about 13 percent of their mail as valuable to them, and they find almost 80 percent of it to be poorly done.[10]

Nonverbal Communication

☐ *Nonverbal communication involves settings, body language, and imagery.*

The last form of interpersonal communication for us to consider is **nonverbal communication**—communication that either does not use words or else uses words to convey more than their literal meaning.[11] Body movements, facial expressions, and gestures all convey meaning. In fact, it has been suggested that 55 percent of a message is transmitted through facial expression and body movement, and that another 38 percent is conveyed by inflection and tone.[12]

In general, people communicate nonverbally in three ways. First, they use the setting, which is where the communication takes place, and the nature of its surroundings. The manager who sits behind a huge desk in a big chair in front of a wall covered with awards, honors, and accolades is clearly in a position of power and authority, and this power and authority will usually influence the communication process. A visitor who sits in a small chair in front of the desk will be in a very different position in the communication process.

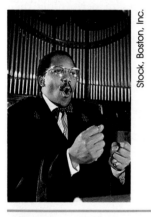

Stock, Boston, Inc.

Much of the content of communication activities is nonverbal. Reverend Charles Stith, of the Union United Methodist Church in Boston, uses gestures and facial expressions to underscore his message.

Second is body language. One element of body language is the distance we stand from someone when we are talking. Close contact can connote intimacy or hostility, and eye contact can convey positive or negative feelings. Body and arm movement, pauses in speech, and style of dress are also important parts of body language.

The third aspect of nonverbal communication is the imagery conjured up by language. A manager such as Sam Walton, who uses colorful language and catchy phrases, conveys a certain image and meaning when he talks. Such a person can transmit messages of confidence, boldness, or aggression or of foolhardiness and recklessness. More mundane, bland language conveys images of cautiousness and thoroughness or of timidity and indecisiveness.

LEARNING CHECK

You should now be able to discuss verbal (oral and written) and nonverbal communication.

Another aspect of nonverbal communication that has become increasingly important in recent years relates to the cultural differences between people of different nations. We have seen that distance between people affects communication. Appropriate distances vary among countries: the English and Germans stand farther apart than Americans do when talking, whereas the Japanese, Mexicans, and Arabs stand closer together.

THE FORMAL COMMUNICATION NETWORK

Managerial communication is a part of the formal organizational hierarchy: that is, it occurs between people in various positions. Three elements of managerial communication are vertical and horizontal communication, management information systems, and the position of chief information officer.

Vertical and Horizontal Communication

☐ Communication in the formal organizational structure may be *vertical* or *horizontal.*

Information flows both up and down and laterally through an organization. These patterns are illustrated in Exhibit 15.3, which uses the example of communication among a vice president and three division heads.

VERTICAL COMMUNICATION   **Vertical communication** takes place between bosses and their subordinates. It can flow both down and up the organization. Downward communication might include the assignment of new job responsibilities, information that will assist subordinates in performing their job duties, or simple information about the organization. Such communication helps subordinates know about aspects of the organization that affect them. Unfortunately, managers don't always do a good job of keeping their subordinates informed.

Upward communication is also a vital part of organizational functioning. Information from employees keeps top management in touch with day-to-day

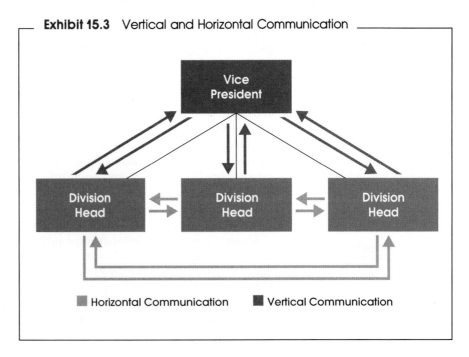

Exhibit 15.3   Vertical and Horizontal Communication

ETHICAL DILEMMAS OF MANAGEMENT

Reward: A Clear Conscience

One of the most troublesome decisions people sometimes have to make is what to do when they find that their employer is breaking the law. The safest course of action is to keep your mouth shut and do your job. Many people aren't able to do this, however, and feel compelled to follow their conscience.

For example, when Jerome LiCari discovered that his employer, Beech-Nut, was claiming its apple juice drink for babies was pure apple juice when in fact it was chemically modified, what was he to do? He went to his boss, who wouldn't listen. Then he went to the president and got the same response. He subsequently resigned and told his story to the media.

In a similar situation a few years ago, David Edwards, a manager at Citicorp, found that the banking giant was guilty of several foreign exchange violations aimed at reducing taxes. He went to his superiors and got no response. Finally, he went to the board of directors. For his troubles he was fired.

This practice, known as whistle-blowing, is becoming increasingly widespread today. Concerns about ethics and social responsibility have become more prominent and the areas in which violations can occur more widespread. But there is still no assurance that a person will get any rewards for such actions—except a clear conscience and a feeling of doing what's right.

SOURCES: Roy Rowan, "The Maverick Who Yelled Foul at Citibank," *Fortune*, January 10, 1983, pp. 46–56; Janet P. Near and Marcia P. Miceli, "Retaliation Against Whistle-Blowers: Predictors and Effects," *Journal of Applied Psychology*, February 1986, pp. 137–145; "What Led Beech-Nut down the Road to Disgrace," *Business Week*, February 22, 1988, pp. 124–128.

operations of the company, significant successes and failures, and potential difficulties. Upward communication is also often associated with the practice called whistle-blowing, as described in *Management Today: Ethical Dilemmas of Management*.

HORIZONTAL COMMUNICATION **Horizontal communication** takes place between two or more colleagues or peers at the same level in the organization. It is critical when there are high demands for coordination and integration. For instance, if the marketing manager is planning a new advertising campaign that will probably increase product demand by 10 percent, the manufacturing manager needs to be aware of this so that he can plan for additional production. Similarly, if a plant manager locates a new supplier who will deliver an important raw material more reliably and at a lower price than current suppliers, it is important for her to pass this information along to other plant managers in the company.

Information Systems

Another important aspect of managerial communication is the various kinds of information systems the organization creates to manage the official flow of information within the business. As you recall, these were covered extensively in Chapter 11. We need only remember that they are an important part of many organizational communications activities and should be as fully institutionalized as possible if they are to be effective.

The Chief Information Officer

☐ The *chief information officer (CIO)* is a new type of executive in charge of information systems within an organization.

A final element of managerial communication, also mentioned in Chapter 11, is the position of **chief information officer,** or **CIO.** Many people have never heard of the CIO because this is a very new executive position that is just being created in many organizations.[13] The CIO position is becoming important because top managers are increasingly recognizing the importance of information to the organization and of having a qualified individual responsible for managing it.

Many managers don't have the title but still fill the role of CIO; others, of course, actually are given the title. This new breed of manager oversees all aspects of information technology, such as computing, office systems, and telecommunications, and reports to the CEO or chairperson. He or she concentrates on long-term strategic issues and leaves the nuts-and-bolts part of the communication job to technicians.

Numerous companies have begun to use the CIO concept, including Firestone, American Airlines, Pillsbury, Aetna Life and Casualty, Northwestern National Life Insurance, and Wells Fargo.

LEARNING CHECK

You should now be able to describe the formal communication network, including vertical and horizontal communication, information systems, and the chief information officer.

MANAGING COMMUNICATION

In addition to using the more formal methods of organizational communication, managers can do several things to enhance communication processes in organizations. In general, these center around understanding the barriers to effective communication and knowing how to overcome those barriers.

Barriers to Effective Communication

☐ Barriers to effective communication are associated with the sender and/or the receiver.

Among the many different kinds of barriers to effective communication, as shown in Exhibit 15.4, some are associated with the sender, some with the receiver, and some with both.[14]

From the standpoint of the sender, problems can arise because of inconsistency, credibility, and reluctance. Inconsistency occurs when the person sends conflicting messages. Credibility problems occur when the individual is considered to be unreliable. When a public official makes statements that are later found to be untrue, he will encounter credibility problems. Finally, people are sometimes simply reluctant to communicate. This may be the case when the news is bad or unpleasant.

From the standpoint of the receiver, poor listening habits and attitudes can be barriers. Not concentrating, letting your attention wander, looking around

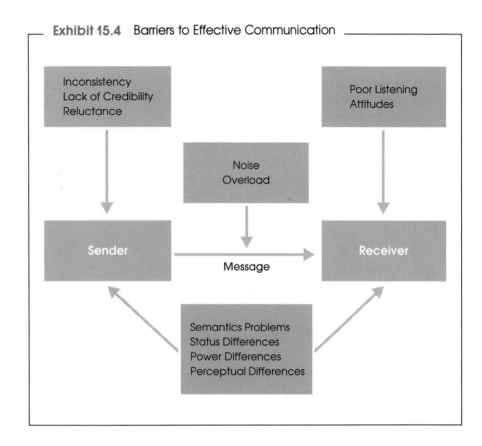

Exhibit 15.4 Barriers to Effective Communication

when someone is talking to you, and daydreaming can all impede effective listening. Sometimes, too, people have already made up their minds about what a speaker is saying, so their attitudes get in the way of listening to the points and arguments being made.

Noise, as we have seen, can also cause difficulties with effective communication. So can **overload,** which occurs when the sender is transmitting too much information for the receiver to process adequately.[15] When a lecturer talks too fast for students to take notes or when someone is trying to watch television while her roommate listens to the stereo, overload can occur.

Other barriers can be attributed to both the sender and the receiver. Semantics problems (problems with word meanings) involve both parties; when an instructor says his course is "challenging and rigorous," the student may hear this as "hard and picky." Status and power differences can also disrupt effective communication. For instance, a janitor may not be able to communicate effectively with a top manager, or a lower-level manager may have problems communicating with a higher-level manager in the same division. And perceptual differences, as described earlier in the chapter, can disrupt communication. If one manager perceives an employee's sloppy work habits as laziness and another manager thinks the same habits indicate creativity, the two managers could have a difficult time discussing the worker's performance.

Improving Communication Effectiveness

☐ Barriers to effective communication can be overcome by the sender, the receiver, or both.

Fortunately, there are things that managers can do to overcome some or all of these problems. As shown in Exhibit 15.5, these techniques can be used by the sender, the receiver, or both.[16]

The sender can be sensitive to the receiver's position. A manager who is telling an employee that her working hours are being reduced might expect the worker to be hostile temporarily; such sensitivity can keep the manager from getting upset if the subordinate says something in anger. The sender should also solicit feedback as a way to facilitate two-way communication. Asking the receiver if he understands, asking for opinions, and other such actions enhance communication effectiveness.

Managers should also be aware of language and meaning. Employees almost always get concerned when they hear about major changes. Hence, a manager should not talk about an impending change as being "big" or "major" if it is, in fact, relatively routine or minor, or if his or her employees will not be affected by it. The sender should also always attempt to maintain credibility. There is nothing wrong with admitting that you don't know something. Of course, it also helps to check facts and stay as up to date as possible.

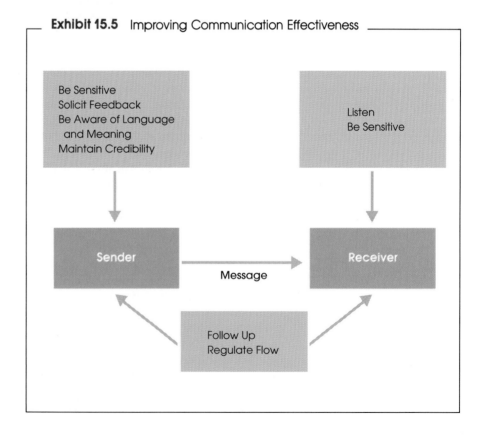

Exhibit 15.5   Improving Communication Effectiveness

Be Sensitive
Solicit Feedback
Be Aware of Language and Meaning
Maintain Credibility

Listen
Be Sensitive

Sender → Message → Receiver

Follow Up
Regulate Flow

Preventing overload is one effective way to manage communication. Managers at Gordon Food Service use voice mail to aid in this approach. People can call them and leave messages electronically, freeing up time for both managers and secretaries.

There are also two things the receiver can do. First, she can work on being a good listener—on concentrating on what is being said, looking at the speaker, being patient, and paying attention to what it all means. Likewise, the receiver should attempt to be sensitive to the sender's perspective. For example, few people enjoy giving bad news, so subordinates who are receiving notice of company layoffs should realize that the manager who is telling them probably is also upset.

Both the sender and the receiver can promote communication effectiveness by following up the communication and by regulating the flow of information. The sender can solicit questions and the receiver can demonstrate understanding. Suppose, for instance, that a sales executive calls a finance executive to schedule a meeting. The finance manager can send a note back to the sales executive confirming the meeting time and location. Both parties can also regulate information flows by working to prevent overload, the sender by making sure that she is not going too fast and the receiver by interrupting and asking the sender to slow down when necessary.

LEARNING CHECK

You should now be able to discuss barriers to effective communication and how to improve communication effectiveness.

PRELUDE CASE UPDATE

Sam Walton was faced with a critical moment in the early days of Wal-Mart that went a long way in determining how he and his employees would communicate in the future. In the early 1960s, a union tried to organize the twenty Wal-Mart stores that had been opened at that time. At the time, his employees were feeling unhappy about their wages and about how Walton was treating them. His lawyer advised him that he could take an adversarial position and probably have labor problems as long as his stores were in operation. Alternatively, he said, Walton could take a collaborative approach and communicate openly and honestly with everyone. He was also advised to be sensitive to their position and to listen to their complaints and suggestions. Walton took the latter option and his employees have generally disdained unions ever since.

THE GRAPEVINE

◻ The *grapevine* is the informal communication network within an organization.

The final element of organizational communication to be addressed in this chapter is the informal communication network that exists in all organizations—the **grapevine**.[17]

The Nature of Grapevines

The nature of organizational grapevines is illustrated in Exhibit 15.6, which shows a hypothetical organization chart and three messages that have wound themselves through the organization. These paths reveal several interesting aspects of the grapevine. First, the grapevine can start anywhere; that is, any individual can start the process simply by telling someone something. Second, some people are included in virtually all of the messages. These people serve as focal points along the grapevine, receiving most messages and passing most of them on to others. Third, the grapevine flows in all directions, messages can go up, down, or laterally in the organization. Finally, not everyone is included; some people neither receive nor pass on informal news.

Why does the grapevine exist? For one thing, being social is human nature. People like to interact with others. Since much of this interaction involves talking, information will naturally be passed among many different people. For another, the grapevine is often used as a way to get power. Controlling information, regardless of its source, makes anyone a more powerful person. And grapevines emerge in response to deficiencies in the formal communication network in the organization. If people are curious about something and don't hear about it officially, they are likely to solicit the information from others.

Advantages and Disadvantages of Grapevines

The grapevine has many attributes, some of them good and some bad. On the plus side, the grapevine can be used to transmit information quickly, it builds

Exhibit 15.6   The Grapevine

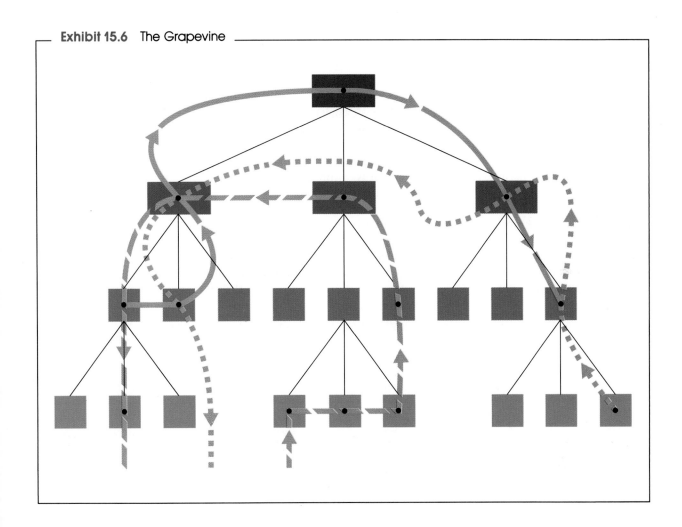

a sense of togetherness and a feeling of being a part of the same team, and managers can use it to try out ideas or get informal reactions to potential decisions.

On the other hand, the grapevine can also be detrimental to the organization. The information carried along the grapevine can be very inaccurate, or it might be information that the manager would prefer to keep confidential. *Management Today: Management in Practice* describes Apple's problems with its grapevine. Employees might distort or otherwise manipulate the grapevine for their own gain.

In sum, managers should be fully aware of the potential benefits and pitfalls of the grapevine. Perhaps the best advice is to maintain open communication with employees at all levels and to respond quickly to inaccurate information. If people can come to their boss and get straight answers, they are less likely to pay attention to gossip and rumors.

LEARNING CHECK

You should now be able to describe the grapevine and discuss its nature, its advantages and its disadvantages.

MANAGEMENT IN PRACTICE

Grapevine Troubles at Apple

Gossip and hall talk are a fact of life in modern corporations. In many cases, the information passed along the grapevine is harmless, and occasionally it is even beneficial to the organization. In other circumstances, however, it can be disastrous. This is especially true in an industry where technology is critical and when the information being passed around involves sensitive secrets about that technology. Information can fall into the wrong hands and end up getting circulated outside the firm.

Apple Computer has recently had to take extreme steps to combat this ever-growing problem. In Silicon Valley, knowing "secrets" is a real status symbol. The company has been plagued by trade secrets leaking to the media and/or to competitors. People carelessly pass information to others, who then tell friends at other companies or interested reporters.

One action taken by Apple was to hire a manager of information security. He has passed out buttons proclaiming "I know a lot but I can keep a secret." Posters with similar messages also festoon the entire building.

Has it worked? Some insiders think it's only made matters worse. They suggest that people who weren't talking before now resent the fact that they apparently aren't trusted and so are even more prone to talk to others than they were before. In one recent very serious breach, an anonymous group of employees mailed a disk containing secret Macintosh software codes to dozens of people working for competing firms.

Apple has scaled back its propaganda campaign about information leaks, but it is still concerned. Managers don't really know where else to turn.

SOURCES: "At Apple Computer Proper Office Attire Includes a Muzzle," *The Wall Street Journal*, October 6, 1989, pp. A1, A5; Brian Dumaine, "Corporate Spies Snoop to Conquer," *Fortune*, November 7, 1988, pp. 68–76; "Mind What You Say; They're Listening," *The Wall Street Journal*, October 25, 1989, p. B1.

Chapter Summary

Interpersonal communication is the process of transmitting information from one person to another. Simple communication is the mere transmission of information; effective communication occurs when the transmission is accurate. Communication is one of the major ingredients of the manager's job.

The communication process involves translating an idea into a message, sending the message in some way, receiving the message, and retranslating it into an idea. Two-way communication occurs when feedback, or repeating the process in reverse, is involved. Noise is anything that disrupts the communication process. The process can also be influenced by a number of important behavioral processes, most notably attitudes and perception.

Interpersonal communication can be verbal—oral, written, or both—or nonverbal, involving the setting, body language, and the like. Effective communication generally involves both forms. Nonverbal communication is also very powerful.

Managerial communication is communication that occurs as a part of the formal organizational hierarchy. Vertical communication occurs between bosses and subordinates and can flow downward or upward. Horizontal communication takes place between two or more colleagues or peers at the same level in the organization. The person who is in charge of information technology in major organizations is the chief information officer, or CIO.

Managing communication involves understanding the numerous barriers to communication and knowing how to overcome them. Overcoming barriers involves recognizing that they exist and being sensitive to the other person in the process.

The grapevine is the informal communication network that exists in all organizations. Managers sometimes use the grapevine to try out new ideas or to get informal reactions to potential decisions. However, the grapevine has disadvantages too.

The Manager's Vocabulary

communication	written communication
interpersonal	nonverbal
communication	communication
sender	vertical communication
receiver	horizontal
noise	communication
attitudes	chief information officer
perception	(CIO)
oral communication	overload
feedback	grapevine

Prelude Case Wrap-Up

This chapter's Prelude Case describes the origins and incredible growth of Wal-Mart, the fastest growing major retailer in the United States. Founded by Sam Walton three decades ago, the discounting giant found early success by establishing itself in the small towns of America's heartland. Today the company has sprawled throughout the Midwest and seems poised to become the world's largest retailer within the next few years.

A real key to the firm's success has been its open and candid approach to communication. Managers recognize that operating employees are the best source of new ideas and opportunities. Thus, they go out of their way to stay in active contact with people throughout the organization.

Consider, for example, David Glass. Glass has worked at Wal-Mart for years and was named CEO in 1988. It was he who pushed Walton to install computers in every store several years ago. In addition to the television system noted in the Prelude Case, Glass also had the company buy a fleet of eleven airplanes. The corporate managers spend much of their time in these planes flying around the country visiting Wal-Mart stores.

He also expects each department manager within a given store to operate that department as though it were his or her own private business. Therefore, he provides each manager with up-to-the-minute information on sales, profit margins, competitive price data, and so forth.

Does Wal-Mart have any weaknesses? A few, perhaps. But if the company doesn't continue its march toward greatness, it won't be because its managers lost touch with their employees.

Prelude Case Questions

1. Identify several examples of interpersonal communication that occur regularly in typical Wal-Mart store.
2. How do attitudes and perception influence communication at a company like Wal-Mart?
3. What barriers to effective communication might exist at Wal-Mart? How could they be overcome?
4. How does nonverbal communication influence the fortunes of a retailer?

Discussion Questions

Review Questions

1. What is the difference between simple communication and effective communication?
2. Summarize the communication model. How do attitudes and perception affect communication?
3. What are the relative advantages and disadvantages of both oral and written communication?
4. What is a CIO? Why is it important?
5. Note four major barriers to effective communication and four important ways to overcome those barriers.

Analysis Questions

1. Which communication form (oral or written) do you prefer? Why?
2. Describe where you have used or observed nonverbal communication taking place.
3. If nonverbal messages contradict verbal statements, which do you believe? Why?
4. Think of the last "message" you picked up from the grapevine. As far as you know, was it accurate or inaccurate?

5. Relate an incident in which your attitude affected communication.

Application Questions and Exercises

1. Identify which arrows on the communication model are most likely to be affected by each of the major barriers to effective communication.
2. Think of a simple message you might need to communicate with a classmate. Time how long it takes for you to write the message, pass it to him or her, and receive a written response. Now think of another message of about the same length. Speak directly to the person and get a response.

How long did this take? Describe any errors that crept into the exchange.
3. Interview a local manager to find out how much of his or her time each day is spent communicating.
4. Designate one person in the class to think of a fairly complicated message. It should involve names, dates, and numbers. In low voices, pass the message from one person to another around the room. When the last person receives it, compare it with the original message.
5. Identify barriers to effective communication that might exist in the classroom. How might an instructor and her or his class overcome them?

ENHANCEMENT CASE

OPEN COMMUNICATION AT HERMAN MILLER, INC.

Who is Herman Miller and what does he do? In perhaps one of the strangest stories in the annals of American business, Herman Miller never worked a day for the company that bears his name. All he did was to loan his son-in-law, D. J. DePree, start-up funds to open a furniture manufacturing business in 1923.

DePree was so grateful he named the business after Miller. And today, Herman Miller, Inc. is a very profitable firm occupying the number two position in the office furniture industry. How it got there, however, is a story in and of itself.

One day in the 1930s, an employee died while working. Because the man had died on the job, DePree felt an obligation to visit the widow and pay his respects. During the visit, she insisted on reading him some poems—poems, it turned out, that had been written by her deceased husband. DePree was moved by the fact that a man whom he had always considered a nameless and faceless cog in the Herman Miller machine had actually had the soul of a poet. In fact, he was so moved that he dedicated himself from that point on to creating a humanistic and open organizational work environment. He vowed that he would treat all his employees with dignity and respect and would give anyone who was interested a real opportunity to contribute and make a difference.

First the elder DePree and now his sons have carried on this unique tradition. The DePrees have always objected to the distinction between managers and nonmanagers. Instead, they argue that management is a function in which everyone at the company needs to participate. Therefore, they stress the need to communicate. When they hire people, they don't look at things like school grades or previous jobs. Instead, they focus on an individual's interest and motivation to contribute and that person's ability to work well with others.

Since 1950, Herman Miller has used the Scanlon method for rewarding its employees. Under this arrangement, employees receive a bonus every quarter based on productivity, cost savings, and other factors. Workers are also organized into work teams. Indeed, Miller was one of the first corporations in America to adopt the team concept.

Every six months, team leaders evaluate their workers. Then the workers evaluate the team leaders. Team representatives regularly meet with higher-level managers to discuss anything from grievances to sales projections. If people are unhappy with what's going on or what they are hearing, they know they can go to increasingly higher levels in the organization for a hearing.

For example, two production managers were recently fired by a vice president. A young assembly-line worker thought an injustice had been committed and took the case to the CEO, Max DePree. DePree heard her out, investigated, and agreed with her. He subsequently rehired the two managers and fired the vice president who had started the whole thing.

Business took a downturn at Herman Miller in the mid-1980s. Downsizing of corporations hurt sales of all office furniture in general, and since Miller is a dominant seller of computer-related furniture, the computer slump of the mid-1980s also hurt. To top it all off, a new line of furniture Miller was pushing ran into production delays and cost overruns.

Unlike many other companies, however, managers at Herman Miller did not panic. They instituted some cost controls and tightened their belts a bit, but they devoted most of their energies to getting out of the hole in which they had fallen. During the worst of it all, they even gave out "silver parachutes"—protection for workers in the event of a takeover.

Miller has indeed turned itself around again. Profits are on the upswing, and sales are increasing nicely. And even though for the first time in history a non-DePree is CEO, his door is still open for anyone who needs to talk.

SOURCES: Kenneth Labich, "Hot Company, Warm Culture," *Fortune*, February 27, 1989, pp. 74–78; "A Comeback in Cubicles," *Forbes*, March 21, 1988, pp. 55–56; Beverly Geber, "Herman Miller—Where Profits and Participation Meet," *Training*, November 1987, pp. 62–66.

Enhancement Case Questions

1. Why do you think more companies don't practice the same kind of open communication as Herman Miller?
2. How do you think attitudes and perception affect communication at Herman Miller?
3. What do you think happened to communication during the downturn at Herman Miller?
4. Speculate on how the grapevine works at Herman Miller.

Chapter Notes

1. Norman B. Sighand and Arthur H. Bell, *Communication for Management and Business* (Glenview, Ill.: Scott, Foresman, 1986).
2. Henry Mintzberg, *The Nature of Managerial Work* (New York: Harper & Row, 1973).
3. Henry Mintzberg, "The Manager's Job: Folklore and Fact," *Harvard Business Review*, July-August 1975, pp. 49–61.
4. Martin Fishbein and I. Ajzen, *Belief, Attitude, and Behavior: An Introduction to Theory and Research* (Reading, Mass.: Addison-Wesley, 1975).
5. E. E. Jones and R. E. Nisbett, *The Actor and the Observer: Divergent Perceptions of the Causes of Behavior* (Morristown, N.J.: General Learning Press, 1971).
6. D. C. Dearborn and H. A. Simon, "Selective Perception: A Note on the Departmental Identification of Executives," *Sociometry*, vol. 21, 1985, p. 143.
7. See James P. Walsh, "Selectivity and Selective Perception: An Investigation of Managers' Belief Structures and Information Processing," *Academy of Management Journal*, December 1988, pp. 873–896, for a recent study of these issues.
8. Mintzberg, *The Nature of Managerial Work.*
9. Walter Kiechel III, "The Big Presentation," *Fortune*, July 26, 1982, pp. 98–100. See also Michael T. Motley, "Taking the Terror out of Talk," *Psychology Today*, January 1988, pp. 46–49.
10. Kiechel, "The Big Presentation."
11. Michael B. McCaskey, "The Hidden Messages Managers Send," *Harvard Business Review*, November-December 1979, pp. 135–148.
12. Ibid.
13. "Management's Newest Star," *Business Week*, October 13, 1986, pp. 160–172.
14. Jerry Wofford, Edwin Gerloff, and Robert Cummins, *Organizational Communication* (New York: McGraw-Hill, 1977).
15. "Information Overload Is Here," *USA Today*, February 20, 1989, pp. 1B–2B.
16. Wofford, Gerloff, and Cummins, *Organizational Communication.*
17. Keith Davis, "Management Communication and the Grapevine," *Harvard Business Review*, September-October 1953, pp. 43–49.

THE ENTREPRENEURIAL SPIRIT

This section of the text has introduced you to the third critical managerial function, leading. First it discussed the leadership process itself, and then it described how and why employees are motivated to perform. The next chapter discussed important interpersonal processes that occur in organizations, and the final chapter analyzed interpersonal communication.

Each of these elements is also important to both small and entrepreneurial businesses. For example, in a small business, the owner, manager, and leader are all likely to be the same individual. Therefore, this person will have direct and personal contact with virtually everyone who works in the organization. In addition, he will probably have more different kinds of power than his counterpart in a larger business. Since this person has so many hats to wear, it is important that he always recognizes that his behavior may have an especially powerful impact on those who work in the business.

In a rapidly growing, entrepreneurial firm, the leadership dynamics are even more complex. For most such firms, there comes a time when the owner-manager-leader has to change her approach to leading. In the early days of a business like Apple or Tandem Computers, the leader knows everyone and can lead with a direct and personal style. As the business grows, though, it will become necessary to create new layers in the organization and pass some of the leadership mantle to others. Managers who fail to recognize this transition may forestall growth and drive away employees seeking opportunities for advancement.

Motivation also plays a big role in both small and entrepreneurial firms. People who aspire to go into business for themselves need to understand their own motives. In general, such people usually have a high need for achievement and can often live without a lot of security. In addition, they want to be independent and responsible for their own destiny and are anxious to make their mark in the world. Nor are they afraid to take risks.

Entrepreneurs who pursue rapid growth also tend to have strong needs for esteem and recognition. At the same time, however, even though they may not like it, they can usually tolerate failure. And many entrepreneurs pursue growth and success as a means to achieve self-actualization.

But owners of small businesses and entrepreneurial firms also need to understand how their employees are motivated. Although many of the same motivational processes that were discussed in Chapter 13 apply to these organizations, there are also a few unique differences.

For one thing, employees of smaller firms must usually be able to handle less job security than their counterparts in larger businesses. Although there are no guarantees and although larger businesses occasionally have to cut back and lay people off, working for IBM or General Motors is still more secure than working for a new and struggling software firm or retail outlet. Thus, managers should do everything they can to assure job continuity, keep their ears to the ground for unfounded rumors about layoffs, and focus on satisfying other needs.

Owners of smaller and/or growing enterprises may also find it necessary to adopt new and innovative reward systems. For example, a new software firm in Texas could not afford to pay the same high salaries that larger firms were paying, but the owner wanted to attract the best people. Therefore, she decided to make up for below-market salaries by giving each employee who remained with her firm for one year a share of the business ownership.

Interpersonal processes, especially group dynamics, must also be understood by the small-business owner-manager-leader and the manager in an entrepreneurial firm. Group cohesiveness and norms are particularly important. For example, consider the case of a group of employees who have worked for a growing business since its formation. They are likely to have developed a strong set of norms and to be relatively cohesive. As the firm grows, however, they may be threatened by a loss of power and may need to adopt new norms. Many such groups are likely to resist efforts to change and may respond with hostility or other negative reactions.

Conflict may also be encountered in special situations. For example, partnerships occasionally dissolve because of conflict among the partners. Thus, all managers in small businesses and entrepreneurial firms need to be especially aware of the potential for conflict and must be prepared to deal with it.

Finally, communication is also important for the small businessperson and entrepreneur. In some ways, communication is easier in these types of orga-

nizations; in other ways, it is more difficult. It may be easier in small firms because people interact more often and are more comfortable with one another. On the other hand, the owner-manager-leader may be either too busy or too threatened to openly share all the information subordinates need to adequately perform their jobs. And grapevines may be especially potent in these kinds of organizations. For example, as noted earlier, rapidly growing businesses tend to encounter unusual levels of environmental complexity. These conditions may increase the activity of informal communication networks throughout the organization as people turn to the grapevine for faster communication than is available through more formal channels.

SOURCES: "Starting from Scratch After a Messy Split with Partners," *The Wall Street Journal*, January 12, 1990, p. B2; "Pursuing a Dream," *The Wall Street Journal*, February 24, 1989, p. B38; Murray B. Low and Ian C. MacMillan, "Entrepreneurship: Past Research and Future Challenges," *Journal of Management*, June 1988, pp. 139–159; Stanley Cromie, "Motivations of Aspiring Male and Female Entrepreneurs," *Journal of Occupational Behaviour*, vol. 8, 1987, pp. 251–261.

FIVE

Controlling

Back in Chapter 1 we saw that controlling was the fourth important managerial function. In the first of the four chapters devoted to this important aspect of the management process, we learn about the nature of organizational control and identify several approaches to it. The chapter also describes the actual steps in establishing a control system, explains how to use control more effectively, and discusses who is responsible for control. Chapter 17 then describes a number of specific control techniques, and Chapter 18 focuses on production and operations control. Chapter 19 concludes by focusing on the important issues of productivity and quality.

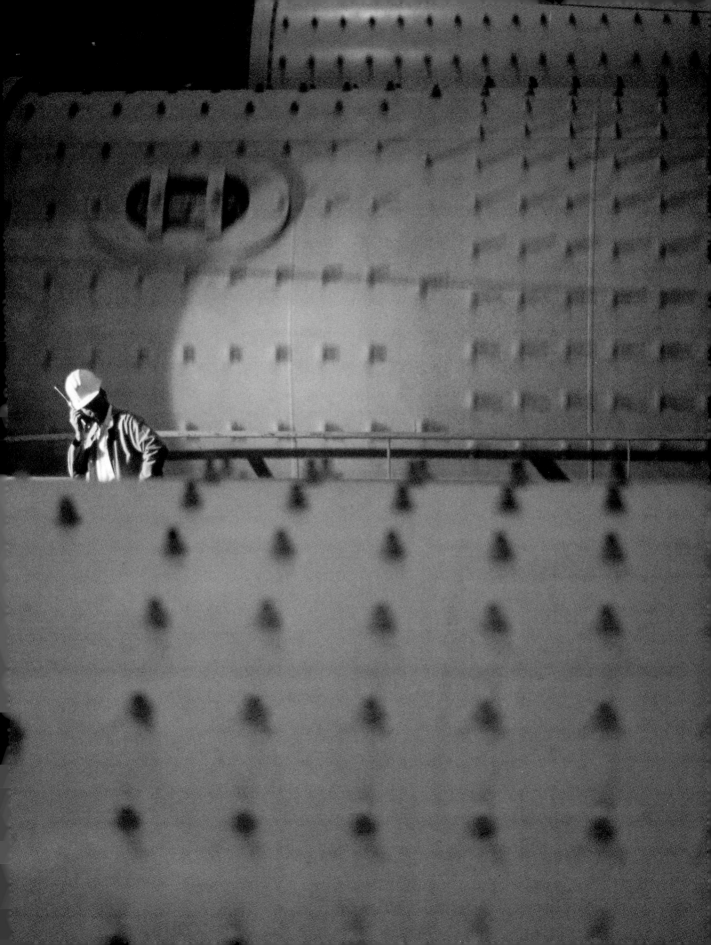

CHAPTER OUTLINE

I. The Nature of Control
A. Reasons for Control
B. Areas of Control
C. The Planning-Control Link

II. Approaches to Control
A. Steering Control
B. Concurrent Control
C. Postaction Control
D. Multiple Controls

III. Establishing a Control System
A. Setting Standards
B. Assessing Performance
C. Comparing Performance with Standards
D. Evaluating and Adjusting

IV. Effective Control
A. Integration
B. Objectivity
C. Accuracy
D. Timeliness
E. Flexibility

V. Managing Control
A. Understanding Resistance to Control
B. Overcoming Resistance to Control

VI. Responsibility for Control
A. Line Managers
B. The Controller

CHAPTER

16

After studying this chapter you should be able to

1. Describe the nature of control and why it is necessary, as well as some areas of control and the planning-control link.

2. Identify and discuss various approaches to control, such as steering, concurrent, postaction, and multiple controls.

3. Identify and discuss the steps in establishing a control system.

4. Describe the characteristics of effective control.

5. Discuss reasons for resistance to control and how to overcome this resistance.

6. Describe the responsibility for control that lies with line managers and the controller.

Organizational Control

REEBOK'S OFF AND RUNNING

The small British firm of Reebok (named after a speedy African antelope) was founded in 1895. Reebok specialized in making top-quality running shoes; the 1924 British Olympic team depicted in the film *Chariots of Fire* used Reeboks. In 1979, Paul B. Fireman was trying to expand his family's Massachusetts hunting and fishing business. He saw a pair of Reebok shoes at a sporting goods trade fair in Chicago and obtained the license to sell them in North America. Racing shoes, however, proved a very small market, and Fireman's American Reebok unit struggled.

In 1982, Fireman's partner, Jim Barclay, proposed an aerobics shoe to appeal to women. A year later, when they started a marketing strategy of having aerobics instructors wear the shoe, sales began to grow rapidly. The American Reebok expanded its lines well beyond those of its British parent, and, as people began to use different shoes for different activities, sales grew even more. The impact of the American unit on that growth was made abundantly clear in 1985, when the American unit bought the British firm. In 1986 Reebok be-

gan to buy other firms—Avia (basketball shoes), Rockport (walking shoes), John A. Frye (boots), and Ellesse (women's sportswear). The firm's annual growth rate from 1983 through 1987 was 155 percent, and although it has slowed a bit, it hasn't stopped.

Reebok's success has been huge. By late 1988 it had nearly half of the market in tennis and basketball shoes and was a strong contender in virtually every product line it carried. The main exception was an attempted invasion into the sportswear market. Reebok failed to monitor the quality of the products being furnished by suppliers and ended up with inferior goods. That effort could have hurt the company badly if poor distribution systems had not prevented most of the merchandise from reaching the market.

In an effort to see that this sort of thing did not recur, Reebok made some changes. It created five separate divisions, each focusing on a different product line. C. Joseph LaBonte, a venture capitalist, was also brought in to instill experienced, professional management into the company, and LaBonte quickly brought in others from outside the shoe in-

dustry to assist him. The company had grown so fast that too many decisions were being made by inexperienced personnel. There was little guidance from the upper levels of management to assist the inexperienced managers. The new structure and executives were to provide the infrastructure that would enable Reebok to continue growing in a more manageable way.

LaBonte quickly cut the size of the apparel group and instituted a series of controls over quality and distribution. He added levels of management to the overall company to control its operations. The result was a highly regimented organization that instilled management discipline into the ranks of a much-needed organizational structure. Finally, cost-cutting programs were instituted to make the products more price competitive.

However, certain limitations to the changes quickly became apparent. Customers and dealers alike began to complain that Reebok was no longer responsive to their needs. Foot Locker, a division of F. W. Woolworth that accounted for about 20 percent of Reebok's sales, found that it could no longer air its views to Reebok's

One way Reebok stays on top is by developing hot new products on a regular basis. For example, The Pump is bringing new revenues into the firm at a record pace.

top management. In 1988 the director of buying for Foot Locker told Reebok that customers would not pay high prices for plain white shoes, but Reebok went that route anyway, and the sales of those shoes were disappointingly low. It was clear that Reebok had gained control over internal production and distribution but had lost control over its marketing knowledge and sensitivity.

Early in 1989, LaBonte resigned and Fireman again took charge.

Fireman sought to retain control over operations while at the same time fostering the entrepreneurial spirit that had inspired the company during its early years. This strategy spirit manifested itself quickly in a rash of new products. In 1989 Reebok introduced its first high-tech shoe using what it called an "energy-return system." That product sold very well. Reebok also introduced a new line of shoes manufactured from Hexalite, which had originally been

developed for the aerospace industry. A new basketball shoe, The Pump, began to sell well, too. The Pump features an ankle collar that the user inflates with an air pump for additional support. These new products and a massive advertising campaign helped Reebok regain some of its lost enthusiasm. Rockport's walking shoe sales increased dramatically during 1989, as did sales of Avia's running shoes. Both became strong contributors to corporate profits.

Nevertheless, going into 1990, Reebok still needed to expand and improve its control processes. It lost its first-place ranking to Nike, which specializes in high-performance shoes, and L. A. Gear eroded Reebok's market share with fashion-conscious women. Fireman's strategy for regaining Reebok's number one position is to continue to introduce new products while also controlling costs, quality, and distribution.

SOURCES: "Paul Fireman Pulls On His Old Running Shoes," *Business Week*, November 6, 1989, p. 46; John Sedgwick, "Treading on Air," *Business Month*, January 1, 1989, pp. 29–34; "Global Distribution: How Reebok Stays One Step Ahead," *Traffic Management*, September 1, 1989, pp. 44–47; Stuart Gannes, "America's Fastest-Growing Companies," *Fortune*, May 23, 1988, pp. 28–40.

THE NATURE OF CONTROL

Controlling is the process of monitoring and adjusting organizational activities toward goal attainment.[1] Why is control necessary? Exactly what is being controlled? How does control relate to other managerial functions? Each of these questions is answered in the following chapter.

□ *Controlling* is the process of monitoring and adjusting organizational activities toward goals.

ontrol was defined in Chapter 1 in terms of monitoring and adjusting organizations so that they can accomplish their goals. In the Prelude Case to this chapter, we see how the lack of monitoring almost led to serious problems at Reebok. But overmonitoring and the use of rules and regulations also caused Reebok problems. Clearly, both too much and too little control can be dangerous to your organization's health.

Reasons for Control

American Greetings instituted financial controls because it had years and years of ups and downs while its major competitor, Hallmark, was almost always profitable.[2] Intel noted that it was spending too much on employee salaries and decided to reduce its work force by 7,600 employees. Ford cut its production costs so that it could make cars more cheaply than General Motors. Weyerhaeuser overhauled its entire management system in order to reduce administrative costs.[3] Each of these examples reflects a company's response to a need for greater control. American Greetings responded to financial fluctuations; Intel responded to increased competition from Japanese manufacturers; Ford saw a need to cut costs in order to remain competitive; and Weyerhaeuser had to confront rising costs and declining profits.

In general, there are three basic reasons for control. One is the environment. We have seen several times how contemporary environments change rapidly and how organizations need to respond to these changes. Intel, for example, was forced to respond because the Japanese were continually increasing the quality of their products while reducing their prices. Control is one of the primary channels for recognizing the need for such responses.

□ The environment, organizational complexity, and compounding—the tendency of small errors to grow—are the chief reasons for control.

A second reason for control is organizational complexity. Contemporary organizations are so complicated that a single manager cannot hope to grasp all of their inner workings, so control can help the manager monitor internal operations. For instance, a properly designed control system can provide data on raw materials inventory, work-in-process inventory, and finished goods inventory. Without such a system, the manager can never get a true fix on what the company's inventory actually is. For example, Emery Air Freight tried to bring in its acquisition of Purolator Courier Corporation without changing its controls, and the new organizational complexity almost destroyed the firm.[4]

A final reason for control is the concept of compounding, which suggests that a small error that is not detected early can become a bigger error. A spaceship en route to Jupiter that is only a little off course at launch time, for example, will miss the planet by millions of miles if the error is not identified and corrected. Similarly, a small deviation in costs in a manufacturing plant can grow significantly if uncorrected. Control can help the manager detect and correct small problems before they grow into bigger ones.

Areas of Control

There are four basic areas of control in most organizations, as shown in Exhibit 16.1: financial resources, physical resources, human resources, and information resources. As the exhibit also shows, financial resources are usually at the center of the controlling process.

Physical resources control includes such areas as inventory control (having neither too much nor too little inventory), quality control (ensuring that products are being made to appropriate quality standards), and equipment control (having the proper equipment to do the job). Quality control is particularly important, as can be seen in *Management Today: The World Of Management*. For that reason, most of Chapter 19 addresses that topic more fully. Human resource control includes such activities as employee selection and placement (hiring the right kinds of employees and assigning them to appropriate jobs within the organization), training (upgrading employee skills), performance appraisal (assessing employee performance), and compensation (paying neither too much nor too little). Information resource control involves making sure that various forecasts and projections are prepared accurately and on a timely basis, that managers have access to the information they need to make decisions effectively, and that the proper image of the organization is projected to the environment.

Finally, as already noted, financial resource control is all-important. First, financial resources themselves must be controlled. For instance, the organiza-

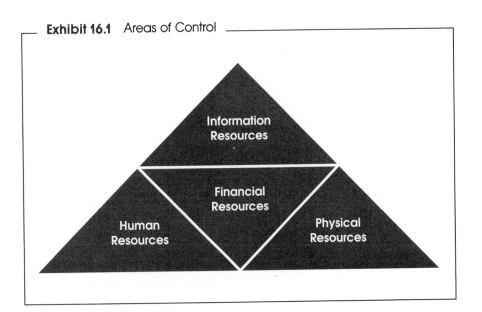

Exhibit 16.1   Areas of Control

THE WORLD OF MANAGEMENT

What Quality Really Means

Small manufacturers in the United States are learning about quality control from the Japanese. Consider the case of Metalloy, a forty-three-year-old family-owned Hudson, Michigan, metal-casting company. It was justifiably proud of its quality control. It had supplied all major U.S. automobile manufacturers with products for years with no major complaints and, indeed, lots of praise. In the late 1980s, Metalloy signed a contract to make engine-seal castings for NOK, a leading Japanese manufacturer of automotive parts. NOK sent rubber rings to Metalloy to be inserted into round metal parts, which Metalloy then shipped to Japan.

In the first shipment of 5,000 parts, NOK reported finding 15 defective ones (about one third of 1 percent of the total). NOK requested a meeting with Metalloy and expressed dissatisfaction with the number of defective parts. The president of Metalloy, David Berlin, countered by having his staff inspect the thousands of rubber rings that NOK had supplied them to calculate the percentage that were defective. When his staff reported to him that there were no defective rings in the thousands, he began to understand what quality really means.

Metalloy then asked NOK officials to help it learn how to improve quality control. Now carefully developed instructions about quality are posted at each work station, and each operator inspects his or her own work as it is finished. The result is that Metalloy's defect rate is fifteen times better than that of other companies in its industry. Quality control pays off, but now Metalloy executives worry that American manufacturers are still more concerned about obtaining lower prices than about obtaining higher quality. The challenge, then, is for companies like Metalloy to be able to reduce costs by increasing quality and thereby compete on both dimensions.

SOURCES: Joel Dreyfuss, "Shaping Up Your Suppliers," *Fortune*, April 10, 1989, pp. 116–122; "New Kid on the Block: We Profile Supplier Fruendenberg-NOK," *Chilton's Automotive Industries*, December 1, 1989, pp. 65–69; Joel Dreyfuss, "Victories in the Quality Crusade," *Fortune*, October 10, 1988, pp. 80–88.

tion needs to have enough cash on hand to be able to function but not so much that resources are being used inefficiently. Second, many of the other areas of control relate to financial resources—improper inventory management costs money, as do poor employee selection, inaccurate forecasts, and so forth.

The Planning-Control Link

☐ *Planning* and *control* are linked in that they continually cycle into one another.

In many respects, controlling is the other side of the planning coin. This **planning-control link** is shown in Exhibit 16.2. Note in particular that planning and control continually cycle into one another, with organizing and leading serving as ways to get the actual work of the organization done.

For example, the normal cycle is for management to determine plans for the future and simultaneously to specify control conditions to keep the organization moving toward achieving those plans. Organizing and leading activities come into play as the organization implements the plans.

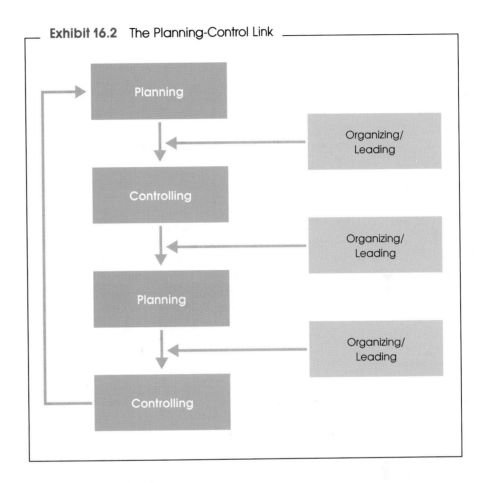

Exhibit 16.2   The Planning-Control Link

Control helps management determine whether to adjust plans. Suppose a firm plans to increase sales by 20 percent over the next ten years. At the end of the first year, an increase of 2 percent suggests that things are on track. No increase in sales during the second year, however, suggests that modifications to plans, such as increasing advertising or lowering the original projection, may be necessary.[5] The Champion Spark Plug Company used just this approach in a recent move to add twenty-one new products to its line.[6] (In a later section we explore how managers can make adjustments if plans are not being achieved as expected.)

APPROACHES TO CONTROL

Another important perspective that we need to consider is approaches to control. Most managers agree that there are three basic approaches: steering, concurrent, and postaction control.[7] As shown in Exhibit 16.3, steering control deals with inputs from the environment, concurrent control focuses on transformation processes, and postaction control is concerned with outputs to the environment.

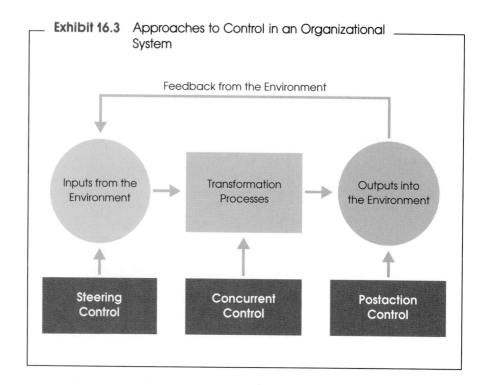

Exhibit 16.3   Approaches to Control in an Organizational System

Feedback from the Environment

Inputs from the Environment → Transformation Processes → Outputs into the Environment

Steering Control   Concurrent Control   Postaction Control

Steering Control

☐ *Steering control* monitors the quality and/or quantity of resources before they enter a company's system.

Steering control, also called *preliminary control* and *feed-forward control,* monitors the quality and/or quantity of various kinds of resources before they enter the system.[8] Firms like General Foods and Procter & Gamble, for instance, pay extra attention to what kinds of people they hire for future management positions. Similarly, when Sears orders merchandise to be sold under its brand, it specifies rigid standards to ensure appropriate levels of quality. Networks such as CBS and NBC monitor the commercials that potential sponsors intend to run to be sure that appropriate standards are being met; financial inputs are thus monitored to the extent that some sponsors are rejected. Of course, some organizations control information inputs by contracting only with the best market research firms and paying attention to only the most valid economic forecasts.

Concurrent Control

☐ *Concurrent control* involves control of the process of transforming resources into products.

Concurrent control, also referred to as *yes/no control* and *screening control,* focuses on activities that occur as inputs are being transformed into outputs. For example, a company might design various inspection stages during a production process to catch problems before too much damage is done. Likewise, the performance of employees is usually assessed at regular intervals. Care is usually taken to ensure that the information about ongoing operations that is provided to managers is accurate. Financial resources are also carefully monitored through periodic audits.

Postaction Control

☐ *Postaction control* monitors the quality and/or quantity of products as they leave a company's system.

Postaction control deals with the quality and/or quantity of an organization's outputs. When General Electric inspects finished goods before they are shipped, it is using postaction control. Rewarding employees after they have done a good job is an example of postaction control of human resources. It is common for top management to screen news bulletins and press releases before they leave the organization; this represents postaction control of information. And payments of dividends to stockholders and investments in the stock market are checked to provide postaction control of financial resources.

Multiple Controls

Each of the various approaches to control is useful in particular circumstances. Indeed, most large organizations find it necessary to establish integrated control systems using multiple approaches.

For example, consider a large manufacturing firm such as Boeing. Boeing carefully screens the engineers it hires, the materials it buys, the smaller firms it subcontracts with, and the financial solvency of airlines that place orders for new planes (steering control).

Postaction control focuses on the outputs created by the organization. This engineer at Textron, a large aerospace business, is inspecting isogrid panels the firm has made before they are shipped to NASA. Thus, he is practicing postaction control.

Courtesy Textron Inc./Photo by Mason Morfit

LEARNING CHECK

You should now be able to identify and discuss various approaches to control, such as steering, concurrent, postaction, and multiple controls.

It also carefully monitors each stage of the construction process as new planes are assembled. Performance of individual managers is assessed regularly, as is cash flow. After each plane is finished, it is again subjected to numerous inspections and checks to make sure that it is flightworthy. Managers get bonuses for completing work ahead of schedule, and the company collects its payment from the airline. Such integrated and comprehensive systems are necessary to provide adequate control for large, complex organizations.[9]

PRELUDE CASE UPDATE

In the Reebok case, the use of only postaction control in its initial foray into sportswear was almost disastrous. Clearly Reebok needed steering and/or concurrent control to maintain quality in its products and to ensure delivery of the products to retail outlets. These forms of control were added, and Reebok now has high-quality sportswear that is distributed to its customers on a timely basis.

ESTABLISHING A CONTROL SYSTEM

Regardless of which approach to control a manager is taking, he or she must follow four basic steps in establishing a **control system** or framework.[10] A control system is a mechanism used to ensure that the organization is achieving its objectives. The four steps in control systems are illustrated in Exhibit 16.4.[11]

Setting Standards

☐ *Standards* should be consistent with the organization's goals and appropriate for the level at which they are being used.

The first step in control is to set **standards,** or targets against which performance will be compared. A Burger King restaurant might set the following standards:

1. Customers will be served within four minutes of their entrance into the restaurant.
2. Drive-through customers will have their orders filled within five minutes of the time they enter the drive-through queue.
3. All tables will be wiped clean within three minutes after a customer has left.

Note that each standard is stated in objective terms, is very clear and specific, and has a specific time frame.

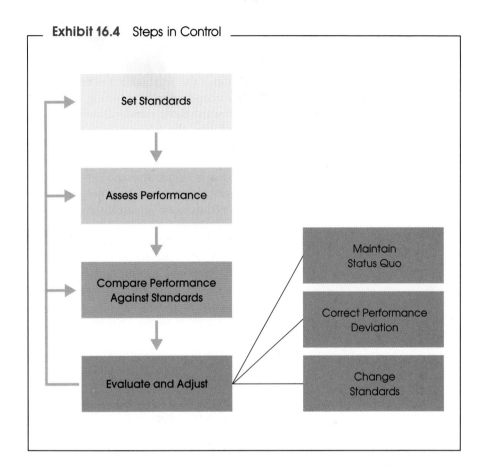

Exhibit 16.4 Steps in Control

Set Standards

Assess Performance

Compare Performance Against Standards

Evaluate and Adjust

Maintain Status Quo

Correct Performance Deviation

Change Standards

Standards are usually derived from, and therefore consistent with, the goals of the organization. Consider the Burger King restaurant. The standards given above are appropriate for an organization whose primary goals are related to customer service and satisfaction. If growth were of paramount importance, the standards might reflect sales increases, increases in the number of customers served, and so forth. In similar fashion, a university coming under criticism for its overemphasis on athletic programs might attempt to offset this criticism by shifting its emphasis back to academics. It might set a standard that 75 percent of all student athletes will graduate within five years of their initial enrollment.

Of course, the specificity of standards will vary according to the level of the organization to which they apply. A single Burger King restaurant has many different standards, all very specific and focused on areas related to customer service, cleanliness, and efficiency. At the corporate level, Burger King's standards are probably fewer and less focused. The corporation probably has standards for sales growth, growth in the number of outlets, menu adjustments, and so forth.

Assessing Performance

The second step in the control process is to assess performance, which relates to those things the organization is attempting to control.

When managers are establishing standards, they should also specify how progress toward those standards will be assessed. Suppose that Safeway has determined that the average customer spends five minutes waiting in the check-out line before being served. Because of increased competition from Kroger, Safeway wants to reduce waiting time to three and a half minutes. Managers might decide that the best way to achieve this is to eliminate a half-minute every six months for eighteen months. In a given store, then, the manager will need to measure current average waiting time, develop techniques for shortening waiting time (such as increasing the number of lines and training checkers to be more efficient), and then monitor progress to ensure continued improvement.

In many situations measuring performance is fairly easy, especially when the standards are objective and specific. In other settings, however, performance assessment is considerably more difficult. A manager taking over a struggling company might need an extended time to turn things around. Or a research and development scientist may not be able to produce consistent breakthroughs that can be immediately evaluated; instead, her or his contributions may come at irregular intervals, and their value may take some time to assess.

Finally, we should note that the appropriate time intervals for assessing performance also vary a great deal. In some areas, such as the strategic goals of General Motors or IBM, performance measurement may be appropriate every six months, or even longer. In others, such as a gambling casino, it is necessary to assess performance every day along several different dimensions.[12]

Comparing Performance with Standards

■ It is difficult to compare performance with standards because some standards are not quantifiable and judgment is often involved.

After setting standards and measuring subsequent relevant performance indicators, the manager must compare the two. Although this sounds fairly easy, it is really quite difficult in many cases.

For instance, some standards are hard to quantify. A standard of increasing customer or employee satisfaction is difficult to assess, as is a standard of achieving technological innovation.

Another difficulty relates to the fact that performance and standards are seldom precisely the same. If the standard is 10 percent and actual performance is 9.7 percent, has the standard been met or not? The answer, of course, is that it depends. The manager needs to draw on his or her experience and insight to determine whether the company needs to attain precisely 10 percent to be successful or whether a range from, say, 9 percent to 11 percent is really the same thing.

Evaluating and Adjusting

The final step in control is to evaluate and adjust standards and performance. In general, three actions may be appropriate.

One response is to do nothing—to keep things the same. This action is clearly most appropriate when the assessed performance meets the standards for performance. For example, if our standard is to increase sales by 12 percent this year and at the end of six months we have achieved an increase of 6.05 percent, we probably do not need to make any changes.

More likely, some action will be needed to correct a deviation in performance from the desired standard. If our standard is to increase sales by 12 percent this year and we only have a 4 percent increase after six months, we are clearly not on track to meet our standard. We may need to advertise more, plan more promotional activities, motivate our sales force, and so on.

Of course, we also have problems if we are exceeding our standards by too much. Suppose our standard is to hire one hundred highly qualified new employees this year. If we end up hiring seventy-five in the first six months, we may need to cut back on recruiting and hiring.

In some situations it may be appropriate to change the standards against which performance is being assessed. Unexpectedly strong competition, for instance, may necessitate lowering an organization's expectations for growth. On the other hand, if all employees are exceeding their standards easily, the standards may have been set too low to begin with. In this case, if the standards are subsequently raised, employees will probably be resentful and angry toward the organization, so it is clearly important to do a good job in setting standards from the beginning.

LEARNING CHECK

You should now be able to identify and discuss the steps in establishing a control system.

EFFECTIVE CONTROL

☐ The five characteristics of effective control are integration, objectivity, accuracy, timeliness, and flexibility.

Clearly, the manager's job would be greatly simplified if establishing organizational controls were easy. However, as we have seen, the control process is actually quite difficult and demanding. What can a manager do to enhance the effectiveness of the organization's control system? In general, effective control has five attributes, which are summarized in Table 16.1.[13]

Integration

First, and perhaps foremost, control systems must be integrated into the overall organizational system. This is most critical in terms of planning. Given the cyclical nature of planning and control, it is logical that the planning and control systems must be properly coordinated and integrated for them to work smoothly.

To see how this works, consider the situation confronted by Knight-Ridder, one of the largest media corporations in the United States. Although Knight-

TABLE 16.1
The Characteristics of
Effective Control

Characteristics	Explanation
1. Integration	Establishing control systems that take into account organizational plans
2. Objectivity	Supplying detailed, verifiable information
3. Accuracy	Providing complete and correct information
4. Timeliness	Providing information when it is needed
5. Flexibility	Establishing control systems that accommodate changes in the organization or the environment

Ridder publishes some of this country's most prestigious newspapers, problems caused the company to take strong action to enhance profitability. Two interdependent actions were used: all of the company's newspapers had to prepare five-year plans aimed at boosting profit margins to 20 percent or higher, and tight controls were implemented to ensure that these targets were met.[14]

Actually, the mechanics involved in achieving proper integration are fairly straightforward. Managers need to consider relevant control elements as they engage in planning, using goals, strategies, and tactics to establish complementary dimensions of the control system. Similarly, results provided by the control system make useful resources for future planning cycles.[15] If managers take these considerations into account, a well-integrated control system will permeate the entire organization.[16]

PRELUDE CASE   UPDATE

We earlier noted how Reebok got into difficulty because it had relied on only postaction control. Adopting a multiple control approach alleviated most of those difficulties. A second problem that Reebok encountered, however, was that it had installed control structures and mechanisms that restricted innovation and input from customers. Reebok had not integrated control with its organizational culture and system strengths. When Fireman took back the top executive position, he immediately moved to bring about that integration.

Objectivity

A second characteristic of effective control systems is objectivity. This simply means that to the greatest extent possible, the control system should use and provide detailed information that can be verified and understood.

For instance, suppose a sales manager asks two sales representatives to assess how their clients feel about the company and its products. One reports that she talked to fifteen customers and that ten of them liked what the com-

Macmillan Bloedel, Canada's largest pulp manufacturing and forest products company, strives for effective control. Using detailed computer-generated charts and close observation to monitor the company's natural resource inventories, surveyors provide objective, accurate, and timely information to company planners on a regular basis.

pany was doing, three were indifferent, and two had complaints. She also reports on the exact nature of the clients' likes and dislikes and provides an estimate of how much each intends to order next quarter. The other sales representative reports that he talked to a few people, that some were happy and some were unhappy with the products (although he isn't too sure of the reasons for their attitudes), and that sales will be okay next quarter. Clearly, the data provided by the first sales representative will be more useful than those provided by the second.

Of course, the manager needs to look beyond simple numbers. A plant manager may appear to be doing a great job of cutting costs, but closer inspection might reveal that he is using substandard materials, pushing his workers too hard, and padding his reports. On balance, the control system should be as objective as possible, but not so dependent on figures that managers lose contact with what is actually going on behind the scenes.[17]

Accuracy

Obviously, the control system must be accurate in order to be effective. If it is providing erroneous information, it may be doing more harm than good. In reality, of course, any number of things can allow inaccuracies to creep into the system. A plant manager might be providing incomplete cost figures to make himself look better, or a sales representative might be padding her expense account and collecting more reimbursement than she is owed.[18] At another level, a human resource manager might overestimate the company's minority recruiting prospects.

The critical nature of such inaccuracies becomes apparent when we consider how managers use the control system. If a manager signs a contract to provide merchandise for a figure below what the true production costs are, the firm will lose money. Hence, managers need to take every precaution to ensure the accuracy of the information they receive from the control system.

Timeliness

It is also important that the information provided by the control system be timely. This means that the manager must have the information when he or she needs it most. The manager of a K mart store, for example, will want and need to know precise sales figures on a daily basis, but she may need inventory figures only every two or three months. And the corporate office will not need daily sales figures but only weekly or monthly figures. Timeliness doesn't necessarily mean speed, but it does mean that information is in the manager's hands when it is needed.

In general, the need for timeliness is related to uncertainty. The more uncertain the situation, the greater the need for timely information. When a new product is introduced, the manager may desire daily sales reports, but for a more established product he may need them only every week or every month.

Flexibility

Finally, effective control systems tend to be flexible—that is, they are able to accommodate adjustments and change in the organization or the environment.[19] Suppose a control system is designed to manage information about two hundred raw materials that go into producing the company's products. A new technological breakthrough allows the company to produce the same products with only half as many materials. If the control system is not flexible, the managers will have to scrap the entire system and develop a new one. However, a flexible system will be able to accommodate the changes.

In summary, effective control systems generally have five basic attributes: they are integrated with other organizational systems, they are objective, they are accurate, they are timely, and they are flexible. In the next section we explore other ways to enhance control system effectiveness.

LEARNING CHECK

You should now be able to describe the characteristics of effective control.

MANAGING CONTROL

In addition to making control systems effective by promoting the attributes described above, managers must deal with resistance issues. Some people tend to resist control in particular, so managers need to understand why resistance

TABLE 16.2
Managing Control

Reasons for Resistance	Ways to Combat Resistance
1. Overcontrol	1. Design the system well
2. Inappropriate focus	2. Encourage employee participation
3. Rewards for inefficiency	3. Use MBO
4. Accountability	4. Provide checks and balances

occurs and what they can do to overcome it. The most common factors under-lying resistance and the best ways to deal with them are summarized in Table 16.2.[20]

Understanding Resistance to Control

Four of the most common reasons that people resist control are overcontrol, inappropriate focus, rewards for inefficiency, and accountability.

□ *Overcontrol* causes resistance by limiting employees' independence and autonomy.

Organizations sometimes make the mistake of practicing **overcontrol,** or too much control. This can be particularly problematic when the control relates to employees. Employees may require a certain degree of control in the work-place, but they also want a reasonable degree of autonomy and freedom. For example, an organization may specify normal working hours and work-related expectations for its employees, but it will probably not be successful in trying to dictate personal behavior such as mannerisms, recreational preferences, and so forth. Attention is increasingly being paid to ways in which managers can get employees to exert personal control and accommodate both individual and organizational goals.[21] Personal control issues can be important to new and growing businesses, too, as indicated in *Management Today: Small Business And Entrepreneurship.*

Another reason for resistance to control is **inappropriate focus,** which oc-curs when the control is too narrowly focused or does not provide a reasonable balance between different outcomes that are important. For instance, if a sales manager concentrates so much on sales increases that nothing else really mat-ters, sales representatives may come to ignore other parts of their jobs. Like-wise, if a university encourages and rewards publication and provides few incentives for professors to be good teachers, its faculty will gradually devote more and more time to research and less and less time to teaching.

In other cases, organizations end up rewarding inefficiency and perhaps not rewarding efficiency. Many departments rush to spend any of their budget that is going to remain at the end of the year because they feel that if they have money left over, management will assume they need less money next year. But if they spend all of their money, and perhaps even report a small loss, their budget might be increased next year. Obviously, this situation re-wards inefficiency.

□ *Accountability* allows a manager to determine how each part of the organization is performing.

A final reason for resistance to control is that control creates **accountability.** That is, a properly designed control system will allow a manager to determine

SMALL BUSINESS AND ENTREPRENEURSHIP

Depending on the Employee

C. C. Creations of College Station, Texas, began its existence as a very small silk-screening establishment. In 1982 it had gross sales of only $60,000. By 1989, however, C. C. Creations had expanded to add embroidered merchandise and trophies to its full line of silk-screened products, and gross sales were in excess of $2.5 million. Once, a good day's production was 200 dozen shirts, but now that would be a bad day; a good day would be closer to 1,500 dozen. This tremendous growth in performance came about not just because the owner, Ford Taylor, had had a focused dream ever since junior high school to run such a store. Nor did it occur just because Taylor works sixty to seventy-five hours each week to make that dream come true. It is also because C. C. Creations is using group participation to ensure quality and production control.

Taylor is careful to hire good people and train them to do their jobs well. They set their own goals so that minimum supervision is necessary. They can function even if Taylor is out of town lining up new contracts or suppliers. Combining the latest technology with trained workers is becoming one of the strongest approaches to quality control for small businesses.

However, growth must always be controlled or quality will suffer with too rapid an expansion. At one point, Taylor purchased equipment from a major customer that had been doing its own silk-screening. The equipment was located in Houston, about ninety miles away. Taylor quickly found that he was spending about 70 percent of his time in Houston supervising the use of the new equipment. That part of the business began to lose money, so Taylor moved it to College Station, hired good people to run the equipment, trained them in proper quality control, and involved them in the entire process. Now, that part of the business, like all the rest, makes money and is under control.

SOURCES: "Integrating Automated PCB Component Assembly with Quality Planning," *Electronic Manufacturing*, January 1, 1990, pp. 22–27; Tracy Staton, "Team Players," *Bryan-College Station Eagle*, May 28, 1989, p. 1E; Ted Cocheu, "Training for Quality Improvement," *Training and Development Journal*, January 1989, pp. 56–62.

how each department, and in many cases how each individual manager, is performing. As a consequence, managers become more accountable for their actions, decisions, and performance. Obviously, some managers will not object to such accountability, but others—especially those who are not doing a good job—will resist.

Overcoming Resistance to Control

As also shown in Table 16.2, managers can at least partially overcome employee resistance to control in a number of ways. One obvious method is to make sure that the control system is properly designed. In particular, if it is designed to have the attributes of effective control already discussed, employees will be less likely to object to it.

Second, employee participation can reduce resistance to control. If employees have a voice in designing the parts of the control system that directly affect them and also have avenues for suggesting modifications, they are more likely to accept the system as fair and reasonable.

A third approach to overcoming resistance to control is to use management by objectives, or MBO, which is described in Chapter 4 as a collaborative goal-setting technique between managers and their subordinates. Employees in a well-conceived and well-managed MBO system know exactly what is expected of them, how they should attempt to achieve those goals, and what their rewards will be if they succeed.

Finally, the control system should have a built-in provision for checks and balances. This simply means that it should provide a mechanism for checking and potentially adjusting for discrepancies. For example, suppose an employee who is dismissed for frequent tardiness denies that he was late very often. If the human resource manager can prove that he was actually late many times, he (and other employees) will be more likely to see the control system as fair and equitable. Or suppose that a sales representative claims that she did not meet her quota because of unexpectedly high levels of competition from other companies. If the sales manager has adequate information to assess the validity of her claim, he can more easily accept or refute that claim.

LEARNING CHECK

You should now be able to discuss reasons for resistance to control and how to overcome this resistance.

Overcoming resistance to control is an important part of effectively managing organizational control. Charles Royer, Mayor of Seattle, Washington, hired a group of experienced managers to help him run the city. One of their accomplishments has been to give business and industry leaders more say in what goes on in the city.

RESPONSIBILITY FOR CONTROL

A final issue to consider is the responsibility for control. Exactly who in the organization needs to be concerned with control? As shown in Exhibit 16.5, this responsibility is shared between line managers and specialized managers called controllers.

Line Managers

In a very real sense, all managers are responsible for control. They all help design the system, are responsible for implementing and using it, and are at least partially governed by it.

As the exhibit illustrates, the CEO is responsible for the overall control of the total organization. Each division head is responsible for control within his or her division. In general, such managers have some degree of autonomy in adjusting the control system to fit their own preferences and views on how control should be executed.[22] No matter what variations they implement, however, the system within each division must mesh and be consistent with the overall system of the organization.

Exhibit 16.5 Responsibility for Control

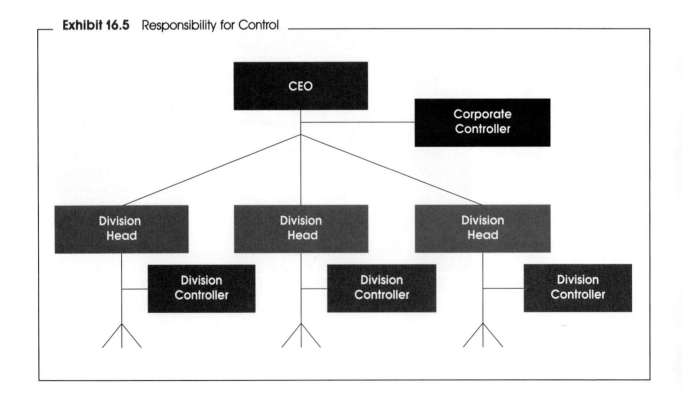

The Controller

In most organizations, control is also the specific responsibility of one or more managers who have the title of **controller.** As shown in the exhibit, a large organization may have a corporate controller as well as other controllers in each division.[23] The controller's job is to help line managers with their control activities, to coordinate the overall control system within the organization, and to gather relevant information and report it to all managers. Monsanto developed a program to train employees in controllership that it claims graduates broad-thinking, line-oriented managers.[24]

Controllers are particularly involved in the control of financial resources. This is consistent with the pervasiveness of financial concerns in control. Because of the increased importance of the control function in recent years, the position of controller has taken on added stature in many organizations, Coors being one example.[25]

Chapter Summary

Controlling is the process of monitoring and adjusting organizational activities toward goal attainment. Most organizations have controls to deal with four areas: financial resources, physical resources, human resources, and information resources.

The planning-control link means that control is the other side of the planning coin; it helps management to ensure that performance conforms to plans.

There are three basic approaches to control: steering control, concurrent control, and postaction control. Steering control monitors the quality and/or quantity of various kinds of resources before they enter the system. Concurrent control focuses on activities that occur as inputs are being transformed into outputs. Postaction control deals with the quality and/or quantity of an organization's outputs. These approaches to control are usually used together as multiple controls.

There are four basic steps to establishing a control system: setting standards, assessing performance, comparing performance with standards, and evaluating and adjusting.

Effective control has five attributes: it is integrated, objective, accurate, timely, and flexible. *Integration* means that the control system must fit into the overall organizational system. *Objectivity* means that everyone who is affected by the control system

must be able to understand it. *Accuracy* means that the control system must be reporting correct information that is pertinent to the company's goals. *Timeliness* means that the information provided by the control system must be available when it can be used. Information that arrives too late is of no value. Finally, *flexibility* means that the control system must be able to accommodate adjustments and change and should not be applied rigidly.

Managing control also involves dealing with resistance to control. There are four basic things a manager can do to overcome such resistance. First, he should make sure that the control system is properly designed and has the characteristics of effective controls. Second, he should encourage participation, which tends to increase acceptance. Third, he can use management by objectives to establish collaborative goals and to enhance acceptance of controls. Finally, he should ensure that the control system has a built-in provision for checks and balances, so that discrepancies do not occur or are corrected if they do.

The ultimate responsibility for control must be shared by everyone in the organization. In more practical terms, the responsibility is shared by line managers and specialized managers called controllers. All managers contribute to the planning process and so also share the responsibility for control. However, control is the specific responsibility of one or more managers who have the title of controller. The controller's job is to assist line managers with their control activities, coordinate the overall control system, and gather relevant information and report it to all managers.

The Manager's Vocabulary

controlling	standards
planning-control link	overcontrol
steering control	inappropriate focus
concurrent control	accountability
postaction control	controller
control system	

Prelude Case Wrap-Up

Our Prelude Case for this chapter describes Reebok, a highly successful and fast-growing company. Too little quality control almost led to serious problems at Reebok. Its abortive sportswear effort could have spilled over into all aspects of the firm's activity and destroyed its product image and sales. But too much control in the form of overmonitoring and the use of rules and regulations also caused problems. The entrepreneurial spirit that had made the company successful was being stifled, and feedback from customers was being ignored. One of Reebok's co-founders then took back control of the firm and is helping it turn around and re-establish itself as the market leader.

Reebok stepped up controls in marketing and distribution. In marketing, for example, Reebok's advertising efforts expanded and the firm employed a number of innovative new advertising campaigns. Reebok also upgraded its materials-handling operations in order to improve its distribution methods and capabilities and it began to listen more closely to its distributors.

Prelude Case Questions

1. Which concepts presented in this chapter are illustrated in the Reebok case? Cite specific examples.
2. What major characteristics of control are described in the Prelude Case?

3. What are the strengths and weaknesses of Reebok's control mechanisms? How might such weaknesses be offset?
4. Do you feel that Reebok will continue to grow as rapidly in the future as it has in the past? Why or why not?

Discussion Questions

Review Questions

1. What is control, and why do organizations need it?
2. In terms of timing, what are the several approaches to control?
3. Discuss each of the steps in establishing a control system.
4. What are the characteristics of effective control?
5. Why do people resist control, and how do managers overcome this resistance?

Analysis Questions

1. Do you ever feel that certain aspects of your life are out of control? Do you wish you could exercise more control over things that affect you? If so, describe some reasons why you might need some control, apart from those given in the text.
2. Which step in the control system is likely to be the most difficult to carry out? Why? Which is likely to meet with the most resistance? Why?
3. Do all of the characteristics of effective controls fit together? Why or why not?
4. Which characteristic of effective control do you feel is most important? Why?
5. Why would it be unwise for an organization to have just one person totally responsible for control? What persons should be responsible for control? Why?

Application Questions and Exercises

1. Interview several local managers to determine which approach to control they seem to use most—steering, concurrent, postaction, or multiple. Share your results with the class.
2. Make up a tabular list of the costs and benefits of each approach to control for routine production

and operations, for hiring and other personnel decisions for clerical workers, for accounting and financial records, and for hiring and other personnel decisions for executives. Which approach would you use in each case? How do your answers here compare with your results in application question 1?

3. Ask different kinds of managers (supervisors, executives, accountants, and so on) to rank the characteristics of effective control. Are the rankings all the same? If not, how can you explain the differences?

4. Sit down with your roommate or family or close friend and discuss how the concepts of control presented in this chapter might be applied to your life to enable you to feel that you have more control over things that affect you.

5. Go to the library and read about how specific companies use control. Share your findings with the class.

ENHANCEMENT CASE

RYDER TRIES TO GET ON THE ROAD AGAIN

For many years the truck-leasing business was dominated by Ryder System, Inc., based in Miami, Florida. Ryder led the way in the consumer one-way rental business and in the full-service commercial leasing business. Success seemed to come easily to Ryder. From 1979 through 1989, its revenues increased fivefold and its earnings grew about 14 percent per year. But in 1989, for the first time in over a decade, earnings dropped. Ryder's stock had been falling since 1987, and the 1989 earnings brought it down even further.

What went out of control and led to this problem? The answer lay partly in the environment. When most people move, they use their own vehicles. The rest are about evenly split between those who use moving companies and those who use rental equipment. Moreover, people tend to move toward areas of economic growth in good times and away from areas of economic decline in bad times. The late 1980s were neither good nor bad; as a result, people did not move as frequently as before. Moving in general had slowed, and Ryder suffered because it had not controlled for this eventuality.

Ryder had been growing so strongly that it had neglected to plan for this slowdown; it had no controls for reductions in operations. The planning-control link had not been established. It, along with other rental companies, had actually increased its fleet size in anticipation of continued growth. This meant that, when the slowdown occurred, Ryder had more trucks but fewer customers, and it was stuck with excess capacity. Thus, at the same time that sales revenues were dropping because people were not moving as much, costs were increasing because more trucks were being brought on line. Clearly profits were going to suffer under those conditions. Steering and concurrent controls did not appear to exist or, if they did, they did not work.

There may have been more to it than that, however. M. Anthony Burns was named CEO at Ryder in 1983 at the age of forty. His strategy was to change Ryder from a truck-leasing company to a major service company and in this way reduce its dependence on seasonal business. To do this, he used the tremendous flow of cash from truck-leasing and rental operations to finance an ambitious series of acquisitions. Burns bought a truck line to haul freight, a freight forwarder, and airplane-leasing and maintenance companies; he also expanded Ryder's insurance management operations.

Burns's strategy did not work. The airplane-leasing unit had trouble leasing all of its planes; in 1988, nine out of forty went unleased. The airplane service unit also had problems; it overstocked airplane parts and so had to carry excessive inventories. The freight business was in even worse shape. And when executives began to concentrate on these new enterprises in an effort to turn them around, Ryder's bread-

Courtesy Ryder System, Inc./Photo by Steve Uzzell

Ryder has to be very concerned with how it manages its control function. By providing vehicles to the food service industry to help meet seasonal demands and last-minute rush orders, Ryder can smooth demand for its trucks. This allows Ryder to maintain a smoother cash flow with a smaller inventory of units.

and-butter businesses of truck leasing and consumer rental got into trouble. However, its full-service business that leases and services truck fleets for corporate clients was quite successful.

Using financial controls, Burns then made a lot of changes to try to regain control. He sold off or put on the market some of the acquisitions he had recently made. He trimmed the truck fleet by several thousand vehicles, eliminated a layer of management,

and reduced the work force by about one thousand in 1988 alone. By mid-1989 Ryder International Freight and Customs Services and U.S. Packing and Shipping were gone, and the insurance services were due to be sold at any time.

Of course, U-Haul did not miss this opportunity to try to gain market share from Ryder. It cut prices and took actions designed to target certain parts of the moving market. Ryder matched the price cuts and target market strategies with those of its own. Recognizing that female heads of households are more mobile than men, Ryder began a series of ads in major women's magazines emphasizing features that might have greater appeal to women drivers—air conditioning, power steering, adjustable seats, and automatic transmissions, for instance. To accommodate "pack-rat" families whose possessions exceed the capacity of most rental trucks, both U-Haul and Ryder introduced larger trucks to compete with commercial moving companies, which were introducing packages by which customers did their own packing, loading, and unloading, leaving only the driving to the company. Ryder also expanded its television advertising, pushing the theme that using Ryder makes moving easier.

Ryder is moving to regain control and to more clearly establish itself as a truck-leasing and renting operation. By divesting itself of units that do not fit relatively well with that concept, it has enabled its management to use knowledge and skills across divisions to control quality, service, and performance. Whether its skid will prove more serious will be determined in the early 1990s.

SOURCES: "Ryder, U-Haul Try to Get Businesses Moving Again," *The Wall Street Journal*, June 14, 1989, p. B1; "Suddenly, Ryder's Engine Is Sputtering," *Business Week*, June 19, 1989, p. 56; "Ryder Detour Won't Wreck Long Haul," *USA Today*, July 25, 1989, p. 3B; "Ryder System, Hurt by Growing Too Fast, Tries to Stop Skidding," *The Wall Street Journal*, July 25, 1989, pp. A1, A4.

Enhancement Case Questions

1. What similarities and differences can you note between the control systems of Ryder and Reebok from the Prelude Case?
2. Describe Ryder's control systems. What concepts discussed in the chapter can you identify? Cite specific examples of each of them.
3. What are the strengths and weaknesses of the controls used by Ryder? How might it reduce the weaknesses?
4. What do you feel that Ryder could do to make its controls function even better in the future? How would your suggestions improve its systems?

Chapter Notes

1. William Newman, *Constructive Control* (Englewood Cliffs, N.J.: Prentice-Hall, 1975).

2. "American Greetings Is Carding Gains," *USA Today*, August 24, 1988, p. 3B; "Flounder," *Forbes*, April 25, 1988.

3. "The Meanest and Leanest Sit Down to Just Desserts," *Business Week*, February 9, 1987, pp. 30–31.

4. "Why Emery Is Biting Its Nails," *Business Week*, August 29, 1988, p. 34.

5. J. M. Horovitz, "Strategic Control: A New Task for Top Management," *Long Range Planning*, June 1979, pp. 28–37.

6. "Champion Is Starting to Show a Little Spark," *Business Week*, March 21, 1988, p. 87; "Champion Spark Plug Agrees to Merge with Dana Corp. for $17.50 a Share," *The Wall Street Journal*, January 26, 1989, p. A4.

7. Newman, *Constructive Control*.

8. Harold Koontz and Robert W. Bradspies, "Managing Through Feedforward Control," *Business Horizons*, June 1972, pp. 25–36.

9. Edward E. Lawler III and John G. Rhode, *Information and Control in Organization* (Pacific Palisades, Calif.: Goodyear, 1976).

10. Robert N. Anthony, *The Management Control Function* (Boston: Harvard Business School Press, 1988).

11. Newman, *Constructive Control*.

12. Daniel Seligman, "Turmoil Time in the Casino Business," *Fortune*, March 2, 1987, pp. 102–116.

13. William G. Ouchi, "The Transmission of Control Through Organizational Hierarchies," *Academy of Management Journal*, June 1978, pp. 173–192.

14. "Knight-Ridder Acts to Boost Bottom Line," *USA Today*, November 11, 1986, pp. 1B–2B.

15. Horovitz, "Strategic Control."

16. Paul G. Makosz and Bruce W. McQuaig, "Is Everything Under Control? A New Approach to Corporate Governance," *Financial Executive*, January 1, 1990, pp. 24–29.

17. Newman, *Constructive Control*.

18. See Walter Kiechel III, "Managing Expense Accounts," *Fortune*, September 16, 1985, pp. 205–208.

19. Peter F. Drucker, *Management: Tasks, Practices, and Responsibilities* (New York: Harper & Row, 1974).

20. See Lawler and Rhode, *Information and Control in Organizations*, for a thorough explanation of resistance to control.

21. David B. Greenberger and Stephen Strasser, "Development and Application of a Model of Personal Control in Organizations," *Academy of Management Review*, January 1988, pp. 164–177.

22. Cortlandt Cammann and David A. Nadler, "Fit Control Systems to Your Management Style," *Harvard Business Review*, January-February 1976, pp. 65–72.

23. Vijay Sathe, "Who Should Control Division Controllers?" *Harvard Business Review*, September-October 1978, pp. 99–104.

24. Michael A. Robinson and Donald T. Hughes, "Controllership Training: A Competitive Weapon," *Management Accounting*, May 1, 1989, pp. 20–24.

25. Al Pipkin, "The 21st Century Controller," *Management Accounting*, February 1, 1989, pp. 21–26; "The Controller—Inflation Gives Him More Clout with Management," *Business Week*, August 15, 1977, pp. 85–87, 90.

CHAPTER OUTLINE

I. The Nature of Control Techniques
   A. The Importance of Control Techniques
   B. Strengths and Weaknesses

II. Budgets
   A. The Budgeting Process
   B. Types of Budgets
   C. Fixed and Variable Costs in Budgeting
   D. Managing the Budgeting Process

III. Financial Analysis
   A. Ratio Analysis
   B. Audits

IV. Other Control Techniques
   A. Human Resource Control
   B. Marketing Control

V. Computers and Control
   A. Kinds of Computers
   B. Contributions to Control
   C. Advantages and Disadvantages

CHAPTER

17

LEARNING OBJECTIVES

After studying this chapter you should be able to

1. Describe the nature and importance of control techniques and indicate their strengths and weaknesses.

2. Discuss the budgeting process, types of budgets, costs used in budgeting, and how to manage the budgeting process.

3. Define financial analysis and discuss ratio analysis and audits.

4. Discuss techniques used to control human resources and marketing.

5. Name several kinds of computers and discuss their contributions to the control process and the advantages and disadvantages of using them.

Control Techniques and Methods

BLOCKBUSTER'S BUSTING OUT

In 1972 H. Wayne Huizenga (pronounced "high-zen-ga") and two partners formed a small trash-hauling company and quickly transformed it into Waste Management Inc., a multibillion-dollar giant enterprise. It was no surprise, then, that when he and some other partners bought the Fort Lauderdale, Florida, Blockbuster video rental chain in 1987, they moved just as quickly to expand it into a national force to be reckoned with in that industry.

In the mid-1980s, many video rental outlets were perceived as fly-by-night operations. They were stuck in little out-of-the-way locations, were dimly lit, carried a limited selection of titles, had no displays other than some furnished by an occasional movie distributor, and were owned and managed by inexperienced people. Huizenga's outlets were in more desirable sites, and they were large and well lighted. Blockbuster also focused on a family-oriented approach, carrying titles for children as well as adults and carefully restricting the rental of rated videos. The typical Blockbuster outlet stocks 7,000 titles

and averages $70,000 a month in revenues, a figure that is much higher than the industry average. Huizenga took Blockbuster from about one hundred outlets to over seven hundred in just two years.

From its base in Fort Lauderdale, Blockbuster has expanded rapidly and has seen its profits and sales skyrocket: 1988 profits were over $15 million on sales of nearly $140 million. The selling price of stock in the firm rose almost sevenfold from 1987 to 1989. Growth was strong and success was clear. For 1990, Blockbuster projected sales of nearly $200 million from about one thousand outlets.

Most of Blockbuster's growth comes from an expansion of retail outlets through the purchase of other video chains. This means, then, that it must keep buying other stores to maintain the growth (although not necessarily the return on investment) that catapulted it into national prominence. Some analysts doubt whether that growth pace can be sustained. Even more significant, there has been some concern about the accounting control

procedures being used by Blockbuster.

Blockbuster uses the maximum period allowed by accounting standards for any goodwill obtained when it buys a chain of video rental stores. Goodwill is the difference between the purchase price and the fair market value of a collection of assets. It is usually attributed to factors such as favorable locations of outlets, a valuable trade name, or the like. Using this approach, Blockbuster can report higher profits in the short term but will have to report lower profits in the long term, especially if revenues drop off.

Another potential problem is that Blockbuster franchisees pay not only a one-time sign-up fee but also a fee to lock in territory, and they must also purchase inventory from Blockbuster. This means that not only are profits overstated in the near term, but revenues also come in large part from these one-time sign-up payments from franchisees (nearly 30 percent in 1988, for instance). As long as Blockbuster keeps signing on new outlets, everything is fine, but if growth slackens, rev-

Blockbuster is a fast-growing video rental chain. H. Wayne Huizenga, Blockbuster's CEO, is shown here with a cutout of Bob Hoskins, star of *Who Framed Roger Rabbit?*

© 1990 photo by Acey Harper

enues will fall precipitously. Couple that with the profit impact later, and future earnings may well be in grave doubt. Moreover, Blockbuster's techniques make it difficult for its investors to make reliable forecasts; if a fall comes, they will not be able to predict it.

Criticism of his methods is not new to Huizenga. He and his partners at Waste Management were charged with fixing prices, improperly influencing government officials, and illegally dumping hazardous wastes. Huizenga, in fact, signed a consent agreement in 1976 not to make illegal contributions to the election campaigns of government officials. At Blockbuster, he has been criticized, too. In 1988 Blockbuster stock prices shot up when it announced a distribution agreement with Walt Disney; however, they quickly came back down when Disney pointed out that the agreement was not exclusive and that

many video rental chains besides Blockbuster had benefited. Blockbuster was then criticized for framing its announcement so that it implied an exclusive arrangement. Again, Blockbuster's practices obviously made stock forecasting difficult for investors.

Several factors suggest that Blockbuster's market may begin to shrink. First, the market for videocassette recorders (VCRs) is becoming saturated. As it becomes saturated, the volume of video rentals will level off. Dual-cassette recorders are coming into production that will enable customers to view one cassette while taping on another from their tele-

vision and to make copies of cassettes easily. What the impact of such dual-deck VCRs will be on video rentals is unclear. Further, more and more cable operators are offering their customers a "pay for only movies that you watch" option that, as it grows, will erode the video rental market. Finally, huge warehouse-sized record stores and even supermarkets are getting into the video rental business. They can offer greater selection or more convenience and, in some cases, both. These three trends, then, might suggest that Blockbuster's growth will soon begin to level off and possibly even decline.

SOURCES: "Fast-Forward Video King," *Business Week*, January 22, 1990, p. 47; "Will This Video Chain Stay on Fast-Forward?" *Business Week*, June 12, 1989, pp. 72,75; "A Booming Blockbuster: This Video Retailer Is Growing like Gangbusters," *Dealerscope Merchandising*, August 1, 1989, p. 24; William P. Barrett, "A Roll of the Dice," *Forbes*, February 20, 1989, p. 81; "Blockbuster's Big Move," *Adweek's Marketing Week*, December 19, 1988, p. 32.

The theme of this chapter is the techniques and methods that managers use to maintain adequate control. In the Prelude Case to this chapter, we see the importance such control techniques and methods can have for a business. If Blockbuster had chosen to use a substantially shorter period of time in which to charge goodwill, its earnings picture would be quite different. Or if it handled one-time franchisee fees more as short streams of payments than as one-time revenue sources, its financial statements would again seem quite different. And, of course, if it did both of these together, the picture a potential investor would get would be radically different from that which is usually portrayed for Blockbuster.

In this chapter we will get a better understanding of these sorts of issues. First we will examine the role of control techniques in management. We then explore one of the most important and widespread techniques, the budget, before going on to investigate financial analysis. Other control techniques are summarized, and the chapter concludes by looking at the relationship between computers and control.

THE NATURE OF CONTROL TECHNIQUES

Chapter 5 uses the analogy between planning techniques and the tools of a carpenter. The same analogy holds true for control techniques; they too are handy tools that managers can use to enhance organizational effectiveness in general and organizational control in particular.

The Importance of Control Techniques

As we have seen, adequate control is important for numerous reasons. The proper use of the right techniques facilitates control and also helps managers communicate with others both inside and outside the organization. Many of the techniques are used by virtually all organizations and so represent standard business practice. The techniques involve different levels of management in the control process and enable managers to know what is happening in the organization.

A plumber who decided to become a plumbing contractor soon went out of business because he forgot that, although he had to pay his workers weekly, he did not get paid until the job was completed. Had he used budgets and financial control techniques, he would have foreseen his cash flow problem and perhaps been able to borrow enough money to keep from going bankrupt. Financial techniques provide the opportunity to keep up with the assets and debts of the firm, and budgetary techniques can ensure that the firm will not overspend its resources. In fact, as indicated in *Management Today: Small Business And Entrepreneurship*, control is particularly important to small businesses.

SMALL BUSINESS AND ENTREPRENEURSHIP

Entrepreneurs May Not Make Managers

Although there has been some debate as to actual failure rates among new businesses, the fact remains that any new venture is risky and that managerial problems are a primary cause of such failure. Those who are successful in starting new businesses are not necessarily always equally successful in developing the proper control mechanisms for operating them. Indeed, there is substantial evidence that many new business failures happen because of poor controls.

Some entrepreneurs do develop proper control mechanisms that ensure success as well as permitting the entrepreneurial spirit of the organization to remain. Some don't. In order to handle the differences between the needs of their organizations and their own personal needs, some entrepreneurs turn over the management of the business to others and retain a position in the part of the organization that uniquely fits their talents. Others sell their businesses and go on to create new ones. All entrepreneurs, however, learn that the control techniques that work when a business is new and relatively small will not continue to work as effectively as the business matures and grows.

One control issue regards who controls. Entrepreneurs learn to delegate to others so that decisions are made quickly by those in the best position to have the necessary information. This is especially important when the entrepreneur is trying to expand rapidly through franchising or when the entrepreneur tries to couple one early success with others. But shared control also occurs when venture capitalists become involved; they are unlikely to risk their funds without some measure of shared control. If the entrepreneur also wants to play less of a role so that she or he can have more time to enjoy the fruits of her or his labors, sharing control may permit some degree of "having your cake and eating it, too."

Studying how others have handled control as they have grown will generally be quite helpful to entrepreneurs. As tools of control, computers can be as valuable to small business owners as they are to owners of large enterprises. The importance of control to entrepreneurs is apparent and even auditors are beginning to stress that importance and to discuss control improvements with their clients.

SOURCES: "Small Business," *Director*, January 1, 1990, pp. 87–88; Terry J. Engle and David M. Dennis, "Benefits of an Internal Control Structure Evaluation in a Small Business Audit," *The Ohio CPA Journal*, Spring 1989, pp. 5–11; "Cashing Out and Maintaining Control; Have Your Cake and Eat it Too," *Small Business Report*, December 1, 1989, pp. 27–41; "Case History: Growing Pains," *Small Business Report*, July 1, 1989, pp. 34–44; Ralph M. Stair, William F. Crittenden, and Vicky L. Crittenden, "The Use, Operation, and Control of the Small Business Computer," *Information and Management*, March 1, 1989, pp. 125–130; A. Shapero and L. Sokol, "Exits and Entries: A Study in Yellow Pages Journalism," in Karl H. Vesper, ed., *Frontiers on Entrepreneurship Research 1982*, (Englewood Cliffs, N.J.: Prentice-Hall, Inc., 1982, pp. 72–90); *The Business Failure Record*, (New York: Dun and Bradstreet, 1981).

PRELUDE CASE UPDATE

In the Blockbuster case, the use of two specific accounting control techniques resulted in a picture of its financial well-being that some investment experts felt was inaccurate. If either or both of those control techniques had been changed, the financial picture of Blockbuster would have also changed. A changed picture, in turn, could have led to very different buying and selling patterns among investors and stockholders. It is important to Blockbuster that it use control techniques that portray its financial health in the best possible light; on the other hand, it is important to investors that they see as accurate a picture as possible.

Strengths and Weaknesses

Like a carpenter's tools, control techniques have various strengths and weaknesses. When used properly, they are a great asset to any manager. When used improperly, however, they can do more harm than good.

On the plus side, control techniques provide objective indicators of an organization's performance. Budgets and various financial ratios, for example, are quantifiable and verifiable indications of the firm's financial situation. Control techniques also provide useful road maps for action; budgets indicate clearly where and how resources are to be allocated.

On the other hand, these techniques can be characterized by two significant weaknesses. For one thing, they can be rigid and uncompromising, especially when managers use them with no regard for flexibility or for the appropriate context. A manager could, for instance, continue to rely on a budget that had been developed on the basis of outdated government regulations. Thus, control techniques must be flexible to be truly effective.[1]

Similarly, control techniques can be misused. In particular, individual managers might be able to distort information in order to mask problems. A manager could report that, historically, personnel recruited from one region of the country turn over more than others. She could use these data to support an argument for not recruiting from that region when, in fact, the turnover stemmed from her treatment of those employees.

Thus, when using control techniques, managers need to remember that they are valuable tools but that they do not replace individual judgment and insight into organizational dynamics.

> **LEARNING CHECK**
>
> You should now be able to describe the nature and importance of control techniques and indicate their strengths and weaknesses.

BUDGETS

> ☐ A *budget*—a plan expressed in quantitative terms—helps coordinate resources, define control standards, provide guidelines for resources, and evaluate performance.

Budgets are perhaps the most widely used and universally known control techniques available.[2] A **budget** is simply a plan expressed in quantitative terms. Budgeting, then, is the process of developing budgets.

Budgets serve four basic purposes. They help coordinate resources and projects; they define standards used in other control systems and activities; they provide clear and unambiguous guidelines about resources; and they facilitate appraisals of managerial and departmental performance.

Because of the importance and pervasiveness of budgets in organizations, we need to explore them in detail. First, let's look at the budgeting process. We can then identify different types of budgets and fixed and variable costs, important parts of most budgets. Finally, we'll see how to manage the budgeting process effectively.

The Budgeting Process

◻ In the typical *budgeting process,* top managers request proposals from lower-level managers and integrate these to develop the overall organizational budget.

The **budgeting process** is unique for every organization—that is, every organization comes to follow a budgeting process that fits its own culture and style. Thus we cannot identify a process that is representative of all organizations. However, many organizations follow the general pattern of budgeting, shown in Exhibit 17.1. [3]

As a starting point, top management usually issues a call for budget requests, a step indicated in the exhibit by arrow 1. As we can see, the first demand usually goes from top to middle-level managers. The top managers usually accompany this call with some indication of what resources are available during the coming time period. For example, they might point out that sales and profits are increasing and therefore encourage requests for budget increases. Alternatively, they could ask for cutbacks. As a part of strategic planning, the top managers might also indicate that some units will have higher or lower priorities than in the past.

Exhibit 17.1 The Budgeting Process

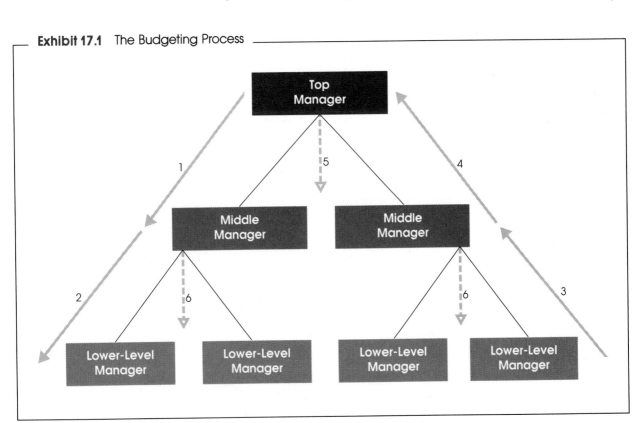

Step two parallels step one in that middle managers request budget proposals from lower-level managers. They provide the same basic information, but it pertains more to individual subunits than to the overall division.

In step three, the lower-level managers prepare budget requests and forward them to the appropriate middle managers. In general, these requests summarize the unit's current resources, account for how those resources have been used, and point out what resources are needed for the next period (usually one year) and how those resources will be used.

The middle manager then coordinates and integrates the various requests. For instance, two department heads in a college of business might each request $10,000 to buy five computers. The dean knows that an order of ten computers carries a 10 percent discount, so the college will request $18,000 to buy ten computers.

As indicated by arrow 4, middle managers then forward their division requests to top management, which in turn coordinates and integrates these requests. Some will be returned to middle management for further work. Others will be approved as is. Still others will be modified by top management, with little or no input from below.

The last step, as indicated by arrows 5 and 6, is to pass final budgets back down the organization. In some cases middle managers will still have the option of modifying their subunits' budgets, whereas in other cases the final budgets are provided all the way down the hierarchy.[4]

Types of Budgets

In most organizations several different types of budgets are produced.[5] The most common of these are shown in Table 17.1.

□ *Financial budgets* detail where the organization intends to get its cash and how it intends to use it.

FINANCIAL BUDGETS **Financial budgets** detail where the organization intends to get its cash for the coming period and how it intends to use it. Most money comes from sales revenues, the sale of assets, loans, and the sale of stock. This money is used to pay for expenses, to repay debt, to purchase new assets, and to pay dividends to stockholders.

A **cash flow budget** outlines precisely where the money will come from and how it will be used for the coming period (usually a quarter or a year). If incoming funds will not cover needs, the organization must make other plans, such as getting loans or deferring payments. Surplus cash, in contrast, can be invested. Martin Marietta, a large defense contractor, uses cash flow budgets effectively as tools to bid for lucrative government contracts.[6]

Capital expenditure budgets are used to plan for the acquisition of such major assets as new equipment, entire plants, and land. Such assets are often paid for with borrowed funds, so even large firms like Ford and AT&T need to control their use carefully.

The **balance sheet budget** is a projection of what the assets and liabilities of the firm will look like at the end of the coming period. The balance sheet is discussed in more detail in a later section.[7]

TABLE 17.1
Types of Budgets

Major Type	Subtypes
Financial budgets	Cash flow budget Capital expenditure budget Balance sheet budget
Operations budgets	Revenue budget Expense budget Profit budget
Nonmonetary budgets	Output budget Labor budget Space budget

☐ *Operations budgets present operational details in financial terms.*

OPERATIONS BUDGETS   **Operations budgets** relate to all or a portion of the organization's operations for the coming period. In particular, they present the various details of operations in financial terms.

A very important budget for all organizations is the **revenue budget.** For a business like Colgate-Palmolive or Avis, revenues come from sales, but a university derives its revenues from legislative appropriations, tuition and fees, and government contracts for research. Regardless of the source, the revenue budget is extremely important because it is the starting point for virtually all other budgeting.

The **expense budget** is the counterpart of the revenue budget. It summarizes the projected expenses for the organization over the coming period. The **profit budget** simply presents the difference between projected revenues and projected expenses.

☐ *Nonmonetary budgets express important variables in terms other than dollars.*

NONMONETARY BUDGETS   **Nonmonetary budgets** are budgets that express important variables in terms other than dollars. For example, an **output budget** may project how many of each of the organization's products will be produced. A **labor budget** details the number of direct hours of labor that are available, and a **space budget** can be used to allocate plant or office space to different divisions or groups within the organization.[8]

Fixed and Variable Costs in Budgeting

In Chapter 5 we noted the distinction between fixed and variable costs. **Fixed costs** are those incurred regardless of the level of operations. Examples include rent, taxes, minimum utility payments, interest payments, and guaranteed salaries. **Variable costs** are those that vary as a function of operations. Raw materials that go into each product, electricity used to operate machines, and commissions paid are all variable costs.

There are also **semivariable costs,** which vary as a function of output but not necessarily in a direct fashion. Advertising, for instance, varies in response to competition and seasonal sales patterns. Equipment repairs, maintenance, and labor are also semivariable costs.

When developing budgets, managers need to try to account for all three kinds of costs. Obviously, fixed costs are the easiest to assess, and semivariable costs the most difficult. If the managers don't give each kind of cost adequate consideration, however, the budget may not serve its intended purpose, and the organization could end up with unexpected cash shortfalls at the end of the period. Because these types of costs are so important, managers are trying to find new ways to control them.[9]

Managing the Budgeting Process

Clearly, budgets are an important facet of organizational life in general and of control in particular. Table 17.2 summarizes the strengths and weaknesses of budgets, which managers must understand if they are to manage the budgeting process effectively.[10]

Budgets can be characterized by four basic strengths. First, they facilitate control, as the foregoing discussion should make obvious. They also facilitate coordination. This stems from the fact that middle managers integrate the budgets of lower-level managers, and top managers subsequently integrate the budgets submitted by the middle managers for the overall organization.

Budgets also aid documentation. They are almost always written down, so there is a permanent record of expectations and actual performance. Finally, budgets help the planning process. As we have seen, planning and control are linked; given the pervasive role of budgeting in control, it is logical that budgets are also an important part of planning. Indeed, a budget has been defined as a plan.

Of course, budgets have certain weaknesses as well. For one thing, some managers make the mistake of using them too rigidly. If the manager fails to consider the situation and looks at the numbers in a mechanical way, he may lose important related information. Budgeting is also a time-consuming process. To do it right, every manager must invest considerable time, effort, and energy in making the budget as effective as possible. Third, budgets occasionally limit innovation. In a company like Texas Instruments, for example, if all funds are allocated to operating groups and divisions, the organization might have trouble raising money for unexpected opportunities.

Andy Freeberg

Many organizations use a Chief Financial Officer (CFO) to help maintain control of the firm's financial resources. Fran Rathke, shown here, is preparing to take over the CFO position at Ben & Jerry's, a fast-growing ice cream concern.

TABLE 17.2
Managing the Budgeting Process

Strengths	Weaknesses
Facilitates control	Subject to rigidity
Facilitates coordination	Time consuming
Facilitates documentation	Limits innovation
Facilitates planning	Reinforces inefficiency

Fourth, the way budgets are used frequently reinforces inefficiency. The manager who is efficient (who spends less than her budget) may find that her budget is reduced in the next cycle. On the other hand, a manager who is inefficient (who spends over his budget) may find his budget increased in the next cycle. This common practice occurs because higher-level managers are not carefully examining the assumptions and conditions under which the budget was developed.

A key method many managers have come to use to enhance the strengths and to minimize the weaknesses inherent in budgeting is participation. The greater the role lower-level managers have in developing their budget, the more likely they are to make sure that it is useful. They will work hard to justify the funds they want and to use those funds wisely. Of course, the same holds true for middle managers as they develop budgets for entire divisions or operating groups.[11]

LEARNING CHECK

You should now be able to discuss the budgeting process, types of budgets, costs used in budgeting, and how to manage the budgeting process.

FINANCIAL ANALYSIS

Another important technique for control is financial analysis. Whereas budgets are used to plan and control an organization's future financial expenditures, financial analysis helps managers study an organization's financial status at a given point in time. Using financial analysis, which consists of several techniques, managers are better able to understand and control the monetary aspects of an organization. Two of the most important techniques are ratio analysis and audits.[12]

Ratio Analysis

☐ Managers use balance sheets and income statements to perform *ratio analysis,* a calculation of various financial possibilities.

☐ A *balance sheet* depicts an organization's financial position at a given time.

BALANCE SHEET AND INCOME STATEMENT **Ratio analysis** involves calculating and evaluating any number of ratios of figures obtained from an organization's balance sheet and income statement. This analysis can be used internally or externally to obtain information about companies' financial positions.[13] A **balance sheet** is a cross-sectional picture of an organization's financial position at a given time. A simplified balance sheet for a small manufacturing firm is presented in Exhibit 17.2.

The left side of the sheet summarizes the **assets,** those things the company has that are of value. Current assets are those that are fairly liquid, or easily convertible into cash, such as cash, accounts receivable, and inventory. Fixed assets are those that are less liquid and that play a longer-term role in the organization, such as land, plant, and equipment.

The right side of the balance sheet summarizes the firm's **liabilities**—debts and other financial obligations—and **owners' equity,** or claims against the assets. Current liabilities are those that must be paid in the near future and include accounts payable and accrued expenses, such as salaries earned by workers but not yet paid. Long-term liabilities are bank loans amortized over a several-year period and payments on bonds. Stockholders' (owners') equity

Exhibit 17.2 A Sample Balance Sheet

		Ajax Manufacturing			
		Balance Sheet			
		December 31, 1990			
Current assets			**Current liabilities**		
Cash	$ 10,000		Accounts payable	$ 60,000	
Receivables	10,000		Accrued expenses	20,000	
Inventory	140,000		Long-term liabilities	150,000	
	160,000			230,000	
Fixed assets			**Stockholders' equity**		
Land	60,000		Common stock	200,000	
Plant equipment	400,000		Retained earnings	190,000	
	460,000			390,000	
Total current and			Total liabilities		
fixed assets	$ 620,000		and equity	$ 620,000	

> □ An *income statement* enables managers to add up the organization's revenues and subtract expenses and liabilities to obtain a profit or loss figure.

consists of common stock and retained earnings. Retained earnings are profits held by the company for expansion, research and development, or debt servicing. As shown in the exhibit, the totals on each side of the balance sheet must be equal.

Whereas the balance sheet reflects a point in time, the **income statement** summarizes several activities over a period of time. In general, a company prepares an income statement on an annual basis and a balance sheet for the point in time at which the income statement ends. For instance, the balance sheet in the exhibit reflects the firm's position as of December 31, 1990. Exhibit 17.3 presents a simplified income statement for the same organization for the year ending December 31, 1990. Essentially, the income statement shows how the accountant adds up all the revenues of the organization and then subtracts all the expenses and other liabilities. The so-called bottom line is the profit or loss realized by the firm.

> □ Commonly used ratios include *liquidity ratios, current ratios, debt ratios, returns on assets, profitability ratios,* and *operating ratios.*

RATIOS Data from both the balance sheet and the income statement provide useful benchmarks for assessing an organization's overall financial health, especially when expressed as any of several commonly used ratios.

Liquidity ratios assess how easily the assets of the organization can be converted into cash. When a bank lends money to a small business, for example, it might be interested in learning how quickly it could recover its money if the business folded. The **current ratio,** the most commonly used liquidity ratio, is determined by dividing current assets by current liabilities. Thus the cur-

Exhibit 17.3   A Sample Income Statement

Ajax Manufacturing
Income Statement
For the Year Ending December 31, 1990

Gross sales		$ 806,000
Less returns	$ 6,000	
Net sales		800,000
Less expenses and cost of goods sold		
—Expenses	120,000	
—Depreciation	40,000	
—Cost of goods sold	400,000	560,000
Operating profit		240,000
Other income		20,000
Interest expense	30,000	
Taxable income		230,000
Less taxes	110,000	
Net income		$ 120,000

rent ratio for Ajax Manufacturing (see Exhibit 17.2) is $160,000 ÷ $80,000, or 2. The ratio is expressed in the form of 2:1, which means that Ajax has two dollars of liquid assets for each dollar of short-term liability. This is considered to be a fairly healthy ratio.

Debt ratios are intended to reflect the firm's ability to handle its long-term debt. The most common debt ratio is found by dividing total liabilities by total assets. This debt ratio for Ajax is $230,000 ÷ $620,000, or .37. This indicates that the organization has .37 dollar in debt for each dollar of assets. The higher the ratio, the poorer the financial health of the organization.

The return on assets (ROA) is usually of more interest to potential investors. It tells them how effectively the organization is using its assets to earn additional profits. The normal method for calculating this ratio is to divide net income by total assets (see Exhibits 17.2 and 17.3). Thus, the ROA for Ajax is $120,000 ÷ $620,000, or .19. This figure is the percentage return achieved by Ajax over the twelve-month period. It means that the company earned 19 cents of profit for each dollar in assets it controlled. Since most savings accounts earn only about 5 percent, an ROA of .19 is very good. Therefore, investors would probably think that Ajax was a good investment.

Other ratios are occasionally used, of course. **Return on equity (ROE)** is net income divided by owners' equity. For Ajax, ROE is $120,000 ÷ $390,000, or .3. This would then be compared with previous figures and to other companies in the industry to get an indication of how well Ajax is doing.

Profitability ratios indicate the relative effectiveness of an organization. For example, $1 million in profits from sales of $10 million (.1) is quite good, whereas a profit of $1 million on sales of $100 million (.01) is not so good.

Operating ratios can also be useful. The index obtained by dividing the total cost of goods sold by the average daily inventory, for instance, provides a good indication of how efficiently the organization is forecasting sales and ordering merchandise.

Audits

☐ An *audit* is an independent appraisal of an organization's accounting, financial, and operational systems.

Another important part of financial analysis is the **audit,** an independent appraisal of an organization's accounting, financial, and operational systems. An audit may be either external or internal,[14] and care must be taken to ensure that audits are of high quality.[15]

EXTERNAL AUDITS   **External audits** are conducted by experts who do not work directly for the organization. Most often these experts are employed by an accounting firm, such as Peat, Marwick, Mitchell & Co. Their purpose is to evaluate closely the appropriateness of the company's controls and reporting procedures and to report their findings to relevant parties such as stockholders and the IRS. Publicly held corporations—that is, corporations whose stock is traded on public markets and can be purchased by anyone—must conduct external audits on a regular basis.

External auditors are extremely thorough. In some cases they even visit warehouses to count inventory in order to verify the accuracy of the firm's balance sheets. Auditors who are found to have made mistakes may lose their reputations and even their licenses, so they are generally very careful. Virtually all smaller firms, and many medium-sized ones, conduct external audits at least on an annual basis.

PRELUDE CASE UPDATE

In the Blockbuster case, the use of an external audit with the results made available directly to investors would probably have done a great deal to alleviate concerns about its accounting control techniques. Such an audit would have verified not only the accuracy of information being presented but also the appropriateness of the specific techniques being used.

INTERNAL AUDITS   **Internal audits** are conducted by people who work directly for the organization. Their purpose is the same as that of external auditors: to verify the accuracy of the organization's reporting system. Internal audits tend to go further, however, and also deal with matters of efficiency. For example, if an organization's accounting system is technically accurate but somewhat inefficient, an external audit will verify the system's accuracy but ignore the efficiency problem, whereas an internal audit will deal with both.

Most large firms have internal auditing staffs. It is considerably cheaper to maintain these staffs than to rely totally on the services of an external accounting firm.[16] Internal auditors spend much of their time auditing various subunits or divisions of the organization.

In many ways, internal auditors are more valuable than external auditors. Besides uncovering a variety of problems, they tend to be very familiar with all the inner workings of the organization. Even when an organization has an internal auditing staff, though, it periodically uses an external auditing group to provide an independent assessment of its practices. And well-kept records are crucial to both internal and external auditors and can influence a company's fortune in many ways.

OTHER CONTROL TECHNIQUES

Although financial and operations control are the primary concerns of most businesses, other important areas of control should not be neglected. Two of these are human resource control and marketing control.

Human Resource Control

Human resource control focuses on the work force of the organization. In particular, it is concerned with the extent to which members of the work force are productive and the extent to which the organization is effectively managing them.

☐ Performance appraisal is a crucial aspect of human resource control.

PERFORMANCE APPRAISAL   The primary way in which an organization controls the performance of its employees is through performance appraisal. As Chapter 10 pointed out, performance appraisal is the way the organization determines individuals' level of performance.[17] From a control standpoint, it helps the manager monitor the performance of employees, compare that performance with desired standards, and address any problems or deficiencies that she finds.

Indeed, the basic steps in performance appraisal parallel those in control very closely. First, using job analysis, the organization determines the exact content of each job and then assesses how much each person should produce. For example, the work of a machine operator might be defined as adjusting machine settings, working metal parts through the machine, and inspecting the final product, and management might further decide that the desired level of output per operator is 144 dozen parts. This standard is then used as a part of the standard performance appraisal—say, the supervisor checks the output of each operator under his control every month.

The actual performance is then measured against the standard, and appropriate action is taken. Jack may be producing more than 160 dozen parts per day, so he should be complimented and perhaps given a small pay raise. Laverne may be producing around 146 dozen parts per day; the supervisor can tell her she's doing a good job and leave it at that. If Joe is found to be producing only 98 dozen parts per day, appropriate action might include counseling, encouraging him to work harder, and training. If things don't improve, the supervisor can transfer him to another job or perhaps even fire him.

HUMAN RESOURCE RATIOS   Managers can also use any of several human resource ratios to assess the degree to which the organization is managing its work force properly. Three of the more important ones are turnover, absenteeism, and work force composition.[18]

□ The percentage of the work force that leaves over a time period is called *turnover;* the percentage that is absent on a given day is called *absenteeism.*

Turnover is the percentage of the organization's work force that leaves and must be replaced over a period of time, usually one year. Companies like McDonald's and Pizza Hut experience high levels of turnover, occasionally as high as 100 percent, whereas companies like K mart have moderate turnover and those like General Motors have relatively little turnover. The manager needs to know what the acceptable turnover is for both her firm and the industry. If turnover increases or is higher than the industry average, she will need to take steps, such as increasing wages to meet the industry standard, to get things back in line.

Absenteeism is the percentage of an organization's work force that is absent on a given day. Absenteeism may range from only a few percent to as high as 20 or 30 percent. It is especially troublesome on Monday and Friday, when employees use sick time to extend their weekends. Again, the key for the manager is to know what the acceptable level of absenteeism is in the organization and the industry and to take steps if it gets out of line. He might issue warnings about excessive absences, for instance, or offer incentives to those who do not call in sick.

□ *Work force composition ratios* tell managers about the demographic characteristics of employees.

Work force composition ratios are indicators of how many of the organization's employees fall into various groups. For example, the manager may need to know how many of the organization's employees are black, Hispanic, female, handicapped, and over the age of forty-five. If the general labor market from which the firm hires its employees contains a higher proportion of such groups, the company may be guilty of discrimination. That is, if blacks make up 25 percent of the potential work force, yet only 10 percent of the firm's employees are black, discrimination may be occurring. The obvious step in this case is to eliminate such discriminatory practices.

Marketing Control

Another area that is important for control is **marketing**—the set of activities involved in getting consumers to want the goods and services provided by the organization.[19] As indicated in *Management Today: The World Of Management,* marketing control can help a troubled organization revive itself. Two common

MANAGEMENT TODAY

THE WORLD OF MANAGEMENT

British Airways Flies Right

While operated as a government-owned enterprise, British Airways (BA) became known as "Bloody Awful." Losses by the early 1980s mounted to nearly $1 billion. Something had to be done, and something was. British Airways was privatized (converted to a private enterprise) in 1987 and put under the control of a new team of managers. Since that time major carriers such as Pan Am, TWA, and Eastern have gone into decline, but BA has taken off. The control techniques employed by the new management team have involved four components: organizational arrangements, technology, costs, and customers.

Organizational arrangements such as acquisitions and joint ventures have been used to match the route structure to the travel patterns of customers. An example is the arrangement with United Airlines in the United States to share ground facilities and customer services and to jointly develop and market vacation packages that involve the use of both carriers.

Advanced technology has been put in place to more effectively control schedules, maintenance, baggage handling, and food service. In addition, marketing programs that use polished techniques and vivid graphics to reach specifically targeted audiences have been implemented.

Costs have been brought under control through the sale of surplus aircraft and a massive reduction of the work force (from around 60,000 to about 36,000 employees). British Airways also switched banks and advertising agencies to obtain new and more favorable contracts to further reduce costs.

The most dramatic control, however, has been its marketing focus on customers. The changes already noted were all directed at achieving market control by more clearly responding to customers' wants and needs, but British Airways did other things as well. Cabin service was upgraded. Business-class lounges were designed to lure business travelers. At selected airport facilities, passengers can videotape comments or criticisms to be viewed later by the company. Hunters have been stationed throughout London's Heathrow Airport to locate and assist passengers having difficulties of any kind. Employees all attend a two-day seminar on "putting people first" to learn to see things from their passengers' perspectives.

The result of these control techniques has been dramatic. By the late 1980s, British Airways' profits and profit margins on sales were among the highest in the industry. Its average revenue per passenger also was among the industry's highest. And its market share had increased; it ranked among the top in terms of passengers carried and passenger miles flown.

SOURCES: "Buttering Up Passengers," *Business Week*, March 12, 1990, p. 94; "High-Flying Image: British Airways Integrates WIIS," *Informationweek*," February 19, 1990, p. 46; "The World's Best Airlines," *Institutional Investor*, June 1, 1989, pp. 195–208; "British Airways Empire," *Business Week*, October 9, 1989, pp. 97–101; Kenneth Labich, "The Big Comeback at British Airways," *Fortune*, December 5, 1988, pp. 163–174.

□ *Test marketing* is introducing a new product on a limited scale to assess customers' reactions to it.

approaches to marketing control are test marketing and assessing important marketing ratios.

TEST MARKETING **Test marketing** involves introducing a new product on a limited basis in order to assess consumer reaction on a small scale. Say that Wendy's creates a new sandwich and sells and advertises it only in Missouri and Kansas. If it is successful, Wendy's will introduce it in all Wendy's restaurants. If it is unsuccessful, the company might decide not to introduce it anywhere else, and it will be dropped from the menu in Missouri and Kansas as well.

The advantage of test marketing is that it minimizes the risk of losing large sums of money by introducing a new product nationally and then watching it fail. Test marketing also allows the firm to make adjustments and refinements based on limited consumer responses before committing itself to national introduction.

In recent years there has been a trend away from test marketing because it is slow and gives competitors time to copy and perhaps get ahead of the company with new products. The new approach being tried by some companies is shown in Exhibit 17.4.

Under the traditional approach, also shown in the exhibit, new products are developed and then test marketed. The results are assessed quantitatively (that is, actual sales are measured), modifications are made, and the product is then introduced via a full-scale marketing effort. Under the new approach, products are developed and then assessed intuitively by the firm's managers and perhaps by very limited consumer panels. If things look positive, the product is introduced full-scale.

Sara Lee, Ralston Purina, and Frito-Lay have all adopted this approach.[20] The risk, of course, is that if the product fails, the company loses a lot of money. On the other hand, the company may be able to get a big jump on the competition and save the expenses of test marketing if it guesses right.

Marketing control is often achieved through such methods as test marketing. Peacock Papers Inc. has set up its own store for use in test marketing. President Sharon P. Cavanaugh, shown here, believes the store allows her company to stay on top of consumer tastes and wants.

© Mark Alcarez 1990

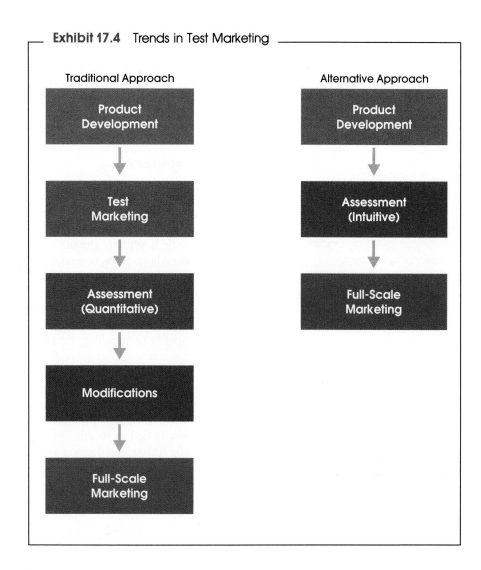

Exhibit 17.4   Trends in Test Marketing

Traditional Approach

Product Development

↓

Test Marketing

↓

Assessment (Quantitative)

↓

Modifications

↓

Full-Scale Marketing

Alternative Approach

Product Development

↓

Assessment (Intuitive)

↓

Full-Scale Marketing

MARKETING RATIOS   There are also several ratios that are useful in marketing control. Perhaps the most common is **market share,** the proportion of the total market controlled by the firm's products. If the total market for a particular product is 1,000,000 units per year and a certain company sells 100,000 units, its market share is 10 percent. A common goal of many organizations is to increase market share through increased advertising, promotion, and so forth. Decreases in market share, of course, are a source of considerable concern.

Profit margin on sales is another useful marketing ratio. This is determined by dividing net income by sales. The higher the ratio is, the more effective the organization is in managing its marketing function. When the profit margin is calculated for each product a firm sells, managers can learn which products are contributing the most in profits.

COMPUTERS AND CONTROL

Perhaps the biggest change ever to affect the control function of management has been prompted by the increased presence of computers in the workplace.[21] They are now being used to perform almost every task conceivable; for instance, they are even being used in interviewing.

Kinds of Computers

□ *Mainframe computers are the largest and most expensive, so most organizations use minicomputers and micro-, or desktop, computers.*

In general, there are three basic kinds of computers. **Mainframe computers** are the very large, very expensive machines most people think of when they hear the word *computer*—the huge monoliths that occupy entire rooms. Such computers can handle enormous amounts of information in fractions of a second. They cost anywhere from several hundreds or thousands of dollars to millions. In reality, only the largest businesses and major research centers and universities are able to buy mainframe computers.

Minicomputers are the type that most medium-sized and large businesses have. Such machines cost from around $25,000 to a few hundred thousand dollars and are capable of handling relatively large amounts of information very efficiently.

Microcomputers, more commonly known as personal computers, are the desk top machines that have become popular in recent years. These machines, which usually cost between several hundred and a few thousand dollars, can often handle all the information processing needs of managers. In addition, they serve as terminals tied in to minicomputers or the company mainframe, and they can also be linked together via an information network.

Contributions to Control

The primary role of the computer in control is to give managers access to more information in ways that are faster and more accurate. For example, Shop 'n Save is a chain of grocery stores in New England. Its managers have precise figures on profit margins for over 17,000 items in sixty-five different stores, thanks to a centralized mainframe computer that is linked to terminals in each of the stores.

Another area of improvement has been in inventory management. In the old days, stores counted their inventory annually, and this was the only time they knew precisely what their total inventory was. Today's computer networks can automatically enter new orders and subtract individual sales; thus the manager has a perpetual inventory and always knows what inventory levels are.[22] And hand-held or other portable computers linked to the company's main computer through telephone devices called modems can provide a better exchange of information between the organization's field or sales personnel and the home office.

Advantages and Disadvantages

Not surprisingly, there are both pluses and minuses to using computers in organizational control.[23] One critical strength is storage capacity. Computers can store enormous amounts of information in a very small space. They are also very fast; they can process information and perform calculations many times faster than people can. And they tend to be extremely accurate. If the computer has the proper operating system and instructions and accurate data, errors are very rare.

But computers are still quite costly. A medium-range personal computer, for instance, costs around $2,000. Another problem is overreliance. As discussed in Chapter 11, managers tend to believe everything the computer "tells" them, without considering their own experience and intuition. A third problem is that computers are complex and difficult for some people to learn to use. Such complexity can serve as a barrier to innovation and limit the potential value of the computer to the organization.

LEARNING CHECK

You should now be able to name several kinds of computers and discuss their contributions to the control process and the advantages and disadvantages of using them.

Chapter Summary

Control techniques are the tools that managers use to enhance organizational effectiveness in general, and organizational control in particular. The major strengths of control techniques are that they provide objective indicators of how the organization is doing and road maps for action. The weaknesses are that they can be rigid and uncompromising and also subject to misuse.

Although the particulars of the budget process are unique for every organization, the process usually starts at the top of the organization with a call for budgets, which is then transmitted downward throughout the whole organization. Working from the lowest levels upward, budget requests are then developed and moved up through the organization. After one or more attempts, the final budgets are sent back down.

There are three basic types of budgets: financial, operations, and nonmonetary. Financial budgets include cash flow budgets, capital expenditure budgets, and balance sheet budgets. Operations budgets include revenue budgets, expense budgets, and profit budgets. Nonmonetary budgets include output budgets, labor budgets, and space budgets.

Budgeting involves fixed, variable, and semivariable costs. Fixed costs are those incurred regardless of the level of operations. Variable costs are those that vary relatively directly with the level of operations. Semivariable costs also vary with the level of operations, but not in a direct fashion. The weaknesses of budgeting are that it can be used too rigidly, can be very time consuming, can limit innovation, and can be used to reward inefficiency. Its strengths are that it makes planning, coordination, and control easier and also provides documentation in case of controversy and for future reference.

Financial analysis refers to techniques and methods used to understand and control the monetary aspects of an organization. The most important types are ratio analysis and audits. Ratio analysis involves calculating and evaluating any number of ratios of figures obtained from an organization's balance sheet and income statement. Audits are independent appraisals of the company's accounting, financial, and operational systems. External audits are performed by experts who do not work directly for the organization. Internal audits are conducted by those who do.

Control techniques have been developed for every area of organizational performance, not just financial and operational performance. Two of the more important areas are human resource control and marketing control. Human resource control focuses on the members of the organization. Marketing refers to those activities that get consumers to want the goods and services of the company.

Computers are used in control because of their ability to handle enormous amounts of information in fractions of a second. Because they are fast and accurate, and have large storage capacities, they are invaluable control aids. However, they can be expensive and difficult to use, and some managers over-rely on computer data.

The Manager's Vocabulary

budget	income statement
budgeting process	liquidity ratio
financial budgets	current ratio
cash flow budget	debt ratio
capital expenditure budget	return on assets (ROA)
	return on equity (ROE)
balance sheet budget	profitability ratio
operations budgets	operating ratio
revenue budget	audit
expense budget	external audit
profit budget	internal audit
nonmonetary budgets	turnover
output budget	absenteeism
labor budget	work force composition
space budget	ratio
fixed costs	marketing
variable costs	test marketing
semivariable costs	market share
ratio analysis	profit margin on sales
balance sheet	mainframe computers
assets	minicomputers
liabilities	microcomputers
owners' equity	

Prelude Case Wrap-Up

Our Prelude Case for this chapter describes Blockbuster, a highly successful video rental chain. Whereas its size in terms of numbers of outlets has been expanding rapidly, the financial picture for Blockbuster has been less clear. Blockbuster uses the maximum allowable accounting period for charging goodwill. Although allowable, that approach has the effect of overstating short-term profits and understat-ing long-term profits. Further, Blockbuster charges its franchisees a one-time fee that it treats completely as revenue in the year of payment. That practice tends to present the maximum interpretation of revenues, which also presents as positive a financial picture as possible. Clearly, the combined impact is to present a very favorable picture of profits, revenues, and growth potential for Blockbuster.

This very favorable picture of Blockbuster's financial health, however, is not the only one that could be drawn. As we have seen, if both methods were altered substantially, investors would have a drastically different picture of the firm's financial health. Some critics of Blockbuster argue that it should take a less optimistic position with regard to these accounting controls and present at least a more intermediate picture. An alternative picture, of course, would have affected the sales of Blockbuster stock and might have even made it more difficult for Blockbuster to continue to obtain the financing that was necessary to sustain its continued rapid growth. Thus the controls Blockbuster uses could have many different effects, both internally and externally.

Prelude Case Questions

1. Which concepts presented in this chapter are illustrated in the Blockbuster case? Cite specific examples.
2. What major control techniques does Blockbuster use?
3. What are the strengths and weaknesses of Block-buster's control techniques? How might the weaknesses be offset?
4. Do you feel that Blockbuster will continue to be as successful in the future as it has in the past? Why or why not?

Discussion Questions

Review Questions

1. What are the strengths and weaknesses of control techniques?
2. Describe the budgeting process. What are the several types of budgets?
3. What is financial analysis, and how is it used by organizations?

4. What are the major types of human resource control? Marketing control?

5. What are the advantages and disadvantages of using computers in control?

Analysis Questions

1. If a frequent misuse of budgets reinforces inefficiency, why do they continue to be misused?

2. Do all organizations have to use all of the different types of budgets? Why or why not?

3. Comment on this statement: "If you want low turnover, hire incompetents and pay them well."

4. Comment on this statement: "The only real test of a product is to offer it for sale."

5. Despite careful market research, many products fail. Why is this true? What does this suggest about marketing controls?

Application Questions and Exercises

1. Interview a manager from a local organization to identify examples of fixed, variable, and semivariable costs in his or her firm. Share those examples with your class.

2. Identify five organizations that you feel are particularly good ones. Obtain information for as many different financial ratios as you can for each of them. Is the same firm strong in all ratios? Why or why not?

3. Interview local managers of a business and a not-for-profit organization about the control techniques they use. How are they similar? How are they different?

4. Would it be as easy to appraise the performance of a typist as of a scientist? A teacher as a brickmason? A telephone line repairer as a steelworker? What difficulties in appraising performance are reflected here?

5. Interview managers who have used computers to obtain their views on the advantages and disadvantages of using computers in control.

ENHANCEMENT CASE

MAKING THE ORIOLES SING

Eli S. Jacobs built himself a fortune through astute investments. Most of those investments involved companies that he was able to turn around into huge successes through the use of careful control. Among the more notable of those companies are Memorex International and Telex Corporation. But, when he bought the Baltimore Orioles baseball team in 1988, many people felt that he had gone too far. The Orioles had begun that season with a twenty-one game losing streak—the longest opening losing streak in baseball history. They went on to spend most of the season at the bottom of the rankings, in the cellar. No one believed that the team could be turned around quickly. The next season, however, saw the Orioles back near the top of their division finishing in second place.

What Jacobs knew but apparently many fans did not was that the organization was not in any financial trouble and that steps had already been taken to improve team performance before he bought it. Even during the team's disastrous 1988 season, the organization was sound financially and earning a profit for its owner. Further, that owner, Edward Bennett Williams, had given the operating executives (President Lawrence Lucchino and General Manager, Roland A. Hemond) permission to begin cutting the player roster drastically.

The openings in the roster were filled with new players and veterans who had been laid off from other clubs. Since most of the cuts were of high-paid veterans, these actions reduced the average salary paid to Orioles players from $425,000 to $234,000, making it the lowest in the league. Further, since these changes were so dramatic, they excited fans (not all of whom agreed with the moves, but all of whom seemed to want to see the results), and season ticket sales increased by 10 percent. When the team of relatively unknown players began to win game after game, ticket sales at the gate set near records—well over two million for the season.

While Jacobs was clearly changing things for a winning season in the future, the team manager, Frank Robinson, was pushing the team to win immediately. He carefully built its enthusiasm by talking about its history, how it had won the pennant in 1966 and the East Division in 1969, '70, '71, '73, '74, '79, and '83. In three of those years (1966, 1970, and 1983) the team had even gone on to win the world championship. Robinson told the players that they could do so again. He noted that they were young and that, with top performance, they could earn more in the future. The players responded to these efforts by pushing themselves to their limits, by becoming highly successful overachievers.

The future for which Jacobs was changing things includes a major new stadium. Due to open in 1992, the new stadium will seat nearly 47,000 and will have 70 luxury suites as well as 5,000 premium seats. Suites will sell for about $60,000, and premium seats will go for $20 per game. If attendance remains high, Jacobs will have demonstrated that he has an almost uncanny knack for investing in successful turnaround efforts. The careful implementation of cost, human resource, and marketing controls contributed in large part to those successes.

Former professional baseball star and Hall-of-Famer Frank Robinson currently serves as manager of the Baltimore Orioles. Like any other organization, the Orioles must practice effective control if it is to survive.

SOURCES: Tracy Ringolsby, "Interview: Frank Robinson," *Inside Sports*, April 1, 1990, pp. 22–29; "For the Orioles, Less Is More—It's First Place," *Business Week*, July 10, 1989, p. 34; Peter Gemmons, "A Flight to the Finish," *Sports Illustrated*, October 2, 1989, pp. 48–51; Steve Wulf, "O You Beautiful Birds," *Sports Illustrated*, June 16, 1989, pp. 26–33; "SPORT: Baseball's Pennant Passion Reaches a Peak," *Time*, October 2, 1989, pp. 96–97.

Enhancement Case Questions

1. What similarities and differences can you note between the control techniques of the Orioles and those of Blockbuster from the Prelude Case?
2. Describe the Orioles' control techniques. What methods described in the chapter can you identify? Cite specific examples of each of them.
3. What might be the weaknesses of the control techniques used by the Orioles? How might it reduce any such weaknesses?
4. What do you feel the Orioles could do to make its control techniques function even better in the future? How or in what way would your suggestions improve its techniques?

Chapter Notes

1. "Flexible Budget System a Practical Approach to Cost Management," *Healthcare Financial Management*, January 1, 1989, pp. 38–53.
2. Belverd E. Needles, Jr., Henry R. Anderson, and James C. Caldwell, *Principles of Accounting*, 4th ed. (Boston: Houghton Mifflin, 1990).
3. Joe Park, "Budget Systems: Make the Right Choice," *Financial Executive*, March 1984, pp. 26–35.
4. Jay W. Lorsch, James P. Baughman, James Reece, and Henry Mintzberg, *Understanding Management* (New York: Harper & Row, 1978).

5. Glenn A. Welsch, *Budgeting: Profit Planning and Control*, 4th ed. (Englewood Cliffs, N.J.: Prentice-Hall, 1976).

6. Thomas Moore, "Why Martin Marietta Loves Mary Cunningham," *Fortune*, March 16, 1987, pp. 66–70.

7. Harry Ernst, "New Balance Sheet for Managing Liquidity and Growth," *Harvard Business Review*, March-April 1984, pp. 122–135.

8. Welsch, *Budgeting*.

9. Robin Cooper, "You Need a New Cost System When . . . ," *Harvard Business Review*, January-February 1989, pp. 77–82.

10. Bess Ritter May, "How Any Supervisor Can Control Company Costs: Be a Budget Watcher," *Supervision*, April 1, 1990, pp. 3–5.

11. Henry L. Tosi, Jr., "The Human Effects of Budgeting Systems on Management," *MSU Business Topics*, Autumn 1974, pp. 53–63.

12. Eugene Brigham, *Financial Management: Theory and Practice*, 4th ed. (Chicago: Dryden, 1985).

13. Raphael Amit and Joshua Livnat, "Grouping of Conglomerates by Their Segments' Economic Attributes: Towards a More Meaningful Ratio Analysis," *Journal of Business Finance & Accounting*, Spring 1990, pp. 85–100.

14. Brigham, *Financial Management*.

15. Douglas A. Clarke and William R. Pasewark, "Establishing Quality Control for Audit Services," *National Public Accountant*, December 1, 1989, pp. 40–44.

16. Wanda Wallace, "Internal Auditors Can Cut Outside CPA Costs," *Harvard Business Review*, March-April 1984, p. 16.

17. Wendell French, *Human Resource Management* (Boston: Houghton Mifflin, 1986).

18. Ibid.

19. William M. Pride and O. C. Ferrell, *Marketing—Concepts and Strategies*, 6th ed. (Boston: Houghton Mifflin, 1989).

20. "Companies Get on Fast Track to Roll Out Hot New Brands," *The Wall Street Journal*, July 10, 1986, p. 25.

21. See Hugh J. Watson and Archie B. Carroll, eds., *Computers for Business* (Plano, Tex.: Business Publications, 1984).

22. "At Today's Supermarket, The Computer Is Doing It All," *Business Week*, August 11, 1986, pp. 64–65.

23. Watson and Carroll, *Computers for Business*.

CHAPTER OUTLINE

I. The Nature of Operations Management
  A. The Meaning of Operations Management
  B. The Importance of Operations Management

II. Planning for Operations
  A. Operations Decisions
  B. Operations Planning

III. Managing Operations
  A. Organizing for Operations
  B. Change and Operations

IV. Operations Control
  A. Inventory Control
  B. Quality Control
  C. Scheduling Control
  D. Cost Control

V. Operations Control Techniques
  A. PERT
  B. MRP

VI. Trends in Operations Management

CHAPTER

18

1. Discuss the nature, meaning, and importance of operations management.

2. Describe operations decisions and operations planning.

3. Indicate what is involved in the management and organization of operations and describe the relationship of change to operations.

4. Discuss operations control in its most important forms—inventory control, quality control, scheduling control, and cost control.

5. Describe operations control techniques, including PERT and MRP.

6. Identify and discuss current trends in operations management.

Operations Management

CUMMINS GRINDS ITS WHEELS FINER

The Cummins Engine Company provides a remarkable case study of how a firm can stand its ground and fight foreign competition. Unfortunately, the jury is still out on whether Cummins is winning or losing its duel.

Cummins was founded in 1919 as a manufacturer of diesel engines. The company struggled to stay afloat for decades: it took eighteen years to even earn a profit. Indeed, it wasn't until World War II that Cummins's future was secured. During the war, the company's engines won rave reviews from the military, and sales skyrocketed.

For the past several years, Cummins has been in the capable hands of Henry B. Schacht. Schacht became vice president of finance in 1964 and promptly turned around Cummins's ailing European division. He was subsequently named president in 1969 and became CEO in 1973.

Schacht toured several Japanese manufacturing facilities shortly after becoming CEO. He quickly saw that the Japanese plants were superior to most U.S. facilities in terms of their layouts, technology, and operating systems. He also saw that if changes were not made at his own firm, the Japanese would someday threaten Cummins's future.

After returning home, Schacht committed more than $1 billion of Cummins's money to overhaul the very fabric of the company's operating systems. Some plants were closed; others were thoroughly modernized. New technology was introduced throughout the organization. Over 3,500 jobs were eliminated, and a variety of productivity improvement measures were implemented.

As it turned out, Cummins's efforts came none too soon. Major Japanese engine manufacturers like Komatsu Ltd. and Nissan Motor Company launched a full-scale assault on the U.S. market in the mid-1980s. Many of Cummins's customers were reporting that the Japanese engines were comparable to those the American firm was manufacturing but were also 25 percent cheaper.

Schacht responded by dropping Cummins's prices by a full one-third. Since quality had never been a problem for Cummins, the Japanese were forced to retreat. Cummins retained its market share and still dominates the market for tractor-trailer trucks.

But Cummins didn't just stand still. Indeed, the company simultaneously launched several generations of new engines. In the past, the firm had concentrated primarily on larger engines. For example, its earliest customers were manufacturers of dump trucks and eighteen-wheelers. More recently, though, the company has developed several midsize and smaller engines. Recent market breakthroughs have included a diesel engine for the Dodge Ram pickup and a line of new motors for pleasure boats and power generators.

Cummins isn't out of the woods yet, however. For one thing, even though the firm has retained its market share and position, its

Cummins Engine Company Photo

Operations management is especially critical to a manufacturing firm such as Cummins Engine Company. The firm's new line of engines, powering such vehicles as the London bus shown here, have greatly increased Cummins's share of the market.

profits are still far below where industry analysts think they should be. For another, although the Japanese retreated, they have not surrendered. Indeed, Komatsu in particular seems to be preparing for another major run at taking market share away from Cummins and establishing itself as a major player in the U.S. market for engines.

But Cummins is also looking to the future. Managers believe that the firm can achieve even greater breakthroughs in quality, costs, and profitability by continuing to refine its manufacturing methods. The centerpiece of their plans is the concept of the flexible factory—a factory that will allow the firm to apply mass-production techniques to the creation of customized products tailored to the needs of individual customers.

SOURCES: Ravi Venkatesian, "Cummins Engine Flexes Its Factory," *Harvard Business Review*, March-April 1990, pp. 120–127; "Was Brierley's Move on Cummins Dumb or Dangerous?" *Business Week*, March 19, 1990, pp. 46–48; "Mr. Rust Belt," *Business Week*, October 17, 1988, pp. 72–78, 82.

B y definition, business organizations provide goods and services to customers. Cummins Engine Company is in the business of manufacturing and selling engines for resale to other manufacturers. In similar fashion, Chevron produces and sells gasoline. Pizza Hut makes and sells pizza. NEC combines thousands of component parts into computers.

The various processes, decisions, and systems involved in the acquisition of resources and the transformation of those resources into the firm's products or services is the domain of operations management. In this chapter we explore the nature of operations management and the connection between planning and operations. The chapter then describes the management of operations, operations control, and a number of operations control techniques. It concludes with a brief description of two important trends in operations management, robotics and automation.

THE NATURE OF OPERATIONS MANAGEMENT

The management of operations is an extremely complex, as well as a very important, function. Indeed, without effective operations management, few organizations could survive for any length of time. Let's now examine both the meaning and the importance of operations management.

The Meaning of Operations Management

□ *Operations management is the total set of managerial activities that an organization uses to transform resources into products and services.*

As already stated in Chapter 2, **operations management** can be defined as the total set of managerial activities used by an organization to transform resource inputs into products and services.[1] Exhibit 18.1 illustrates the true nature of operations management. Recall the discussion of systems theory in Chapter 2. Systems theory holds that organizations consist of four basic parts—inputs, transformation processes, outputs, and feedback. As shown in the exhibit, operations management is primarily concerned with the processes that transform inputs into outputs. At a secondary level, it is also concerned with inputs, outputs, and feedback.

Because of its focus on transformation processes, this aspect of management was historically referred to as production management. In recent years, however, managers have come to realize that many of the basic concepts and approaches previously used in manufacturing were just as applicable to service firms, restaurants, government organizations, not-for-profit organizations, and so forth. Thus, the term *operations* has gradually supplanted *production* because it indicates a broader view.

The Importance of Operations Management

Operations management is a critically important function for all organizations. Cummins faced problems because it could not produce engines as efficiently as

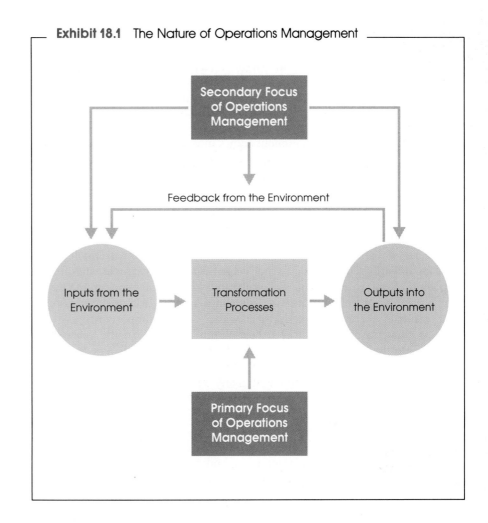

Exhibit 18.1 The Nature of Operations Management

its foreign competitors. Sears has problems if it has too much inventory (carrying costs, spoilage, warehousing expenses) or too little inventory (customer complaints, lost sales) on hand. It also has problems if it has the wrong merchandise or pays too much for its merchandise. Chevron has problems if it cannot refine gasoline efficiently, if it cannot deliver the gas to service stations efficiently, or if it must charge too much for its products. A Pizza Hut restaurant has problems if it has too many or too few ingredients to make pizza, if it produces poor-quality pizzas, or if its service is bad.

The hallmarks of operations management, then, are efficiency and effectiveness—doing things in a way that gets the maximum value from resources, and doing the right things to begin with. Operations management helps Ford determine what parts to make and what parts to buy, when to have them delivered, how they should be combined, and how the finished product will be delivered to the showroom floor. Without an effective operations management system, few organizations would survive.[2]

ETHICAL DILEMMAS OF MANAGEMENT

Responsible Operations Management

Dirty smokestacks belching poisonous fumes into the atmosphere. Massive pipes pumping waste and raw sewage into rivers and streams. Truckloads of dangerous chemical by-products being buried indiscriminantly. Sounds pretty offensive, doesn't it? Yet, firms around the world did just these things for decades. And unfortunately, some still do.

In many ways, technology in general and manufacturing in particular have been major culprits in the despoiling of our environment. For years and years, there were few or no constraints or guidelines as to what companies could do with their waste. The cheapest thing to do, then, was to just dump it—dump it into the air, the water, or underground.

A combination of legislation, public pressure, and enlightened management has brought many of the most dangerous problems at least partially under control. For example, the Environmental Protection Agency helps police businesses to guard against indiscriminate pollution. Public interest groups like the Sierra Club also play an important role. And managers at companies like Dow Chemical and General Electric often go far beyond their legal obligation in protecting the environment. In general, for example, most forms of air pollution have decreased over the past several years. And the ocean dumping of sewage sludge is the only major form of water pollution on the upswing.

Many of the changes made by organizations to address environmental concerns relate to operations. New technology and manufacturing processes, for example, are often designed with environmental protection in mind. The location of facilities and the technologies associated with waste disposal are also important.

In the years ahead, organizations will have other challenges to address. For example, industry is increasingly being pressured to help cope with acid rain, ground-level ozone, global warming, and toxic waste problems. As always, however, managers will have to come to grips with the basic ethical dilemmas that have dogged them for decades—where to draw the line between doing the socially responsible thing and overcommitting profits to environmental cleanup activities.

SOURCES: Jeremy Main, "Here Comes the Big New Cleanup," *Fortune,* November 21, 1988, pp. 102–118; David Kirkpatrick, "Environmentalism: The New Crusade," *Fortune,* February 12, 1990, pp. 44–52; "Environmentalists, State Officers See Red As Firms Rush to Market 'Green' Products," *The Wall Street Journal,* March 13, 1990, p. B1.

LEARNING CHECK

You should now be able to discuss the nature, meaning, and importance of operations management.

Another reason for the importance of operations management is the relationship between an organization and its natural environment. As described more fully in *Management Today: Ethical Dilemmas of Management,* operations systems are an important ingredient in how a firm treats its environment.

PLANNING FOR OPERATIONS

The first stage in effective operations management is planning for operations. This aspect of operations management includes both operations decisions and operations planning.[3]

Operations Decisions

Operations decisions encompass virtually all aspects of the operations management system. There are eight primary areas of decision making. These decisions relate primarily to transformation processes and secondarily to inputs and outputs.

□ An organization's *product/ service line* is the set of products and/or services it sells.

PRODUCT/SERVICE LINE   The **product** or **service line** decision is one of the most crucial decisions an organization makes. It is almost always made by top managers from all relevant functional areas, because the organization's overall strategy determines the general products and/or services on which it will concentrate. That is, Sony deals in consumer electronics, whereas Pepperidge Farm concentrates on baked goods.

Marketing and operations managers then work together to define more precisely what the product line should, can, and will be. Marketing managers at Pepperidge Farm might use consumer research to get information about what products customers want and might then ask operations managers to figure out how best to produce those products. Similarly, operations managers at Sony might realize that producing another version of an existing VCR or stereo system would be very easy and efficient. They would then ask marketing managers to find out whether such a variation would sell at acceptable levels. Thus, product or service line decisions are almost always made jointly by managers from different areas.[4]

□ *Capacity* refers to the space the organization has available to create products and/or services.

CAPACITY   Capacity decisions, which involve determining how much space the organization needs to meet the demand for its products or services most efficiently and effectively, are also an important part of operations management. For example, how many automobiles does Mazda want to produce each year? How much floor space does K mart want to devote to various kinds of merchandise? How many tables does a certain McDonald's restaurant need? These are capacity decisions.

Capacity decisions must be made with great care. If a firm has too much capacity, the result can be a dramatic underutilization of resources. If K mart builds a new store with 150,000 square feet of floor space when 100,000 would have sufficed, the company will have to find uses for the extra space, maintain it, and keep it heated and cooled. Many recent plant closings and cutbacks have been the result of excess capacity.

Too little capacity can be just as damaging, however. For example, a manufacturing plant with insufficient capacity cannot provide an adequate quantity of merchandise and will subsequently lose customers to competitors. Likewise, if retail customers have to wait in line too long, they will get discouraged and shop elsewhere.

In general, the key is to optimize. In most cases demand fluctuates. A restaurant, for instance, might be able to fill eighty tables on Friday night and one hundred on Saturday night. The rest of the week, however, only thirty tables will be filled. Having one hundred tables is probably not efficient; instead, the restaurant should probably have fifty or sixty tables. The excess capacity during the week will probably not be a problem, and on weekends the tables will be filled, although some people will have to wait to be seated and a few will leave. On balance, the organization will probably be most effective if it has more than the minimum capacity it needs but less than the maximum it occasionally will be able to use.

PLANNING SYSTEM   The planning system decision involves determining how operations managers will get the information they need and how they will provide information to other managers. For example, assume an organization uses sales forecasts as a basis for deciding how much of a particular product to make. In the middle of January the operations manager receives a sales forecast for the month of February. He then needs to check current inventory, including work-in-process, and set production levels for February. The information can also go in the other direction—the operations manager may need to keep the marketing manager informed about current cost and inventory levels. These figures will help the marketing manager decide what discounts to grant, what products to push, and so forth.

> A planning system determines how the operations managers get the information they need and how they provide information to others.

ORGANIZATION   Another operations management decision involves the organization of the operations function—that is, where in the overall design of the organization operations activities should be housed. These issues are explored in a later section.

HUMAN RESOURCES   Working in conjunction with human resource managers, operations managers must decide what kinds of employees they need. These decisions involve both the quantity and the quality of the work force. For example, suppose a toy manufacturer needs to increase its work force as it builds toys for the Christmas season. Its managers need to decide how many new workers will be needed, what skills they should have, and when they should be hired. Recent trends toward automation and high-tech manufacturing have made these decisions even more critical, in that managers must take greater care to select just the right kinds of employees to work in such high-tech settings.[5]

TECHNOLOGY   **Technology** involves the actual processes used in transforming raw materials and other inputs into appropriate outputs. Some organizations, such as home cleaning services and athletic teams, tend to be **labor-intensive**, which means that people do most of the work. Other firms, such as General Electric, are **capital-intensive**, which means that machines do almost all of the work. Still other companies use a balance of people and machines. Decisions related to what form of technology to use and when to change technology are critical parts of operations management.

> *Technology* is the set of processes used by an organization to transform raw materials and other inputs into appropriate outputs.

FACILITIES   Another important decision, which is actually a set of interrelated decisions, involves **facilities**—the physical means of accomplishing production. Should a firm have one or two large plants or several smaller plants? Should it make all its own components and then assemble them, or buy some or all of them from other manufacturers? Where should the plants be located? And how should they be arranged?

> *Facilities* are the physical means the organization uses to create products and/or services.

Each of these decisions requires considerable research and consideration. Suppose that a company is searching for a site for a new plant. It might be efficient to locate the plant near major suppliers, or it might be more efficient to put it close to major customers. The company also needs information about land costs, the supply of labor, construction costs, tax rates, utility rates, the quality of life for employees, and so forth. And considerable pressure is often put on companies to locate plants in certain cities. Small towns throughout the United States have engaged in high-stakes competition as potential sites for new manufacturing facilities. To get the predicted economic benefits, such communities offer reduced tax rates, free land, and other incentives.[6]

CONTROLS   Decisions also must be made about operations control, including inventory control, quality control, and scheduling control. Each of these is discussed in more detail later in this chapter.

Operations Planning

Operations planning relates to the more day-to-day activities of operations management. There are many questions that have to be answered by managers responsible for carrying out operations activities. For example, how

Planning for operations often includes day-to-day scheduling. For example, during the winter Baltimore Gas & Electric Co. has to thaw the coal it receives directly from mines before it can be used. Planning and scheduling such thawing activities is necessary to ensure a steady supply of fuel.

Baltimore Gas & Electric Company

much should the organization produce? When should it be produced? How often should it be produced? In general, there are four basic steps are involved in operations planning.

The first step is to select a **planning horizon,** or time span across which to plan. This decision will vary, of course, depending on what kind of company is involved. A manufacturer of heavy equipment may plan over a twelve-month cycle, whereas a restaurant manager might plan seven days ahead.

Once the appropriate horizon has been chosen, the manager needs to estimate demand for that period. For example, the manufacturer's plant manager might use marketing data to estimate equipment demand for each month of the next year. The restaurant manager, in contrast, will forecast customers for each meal for each of the next seven days.

The third step is to compare projected demand with current capacity for each meaningful block of time. In the plant, this might mean that comparisons are made on a monthly basis; in the restaurant, they might be made for each meal.

The last step is to try to adjust capacity to demand. If demand exceeds capacity in the plant, the manager has several options: she can schedule overtime, add more workers, or add another shift, or she might subcontract some of the work out to other manufacturers or shift it to other plants in the same company. If capacity exceeds demand, she can lay off some workers and/or shut down some of the plant. Similarly, the restaurant manager might increase or decrease staff, order more or less food, and so on.

■ The *planning horizon* is the time span across which operations managers plan.

LEARNING CHECK

You should now be able to describe operations decisions and operations planning.

PRELUDE CASE U P D A T E

Cummins Engine Company clearly had to address each of the major operations decisions as it formulated its strategy for dealing with foreign competition. For example, at one point managers considered moving away from engine production to avoid the increased competition. The decision was subsequently made, however, to keep the product line focused on engine production. Excess capacity was eliminated, and new planning systems were developed to compete more effectively. The organization itself and its human resources were also adjusted to better cope with the new competitive environment of the organization. Finally, technology, facilities, and controls became an even more central part of the firm's operations.

MANAGING OPERATIONS

Clearly, managing the various elements of an organization's operations systems is an important consideration for managers. In addition to the elements already discussed, two major areas of concern in managing operations are organizing and organizational change.

Organizing for Operations

The principal issue in organizing for operations is defining where the operations management function fits into the overall structure and design of the organization.[7] Directly or indirectly, operations management affects and is affected by all of the dimensions of organizational design described in Chapters 8 and 9.

For example, job design considerations permeate operations management. Specialization is one approach to designing jobs, but operations management is affected when managers turn to alternative approaches, such as rotation, enlargement, or enrichment.

Perhaps even more significant is the link between departmentalization and operations management. How the operations function looks when the organization is departmentalized by function and by product is shown in Exhibit 18.2. As we can see, operations are centralized at the top under the control of a vice president or similar top manager when departmentalization is functional. When departmentalization is by product, as in a divisional structure,

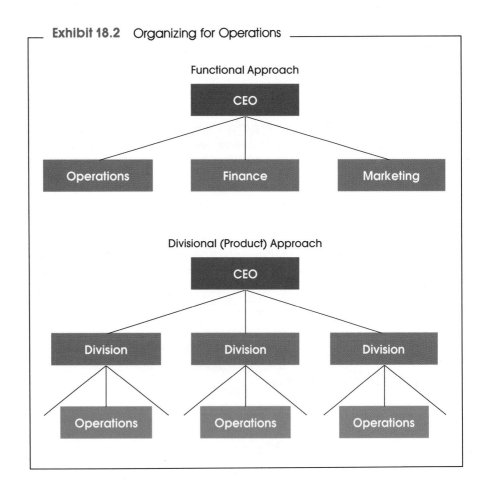

Exhibit 18.2   Organizing for Operations

Functional Approach

CEO

Operations   Finance   Marketing

Divisional (Product) Approach

CEO

Division   Division   Division

Operations   Operations   Operations

operations for each product group or division are decentralized under the manager responsible for the division. Other variations are also possible. Each plant might be thought of as a separate department (departmentalization by location), or departmentalization by time might be used for different shifts within a plant.

Operations management must also address delegation and decentralization issues. Firms like General Electric and Westinghouse have relatively high levels of decentralization, and their plant managers have considerable discretion and autonomy and can make fairly significant decisions without approval from corporate managers. In settings like the distribution division of K mart, more centralization is the norm. Warehouse managers, for example, have relatively little discretion in decision making. In most cases they have to follow established procedures and regulations or must consult with higher-level managers before making decisions.[8]

In recent years, managers have begun to be increasingly interested in how to structure their organizations to facilitate operations management, especially new product development. For example, innovation and the creation of both new products and services and the ways to create those products and services are becoming ever more critical.

Change and Operations

Another important dimension of the management of operations relates to organizational change. As we will see more fully in Chapter 20, two of the major reasons for change are technology and competition. Technology, of course, relates directly to operations management, so being aware of new technology and adopting it when it is appropriate are important to operations managers. Similarly, many (but not all) of the reasons for responding to competitors involve operations. Changes in packaging, product design, product quality, and so forth might be undertaken for competitive reasons.

Technology also provides a major way in which to change organizations. Changes in work processes and sequences, for instance, are common forms of organizational change that have direct implications for operations management. Several structural (for example, coordination and decentralization) and people-focused (such as selection and training) change techniques are also related to operations management.[9]

LEARNING CHECK

You should now be able to indicate what is involved in the management and organization of operations and describe the relationship of change to operations.

PRELUDE CASE UPDATE

The circumstances faced by Cummins clearly demonstrate relationships among both organizational and change issues and operations management. For instance, increased competition from abroad was a primary catalyst to the actions Cummins had to take to survive. And of course, the transformation Cummins went through was a major change itself. A key focus of these change activities involved the organizational context of operations at Cummins. Managers reaffirmed the primacy of operations to the success of Cummins and kept it as a central dimension of the organization. Decentralization was undertaken to increase managerial autonomy on the shop floor, and steps were undertaken to promote innovation as well.

OPERATIONS CONTROL

A major concern of operations management is the control function—in fact, many people consider operations management to be almost totally concerned with control. Although this view may be too narrow, operations and control are certainly interrelated.[10] Four areas of operations management that are especially critical are inventory control, quality control, scheduling control, and cost control.

Inventory Control

❑ *Inventory control* is making sure the organization has an adequate supply of raw materials to transform into products, that there are enough finished goods to ship to customers, and that inventory in process is adequate.

Inventory control is essential for effective operations management because inventories represent a major investment for all organizations. The goals of **inventory control** are to make sure the organization has an adequate supply of raw materials to transform into products, that there are enough finished goods to ship to customers, and that inventory in process is adequate to meet future needs.[11]

As shown in Exhibit 18.3, there are four basic forms of inventory. **Raw materials inventory** is the supply of materials, parts, and supplies the organization needs to do its work. Ford's raw materials include mechanical parts, electrical parts, paint, belts and hoses, upholstery fabric, and so forth; Pizza Hut's raw materials include flour, sausage, tomato paste, cheese, and other ingredients. The most important thing in raw materials inventory is to make sure that enough materials are on hand to meet production needs but not so much that materials spoil, get broken, or are stolen.

Work-in-process inventory refers to the inventory of parts and supplies that are currently being used to produce the final product or service, which is not yet complete. For example, at any given point in time Ford has millions of dollars' worth of materials at various stages of completion on the assembly lines of its factories. At Pizza Hut, in contrast, work-in-process is fairly minimal.

Finished goods inventory is the set of products that have been completely assembled but have not yet been shipped. The key concern here is to have enough goods on hand to meet customer demands but not so much that the products become obsolete, spoiled, or damaged. Boeing does not maintain an inventory of 747 jumbo jets, but instead makes each plane to customer specifications, whereas Ford often has thousands of automobiles in finished goods inventory, awaiting dealer orders.

Exhibit 18.3 Kinds of Inventory

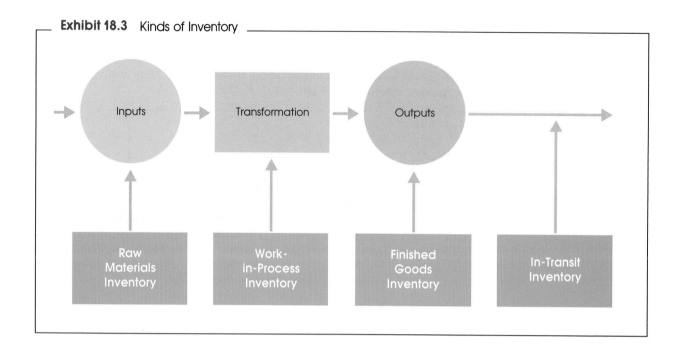

Finally, **in-transit inventory** includes goods that have been shipped from the company but have not yet been delivered to the customer. Again, Ford is always likely to have a lot of automobiles on trains and trucks, heading for dealer showrooms.

Quality Control

□ *Quality control* is the attempt to make sure that inputs and outputs meet desired levels of quality.

Another important part of operations management control is **quality control**—ensuring that the inputs and outputs of the organization meet desired levels of quality. Quality control has become increasingly important in recent years, primarily because of the growing recognition that Japanese success is often due to the quality of their products.[12]

Quality control begins with strategic planning. A strategic issue for most firms is determining how they want their products to be perceived in the marketplace. Mercedes-Benz, F. A. O. Schwarz, Rolex, Neiman-Marcus, and Yale University have all decided that quality is to be their hallmark. Thus price becomes a secondary consideration. Honda, Seiko, Sears, Ford, and Sony have all determined to strike a balance between good quality and reasonable price. At the low end, K mart, Timex, and Radio Shack don't focus too much on quality but instead stress low price.

Quality control systems can usually parallel inventory control systems. For example, it is quite common for companies to specify certain quality standards when they buy raw materials or supplies. The supplies are checked carefully when they are delivered, and if the standards haven't been met or if the shipment is damaged, the company either refuses the materials or accepts them subject to further review.

Work-in-process is generally the time when desired levels of product or service quality are achieved. Managers in an automobile plant make numerous checks as various parts are assembled. If the company has decided that sheet metal parts like fenders and doors cannot deviate more than half an inch from target fittings in order to be acceptable, the managers can detect and correct a problem in a fender or door before it is compounded.

Finished goods are also checked for quality. Say that each car at an auto plant is driven from the end of the line to a holding area. During the drive, the worker can check things like the lights, radio, and brakes. In other instances, the quality of finished goods can only be assessed via sampling. Obviously, checking a flash cube or a bottle of wine makes the product unusable, so managers check samples to determine overall quality.

We should also note that quality control is as important for service companies as it is for manufacturers. A restaurant that sells poor-quality foods, a barber who gives bad haircuts, or a university that doesn't care about teaching will have problems. We will return to quality again in Chapter 19.

Scheduling Control

❏ Making sure that the right things arrive at and depart from the organization at the right time is *scheduling control.*

Still another important aspect of operations management control is **scheduling control**—having the right things arrive at and depart from the organization at

Courtesy Echlin Inc./Photo by Gary Gladstone © 1989

Scheduling control is especially important when organizations adopt computer integrated manufacturing. For example, Echlin Inc., a major supplier of auto parts, relies on materials resource planning techniques to assure availability and proper inventory levels throughout its computerized assembly plant.

the right time.[13] Consider the case of a contractor who is building a new house. He will need a supply of two-by-four studs to use in framing the house. If the shipment arrives too soon, the wood might be stolen or scattered, but if it arrives too late, work will be delayed. Thus, one of the contractor's scheduling control problems is to have the lumber delivered on time.

A technique in scheduling control similar to that used in the construction of the Panama Canal is the **just-in-time method,** or **JIT.**[14] JIT has been used extensively by the Japanese and is also increasingly useful in the United States.[15] As illustrated in Exhibit 18.4, the traditional approach to scheduling incoming materials is to order a relatively few large shipments of materials, which are then stored in warehouses until they are needed for production. The traditional American automobile plant capable of producing one thousand cars a day requires two million square feet of space, much of it devoted to storage space, and $775 in inventory per car.

Under a JIT system, the company makes more frequent, and therefore smaller, orders of raw materials. The idea is to have resources arrive just as they are needed—just in time. Some materials go straight to the plant, and others are maintained (at a low level) in small warehouse facilities. A Japanese plant designed to produce one thousand cars a day is around one million square feet in size and uses only $150 in inventory per car.

For obvious reasons, American firms have begun to copy this system. Today, automobile engines at many Ford plants are delivered daily and taken straight to the assembly line. Computers and advanced communication systems facilitate this practice a great deal.

Another dimension of scheduling applies to manufacturing itself. In traditional systems, machines in a plant are fixed, in terms of both where they are

> ☐ *JIT (just-in-time)* scheduling involves having things arrive at designated spots just as they are needed.

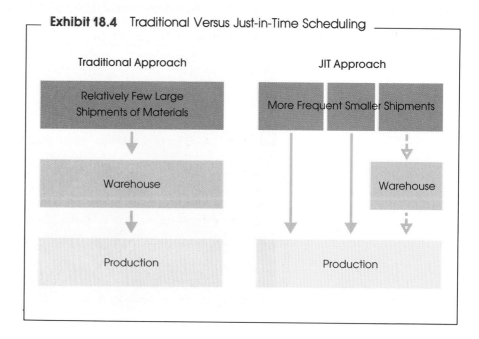

Exhibit 18.4 Traditional Versus Just-in-Time Scheduling

THE WORLD OF MANAGEMENT

Ford and Mazda Team Up for Profits

In 1983, Ford and Mazda entered into a long-range agreement to jointly plan the next generation of Ford's Escort. Their goal was to produce the first "world car"—a car that could be made and sold anywhere in the world with relatively few modifications.

For years, the consensus has been that U.S. automakers know how to style automobiles but that the Japanese know how to build them. Thus, the plan developed by Ford called for Ford to design the outside of the car, with Mazda designing everything else. That is, Ford relied on heavy involvement by its Japanese partners in developing the technical specifications for the Escort.

At numerous stages throughout the process, Ford engineers came up with problems, issues, ideas, or concerns that threatened to stall the schedule. At every juncture, however, their Mazda counterparts applied relentless pressure to keep development moving forward so as to not get off schedule. Their

thinking was that the issues Ford wanted to address could be handled, but that they should not detract from the schedule that both parties had agreed to. Mazda's pressure forced managers to always do things within the context of time and cost considerations.

How did the partnership work out? The first new Escort was produced almost to the day it was projected over seven years earlier. In addition, costs were lower than planned, gasoline mileage was higher than planned, and quality better than Ford had ever expected. Indeed, managers estimated that Mazda's involvement had already saved Ford over $1 billion. Much of the savings was attributable to the fact that Mazda continually kept everyone's attention on the schedule and the costs involved. Thus, each decision was routinely scrutinized more closely than normal.

SOURCES: "How Ford and Mazda Shared the Driver's Seat," *Business Week,* March 26, 1990, pp. 94–95; Alex Taylor III, "Ford's for the Future," *Fortune,* January 16, 1989, pp. 36–49; Louis Kraar, "Japan's Gung-Ho U.S. Car Plants," *Fortune,* January 30, 1989, pp. 98–108; "Shaking Up Detroit," *Business Week,* August 14, 1989, pp. 74–80.

and what they do. Parts flow through the plant and are assembled into a certain final product. Changes in products necessitate major changes in the plant as well. Innovations called computer-integrated manufacturing systems (CIM) promise to change this approach, however. In a CIM system, computers adjust machine placements and settings automatically. This greatly enhances both the complexity and the flexibility of scheduling in a manufacturing system.[16] *Management Today: The World of Management* describes how Mazda taught Ford some new lessons about the value of scheduling.

Cost Control

☐ *Cost control* involves the management of expenses.

Finally, operations management control also gives considerable attention to **cost control**. Costs are the expenses incurred by the organization as it con-

ducts its business. Obviously, payments for labor and materials frequently
represent major costs, so managers using cost control attempt to identify areas
in which costs are excessive and to find ways to reduce them appropriately.

Cost control has become a major area of managerial attention. AT&T, Xerox, Celanese, and Burlington have all undertaken major cost-cutting programs in recent years,[17] and Honeywell has also recently cut costs in order to
enhance its profitability.[18]

OPERATIONS CONTROL TECHNIQUES

Managers can use numerous techniques to help them control operations in an
organization. Chapter 5 described forecasting, linear programming, and break-
even analysis, and Chapter 7 discussed payoff matrices and decision trees.
Each of these techniques is also useful in operations management. Two other
techniques that are especially relevant for operations control are PERT and
MRP.

Courtesy Textron Inc./Photo by Mason Morfit

PERT is a powerful control technique used by many different organizations. Textron, for
example, used PERT to figure out how to increase production volume and improve the
quality of its two-color automobile bumpers.

PERT

PERT stands for *p*rogram *e*valuation and *r*eview *t*echnique.[19] It was developed in the late 1950s to assist the Navy in scheduling, coordinating, and controlling the Polaris nuclear submarine project. Thanks to PERT, the Navy saved two years in the development of the submarine.

PERT involves identifying the various activities necessary in a project, developing a network that specifies the interrelationships among those activities, determining how much time each activity will take, and refining and controlling the implementation of the project using the network.

A PERT diagram is shown in Exhibit 18.5. The circles with numbers in them represent events that are specific, definable accomplishments. The arrows identified by letters are activities or tasks necessary to complete the various events, and the numbers beside each activity are estimates of how much time will be needed to complete the activity.

Note that some activities can be worked on simultaneously, whereas others must be completed in sequence. For example, contractors cannot do anything toward building a house until the foundation has been poured. After the framing is complete, however, one crew can be putting on the roof while an electrical crew is wiring the walls and a plumbing crew is working on the pipes. In the PERT diagram in the exhibit, activities a, b, and c can all be undertaken after Event 1 is completed. Similarly, at the other end of the network, all other events must be completed before Event 8 can be attained.

A particularly useful part of a PERT network is the determination of the **critical path**, the longest path through the entire network. In the exhibit, the critical path is 1-2-5-6-7-8. This series of activities will take twenty units of

Exhibit 18.5   A PERT Diagram

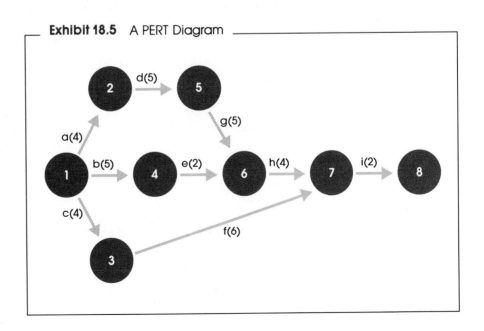

time to complete. In contrast, path 1-4-6-7-8 takes thirteen units of time, and 1-3-7-8 takes twelve units of time.

An understanding of the critical path helps managers in two ways. First, the manager recognizes that a delay in any activity along the critical path delays the entire project. If activity c takes five days instead of four, no real harm has been done. On the other hand, if activity d takes six days instead of five, the entire project has been delayed by one day. Of course, the manager may be able to regain the lost time by working overtime, hiring extra help, and so on.

Understanding the critical path also allows managers to reallocate resources to shorten the overall project. For example, after seeing the PERT diagram in Exhibit 18.5, the manager might decide to move some workers from activity e to activity d. As a result, activity e now takes three days to complete, but activity d is finished in four days. The overall time of completion—that is, the critical path—has therefore been reduced by one day.

MRP

◻ *MRP is a computer method for managing complex delivery schedules.*

Another useful control technique for operations management is **MRP**, which stands for *material requirements planning*.[20] MRP is used to manage complex delivery schedules so that materials arrive as needed and in the proper quantities. Table 18.1 outlines the steps in the MRP process.

TABLE 18.1
The MRP Process

Step	Example
1. Manager specifies the needed resources and decides when they must be available.	A plant manager determines that 240 steel wire casings as well as component nuts, bolts, wires, and screws are needed to make 240 products during the next six weeks. Production is to be spaced evenly throughout the period.
2. Manager determines the existing inventory.	Current inventory includes 17 wire castings as well as specified numbers of nuts and bolts, wire, and screws.
3. Computer specifies an ordering and delivery system for parts not currently in inventory.	The specifications include details as to amounts needed, suppliers, schedules, and the like. The suppliers are all local.
4. Computer generates reports that tell the manager what and when to order.	The manager gets a report summarizing orders for 23 casings and sets of component items to be delivered next Monday, and 40 additional casings and sets of component items to be delivered each of the following Mondays.

MRP is undertaken with a computer program. First the manager specifies the parts and supplies that are needed for a project and figures out when they should arrive. Then he determines existing inventories. The MRP system then specifies an ordering and delivery system for materials and parts that are not currently in inventory. Finally, the computer generates reports that tell the manager when to place orders and what quantities of each material and part to specify in each order.

Perhaps the greatest value of MRP is its ability to handle different delivery systems and lead times effectively. When a company needs hundreds of parts in vastly different quantities and when delivery times range from a day to several months in the future, coordination by an individual manager may well be impossible. A properly designed MRP system, however, can cope with such factors fairly easily.

LEARNING CHECK

You should now be able to describe operations control techniques, including PERT and MRP.

P R E L U D E   C A S E   U P D A T E

Cummins Engine Company makes frequent and extensive use of techniques such as PERT and MRP. PERT is used in the planning of new products and product extensions, for example. Similarly, MRP is used in each of Cummins's plants to plan and schedule the various materials that are needed to carry out various projects.

TRENDS IN OPERATIONS MANAGEMENT

Like all other areas of management, operations management is complex and dynamic. Things are not the same today as they were yesterday, and they will be different again tomorrow. Many of the changes in this field are likely to be related to computers, automation, and robotics.

As we have seen, computers are bringing increased flexibility to a wide variety of operating settings, ranging from manufacturing plants to information and service firms. Automation is the process of designing work so that it can be done by machines, and increasingly those machines are robots.

Many people are familiar with the increased use of computers and robots in the automobile industry, but their use is considerably more widespread than that. For example, Farley, Inc., the maker of Arrow shirts, has taken major steps toward automation in its plants, which have resulted in a 25 percent increase in productivity. Today, one worker operating two machines can attach plackets to ninety-five dozen shirts in one hour. Under the old system, she would have taken almost five hours to do the same amount of work.[21]

LEARNING CHECK

You should now be able to identify and discuss current trends in operations management.

More and more firms are beginning to realize the advantages of automation. In all likelihood, these trends will continue and perhaps even gain additional momentum. Thus operations managers will function in an increasingly complex, dynamic, and exciting world.

Chapter Summary

Operations management deals with the transformation of inputs into outputs; the inputs and outputs themselves are secondary components. Because it affects so many other parts of the organization, operations management is critically important.

Planning for operations is the first stage in effective operations management. It involves both operations decisions and operations planning. Operations decisions must be made in eight primary areas, which affect all aspects of operations management but relate most significantly to the transformation process. Operations planning relates to the more day-to-day activities of operations management. There are four basic steps in operations management.

The management and organization of operations involve all of the aspects discussed under planning for operations. In addition, the positioning of operations activities within the broader organization design, job design, and other specific structural components are also important. There is also a very important link between change and operations management.

Operations management also involves control, particularly in four areas: inventory, quality, scheduling, and costs. Inventories represent a major investment for an organization and so must be carefully controlled. Quality is also important; indeed, many firms now compete primarily on the basis of the quality of their products or services. Scheduling control involves having the right things arrive and depart from the organization at the right time. Cost control deals with the expenses incurred by the organization in conducting its business.

Managers can use numerous techniques in operations management. The major tools and techniques are forecasting, linear programming, break-even analysis, payoff matrices, decision trees, PERT, and MRP.

The most obvious trends in operations management today involve the increasing use of computers, automation, and robotics.

The Manager's Vocabulary

operations management
product/service line
capacity
technology
labor-intensive
capital-intensive
facilities
planning horizon
inventory control
raw materials inventory
work-in-process
 inventory
finished goods inventory
in-transit inventory
quality control
scheduling control
JIT (just-in-time)
 method
cost control
PERT
critical path
MRP

Prelude Case Wrap-Up

Our Prelude Case for this chapter describes the Cummins Engine Company and its attempt to succeed in an increasingly competitive world. Over a decade ago, Cummins began laying the foundation it felt it needed to compete effectively against foreign competition. Although considerable progress has been made, Cummins still faces challenges in the years to come.

Today, many of Cummins's hopes depend on the success of its so-called flexible factories. In the past, Cummins made extensive use of traditional manufacturing work flows called "process layouts" in its factories. In a process system, the same kinds of machines are installed in fixed positions all together, and work-in-process flows from group to group as it needs various operations. For example, one part might flow from grinders to lathes to milling machines arranged around the entire shop floor.

Now, however, similar machines are separated from one another and are instead grouped with different kinds of machines. Thus, a grinder, lathe, and milling machine might all be grouped together in one small area. These clusters allow work-in-process to flow through a much smaller area. Thus, they form mini assembly lines within a larger job shop system.

This clustering arrangement provides considerably more flexibility than in the past. For example, the machines and/or procedures used to produce one family of products can be changed or completely rearranged without disrupting other production processes in the organization.

Managers at Cummins are currently looking for further refinements to the flexible manufacturing systems they have pioneered. Their goal is to eventually be able to change work setups and component part designs in as little as a few hours. If they can succeed, they may well have achieved the competitive edge they have been seeking.

Prelude Case Questions

1. What operations decisions can you identify at Cummins?
2. What role does operations management play in the overall organization design at Cummins?
3. How has change been managed at Cummins?
4. How are the various forms of operations control used at Cummins?

Discussion Questions

Review Questions

1. Why has the term *operations management* gradually replaced the term *production management*?
2. What are the eight key operations decisions managers must make?
3. Identify the four key areas of operations control.
4. Name and define the four types of inventory most organizations maintain.
5. What is meant by "just-in-time scheduling"?

Analysis Questions

1. How do you use operations management in your day-to-day activities?
2. Which operations decisions are most related to other managerial activities, and which are "purely" operations management?

3. How is operations planning similar to and different from more general types of planning activities as described earlier in Chapter 5?
4. Are some forms of operations control more important for some businesses than for others? Support your answer with examples.
5. What steps might an organization go through in converting from a traditional to a just-in-time scheduling system?

Application Questions and Exercises

1. Visit a local pizza parlor or hamburger joint. On the basis of your observations, infer how the organization has addressed the various operations decisions described in the chapter.
2. Interview a manager from a local manufacturer. Ask him or her about new breakthroughs in operations management that his or her company is using or is considering.
3. Assume you are the manager of a manufacturer that needs extra capacity. Identify as many different examples as you can of how to increase capacity *without* adding on to your existing plant.
4. List five very different kinds of businesses. Then identify potential environmental changes that might affect their operations management.
5. Use PERT to plan a project in which you are involved (for example, a term paper or group project).

ENHANCEMENT CASE

BETHLEHEM SHAPES UP FAST

During the 1970s, being a manager for a big U.S. steel company was almost like belonging to a country club. Big steel had a virtual monopoly and could almost tell customers what to buy and charge them whatever they wanted. Top steel executives, in particular, led the good life. They routinely enjoyed limousines, company jets, lavish offices, and various other perks. Unfortunately, this good life led to complacency, which in turn resulted in poor-quality products and even worse service.

Two things happened in the early 1980s, however, that brought big steel to its knees. First of all, a major worldwide recession brought on the biggest drop in the demand for steel in forty years. At the same time, a flood of high-quality and low-cost steel from Japan captured much of what was left of the declining market.

Bethlehem Steel Corporation, in particular, was crippled by this one-two punch. Among the most inefficient steel companies in the United States,

Courtesy Bethlehem Steel/Photo by Mason Morfit

Bethlehem Steel has regained its competitive edge by stressing quality as part of its operations management function. For example, the sheet metal parts Bethlehem supplies to General Motors are inspected regularly and now fit together much better than they did in the past.

Bethlehem's sales and profits plummeted until the company was on the brink of bankruptcy.

To compound the problem, the newly available sources of higher-quality steel resulted in many customers threatening to jump ship altogether. For example, Ford was returning over 8 percent of its sheet steel to Bethlehem because of its poor quality. Campbell was complaining because the tin plate it was buying for cans was wavy and prone to rusting. Caterpillar and Firestone were also complaining bitterly about quality.

CEO Donald H. Trautlein recognized that he had a formidable challenge and set to work to turn things around. Between 1982 and 1985, he and his executive team cut 39,000 jobs, installed the firm's first real accounting control systems, shut down inefficient mills, and spent several billion dollars upgrading the rest. In particular, he optimized capacity, installed new planning systems, and installed new operations control procedures.

Trautlein's efforts were an excellent start, but the turnaround job was far from complete. In 1986 he

was succeeded by Walter F. Williams. Williams had joined the company in 1951 as a civil engineer and had worked himself through the hierarchy by hard work, dedication, and a commitment to excellence.

Thus, it came as no surprise when he applied these same standards of excellence to the top job. As a starting point, he cut several thousand more jobs and continued to refurbish Bethlehem's existing mills. Some jobs were automated and newer technology was installed. He also negotiated important wage concessions. By delaying major wage increases for several years, he was able to improve the company's cash-flow situation dramatically. Finally, scheduling, inventory, and cost controls were all tightened.

In addition, Williams also had to re-establish good relations with the banks that were underwriting the company's operations. Several of them still feared for the firm's future and refused to extend additional credit. Williams convinced them that Bethlehem had a viable future and that their investment was relatively secure.

Most important, though, have been Williams's efforts with Bethlehem's customers and his efforts to boost quality and productivity. Quality and productivity have both rebounded to the point that the Japanese are now copying Bethlehem. Whereas it used to take eight hours of labor to make a ton of steel, it now takes Bethlehem only four hours. And at one ultramodern Bethlehem facility, it can be done with less than three hours of labor.

Customers have responded favorably to Williams's initiatives. Many report that quality now exceeds that available from the Japanese. Moreover, the company is far more profitable than it was in years past, even though it has lower sales and fewer employees.

Williams cautions, however, that the past is not totally conquered. Some observers believe that the boom that propelled recent steel sales has peaked and that demand will start dropping now. In addition, Bethlehem is still heavily leveraged and must repay over $1 billion to its pension fund. Given the sorry state of the firm just a few years ago, however, many managers are in awe of Bethlehem's successes.

SOURCES: "Forging the New Bethlehem," *Business Week*, June 15, 1989, pp. 108–110; "Bessie's Blessings," *Forbes*, January 8, 1990, pp. 40–42; Nathaniel Gilbert, "Global Strategies: Foreign Firms' Resources Drive U.S. Steel Revival," *Management Review*, September 1989, pp. 52–56.

Enhancement Case Questions

1. What elements of operations management have contributed to Bethlehem's success?
2. How can managers avoid the problems encountered by Bethlehem in the 1980s?
3. Do you think Bethlehem did anything wrong during its recovery? If so, explain.
4. How does a firm like Bethlehem use the various operations control techniques?

Chapter Notes

1. Everett E. Adam, Jr., and Ronald J. Ebert, *Production and Operations Management*, 4th ed. (Englewood Cliffs, N.J.: Prentice-Hall, 1989).

2. Everett E. Adam, Jr., "Towards a Typology of Production and Operations Management Systems," *Academy of Management Review*, July 1983, pp. 365–375. See also Everett E. Adam, Jr., and Paul M. Swamidass, "Assessing Operations Management from a Strategic Perspective," *Journal of Management*, June 1989, pp. 181–204.

3. John O. McClain and L. Joseph Thomas, *Operations Management: Production of Goods and Services*, 2nd ed. (Englewood Cliffs, N.J.: Prentice-Hall, 1985).

4. Adam and Ebert, *Production and Operations Management*.

5. Cynthia Fisher, Lyle Schoenfeldt, and James Shaw, *Human Resource Management* (Boston: Houghton Mifflin, 1990).

6. See Louis Kraar, "Japan's Gung-Ho U.S. Car Plants," *Fortune*, January 30, 1989, pp. 98–108.

7. See Ricky W. Griffin, *Management*, 3rd ed. (Boston: Houghton Mifflin, 1990).

8. See Richard Daft, *Organization Theory and Design*, 3rd ed. (St. Paul, Minn.: West, 1989), for a detailed discussion of other organization design issues that are applicable to operations management.

9. See Michael Beer, *Organizational Change and Development—A System View* (Santa Monica, Calif.: Goodyear, 1980), for a more detailed discussion of change and its relationship to operations management.

10. Adam and Ebert, *Production and Operations Management*.

11. See John Kanet, "Inventory Planning at Black and Decker," *Production and Inventory Management*, 3rd quarter 1984, pp. 9–22, for an example of inventory management.

12. David Garvin, "Product Quality: An Important Strategic Weapon," *Business Horizons*, March-April 1984, pp. 31–36.

13. Adam and Ebert, *Production and Operations Management*.

14. James C. Worthy, *Shaping an American Institution* (Urbana, Ill.: University of Illinois Press, 1984), p. 7.

15. Charles G. Burck, "Can Detroit Catch Up?" *Fortune*, February 8, 1982, pp. 43–49.

16. See Bill Saporito, "IBM's No-Hands Assembly Line," *Fortune*, September 15, 1986, pp. 105–109, for an example.

17. Maggie McComas, "Cutting Costs Without Killing the Business," *Fortune*, October 13, 1986, pp. 70–78, and Ronald Henkoff, "Cost Cutting: How to Do It Right," *Fortune*, April 9, 1990, pp. 40–49.

18. "Honeywell Says Cost Controls to Account for Most of Year's Improvement in Profit," *The Wall Street Journal*, February 19, 1987, p. 6.

19. Adam and Ebert, *Production and Operations Management*. See also Harold Fearon, William Ruch, Patrick Decker, Ross Reck, Vincent Renter, and David Wieters, *Fundamentals of Production/Operations Management* (St. Paul, Minn.: West, 1979).

20. Ibid.

21. "Some Firms Resume Manufacturing in U.S. After Foreign Fiascoes," *The Wall Street Journal*, October 14, 1986, pp. 1, 27.

CHAPTER OUTLINE

I. The Nature of Productivity
  A. The Meaning of Productivity
  B. Levels and Forms of
     Productivity
  C. The Importance of
     Productivity

II. Productivity Trends
  A. Trends in the United States
  B. International Trends

III. Improving Productivity
  A. Operations and
     Management
  B. Motivation and Involvement
  C. The Productivity-Quality Link

IV. The Nature of Quality
  A. The Meaning of Quality
  B. The Importance of Quality

V. Improving Quality
  A. Quality Assurance
  B. Operational Techniques

VI. Related Control Issues
  A. Speed and Time
  B. Flexibility

CHAPTER

19

After reading this chapter you should be able to

1. Describe the nature of productivity, including its meaning, levels and forms, and importance.

2. Characterize productivity trends both in the United States and in other countries.

3. Identify ways to improve productivity.

4. Describe the nature of quality, including its meaning and importance.

5. Identify ways to improve quality through quality assurance and specific operational techniques.

6. Discuss the related control issues of speed and time and flexibility.

Productivity and Quality

CORNING TAKES NOTHING FOR GRANTED

Corning Glass Works, a New York–based corporation, is perhaps best known for its various cookware product lines such as Pyrex and Visions. Corning has a rich and significant heritage, however, having blown the glass for Thomas Edison's original light bulb, for the first television picture tube, and for the first vacuum tube.

The corporation was founded by the Houghton family over one hundred years ago. The family still controls 25 percent of the company's stock today. Indeed, the company's current CEO is James R. Houghton, the great-great-grandson of the founder.

Corning makes far more things than dishes. One of its major divisions is a world leader in medical technology. Another is a major player in fiber optics. Still another is the only remaining television glassmaker left in the United States. Corning also has several joint ventures under way with other firms.

At the time James Houghton took over—in 1983—the firm was not doing so well, however. Corning had several unproductive divisions, and profits for the overall company were meager. Since Houghton had already been preparing for the increasingly competitive environment he knew he would face, he was ready to take decisive action.

His first action was to sell several of the company's unproductive divisions. He then turned his attention to changing the corporate culture so as to make productivity and quality central themes. Corning had not really been having major problems with either its productivity or its quality, but Houghton reasoned that they should be a strength, rather than just not being a weakness.

A good example is the firm's television glass business. In 1983, Corning was forced to shut down one of its two remaining plants. The sole survivor, located in State College, Pennsylvania, was not expected to last more than two or three years.

The biggest problem in making television glass is to avoid bubbles and other imperfections. A tiny bubble—as small as a few thousandths of an inch in diameter—can render a forty-pound television glass unacceptable. Before Houghton's initiatives to improve quality, Corning's customers were returning around 4 percent of all the glass parts they received. Since Houghton's program was implemented, however, defects have dropped to .3 percent.

How was such a dramatic change brought about? For one thing, each employee involved in making the screens was made responsible for his or her own efforts. Previously, screens had been tested only once, at the end

of the production process. Now they are inspected at each step of the way. And the person who inspects them is the individual who performed that step and who is now personally responsible for seeing that it was done correctly.

The payoffs from such breakthroughs are dramatic. For example, Corning has expanded the plant's capacity by 40 percent. And 150 new hourly workers have been hired. Today the company sells television glass to both Japanese and European manufacturers and has recently entered into a joint venture with Ashai Glass, the major Japanese television glassmaker.

Of course, such breakthroughs aren't achieved by Houghton visiting a plant and waving a magic wand. They are the result of careful planning and a logical and systematic effort to make quality improvement a major element in everything the firm does.

Corning Glass has dramatically enhanced its effectiveness by making a true commitment to quality. Workers now inspect parts such as this television picture tube screen themselves and decide when to have them reworked.

SOURCES: "At Corning, A Vision of Quality," *Fortune*, October 24, 1988, p. 64; Joel Dreyfuss, "Victories in the Quality Crusade," *Fortune*, October 10, 1988, pp. 80–88; "Talk Has Corning Stock Cooking," *USA Today*, March 11, 1987, p. 3B; William H. Miller, "Mr. Houghton Goes to Washington," *Industry Week*, June 5, 1989, pp. 65–68.

T

he actions taken by James Houghton and Corning Glass Works clearly demonstrate both a major problem and the best way of addressing it. The problem is a corporate culture that allows productivity and quality to be secondary considerations. The solution is a renewed dedication to making productivity and quality a cornerstone for managerial decisions and activities.

This chapter explores the concepts of productivity and quality in detail. First it describes the nature of productivity. It then discusses productivity trends and ways that productivity can be improved. The nature of quality is addressed next. After considering ways to improve quality, the chapter concludes by noting the related issues of speed, time, and flexibility.

THE NATURE OF PRODUCTIVITY

Most people have a general sense of what productivity means. As we will see, however, it is actually more complex than most people imagine. This section explores the general meaning of productivity, identifies several levels and forms of productivity, and then considers its importance.

The Meaning of Productivity

☐ *Productivity is a measure of efficiency that indicates what is created relative to the resources used to create it.*

In a very general sense, **productivity** is a measure of efficiency. More specifically, it is an economic index of the value or amount of what is created relative to the value or amount of resources used to create it. For example, assume two workers each spend eight hours assembling toasters. One assembles 100 toasters that meet standard quality tests, and the other produces 125 toasters of the same quality. Clearly, the worker that makes 125 toasters is more productive than the one that makes only 100 toasters within the same period of time.

Similarly, assume two manufacturing plants are of the same size, have identical production equipment, and have the same type of work force. One plant, however, is able to manufacture 5,000 CD players per day, whereas the other can make only 4,500 players per day. The former plant is more productive than the latter. As we will explore more fully in the next section, then, there are different levels and forms of productivity.

Levels and Forms of Productivity

☐ *Productivity can be assessed at the level of the individual, unit, company, industry, and country.*

The examples above illustrate two levels of productivity—individual and plant. However, there are actually several different levels of productivity that can be identified.[1]

LEVELS OF PRODUCTIVITY Exhibit 19.1 illustrates some of the more general levels of productivity that are of interest and concern to managers. The most basic level is **individual productivity**—the amount produced or cre-

Exhibit 19.1   Levels of Productivity

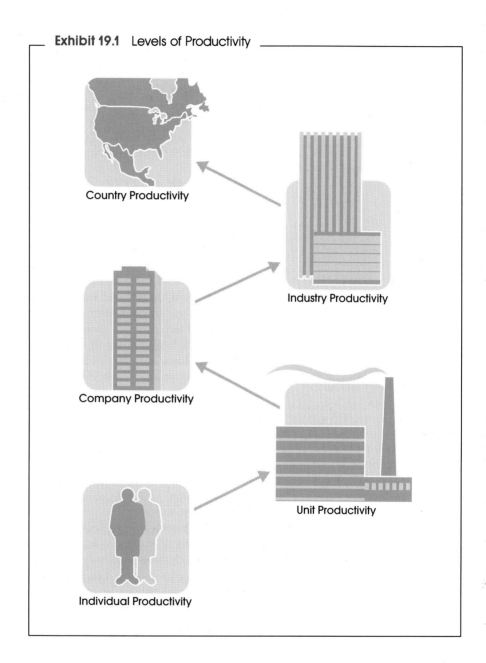

Country Productivity

Industry Productivity

Company Productivity

Unit Productivity

Individual Productivity

ated by a single individual relative to his or her costs to the organization. For example, Glen May works in a K mart distribution center in Texas. His productivity reflects the value of the orders he fills each day relative to his wages.

One step higher is **unit productivity.** Unit productivity might be the productivity of a manufacturing plant (as shown in the exhibit), a single restaurant, or a group of workers within a single facility. K mart determines the unit productivity of each of its distribution centers. **Company productivity,** in turn, is the total level of productivity achieved by all the company's employees and/or units combined. All of K mart's distributions centers, retail stores, and other operations combine to determine the corporation's overall productivity.

Industry productivity is that achieved by all companies in a particular industry. K mart, Sears, Wal-Mart, and other retailers contribute to the retailing industry's aggregate level of productivity. Finally, **country productivity** refers to the productivity levels achieved by entire countries. The retailing industry in the United States contributes to this country's total productivity.

FORMS OF PRODUCTIVITY   In many instances it also makes sense to consider different forms of productivity. For example, overall productivity—technically called **total factor productivity**—is determined by dividing outputs by the sum of labor, capital, materials, information, and energy costs. That is, it includes all the inputs used by the organization.

In many instances, however, it makes sense to evaluate productivity in terms of only some of the resources used by the organization. For example, labor productivity is determined by dividing outputs by direct labor. Such a partial productivity index has several advantages. For one thing, resources can be expressed in different terms (hours of labor, units of raw materials, and so forth), rather than having to all be transformed into a common base (such as dollars). It also allows managers to focus on improving productivity in specific areas and to be better able to directly assess their results.

The Importance of Productivity

☐ Productivity is important because of its impact on profitability as well as on our quality of life and standard of living.

Productivity is important for both obvious and less obvious reasons. For example, a firm's level of productivity will contribute directly to its profitability and, thus, to its ability to survive. Likewise, unit productivity can help the organization determine where resources are being used wisely and where they are being used less wisely.

Less obvious, but also very important, is the fact that productivity contributes to our overall quality of life and standard of living. For example, the more goods and services a country can create with its resources, the more goods and services its citizens will have to consume. And if those goods and services are produced efficiently enough, it will also be possible to ship them to foreign markets. The money that flows back will also add to the overall standard of living. Thus, the citizens of a highly productive country will have a better standard of living than people in a less productive country.

LEARNING CHECK

You should now be able to describe the nature of productivity, including its meaning, levels and forms, and importance.

PRODUCTIVITY TRENDS

The preceding section documented the clear importance of productivity. Given that importance, it is critical that we understand trends and patterns in how productivity is changing.[2]

Trends in the United States

As far as managers in the United States are concerned, there is both good and bad news about productivity. On the plus side, the United States has the highest level of productivity in the world. For example, the typical American worker produces goods or services worth almost $40,000 each year.[3] Canadian workers are the second most productive workers in the world. Moreover, there is little chance that our absolute leadership in this area will disappear anytime in the near future.[4]

◻ U.S. productivity growth in the manufacturing sector is increasing now after a period of stagnation.

On the other hand, productivity growth rates in the United States have been somewhat erratic in recent years. For example, during much of the 1960s and 1970s, U.S. productivity increased at a very slow pace—sometimes as little as 0.7 percent a year. Several factors accounted for this slowdown in growth as we shall see shortly. Since the early 1980s, though, manufacturing productivity has started to increase at a faster pace. Exhibit 19.2 shows manufacturing productivity in the United States since 1983.

Exhibit 19.2   Manufacturing and Service Productivity in the United States

Index: 1977=100

Manufacturing

Services

Productivity

145

130

115

100

1983   1984   1985   1986   1987   1988   1989

Quarterly

SOURCE: "Rising Factory Productivity Is Giving the Expansion Room to Run," *Fortune*, August 1, 1988, p. 25. © 1989 The Time Inc. Magazine Company. All rights reserved. Used by permission.

☐ Productivity growth in the service sector still remains slow.

Although manufacturing productivity has risen continuously since the early 1980s, productivity in the service sector has remained essentially flat. This pattern is also shown in the exhibit. And since the service sector has become such an important part of our total economy, the stagnation in productivity in this sector has kept overall productivity from growing as much as it would have otherwise.

Why did overall U.S. productivity slow down to begin with? Several factors contributed to this pattern. For one thing, because of booming production levels and relatively little foreign competition, American manufacturing facilities deteriorated badly during the 1950s. This resulted in less efficient production in the 1960s. For another, the work force absorbed many new and inexperienced employees, as more and more women and younger workers joined the work force for the first time during the 1960s and 1970s. Finally, American business started spending less and less on research and development, and the result was fewer breakthroughs in technology.

As far as the service sector is concerned, there are also several explanations as to why its productivity levels have lagged. For one thing, the rapid growth in services has carried with it some inefficiencies due to rapid start-up, lack of training, poorly designed operations, and so forth. For another, measuring output in many service areas is difficult. The output of a lawyer or accountant, for example, is more difficult to assess than that of an assembly-line worker. Hence, accurate measures of output are harder to obtain. Finally, many of the operational innovations (for example, robotics and automation) of the 1970s and 1980s were directed at the manufacturing sector; fewer were produced for the service sector. Managers now have a clearer understanding of the causes of the situation, however, and more and more attention is being focused on finding ways to increase productivity in the service sector in the 1990s.

International Trends

A major reason that people are concerned about productivity growth rates in the United States is that workers in many other countries are becoming more and more productive. Indeed, over the last several decades, productivity growth in several industrial countries—including Japan, France, and Great Britain—has outstripped productivity growth in the United States.[5] Exhibit 19.3 shows productivity growth rates for several industrial countries from 1984 to 1988.

Since many of the countries shown in the exhibit are our major competitors in the world marketplace, concerns about their productivity growth rates are clearly well founded. Increased awareness of these trends has galvanized many American business leaders to try to stem the tide. Through a variety of actions, many of which are noted in the following sections, American businesses are working harder than ever to maintain their productivity and position in the world economy.[6]

LEARNING CHECK

You should now be able to characterize productivity trends both in the United States and in other countries.

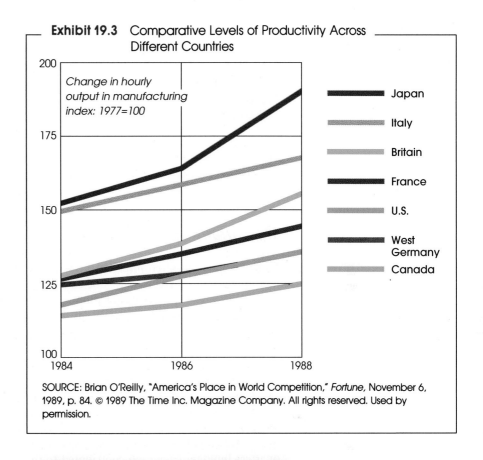

Exhibit 19.3 Comparative Levels of Productivity Across Different Countries

Change in hourly output in manufacturing index: 1977=100

Japan
Italy
Britain
France
U.S.
West Germany
Canada

PRELUDE CASE UPDATE

Corning Glass Works provides a perfect example of the cycle through which many American businesses have progressed during the past several decades. Because of plentiful business opportunities and few competitors, managers at Corning grew lax. Consequently, productivity began to slip. Eventually, however, the company woke up and recognized that it had a problem. New initiatives and a concerted effort have allowed Corning to partially regain its lost advantages. Of course, more challenges remain to be addressed in the future.

IMPROVING PRODUCTIVITY

Organizations that wish to enhance productivity at one or more levels can take several different approaches. As shown in Table 19.1, some of these methods are based on operations and management, and others focus on greater employee motivation and involvement.

TABLE 19.1
Methods for Enhancing
Productivity

Through Operations and Management	Through Motivation and Involvement
Improve technology and facilities	Increase training
Increase research and development spending	Increase employee participation
Adopt automated and robotic systems	Improve reward systems
Enhance speed	
Enhance flexibility	

Operations and Management

☐ Productivity can often be improved through a variety of operations and management techniques.

Organizations can often improve productivity through various operations and basic management techniques. For example, improved technological methods and facilities can be a big contributor. In 1980, the average American plant was fifteen years old. In contrast, its Japanese counterpart was less than ten years old. In many cases, the older a plant is, the less efficient it is likely to be. Thus, by building new plants and installing new technology, a company may well increase its productivity. Ford and Caterpillar have both improved productivity by constructing new facilities.

Likewise, new distribution systems, communication systems, and office buildings may also boost productivity if they help employees do their jobs more efficiently. Wal-Mart's modern distribution centers, Federal Express's marvelous communication network, and Union Carbide's efficient new headquarters building have each contributed to the productivity of their respective organizations.

Another approach to enhancing productivity is increasing spending on research and development (R&D). R&D can create new products, new uses for current products, and new methods for making products. Each of these breakthroughs results in improved productivity.[7] Bausch & Lomb, Merck, and IBM all credit R&D with being a key ingredient in their overall level of organizational effectiveness.

Unfortunately, R&D is often a prime target for cutbacks when a business faces a downturn. Since R&D's dividends are usually paid "tomorrow," shortsighted managers worried about today's bottom line may inadvertently hurt a firm's future by trying to maximize short-term profits.[8] Avon, USX, and Texaco have all cut R&D spending at least once in the last decade.

Organizations can also increase productivity by investing in automation and/or robotics, which are related to both technology and R&D. Automated production systems, for example, can make products with much higher levels of precision and at more exacting tolerance standards than can human workers. Similarly, robots don't tire and let their concentration slip.

Finally, an increased emphasis on speed and flexibility can also increase productivity. These methods are discussed more fully later in this chapter.

Motivation and Involvement

□ Employee motivation and involvement can also lead to higher productivity.

Managers can also improve productivity by improving the motivation and involvement of their employees. Common methods for doing this are also noted in Table 19.1.

One approach is to increase training. Sometimes workers don't perform at their maximum efficiency simply because they don't know how. Training is especially important in conjunction with the operations improvements already noted. For example, installing new production technology and not appropriately training employees in how to use it accomplishes very little. Indeed, some experts speculate that service productivity has lagged because companies have invested billions of dollars in sophisticated computer systems, networks, and work stations but have not adequately trained employees and managers in how to effectively use them.[9]

Increased employee participation is also often cited as a key to improving productivity. Japanese firms like Samsung, Sony, and Honda are held up as examples of how important employee participation can be to productivity growth. American firms like Westinghouse, Ford, and General Electric have learned valuable lessons from the Japanese and have taken steps to dramatically improve the level of participation among their employees. For example, each now gives operating employees considerably more control over how they

Employee involvement is one important way organizations can enhance productivity and quality. The two employees shown here work for Dana Corporation. They are checking the idea board, a new program suggested by Dana employees. Overall, the firm reports outstanding results from its involvement activities.

THE WORLD OF MANAGEMENT

Harley-Davidson's Long Ride Back

Harley-Davidson was a company going nowhere fast. Motorcycles had a bad image to the average American, Japanese firms like Yamaha and Honda were gobbling market share, and Harley in particular was stereotypically linked with black-jacketed bandits.

In 1975, about half of all the motorcycles Harley made came off the assembly line with parts missing. The engines leaked oil, the bikes vibrated badly, and starting them was often an adventure. In 1981, the company's management bought Harley from its parent company, AMF, and set about turning things around.

The keystone to Harley's efforts was employee involvement. Each worker was given a small ownership stake in the company. And much of the new technology that had just been installed to automate production was actually ripped out. Every single worker was challenged to do a better job and produce a better product. People on the assembly line were asked their opinions, and they were listened to.

Change didn't occur overnight, of course. Indeed, it took about four years before Harley got productivity and quality where they needed to be to compete with the Japanese. And since that time, the company has made major strides in regaining its market share from the Japanese. Productivity and quality have continued to increase, and some experts are now holding Harley-Davidson up as an American success story.

SOURCES: Peter C. Reid, "How Harley Beat Back the Japanese," *Fortune*, September 25, 1989, pp. 155–164; Rod Willis, "Harley-Davidson Comes Roaring Back," *Management Review*, March 1988, pp. 20–27; Vaughn Deals, "Harley-Davidson: An American Success Story," *Journal of Quality & Productivity*, June 1988, pp. A10, A23.

do their jobs and has made them directly responsible for monitoring the quality of their work and correcting any defects that they happen to observe. As a result, their productivity has improved. *Management Today: The World of Management* illustrates how employee participation at Harley-Davidson saved that company.

Finally, organizations can also improve productivity by modifying their reward systems. All too often, workers receive the same rewards regardless of the quality of work they perform. Thus, there are no incentives to work hard or to worry about how much one is producing. On the other hand, firms that tie significant rewards to improvements in productivity often see significant improvements. For example, Du Pont has recently implemented a new incentive system whereby employees receive bonuses if unit productivity exceeds previously agreed-upon levels. Although it's too early to know the results of this program, it seems to hold considerable promise for the future.

The Productivity-Quality Link

Productivity is also important because of its common link with quality. In the past, managers often assumed incorrectly that productivity and quality were inversely related: that is, they thought you could only increase output by lowering quality.

More recently, however, many managers have come to realize that productivity and quality are actually related in a positive way: increased productivity often means higher quality, and higher quality results in higher productivity. How this happens is explained a little later. We turn our attention now to a detailed discussion of quality.

THE NATURE OF QUALITY

As with productivity, many people have a general sense of what quality means. This section will first define the concept of quality more precisely and then will document its importance.

The Meaning of Quality

Suppose someone goes to a store and buys two pens. It turns out that one pen writes for thirty hours and the other writes for sixty hours. However, the latter is not necessarily of higher quality than the former. For example, if the first pen costs the consumer $.69 and has a stated manufacturer's expectation of being able to write for twenty-five hours, it actually looks pretty good. And if the second pen costs $5.00 and was intended to write for eighty-five hours, it isn't such a good deal after all. Thus, quality has both an absolute and a relative meaning.

□ *Quality* is the total set of features of a product or service that bear on its ability to satisfy stated or implied needs.

Following guidelines established by the American Society for Quality Control, **quality** can be defined as the total set of features and characteristics of a product or service that bear on its ability to satisfy stated or implied needs.[10] Thus, assuming that the two pens noted above are equivalent in all other respects, the cheaper pen that writes for thirty hours is of higher quality than the pen that costs more and writes for a while longer.

Table 19.2 lists eight specific characteristics that can be used to assess quality. For example, all else being equal, the more desirable features a product or service has, the higher its quality. Likewise, all else being equal, the more aesthetically pleasing the product or service, the higher its quality. Note here again, however, the notion of "all else being equal." If a product has an abundance of features and looks beautiful but seldom works the way it is supposed to, its quality obviously suffers.

□ Quality can be assessed in both absolute and relative terms.

Moreover, we need to relate these ideas to the previously noted dimensions of *absolute* and *relative quality*. Suppose you want to buy a new stereo system. You go to an electronics store and look at a portable Sony system for $350, a Sony rack system for $1,000, and another Sony rack system for $2,000. Regardless of which system you buy, you expect it to play a cassette tape when you push the play button, to pick up the local transmission from your favorite FM radio station, and so forth. You also expect it to do so for a reasonable period of time (longer than a few days, but not necessarily twenty years). Thus,

TABLE 19.2
Eight Dimensions of Quality

Dimension	Explanation
1. *Performance*	A product's primary operating characteristic. Examples are automobile acceleration and a television set's picture clarity.
2. *Features*	Supplement to a product's basic functioning characteristics, such as power windows on a car.
3. *Reliability*	A probability of not malfunctioning during a specified period.
4. *Conformance*	The degree to which a product's design and operating characteristics meet established standards.
5. *Durability*	A measure of product life.
6. *Serviceability*	The speed and ease of repair.
7. *Aesthetics*	How a product looks, feels, tastes, and smells.
8. *Perceived quality*	As seen by a customer.

SOURCE: Adapted and reprinted by permission of *Harvard Business Review*. An excerpt from "Competing on the Eight Dimensions of Quality" by David A. Garvin, (November/December 1987). Copyright © 1987 by the President and Fellows of Harvard College; all rights reserved.

each system is evaluated in terms of some generally understood absolute level: a product or system needs to be capable of fulfilling its intended purpose.

At the same time, you also are likely to recognize that the $350 system will not perform as well in several ways as will the other systems. The portable system may have a limited range for FM reception, may not reproduce the bass tracks as well, does not have the same volume capabilities, may not have remote control, and may only be expected to last two or three years. On the other hand, the more expensive systems will pick up more stations, have louder and better sound, have remote control, last much longer, and so forth.

Thus, the relative component of quality must be interpreted in comparison to other alternatives in several ways. All three Sony systems may be high quality relative to the standards they are expected to meet. The question becomes how much you want to pay in terms of what you will get. And you will need to compare each system with systems made by other manufacturers.

PRELUDE CASE   UPDATE

Corning Glass Works has attacked its quality problems on both dimensions. For example, virtually every product it makes has higher absolute quality standards and expectations than it did just a few years ago. Similarly, the firm also strives to make each of its products as good as or (preferably) better than comparable products available from other manufacturers.

The Importance of Quality

□ Quality is important because of its impact on productivity, competition, and costs.

Although quality is important for a variety of obvious reasons, three specific reasons warrant additional discussion. These are productivity, competition, and cost.[11]

PRODUCTIVITY   We have already seen the link between productivity and quality. To expand on that point a bit more here, if a firm can enhance its quality, several things will happen. First of all, since defects are almost certain to decrease, there will be fewer returns from unhappy customers. Second, because there are fewer defects, fewer resources will need to be dedicated to reworking or repairing defective products. And finally, since there are fewer defective units being produced and since operating employees will be more involved in quality enhancement, fewer quality control inspectors will be needed. Overall, then, since fewer resources are being used to produce products and services, productivity (by definition) increases.

COMPETITION   Quality has also become an important point of competition. Consumers around the world are increasingly demanding higher-quality products and services. Thus, a firm that can argue or demonstrate that its products or services are as good as or better than those offered by competitors will have an upper hand in the marketplace. In recent years, quality has become a major point of competition in the automobile, computer, airline, and electronics industry. For example, Ford has always promoted its Escort line on the basis of low price. However, the company has decided to promote its new 1990 Escorts on the basis that they are as good as or better than Japanese

Quality is important for several reasons. One key reason is that it can give a firm a competitive edge. University National Bank & Trust Co., in Palo Alto, California, uses all of its staff members to send out customer statements on the first day of each month. This approach improves service quality by getting statements out faster.

© Robert Holmgren

SMALL BUSINESS AND ENTREPRENEURSHIP

Ben and Jerry's Spells Success Q-U-A-L-I-T-Y

Ben Cohen and Jerry Greenfield met in the seventh grade and have been inseparable ever since. After taking a $5 correspondence course in making ice cream from the University of Pennsylvania, the two friends decided to go into business for themselves.

From the beginning, Cohen and Greenfield were committed to quality as a primary ingredient in their business. Thus, they insisted on using only natural ingredients. They also blend their ice cream to minimize the air that is retained. The result is a rich, high-quality ice cream that is thick and tasty—and very popular.

Ben & Jerry's started out in a converted gas station in Vermont. The start-up funds consisted of $12,000 the two friends were able to borrow from family and friends. They made their ice cream themselves and delivered it to local supermarkets in the back seat of their car.

Today, Ben & Jerry's has annual revenues of over $45 million. Its ice cream is sold in over thirty-five states and is due to be introduced into the Soviet Union in the near future. An interesting sidenote is the owner's commitment to society. For example, they pledge 7.5 percent of all pretax profits to social causes and have won numerous awards for their contributions to the general welfare.

The two owners have maintained their simple business philosophies and commitment to quality throughout their rapid growth, however, and most observers feel that both they and their products are exactly as they were in the beginning. And Ben and Jerry profess that the only changes on the horizon involve even higher quality standards and new and more exotic flavors.

SOURCES: "Vermont Ice Cream Makers Try Marketing World Peace," *Mobile Press Register,* February 5, 1989, p. 16A; Jonathan Adolph and Florence Graves, "Ben & Jerry: Two Real Guys," *New Age Journal,* March-April 1988, p. 32; "Food Firms Aim to Emulate Ben & Jerry's But Find Kitchen Hotter Than Expected," *The Wall Street Journal,* March 21, 1990, p. B1.

imports. And *Management Today: Small Business and Entrepreneurship* describes how one small firm used its commitment to quality to become a major player in its industry.

LEARNING CHECK

You should now be able to describe the nature of quality, including its meaning and importance.

COSTS Improved quality also results in lower costs. The earlier discussion of productivity noted several ways that productivity can be enhanced. Since productivity and quality are linked, lower costs from productivity gains should also logically follow quality gains as well. Improved quality also cuts down on shipping replacement products to customers, lowers the costs of servicing warranties, and minimizes lawsuits from disgruntled customers or customers that are injured by poorly made products. At one time, Whistler Corporation was using 100 of its 250 employees to repair radar detectors that would not work. After a quality improvement program was implemented, the company was able to transfer most of the workers back to the original production department, substantially lowering its labor costs.

IMPROVING QUALITY

As with productivity, managers have a number of methods they can draw upon to improve quality. Some of these fall under the general area called quality assurance, whereas others are more specific operational techniques. Both categories are discussed in the sections that follow.

Quality Assurance

☐ *Quality assurance is achieved through a combination of strategic commitment and improvements in employee involvement, materials, methods, and technology.*

The term **quality assurance** is a general label applied to an overall effort by an organization to enhance the quality of its products and/or services. The basic components of most quality assurance programs are illustrated in Exhibit 19.4.

STRATEGIC COMMITMENT   The starting point for any real quality assurance effort is a strategic commitment by the top management of an organization to make quality a top priority in every aspect of operations. Without such a commitment, quality is most likely to get only superficial consideration. And if a firm tries to promote itself on the basis of quality but that quality is eventually found to be lacking, more harm than good will have been done.

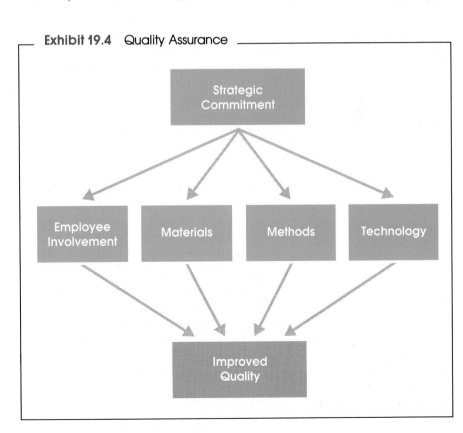

Exhibit 19.4   Quality Assurance

When James Houghton took over at Corning, he stated publicly, clearly, and without equivocation that quality was a top priority. He then proceeded to back up his assertion by committing the funds necessary to increase quality, rewarding other managers on the basis of their quality improvement, and so forth. Thus, his strategic commitment to quality was a key ingredient to everything Corning has been able to accomplish. Moreover, as shown in Exhibit 19.4, this commitment is generally operationalized in four specific areas.

EMPLOYEE INVOLVEMENT   We saw earlier that employee involvement is often used to increase productivity. In similar fashion, employee involvement and participation are also necessary to improve quality. Without such involvement, and without the commitment and acceptance of the program by employees, any attempt to enhance quality is not likely to succeed.

MATERIALS   Another part of improving quality is using higher-quality materials. It stands to reason, for example, that if a stereo maker uses poor-quality circuitry in its stereo systems, they are likely to fail. But if the company demands better circuits from suppliers, the systems will improve.

METHODS   In similar fashion, quality can also be enhanced through the use of more efficient and effective methods of operation. For example, L.L. Bean has an enviable reputation of gaining customer loyalty and satisfaction. Part of the reason, as we saw in an earlier chapter, is that its telephone operators are trained to listen carefully to what customers want and to then do everything possible to satisfy those needs. In contrast, other mail-order houses have suffered because their operators are rude, ill-informed, and otherwise unable to help customers. Such businesses might make improving their telephone assistance methods a first step in enhancing quality.[12]

TECHNOLOGY   Related to methods, but also a distinct area, is technology. Firms can improve quality by buying new equipment, investing in automation, and taking other such actions. Better technology provides a higher degree of standardization with fewer defective units or incomplete assemblies.

Of course, achieving quality assurance is more difficult than it might sound from reading these steps. For example, *Management Today: Management in Practice* describes the hurdles Dairy Queen has faced in its effort to upgrade quality. Still, the guidelines noted here provide a good framework for understanding quality assurance and are a good starting point in any effort to enhance quality by an organization.

Operational Techniques

Organizations striving for quality improvement also have an array of operational techniques they can draw upon. One important category of techniques

MANAGEMENT IN PRACTICE

Dairy Queen's Struggling Empire

Sometimes the struggle for quality runs into unusual barriers. Such is the case of Dairy Queen. International Dairy Queen, Inc. (IDQ) is one of the world's largest franchised organizations, and also one of its most troubled.

Dairy Queen restaurants sell a wide array of soft-serve ice cream, hamburger, hot dog, soft drink, and regional specialty items. There are over 5,000 Dairy Queen restaurants around the world, but most are unlike any of the others. Modern franchising successes like McDonald's and Pizza Hut have built their achievements on a strict standardization of menus, methods, and so forth. However, Dairy Queen established its network years before the importance of this premise was recognized. Consequently, its franchisees are accustomed to running their business however they see fit, including adding or dropping menu items, modifying formulas, and developing local or regional advertising campaigns without corporate oversight.

Unfortunately, corporate managers at IDQ have discovered serious quality problems. For example, customers don't think most Dairy Queen restaurants are as clean or as well managed as their competitors. But many franchisees still have so much power that they can resist IDQ's efforts to make them change.

To combat this resistance, IDQ has begun an aggressive campaign to buy back its restaurants from the franchisees. It then installs more standardized procedures, menus, and so forth in an effort to boost quality. It also makes low-interest loans available to franchisees who want to follow the new guidelines for quality. Still, IDQ has a long way to go to achieve the companywide levels of productivity and quality it has set as a target.

SOURCES: "When Franchisees Go Their Own Way," *The Wall Street Journal,* July 6, 1989, p. B1; "The Proof Is in the Eating," *Forbes,* March 21, 1988, p. 109; Leslie Schultz, "Frozen Assets," *CFO,* April 1988, pp. 62–64.

☐ *Statistical quality control is a set of statistical techniques for improving quality.*

is called **statistical quality control,** which consists of a set of mathematical and/or statistical methods for measuring and adjusting quality levels.

For example, **acceptance sampling** is a process whereby finished goods are sampled to determine what proportion are of acceptable quality. By pre-establishing the desired quality level and then statistically determining confidence levels, the manager can determine what percentage of finished goods must be checked to achieve the target level of quality.

Similarly, **in-process sampling** involves testing products as they are being made, rather than after they are finished. In-process sampling works best for products like chemicals, paint, and so forth that go through various transformation steps.

Beyond the various statistical quality control techniques, other useful operational procedures for enhancing quality can be drawn from any of the different decision-making, control, and operations management methods discussed in Chapters 7, 17, and 18, respectively. The key, of course, is always to match the technique with the situation.

LEARNING CHECK

You should now be able to identify ways to improve quality through quality assurance and specific operational techniques.

RELATED CONTROL ISSUES

☐ Speed, time, and flexibility are important factors in improving productivity and quality.

In recent years, two related control concepts have been developed that may also play a role in improving productivity and quality. These are speed and time, and flexibility.

Speed and Time

Obviously, speed and time make a difference in productivity. If one organization can fill a customer's order in three days and another takes three weeks, the former is clearly at a competitive advantage.[13]

A recent survey of executives identified speed and time as the number one competitive issue of the 1990s.[14] It should come as no surprise, then, that many organizations are searching for ways to get things done faster. General Electric provides a good case in point. In 1985, the company needed three weeks to deliver a custom-made circuit breaker from the time the order was received. At the time, GE had six plants and several hundred workers involved. Now the same order can be delivered in only three days—using only one plant and 129 workers.[15]

GE accomplished this turnaround primarily by following the six guidelines listed in Table 19.3. For example, it totally revamped one of its plants (started from scratch) and eliminated most supervisory jobs (minimized the number of approvals). Given the dramatic successes achieved by GE and similar organi-

TABLE 19.3
Increasing the Speed of Operations

Strategy	Explanation
1. Start from scratch.	It's usually easier than trying to do what the organization does now but in a faster way.
2. Minimize the number of approvals needed to do something.	The fewer people who have to approve something, the faster it will get done.
3. Use work teams as a basis for organization.	Teamwork and cooperation work better than individual effort and conflict.
4. Develop and adhere to a schedule.	A properly designed schedule can greatly increase speed.
5. Don't ignore distribution.	Making something faster is only part of the battle.
6. Integrate speed into the organization's culture.	If everyone understands the importance of speed, things will naturally get done quicker.

SOURCE: Adapted from Brian Dumaine, "How Managers Can Succeed Through Speed," *Fortune*, February 13, 1989, pp. 54–59. © 1989 The Time Inc. Magazine Company. All rights reserved.

Organizations must often control the means by which their products are distributed. Coca-Cola uses pushcarts in remote areas like Jakarta to expand the availability of its beverages and get them in the hands of consumers in as little time as possible.

zations that have also promoted speed and time as major concerns, it is very likely that these issues will be of major importance in the years ahead.

Flexibility

Finally, organizations are also realizing that the greater the flexibility they maintain, the easier it is for them to adopt new methods and approaches and to respond to shifts in technology, consumer tastes, and so forth. For example, if a firm invests millions of dollars in a plant that is capable of making only a single product and of making it in only one way, it will be very vulnerable to obsolescence. If a new and cheaper method of making the same product is discovered, for example, the firm will either have to continue to produce at a cost disadvantage or else scrap the plant and start over.

Flexibility can be achieved in several different ways. For example, manufacturing technology can be installed that will enable the firm to alter work flow, add new equipment, or delete equipment without altering the overall production system too extensively. Another method is to train workers to be able to perform several different tasks so that the organization can easily shift employees between different jobs when demand shifts too much. Like speed and time, flexibility is likely to become increasingly important in the future.

LEARNING CHECK

You should now be able to discuss the related issues of speed and time and flexibility.

Chapter Summary

Productivity is an efficiency measure of how much is produced from inputs into the organization. It occurs at the level of the individual, the work unit, the entire organization, the industry, and the country. Productivity is important because it impacts on profitability and also determines standards of living.

Manufacturing productivity growth in the United States has started increasing again, following several years of stagnation. However, productivity in the service sector continues to grow slowly. In contrast, productivity rates are growing rapidly in many other countries.

Productivity can be improved through a variety of methods. Some of these are operations and management techniques, and others are based on motivation and involvement. Productivity is also related to quality.

Quality is assessed both in absolute and relative terms. It is important because of its relation to productivity, its role in competition, and its ability to lower costs.

Quality can also be improved in different ways. Quality assurance is a general managerial approach to quality improvement. In addition, various operational techniques can be used.

There are also other related control issues that affect productivity and quality. Some of these are speed and time and flexibility.

The Manager's Vocabulary

productivity	total factor productivity
individual productivity	quality
unit productivity	quality assurance
company productivity	statistical quality control
industry productivity	acceptance sampling
country productivity	in-process sampling

Prelude Case Wrap-Up

The Prelude Case for this chapter focuses on Corning Glass Works. When the current CEO, James Houghton, took over in 1983, he was concerned about productivity and quality. Consequently, he took a series of steps to improve both of these important areas.

As already noted, significant improvements have been made in both productivity and quality. These were accomplished through employee involvement and similar techniques. At a more general level, Houghton has turned things around through his own personal strategic commitment to enhancing the firm's reputation. He makes forty to fifty trips a year to the various Corning facilities to see that his goals are met.

Houghton thinks the costs of preventing, detecting, and paying for errors run between 20 and 30 percent of total sales. Given that level, it is obviously important that those costs be kept as low as possible. Houghton also believes employees can make even greater contributions than they currently do. Therefore, in 1991 Corning workers will have their ongoing program training increased to a full two weeks a year. Much of the additional training will be targeted at the productivity and quality areas.

We have already seen some specific payoffs of Houghton's efforts. At a more general level, many managers agree that the company's entire culture has started to shift. Participation, for example, is now more than just a suggestion box in the plant. More and more people at Corning are starting to realize that their opinions matter, that people will listen to their ideas, and that their team can be a winner.

Prelude Case Questions

1. What levels of productivity are most relevant for a company such as Corning?
2. Have operations or motivation and involvement been the primary contributors to change at Corning?
3. Describe how productivity and quality seem to be related at Corning.
4. How might speed and time and flexibility become more central to Corning?

Discussion Questions

Review Questions

1. What are some examples of different levels of productivity?

2. What has been the trend in productivity growth in the United States, compared with that of other countries, in recent years? What differences exist within the U.S. economy?

3. How are productivity and quality related to one another?

4. How can managers go about trying to increase productivity? Quality?

5. What role do speed, time, and flexibility play in productivity and quality?

Analysis Questions

1. Think of a few manufacturing jobs and a few service jobs with which you are familiar. What factors can you identify that might account for productivity differences between them?

2. Since productivity and quality are related, efforts to improve them might also be related. Identify compatible ways in which managers might try to boost productivity and quality simultaneously.

3. Brainstorm a list of products that American companies seem to make better than foreign competitors. Now do the same for products that foreign manufacturers seem to make better. Describe any trends you see.

4. Are there limits to productivity growth: that is, is it always possible to increase productivity? Why or why not?

5. Describe instances in which productivity and quality are *not* related.

Application Questions and Exercises

1. Working alone, develop three to five measures of productivity and quality for an airline, a hamburger restaurant, and a retail clothing shop. Compare your measures with those of some of your classmates.

2. Visit a local restaurant, barbershop or hair salon, or video rental store. Unobtrusively observe ways that productivity and quality might be improved.

3. Is it ever okay for a manager to make a conscious decision that productivity and quality are satisfactory and that no attention need be devoted to these areas? If so, how prevalent is this situation? Describe with specific examples.

4. Visit your library and update the productivity growth trends in the chapter. Are the trends changing? If so, how?

5. Interview a local businessperson and find out what she or he is doing to enhance productivity and quality.

ENHANCEMENT CASE

WESTINGHOUSE GETS SOME RESPECT

In the mid-1970s, Westinghouse was a mess. The firm consisted of a hodgepodge of businesses ranging from a record club to a low-income housing construction firm to a light bulb manufacturer. Profits were slim, return to stockholders abysmal, and the company a laughing stock in its industry.

When Robert Kirby was named CEO in 1975, he recognized that he had a formidable array of challenges before him. Wasting little time, he first opened communication channels. He proclaimed that if there was a problem in the company, he wanted to be the second person to know about it. Kirby also laid the groundwork for divesting many of Westinghouse's more unprofitable businesses.

Kirby resigned in 1983, and his successor, Douglas Danforth, actually ended up carrying out many of his plans and decisions. Between 1985 and 1987, Danforth sold seventy different businesses within Westinghouse and made fifty-five acquisitions. Throughout this turbulent period, sales remained constant. Even today, Westinghouse continues to shed unprofitable businesses and search for new opportunities.

One element in Westinghouse's new approach to doing business is its strategic planning system. The company calls its approach VABASTRAM (an acronym for *value-based strategic management*). The basis for VABASTRAM is to evaluate every business in terms of its real and potential contribution to shareholder value. Management then tries to optimize this value across a set of businesses.

In the United States today, there is a marked trend for companies to remain in a small set of core businesses central to their preferred markets. Thus, many large corporations are selling off businesses that are unrelated to their primary operations. Westinghouse, in contrast, continues to practice diversification.

For example, Westinghouse has seventy-five different businesses arranged in seven basic groups. The groups are industries (circuit breakers, motors, etc.), energy and utility systems (nuclear power, turbines, etc.), electronic systems (defense electronics, radar, etc.), Wesco (a chain of commercial electrical supply stores), commercial products (beverage bottling, office furniture, etc.), financial services (land development, real estate financing, etc.), and broadcasting (radio and television stations, satellite communications, etc.).

A critical part of Westinghouse's ability to make VABASTRAM work is a unique and sophisticated approach to managing productivity and quality. In the early 1980s, the company established a unit called the Productivity Center. The center was to serve as a resource for any manager or unit that had a productivity problem or that was having trouble reaching its desired levels of productivity.

Within months, managers working at the Productivity Center realized how intricately related productivity is to quality. Thus, almost immediately the unit was renamed the Productivity and Quality Center, and today many people call it the Quality Center for short.

The center is housed in a former Chrysler warehouse outside Pittsburgh (Westinghouse's headquarters). Although its composition is fluid, there are usually around 130 computer experts, engineers, and consultants on staff at any one time. The focus of the group is on improving the quality of both technological processes and final products and services so as to better meet customer needs.

Whenever it feels the need, a business unit can request a "total quality fitness review" from the center. (At present, the center gets around one hundred of these a year.) When such a call comes in, the center assembles a team and sends it out to help. The team conducts interviews with employees and customers, analyzes productivity and quality data, and tries to identify areas of training, manufacturing, and product design that are deficient.

The results are not passed up the hierarchy in a control sense. Instead, both the results and a set of recommendations are given to the manager who initially requested the review. The center's team is also available to work with the manager in implementing its recommendations.

The center has been an enormous success. Even in the normally sluggish service side, Westinghouse is increasing its productivity at a rate of 6 percent a year. Other companies have begun to notice the successes Westinghouse has achieved. Indeed, more than 2,000 organizations have sent representatives to visit the center during the last ten years. In all likelihood, it will become a model of how to enhance productivity and quality throughout the United States during the years ahead.

SOURCES: "Westinghouse Relies on Ruthlessly Rational Pruning," *The Wall Street Journal*, January 24, 1990, p. A4; Thomas A. Stewart, "Westinghouse Gets Respect at Last," *Fortune*, July 3, 1989, pp. 92–98; "How Westinghouse Is Revving Up After the Rebound," *Business Week*, March 28, 1988, pp. 46–52.

Enhancement Case Questions

1. Why would a company like Westinghouse be willing to open the doors of its center to other companies?
2. What advantages and disadvantages do you see in the center concept as used by Westinghouse?
3. How might the center help Westinghouse manage speed, time, and flexibility?
4. Do you think Westinghouse can continue to use the center as it has been, or will it need to change how it operates? Why?

Chapter Notes

1. See John W. Kendrick, *Understanding Productivity: An Introduction to the Dynamics of Productivity* (Baltimore, Md.: Johns Hopkins, 1977).

2. Brian O'Reilly, "America's Place in World Competition," *Fortune*, November 6, 1989, pp. 83–88.

3. "Faster May Soon Mean Foreign," *Industry Week*, November 30, 1987, p. 15.

4. Louis S. Richman, "How America Can Triumph," *Fortune*, December 18, 1989, pp. 52–66.

5. See Michael E. Porter, "The Competitive Advantage of Nations," *Harvard Business Review*, March-April 1990, pp. 73–93.

6. Michael E. Porter, "Why Nations Triumph," *Fortune*, March 12, 1990, pp. 94–108.

7. "How to Regain the Productive Edge," *Fortune*, May 22, 1989, pp. 92–104.

8. Gary Hector, "Yes, You *Can* Manage Long Term," *Fortune*, November 21, 1988, pp. 64–76.

9. William Bowen, "The Puny Payoff from Office Computers," *Fortune*, May 26, 1986, pp. 20–24.

10. Ross Johnson and William O. Winchell, *Management and Quality* (Milwaukee, Wisc.: American Society for Quality Control, 1989).

11. See Genichi Taguchi and Don Clausing, "Robust Quality," *Harvard Business Review*, January-February 1990, pp. 65–75.

12. "King Customer," *Business Week*, March 12, 1990, pp. 88–94.

13. George Stalk, Jr., and Thomas M. Hout, *Competing Against Time* (New York: Free Press, 1990).

14. Brian Dumaine, "How Managers Can Succeed Through Speed," *Fortune*, February 13, 1989, pp. 54–59.

15. Ibid.

THE ENTREPRENEURIAL SPIRIT

This fifth part of the book has introduced you to the last managerial function, that of controlling. You were first provided with an overview of the control function, including how to establish a control system and how to attain effective control. Specific control techniques, including budgets, financial analysis, human resource control, and marketing control, were next presented. Operations control was discussed in some detail, and the part concluded with a special chapter on the key issues of productivity and quality control.

Throughout these chapters you have been presented with examples of particular control problems and approaches of small businesses. Ben & Jerry's was used to illustrate the successful dedication to quality that many entrepreneurs have built into their organizations. In the case of C. C. Creations, a different point was made. Here the entrepreneur found himself using all of his personal time to try to control the use of new equipment. He then trained his work force as a team and delegated the operation to them so that he could use his time more wisely. We have seen several times that there is substantial evidence that many new business failures occur because the founding entrepreneur cannot make the transition to professional manager.

In many ways, control is a particularly critical function for entrepreneurs. Too much control can stifle the creativity and innovation so necessary to the success of a truly entrepreneurial organization. But too little control can so undermine performance that even the most innovative companies cannot survive because of poor quality or a lack of funds due to low sales. The support for continuing creativity and innovation throughout the entrepreneurial organization is frequently seen as more important than any other consideration. Yet, example after example can be given of innovative, entrepreneurial organizations that have gone bankrupt because of a lack of professional managerial control. This has been particularly true among high technology organizations where rapid growth and high sales can mask fatal financial weaknesses for some time. However, even among such organizations there are examples of success. Consider the case of Intel.

Andrew S. Grove was one of the founders of Intel and is currently its CEO. His company is a premier high-technology organization and a leader in innovation, and its success shows that keeping a balance between preserving the entrepreneurial spirit and ensuring that objectives are met is difficult but not impossible. Grove offers some sound advice on this issue. He maintains that in an environment where complexity, uncertainty, and ambiguity are high, management must ensure that individual motivation is based on group interest, because appealing to self-interest simply does not work under those conditions. In those circumstances, then, control is achieved through cultural values: workers achieve both high quantity and high quality because they believe that is the right thing to do.

If cultural values are the key to success, Grove feels that management has to develop and maintain those values by building trust through clarification and example. Clarification involves identifying the objectives and explaining how to achieve them, making certain that everyone knows what has to be done to accomplish those objectives, making certain that everyone knows how to do his or her part, and so on. Example means that management provides a model for everyone else in the organization. At Intel, then, managers, not just employees, work hard to perform well.

In many ways, this is like what C. C. Creations did. (See *Management Today: Small Business and Entrepreneurship* in Chapter 16.) The entrepreneur, Ford Taylor, created a culture in which the interests of his workers were linked to those of the organization. This ensured that people performed even if he was not there to "check up on them." Although there may be more risks with such approaches to control, they seem particularly effective in entrepreneurial organizations. In such a circumstance, the entrepreneur is able to spend his or her time and energy developing the organization rather than just running it.

Such sharing of control is, however, quite difficult for many entrepreneurs. Flexibility should be more important to the entrepreneurial organization than control, but nonetheless many entrepreneurs fear loss of control when their organizations grow and are, therefore, very reluctant to let go. It is important to create a culture and maintain a balance so that the organization does not get out of control and yet is not overly controlled.

SOURCES: Barbara J. Bird, *Entrepreneurial Behavior* (Glenview, Ill.: Scott, Foresman, 1989); Adam Osborne and John C. Dvorak, *Hypergrowth* (Berkeley, Calif.: Idthekkethan Publishing, 1984); Andrew S. Grove, *High Output Management* (New York: Random House, 1983); S. P. Robbins, *Organization Theory: The Structure and Design of Organizations* (Englewood Cliffs, N.J.: Prentice-Hall, 1983); J. Hage and R. Dewar, "Elite Values Versus Organizational Structure in Predicting Innovation," *Administrative Science Quarterly*, vol. 18, no. 3 (1973), pp. 279–290.

Special Challenges of Management

This section is devoted to a variety of special challenges managers face in all aspects of their work. Chapter 20 explores organization change and development. The increasing importance of the international arena is the topic of Chapter 21. Finally, Chapter 22 notes a number of future challenges managers must be prepared to confront.

CHAPTER OUTLINE

I. The Nature of Organization Change
  A. Reasons for Change
  B. Planned Organization Change
  C. Steps in Planned Change

II. Managing Organization Change
  A. Resistance to Change
  B. Overcoming Resistance to Change

III. Areas of Organization Change
  A. Strategic Change
  B. Structural Change
  C. Technological Change
  D. People-Focused Change

IV. Organization Development
  A. The Nature of Organization Development
  B. Organization Development Techniques

V. Organization Revitalization
  A. Reasons for Revitalization
  B. Stages in Revitalization

CHAPTER

20

After studying this chapter you should be able to

1. Discuss the nature of change, including the reasons and need for change, planned organization change, and the steps involved in planned change.

2. Explain why people resist change and how to overcome that resistance.

3. Identify strategic, structural, technological, and people-focused approaches to change.

4. Define and discuss the nature and techniques of organization development.

5. Explain why organizations may need to undergo revitalization and the general growth pattern they often follow.

Organization Change and Development

DOUBLE TROUBLE AT UNISYS

It seemed like a marriage made in heaven—two large (but ailing) computer giants merging to form an industry colossus. This was the picture being painted in 1986 when the Sperry Corporation and the Burroughs Corporation merged to create the third largest computer manufacturer in the United States. The new firm was named Unisys.

Unfortunately, many of the anticipated advantages of the merger have never materialized. Moreover, the company has continued to struggle with how to truly become one firm instead of two operating out of the same building. Few managers at either company anticipated the difficulties they would encounter in trying to pull off one of the largest planned change efforts in history.

At one time, Sperry (originally named Sperry-Rand) dominated the computer industry. It made the famous Univac computer and was predicting as early as 1952 that managers would one day have computers that would fit inside a briefcase. Unfortunately, Sperry lost ground to IBM and eventually dropped behind both IBM and Digital in the mainframe market.

Burroughs achieved its greatest successes by being a follower. The company focused its marketing research efforts in highly select areas. At the same time, it waited for others to achieve significant technological breakthroughs and then copied or imitated those successes. Burroughs eventually fell behind as well, however.

In the early 1980s, both Sperry and Burroughs were clearly slipping. Both were losing market share, both had quality problems, and both were introducing new products later and later. One key error both firms made was to stay primarily in the main-frame market. Companies like IBM were succeeding with both main-frames and personal computers; others, like Apple, were concentrating on personal computers only. Sperry and Burroughs, however, decided to stay away from minicomputers and personal computers.

Top management at each firm made several efforts to turn things around. For example, each company went through periods of major cutbacks. Each eliminated employees, each changed its strategy, each altered its organization design, and each changed top-management teams at least once. But nothing helped. Traditional rivals like IBM and Digital continued to pull away, and new competitors like Compaq, Tandem, and others were coming onto the scene.

Gerald Probst, CEO of Sperry, and Michael Blumenthal, CEO of Burroughs, decided that the only way either firm could regain its standing in the industry was to merge. Neither firm had the resources to fight back against its emerging competitors. At the same time, though, each did have a loyal customer base and an established product line to sustain itself. By merging, Probst and Blumenthal reasoned, they could essentially add together the market shares and customer bases of each firm, creating a far bigger company.

Several task forces were created to help facilitate the merger. A new organization design was created to accommodate Unisys. Psychologists were hired to help key people make the transition to a new type of organization. And the new name was selected so that neither of the existing companies could be identified as either a "winner" or a "loser" as a result of the merger.

Probst retired when the merger was almost finished, leaving Blumenthal to run the new firm. At first, things seemed to go about as well as might have been expected. There were tensions and conflicts. People quarreled, and there was a period of inefficiency during which the firm did not function well. Overall, however, the merger was generally seen as a success.

However, in late 1989, problems began to surface. Profits were lower than projected. Several key top managers had left the organization for a variety of reasons. Some insiders grumbled that Unisys was still just two different companies with a common name and CEO. And opinions varied greatly as to the future of the firm.

Sarah Leen

Michael Blumenthal is CEO of Unisys. He oversaw the creation of Unisys through the merger of Burroughs and Sperry and is today trying to steer the computer firm back to the top of its industry.

SOURCES: "This Is Hardly the Turning Point Unisys Had in Mind," *Business Week*, August 28, 1989, pp. 82–84; "Unisys Struggles with Double Trouble," *USA Today*, August 30, 1989, p. 3B; "How Burroughs Finally Won Sperry," *Business Week*, June 9, 1986, pp. 28–29; "Unisys: So Far, So Good—But the Real Test is Yet to Come," *Business Week*, March 2, 1987, pp. 84–86.

Unisys presents a vivid portrait of the complexities and issues involved in the management of organization change. Sperry and Burroughs each underwent several changes independently and then changed again through a full-scale merger. And Unisys continues to change today. All organizations must change if they are to survive. Indeed, their ability to effectively manage change is often a critical ingredient to their survival.

This chapter explores organization change and two of its related areas, organization development and revitalization. First it discusses the nature of change. Then it describes ways that change can be more effectively managed, highlighting why people resist change and ways to overcome that resistance. Four general areas of organization change are then identified. The final two sections focus on organization development and organization revitalization.

THE NATURE OF ORGANIZATION CHANGE

□ *Organization change* is a fundamental change in some aspect of the organization.

Disney has dramatically increased the number of new movies it will make each year. Unisys recently announced that it would reduce its work force by 8,000 employees. Apple Computer has changed its organization design several times in recent years. Westinghouse has eliminated typewriters from its corporate offices and replaced them with computers.[1] All these examples represent a fundamental change in some aspect of the organization—a form of **organization change.** Disney has changed its strategy and is trying to make movies a more important part of its business. Unisys is currently changing its human resource system. Apple is changing its structure. And Westinghouse has implemented a technological change. Why were these changes felt to be necessary? To answer this question, we must explore some of the reasons for organization change and look at the steps that managers usually follow in making such changes.

Reasons for Change

□ Reasons for change are associated with forces in the organization's task and/or general environments.

An organization might find it necessary to change for a variety of different reasons. As shown in Exhibit 20.1, the most common reasons for change stem from one or more forces in the organization's general and/or task environments, as discussed previously in Chapter 4.[2]

Consider, for example, how shifts in an organization's general environment might force it to respond. Technological forces might provide new equipment or make existing technology obsolete. For example, newly automated work processes might have to be implemented to reduce labor costs and improve quality and productivity. Political-legal forces might introduce new legislation or regulations that affect the organization. For example, a new law that increases safety standards for the firm's products might alter the parts the firm uses in assembling the product.

Exhibit 20.1 Reasons for Change

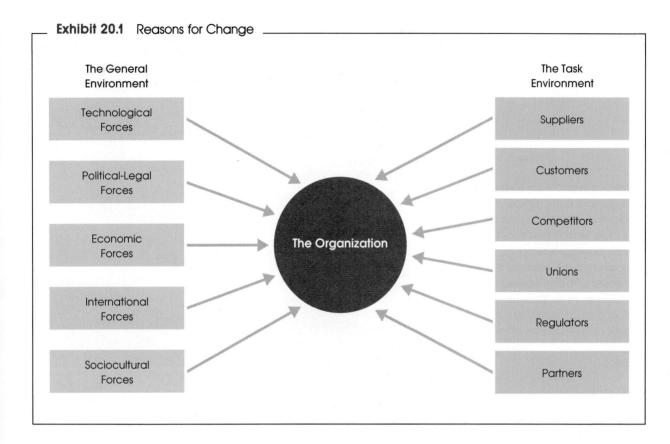

Economic forces could impact an organization in several different ways. For example, inflation or changes in unemployment might affect how the organization hires new employees. Similarly, shifts in interest rates might change a firm's ability or willingness to borrow money. International forces are also becoming increasingly important. For example, new markets and/or competition might emerge in other countries. Finally, sociocultural forces are also important in many different circumstances. For example, general shifts in consumer values and preferences about alcohol are changing how alcohol-producing companies like Miller and Coors do business.

In similar fashion, the task environment can also bring about organization change. Suppliers can raise or lower prices, alter quality standards, or change delivery schedules. Customers might turn to alternative products or demand higher quality or lower prices. Competitors might raise or lower prices, introduce new products or services, or adjust their advertising techniques. Unions might demand higher wages, better working conditions, or a greater voice in making decisions. Regulators might impose new restrictions on how the organization does business or modify the ways the organization can do certain things. And partners might want to negotiate new joint venture agreements or modify or cancel existing ones.

Terry Husebye

Some organizations are finding that changes in the general and/or task environments are providing new business opportunities. Westinghouse, for example, has adapted radar systems from military applications for use on dirigibles to detect drug smugglers' airplanes as they cross the border from Mexico into the United States.

P R E L U D E   C A S E   U P D A T E

Many of the forces that led to the creation of Unisys grew from the general and task environments faced by Sperry and Burroughs. For example, technological forces increased both the role of computers in organizations and the methods by which they could be produced. And economies of scale also led to lower and lower prices for computers. From the task environment, competitors like IBM and Digital clearly played important roles. And in some ways, the merger that created Unisys resulted from a new partnership between the two original companies.

Planned Organization Change

☐ *Planned organization change* is the anticipation of possible changes in the environment and a consideration of how the organization should most likely respond to those changes.

One of the ways in which organizations can deal with these forces in the general and task environments is to try to anticipate them ahead of time. In most cases, the company that senses the need for a change before the change is actually needed and then plans for that change in a careful and systematic fashion will be more effective than the company that waits to be forced to respond.[3]

The former approach is called **planned organization change.** In general, planned organization change involves the anticipation of possible changes in the environment to which the organization will have to respond and some consideration of how that response will occur. Of course, managers cannot always accurately predict the future. Even an imperfect vision of what the future holds for a business, however, is almost certain to be better than no vision at all.

In contrast, **reactive change** is when the organization pays little attention to anticipating environmental shifts and must consequently react to the environmental change when it occurs. For example, as noted in the Prelude Case, Burroughs tended to wait and see what new technology its competitors developed and then tried to respond to those changes. And as you might infer, such a reactive approach is probably one thing that hurt Burroughs.

☐ *Reactive change* is an unplanned response to environmental changes as they occur.

Steps in Planned Change

When an organization is successful in its efforts to anticipate the need for change, it will be able to manage that change in a comparatively rational and logical way. Exhibit 20.2 summarizes the steps that can be followed.[4]

First, logically, the process must start with the recognition of a need for change. This recognition might come in the form of an anticipated event. For example, a manager may read about a new technological breakthrough that will soon be available and that she believes will be applicable to her organization. Or an employee might casually mention that workers in the organization would greatly appreciate an on-site child-care facility.

After deciding that a change is needed, the manager must set goals for the change. That is, she must consider why the change is being considered and what should be gained from it. For instance, she might decide that adopting

Exhibit 20.2 Planned Organization Change

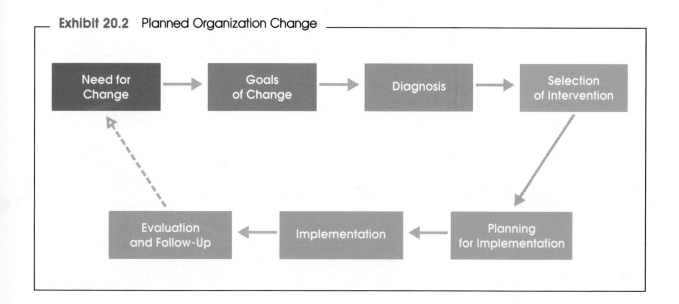

the new technology should cut costs or that the on-site day-care facility should lower employee absenteeism. Obviously, if the change will not benefit the organization in some way, it might be advisable to delay making it until it has more potential.

The third step is diagnosis. This means that the manager should look carefully at the organizational system to identify all of the possible effects of the change. The new technology she is considering might call for employee training, a new performance appraisal system, and higher pay. The child-care facility might require the services of a full-time nurse and other personnel.

Next, the manager chooses the actual intervention to use. For example, several forms of the technology might be available, and it might be possible to buy or lease it. The child-care facility could be operated by the organization itself or managed by an outside company. Each of these options, as well as others, needs to be considered.

The dynamics associated with the intervention must also be carefully planned. The manager must ask herself when the technology will be introduced, whether it will be introduced in stages or all at once, and whether it will be installed in all plants or just in one, as a pilot. When will the training be done, who will do it, and who will be eligible for the training? When will the child-care center be opened, what are its potential hours of operation, how much will employees pay, and what are the insurance implications?

When these and a myriad of other questions have been answered, implementation can take place. Of course, some period of time will probably be necessary to get things fully operational, and some problems will probably have to be worked out. The manager should anticipate and expect these so as not to abandon the change before it has had ample time to demonstrate its usefulness. The day-care center, for example, might need to be phased in gradually over a period of time.

Finally, after the change has been fully installed and is operating smoothly, the manager should evaluate it carefully to ensure that it has met its original goals. After the new technology has been installed, productivity should go up and costs should go down. Absenteeism should also go down once the child-care facility is in place. Assuming that the goals have been reasonably met, the process is essentially complete, and the manager can wait for the next opportunity for change. If the goals are not being met (for example, if the child-care facility is not being used or absenteeism has not dropped), additional fine-tuning may be in order.

LEARNING CHECK

You should now be able to discuss the nature of change, including the reasons and need for change, planned organization change, and the steps involved in planned change.

MANAGING ORGANIZATION CHANGE

Obviously, many of these points relate to the management of organization change, but there are also other aspects of the process. Two that are especially critical are recognizing that people often resist change and understanding ways to overcome this resistance.[5]

Resistance to Change

☐ People resist change because of uncertainty, self-interests, differing perceptions, and feelings of loss.

People in organizations resist change for a variety of reasons. As summarized in Table 20.1, the four most common reasons are uncertainty, self-interests, differing perceptions, and feelings of loss.

First, for a variety of reasons, change breeds uncertainty. People may fear for their place in the organization. They may worry that they cannot meet new job demands or that their job will be eliminated. They may dread the ambiguity that frequently accompanies change. As a result of this uncertainty, they may also feel anxious and nervous. They resist the change in order to cope better with these feelings. Many U.S. government workers are apparently resisting efforts to automate their work because of their uncertainty about the new technology they are having to learn to use.[6]

People also resist change because it threatens their own self-interests. A plant manager might resist a change to automate his plant because he fears it threatens his control of personnel. Likewise, another manager may resist a new automated information network because it will give others access to information that he alone previously controlled.

Differing perceptions also cause resistance to change. For example, a manager with a marketing background might conduct the diagnostic phase of the change process and conclude that a change in promotion and advertising is needed. However, a manager with an operations background might see the problem in terms of quality and productivity. Thus, he sees the situation in a different light and will likely conclude that a different intervention is needed. Consequently, he might resist the change as first proposed by the marketing manager because he perceives the situation differently.

Finally, an individual might resist change because of feelings of loss. Many changes involve alterations in work assignments and work schedules and thus break up informal groups and close working relationships among peers. Loss of power, status, security, or familiarity with existing procedures can also be a problem. *Management Today: The World of Management* illustrates how people at one organization have resisted change.

Overcoming Resistance to Change

☐ Resistance to change can sometimes be overcome through participation, communication, facilitation, and *force-field analysis.*

Fortunately, managers can at least partially overcome resistance to change in several ways. Four especially useful ones are also noted in Table 20.1.

TABLE 20.1
Resistance to Change

Common Reasons for Resistance	Ways to Overcome Resistance
1. Uncertainty	1. Participation
2. Self-interests	2. Communication
3. Differing Perceptions	3. Facilitation
4. Feelings of Loss	4. Force-Field Analysis

THE WORLD OF MANAGEMENT

Beecham Changes with the Times

The Beecham Group PLC is a staid, old-line British company. Although many consumers are familiar with its products (including Tums, Geritol, Sominex, Sucrets, Brylcreem, Cling Free, Calgon, Massengill, and Aqua-Fresh), few know much about the business behind them.

A few years ago, Beecham's directors decided that the firm was ill-prepared to compete in what they saw as an increasingly competitive global market. They also felt that the best source of relief was from outside. Accordingly, they hired an American CEO, Robert Bauman, and instructed him to impart an American culture to the firm.

Bauman took his instructions to heart. First of all, he led in the development of Beecham's first-ever strategic plan. He also fired fifteen top executives and replaced eleven of them with outsiders. Bauman also initiated several new product development ventures.

Not every change has gone smoothly, however. For one thing, he had to drop his plan to have an American consulting firm review all of Beecham's operations because his top-management team fought it. He also had to drop his plan of implementing an American-style incentive pay plan because workers threatened to strike.

Overall, however, Bauman has been successful in his efforts to transform Beecham into a world-class competitor. Indeed, when Beecham recently merged with the American drug company SmithKline, he was tapped for the top job in the combined firm. Thus, although not all his ideas have been adopted, he is still apparently held in high regard.

SOURCES: "Beecham's Chief Imports American Ways," *The Wall Street Journal,* October 27, 1988, p. B9; Robert Teitelman, "Reverse English," *Financial World,* November 15, 1988, pp. 24–27; "SmithKline Beecham's Synergy Sputters," *The Wall Street Journal,* March 14, 1990, p. A5.

One key approach is to encourage participation. When people participate, they feel less threatened, recognize that they have a say in what happens, and are less concerned about feelings of loss. Logically, then, they will come to lower their resistance to the change.

Open communication also helps overcome resistance. Complete and accurate information helps remove the uncertainty that so often accompanies change. Managers should provide information that is relevant to the change as often as they can.

Facilitation, which means simply recognizing that resistance may be present and actively working to manage it, can also reduce resistance. For example, introducing change gradually helps minimize its impact. Being sensitive to people's concerns and helping them resolve those concerns rationally can also be effective.

Another management approach to overcoming resistance to change is the use of **force-field analysis.** The first step in using force-field analysis is to systematically look at the pluses and minuses associated with the change from the standpoint of the employees. Next, the manager should try to increase the pluses and decrease the minuses in order to tip the scales toward acceptance. For example, if a major barrier to an impending change is that a certain work group will be broken up, the manager might try to figure out a way to keep the group intact. If that can be arranged, one minus has been eliminated. Likewise, if one thing working in favor of the change is greater autonomy over how the job is done, providing even more autonomy and making sure employees see how this will benefit them will further increase acceptance of the impending change.

AREAS OF ORGANIZATION CHANGE

So far this chapter has talked a lot about organization change but has not really focused on exactly what the organization might actually be changing. This section identifies the four major areas of organization change. As shown in Table 20.2, these are strategy, structure, technology, and people.[7]

Strategic Change

☐ *Strategic change* occurs when the organization modifies or adopts a new strategy.

Whenever an organization modifies its strategy or adopts a new strategy, it has engaged in **strategic change.** At the corporate level (as discussed in Chapter 6), for example, a firm might move from a growth to a retrenchment strategy. Or it might move from a retrenchment strategy to one of stability. From a portfolio perspective, a corporation might eliminate one or more strategic business units and/or acquire new ones.

At the business level, an organization might shift between the defending, prospecting, and analyzing approaches. Likewise, it might move from a differentiation strategy to one of cost leadership, or from cost leadership to targeting.

TABLE 20.2
Areas of Organization Change

Strategic Change	Structural Change	Technological Change	People-Focused Change
Corporate Strategy	Components of Structure	Equipment	Skills
Business Strategy	Organization Design	Work Processes	Performance
Functional Strategy	Reward System	Work Sequence	Attitudes
	Performance Appraisal System	Automation	Perceptions
	Control System	Information Processing System	Behaviors
			Expectations

Organizations sometimes have to adopt strategic changes in order to remain competitive. McDonald's, for example, is experimenting with serving pizzas in some of its restaurants. The move was prompted by a combination of aggressive advertising by Pizza Hut and McDonald's fear that growing health concerns would drive consumers away from its sandwiches.

Finally, the organization might also change one or more of its functional strategies. These changes might occur in any or all of the areas of marketing, finance, production, research and development, human resources, or organization design.

PRELUDE CASE UPDATE

Unisys represents an example of two organizations (Sperry and Burroughs) that made the decision to dramatically change their strategies. Each decided that it lacked the resources and clout to be a dominant firm in the computer industry. Rather than look for other markets to enter, the two companies decided to merge. And as a direct result of this change in corporate strategy, each functional strategy has also had to be modified. Although such actions are perhaps less common than other strategic changes, for these firms they nevertheless represented a new approach to improving an environmental position.

Structural Change

□ *Structural change* focuses on part of the formal organization itself.

Structural change is any change directed at a part of the formal organizational system.[8] In general, such changes relate to structural components, overall organization design, or other aspects of the organization.

MANAGEMENT IN PRACTICE

Cutting Out Layers at the Franklin Mint

The Franklin Mint is not a mint at all. Instead, the firm makes collectible objects like leather-bound books, commemorative coins, and collector's plates. It does about $500 million in business each year.

Stewart Resnick was promoted to the position of CEO at Franklin Mint about four years ago. One of his first observations was that the company was sluggish in how it responded to its environment. He attributed these characteristics to the fact that Franklin had an unusually tall organization design with narrow spans of management.

Therefore, Resnick set out to change the basic structure of the firm to make it more responsive to its environment. His most significant change was to reduce the number of layers in the organization's hierarchy from six to four. This action improved communication and coordination while also making it easier for managers to get things done. Resnick also doubled the number of people who report directly to him from six to twelve. Moreover, he plans to double it again in the next five years.

What effect have these changes had? Franklin's profits continue to surge, the number of new products being introduced increases each year, and the company's stock price continues to escalate.

SOURCES: Jeremy Main, "The Winning Organization," *Fortune,* September 26, 1988, pp. 50–60; Ruth Podems, "The Mint Man Does it Again," *Target Marketing,* October 1988, pp. 39–40; Karen Gillick, "Success²," *Direct Marketing,* January 1988, pp. 84–101.

Chapter 8 identified several basic components of organization structure. Logically, one or more of these components will need to be changed from time to time. That is, the organization might change its degree of decentralization, its span of management, or its bases of departmentalization. Other structural components can also change—the organization may adopt new methods of coordination, change the degree of job specialization, or modify working hours for employees.

On a larger scale, the company might need to change its overall design. It has been estimated that most companies need changes of this magnitude every five years or so.[9] In Chapter 9, we looked at several forms of organization design. Whenever a firm changes its design, it is embarking on a major organization change. In the late 1970s, for instance, Texas Instruments changed from a functionally organized firm to a matrix organization. In the early 1980s it modified its matrix design.[10] And more recently, the firm decided to alter its design once again to more effectively compete in the international arena.[11] *Management Today: Management in Practice* describes another structural change recently made by another firm.

Of course, there are also other areas in which structural changes may be made. Common changes in this category include changes in the organization's reward system, its performance appraisal system, and/or its control system.

557

Technological Change

A third major type of change is that related to technology. **Technological change** has been increasingly widespread in the last few years.[12] Like strategic and structural change, it comes in many forms. One obvious area is new equipment. As new and more efficient machines are introduced into the market, manufacturers occasionally need to upgrade in order to keep pace.

Changes may also affect work processes or sequences. For instance, a decision to produce plastic flashlight casings instead of metal ones necessitates major changes in the work processes. Similarly, the sequence of work can change as management considers new ways of arranging the workplace. This area will become increasingly important as flexible manufacturing systems come to replace traditional assembly lines.

Automation is a major form of technological change. Such changes as those made by Nissan, which recently installed over two hundred computer-controlled robots in its Tennessee plant, greatly increase productivity but also represent a major capital investment.

Finally, significant changes can also be made in the organization's information processing system. As we have noted, typewriters are increasingly being replaced with word processors, and managers are now provided with personal computers. Each individual piece of equipment can be tied with the others in an integrated network to provide access to large blocks of data. Such data processing capabilities represent major changes.

People-Focused Change

Finally, change can be focused on people within the organization. **People-focused change** can actually affect two distinct areas: (1) skills and performance and (2) attitudes, perceptions, behaviors, and expectations.

In general, managers can take three approaches to upgrading skills and performance. First, current employees can be replaced. This is clearly a difficult route to choose and usually should be taken only when no other options are available. Alternatively, managers can gradually upgrade selection standards. With this approach, existing employees are not dismissed, but when someone leaves for a better job, retires, or is fired, his or her replacement is selected with higher standards. A third option is to train existing employees so as to upgrade their performance-related skills.

Change focused more on attitudes, perceptions, behaviors, and expectations is often undertaken from the perspective of organization development. This area is discussed in more detail in the next section.

ORGANIZATION DEVELOPMENT

As already noted, organization development focuses on changing attitudes, perceptions, behaviors, and expectations.

The Nature of Organization Development

☐ *Organization development is a planned, organization-wide effort to improve the health of the organization by systematically applying behavioral science techniques.*

Organization development can be defined as a planned, organization-wide effort to enhance organizational health and effectiveness through the systematic application of behavioral science techniques.[13] Rather than being a single, isolated change, organization development actually represents a complete philosophy of management. It assumes that people want to grow and develop, that they are capable of making useful contributions, and that one of the missions of the organization is to help facilitate personal growth as a way of enhancing employees' contributions.

Many large organizations practice organization development on a regular basis. For example, American Airlines, Federated Department Stores, ITT, Polaroid, Procter & Gamble, and B. F. Goodrich have major organization development programs under way at all times. Goodrich, in fact, has trained sixty people in organization development processes and techniques. They serve as internal consultants, helping other managers who feel a need to use organization development.

Team building is one very popular form of organization development. The group shown here is comprised of three employees of Gannett, publisher of *USA Today*. As part of their team-building exercise, the group has been given one hour to devise a hypothetical direct-mail campaign for a potential client. After they are finished, a group facilitator will help them understand how they did and did not work well together.

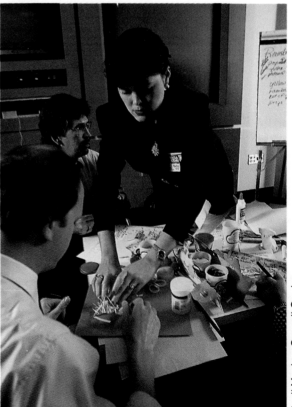

Scott Maclay, Gannett Co., Inc.

Organization Development Techniques

☐ Common organization development techniques include the *Managerial Grid®*, *team building*, *survey feedback*, *third-party peace making*, and *process consultation*.

A number of change techniques fall under the organization development umbrella. One of the best known is the **Managerial Grid®**, which is used to assess current leadership styles in an organization and then to train leaders to practice an ideal style of behavior.[14]

The basic Grid framework is shown in Exhibit 20.3. The axes of the Grid represent concern for people and concern for production. Each leader is scored from one to nine along each dimension. The five main leadership styles (1,1; 1,9; 9,1; 5,5; and 9,9) are shown in the exhibit.

Exhibit 20.3   The Managerial Grid®

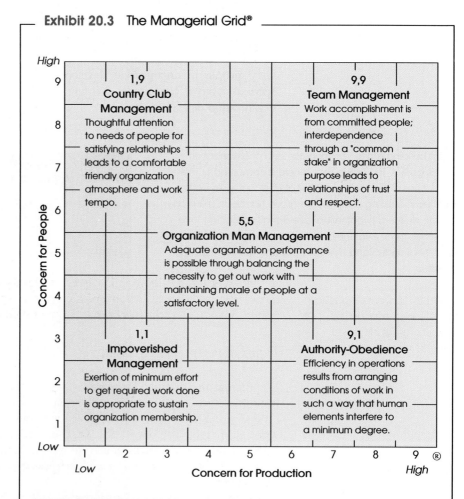

SOURCE: The Managerial Grid Figure from *The Managerial Grid III: The Key to Leadership Excellence*, by Robert R. Blake and Jane Srygley Mouton. Houston: Gulf Publishing Company, Copyright © 1985, page 12. Reproduced by permission.

The Grid assumes that the 9,9 combination is the ideal style of behavior for leaders. Managers in the organizations that use the Grid go through a six-phase training program that moves them in the general direction of the 9,9 co-ordinates. Although some people are critical of the Grid's effectiveness, others claim it has been quite beneficial.

In addition to the Grid, of course, other organization development techniques are used by many organizations.[15] **Team building,** for example, is used to enhance the motivation and satisfaction of people in groups. It is a series of activities and exercises designed to foster mutual understanding, acceptance, and group cohesion. **Survey feedback,** surveying subordinates about their perceptions of their leader and then providing feedback to the entire group, is used to increase communication between leaders and their subordinates.

A separate set of organization development activities focuses on improving coordination and communication among different groups. **Third-party peace making** is an organization development effort concentrated on resolving conflict, especially conflict that is quite strong and that has existed for a long time. A neutral observer, often a trained behavioral scientist from outside the firm, acts as a mediator. He or she listens to all sides and then helps the relevant parties process the issues until the conflict is resolved.

Process consultation involves having an organization development expert observe communication, decision-making, and leadership processes in the organization and then suggest ways to improve them. Other activities are directed at specific areas, such as assisting in life and career planning and individual goal setting.

> **LEARNING CHECK**
>
> You should now be able to define and discuss the nature and techniques of organization development.

ORGANIZATION REVITALIZATION

> ☐ *Organization revitalization is a planned effort to bring new energy, vitality, and strength to an organization.*

A final aspect of organization change that organizations occasionally must use is revitalization. **Organization revitalization** is a planned effort to infuse new energy, vitality, and strength into an organization.

Reasons for Revitalization

Why is revitalization necessary? For the most part, organizations do an imperfect job of staying in touch with their environments. Since environments change rapidly, the best most organizations can do is to approximate the best strategy, design, and so forth that fits their particularly unique situation. Even such well-managed organizations as Disney and American Airlines must occasionally step back and work to improve their relationship with their environments.

Sometimes, however, an organization falls so far out of alignment with its environment that simple adjustments and shifts are not enough. When this happens, the organization must undergo a major change in order to get back in touch with the environment.

P R E L U D E   C A S E   U P D A T E

Both Sperry and Burroughs failed to maintain a good fit with their environment. Although each was a strong company in its own right at one time, each also lost touch and began to encounter serious difficulties. As noted in the text, this sometimes happens to almost all companies. IBM and Digital, for example, have both had their ups and downs. However, these two firms saw the down times coming and were able to take action to turn things around quickly. Sperry and Burroughs, on the other hand, failed to properly anticipate their problems and then failed to take sufficient actions to get back on track. As a result, they fell so far out of alignment that a major revitalization effort was necessary.

Stages in Revitalization

Exhibit 20.4 illustrates the general pattern of growth that many companies undergo. First of all, an organization has what might be called normal "momentum"—it is growing and effectively reaching its goals regularly. At

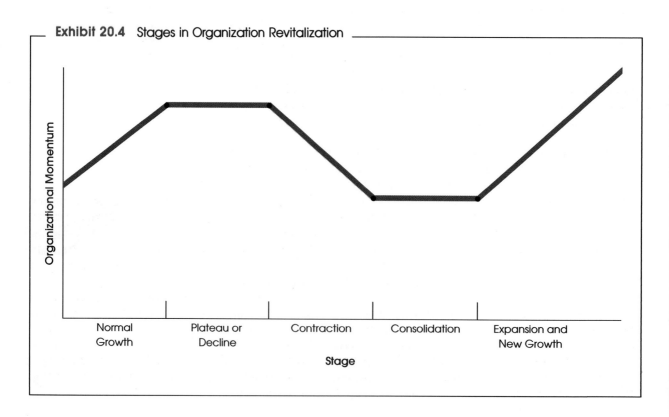

Exhibit 20.4   Stages in Organization Revitalization

some point, however, the organization falls so far out of alignment with its environment that its growth plateaus or goes into a decline.

If this happens and the firm can't turn things around, it may have to enter a planned period of contraction. During this stage, the organization cuts back on its operations, eliminates unnecessary facilities, and so forth.

Next comes consolidation. During this phase, the organization learns to live with a leaner and tighter budget. Eventually, if things go well, the organization will be able to start expanding and growing once again.

During these various stages, the company may undertake a number of initiatives to facilitate its revitalization. For example, it may bring in a new management team. It may also seek an infusion of new capital through extended bank loans or new investment. Some firms even go so far as to change their names. International Harvester became Navistar, U.S. Steel became USX, and the Sperry-Burroughs combination became Unisys.

LEARNING CHECK

You should now be able to explain why organizations may need to undergo revitalization and the general growth pattern they often follow.

Chapter Summary

Organization change is a meaningful alteration in some part of the organization. Forces in the general and task environments can prompt the need for change. Whenever possible, organizations should plan for change. Planned change can be pursued through a series of rational and logical steps.

People resist change for a variety of reasons, including uncertainty, self-interests, differing perceptions, and feelings of loss. There are four common methods of overcoming this resistance: participation, open communication, facilitation, and force-field analysis.

Organization change generally takes place in one or more of four areas: strategy, structure, technology, and people. Strategic change can occur at the corporate, business, or functional levels. Structural change involves changes in the formal organizational system. Technological change might involve new and different machines or work processes. People-focused change involves changes in the skills, performance, attitudes, perceptions, behaviors, and expectations of the people in the organization.

Organization development is a planned, organization-wide effort to enhance organizational health and effectiveness through the systematic application of behavioral science techniques. Organization revitalization is a planned effort to infuse new energy, vitality, and strength into an organization.

The Manager's Vocabulary

organization change
planned organization
  change
reactive change
force-field analysis
strategic change
structural change
technological change
people-focused change
organization
  development

Managerial Grid®
team building
survey feedback
third-party peace
  making
process consultation
organization
  revitalization

Prelude Case Wrap-Up

The Prelude Case for this chapter explains how Sperry and Burroughs combined to form a new firm called Unisys. As detailed in the case, each firm underwent a series of changes before the merger, experienced the merger itself, and has undergone still other changes since that time.

As noted in the chapter itself, the reasons for the various changes relate to various shifts in the general and task environments of the two original companies. Today, Unisys still has to deal with competitive pressures from IBM (task environment) and a slump in the overall demand for mainframe computers (general environment).

Unisys responds to these pressures in a variety of ways. For one thing, Blumenthal recently imposed a salary and hiring freeze. He also announced that the company's total work force of 88,000 employees would be cut by 7 or 8 percent. Finally, he announced that some plants would be closed and operations merged into existing facilities.

What kind of future does Unisys have? There are very different opinions. Blumenthal believes that Unisys will again be a dominant competitor in the computer industry by 1993. He projects substantial growth in both overall sales and profitability by that time.

Other observers, however, are more pessimistic. They claim that Blumenthal is so distracted by politics and other interests that he is neglecting the company. They also note that the company continues to run late in delivering new products and that its recent announcement that it is entering the personal computer market may be too late. There is also speculation that Unisys may be a prime takeover candidate for another company eager to acquire its technology.

Prelude Case Questions

1. Have the changes at Unisys been primarily planned or reactive?
2. How might Blumenthal have applied the planned change steps in merging Sperry and Burroughs?
3. Why might employees at both firms have resisted the merger? What could have been done to overcome that resistance?
4. Do you think Unisys is a candidate for revitalization? Why or why not?

Discussion Questions

Review Questions

1. What are the basic steps to be followed in planned change?
2. Identify the basic reasons people resist change and the most common methods of overcoming that resistance.
3. Provide at least two examples of each area of organization change.

4. What is organization development? What are some of its more common techniques?
5. Why do organizations sometimes find it necessary to go through a period of revitalization?

Analysis Questions

1. Heraclitus once said, "There is nothing permanent except change." Do you think change is, in fact, inevitable? Why or why not?
2. The text notes that people tend to resist change. Are there some people who like change? Who are they, and why do they like it? Is it possible for people to initiate too much change? Why or why not?
3. What changes have you experienced lately? How did you handle them?
4. Which type of change is most likely to affect the average operating employee? The average middle manager? The average top manager?
5. Identify an organization that has had to go through a period of revitalization. Was it successful? Why or why not?

Application Questions and Exercises

1. The various areas of change are likely to be interrelated. Think of a hypothetical change in one area. Diagram how that change might lead to the need for other changes.
2. Think of a change situation you recently observed or experienced. Diagram how a force-field analysis might have facilitated the change.
3. Interview a local manager and find out about a change her or his organization has recently undergone. Find out how the change was managed.
4. Interview an employee who works for a local company. Identify a change the employee has experienced at work, and determine how the individual felt about it (if he or she resisted the change, why or why not, and so forth).
5. Many management and psychology departments have faculty members who serve as organization development consultants. Find out if there is such a person at your college or university and, if so, invite him or her to class to discuss his or her experiences.

ENHANCEMENT CASE

CATERPILLAR SHEDS ITS COCOON

In many ways, Caterpillar had become an American institution. Indeed, managers at the company and outside observers alike had come to believe that the firm was almost invulnerable. After all, Caterpillar had posted profits for fifty consecutive years and had provided investors with exceptional returns for just as long. And the firm's trademark yellow bulldozers and other construction machinery were just as much a part of the American countryside as were Sunday picnics and kites.

Caterpillar dominated its markets. And the markets seemed never-ending: Cat machines rebuilt the infrastructures of war-torn countries following World War II; they provided the muscle that built the U.S. interstate highway system in the 1950s and 1960s; then they were put to work building dams and highways in Third World countries in the 1970s; and when oil prices shot through the roof, Caterpillar provided machines to energy-producers worldwide.

All the while, customers willingly paid premium prices for Caterpillar's superior quality. There were competitors—but they just couldn't seem to measure up.

Although there were occasional labor troubles (strikes were common, but short, at contract time), the company developed a reputation for generosity toward its employees, paying out benefits that rivaled some of the best in the country. The goal of many high school students in Caterpillar's hometown of Peoria, Illinois, was to "graduate and get a job at Caterpillar."

Then, as former chairman George A. Schaefer put it "we met our Waterloo." In 1982, a worldwide recession dramatically cut demand for the heavy construction equipment on which Caterpillar had built its business. Big Japanese competitors—most notably Komatsu—began to aggressively attack Caterpillar's markets. To top it all off, workers went on strike in late 1982 and stayed out for seven months. And so ended the company's profit machine. Indeed, Caterpillar lost almost $1 billion over the next three years.

It was as though Caterpillar's executives had been blindsided. In fact, many have said they hadn't seen the fall coming, and when things started looking bad, no one predicted the extent of the damage.

But, Caterpillar responded quickly and decisively.

There were some tough decisions made in a short period of time. Nine different plants were closed around the world, thirty thousand people were cut from the payroll, many parts and components that had been made in-house were sourced to outside sup-

Caterpillar has had to make many significant changes to regain its competitive position. American and Japanese engineers are working together to enhance quality and productivity as part of Caterpillar's overhaul.

pliers, salaries were reduced, and spending was drastically cut.

That got the company through the recession. But its leaders knew that to survive in the competitive future that lay ahead, they had to lower costs, maintain and improve quality, and perhaps most importantly, get closer to their customers.

As part of its strategy, Caterpillar cut its costs by twenty percent by 1985. Then it diversified, expanding into financial services, insurance, logistics, venture capital, world trading—ancillary services that broadened its base while capitalizing on its strengths. It significantly expanded its product line—from 150 to over 300 models.

A key part of the Cat strategy was a massive program to upgrade all its manufacturing facilities to state-of-the-art capability. Called Plant With a Future, the $1.5 billion program resulted in the rearrangement of 36 million square feet of factory space, the installation of advanced systems technology, an extensive retraining program for its employees, and a change to just-in-time manufacturing.

As a result, the company has been able to reduce costly inventories, speed up assembly time, and improve quality all at the same time. For example, it used to take Caterpillar almost twenty days to assemble a clutch housing from beginning to end. The same housing is now in and out of the plant in four hours. Similarly, it once took eleven workers to machine the basic parts of a transmission. Today, two workers perform the same work in the same amount of time.

To overcome the obstacles facing Caterpillar, Schaefer and his managers realized that workers and managers had to be on the same team, i.e., share a common goal and work together to achieve it. Accordingly, they have worked to transform the company's culture to one of openness and participation. In cooperation with the union (United Auto Workers), union workers and managers sat down together at weekly meetings to identify problems and come up with solutions. In fact, the company moved to a team approach in virtually all aspects of its operation: new product development, quality improvement, machine maintenance, etc. Workers who had been accustomed to having little voice in the company's operations found that their ideas and opinions now mattered, and that their managers were willing to listen to them.

Although much remains to be done, Caterpillar appears to have turned the corner. Its market share has rebounded, while that of Komatsu has started to decline. And profits are also increasing again. Thus, Caterpillar seems to be well on its way back to a healthy and prosperous existence.

SOURCES: Ronald Henkoff, "This Cat Is Acting Like a Tiger," *Fortune*, December 19, 1988, pp. 69–76; "Can Caterpillar Inch Its Way Back to Heftier Profits?" *Business Week*, September 25, 1989, pp. 75–78; Robert S. Eckley, "Caterpillar's Ordeal: Foreign Competition in Capital Goods," *Business Horizons*, March-April 1989, pp. 80–86; "Going for the Lion's Share," *Business Week*, July 18, 1988, pp. 70–72; "Caterpillar Sees Gains in Efficiency Imperiled by Strength of Dollar," *The Wall Street Journal*, April 6, 1990, pp. A1, A8.

Enhancement Case Questions

1. What specific forces for change affected Caterpillar?
2. Identify as many areas of change as you can in this case.
3. How do you think managers at Caterpillar most likely enlisted the union's help in their change efforts?
4. Does the transformation undergone at Caterpillar qualify as revitalization? Why or why not?

Chapter Notes

1. "Unisys Raises Number of Jobs It Plans to Cut to About 8,000 in Restructuring," *The Wall Street Journal*, October 4, 1989, p. A3; "Sculley Slices Apple Computer into 4 Divisions," *USA Today*, August 23, 1988, p. 3B; Jeremy Main, "Work Won't Be the Same Again," *Fortune*, June 28, 1982, pp. 58–65.
2. See Roy McLennan, *Managing Organizational Change* (Englewood Cliffs, N.J.: Prentice-Hall, 1989).

3. Walter Kiechel III, "The Organization That Learns," *Fortune*, March 12, 1990, pp. 133–136.

4. Michael Beer, *Organization Change and Development: A System View* (Santa Monica, Calif.: Goodyear, 1980).

5. See Paul R. Lawrence, "How to Deal with Resistance to Change," *Harvard Business Review*, March-April, 1979, pp. 106–114.

6. "Revolt of Uncle Sam's Paper Pushers," *Business Week*, October 30, 1989, p. 156.

7. John P. Kotter and Leonard A. Schlesinger, "Choosing Strategies for Change," *Harvard Business Review*, March-April, 1979, pp. 106–114.

8. Harold J. Leavitt, "Applied Organizational Change in Industry: Structural, Technical, and Human Approaches," in W. W. Cooper, H. J. Leavitt, and M. W. Shelly, eds., *New Perspectives in Organization Research* (New York: Wiley, 1964), pp. 55–71.

9. Kotter and Schlesinger, "Choosing Strategies for Change."

10. Bro Uttal, "Texas Instruments Regroups," *Fortune*, August 9, 1982, pp. 40–45.

11. "U.S. Exporters That Aren't American," *Business Week*, February 20, 1988, pp. 70–71; "What's Behind the Texas Instruments-Hitachi Deal," *Business Week*, January 16, 1989, pp. 93–96.

12. Dorothy Leonard-Barton and William A. Kraus, "Implementing New Technology," *Harvard Business Review*, November-December 1985, pp. 102–110.

13. Richard Beckhard, *Organization Development: Strategies and Models* (Reading, Mass.: Addison-Wesley, 1969).

14. Robert R. Blake and Jane S. Mouton, *The Managerial Grid III: The Key to Leadership Excellence* (Houston, Tex.: Gulf, 1985).

15. Wendell L. French and Cecil H. Bell, Jr., *Organization Development: Behavioral Science Interventions for Organization Improvement*, 2nd ed. (Englewood Cliffs, N.J.: Prentice-Hall, 1978).

CHAPTER OUTLINE

I. The Nature of International Management
   A. The Meaning of International Business
   B. The Growth of International Business

II. The International Environment
   A. The General Environment
   B. The Task Environment

III. Planning for International Business
   A. The Decision to Go International
   B. International Strategies

IV. Organizing an International Business
   A. Organization Design
   B. Staffing
   C. Information Systems and Communication

V. Leading in an International Business

VI. Controlling in International Business

CHAPTER

21

After studying this chapter you should be able to

1. Define international business and discuss its nature and growth.

2. Describe the international environment, including both the general and the task environment.

3. Discuss what is involved in the decision to go international, as well as various international strategies.

4. Identify the major factors that influence organization design, staffing, and information systems in an international business.

5. Discuss some aspects of leading in international business.

6. Describe the major aspects of controlling in international business.

International Management

TEXAS INSTRUMENTS GOES GLOBAL

The name of the company says it all—Texas Instruments. Texas Instruments, or TI, is a Dallas-based company that got its start making instruments. For years, the firm was an average player in the market for aircraft instruments, medical equipment, and similar product lines.

In 1960, however, a TI engineer named Jack Kilby created the world's first integrated circuit. That breakthrough launched TI into the upper ranks of the world's electronics industry. A little over a decade later, TI also pioneered the microprocessor—a computer on a chip that would eventually power the first personal computers.

For years, TI was one of the fastest-growing and most influential firms in the electronics industry. It was also run by a group of dedicated but single-minded engineers. TI always had what its managers called a "shirt-sleeve" culture. Employees rolled up their sleeves and took off their ties when they went to work each day. Offices and other facilities were modest, and only a few symbols of power separated the top from the bottom.

TI managers began to think the company could accomplish anything. Whenever a new product was created, they relentlessly looked for ways to make it as cheaply as possible so that they could capture more and more market share. They also held themselves aloof from other firms, never assessing how they might capitalize on the work of others.

Unfortunately, their stubbornness cost them dearly. For example, they were very well positioned to compete in the personal computer market. However, they refused to adopt the IBM standard for their machines and consequently never made much of a dent in that market. Frustrated, a group of TI engineers left the firm to start their own computer firm. That company, Compaq, generated annual sales of over $3 billion in just three years.

TI has also taken its lumps in consumer electronics. Its line of digital watches collapsed because managers refused to worry about design and appearance. Only a few of their electronic toys and a few calculators remain from a once-promising consumer electronics division.

In 1985, the world market for integrated circuits collapsed. TI was not well positioned for this turn of events and lost both money and market share by the truckload. During what is now called the company's darkest era, a new CEO, Jerry Junkins, was appointed and managers had to take a long, hard look at where the company was headed. They didn't like what they saw.

One of the things they realized was that Dallas was not the hub of the universe. While the electronics industry had become global, TI had remained essentially domestic in its orientation and approach. Thus, Junkins made globalization one of the firm's highest priorities.

TI has also returned to its roots, making integrated circuits the heart of its operations. Consumer electronics are being scaled

Texas Instruments has had to adopt a global strategy in order to maintain its position in the electronics industry. The employee at the left is working at a TI wafer fabrication facility, where electronic circuitry that can be used around the world is created. In Dallas, the work force has become more international with the addition of engineers such as these from Japan and India.

back, and little growth is foreseen in the firm's military defense business. Managers at TI have decided that their future lies in the rapidly changing and expanding worldwide market for chips. To keep pace, TI is building or converting existing facilities to produce nothing but integrated circuits and derivative products. By 1991, the firm intends to have nine state-of-the-art plants making the chips. But only two will be in Dallas. Four of them will be in Japan, one in Taiwan, one in Italy, and one in France.

In addition to building plants in other countries, TI is making a major effort to line up joint ventures and other cooperative relationships with foreign firms. For example, it struck deals with Hitachi in 1988 and with Kobe Steel in 1990.

SOURCES: "TI Bets Most of Its Marbles on Chips," *Business Week*, January 29, 1990, pp. 73–74; Jeremy Main, "How to Go Global—And Why," *Fortune*, August 28, 1989, pp. 70–76; Brian O'Reilly, "Texas Instruments: New Boss, Big Job," *Fortune*, July 8, 1985, pp. 60–64; "What's Behind the Texas Instruments-Hitachi Deal," *Business Week*, January 16, 1989, pp. 93–96; "Texas Instruments, Japan's Kobe Steel Form Venture to Make Semiconductors," *The Wall Street Journal*, March 20, 1990, p. B4.

exas Instruments is following a course of action that is becoming increasingly common around the world. This course has been prompted by the realization that few large companies can survive by manufacturing or marketing products or services in a single country. And even medium-sized and small firms that do operate within a single country are still increasingly being affected by international business forces.

Throughout this book we have considered the international dimension of business through boxed inserts called *The World of Management*. We have also used dozens of international examples; many of the companies in the cases are international in scope as well. In this chapter we look at international management in more detail. First we examine the nature of international management and the environment of international business. Subsequent sections relate international management to the four basic managerial functions of planning, organizing, leading, and controlling.

THE NATURE OF INTERNATIONAL MANAGEMENT

◻ *Globalization* is moving us to an integrated economy composed of interrelated markets.

All business today has been affected by the process of **globalization:** the gradual evolution to an integrated global economy composed of interrelated markets. This evolutionary process started decades ago, but, as we will see, it is now moving forward at an increasingly fast pace.[1] Exhibit 21.1 shows two of the major markets and business centers of the world.

The Meaning of International Business

◻ *International business* takes place across national boundaries.

What is international business? Is it simply domestic business as practiced in different countries, or is it something else altogether? We can define **international business** as business activity that takes place across national boundaries.[2] When Boeing sells an airplane to Air India, when Compaq Computer buys microchips from a Japanese manufacturer, and when General Foods buys coffee beans from a South American coffee grower, international business is taking place.

International business, then, can involve buying or selling products or services between countries. It can also involve borrowing money from a lender in another country. When companies in different countries undertake joint ventures, international business is also occurring.

◻ A *multinational* is a firm that operates in many different countries simultaneously.

Virtually all large organizations engage in international business. When a company's international involvement reaches a fairly high level, it becomes a **multinational**—a company that operates in many different countries at the same time. For example, Unilever is based jointly in London and Rotterdam. It consists of over two hundred individually defined subsidiaries doing business in eighty countries.[3] Obviously, this organization's level of international involvement is quite different from that of a firm that manufactures all its products at home and exports to two or three other major markets.

Exhibit 21.1   Major Markets and Business Centers

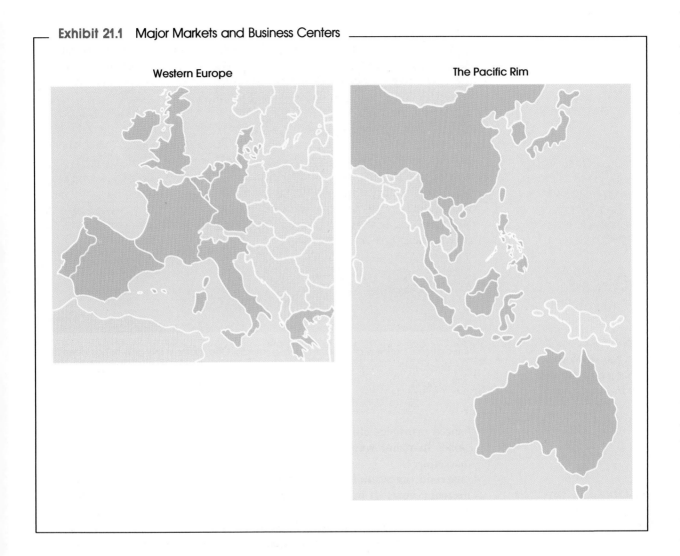

Western Europe

The Pacific Rim

The Growth of International Business

☐ International business activity has been increasing at a rapid pace during the last several years.

International business has grown at an extraordinary rate over the past several years. The volume of international trade in 1990, for instance, measured in current dollars, is around forty times larger than the amount in 1960. In addition, U.S. firms have around $327 billion invested in other countries, and foreign firms have around $329 billion invested in the United States. These figures, too, are expected to continue to climb.[4]

What accounts for this growth? Actually, several factors have served to spur growth in international business. First, breakthroughs in transportation and communication have made worldwide business much easier. Managers can now travel between New York and Europe in only a few hours. Similarly, electronic communication and improved telephone networks have greatly en-

International business at AT&T is growing rapidly. One factor in this growth has been training employees such as these to provide on-line translation services in 140 languages for AT&T clients.

hanced managers' ability to keep in touch with colleagues located around the globe. In many ways, we have evolved to a world economy and a world marketplace.[5]

Second, international business has actually been developing at a rapid pace for many years. It just seems newer to many in the United States because in some respects we are latecomers. Companies located in very small markets, such as Nestlé in Switzerland, Shell in the Netherlands, and Nissan in Japan, recognized long ago that they needed to become international in order to grow and prosper. American firms, in contrast, often had a large enough market at home to satisfy current growth patterns. Only when the domestic market began to falter did many firms recognize that there were other markets to pursue.

A third factor accounting for the rise in international business is the cost of production and transportation. Suppose that Union Carbide wants to increase its market share in the worldwide market for a certain chemical. If the company knows that the minerals it needs to make the chemical are readily available in Australia, it may make economic sense to build a refinery in Australia. The refinery will buy the minerals locally and ship the finished goods to customers in the Pacific basin. In other words, the availability of inexpensive materials and labor and proximity to customers often suggest the need for international expansion.

LEARNING CHECK

You should now be able to define international business and discuss its nature and growth.

PRELUDE CASE UPDATE

Texas Instruments has clearly been affected by international business conditions and opportunities. In many ways, the Japanese consumer electronics industry has spurred much of the growth that has made integrated circuits so profitable. At the same time, Japanese chip makers have squeezed profits from many American firms in that industry, forcing many to drop out altogether. Texas Instruments has hung on, however, and is now moving aggressively to recapture its market share and make inroads in Japan itself. Obviously, factors such as improved communication and transportation capabilities have facilitated the company's efforts.

THE INTERNATIONAL ENVIRONMENT

In numerous places throughout this book we have noted the importance of the organizational environment. Chapter 4 describes the general and task environments, which we can now relate to international business.

The General Environment

□ The political-legal, economic, sociocultural, and technological dimensions of the general environment are all important for an international business.

Recall that the general environment consists of five dimensions: political-legal, economic, international, sociocultural, and technological. Since we are interested here in the international dimension, we need to investigate the other four dimensions and their effect on international forces.[6]

POLITICAL-LEGAL   The political-legal dimension is obviously important to all international businesses. The stability of the government in foreign markets is extremely critical. Countries such as the United States, Great Britain, France, and Japan enjoy considerable government stability, so a firm choosing to conduct business there can be relatively certain of what its rights, privileges, and obligations are. But political conditions in countries such as Iran, Argentina, Libya, and El Salvador have often been less stable. A firm that chooses to invest in these countries runs the risk of considerable loss if there are dramatic changes in government policies and receptivity to foreign trade. The recent political changes in Eastern European countries and the Soviet Union seem destined to improve the business climate in those countries.[7]

Another aspect of the political-legal dimension is that some countries actively seek foreign investment whereas others are indifferent or perhaps even hostile. Common incentives for investment include tax breaks, construction subsidies, and reduced interest on loans. Brazil and India have been particularly aggressive in this area.[8]

Jacques Witt/SIPA

The political-legal environment has seen profound changes during the last few years. For example, the fall of the iron curtain and the dismantling of the Berlin Wall carry enormous implications for business in both Western and Eastern Europe.

☐ *Protectionist techniques* such as quotas, tariffs, export restraint agreements, and "buy national" laws are intended to protect domestic business from foreign competition.

A company considering doing business in another country also needs to consider how much that country attempts to control international trade across its borders. For example, the United States limits the number of automobiles that can be produced in Japan and shipped in this country, which is a major reason that Japanese firms such as Honda and Nissan are building plants in the United States—cars produced here do not count against the quota. Other **protectionist techniques** include tariffs (a tax levied on incoming products), export restraint agreements, and "buy national" laws such as the one that requires the U.S. military to buy uniforms made by American firms.

ECONOMIC   The economic dimension is also important to a company considering international involvement. For one thing, the firm should consider the basic economic system of the country in which it is thinking of doing business.[9] Factors such as governmental regulation of industries, property rights, and so forth are influenced by the prevailing economic system. For example, some governments heavily regulate business activity, whereas others take a more casual approach. Likewise, some countries require that local investors control some part of foreign businesses that are operating local facilities.

Again, the decline of communism around the world is altering this aspect of the general environment as well.

The country's infrastructure is also important. Most developed countries already have adequate utilities, schools, hospitals, highways, airfields, housing, railroads, recreational facilities, ports, and so forth, but less developed countries often are deficient in one or more of these areas. Companies doing business in some African nations must routinely deal with power cuts on a daily basis. Communication breakdowns also occur frequently. Companies may even have to go so far as to build entirely new towns for employees, provide schools and clinics, and construct connecting highways. Obviously, any organization must carefully weigh such costs against the potential benefits before proceeding with this level of investment.

The monetary and fiscal policies of the potential host country must also be considered. Mexico's foreign debt was approaching $140 billion in late 1989, and as a consequence local facilities were neglected, inflation was rampant, and unemployment was high. These indicators of poor economic conditions would cause potential investors to go elsewhere.

SOCIOCULTURAL   The human, cultural, and physical characteristics—the sociocultural dimension—of a country are also important. Age distribution, for example, helps to determine the potential demand for products such as disposable baby diapers or denture cream. Literacy rates play a role in determining both the quality of employees available in the country and the kinds of products that are in demand; if a country has a low literacy rate, its citizens will demand fewer published products, like books and magazines.

In a similar way, it is often necessary to account for physical differences between people of various countries. Japanese, for instance, are generally smaller and thinner than Americans, so when Levi Strauss exports jeans and shirts to Japan, it must send a larger proportion of smaller products.

There may also be significant differences in values across national boundaries. Daily shopping at fresh food markets is still widely practiced in Europe, whereas most Americans shop at large food stores once or twice a week. Local tastes, preferences, and customs must also be accommodated. For example, McDonald's restaurants in France and West Germany sell beer, and workers in England expect to receive several more paid holidays each year than their American counterparts do. *Management Today: Ethical Dilemmas of Management* describes one of the issues Mobil and other U.S. firms have had to confront.

Finally, the physical characteristics of the country need to be considered. A large U.S. firm made a mistake in this respect when it built a pineapple cannery in Mexico a few years ago. It expected to transport raw pineapple from the field to the cannery by barge, but it later learned that the river currents were too strong at harvest time for barges to carry their load. Since no transportation alternatives were available, the company had to abandon the cannery.[10] Climate and topography are among the aspects of the physical area that companies need to assess.

ETHICAL DILEMMAS OF MANAGEMENT

Protest or Profits?

Mobil Corporation has for years taken a stance that corporations exist for reasons beyond pure profits. For example, the big oil company regularly sponsors print ads presenting its views on topics ranging from capitalism in general to free enterprise to the excessive regulation of business activity by government. Mobil is also a big sponsor of public television.

Mobil recently made another big decision that relates to the issues of ethics and social responsibility. South Africa is a relatively large and prosperous marketplace. Not surprisingly, then, many large firms have had operations in South Africa for years. In recent times, however, many people have protested the apartheid practices of the South African government. These same protestors have called for the United States to do as much as possible to change that government's position regarding racial equality.

Many U.S. firms—Kodak and IBM, for example—have sold or simply closed down their operations in South Africa. Through 1986, over 190 U.S. firms left South Africa. Mobil made the same decision recently and sold its operations, valued at $400 million, for only $150 million.

Critics have been quick to note, however, that Mobil may have still been pursuing a profit-driven strategy in reaching its difficult decision to sell its South African operations at such a low price. The U.S. Congress recently eliminated tax credits for taxes paid to the government of South Africa. Thus, Mobil's decision may have been partially made to support anti-apartheid forces and partially to increase its own profits. In either case, of course, it was a tough decision for managers to make.

SOURCES: "Mobil May Unload Its Last Millstone," *Business Week,* February 29, 1988, p. 33; "Mobil Corp., With $4.4 Billion Less Debt Than 3 Years Ago, Gets Ready to Spend," *The Wall Street Journal,* February 17, 1988, p. 4; "Mobil's Big Pullout," *Newsweek,* May 8, 1989, p. 42.

TECHNOLOGICAL   The multinational firm needs to account for technological factors, of course. In many ways the technological dimension relates to the notion of infrastructure, but there are other issues to consider as well, such as the availability of equipment, machinery, and components in a potential host country. Japanese car makers in the United States often continue to buy parts from Japanese companies back home rather than from local companies because they claim the quality of locally manufactured parts is not good enough.[11] Similarly, a company that wanted to build an automated plant in another country could save a lot if the robots could be obtained locally. On the other hand, if it had to acquire the robots elsewhere, costs would be higher.

A final aspect of technology involves an interaction with the sociocultural dimension. Suppose that a company needs hundreds of technical employees such as engineers, computer programmers, and so forth. If qualified people are available locally, the business will incur lower human resource costs and establish good relations with the local citizenry. If no qualified people are available, however, the company must reassign them from other locations, which can drive costs up and engender resentment.

Clearly, the environment of any business is complex, and that faced by the international business is especially complex. Consider the situation faced by the firm represented in Exhibit 21.2. It is actively involved in doing business in three countries, so it operates in three general environments and three task environments (discussed next). Moreover, these three units, as well as their respective environments, are interrelated. The manager in such a setting must address an enormously intricate set of forces.

Exhibit 21.2   The International Environment

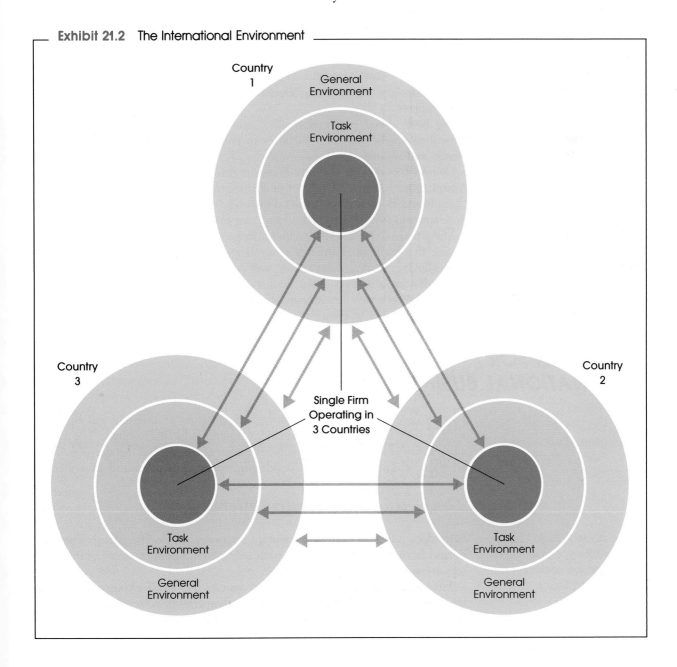

The Task Environment

☐ Each dimension of the task environment is important to an international business.

As Chapter 4 notes, the task environment of an organization is the specific set of other organizations and groups with which the organization must interact. Common dimensions of the task environment include customers, suppliers, competitors, partners, regulators, and unions. In many ways the basic influences of the task environment appear within the major general environment dimensions. There are, however, a few additional points to consider.

For one thing, customers may need to be treated differently. We have already seen how organizations need to modify their products to meet different consumer preferences. In addition, people in poor countries may not be able to buy luxury goods. In some countries, such as the United States, some people feel strongly that everyone should buy from domestic companies instead of foreign firms.

We have noted potential quality problems with local suppliers. Other difficulties might include differences in payment expectations, legal arrangements, and so forth.

Competitors include not only domestic firms but also other foreign firms. In America, for example, Unilever (a European firm) competes with Procter & Gamble and Borden (U.S. firms). However, it also competes with SmithKline Beecham and Nestlé (two other European firms).

Many firms today are also seeking foreign partners for joint venture arrangements. For example, Ford has a number of joint ventures around the globe with Mazda, Nissan, Volkswagon, and other firms.

Regulations also vary from country to country, as do union influences. Unions are relatively uninfluential in Japan, where work is exemplified by a cooperative spirit. In contrast, unions are often very strong in England.

LEARNING CHECK

You should now be able to describe the international environment, including both the general and the task environment.

PLANNING FOR INTERNATIONAL BUSINESS

Having investigated the environmental foundation of international business, we can now focus on the management functions in that context. The crucial elements of planning for international business are making the decision to enter the world marketplace and developing appropriate plans and strategies.

The Decision to Go International

☐ The decision to go international is influenced by market, production, competitive, and governmental factors.

Why does a firm decide to become international in the first place? There are several factors that might lead to such a decision. The four most common factors are summarized in Table 21.1.[12]

First, and perhaps most common, are market factors. If a company's domestic market is saturated, the only alternative for growth is to enter foreign markets. (This was the situation that originally led Nestlé to go international). Even if the domestic market is still growing, a firm with sufficient resources might decide that major markets for its products exist in other countries.

TABLE 21.1
Factors Influencing the
Decision to Go
International

Factors	Examples
1. Market Factors	Saturation of domestic market; recognition of the possibilities of foreign markets
2. Production Factors	Lower labor costs abroad; lower cost of producing near the source of raw materials
3. Competitive Factors	A major competitor enters the international market
4. Governmental Factors	Foreign government incentives to invest; favorable political climate

A second major group of influences is production factors. Many companies have discovered that lower labor costs in other countries can lower their overall production costs. For example, Zenith's electronics plant in Reynosa, Mexico, pays individual labor costs of only 75 cents an hour. Similar costs are available in Taiwan and some Central African nations.

Third, a firm may contemplate international involvement because of competitive factors. If a major competitor decides to go international, it may enjoy additional sales and lower costs as a result. Thus the company it is competing with may have to follow suit to not fall further and further behind.

A final set of influences to consider is governmental factors, which was discussed as a general environmental dimension. Specifically, the firm contemplating an international venture needs to consider the extent to which the relevant foreign government will take a friendly or a hostile stance. Likewise, it must consider the extent to which the government will provide incentives or other concessions to attract the firm and possible competitors.

International Strategies

After considering many factors, a company may decide to stay at home. If it decides to go international, it can take any of several approaches. The most common options are shown in Exhibit 21.3.

❏ A *pure domestic strategy*
focuses on the home country's
marketplace.

PURE DOMESTIC STRATEGY   The organization that chooses not to enter the international market is using a **pure domestic strategy**. It buys its materials in its home country, produces its products there, and sells its products there. Although some of its materials may have been made in other countries, they are purchased from a domestic distributor. Many smaller firms practice this strategy, although many are also finding that they, too, can compete internationally. Examples are described in *Management Today: Small Business and Entrepreneurship*.

❏ *Exporting* involves shipping
a firm's products to other
countries for resale.

IMPORTING/EXPORTING STRATEGY   Importing and exporting are the least intense levels of international business. When **exporting**, a firm simply

SMALL BUSINESS AND ENTREPRENEURSHIP

International Niches

A firm does not have to be a giant to compete in the international arena. Increasingly, managers of such firms are finding that they can find niches for themselves in foreign markets.

For example, Bilco Tools is a small Louisiana-based manufacturer of oil field equipment. During the oil bust in the 1980s, the firm's owner, William Coyle, thought he was going to have to shut down. At the last minute, though, he set out to see if he could locate any buyers overseas. As it turned out, he found a graduate of Louisiana State University working in the Middle East and persuaded him to try Bilco's products. Other sales resulted, and the company now exports over 60 percent of its products.

Dorr-Oliver is a small New England maker of food-processing equipment. The company has been able to successfully build its business in China, exporting around 30 percent of its products to that country.

Nor is international small-business success limited to the United States. Several small businesses from Hong Kong, Italy, and Great Britain have been successful in exporting their products to other countries. If a manager is willing to be patient and is careful in selecting appropriate markets, there will always be opportunities to grow, even if that growth comes from abroad.

SOURCES: "The Long Arm of Small Business," *Business Week,* February 29, 1988, pp. 63–66; "Simplifying Global Trading," *Venture,* April 1988, p. 12; "Hot Startups Abroad: The World is Their Market," *Business Week,* May 22, 1989, pp. 110–115.

sells its products to an organization in another country, as American wheat farmers sometimes sell grain to the Soviet Union and Mercedes-Benz exports cars from West Germany to the United States.

Importing involves buying products or materials from another country for use or sale in the company's own country. Many American wine distributors, for instance, buy wine from French and Italian distributors for resale here.

☐ *Importing* is buying products from another country and bringing them into one's own country for resale.

The importing/exporting strategy requires little initial investment. However, it is heavily regulated, and products must typically be taken "as is"— there is no opportunity to modify them for local conditions.

☐ *Licensing* is a strategy whereby a firm in another country produces goods or services for the contracting company.

LICENSING STRATEGY Licensing involves a slightly stronger commitment to international business. The **licensing strategy** uses contractual relationships in which a firm in another country produces goods or services for the contracting company, often using that company's name on the finished goods. Actual goods do not pass from one country to another. Rather, permission to use a company's name is conveyed. Thus, a dotted line is used to show this relationship in Exhibit 21.3. An example is provided by General Instruments, which recently licensed Hyundai Electronics of South Korea to produce integrated circuits using General Instruments' design and product specifications and carrying General Instruments' trademark and name.[13]

Exhibit 21.3 International Strategies

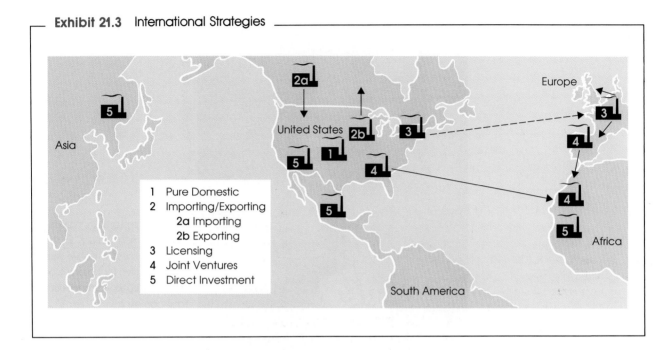

1 Pure Domestic
2 Importing/Exporting
    2a Importing
    2b Exporting
3 Licensing
4 Joint Ventures
5 Direct Investment

Licensing is a good initial step for introducing a company's products into a foreign market or for helping domestic manufacturing facilities to meet demand. However, the company gives up a certain degree of control and is often constrained from other activity during the course of the licensing agreement.

☐ *Joint ventures* occur when two or more companies work together to produce goods or services.

JOINT VENTURES **Joint ventures** are partnerships between two or more companies. In the international context, common types of joint ventures include agreements between a foreign company and a domestic company to work together on a project in the domestic market, to work together in the foreign market, or to work together in a third market. As noted in the Prelude Case, Texas Instruments has several joint ventures under way.

Joint ventures can allow an organization to enter a new market quickly and to draw upon the expertise of its partner, which is already in that market. They can also be used to acquire new technology and information. At the same time, they usually carry long-term commitments and involve sharing decision making and control.

☐ *Direct investment* involves buying or building operations facilities in other countries.

DIRECT INVESTMENT STRATEGY **Direct investment** is typically the highest level of international involvement. The company taking this approach builds plants in other countries, develops its own distribution and marketing networks in those countries, and takes a global view of the marketplace. It is a multinational, as already defined.

It is relatively rare for a firm to change immediately from a pure domestic strategy to direct investment abroad. The initial decision to enter the interna-

Courtesy of The Upjohn Co.

Joint ventures are an increasingly common strategy in global business. A native sales representative for Upjohn Company (a large pharmaceutical firm) can explain the firm's new medicine, Motrin, to a pharmacist in Seoul, South Korea. The marketing of Motrin is part of a joint venture between Upjohn and Yu Yu Industrial, a Korean firm.

LEARNING CHECK

You should now be able to discuss what is involved in the decision to go international, as well as various international strategies.

tional market is often based on such factors as costs, opportunities, experience, the risk involved, and so forth. The organization that decides to take this course usually progresses through the various levels of involvement, using importing and exporting as the first step, licensing as the next step, and joint ventures as a third step. Direct investment represents the most significant level and is reached only by large firms.[14]

ORGANIZING AN INTERNATIONAL BUSINESS

A company that makes the decision to go international must almost certainly reorganize its operational systems in order to handle the increased complexity of its environment. Our major concern is with organization design in the international context. The other two dimensions of organizing, staffing and information systems, are only briefly noted here.[15]

Organization Design

A number of factors influence the design of an international business. One major one is the level of international involvement, as determined by the company's strategy. Others include the magnitude of the investment, the nature of the product, and location. For example, many companies locate their international operations in New York because it is easy to travel abroad through that city's airports. Companies doing a lot of business in South America, like Dow Chemical and Pfizer, in contrast, put their major centers in Miami in order to facilitate travel. Still others, like Bendix (in Southfield, just outside of Detroit) and Coca-Cola (in Atlanta), simply integrate their international operations with their existing corporate headquarters.

As the level of a company's international involvement increases, its design is also likely to change. When the organization is simply exporting or importing, it will probably have an exporting manager, who oversees this aspect of its operations, and an importing manager, probably located in the purchasing department. When the dominant strategy is licensing, a single manager or perhaps a small department will be sufficient to handle most of the firm's international activities.

□ An *international divisional design* involves setting up a special division to handle international activities.

When a firm begins joint ventures or direct investment, however, major structural changes are often needed. A common early form of organization design for the emerging international business, the **international divisional design,** is illustrated in Exhibit 21.4. Domestic operations, which are probably still the company's major area of concern, are designed in one of the basic forms described in Chapter 9. But the organization also creates a new international division, usually headed by a vice president or some other top-level manager. This division can take any of a number of different designs. For example, within Levi Strauss's overall corporate structure is a major division

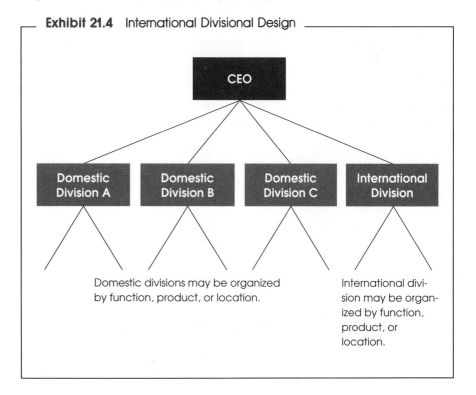

Exhibit 21.4   International Divisional Design

CEO

Domestic Division A | Domestic Division B | Domestic Division C | International Division

Domestic divisions may be organized by function, product, or location.

International division may be organized by function, product, or location.

called Levi Strauss International, which has units based in Europe, Latin America, Canada, and the Pacific basin. Each of these units, in turn, is organized by products.[16]

Several other international designs are also used. Some companies, like Ford and Union Carbide, use a modified type of product design. Many foreign firms use a location-based or geographical design, which is useful when foreign markets are extremely large and there is no single dominant market to consider. Lever Brothers, based in Rotterdam, uses this approach. Few American firms have followed suit, though, because our domestic market is so large.

The most sophisticated form of international organization design is the **international matrix,** which is illustrated in Exhibit 21.5. As in a normal matrix, the international matrix employs two bases of departmentalization. Product managers are arrayed across one side of the matrix, and location-based division managers are arrayed along the other dimension. Thus, a plant manager in Italy may be accountable to a product manager based in France and a

▢ An *international matrix* is a normal matrix with one dimension arrayed by country or region.

Exhibit 21.5 International Matrix Design

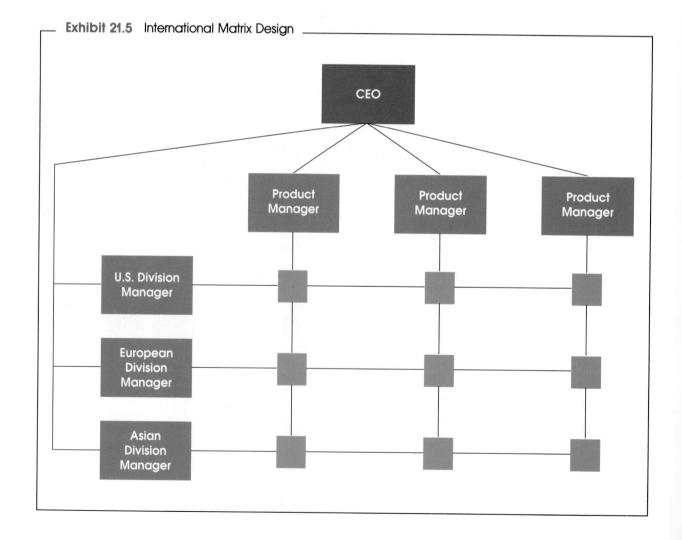

division manager based in England. Several larger, truly multinational corporations, like Royal Dutch Shell and Nestlé, have also used this form of organization design.

Staffing

Another important aspect of international management is staffing. We have already considered several of the issues confronting managers in this area. For instance, they must decide how many employees to hire locally and how many to transfer from domestic operations. Hiring locally increases good will and is usually cheaper, but local employees may not have the skills they need to do the job and may be more loyal to their country than to the business. Transferring employees from domestic operations is often expensive and can lead to local hostility, but the employees are usually skilled, and their loyalty is more clearly defined.

Information Systems and Communications

A final aspect of organizing in the international sector is information systems and communication. As we have noted, communication breakthroughs have been a major catalyst for the growth of international business. At the same

Many firms are seeking ways to better compete in a global economy. Firms from five different countries recently sent top managers to a training program sponsored by the University of Michigan. By using methods such as having teams work together to build rafts, communication among managers from different cultures was improved.

Jeremy Main

time, however, communication remains a major chore for the international company. Three things in particular are problematic.

First, time differences can hinder communication. Managers located on opposite sides of the globe find telephone calls difficult because of the twelve-hour time difference. Second, language barriers can be a problem. Managers need to be able to communicate in the local language as well as in the official language of the company. Finally, currency differences can cause confusion. A manager overseeing operations for an American firm in England, France, West Germany, and Switzerland, for instance, must understand the basic proportional differences among English pounds, French francs, German marks, Swiss francs, and American dollars, as well as fluctuations in exchange rates.

> **LEARNING CHECK**
>
> You should now be able to identify the major factors that influence organization design, staffing, and information systems in an international business.

PRELUDE CASE UPDATE

Texas Instruments has had to confront each of the major components of the organizing process as it has become more global. In terms of organization design, the firm has created a special, but temporary, international division that is focusing attention and resources on the company's commitment to international operations. Once full-scale globalization has been achieved, the special division will be eliminated and international operations will be merged into all ongoing aspects of the firm. In terms of staffing, Texas Instruments generally prefers to hire local employees. However, it has begun to systematically rotate key managers through a series of international assignments. Finally, in order to promote communication, the firm is linking all of its plants into a single information system serviced by satellite time it leases from AT&T.

LEADING IN AN INTERNATIONAL BUSINESS

☐ An international context can influence each aspect of the leadership function of management.

Obviously, it is important for a manager in an international setting to understand how that context should affect his or her approach to leadership. One significant area is the leadership process itself, which carries implications for motivation, groups, and conflict and change.

Appropriate leadership behavior in an international setting is determined in part by three basic factors.[17] First, the leader needs at least a basic familiarity with the host country's language. Although it is possible to survive in many international settings using only English, many things can slip by if the manager doesn't understand the local language. Moreover, insisting that everyone communicate in English can be interpreted as a lack of respect for the host country and its people.

Second, the manager needs to understand and appreciate the basic prevailing work-related attitudes held by the people of the host country. For example, Americans generally take a positive view of competition and place a premium on winning. In many European countries, as well as Japan, competition is seen in a different light. Although it is recognized as a necessary ingredient in business in these countries, managers there tend to assume that it should be restrained so as not to become too destructive.[18] In a similar way, there are dramatic differences in people's perceptions of the proper role of business in society, of the role of the individual in the organization, and so forth.

Third, managers need to recognize that individual needs and reasons for working often vary among countries. People in Japan and Switzerland have strong needs for security and can often best be motivated by opportunities to achieve this security. In contrast, employees in the Scandinavian countries of Norway and Sweden place a greater premium on social needs, so opportunities for social interaction are important to these workers. American, Canadian, and Australian workers often want opportunities to grow and to expand their personal and professional capabilities.[19]

Clear implications for motivation can be drawn from these observations. In particular, the manager must recognize that people in different countries are motivated by different incentives. The key, then, is to understand the factors that motivate people in a given setting and to establish a reward system that gives them what they value most.

The manager also must not neglect the role of the group in different settings. Just as social factors are important in Scandinavian countries, clan or tribal affiliation is important in many African nations, and the caste system in India, which is technically illegal, still plays a role in many places.

Reactions to conflict and change also vary among cultures. In the United States, most people accept a certain degree of both conflict and change as a fact of business life. In British settings, however, there is often more conflict, whereas change is less acceptable. The exact opposite is true in Japan: conflict is seldom tolerated, but change is relatively acceptable.

LEARNING CHECK

You should now be able to discuss some aspects of leading in international business.

PRELUDE CASE UPDATE

Texas Instruments has had to respond to international circumstances in the leadership area in several different ways. For one thing, the firm has had to create specialized performance appraisal systems for plants in each country. It has also been necessary to modify the reward system in each plant to account for cultural nuances. Finally, Texas Instruments has had to establish special training programs for its managers at all plants to help them better understand how interpersonal dynamics vary across cultural boundaries.

CONTROLLING IN INTERNATIONAL BUSINESS

☐ The controlling function is very important for an international business.

In several places we have seen the implications for control in international business. Perhaps the most significant factor associated with this topic is its extreme difficulty and complexity. For instance, a few years ago Nestlé lost over

$100 million in Argentina simply because its control system was not providing the corporate headquarters in Switzerland with timely and accurate information.[20]

Several things account for such problems. For one, language and communication differences and barriers occasionally make control difficult to implement and manage. Exchange rate fluctuations and transfer pricing differences make it hard to assess unit profits in various countries. Cultural factors also come into play; just as different cultures respond to leadership in different ways, so too they respond to control in different ways. People in some countries are accustomed to tight controls and have little difficulty working within them, but in other places employees will react very negatively to attempts to implement appropriate controls.[21]

There are two basic strategies managers can adopt to deal with these difficulties. First, they should simply recognize that there are difficulties and complexities and develop control systems that can provide the necessary control-related information. Citicorp, for example, has a worldwide computer network that keeps its managers abreast of relevant information, facts, trends, and unit performance on a constant basis.[22]

The second strategy is to maintain headquarters and foreign affiliates, as Unilever does. This organization regularly rotates corporate-level managers through its various units around the globe in order to maintain effective communication among the various units and between the units and corporate headquarters.

LEARNING CHECK

You should now be able to describe the major aspects of controlling in international business.

Chapter Summary

International business is business activity that takes place across national boundaries. International business has grown spectacularly in recent years, for several reasons.

As with any organization, the international business's environment consists of a general and a task environment. The general environment consists of political-legal forces, economic forces, international forces, sociocultural forces, and technological forces. The task environment consists of customers, suppliers, competitors, partners, regulators, and unions. Each dimension of each environment has special implications for the business competing in the international arena.

A company considering becoming international must consider four factors: market factors, production factors, competition, and government. Once the decision to go international has been made, several strategies are available: exporting (selling overseas), importing (buying from overseas), licensing, joint ventures, and direct investment in foreign operations are the basic options.

Several major factors influence organization design for the international business. Two common arrangements for fairly high levels of involvement are the international divisional design and the international matrix design. Staffing is an important aspect of international management, and information systems and communication problems must also be considered.

Appropriate leadership behavior in an international setting is determined by three basic factors. First, the extent of the leader's knowledge of the host country's language is important. The second factor is the extent of the manager's understanding and appreciation of the work-related attitudes of the people in the host country, including attitudes toward competition. The final factor is the extent to which managers recognize that individual needs and motives vary among countries.

The dominant nature of controlling in international business is its difficulty and complexity. Language and communication differences make control more difficult, as do fluctuating exchange rates and transfer pricing differences. Cultural factors also play a part in control.

The Manager's Vocabulary

globalization
international business
multinational
protectionist techniques
pure domestic strategy
exporting
importing

licensing strategy
joint ventures
direct investment
international divisional
  design
international matrix

Prelude Case Wrap-Up

The Prelude Case for this chapter explains how Texas Instruments has been forced to adopt an international strategy. Faced with high costs and a declining market, the company has had to develop new approaches to management and search for new opportunities for growth.

Two of the firm's recent joint venture agreements provide special insights into what the company is trying to accomplish. A few years ago, Motorola, one of Texas Instruments' largest domestic competitors, announced that it had reached an agreement with Toshiba to buy that company's technology for making a new generation of chips.

In response, Texas Instruments soon thereafter structured a deal with Hitachi. Under the terms of the agreement, the two companies would work together toward the construction of a chip capable of storing sixteen million bits of data. Since a plant to build such a chip will cost over $400 million, the two companies working together are sharing the risks. And each has something to contribute, making the entire project a potential winner for each firm.

Texas Instruments' newest joint venture is with Kobe Steel. In recent years, several Japanese steel companies have taken steps to enter the electronics industry. Under the terms of the new agreement, Kobe Steel is paying more than half the cost of constructing a new plant in Japan that will cost at least $350 million. Texas Instruments will pay the rest and will tutor Kobe managers in how to function in

the electronics market. Kobe will get most of the profits, but Texas Instruments also has the option of increasing its ownership—and thus profits—in the future.

Prelude Case Questions

1. What things do you think Texas Instruments is doing right in its efforts to become more international?
2. Do you think Texas Instruments is making any mistakes in its efforts to become more international? If so, what?
3. Several other joint ventures between U.S. and Japanese electronics firms have been established recently. Do you think this trend will continue? Why or why not?
4. Why don't more firms build plants in Japan?

Discussion Questions

Review Questions

1. What environmental forces affect businesses engaged in international operations?
2. What are the basic factors that must be considered in making the decision to go international?
3. What are the basic strategies a firm competing internationally might adopt?
4. What organization design options must be considered as a firm becomes more international?
5. What aspects of leading are especially important in international business?

Analysis Questions

1. How has international business affected your life?
2. Businesses today need to better acquaint their managers with international issues. In what ways might this be most effectively done?
3. Analyze what the consequences of choosing the wrong international strategy are likely to be.
4. Do you have any interest in international job assignments? Why or why not?
5. Suppose you were asked to accept an international assignment. What factors would enter into your decision about whether or not to accept it (assuming your career will not suffer if you reject the offer)?

Application Questions and Exercises

1. Identify the major industries or companies in your neighborhood or community that have international operations.
2. Make a list of all the companies used as cases in this text. Classify them as domestic, international, or multinational. Pick two or three of the international or multinational companies and read more about their operations.
3. International activities aren't limited to businesses. Make a list of other kinds of organizations that interact with other countries.
4. Many colleges and universities offer international programs. Find out about options that might exist on your campus.
5. Assume you are in charge of international training for a big company. Sketch a training plan for managers who will be given international assignments in the near future.

ENHANCEMENT CASE

NESTLÉ CONQUERS THE WORLD

Two American brothers, Charles and George Page, started the Anglo-Swiss Condensed Milk Company in Cham, Switzerland, in 1866. The very next year, Henri Nestlé, a German chemist, started a business to make artificial milk for babies in Vevey, Switzerland. The two firms were bitter rivals for years but eventually merged in 1905 to form the Nestlé Corporation.

In many ways, Nestlé was one of the world's first companies to use an international strategy. Managers saw very quickly that, given the relatively small population in Switzerland, they had to pursue larger markets if they wanted to grow.

Rather than expand their domestic business into foreign markets, however, Nestlé executives have usually chosen to buy foreign firms and then have modified them to fit the Nestlé way of doing business. A recent acquisition, for example, was the Carnation milk company in the United States.

Today, Nestlé has around two hundred separate operating units scattered around the globe. Each unit operates with a relatively high level of autonomy, and each contributes significantly to Nestlé's bottom line. For example, Nestlé gets around 43 percent of its revenues in Europe, 29 percent in North America, 13 percent in Asia, 10 percent in Latin America, 3 percent in Africa, and the rest in Oceania.

Nestlé does have a few international brands. Most notable from this list are Nescafé instant coffee and Nestlé candies. More common, however, are brands that are specific to local markets. For example,

Nestlé sells Stouffer's frozen foods only in the United States, Maggi chili powder only in Asia, Chambourcy yogurt only in Europe, and Milo malt-flavored beverages only in Africa.

Nestlé follows a few simple principles in its strategy. First of all, managers stress the long term. Quarterly profits are scanned, but little emphasis is placed on short-term results. Indeed, managers are given an unusually long time period in which to demonstrate results.

Another facet of Nestlé's strategy is to adapt food products to meet local cultural norms. For example, even though Nescafe coffee is sold worldwide, its formula varies to meet local tastes. Thus, the coffee is dark and rich in Latin America, lighter in the United States, and stronger in Europe.

The final prong of Nestlé's strategy is to build market share. Thus, the firm is willing to sustain losses for a long time while it is enhancing market share. Its reasoning is that once it dominates a market, profits can be increased over the long term.

Nestlé uses a decentralized organization design to manage its operations. Even though the firm has over 160,000 employees worldwide, only about 7,000 of them are based in Switzerland. Each operating unit is managed like an independent small company. Managers submit one-page progress reports each quarter and provide more detailed financial data only on an annual basis.

The company uses a fairly complex financial structure for its operations. It tries to finance acquisitions from local investors, but it maintains all liquid assets back in Switzerland. Nestlé also tries to use local managers whenever possible.

Because of its rich international heritage, Nestlé prides itself on how it develops new managers for international assignments. Candidates for these positions are selected on the basis of their interest, leadership skills, language fluency, and interpersonal mannerisms. They subsequently go through an intense training regimen designed to allow them to function in almost any situation anywhere in the world.

Nestlé today is the largest food company in the world. However, managers are not resting on their laurels. Indeed, they are in the midst of a new and very aggressive growth program aimed at acquiring new firms from around the globe. Thus, there is no end in sight for the little milk company from Switzerland.

SOURCES: Nestlé Public Affairs Department, *Nestlé: A Long Adventure* (Vevey, Switzerland: Nestlé S.A., 1986); Shawn Tully, "Nestlé Shows How to Gobble Markets," *Fortune*, January 16, 1989, pp. 74–78; "Nestlé to Help General Mills Sell Cereals in Europe, *The Wall Street Journal*, December 1, 1989, p. B5; "Nestlé's Bid to Crash Baby-Formula Market in the U.S. Stirs a Row," *The Wall Street Journal*, February 16, 1989, pp. A1, A6.

Enhancement Case Questions

1. What threats or weaknesses might Nestlé have to overcome in the future?
2. Research the infant formula problems Nestlé has had and relate them to issues of ethics and social responsibility.
3. Nestlé recently announced a joint venture with General Mills to distribute that firm's cereals in Europe. What do you think might have prompted each company to be interested in such an arrangement?
4. Under what circumstances might Nestlé find it necessary to become more centralized?

Chapter Notes

1. See Richard I. Kirkland, Jr., "Entering a New Age of Boundless Competition," *Fortune*, March 14, 1988, pp. 40–48.
2. See Christopher Korth, *International Business*. 2nd ed. (Englewood Cliffs, N.J.: Prentice-Hall, 1985).
3. Andrew C. Brown, "Unilever Fights Back in the U.S.," *Fortune*, May 26, 1986, pp. 32–38.
4. "Where Global Growth Is Going," *Fortune*, July 31, 1989, pp. 71–92.
5. John Naisbett, *Megatrends: Ten New Directions Transforming Our Lives* (New York: Warner Books, 1982).
6. Korth, *International Business*.
7. "For Gorbachev, Perestroika II May Mean Survival," *Business Week*, September 25, 1989, pp. 60–62.

8. James E. Austin, *Managing in Developing Countries* (New York: Free Press, 1990).
9. John D. Daniels and Lee H. Radebaugh, *International Business*, 5th ed. (Reading, Mass.: Addison-Wesley, 1990).
10. David Ricks, *Big Business Blunders: Mistakes in Multinational Marketing* (Homewood, Ill.: Dow Jones-Irwin, 1983), p. 4.
11. Edward Boyer, "Are Japanese Managers Biased Against Americans?" *Fortune*, September 1, 1986, pp. 72–75.
12. Korth, *International Business*, and Daniels and Radebaugh, *International Business*.
13. "General Instrument, Hyundai Sign Accord," *The Wall Street Journal*, March 5, 1986, p. 34.
14. See Korth, *International Business*.
15. Daniels and Radebaugh, *International Business*.
16. John Quirt, "Levi Strauss Is Stretching Its Wardrobe," *Fortune*, November 19, 1979, pp. 88–89.
17. See Geert Hofstede, "Motivation, Leadership, and Organizations: Do American Theories Apply Abroad?" *Organizational Dynamics*, Summer 1980, pp. 42–63.
18. Ibid.
19. Ibid.
20. Robert Ball, "A 'Shopkeeper' Shakes Up Nestlé," *Fortune*, December 27, 1982, pp. 103–106.
21. Hofstede, "Motivation, Leadership, and Organizations."
22. "Citicorp's Gutsy Campaign to Conquer Europe," *Business Week*, July 15, 1985, p. 46.

CHAPTER OUTLINE

I. The Changing Role of Management
   A. Forces for Change
   B. Effects of Change

II. General Issues
   A. Organizational Governance
   B. Global Interdependence
   C. Information Technology
   D. Organizational Dynamics

III. Specific Issues
   A. Stress
   B. Career Issues
   C. Changing Demographics at Work
   D. Drugs and Drug Testing
   E. Alcoholism and Smoking

IV. Preparing for the Future
   A. Be Aware
   B. Continue to Learn
   C. Be Adaptable
   D. Be Professional

CHAPTER

22

After studying this chapter you should be able to

1. Delineate the reasons for and effects of the changing role of management.

2. Discuss the general issues likely to bring about more changes in business and management, particularly organizational governance, global interdependence, information technology, and organizational dynamics.

3. Discuss several specific issues concerning which fundamental changes are already occurring, such as stress, career issues, changing demographics at work, drugs and drug testing, and alcoholism and smoking.

4. Describe what managers must do to be prepared for the future.

Management in the Future

BIOTECH: A WHOLE NEW FRONTIER

One of the more exciting types of business organizations of the future is the company dealing with biotechnology, or biotech. *Biotech* refers to the application of chemical, physical, and engineering principles and techniques to biological systems. As an industry, it encompasses those organizations that are developing new biological products through the application of advanced technology. Although the early developments in biotech occurred in the United States, in the 1980s biotech emerged in Japan as a billion-dollar industry involving over three hundred firms.

The Japanese presence in biotech began in 1983, when Mitsui Petrochemical Industries made a red dye from the cells of a medicinal plant. Mitsui successfully mass-produced the dye for use in cosmetics. The company then began to work on flowers and was able to develop tank-grown, nearly perfect lilies with which it plans to capture the whole lily market.

Whereas the major U.S. and European biotech companies have stayed almost exclusively in drugs and agriculture, the Japanese have branched out into an amazing array of experiments, including trying to make microcircuits of living tissue. In 1989 Kirin Brewery Company spent nearly 80 percent of its research budget on the use of gene-splicing to develop new beverages, vegetables, and drugs. That same year Mitsubishi Kasei used about 50 percent of its research monies on improved rice and biodegradable plastics.

A listing of companies and what they are doing in this industry is staggering:

• *Ajinomoto*—With over $3 billion in sales, the leading food processor in Japan spends about 50 percent of its research budget on biotech, is a leader in amino and nucleic acids, and is developing a strong presence in pharmaceuticals.
• *Takeda*—Sales are over $5 billion, and it has alliances in West Germany, France, Italy, and the United States to develop and market prescription drugs.
• *Kyowa Hakko Kogyo*—Sales are nearly $2 billion, and it spends about 70 percent of its research monies on biotech, where it leads in amino acids; it is also working on fish growth hormones, plants and vegetables, wine, bread yeast, and pharmaceuticals.
• *Fujisawa*—Sales are nearly $2 billion; the company owns about three-fourths of Klinge Pharma in West Germany and has U.S. interests as well for its highly promising organ transplant drug.
• *Mitsui Toatsu Chemicals*—With nearly $3 billion in sales, it spends only about 15 percent of its research monies on biotech but is strong in pharmaceuticals, amino acids, hydroponics, and plant cell culture.
• *Yamanouchi*—With sales of about $1.5 billion, it has interests in the United States and Ireland for its ulcer drugs and cell biology work.
• *Kirin Brewery*—Sales are over $8 billion, and 80 percent of its

Biotechnology is likely to grow rapidly throughout this decade. The Japanese shopper shown here is buying a bioengineered detergent in Tokyo.

research is in biotech; it also has a strong presence in pharmaceuticals, fruits, rice, vegetables, and artificial seeds.
• *Chugai*—It has sales just under $1 billion and is developing British and U.S. connections for its work on ulcer drugs and a drug to treat anemia caused by kidney failure.
• *Mitsubishi Kasei*—With nearly $2.5 billion in sales, the leading chemical company in Japan spends about 50 percent of its research budget on biotech; it has developed a hepatitis-B vaccine as well as other pharmaceuticals, seeds, and biochips.

Numerous other companies and developments abound. Toto Ltd. is using biosensors to develop an intelligent toilet that can run checks on the user's health. Aji-nomoto developed an elastic paper that Sony uses in its top-of-the-line headphones. Eisai is marketing an improved version of a drug that dissolves blood clots. Aji-nomoto is licensing Interleukin 2, which treats breakdowns of the immune system.

Clearly, this industry represents a major wave of the future for Japan, as well as for the rest of the world. In pharmaceuticals, where Japan has been second in the world and in which the United States maintains a favorable balance of trade with Japan, biotechnology may have a tremendous impact, although in just what way it is probably too early to speculate.

SOURCES: "Japanese Biotech's Overnight Evolution," *Business Week*, March 12, 1990, pp. 69, 72; "Japan's Next Battleground: The Medicine Chest," *Business Week*, March 12, 1990, pp. 68–69; "U.S. Leads Japan in Development of Biotech Drugs," *Drug Topics*, June 19, 1989, pp. 29–33; Motoyuki Fujii, "Biotechnology R&D Intensifies," *Business Japan*, July 1, 1989, pp. 74–76; Aki Yoshikawa, "The Other Drug War: U.S–Japan Trade in Pharmaceuticals," *California Management Review*, Winter 1989, pp. 76–90.

T he application of the latest technology in organizations represents one of the more exciting aspects of the future of management. Advanced-technology organizations are springing up in all areas of business, in services as well as in manufacturing. Biotechnology and information technology are two of the more obvious areas, but robotics and computers are others that could quickly come to mind. This chapter focuses on the future of management in a world in which these changes are taking place.

In Chapter 2, we saw that interest in management is only a few decades old. Its brief history has unfolded within the context of profound social and cultural change. The human race has existed for tens of thousands of years, but only within the past hundred years have we come to accept the automobile, the airplane, the telephone, and electricity as a part of our daily lives. Only within the past fifty years have motion pictures, x-rays, and televisions become anything more than curiosities. Large computers, nuclear power, and space exploration have emerged within the past thirty years, and personal computers and home video recorders have appeared only within the past decade.

As our daily lives change, so does the world of management. The managers of today must function within an environment several times more complex and challenging than that of their predecessors. The managers of tomorrow will have to deal with even more complexity and challenge.[1]

In this, the last chapter of the book, we look at the managerial world of the future. The chapter first discusses the changing role of management. It then identifies and describes four general and five specific issues that will increasingly affect management. To conclude, it summarizes four things that today's manager can do to become better equipped for tomorrow.

THE CHANGING ROLE OF MANAGEMENT

No one can deny that the role of management in contemporary society is changing. Why is this true? And what are the effects of these changes? The following sections provide answers to these questions.

Forces for Change

In general, four basic forces currently shape the manager's job.[2] First, more and more firms are recognizing the need to cut back and retrench. Organizations such as AT&T, IBM, Xerox, Chrysler, and American Can Company have already undergone enormous changes aimed at eliminating unnecessary costs and unprofitable operations. In addition, many firms are flattening their structures by eliminating levels of management. This practice, often called **downsizing,** is likely to become even more prevalent over the next few years.

Second, advances in computers and communications technology are greatly altering the nature of managerial work. Machines can now perform many basic

☐ *Downsizing* refers to the flattening of organizational structures through the elimination of levels of management.

SMALL BUSINESS AND ENTREPRENEURSHIP

Cetus Joins the Fight

Cetus Corporation of Emeryville, California, is one of many emerging small biotechnology firms in the United States concentrating on cancer. One of the newest developments in the field originated at Cetus. It is a technique called the polymerase chain reaction (PCR), which lets researchers identify and make copies of a single gene in a DNA sample. The millions of copies produced by the technique make it much easier to remove the particular gene from the tens of thousands of other genes, so much so that it can be done in just a few hours.

This development has already led to important results. An early diagnostic test using it is available for chronic myelogenous leukemia (CML), and one is in clinical trials for breast cancer. Others are being developed for genital cancer and colon cancer. The importance of these tests rests on the fact that many of these cancers are highly treatable or even curable if detected early enough.

Along with Cetus, small firms such as Triton Biosciences, Oncogene Science, Oncor, Lifecodes, and Applied Biotechnology are working on diagnostic tests for breast, cervical, colon, CML, retinoblastoma (eye cancer), and many other forms of cancer. Although progress may be disappointingly slow, the future continues to appear bright, despite the occasional overly optimistic statements of biotech companies.

SOURCES: "Stopping Cancer in the Starting Blocks," *Business Week,* April 2, 1990, pp. 82–83, 86; "The Hope Doctors: A Biotech Institute Joins the Race for a Cancer Cure," *Hispanic Business,* March 1, 1990, pp. 30–31; Linda Hembree, "Business Forum: Cancer Treatment and the Economy," *Business and Economic Review,* October 1, 1989, pp. 30–31; Gary Slutsker, "Look Before You Speak," *Forbes,* December 6, 1988, pp. 116–121.

organizational tasks more efficiently than people can, and software is being developed that can significantly aid managers in their jobs.[3]

Third, the rapid growth in the service sector promises to continue. This means that a greater array of services will be available for all types of consumers, more and different kinds of managerial positions will be available within service firms, and new services not yet imaginable will emerge. In fact, the Bureau of Labor Statistics estimates that 14.5 million new jobs will be created in the service sector by 1995 and that one-sixth of these positions will be managerial or executive-level jobs.[4]

Finally, the emerging importance of small businesses and entrepreneurship will play a major role in shaping the future of management. More people than ever before are choosing to work for themselves. Small-business growth is mushrooming, and successful entrepreneurs such as Steve Jobs, Bill Gates, and Sam Walton have increasingly become popular figures in the United States and the world. Indeed, entrepreneurship is perhaps even more pronounced in Europe than it is here. Many small businesses are emerging in high-technology areas; one example is presented in *Management Today: Small Business and Entrepreneurship.*

Effects of Change

The effects of these changes manifest themselves along two dimensions, which in turn directly affect the degree of uncertainty that managers and organizations face. Exhibit 22.1 illustrates how this occurs.

☐ Organizational environments are becoming more *dynamic* and *complex*.

One dimension is increased **dynamism**—that is, an increase in the rate of change. Things have always changed. Now, however, more things are changing than ever before, the changes are occurring more frequently than ever before, and more and more changes are taking place simultaneously. Thus the manager's world is becoming increasingly dynamic.

It is also becoming increasingly complex. **Complexity** refers to the sheer number of issues, problems, opportunities, and threats that must be considered. In the past most managers needed to concern themselves with only a limited number of environmental elements. Now the number of competitors, regulators, suppliers, and customers continues to increase rapidly. This combination often results in surprising relationships; General Motors and Toyota are competitors in the world marketplace for automobiles, for example, but they are collaborating in a venture in California.

Taken together, the complexity and dynamism faced by managers dramatically increase the uncertainty that those managers must address. In some industries, new technological developments occur almost daily. Competitors appear and disappear overnight. New governmental regulations sometimes take years to untangle. Union demands are hard to predict. Consumer tastes are fickle and change so fast that some companies cannot adjust.

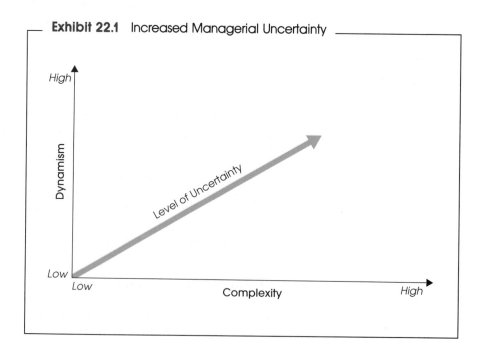

Exhibit 22.1   Increased Managerial Uncertainty

It is evident, then, that managers have many obstacles to overcome to enhance organizational effectiveness. Several forces beyond the individual's control are dictating myriad changes in organizational life. These changes lead ultimately to a high degree of uncertainty as to how best to compete in an ever-changing world.

GENERAL ISSUES

The four most pervasive issues that affect the world of management are shown in Exhibit 22.2.[5] As suggested by the solid and dashed arrows, the effects of these issues are felt most directly at the overall organizational level and secondarily at the level of the individual manager.

Organizational Governance

☐ *Organizational governance* refers to the rights and privileges of organizations and the individuals in those organizations.

Questions of **organizational governance**—the questions associated with the rights and privileges of organizations and of the individuals within those organizations—are becoming more and more critical.[6] The trend toward even more employee participation in decision making through such arrangements as semi-autonomous work teams and quality circles suggests that workers will have increasing influence on what occurs in the workplace.[7]

Other issues involve the constitutional rights of employees while they are at work. For instance, if an employee tells the press that the company is committing a crime, can the company fire her? Such whistle-blowing does occasionally lead to dismissal, but employees recognize more and more often that they may be able to pursue reinstatement.[8]

☐ *Employment at will* means that organizations can hire and fire at any time for any reason.

Still another governance question involves the employee's legal claim to his job. Before 1980 the doctrine of **employment at will** generally governed the implied employment contract between the worker and the organization. This doctrine held that the organization was free to employ someone at will and could therefore dismiss the employee at any time for any reason. Several courts have ruled since then, however, that claims made in employee handbooks or by managers can guarantee an employee his job in a variety of circumstances. An example occurred at Safeway, which fired hundreds of employees in 1986 during a major cost-cutting program. Two hundred and fifty of them filed a lawsuit for $400 million, arguing that the company essentially guaranteed them their jobs. Other suits have been brought against AT&T, TWA, Sears, Caterpillar, and McGraw-Hill.[9] The resolution of these cases will dramatically affect management practices in the future.[10]

Global Interdependence

Throughout the book, but particularly in Chapter 21, we have seen the increased importance of international business. This trend will have significant

Exhibit 22.2   General Issues for the Manager of the Future

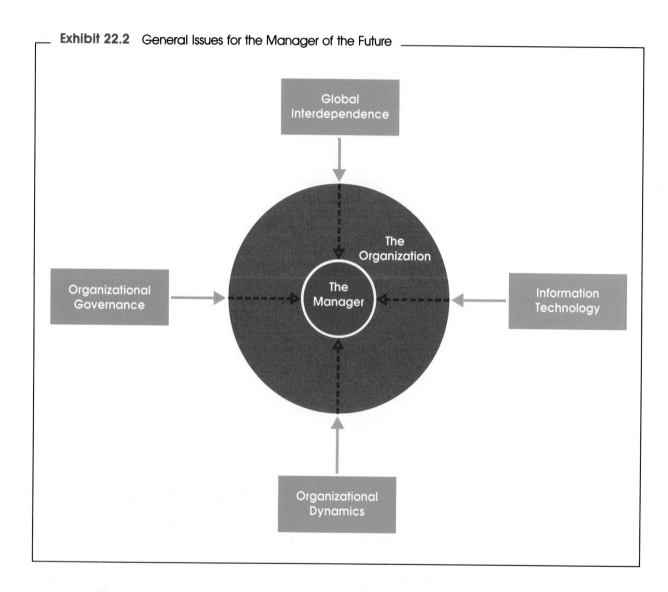

consequences for the business world of tomorrow. We have already considered many of the implications of this pattern for the manager of the future; for instance, the increase in international competition and movement toward a truly global economy will mean that many future managers will need to be fluent in more than one language.

At another level, however, there are other implications. These involve the heightened level of uncertainty and complexity managers will face in the future. We often hear about the "balance of payments deficit" and "international trade wars," but these areas are fraught with ambiguities and misunderstandings. For example, Japanese products may indeed be invading the American marketplace, yet for years American firms have been moving aggressively into Japanese markets. IBM Japan Ltd. had sales of $650 million in Japan in 1985.[11]

Moreover, the distinctions between companies and country boundaries are becoming increasingly blurred. General Motors of Canada and Ford–West Germany, two of the largest firms in the world, are considered foreign companies. Japanese firms are trying to use names in the United States that sound more English than Japanese, and young Japanese consumers increasingly want American goods and services.[12] Thus, the question of what is domestic and what is foreign is growing more and more difficult to answer as **global interdependence** increases. In all likelihood this trend will continue and will greatly affect managers in the future.

⬛ With *global interdependence* the distinction between what is domestic and what is foreign is becoming blurred.

PRELUDE CASE UPDATE

The Japanese biotech case clearly illustrates many of these points. Many of the companies have such extensive interrelationships with other companies in the United States and Europe that it is increasingly difficult to identify whether it is, indeed, a Japanese company, an American company, a European company, or a truly global company.

Information Technology

We have also considered some of the dramatic changes and effects on management caused by innovations in information technology in general and computers in particular. In terms of managerial practice, three basic implications are especially relevant.

Advances in communication technology will likely change the way many people work. Carol D'Agostino, shown here, is a researcher and editor who does much of her work from her home office. Such work arrangements are increasingly common as people have access to computers, facsimile machines, voice mailboxes, information networks, and other information technology innovations.

Photo © Alan Dorow

THE WORLD OF MANAGEMENT

Lasers In Our Lives

Lasers are entering industry in a wide variety of ways: they are used in machine shops for metalworking, in hospitals for surgery, and in dentists' offices for drilling. New developments in diode lasers should expand those applications. Diode lasers are already being used in an amazing array of applications, such as in the ranging devices used by border patrol officers to quickly check the interior length of vehicles to see if it matches the exterior length as part of their search for hidden compartments. Other applications involve compact disc players and the fiber-optic networks used by phone companies. The prediction is that such diode lasers will replace gas lasers and double the sales of the industry (from just under $900 million to over $1.7 billion). The reason for this is a major development known as the quantum well.

Quantum well lasers are being developed by AT&T, Philips, several other smaller American companies, and numerous Japanese companies. The quantum well is an area between layers of gallium arsenide and ultrathin layers of aluminum gallium arsenide where electrons are so closely packed that far less energy is needed to emit light. Less energy means a more efficient laser that generates less heat.

In early 1990, Sony announced a diode laser fifty times more powerful than previous ones. Work at the Sarnoff Research Center in Princeton, New Jersey, could potentially enable a cable television operator to send two hundred channels using fiber-optic cable instead of the forty to eighty channels in use today. Companies like NEC and Laser Magnetic Storage International are working to develop shorter-wavelength lasers for use in compact and video disc players as well as in computer storage devices. Other companies, such as Coherent Inc., Candela Laser Corp., and Micracor Inc., are also pushing this emerging technology to new uses and promise to reshape our communications and information storage capabilities substantially.

SOURCES: "The Business of Laser," *Modern Machine Shop*, April 1, 1990, pp. 54–65; "The Laser Marketplace—Forecast 1990," *Lasers and Optronics*, January 1, 1990, pp. 39–58; "The Burning-Bright Future of Lasers," *Business Week*, April 16, 1990, pp. 88–89; "Tooth Tech: The New Dentistry," *High Technology Business*, April 1, 1989, pp. 28–33.

First, the advent of computers, computer networks, and electronic mail promises to greatly enhance productivity in the workplace. Managers will have much greater access to information, will be able to sort and process that information rapidly, and will be able to communicate with others very quickly. New developments in laser technology will further accelerate and expand our communication ability, as indicated in *Management Today: The World of Management*.

Second, it will become even more important for managers to remain abreast of breakthroughs and changes. As each new generation of computer is unveiled and each new application is developed, managers will need to assess how and to what degree their organization can effectively use these innovations.

Third, every organization will have to contend with issues of supervision and coordination. For instance, the Hartford Insurance Group tried a program that allowed employees to work at home on computers, but it was soon abandoned because supervisors had trouble coordinating work and complained that they were losing touch with their work groups. Although widespread telecommuting has been slow to develop, its potential advantages—it allows the disabled to work, calls for less office space, provides greater work flexibility, and so forth—suggest that managers will have to work even harder in the future to make it possible.[13]

Organizational Dynamics

☐ The way in which organizations structure themselves and manage their employees is termed *organizational dynamics*.

Organizational dynamics—the way in which organizations structure themselves and manage their employees—will also continue to shape the manager's world. Several issues can readily be identified in this field.[14]

For example, the distinction between line and staff workers is already becoming blurred. Employees are better educated, and more and more women and members of minority groups are entering the workplace and competing effectively for higher-level positions.

Organizations find that they must explore a variety of compensation arrangements, benefit offerings, and flexible work schedules. They must give more consideration to dual-career situations and alternative lifestyles. Union-management relations will continue a trend toward collaboration rather than conflict. There are also a number of specific work-related issues, which we consider in the next section.

LEARNING CHECK

You should now be able to discuss the general issues likely to bring about more changes in business and management, particularly organizational governance, global interdependence, information technology, and organizational dynamics.

SPECIFIC ISSUES

As we have noted, the general issues just described usually affect the organization first and the individual second. A set of more specific issues affect the individual first and the organization second; these are illustrated in Exhibit 22.3.

Stress

☐ *Stress* occurs when a person is subjected to unusual situations, demands that are difficult to handle, or extreme expectations or pressures.

The problem of occupational **stress** has emerged as an important concern for individual managers and organizations alike.[15] Stress, or physical or emotional tension, occurs when a person is subjected to unusual situations, to demands that are difficult to handle, or to extreme expectations or pressures. Starting a new job, trying to win a promotion, working long hours, being pressured by a demanding boss, and similar situations all induce stress. Positive events can cause stress too. Winning a contest, achieving the desired promotion, and getting a big pay increase are stress-inducing situations.

The demands associated with a person's job, such as having to satisfy many people simultaneously, can increase stress, as can physical conditions like frequent international travel (jet lag). Interpersonal demands, such as group pressure and disagreements with others, are also a possible cause of tension.

Exhibit 22.3   Specific Issues for the Manager of the Future

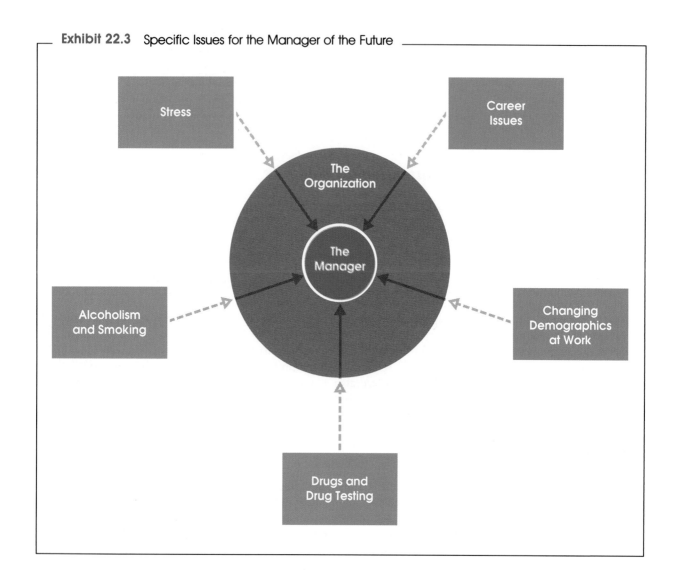

Of course, a moderate level of stress is normal, and in fact healthy. It causes us to feel excited about what we're doing, increases motivation, and sparks creativity. Too much stress, however, can cause physical problems such as heart attacks, high blood pressure, and high cholesterol levels and psychological problems such as sleep disturbances and depression. Behavioral problems—alcohol abuse or violence—can also result. From the organization's perspective, employees who are experiencing too much stress might be absent from work too often, perform at a low level, and generally be incapable of doing their jobs in the most effective fashion.

One interesting line of research has proposed two "stress profiles" that describe many people.[16] As shown in Table 22.1, **Type A people** tend to be

TABLE 22.1
Stress-Related Behavior
Patterns

Stress Profile	Behavior	Consequences
Type A	Competitive Devoted to work Strong sense of urgency	Heart problems High blood pressure Relative unconcern with health
Type B	Less competitive Less devoted to work Weaker sense of urgency	Fewer heart problems Lower blood pressure More concern with health

very competitive and devoted to work, and they have a strong sense of urgency. As a result, they experience heart problems and high blood pressure and are relatively unconcerned with their health. These are symptoms of stress. **Type B people,** in contrast, are less competitive and less devoted to their work and have a weaker sense of urgency. They also have fewer heart problems, lower blood pressure, and are more concerned with their health.

Although there is conflicting evidence about the importance of Type A and Type B behavior patterns, the fact remains that more people than ever before are concerned about stress.[17] Similarly, more and more organizations are taking steps to help their employees cope better with the stress they encounter in their jobs.

Career Issues

□ *Forced mobility* refers to frequent changes of jobs and companies brought about by organizational changes such as downsizing and retrenchment.

Other significant issues in the manager's future relate to her career, particularly to what might be called **forced mobility.** In the past people started working for a company right after college. One or more job changes in the early years were normal, but by midcareer most people had settled with one company. In this age of retrenchment and downsizing, however, it is becoming increasingly common for organizations to fire people in the middle of their careers or later. It is also becoming more common for managers to move frequently, some to get extra pay, some to accelerate advancement, and others to find new challenges.[18]

These and other changes suggest that managers need to take a new view of their careers.[19] In particular, they must do two things. First, they must understand that they will be held more accountable for their contributions to the organization—for the "value added" to the company. Today, companies want tangible evidence of what an individual is contributing to the bottom line. For example, Citibank terminated several dozen managers who did nothing but supervise the work of others because it felt that these people added nothing specific to the company's profitability.[20]

Second, managers will have to recognize that they are very likely to experience job changes, regardless of their preferences. It used to be that a manager who was fired had reason to be embarrassed. Now, however, more and more people are coming to see that forced mobility is nothing to be ashamed of. In fact, it has become the rule rather than the exception.[21]

Changing Demographics at Work

⬛ *Organizational demographics refers to the age, sex, education, race, ethnic background, country of national origin, and experience of the work force.*

Organizational demographics—the age, sex, education, race, ethnic background, country of national origin, and experience of the work force—have begun to change.[22] The more obvious aspects of that change are reflected in the increasing presence of women and minority-group members in management.[23] Many aspects of organizational culture have arisen in a white, male, Protestant social culture and hence reflect images, expressions, and attitudes from that social culture. Clearly, those aspects of organizational culture will have to undergo massive change.

Communication patterns will also change.[24] Mobility and dual-career problems will increase, and this complexity will further contribute to the stress problem. Issues concerning the language to use in manuals, reports, and the like will grow, not just with the impact of globalization but also with the diversity of ethnic groups that will become more common.

Ed Lallo

The changing demographics of society will present many challenges to businesses in the future. R. Roosevelt Thomas, shown here, runs the Institute for Managing Diversity. His programs help organizations better manage and retain an effective, multicultural work force.

Drugs and Drug Testing

☐ Drugs and drug use, including the use of alcohol and tobacco, are becoming more of an issue in organizations.

An issue that has emerged in the last decade as a major factor in the manager's job is drugs and drug testing. The stress inherent in management, high salaries in the executive ranks, freedom of movement, and peer pressure have combined to cause many managers to experiment with painkillers and stimulants as well as with cocaine and even heroin.[25]

Because of the high costs to both the individual and the organization, some companies have begun to experiment with drug testing in the workplace as a way to cope with the problem. General Electric and Kodak have started testing new job applicants for drug use.[26] But the legality of such mandatory testing is still open to debate. Some people argue that testing is necessary for control in the organization as well as for the well-being of individual managers. Others feel just as strongly that drug testing is an invasion of privacy and is not justified under most circumstances.[27]

PRELUDE CASE UPDATE

Biotech developments may make testing far simpler and accurate, less obtrusive and invasive, and hence easier. Nevertheless, the legal and ethical aspects will remain and may even become more complex if technological developments make covert testing possible.

Alcoholism and Smoking

Strictly speaking, alcohol and tobacco are drugs too, but their legality and the fact that they have been an issue for a longer period of time generally set them apart from drug abuse problems.

Alcoholism has been recognized as a problem among managers for many years. In general, although major difficulties associated with alcohol in the workplace are still evident, some experts feel that the corner has been turned in dealing with alcohol abuse. There has been a trend toward lighter drinking among the general population, and this trend appears to exist among the managerial ranks as well. In 1985 estimates put alcohol abusers among managers at about 10 percent of the total, which represented a decline from over 15 percent just a few years earlier and was about the same level as among the general population.[28] Progress is still needed.

A different situation characterizes smoking. Most people now accept that smoking is dangerous, but excessive smoking does not have the same kinds of behavioral and performance-related effects as excessive drinking. The issue has emerged in terms of the conflict between the rights of smokers and those of nonsmokers. In particular, nonsmokers are becoming more aggressive in trying to get smokers to break their habit or at least to smoke in a setting away from those who do not smoke. Nevertheless, smoking creates fire hazards leading to higher insurance costs and affects others in organizations so that more and more organizations are banning or limiting it.

One survey has found that one-third of American businesses restrict or prohibit smoking altogether and that another 20 percent are investigating such policies. Evidence from the same survey suggests that more and more smokers are finding that their habit limits their career opportunities.[29] Texas Instruments allows smokers to light up only in certain areas (a barrier in the cafeteria separates the smoking and nonsmoking sections, for instance), and Boeing and Greyhound prohibit smoking in the workplace altogether.[30] Since this is an emotional issue involving deeply felt convictions, smoking is quite likely to play an important role in the manager's future.

Alcohol and tobacco are drugs even if they are more socially acceptable. They have subtle but substantial costs to organizatioins particularly in terms of health-care claims, absenteeism, and tardiness.

PREPARING FOR THE FUTURE

Predicting the future is hardly a precise science.[31] This chapter has attempted to spotlight several of the most significant issues that promise to characterize the managerial world of tomorrow. If we knew with certainty what tomorrow would bring, we could all be better prepared to cope with it. However, all too often we don't really know and can only speculate about the future.[32]

This is certainly the case in the business world. It is possible that some of the issues noted throughout this chapter will quickly fade away and be of little concern to anyone in the future. And issues that are totally unexpected and unknown today might arise and come to dominate the job of tomorrow's manager.

How, then, should managers behave? Even if the issues noted here are the only ones managers will face, they are complex, ambiguous, and difficult to address. When we're not even sure of the issues, complexity is greatly magnified. Therefore, although the real issues will most closely dictate how managers should prepare for them, all managers must do four things to become better equipped for the future.

☐ To become better equipped for the future, managers must develop an awareness of change, continue to train for changes, learn to adapt, and develop a professional view of their work.

Be Aware

First, every manager simply needs to be aware that things are changing. When a new manager starts to work at his first job, he should not assume that what he is being told today is the same thing he will be told tomorrow, that he and the organization are unchanging, and that today's problems and solutions will be tomorrow's problems and solutions. Instead he must recognize that today's message will change, that neither he nor the organization will remain the same, and that the problems and their solutions will be different. Being aware that change is inevitable helps a person cope better with that change, whatever its form.

The manager of tomorrow may do well to consider the challenge expressed in this statement by the founder and executive adviser for Matsushita Electric Industrial Co. (Osaka, Japan):

> *We will win and you will lose. You cannot do anything about it because your failure is an internal one . . . . You firmly believe that sound management means executives on one side and workers on the other . . . . For you, management is the art of smoothly transferring the executives' ideas to the workers' hands . . . . We are aware that business has become terribly complex. Survival is very uncertain in an environment increasingly filled with risk, the unexpected, and competition. Therefore, a company must have the constant commitment of the minds of all of its employees to survive. For us, management is the entire work force's intellectual commitment at the service of the company . . . .*[33]

Continue to Learn

Likewise, when an individual leaves school, she should not assume that her education is complete. As noted in Chapter 1, education is a lifelong experience for the manager. Throughout her career she will learn new things from her job, and she will participate in training and development programs. She may even return to school full- or part-time for an advanced degree.

Training and experience are intertwined. We learn, we apply what we have learned, we learn from that experience, and then we learn some more. The manager's job today is profoundly different from the manager's job yesterday, and it will probably be even more different tomorrow. Taking a lifelong learning perspective, recognizing the importance of learning, and seeking new opportunities to learn will all serve tomorrow's manager in good stead.[34]

Be Adaptable

Following logically from the concepts of awareness and training is **adaptation,** one of the key skills tomorrow's manager will need. If we expect change (are aware) and are able to deal with it objectively (have the necessary training), almost by definition we are more adaptable. But if we assume things will always stay as they are today and we don't prepare for tomorrow's changes, we will not be able to adapt to those changes easily when they occur.

Of course there are no hard and fast guidelines for becoming more adaptable. The manager simply needs to be prepared to work in different situations and under different circumstances. The rules of work will change, the workplace will change, and the people in the workplace will change. Being willing and able to adapt to those changes is a crucial attribute of tomorrow's successful manager.

In the future, managers will increasingly have to adapt and adjust to a changing world. J. R. Simplot is CEO of a privately held company that bears his name. He has built a fortune on his ability to find creative uses for the potato. For example, his firm uses the waste from potato processing to make livestock feed, ethanol, low-cost fish food, and other unusual products. Simplot's ability to find new business opportunities will need to be increasingly emulated by other managers.

Be Professional

Finally, the manager of tomorrow needs to take a professional view of his or her work. At one time managers were considered second-class citizens. Increasingly, however, corporate leaders are being accorded the same level of status as doctors, attorneys, and others in the traditional professions.

Tomorrow's managers need to capitalize and build on these changes in status. Heightened **professionalism** will give managers greater access to the information they need to carry out their job, more respect from government leaders, and better standing among the general public. *Professionalism* refers to a belief in self-regulation based on expertise in some particular field, in this case, the field of management.

Managers can continue the current trend toward getting more education; they can join professional associations such as the American Management Association and the Academy of Management, and they can behave in socially responsible ways. Each of these activities can serve only to increase the level of professionalism within the field.

Above all, however, managers should take pride in their work. When they work within the legal and cultural framework of our society, they provide a great service to everyone. They continue to raise our standard of living, to enhance our ability to confront social problems, and to play a fundamental role in maintaining the basic rights and privileges of the individual.

Chapter Summary

The role of management is changing for many reasons. Among the more important are downsizing, advances in computers and related technology, the rapid growth and changing composition of the service sector, and the increased importance of small businesses and entrepreneurship. The effects of these changes show up in two general ways: through an increasing rate of change in organizations and their environments, and through an increase in the complexity of managers' roles. These two in turn increase the uncertainty associated with the management of organizations so that management in the future will be more challenging than it has been in the past.

Four general issues affect organizations today. *Organizational governance* refers to the rights and privileges of organizations and the individuals within those organizations. *Global interdependence* means that the boundaries between domestic and international companies and between countries are becoming increasingly blurred, so that the distinction between domestic and foreign trade is less clear than it used to be. Information technology is developing at an increasing rate; some employees can work at home with computers, and communication, including mail, can be handled electronically. Finally, the rapid rate of change in organizational dynamics suggests that simple rules, procedures, and processes will be replaced with complex ones.

Five specific issues will affect individuals primarily and organizations in a related way. Stress occurs when a person is subjected to unusual situations, to demands that are difficult to handle, or to extreme expectations or pressures. A moderate level of stress is normal and healthy; too much stress is detrimental. Managers are beginning to implement stress management programs within their organizations.

Career issues include forced mobility and accountability as well as changing career paths. Changing organizational demographics will also influence the way organizations function in the future.

The real and potential effects of drug use on the performance of managers and nonmanagers, as well as the illegality of many drugs, are causing many organizations to test their employees for drug use. The legality and ethics of such testing are now being questioned in the courts and in public opinion, but the problem will be around for some time. The impact of alcohol and tobacco on performance and costs, particularly in terms of health care claims, absenteeism, and tardiness, are causing organizations to closely examine their policies regarding the use of these substances.

To be prepared for the future, managers must become aware of the forces and issues that are bringing about change. They must realize that change is inevitable and perhaps even necessary if companies are to compete effectively. They should also recognize that their training and education do not stop with formal graduation from school. What this means is that managers must learn to adapt; they must learn to be flexible and tolerant. Managers must also take a professional view of their work. They might join and participate in professional associations such as the American Management Association and the Academy of Management, which help managers keep up to date through publications and programs and also help instill a professional identity.

The Manager's Vocabulary

downsizing	employment at will
dynamism	global interdependence
complexity	organizational dynamics
organizational governance	stress
	Type A people

Type B people   adaptation
forced mobility   professionalism
organizational
  demographics

Prelude Case Wrap-Up

Our Prelude Case for this chapter describes the developing biotech industry in Japan. Developments in that industry promise to reshape our world. Food supplies may be markedly increased as new varieties of plants and animals are developed that can withstand harsher, drier climates and/or that have greater yields per unit of resource (land, water, and so forth). Medical and pharmaceutical products will be improved, and our capacity to combat sickness and disease will substantially increase.

Managing advanced-technology organizations is more challenging than managing less varied, more slowly changing organizations. The entrepreneurial spirit must be fostered so that companies can continue to produce new products and take advantage of the very latest developments in technology. Information must be accurate, timely, open, and accessible to everyone to facilitate that spirit. Reward and control systems must be carefully tailored to the organization and its objectives. All of the concepts discussed in the preceding chapters must be more carefully and flexibly applied in these organizations. Clearly, managing these types of organizations will be among the more challenging tasks facing managers in the future.

Prelude Case Questions

1. Which are the major forces for change illustrated in the Japanese biotech case? Cite specific examples.
2. What are the effects of those changes?
3. There are those who feel that biotech is dangerous and should not be permitted to develop and expand. What are the strengths and weaknesses of the arguments on both sides of this issue?
4. What will likely happen to trade relations between the United States and Japan if Japan's biotech industry continues to expand as rapidly as it is now doing? Why?

Discussion Questions

Review Questions

1. What are the major forces bringing about change in management and organizations?
2. What are the four general issues surrounding the future of management?
3. What are the five specific issues noted in the text that will impact upon management in the future?
4. How should managers prepare themselves and their organizations for the future?

Analysis Questions

1. Comment on this statement: "All members of an organization should share in the governance of that organization."
2. What can managers do to control the dynamics of their organizations?
3. What can managers do to manage stress in their organizations?
4. Do you feel employees should be permitted to smoke on company premises on company time? Why or why not?
5. How could an organization help its managers prepare for the changing world of the future?

Application Questions and Exercises

1. Go to the library and find an example of an organization that has recently downsized. Prepare a two-page description of it to share with your class.
2. Go to the library and determine whether your state has enacted any legislation dealing with employment at will. If it has, what was the nature of the legislation? If not, do you feel it should? Why?
3. What changes in organizational demographics are taking place in your area? Interview local managers to obtain their reaction to these changes.
4. Interview managers of local businesses to determine their use of women and minorities in their organizations. Do any of them have women or minorities in management?
5. Interview managers of local businesses to determine their policies, rules, regulations, and the like with regard to drugs, including alcohol and tobacco. Share your results with the class.

ENHANCEMENT CASE

CYPRESS: A MODEL COMPANY FOR THE FUTURE

Cypress Semiconductor Corporation was founded in 1983 by Thurman John Rodgers when he was thirty-five years old. Since 1984, Cypress has been consistently profitable, even in an industry that has been characterized by extreme fluctuations in sales and profits during this same period of time. One reason for Cypress's success has been the technology it has developed to produce its products—chips, central processing units (CPUs), and other forms of processors. In turn, those products are of very high quality and among the fastest in the industry, operating at speeds of up to 33 MHz (megahertz) as of 1989. But technological innovation isn't everything. The other major reason for Cypress's success is the quality of its management.

Rodgers believes strongly that, as an organization grows, the control mechanisms that must be put into place inevitably bring about a bureaucratic inertia that stifles creativity and innovation. To avoid this situation, Rodgers uses a flattened, highly decentralized form of organization. Therefore, whenever new products are developed at Cypress, he creates a new, separate start-up company under the Cypress "umbrella." His approach ensures that the new company will be small, nonbureaucratic, and, hopefully, aggressively innovative. Four such units currently exist. Three of them have developed new semiconductors, and another is a chip factory that acts as a supplier to both units of Cypress as well as to outsiders; this organizational scheme keeps it competitive with outside suppliers.

Each of these start-up companies is headed by a president who has more authority than the typical division manager. Each president can change product design, issue stock, make major investment decisions such as whether to build a factory, raise money, change wages, and make personnel decisions such as hiring and firing. All the presidents meet with Rodgers once a week to see if Rodgers and the Cypress organization can do anything to help them reach their objectives. Although the presidents have

enormous power, at least 81 percent of the stock is owned by Cypress, so Rodgers can replace a president if that person does not seem able to do the job, and he has occasionally done so.

In addition to this unique organization structure, Cypress has a detailed goal-setting and planning system known as a "Turbo MBO." As discussed in Chapter 4, the Turbo MBO is a computerized management-by-objectives (MBO) system that was developed by Rodgers. Thousands of goals for the several hundred employees are set each week and then monitored to ensure their successful and timely completion. Although it in no way prevents mistakes from occurring, the system can quickly identify mistakes early so that their impact can be greatly lessened.

The first thing each Monday morning, project groups meet and plan everything that has to be completed during that week. They then enter that information into the computer system and begin their work. On Tuesdays, managers (the next-higher level in the organization) use their computers to review the goals of their subordinates and adjust them to ensure equity in workloads. On Wednesdays, the presidents and vice presidents review the status of all goals within their units. If a manager is behind in several of them, a vice president will work with him or her to bring performance up to standard; if the vice president is unable to do so, the president investigates the problem to seek a more permanent solution, which might involve the allocation of more resources (such as personnel or equipment).

This process occurs every week, and, although it involves an enormous number of goals (over 3,500 in 1987, for instance), it takes only about six hours of any given manager's or vice president's time. Using this system has cut in half the time it used to take for Cypress to develop and deliver a new product. Cypress, then, can start earning money more quickly and can use that advantage to continually keep in front of competitors. Moreover, the system does not require highly complex hardware or software.

Managers and higher-level executives all have micro-computers that are linked together through the company's minicomputer.

Turbo MBO is a high-performance system that puts everyone under pressure to perform, and perform they do. The success of Cypress is apparent. Its sales rose from about $3 million in 1984 to over $200 million in 1989. Profits have been consistently high, as have profit margins. The book value per share of stock has risen by a multiple of around eight, and other measures of performance are also quite good.

SOURCES: "SPARC Chip Looks for Fresh Cache," *ESD: The Electronic System Design Magazine*, March 1, 1989, p. 20; Julie Pitta, "Rodgers' Regiment," *Venture*, April 1, 1989, pp. 48 ; Brian Dumaine, "What the Leaders of Tomorrow See," *Fortune*, July 3, 1989, pp. 48–62; "Why Cypress and IDT May Have a Fight on their Hands," *Electronic Business*, February 6, 1989, p. 13; Steven B. Kaufman, "The Goal System That Drives Cypress," *Business Month*, July 1987, pp. 30–32.

Enhancement Case Questions

1. What similarities and differences can you note between the industry in which Cypress operates and the biotech industry discussed in the Prelude Case?
2. Describe the Cypress organization. What are the strengths of Cypress?
3. Would you want to invest your money in Cypress? Why or why not? Would you want to work for Cypress? Why or why not?
4. Do you feel that Cypress will continue to be successful? Why or why not?

Chapter Notes

1. See "Managing in the 1990s," *Business Horizons*, January 1, 1990, pp. 50–61, and Harold E. Edmondson, "Outstanding Manufacturing in the Coming Decade," *California Management Review*, Summer 1989, pp. 70–90.
2. Peter Nulty, "How Managers Will Manage," *Fortune*, February 2, 1987, pp. 47–50.
3. Jeremy Main, "At Last, Software CEOs Can Use," *Fortune*, March 13, 1989, pp. 77–83, and K. Jones, "Executive Support Systems Come of Age," *Modern Office Technology*, October 1989, pp. 78–79, 82.
4. Nulty, "How Managers Will Manage."
5. For a related presentation, see Brian Dumaine, "What the Leaders of Tomorrow See," *Fortune*, July 3, 1989, pp. 48–62.
6. Jerald Greenberg, "Organizational Justice: Yesterday, Today, and Tomorrow," *Journal of Management*, June 1990, and Jerald Greenberg, "A Taxonomy of Organizational Justice Theories," *Academy of Management Review*, January 1987, pp. 9–22.
7. Peter F. Drucker, "The Coming of the New Organization," *Harvard Business Review*, January-February 1988, pp. 45–53.
8. For a review of such practices, see Janet P. Near and Marcia P. Miceli, "Whistle-Blowers in Organizations: Dissidents or Reformers?" in L. L. Cummings and B. M. Staw, eds., *Research in Organizational Behavior* (Greenwich, Conn.: JAI Press, 1987), vol. 9, pp. 321–368.
9. See "More Workers Are Saying, 'Take This Job Cut and Shove It,' *Business Week*, December 29, 1986. See also Peter Nulty, "Pushed Out at 45—Now What?" *Fortune*, March 2, 1987, pp. 26–34.
10. J. Hoerr, "It's Getting Harder to Pass Out Pink Slips," *Business Week*, March 28, 1988, p. 68.
11. "The Myth of a Trade War," *Newsweek*, April 13, 1987, pp. 40–41.
12. See "The Sin of 'Smelling Japanese,'" *Newsweek*, April 27, 1987, p. 55, and "Japan's Prodigal Young Are Dippy About Imports," *Fortune*, May 11, 1987, p. 118.
13. "When Employees Work at Home, Management Problems Often Arise," *The Wall Street Journal*, April 20, 1987, p. 21.
14. See Nulty, "How Managers Will Manage."
15. For a thorough review, see James C. Quick and Jonathan D. Quick, *Organizational Stress and Preventive Management* (New York: McGraw-Hill, 1984). For another viewpoint, see Stephan J. Motowidlo, John S. Packard, and Michael R. Manning, "Occupational

Stress: Its Causes and Consequences for Job Performance," *Journal of Applied Psychology*, December 1986, pp. 618–629.

16. M. D. Friedman and R. H. Rosemann, *Type A Behavior and Your Heart* (New York: Knopf, 1974).

17. Joshua Friedman and R. H. Roseman, "Type A on Trial," *Psychology Today*, February 1987, pp. 42–50.

18. See "Job-Hopping Your Way to More Money," *Business Week*, January 19, 1987, p. 108, "More Executives Finding Changes in Traditional Corporate Ladder . . . ," *The Wall Street Journal*, November 14, 1986, p. 25, and "Laid-Off Managers of Big Firms Increasingly Move to Small Ones . . . ," *The Wall Street Journal*, August 25, 1986, p. 17.

19. Daniel C. Feldman, "Careers in Organizations: Recent Trends and Future Directions," *Operations Research/Management Science*, March 1, 1990, pp. 151–163.

20. Nulty, "How Managers Will Manage."

21. Janina C. Latack and Janelle B. Dozier, "After the Ax Falls: Job Loss as a Career Transition," *Academy of Management Review*, April 1986, pp. 375–392.

22. L. Silk, "Economic Scene: Changes in Labor by the Year 2000," *New York Times*, January 6, 1988, p. D2.

23. A. M. Morrison, R. P. White, E. Van Velsor, and Center for Creative Leadership, *Breaking the Glass Ceiling: Can Women Reach the Top of America's Largest Corporations?* (Reading, Mass.: Addison-Wesley, 1987).

24. Jeffrey Pfeffer, "Organizational Demography: Implications for Management," *California Management Review*, Fall 1985, pp. 67–81.

25. Steven Flax, "The Executive Addict," *Fortune*, June 24, 1985, pp. 24–31.

26. See "Drug Tests," *USA Today*, September 4, 1986, p. 1B.

27. "Drug Testing in the Workplace: Whose Rights Take Precedence?" *The Wall Street Journal*, November 11, 1986, p. 35.

28. Flax, "The Executive Addict."

29. "Cigarette Smoking Is Growing Hazardous to Careers in Business," *The Wall Street Journal*, April 23, 1987, pp. 1, 14.

30. Dexter Hutchins, "The Drive to Kick Smoking at Work," *Fortune*, September 15, 1986, pp. 42–43.

31. P. Narayan Pant and William H. Starbuck, "It Is Written in the Stars," *Journal of Management*, June 1990.

32. Yvan Allaire and Mihaela E. Firsirotu, "Coping with Strategic Uncertainty," *Sloan Management Review*, Spring 1989, pp. 7–16.

33. As quoted in "A Secret Is Shared," *Manufacturing Engineering*, February 1988, p. 15.

34. See William R. Torbert, "Management Education for the Twenty-First Century," *Selections*, Winter 1987, pp. 31–36, for additional thoughts on this subject.

THE ENTREPRENEURIAL SPIRIT

This final part of the book has introduced you to special challenges of management. Organization change was discussed because it is important for organizations to be adaptable to changes in their environments. The increasing globalization of organizations was also discussed, even though it has been stressed in virtually every chapter throughout the book. Finally, management in the future was discussed to help you prepare for what is to come.

Entrepreneurs are by definition agents of change, yet many of them are not so amenable to change within their own organizations. In part this is because they want to maintain personal control. They may also be afraid that the little success they have may be jeopardized. Nevertheless, change comes to all organizations, and all managers must be ready to plan for and manage it. A critical element, of course, is to balance the management of change and the need for conformity against the management of innovation and the need to maintain the entrepreneurial spirit.

The rapid growth of international business presents opportunities for entrepreneurs, both in the near future and in the long term. Entrepreneurs must choose from the strategies already discussed. They may remain purely domestic, go into importing or exporting or both, license goods or services to others overseas, engage in joint ventures, or make direct investments overseas. And, of course, they could use a combination of these. Changes in the European Common Market taking place in 1992, the opening up of trade and investment alternatives in the communist countries of Eastern Europe as well as in China and the Soviet Union, and continual Third World needs also present growth opportunities for entrepreneurs.

The increase in stress in organizations presents a great opportunity for the sale and service of stress reduction equipment. Downsizing leads to numbers of workers and managers in need of job placement and training. Drug-testing firms have growing markets as companies move to test more personnel. Canteen companies offering alternatives to drinks and commodities high in caffeine, cholesterol, sugar, and the like may be able to move into firms that are trying to improve the health of their personnel. Companies offering products that link diverse computer equipment together or computer software that aids in performing one's job also have expanding markets. All of these represent opportunities for entrepreneurs.

An interesting aspect of change and the future was revealed in a recent survey of students in graduate schools of business. Forty-four percent of those surveyed stated that their long-term career goal was to become an independent entrepreneur. Yet, when asked how well prepared they were for different tasks, managing their own businesses finished last. They wanted to be entrepreneurs and run their own businesses but felt unprepared to do so!

Of course, once they experience jobs in major corporations, these students may conclude that they are happy in those jobs and may decide not to pursue owning and running their own businesses. But they may also be prepared (or as prepared as most entrepreneurs ever are) and just don't know it. In either event, it seems clear that they need more information and experience before they embark upon an entrepreneurial career. The Appendix to this book is designed to assist you in thinking about your career.

SOURCES: Kurt Sandholtz, "M.B.A. Attitudes," *The Wall Street Journal, The College Edition of the National Business Employment Weekly*, Spring 1990, pp. 14–15; "Keeping the Fires Lit Under the Innovators," *Fortune*, March 28, 1988, p. 45; Richard M. Steers and Edwin L. Miller, "Management in the 1990s: The International Challenge," *Academy of Management Executive*, February 1988, pp. 21–22.

Managerial Careers

Some people spend their whole lives pursuing a single business career; others begin one career only to switch to another later in life. Some people work for others throughout their entire careers; others operate their own businesses. There is no single career path that leads to success. Each of you must find that which best suits yourself.

You have learned that managers exist at all levels of organizations and in all areas. To more fully understand who managers are and what they do at a more personal level, you need to know about managerial careers. Managers work long hours; their tasks are fragmented; the activities in which they engage are brief; they are involved with other people; and most of their communications are oral.[1] They function in all walks of life, all organizations, and all environments, including foreign countries. Indeed, many young managers are deciding to pursue part or all of their careers outside the United States, since there are many career opportunities in both developed and developing economies.

What Is a Career?

Hard work, long hours, and difficult personal adjustments are all part of a managerial career, and challenge, recognition, and a good income are usually also part of the package. If that sounds interesting, perhaps a managerial career is for you. But exactly what do we mean when we talk about a career?

Many people think of themselves as having jobs, not careers. Yet they do have careers. A **career** is the sequence of attitudes and behaviors that you perceive to be related to work experience during your life.[2] The term *career* can be applied to every walk of life; everyone can have a career. A secretary who considers how she can improve her current position and what that might lead to in a few years has a career in mind. A cook who is learning new recipes and trying to better his work situation has a career.

Careers are important because they help people shape their lives, as an ancient proverb implies: "Give me a fish, and I will eat for today; teach me to fish, and I will eat for the rest of my life."[3] Having a career enables us to respond to changing conditions in our work. It also enables us to tolerate some of the more boring and frustrating parts of our jobs because they are necessary to move us to the next stage of our career.

Career Choice

Your choice of a career is important, but you must remember that careers can and do change, so no choice is forever. The career you decide to prepare for and follow when you are sixteen may very well be different from the one you select when you are twenty-six. That one in turn may be different from the one that you choose at thirty-six.

One career choice is which **economic sector** in which to work. Every sector of our economy needs qualified managers. Employment in agriculture has fallen, but in other sectors it has grown or fluctuated. The service sector, wholesale and retail trade, and state and local government have seen substantial increases in employment during the past forty years. Employment in mining and the federal government has stayed relatively stable over that same period. But no matter what the employment opportunities are, managers are needed everywhere.

You can also choose the military for part or all of your career. Military employment is substantial even in times of peace, so there is an ever-present need for competent managers in all branches of the service, as well as in the Coast Guard and the Merchant Marines.

Not-for-profit organizations, which have goals other than making a profit, need managers too. Religious, social service, and charitable organizations and foundations must be managed even though making a profit is not their fundamental purpose. You need to

619

consider these organizations when you are making a career choice.

Another career decision that you may face, at least for a time, is whether to pursue your managerial career overseas. To find out more about employment outside the United States, contact the addresses shown in Table A.1.

A great many people in the United States want more than anything else to be their own boss—to own and operate a business.[4] This is part of the American dream. Owning and operating a business (usually a small one) clearly involves management, so another choice you have is whether to pursue your managerial career in this field. Small-business activ-

TABLE A.1 Finding Jobs Abroad

Government

Department of State

For some jobs you must first pass the Foreign Service examination. Inquiries about employment in the Foreign Service should be directed to:
PER/REE/REC
P.O. Box 9317
Rosslyn Station
Arlington, VA 22209

Department of Defense

Contact the Civilian Personnel Office at any Defense installation and they can put you in touch with the Department of Defense Automated Overseas Employment Referral Program.

Peace Corps

Call toll free 1-800-424-8580.

Other Federal Agencies

Department of Commerce
Office of Foreign Service Personnel
Room 3813
14th & Constitution Avenues, NW
Washington, D.C. 20230

Voice of America
300 Independence Ave., SW
Washington, D.C. 20547

Agency for International Development (AID)
2201 C St., NW
Washington, D.C. 20523

Business

International Employment Hotline
P.O. Box 6170
McLean, VA 22106
tel. (703) 573-1628

Chamber of Commerce of the U.S.
1615 H St., NW
Washington, D.C. 20062

The Whole World Handbook (New York: Council on International Educational Exchange, published every two years).

General Reference

Aulick, June L., *Looking for Employment in Foreign Countries*, 7th ed. (New York: World Trade Academy Press, 1985).

SOURCE: Excerpted from Gary Dessler, "How to Find Employment Outside the United States," *Bryan-College Station Eagle*, August 24, 1986, p. 5F. Reprinted by permission: Tribune Media Services.

Exhibit A.1 Making Your Career Choice

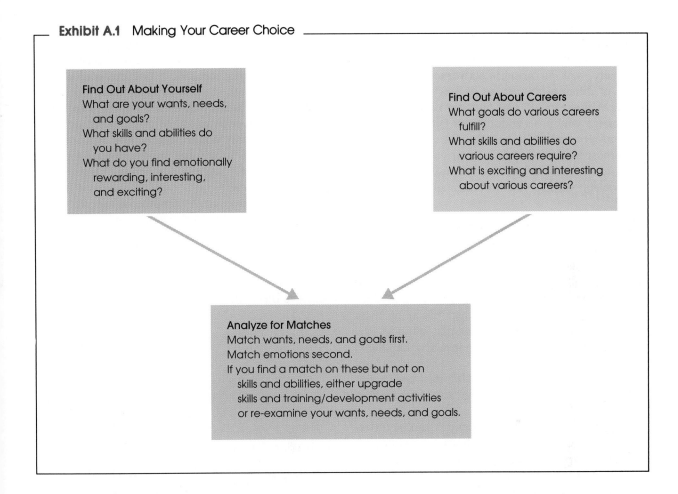

Find Out About Yourself
What are your wants, needs, and goals?
What skills and abilities do you have?
What do you find emotionally rewarding, interesting, and exciting?

Find Out About Careers
What goals do various careers fulfill?
What skills and abilities do various careers require?
What is exciting and interesting about various careers?

Analyze for Matches
Match wants, needs, and goals first.
Match emotions second.
If you find a match on these but not on skills and abilities, either upgrade skills and training/development activities or re-examine your wants, needs, and goals.

ity has increased during the late 1970s and l980s, and pursuing a managerial career in this area is something that many people will choose.

Managers also manage different groups of people: clerical personnel, technical personnel, and even professionals such as engineers, scientists, and physicians. If you choose to pursue your managerial career in one of these areas, you may find that specialized training is valuable. Office administration deals primarily with the management of clerical personnel, whereas hospital administration, obviously, focuses on hospitals.

Choosing a Career

As indicated in Exhibit A.1, making a career choice involves three steps. First you must find out about yourself.[5] Next you must research possible careers.

Finally, you must match yourself with a career. Simple as this seems, it can be difficult to do, but you should try to go through this process periodically during your life.

Ask yourself what you really want out of life. What are your overall goals and aspirations? Do you want to lead a peaceful life? Do you want to invent something? Do you want to be rich? Determine what it would take to achieve those goals. Do you have the necessary skills and abilities? Finally, you need to ask yourself what you find interesting and exciting. What do you like to do?

Now you need to ask these same questions about many possible careers. What are the goals associated with various careers? A career as a professional forester may lead to very different accomplishments than a career as a politician. What do the careers you choose require in terms of skills and abilities? What do they provide people in terms of emotional involvement and excitement?

Finally, look for matches between your goals and those of different careers, as well as for matches in terms of interests. If you find one or more careers that match your goals and interests fairly well, examine the required skills and abilities. If you do not have those skills and abilities, can you get them by going to school or by reading? Counselors and books are available to help you work through these steps.[6]

Life Stages and Career Stages

Life Stages We can think of our lives as taking place in a series of **life stages:** childhood (which consists of infancy, early childhood, play age, and school age), adolescence, young adulthood, adulthood, and senescence or old age.[7] Each of these stages is associated with an age range, although the years are only approximate. For instance, childhood lasts until about age thirteen, adolescence until around age twenty-five, young adulthood until about age forty-five, adulthood until age sixty-five, and old age until we die.

Movement from one stage to another can be turbulent, but things generally settle down again after each transition. Obviously, physiological needs are critical in infancy, whereas esteem and security may be more important in old age. Individual needs vary in these stages, although not in well-understood or predictable ways.

Career Stages Closely related to life stages is the concept of **career stages.** There is no career stage that corresponds to childhood, but each of the others has a counterpart. Career stages are even less exact than life stages in terms of the age at which they occur. As indicated in Exhibit A.2, there are four career stages: exploration, establishment, maintenance, and decline.

The **exploration stage** is a period of self-examination and occupational exploration. People at this stage are usually young, eager to succeed, and ready to upgrade their skills. The exploration stage begins with commitment to training of some kind—vocational school, college, or the military, for instance—and people frequently take part-time employment

while they are still in school. Some schools give special help during this stage; for example, Baldwin-Wallace College runs an assessment center to help students in career planning.[8] The exploration stage continues through the first or entry-level job, which is usually nonmanagerial, even for those who have a managerial career in mind. After all, there are about five times as many nonmanagerial jobs as managerial ones for people in the age groups usually found at this career stage.[9] Sometimes a period of learning the actual work of certain jobs is useful or even necessary before an employee moves into the managerial role in an organization. The exploration stage may also involve beginning one's own business. The dotted line in Exhibit A.2 suggests that performance is unpredictable in this stage, although some companies, such as the New York Telephone Company, are trying to improve this situation.[10]

During the exploration stage of career development, career changes are common. For example, several of these Pitney Bowes managers have altered their career paths one or more times. One studied anthropology and taught in a high school before deciding on a business career. Another worked in government and as a Vista volunteer before joining the firm.

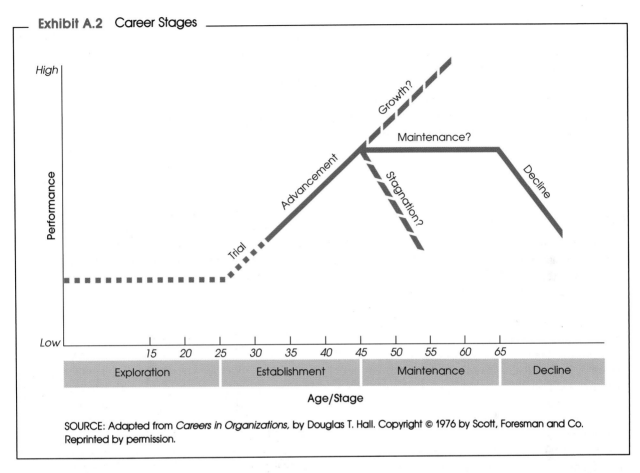

Exhibit A.2 Career Stages

Performance — High / Low

Trial · Advancement · Growth? · Maintenance? · Stagnation? · Decline

Age/Stage: 15 20 25 30 35 40 45 50 55 60 65

Exploration · Establishment · Maintenance · Decline

SOURCE: Adapted from *Careers in Organizations*, by Douglas T. Hall. Copyright © 1976 by Scott, Foresman and Co. Reprinted by permission.

The **establishment stage** begins with a trial period, shown by the continuation of the dotted line from the exploration stage. During this period the person might hold several jobs as he learns more about the occupational choices available to him. After the trial period, accomplishment and advancement occur. Now the person is settling down in a career, learning it, and performing well. He is becoming less dependent on others and more independent. He is now forming an occupational identity, establishing relationships with those in the organization, and perhaps also developing a pattern of love, marriage, and/or family relationships.

Job hopping becomes even more common throughout this stage, and many people find that they can move up faster and earn more money by changing jobs. A former top executive at Wal-Mart, Jack Shewmaker, held eight jobs in 11 years before joining Wal-Mart. Afterwards, he stayed with Wal-

Mart, and rose from district manager in 1970, when he joined the firm, to president, a position he held from 1978 until 1984.[11] Job hopping is partly a function of companies going outside for top leaders. For example, Gould, Inc. recruited James F. McDonald from IBM to be its new CEO. In 1984, Digital Equipment Corporation brought in its new finance vice president from Ford Motor Company. A major consulting firm, the Hay Group Inc., found that companies using outsiders in key jobs exceeded rate-of-return goals more often than those that relied on insiders.[12]

The **maintenance stage** can follow one or more patterns. Individuals who are "making it" may simply extend the establishment stage by continuing growth in performance. This stage can also be a period of maintenance or leveling off, or of stagnation and early decline. Career changes may result from either of these latter two patterns, and the person will start over again. People at this stage of their careers frequently begin to act as mentors for younger members of the organization, showing them the ropes and helping them along. They usually begin to re-examine their goals in life and to rethink their long-term career plans. Many managers are eager for continued success but are deeply troubled by the values they have to abandon along the way. The only solution is to balance the demands of their career with the satisfaction derived from skills and sources of pleasure that do not revolve around money and power. This may mean quitting a job or passing up the chance for promotion.[13]

In the **decline stage,** which usually means the end of full-time employment, the person faces retirement and other end-of-career options. The overriding question is "What do I do now?" Some people begin new careers and others level off, but an all-too-frequent pattern is one of decreasing performance. Individuals at this stage generally begin to recognize that they are growing old and adjust in a variety of ways—some positive, such as helping others, and some not so positive, such as becoming indifferent or even giving up.

Career Development

Your career is important to you, and the careers of members of organizations are important to the success of those organizations. **Career development** refers to a careful, systematic approach to ensuring that sound career choices are made. It involves both an individual element, career planning, and an organizational element, career management.[14]

Career Planning

Career planning is much like career choice, but it is more detailed and involves carefully specifying how to move within a career once the choice has been made. If you decide on a managerial career and want to achieve an executive-level position, just how do you go about it? What is the route to the top? Does the area in which you begin matter? Are there certain positions in which you must be sure to gain experience? Some companies, such as the accounting firm of William Younger, provide formal assistance in career planning.[15]

The first thing you should do is develop a written plan. Think in terms of where you want to be at the end of some long time period—say, twenty years. Now, in order to be at that point in twenty years, where do you need to be in ten years? Work backward to develop an answer; then work backward again to see where you need to be in five years and in one year. Knowing where you need to be in one year to achieve your twenty-year goal should be vital information for shaping your decision today.

As you plan your career, you may become aware of deficiencies in your skills, experience, or abilities. You may discover, for instance, that in order to accomplish your ten-year objectives, you need to acquire a foreign language. You can start learning now. Recognizing what your deficiencies are provides you with the opportunity to rectify them through training or by moving to a new job to gain additional experience.

You should review your career plan from time to time—perhaps every three or four years, but no less frequently than every five years. This will enable you to see whether you are accomplishing your objectives, whether you need to work harder, whether you need more training, development, and experience, or whether you need to rethink your objectives. This periodic review also serves to keep your long-term objectives in your mind so that they are not driven out by short-term crises.

If you are pursuing your career within an organization, you must develop your plan in conjunction with others in the organization. Talk with your superior to get his or her advice. If your company has a formal career management system, check with those who administer it to see whether your plan makes sense within the organization.

Career Management

Career management, the organizational element of career development, is being undertaken by an increasingly large number of firms, including AT&T, Bank of America, General Electric, General Foods, General Motors, and Sears.[16] Career management is distinct from training and development programs, which most companies provide either in house (that is, they do the training themselves) or by sending employees to programs conducted by trade groups, universities, or consulting firms. Career management

During the course of a career, people usually advance through a number of positions. When these are planned and orderly, they can contribute greatly to the individual's value to the organization. Brenda Roberts-Branch has advanced to the number two spot at Gourmet Companies Inc. through a series of promotions over a twenty-year period.

includes career counseling, career pathing, career resources planning, and career information systems.

Career counseling can be informal or formal. Informal advice provided by a superior to a subordinate is one form; another is that provided in interviews and performance evaluation sessions. A more formal method is to have special career counseling, provided by a personnel department, that is available to all personnel or only to those who are being moved down, up, or out of the organization.[17]

Career pathing refers to the identification of coherent progressions of jobs—tracks, routes, or career paths—that are of particular interest to the organization. As with counseling, these may be either formal or informal. The organization may specify a path that follows a particular sequence; an example is a university that states that the positions of assistant professor and associate professor are the normal progression toward becoming a full professor. Or the path may be informal, in which case "everyone

knows" that you must first hold jobs A and B to get to job C.

Although they are useful for planning purposes, career paths should not be taken as absolutes. The organization that changes *normally* to *must* is unable to recognize unique situations and exceptional talent when they occur. In the past, for instance, most executives got to the top by working in only a single firm, whereas today many executives have been with several companies on their way to the top. The increasing number of women in executive positions is also bringing changes in traditional career paths.[18] A system that is not flexible enough to permit this will prevent some extremely talented people from reaching the top.

As indicated in Table A.2, there is evidence that the new generation of executives is quite different

TABLE A.2 Changing Characteristics of Managers

The Old Generation	The New Generation
Cautious	Eager to take risks
Insecure	Optimistic
Resistant to change	Flexible
Loyal to company	Willing to job hop
Values job security	Wants to make impact
Male	Male or female
White	Ethnically diverse
A good day's work	Workaholic
Comfortable in bureaucracies	Craves autonomy, power
Conservative Republican	Independent
People-oriented	Numbers-oriented
Slide rules, legal pads	Computers, data networks
College degree	Advanced degree
Twenty-five-year career plan	Instant gratification

SOURCE: Teresa Carson and John A. Byrne, "Fast-Track Kids," Reprinted from November 10, 1986 issue of *Business Week* by special permission, © 1986 by McGraw-Hill, Inc.

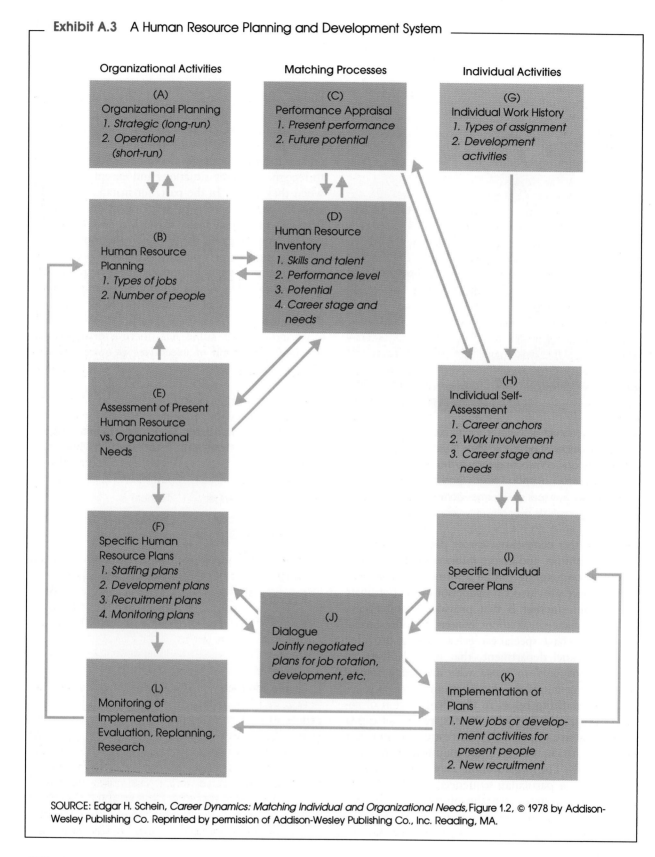

Exhibit A.3 A Human Resource Planning and Development System

Organizational Activities

(A)
Organizational Planning
1. *Strategic (long-run)*
2. *Operational (short-run)*

(B)
Human Resource Planning
1. *Types of jobs*
2. *Number of people*

(E)
Assessment of Present Human Resource vs. Organizational Needs

(F)
Specific Human Resource Plans
1. *Staffing plans*
2. *Development plans*
3. *Recruitment plans*
4. *Monitoring plans*

(L)
Monitoring of Implementation Evaluation, Replanning, Research

Matching Processes

(C)
Performance Appraisal
1. *Present performance*
2. *Future potential*

(D)
Human Resource Inventory
1. *Skills and talent*
2. *Performance level*
3. *Potential*
4. *Career stage and needs*

(J)
Dialogue
Jointly negotiated plans for job rotation, development, etc.

Individual Activities

(G)
Individual Work History
1. *Types of assignment*
2. *Development activities*

(H)
Individual Self-Assessment
1. *Career anchors*
2. *Work involvement*
3. *Career stage and needs*

(I)
Specific Individual Career Plans

(K)
Implementation of Plans
1. *New jobs or development activities for present people*
2. *New recruitment*

SOURCE: Edgar H. Schein, *Career Dynamics: Matching Individual and Organizational Needs,* Figure 1.2, © 1978 by Addison-Wesley Publishing Co. Reprinted by permission of Addison-Wesley Publishing Co., Inc. Reading, MA.

from the old one. Career management systems must be prepared to deal with those differences. In addition, career paths are not always clear and predictable. Take, for example, the career of Robert C. Wright. Wright graduated from law school and served as an infantry lieutenant before joining General Electric as a staff lawyer. He soon left GE to join first one law firm and then another, but in two years he was back at GE, where he moved into manufacturing, then sales, and then finance; most recently, he became chief executive of NBC. Wright is the kind of executive most corporations want, but his career would have been difficult to predict.[19]

Career resources planning refers to the use of careful planning techniques in career management. The organization makes plans and forecasts of personnel needs, develops charts that show the planned progressions of employees, prepares inventories of human resource needs based on assessments of existing personnel, and monitors the implementation of these plans. As shown in Exhibit A.3, such a system can be very complex.

Career information systems are more than just internal job markets (which means that openings within the organization are announced on bulletin boards or in newsletters and memoranda, and members of the organization have a first shot at getting these jobs). Career information systems combine internal job markets with formal career counseling and the maintenance of a career information center for employees. Thus a career information system can help to motivate as well as develop the organization's employees.

Women and Minorities

All too frequently, members of some groups have felt that managerial careers were closed to them, most often because people from that group had not yet entered the managerial ranks in sufficient numbers to set an example for others. When the potential pool of managerial talent is artificially or arbitrarily reduced in some way, our country suffers, because organizational effectiveness is not what it might be. Therefore, it is important to recognize that members of any group can and do become managers. Two groups—women and minorities—merit particular attention.

Photo by Tom Wolff

Although women have made significant strides in corporate America in recent years, many have still had to seek unusual paths to success. For example, Lisa Renshaw leased a failing parking lot near an airport, hoping to turn the business around. For the first two years, she slept in the back of the office for less than five hours a day. Now, though, she has four lots and grosses over $1 million a year.

Managerial Careers for Women

As shown in Exhibit A.4, more and more women work every year. Over half of the females over sixteen years old are now employed, and almost half of the working population now consists of women. Both of these statistics represent huge increases from conditions at the start of this century. For that matter, there has been significant growth over the past twenty years.

As the number of working women has grown, so has the number of women managers. Many of these people own their own businesses. In fact, women-owned businesses were one of the fastest-growing parts of the American economic scene during the 1970s and 1980s. Despite the rapid growth and the fact that nearly three million businesses are owned by women, relatively little is known about the career pattern of successful businesswomen.[20] They certainly are not confined to small businesses; some

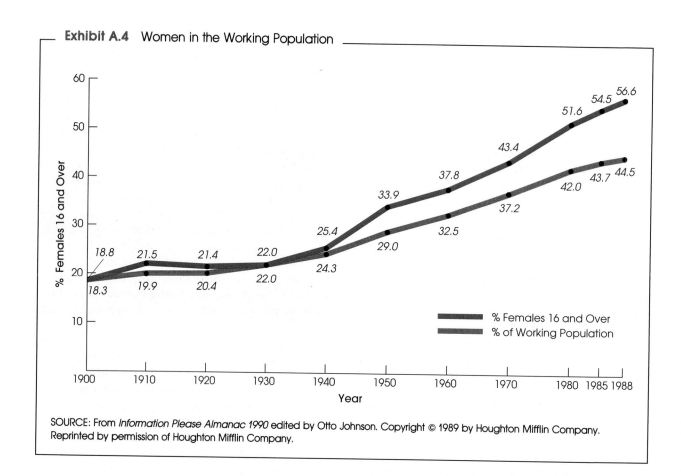

Exhibit A.4 Women in the Working Population

SOURCE: From *Information Please Almanac 1990* edited by Otto Johnson. Copyright © 1989 by Houghton Mifflin Company. Reprinted by permission of Houghton Mifflin Company.

women have excelled in some of the largest corporations in the United States.[21]

Executive search firms have suggested that there are career differences between male and female corporate officers.[22] The men tend to be older and have been with their companies longer. One study found that both groups worked fifty-five-hour weeks, although the men earned substantially more than the women. Further, most of the women felt that they had made great personal sacrifices to get where they were. Twenty percent had never married, as opposed to less than 1 percent of the men; 20 percent were separated or divorced, as opposed to about 4 percent of the men; 95 percent of the men had children, but more than half of the women were childless. Nevertheless, the number of women officers has dramatically risen over the past decade or so, and women have joined the boards of companies such as

Black & Decker and SmithKline Beecham Corporation.[23] These women are experienced managers, and do not hold these positions because they own or control the firms.

However, discrimination continues to plague women, especially in terms of salaries.[24] Only 2 percent of top executives were women as of 1990, and female vice presidents earned 42 percent less than their male counterparts.[25] Indeed, by the mid-1980s women were dropping out of managerial positions more frequently than men. Lower salaries, smaller chances of making it to the top, unexciting job assignments (women most often end up in "the three p's"—purchasing, personnel, and public relations), and less autonomy than they desire seem to be the most common reasons.[26]

Companies such as Corning Glass, General Foods, General Motors, Honeywell, IBM, Mellon Bank,

Procter & Gamble, Peat, Marwick, Mitchell & Co., Mutual of Omaha Insurance, Lotus Development, and Gannett are trying to do something to keep women in management. They are instituting flexible working hours and improving leave policies. Some allow employees to work at home; others help get a manager's spouse a new job when the employee is relocated. The recognition that the problem continues is itself a step toward improving conditions for women in managerial careers.[27] The number of women holding managerial positions attests to the success of such efforts.

Managerial Careers for Minorities

Members of minority groups also succeed as managers and owners.[28] Table A.3 indicates the number of businesses owned by members of minority groups. As we can see, Spanish-owned businesses slightly outnumber those of blacks, although blacks own more corporations and have more sole proprietorships. The corporation is the most common legal arrangement for these minority-owned businesses, and partnerships are the least common form.

Government assistance exists in a variety of forms to help members of minority groups who are interested in starting and running their own businesses. The Minority Business Development Agency was begun in the Department of Commerce in 1969. The U.S. Department of the Interior, through the Bureau of Indian Affairs, began the Indian Business Development Fund in 1970 to help American Indians secure funds for starting businesses. The Economic Development Administration began a Minority Contractors Assistance Program in 1971 to help minorities in the construction industry. Professional and technical assistance such as accounting and engineering help is provided under Section 406 of the Equal Opportunity Act. Some private groups, like the Cuban American Foundation, are also available to assist minorities in owning their own businesses.[29]

Such government assistance exists because long-standing biases against minorities have made it especially difficult for these people to enter the owner and managerial ranks. Despite these programs and a recognition of the problem, however, difficulties remain. Black M.B.A.'s report that many in the business world are "indifferent," "patronizing," and "reluctant to accept blacks."[30]

Of course, although the route to a successful managerial career for a minority member might be circuitous, it can be followed, and the outlook is not dismal.[31] In 1986 the president and chief operating officer of AM International was black, Jerry O. Williams. SmithKline Beecham that same year had four blacks in top-ranking positions, including Frederick C. Foard, director of marketing communications. The director of corporate resources for Xerox, John L. Jones, is black too.[32]

TABLE A.3 Number and Type of Businesses Owned by Minorities

Race	Type of Business			
	Corporation	Partnership	Sole Proprietorship	Total
Spanish	47.0*	26.2	56.9	130.1
Asian	41.0	6.0	30.5	77.5
Black	51.4	0.6	66.3	118.3
Other	36.6	10.8	9.4	56.8
Total	176.0	43.6	163.1	382.7

* Figures are in thousands.

SOURCE: *The State of Small Business: A Report of the President* (Washington, D.C.: U.S. Government Printing Office, 1985), p. 356.

In sum, women and minorities can and do have managerial careers. Perhaps they do have particular troubles, but difficulties exist for men and whites as well. In recent years it has been suggested that the most important action is to be seen, to be visible, noticed, and appreciated by your superiors.[33]

Special Career Issues

Companies that have formal career development programs are generally more effective in utilizing their human resources than those that do not have such programs. And these programs enable organizations to cope with the numerous government regulations concerning human resources, and to recognize and respond to a wide variety of career issues.

Two basic dimensions affect every individual. The more obvious one is the work versus society dimension, in which work (career or job demands) pulls one way and society (family and friends) pulls another.[34] You can advance your career by putting in long hours and focusing on nothing else, but you might not be able to maintain friendships or family under those conditions. The second dimension is the internal versus external one, in which internal, personal demands pull one way while external demands (such as religion and citizenship) pull the other. People must reconcile these multiple issues, and organizations must make that reconciliation easier. The next two sections of this chapter examine some specific examples of such issues.

Dual Incomes and Dual Careers

As we have seen, more than half of all adult females now work. Since many of these women are married, this means that large numbers of households now have two sources of income; they are **dual-income families.** The economic advantages of this system are obvious. Indeed, in the absence of children, there are few, if any, financial disadvantages. Problems do occur when there are children, but, as noted earlier, many companies are taking steps to alleviate some of them by providing flexible hours, more generous personal leaves, day-care centers, and the like.

Perhaps most of the problems of dual-*income* families can be worked out. If a problem arises—say,

a child is stricken with a long-term illness—one partner can drop out of the work force and stay at home to nurse the child back to health. If both partners are pursuing *careers*, however, as opposed to merely earning income, the situation changes radically. Interrupting a career is far more devastating than interrupting a series of jobs. Which career should suffer? Whose career is less important? The adjustment for the **dual-career family** is not easy or obvious, and sometimes one or both partners must make a serious sacrifice of long-term goals. Even such things as scheduling vacations can become a severe problem because both parties must be able to get off at the same time.[35]

The long-term illness of a child is not a problem faced by most dual-career couples, of course. Promotions and reassignments that involve transfers to new locations are far more common and can be extremely disruptive. One partner's career may best be served by taking the new assignment, but the other partner's career may best be served by remaining. Which career is more important?

What if both people are employed by the same organization, and one is a far better performer? That one is moving up rapidly, while the other moves slowly or not at all (or, even worse, gets fired). This kind of friction can tear a marriage apart.

Resolving these conflicts is not easy. It is particularly difficult now because not many people are experienced enough to offer advice, although some tentative advice is becoming available.[36] Obviously, a key element in dual-career families is to adopt a "family" or "we/us" view rather than an "I/me" view. This might mean deciding to relocate to help partner A now with the understanding that the next major career decision will help partner B. (Of course, when partner B's turn comes, partner A may get cold feet.)

Affirmative Action

Affirmative action refers to plans of action undertaken by organizations to comply with the letter and the intent of human rights legislation, part of the responsibility associated with organizational citizenship. Organizations that are acting affirmatively go beyond equal opportunity. Equal opportunity means that they avoid discrimination, as they must under the law, on the basis of race, sex, religion, color, or

Exhibit A.5 Issues Surrounding Corporate Career Planning

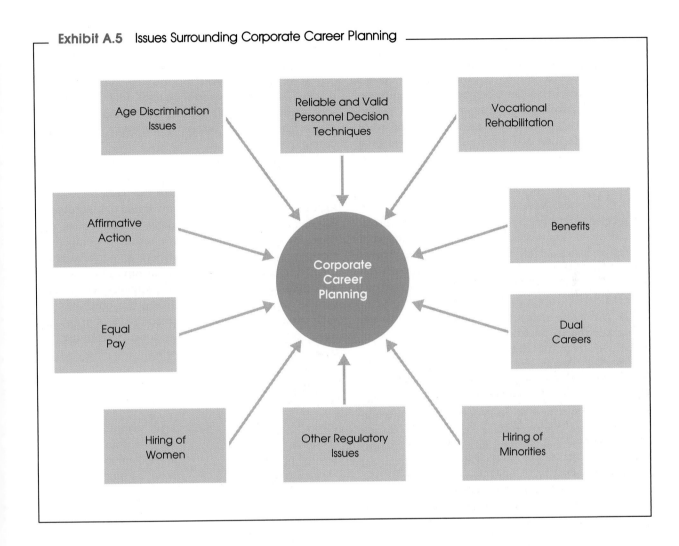

national origin (and age, under certain conditions). Affirmative action means that companies actively strive to recruit, hire, train, develop, and promote women and members of minority groups. This requires a careful balance of the personal wants of individuals against the external responsibilities of citizenship.

In terms of career development, affirmative action dictates that companies give special attention to race, sex, religion, color, national origin, and age to ensure that members of certain groups have equal access to training and development programs. Further, it ensures that they will be helped and counseled formally with their career plans.

These and other issues surround corporate career planning, just as they surround individual career planning. Companies must consider the impact of dual careers as they strive to facilitate managerial succession. Individuals must also consider the impact of dual careers on each of those careers. Affirmative action plans must be taken into account in corporate plans for managerial succession, too. From an individual viewpoint, a company with an affirmative action plan may well provide more career opportunities for women and minorities. Exhibit A.5 indicates some of these issues, with particular emphasis on human rights and related concerns.

Summary

This appendix introduces you to the many possibilities of a managerial career. A career is the sequence of attitudes and behaviors that you perceive to be related to work experience during your life. A person may choose to pursue a managerial career in every kind of organization and environment. Careers exist in all sectors of the economy. Many not-for-profit organizations also employ full-time managers. Increasingly, people are pursuing managerial careers in small businesses. Virtually every position may call for specialized managers, so that office administration, hospital administration, and other managerial careers are also available. Career choice is the process of finding out about yourself and possible careers and then trying to match your goals, skills, and interests with the demands of a particular career.

The major life stages are childhood, adolescence, young adulthood, adulthood, and senescence. Associated with them, but not exactly matching them, are career stages, which include exploration, establishment, maintenance, and decline. The exploration stage involves finding out about yourself and possible careers and your first or entry-level job. The establishment stage begins with a trial period, during which you may hold several different kinds of jobs. After that, you begin to develop an occupational identity and settle into your career and personal life. In the maintenance stage, individuals continue to move upward in their careers, level off, or even begin to decline. Re-examination occurs in this stage, and frequently people begin new careers. The decline stage involves retirement and other end-of-career options. Usually this means the end of full-time employment, but sometimes people begin new careers at this point.

Career development refers to a careful, systematic approach to ensuring that sound career choices are made. It involves both an individual element, career planning, and an organizational element, career management. Career planning carefully specifies how to move within a career once the choice has been made. Career management involves career counseling, career pathing, career resources planning, and career information systems. Career counseling is advising people either formally or informally about their careers. Career pathing refers to the identification of coherent progressions of jobs that are of special interest to the organization. Career resources planning refers to human resources planning applied to careers. Career information systems include internal job markets, formal career counseling, and the maintenance of a career information center for employees.

There are many managerial career opportunities for both women and minorities. Each of these groups makes up a growing segment of the work force, and members from each group are found in increasing numbers in managerial positions. Career issues are those concerns that arise as a result of competing forces such as work versus society or personal concerns versus religion and citizenship. Dual-income and dual-career families have problems with child care as well as a conflict between the objectives of each career. Affirmative action complicates organizational career planning but may provide more opportunities for women and minorities.

The Manager's Vocabulary

career	career planning
economic sector	career management
not-for-profit	career counseling
organizations	career pathing
life stages	career resources
career stages	planning
exploration stage	career information
establishment stage	systems
maintenance stage	dual-income family
decline stage	dual-career family
career development	affirmative action

Discussion Questions

Review Questions

1. What is a career, and what is involved in a career choice?
2. Describe career development.
3. Discuss some career issues.
4. What career opportunities exist for women and minorities?

Analysis Questions

1. In what life stage are you? In what life stage is your instructor? How do you determine which stage you are in?
2. In what career stage are you? In what career stage is your instructor? How do you determine which stage you are in?
3. Where do you want to be in your career in twenty years? Ten years? Five years? One year? Does each of your answers lead you logically to the next?
4. What strengths do you have that will help you achieve your career goals? How can you focus these strengths more clearly on a particular career?
5. What weaknesses do you have that you will have to overcome in order to reach your career goals? How can you accomplish this?

Application Questions and Exercises

1. Go to the library and find out how many women were in managerial positions in business in 1990, 1985, 1980, 1975, and 1970. Do the same for minorities. What changes (if any) have taken place?
2. Repeat question 1 for managerial positions in government (local, state, and federal) and compare your results.
3. Interview local managers about career opportunities in their firms. What careers seem most open to you? Why?

Notes

1. M. W. McCall, Jr., A. M. Morrison, and R. L. Hannan, *Studies of Managerial Work: Results and Methods* (Greensboro, N.C.: Center for Creative Leadership, 1978).
2. Douglas T. Hall, *Careers in Organizations* (Santa Monica, Calif.: Goodyear, 1976).
3. See "Why This Book Was Written" in R. N. Bolles, *What Color Is Your Parachute?* (Berkeley, Calif.: Ten Speed Press, 1980).
4. S. L. Jacobs, "Aspiring Entrepreneurs Learn Intricacies of Going It Alone," *The Wall Street Journal*, March 23, 1981, p. 25.
5. Diane Cole, "Assess Your Skills to Reduce Career Doubts," *The Wall Street Journal, The College Edition of the National Business Employment Weekly*, Spring 1990, pp. 7–8.
6. One excellent book is Bolles, *What Color Is Your Parachute?* For a more academic treatment, see Edgar H. Schein, *Career Dynamics: Matching Individual and Organizational Needs* (Reading, Mass.: Addison-Wesley, 1978).
7. D. J. Levinson, *The Seasons of a Man's Life* (New York: Knopf, 1978), and E. H. Erickson, *Childhood and Society* (New York: Norton, 1963).
8. Peter Rea, Julie Rea, and Charles Moomaw, "Skills Development," *Personnel Journal*, April 1, 1990, pp. 126–131.
9. Michael Brody, "Meet Today's Young American Worker," *Fortune*, November 11, 1985, pp. 90–98.
10. Beverly McQuigg-Martinez and Edward E. Sutton, "New York Telephone Connects Training to Development," *Personnel Journal*, January 1, 1990, pp. 64–73.
11. H. Gilman and K. Blumenthal, "Two Wal-Mart Officials Vie for Top Post," *The Wall Street Journal*, July 23, 1986, p. 6.
12. J. A. Byrne and A. L. Cowan, "Should Companies Groom New Leaders or Buy Them?" *Business Week*, September 22, 1986, pp. 94–96.
13. Douglas LaBier, "Madness Stalks the Ladder Climbers," *Fortune*, September 1, 1986, pp. 79–84.
14. K. R. Brousseau, "Job-Person Dynamics and Career Development," *Personnel and Human Resources Management*, vol. 2, 1984, pp. 125–154, Mariann Jelinek, *Career Management for the Individual and the Organization* (Chicago: St. Clair Press, 1979), and J. C. Arpin and D. K. Gerster, "Career Development: An Integration of Individual and Organizational Needs," *Personnel*, March-April 1978, pp. 23–29.
15. Jane Champion, "Career Planning and Development at William Younger," *Management Accounting*, February 1, 1990, pp. 50–52.
16. B. A. Duval and R. S. Courtney, "Upward Mobility: The GF Way of Opening Employee Advancement Opportunities," *Personnel*, May-June 1978, pp. 43–53, and P. G. Benson and G. C. Thornton III, "A Model Career Planning Program," *Personnel*, March-April 1978, pp. 30–39.
17. W. Kiechel III, "Passed Over," *Fortune*, October 13, 1986, pp. 189–191, J. C. Latack and J. B. Dozier, "After the Ax Falls: Job Loss as a Career Transition," *Academy of Management Review*, vol. 11, no. 2 (1986),

pp. 375–392, and A. Bennett, "Laid-Off Managers of Big Firms Increasingly Move to Small Ones," *The Wall Street Journal*, July 25, 1986, p. 17.

18. Carol Hymowitz, "More Executives Finding Changes in Traditional Corporate Ladder," *The Wall Street Journal*, November 14, 1986, p. 25.

19. A. Taylor III, "GE's Hard Driver at NBC," *Fortune*, March 16, 1987, pp. 97–104.

20. D. D. Bowen and R. D. Hisrich, "The Female Entrepreneur: A Career Development Perspective," *Academy of Management Review*, vol. 11, no. 2 (1986), pp. 393–407.

21. Anne M. Russell, "High-Tech Corporate Careers: Where Career Ladders Are like Roller Coasters," *Working Woman*, May 1, 1989, pp. 55–86.

22. "Male vs. Female: What a Difference It Makes in Business Careers," *The Wall Street Journal*, December 9, 1986, p. 1.

23. "Women Directors Now Bring Strong Management Credentials to Boards," *The Wall Street Journal*, August 19, 1986, p. 1.

24. D. D. Van Fleet and J. Saurage, "Recent Research on Women in Leadership and Management," *Akron Business and Economic Review*, vol. 15, no. 2 (1984), pp. 15–24.

25. Charlene M. Solomon, "Careers Under Glass," *Personnel Journal*, April 1, 1990, pp. 96–107.

26. Alex Taylor III, "Why Women Managers Are Bailing Out," *Fortune*, August 18, 1986, pp. 16–23.

27. Kathleen Gerson, "Briefcase, Baby or Both?" *Psychology Today*, November 1986, pp. 30–36.

28. E. M. Van Fleet and D. D. Van Fleet, "Entrepreneurship and Black Capitalism," *American Journal of Small Business*, vol. 10, no. 2 (Fall 1985), pp. 31–40. See also Erika Kotite, "The Small-Business Melting Pot," *Entrepreneur*, July 1, 1989, pp. 158–165.

29. "Winning Friends and Influencing People," *Hispanic Business*, July 1, 1989, pp. 20–25.

30. Jeffrey H. Greenhaus, Saroj Parasuraman, and Wayne M. Wormley, "Effects of Race on Organizational Experiences, Job Performance Evaluations, and Career Options," *Academy of Management Journal*, March 1, 1990, pp. 64–86, and Larry Rebstein, "Many Hurdles, Old and New, Keep Black Managers Out of Top Jobs," *The Wall Street Journal*, July 10, 1986, p. 25.

31. "Economic Trends," *Business Week*, January 8, 1990, p. 26.

32. Rebstein, "Many Hurdles, Old and New."

33. Walter Kiechel III, "The Importance of Being Visible," *Fortune*, June 24, 1985, pp. 141–143.

34. J. H. Greenhaus and N. J. Beutell, "Sources of Conflict Between Work and Family Roles," *Academy of Management Review*, vol. 10, no. 1 (1985), pp. 76–88, and S. E. Jackson, S. Zedeck, and E. Summers, "Family Life Disruptions: Effects of Job-Induced Structural and Emotional Interference," *Academy of Management Journal*, vol. 28, no. 3 (1985), pp. 547–586.

35. Constanza Montana, "Career Couples Find Vacations Hard to Plan," *The Wall Street Journal*, August 4, 1986, p. 15.

36. Ronya Kozmetsky and George Kozmetsky, *Making It Together: A Survival Manual for the Executive Family* (New York: Free Press, 1981).

Glossary

absenteeism Percentage of the organization's work force that is absent on a given day. (p. 478)

absolute quality The generally understood level of quality a product or system needs to be capable of to fulfill its intended purpose. (p. 527)

acceptance sampling Process whereby finished goods are sampled to determine what proportion are of acceptable quality. (p. 533)

accountability Answerability for actions, decisions, and performance. (pp. 220, 453)

achievement need The desire to excel or to accomplish some goal or task more effectively than in the past. (p. 359)

adaptation Changes in one's behavior in adjustment to new or modified surroundings. (p. 611)

adaptation model The most popular view of business strategy, which suggests that managers should solve entrepreneurial, engineering, and administrative problems by either defending, prospecting, or analyzing markets. (p. 163)

administrative management The subarea of classical management theory that is concerned with how organizations should be put together, with consideration given to factors such as authority and power distribution in the organization, goal setting, and conflict resolution. (p. 43)

administrative managers Generalists who oversee a variety of activities in several different areas of the organization. (p. 14)

administrative problem The managerial problem in strategic planning that involves structuring the organization. (p. 164)

affiliation need The need to work with others, to interact, and to have friends. (p. 359)

affirmative action Plans of action undertaken by organizations to comply with human rights legislation by actively striving to recruit, hire, train, develop, and promote women and members of minority groups. (p. 630)

analyzing A strategic business alternative that involves keeping a core set of products that provide predictable revenues while systematically looking for new opportunities. (p. 165)

ancient management The management concepts and techniques that were used by many ancient civilizations. (p. 38)

applications blanks Printed forms that ask job applicants for information about background, education, experience, etc. (p. 273)

arbitrator A labor law specialist paid jointly by the union and the organization to listen to both sides of a labor dispute and then decide how the dispute should be settled. (p. 287)

artificial intelligence (AI) Attempts to have computers simulate human decision processes. (p. 312)

assessment center An employee selection technique that allows human resource managers to observe and evaluate a prospective employee's performance on simulated tasks such as decision making and time management. (p. 273)

assets Items of value owned by the company. (p. 473)

attitudes Predispositions to respond favorably or unfavorably to something. (p. 415)

audit An independent appraisal of an organization's accounting, financial, and operational systems. (p. 476)

authority The power to carry out an assignment. (p. 219)

avoidance 1) A method of reinforcement that allows an employee, because of good performance, to escape from an unpleasant situation. 2) Ignoring the problem, thing, or situation. (p. 367)

---

b

---

balance sheet A summary statement of assets, liabilities, and equity to reveal an organization's financial position at a given time. (p. 473)

balance sheet budget A projection of what assets and liabilities of the firm will look like at the end of the coming period. (p. 470)

behavioral model An approach to decision making that assumes the manager has imperfect information, an incomplete set of alternatives, bounded rationality, and a tendency to engage in satisficing. (p. 184)

behavioral school School of management thought that focuses on the role of the individual in the workplace. (p. 45)

belongingness needs The needs for love and affection and to be accepted. (p. 357)

benefits Indirect compensation (payments other than wages and salaries) paid to employees, such as health-care, life insurance, vacations, sick leave. (p. 282)

bounded rationality Attempts to be rational are limited (bounded) by the decision maker's values and experience. (p. 185)

brainstorming A process of generating alternatives by asking people to come up with as many ideas as they can. (p. 188)

break-even analysis Determines the point at which revenues and costs will be equal. (p. 142)

budget A plan expressed in quantitative terms. (p. 468)

budgeting process The activities involved in developing a budget for the organization. (p. 469)

bureaucracy A form of organization that is based on a comprehensive set of rational rules and guidelines. (p. 43)

business strategy Strategic plans that chart the course for each individual business or division within a company. (p. 154)

C

capacity The space an organization has available to create products and/or services. (p. 495)

capital expenditure budget A financial budget that outlines when and how much money will be spent for major assets such as equipment, plants, and land. (p. 470)

capital-intensive Machines, not people, do almost all of the work. (p. 496)

career A sequence of attitudes and behaviors that a person perceives to be related to work experience during his or her life. (p. 619)

career counseling Advice and assistance provided informally or formally to the individual regarding his career development and planning. (p. 625)

career development A careful, systematic approach to assuring that sound career choices are made; involves both career planning (an individual element) and career management (an organizational element). (p. 624)

career information systems The combination of internal job markets with formal career counseling and the maintenance of a career information center for employees. (p. 627)

career management The organizational element of career development, involving career counseling, career pathing, career resources planning, and career information systems. (p. 624)

career pathing Identifying coherent progressions of jobs (tracks, routes, or paths) that are of particular interest to the organization. (p. 625)

career planning Making detailed and specific decisions and plans about career goals and how to achieve them. (p. 624)

career resources planning Use of careful planning techniques in career management, including forecasting personnel needs, illustrating the planned progressions of employees, preparing inventories of human resource needs, and monitoring the implementation of these plans. (p. 627)

career stages Spans of years during which an individual has different types of concerns about job and career, sometimes labeled as the stages of career exploration, establishment, maintenance, and decline. (p. 622)

cash cow A product that controls a large share of a low-growth market, thus generating large amounts of cash with relatively little support. (p. 161)

cash flow budget A precise outline of where the money for the coming period will come from and when, plus how the money will be used and when. (p. 470)

centralization Keeping power and control at the top level of the organization. (p. 221)

central processor That part of a system where the analysis and process is done. (p. 298)

certainty Knowing exactly what the alternatives are and that the probabilities associated with each are guaranteed. (p. 181)

channels The means of transmitting an idea, such as a face-to-face meeting, a letter, a telephone call, or a facial expression. (p. 414)

charisma An intangible attribute in the leader's personality that inspires loyalty and enthusiasm. (p. 343)

chief information officer (CIO) The executive who oversees all aspects of information technology, such as computing, office systems, and telecommunications. (p. 422)

classical school School of management thought that emerged around the turn of the century and that led to the application of scientific approaches to the study of management. (p. 40)

codes of conduct Meaningful symbolic statements about the importance of adhering to high ethical standards in business. (p. 73)

coercive power Power to force compliance through psychological, emotional, or physical threat. (p. 328)

cohesiveness The extent to which members of the group are motivated to remain together. (p. 390)

collective bargaining Negotiating a written contract covering all relevant aspects of the relationships among the organization and members of a union. (p. 285)

commitment The favorable response of persons confronted with an attempt by their leader to influence them. (p. 331)

committee Special kind of task group. (p. 394)

communication The process of transmitting information from one person to another. (p. 412)

communication model An illustration showing the route of a message from its beginning as an idea to its termination with the receiver. (p. 414)

company productivity The amount produced or created by all organization members and/or units combined. (p. 519)

compensation Wages and salaries paid to employees for their services. (p. 280)

competitive advantage The component of strategy that specifies the advantages that the organization holds relative to its competitors. (p. 153)

competitors Those organizations that offer similar or alternative products or services to potential customers; part of the task environment. (p. 104)

complexity Number of issues, problems, opportunities, and threats. (p. 600)

compliance Going along with the boss's request but without any stake in the result. (p. 331)

compounding Adding to and increasing, as in the tendency of a small error or deviation to become large if not detected and corrected. (p. 440)

compromise Reaching an agreement between what each of the conflicting parties wants, without either party feeling it has won everything or lost everything. (p. 402)

conceptual skills The skills a manager needs for thinking in the abstract, such as seeing relationships between forces, understanding how a variety of factors are interrelated, and taking a global perspective of the organization and its environment. (p. 20)

concurrent control Monitoring the activities that occur as inputs are being transformed into outputs; also known as yes/no control and screening control. (p. 444)

conflict of interest A situation where the employee's decision may be compromised because of competing loyalties. (pp. 69, 399)

confrontation Addressing a problem or conflict directly and working together to resolve it. (p. 403)

consumer protection Buyer-oriented safeguards from unscrupulous seller practices in advertising, pricing, and warranties. (p. 83)

contingency approaches An approach to leadership definition that recognizes that the same form of leadership is not appropriate in all circumstances. (p. 334)

contingency events The possible conditions or events that could arise and would necessitate the use of alternative or contingency plans. (p. 136)

contingency planning Part of the planning process in which managers identify alternative courses of action that the organization might take if various conditions arise. (p. 134)

contingency theory A management theory that argues that the most appropriate managerial actions in groups of situations depend on, or are contingent on, the elements of each of those particular situational groupings. (p. 53)

continuous-process technology The set of processes used when the making of a product requires that the composition of the raw materials be changed mechanically or chemically. (p. 245)

continuous reinforcement schedule Providing reinforcement after every occurrence of the desired behavior. (p. 369)

controller A manager who has specific responsibility for control; helps line managers, coordinates the overall control system, and gathers important information from and relays it to all managers. (p. 457)

controlling The process of monitoring and adjusting organizational activities toward goal attainment. (pp. 17, 440)

control system A mechanism used to assure that the organization is achieving its objectives; involves setting standards, assessing performance, comparing performance with standards, and evaluating and adjusting. (p. 446)

corporate culture The shared experiences, stories, beliefs, norms, and actions that characterize an organization. (p. 253)

corporate strategy Strategic plans that chart the course for the entire organization and attempt to answer the question "What business are we in?"; also known as grand strategy. (p. 154)

cost control Identifying areas in which costs are too high and reducing them appropriately. (p. 505)

country productivity The amount produced or created by entire countries. (p. 520)

credibility Reputation as to believability. (p. 422)

critical path The longest path through the entire PERT network. (p. 507)

current ratio A liquidity ratio determined by dividing current assets by current liabilities. (p. 474)

customers Those people or groups that buy the goods or services produced by an organization; part of the task environment. (p. 104)

d

data Facts and figures; unorganized pieces of information. (p. 296)

debt ratios Ratios that reflect the firm's ability to cover its long-term debt. (p. 475)

decentralization Shifting, through delegation, some power and control from the top level to the lower levels of the organization. (p. 221)

decision making 1) Choosing one alternative from among a set of options. 2) Choosing among alternatives, as in deciding which goals the organization should pursue and how best to achieve them. (pp. 15, 180)

decision support system (DSS) Form of information system that automatically searches for, analyzes, and reports information needed by a manager for a particular decision. (p. 302)

decision tree A decision-making technique, basically an extension of payoff matrices, that helps managers define the second- and third-level outcomes that can result from an alternative. (p. 196)

decisional roles The roles that a manager plays when making decisions while acting as an entrepreneur, a disturbance handler, a resource allocator, or a negotiator. (p. 18)

decline stage The final career stage, which usually means the end of full-time employment and could mean retirement. (p. 624)

defending A strategic business alternative that involves defining a market niche and protecting it from competitors. (p. 164)

degree of participation The extent to which subordinates are allowed to participate in decision making. (p. 340)

delegation Assigning a portion of one's task to subordinates. (p. 219)

Delphi forecasting The systematic refinement of expert opinion to make predictions. (p. 141)

Delphi technique Use of a group of experts to make predictions. (p. 399)

departmentalization Grouping jobs according to function, product, or location. (p. 215)

devil's advocate strategy Assigning a group member the role of taking issue with the actions of the rest of the group in order to prevent groupthink. (p. 399)

diagnosis Looking carefully at the system to identify all the possible consequences of a potential organizational change. (p. 552)

diagnostic skills The skills a manager needs for defining and understanding situations; includes defining a problem, determining the cause, and identifying ways to reduce it. (p. 21)

differentiation Setting a company's products apart from those of competitors in terms of quality, style, or service. (p. 165)

direct investment In international business, building plants in other countries and developing a distribution and marketing network in those countries. (p. 583)

disseminator The role that a manager plays when relaying to the appropriate people the information that was obtained through monitoring. (p. 18)

distribution model A quantitative decision-making technique that helps managers plan routes for distributing

products by minimizing travel time, fuel expenses, etc. (p. 193)

disturbance handler The role that a manager plays when resolving conflicts between groups of employees, between a sales representative and an important customer, or between another manager and a union representative. (p. 19)

divisional design An organization design that establishes fairly autonomous product departments that operate as strategic business units. (p. 250)

dog A product or business with a small share of a stable market, which makes it difficult to salvage since its growth must come at the expense of competing products or businesses. (p. 162)

downsizing Changes that an organization undertakes to eliminate unnecessary costs and unprofitable operations; also known as cutback and retrenchment. (p. 598)

dual-career family Household in which both the husband and the wife are pursuing careers, not merely earning incomes. (p. 630)

dual-income family Household in which both the husband and the wife earn a paycheck. (p. 630)

dynamism Changing fast, frequently, and in many ways. (p. 600)

e

economic dimension The dimension of the international environment that includes a country's economic system, financial laws, infrastructure, and economic health. (p. 576)

economic forces Forces of the general environment associated with economic conditions—inflation, interest rates, and unemployment, for example. (p. 102)

economic sector A portion or section of the overall business world that produces, distributes, and sells the goods and services of a country. There are, for example, the private sector and the public sector; the profit and the nonprofit sectors; the agricultural, retail, wholesale, mining, and manufacturing sectors. (p. 619)

effective control Organizational control that is characterized by integration, objectivity, accuracy, timeliness, and flexibility. (p. 449)

effectiveness Doing the right things in the right way at the right times. (p. 23)

efficiency Operating in such a way that resources are not wasted. (p. 22)

employee stock ownership plans (ESOPs) The transfer of stock ownership to employees in an effort to increase their commitment, involvement, and motivation. (p. 253)

employment at will Freedom of the organization to employ someone when it desires and therefore to dismiss the employee at any time for any reason. (p. 601)

enacted role How the person in a group actually behaves. (p. 388)

engineering problem The managerial problem in strategic planning that involves decisions regarding production and distribution of goods and services. (p. 164)

entrepreneur The role that a manager plays when taking the lead in looking for new or different opportunities that the organization can pursue. (p. 19)

entrepreneurial leadership Leadership of managers who tend always to be at the forefront of innovation and vision in shaping their organization for the future. (p. 344)

entrepreneurial problem The managerial problem in strategic planning that involves determining which business opportunities to undertake, which to ignore, and so forth. (p. 164)

entropy The negative result, faltering and dying, that occurs when an organization takes a closed system perspective. (p. 52)

environmental analysis An investigation of the ways in which an organization and its environment affect one another. (p. 155)

environmental change The extent to which forces outside the organization alter and the rate of such alterations. (p. 246)

environmental characteristics Nonpersonal factors such as the extent to which a task is highly structured, the nature of the work group, and the authority system within the organization. (p. 338)

environmental complexity Having many different elements in the organizational environment. (p. 247)

environmental context Such situational factors as competition, government regulation, and sociocultural norms. (p. 73)

environmental forces Critical elements of the environment that must be considered in strategic planning; namely, threat of new entrants, power of suppliers, jockeying among contestants, threat of substitute products, and power of buyers. (p. 155)

environmental protection Safeguards pertaining to air and water pollution. (p. 83)

environmental uncertainty The condition that exists when the organizational environment is changing frequently or contains many different elements. (p. 246)

equifinality The idea that two or more paths may lead to the same place, or organizations may achieve similar success by pursuing different objectives. (p. 52)

equity Fairness in the workplace. (p. 364)

equity positions Ownership positions obtained through the purchase of significant portions of stock. (p. 253)

escalation of commitment Making a decision and then becoming so committed to it that one fails to see that it was an incorrect decision. (p. 185)

establishment stage The second career stage, during which time the individual may hold several jobs while learning more about occupational choices; job hopping is common during this stage. (p. 623)

esteem needs The need for recognition and respect from others, and the needs for self-respect and a positive self-image. (p. 357)

ethical dilemma The situation that occurs when a manager is faced with two or more conflicting ethical issues. (p. 68)

ethics Standards or morals that a person sets for himself or herself regarding what is good and bad or right and wrong. (p. 66)

expectancy model A comprehensive model of employee motivation based on the assumption that motivation is a function of how much people want something and how likely they think they are to get it. (p. 361)

expected role How others in a group expect a given person to behave. (p. 388)

expected value The sum of all the possible outcomes of alternatives multiplied by their respective probabilities. (p. 195)

expense budget An operations budget that projects the use and timing of outgoing funds for the coming period. (p. 471)

expert power Power based on knowledge and expertise. (p. 328)

expert systems Systems that build on series of rules—frequently if-then rules—to move from a set of data to a decision recommendation. (p. 312)

exploration stage The first career stage, during which time the individual undergoes self-examination and explores different occupations; begins with school training and continues through first job. (p. 622)

exporting Selling products or materials to persons or organizations in another country. (p. 581)

external audit Audit conducted by experts who do not work directly for the organization. (p. 476)

extinction No longer reinforcing (ignoring) previously reinforced behavior; used to weaken behavior. (p. 367)

f

facilities The physical means of accomplishing production. (p. 496)

factory system Systematic approaches developed by managers of the early factories to cope with the new coordinating and supervisory problems that evolved with the Industrial Revolution. (p. 40)

fair labor practices Equitable practices concerning hiring, wages, union relations, etc. (p. 83)

feedback Response from the receiver of a message to the sender of that message; for instance, telling the employee the results of his or her performance appraisal. (pp. 280, 417)

figurehead The role that a manager plays when simply appearing as a representative of the organization, as in taking a visitor to dinner or attending a ribbon-cutting ceremony. (p. 18)

finance managers Individuals who are responsible for the financial assets of the organization, including overseeing the accounting systems, managing investments, controlling disbursements, and providing relevant information to the CEO about the firm's financial condition. (p. 13)

financial budgets A budget that details where the organization intends to get its cash for the coming period and how it intends to use it. (p. 470)

financial strategy The functional strategy related to monetary matters such as dividends, retained earnings, debt financing, and equity financing. (p. 166)

finished goods inventory The set of products that have been completely assembled but not yet shipped. (p. 501)

first-line managers Those who supervise operating employees. (p. 11)

fixed costs Costs that are incurred regardless of the level of operations; e.g., rent, taxes, minimum utility payments, and interest payments. (p. 471)

fixed interval schedule Providing reinforcement on a periodic basis, regardless of performance (e.g., giving a paycheck every Friday). (p. 369)

fixed ratio schedule Providing reinforcement on the basis of number of behaviors rather than on the basis of time. (p. 369)

flat organization An organization that has relatively few levels of management. (p. 224)

flexibility The ability of an individual or firm to respond or conform to changing or new situations. (p. 452)

force-field analysis Systematically looking at the pluses and minuses associated with a planned organizational change from the standpoint of the employees, and then attempting to increase the pluses and decrease the minuses. (p. 554)

forced mobility The changing of jobs due to events over which the individual has no control, such as firing or lay-off. (p. 607)

forecasting The systematic development of predictions about the future. (p. 140)

forming The initial stage of group information; involves the coming together of would-be members to form a group. (p. 387)

functional departmentalization Grouping together those employees who are involved in the same or very similar functions. (p. 216)

functional group A group created by the organization to accomplish a range of goals with an indefinite time horizon. (p. 383)

functional strategy Strategic plans that correspond to each of the functional areas within the organization: financial, production, human resource, organization design, and research and development. (p. 154)

g

general environment 1) The set of forces that characterize the general setting of an organization. 2) The organizational environment consisting of political-legal, economic, international, sociocultural, and technological dimensions. (p. 101)

global interdependence The situation that exists as the sharp distinctions between companies and country boundaries become blurred, making it difficult to answer the question of what is domestic and what is foreign. (p. 603)

globalization The gradual evolution to an integrated global economy composed of interrelated markets. (p. 572)

goal A desired state or condition that the organization wants to achieve. (p. 98)

goal consistency Goals should be consistent both horizontally (between functions or areas) and vertically (between levels of management) to enhance the effectiveness of goal setting. (p. 114)

goal optimization The process of balancing and trading off between different goals for the sake of organizational effectiveness. (p. 110)

goals Targets for which the organization aims. (p. 9)

goal setting Process involving scanning the environment for opportunities and threats, assessing organizational strengths and weaknesses, establishing general organizational goals, setting unit and subunit goals, and monitoring programs toward goal attainment at all organizational levels. (p. 98)

goal setting theory Use of goal setting to increase individual motivation. (p. 365)

government regulation Federal laws, concerned primarily with enhancing the social responsiveness and awareness of business, and with protecting the best interests of society from abuse by big business. (p. 83)

governmental factors Characteristics or conditions pertaining to the government's influence on or regulations of the business environment, especially as they pertain to foreign governments. (p. 581)

grand strategy An overall framework for action developed at the corporate level. (p. 158)

grapevine Informal communication network. (p. 426)

grievance A written statement or complaint filed by an employee with the union concerning the employee's alleged mistreatment by the company. (p. 287)

group Two or more people who interact regularly to accomplish a common goal. (p. 383)

group decision making Choosing among alternatives by teams, committees, or other types of groups rather than by one individual. (p. 397)

groupthink Phenomenon that happens when the maintenance of cohesion and good feelings overwhelm the purpose of the group. (p. 398)

growth strategy A strategic plan of actively seeking to acquire other related businesses. (p. 158)

h

Hawthorne studies A series of early research studies of the human element in the workplace, conducted at the Hawthorne plant of Western Electric between 1927 and 1932. (p. 45)

horizontal communication Transmission of messages between two or more colleagues or peers at the same level in the organization. (p. 421)

hostility Animosity, bitterness, resentment, or even hatred. (p. 401)

human relations Consideration of workers as individuals with unique needs and motives that affect their satisfaction and performance in the workplace. (p. 46)

human resource control Concerned with the extent to which members of the work force are productive and the extent to which the organization is effectively managing them. (p. 477)

human resource managers Individuals who are responsible for determining future human resource needs, recruiting and hiring the right kind of people to fill those needs, designing effective compensation and performance appraisal systems, and ensuring that legal guidelines and regulations are followed. (p. 13)

human resource ratios Quantitative assessments of the degree to which the organization is managing its work force properly; commonly includes employee turnover, absenteeism, and work force composition. (p. 478)

human resource strategy The functional strategy that deals with employee-related issues such as hiring and retention options, unions, employee development, and compliance with federal employment regulations. (p. 169)

i

importing Buying products or materials from persons or organizations in another country for use or sale in the company's country. (p. 582)

importing/exporting strategy A planned decision to buy from or sell to companies in another country. (p. 581)

in-process sampling Testing products as they are being made rather than after they are finished. (p. 533)

in-transit inventory Goods that have been shipped from the company but have not yet reached the customer. (p. 502)

inappropriate focus Control is too narrowly concentrated or fails to balance essential factors. (p. 453)

income statement A summary statement of the revenues, expenses, and profit or loss of a company during a period of time. (p. 474)

inconsistency A communication problem that exists when a person sends conflicting messages. (p. 421)

individual productivity The amount produced or created by a single individual relative to his or her costs to the organization. (p. 518)

industry productivity The amount produced or created by all companies in a particular industry. (p. 520)

informal group A group created by members of the organization for purposes that may or may not be related to the organization and has an unspecified time horizon; also called an interest group. (p. 383)

informal organization The overall pattern of influence and interaction defined by all the informal groups within an organization. (p. 388)

information Data organized in a meaningful way. (p. 296)

information requirements analysis Process of determining what information each individual needs to perform his or her job. (p. 300)

information system needs Needs of an organization for an information system of one kind or another. (p. 299)

information technology Scientific developments related to the manner and speed with which data are accessed, processed, and communicated. (p. 603)

informational roles The roles that a manager plays when serving as monitor, disseminator of information, or spokesperson. (p. 18)

innovation Identification and utilization of new, unusual, and/or creative solutions and alternatives to problems. (p. 192)

input devices Means used to get data into a system. (p. 298)

instrumental benefits Benefits that may accrue as the result of some other action; e.g., making useful business contacts by playing golf as a member of the country club. (p. 386)

interdependency Unable to perform effectively or efficiently without the aid or output of one another. (p. 402)

intermediate planning Planning for a time perspective between one and five years. Intermediate plans are developed by top managers working with middle managers and are building blocks for long-range plans. (p. 133)

internal audit Audit conducted by people who work directly for the organization. (p. 476)

international business Business activity that takes place across national boundaries. (p. 572)

international divisional design A common early form of organization design for the emerging international business, which involves adding a new international division, usually headed by a vice president or other top-level manager. (p. 585)

international forces Forces of the general environment associated with the impact of international and multinational organizations. (p. 103)

international matrix design A form of organization design, especially useful for multinational firms, that employs two bases of departmentalization: product managers arrayed across one side of the matrix and location-based division managers along the other dimension. (p. 586)

interpersonal attraction Attraction to others because of similar interests and attitudes. (p. 385)

interpersonal communication Communication between people, especially small numbers of people, either orally, in writing, or nonverbally. (p. 412)

interpersonal roles The roles that a manager plays when serving as figurehead, leader, or liaison. (p. 18)

interpersonal skills The skills a manager needs to work well with other people, including the ability to understand someone else's position, to present one's own position, to compromise, and to deal effectively with conflict. (p. 20)

intervention The option chosen to implement an organizational change. (p. 552)

interview Face-to-face talk between a manager and a prospective employee during the employee selection process. (p. 273)

inventory control Monitoring inventory to ensure that the supply is adequate but not excessive. (p. 501)

inventory model A quantitative decision-making technique that helps the manager plan the optimal level of inventory to carry. (p. 197)

j

job analysis 1) The systematic collection and recording of information about jobs in the organization. 2) Determining the exact content of each job and making assessments about how much each person should produce. (pp. 268, 477)

job description A summarization of the duties encompassed by the job, the working conditions where the job is performed, and the tools, materials, and equipment used on the job. (p. 268)

job design Determining what procedures and operations are to be performed by the employee in each position. (p. 211)

job enlargement Adding more activities to a worker's job. (p. 213)

job enrichment Giving a worker more activities to perform and more discretion as to how to perform them. (p. 214)

job evaluation Determining the relative value of jobs within the organization, primarily to establish the proper wage structure. (p. 281)

job rotation Systematically moving employees from one job to another. (p. 213)

job specialization Defining the tasks that set one job apart from others. (p. 212)

job specification A description of the skills, abilities, and other credentials necessary to perform the job. (p. 269)

jockeying among contestants The extent to which major competitors in a market are constantly trying to outmaneuver one another. (p. 156)

joint ventures Partnerships between two or more companies to produce a new product. (pp. 253, 583)

judgmental methods of performance appraisal Nonquantifiable, or subjective, evaluations of how well an employee is doing in his or her job. (p. 278)

just-in-time method (JIT) Making frequent but small orders of raw materials to arrive just as they are needed, with most or all of the materials going straight to the plant instead of warehouses. (p. 504)

l

labor budget A nonmonetary budget that details the number of direct hours of labor that are available during the coming period. (p. 471)

labor-intensive People, not machines, do most of the work. (p. 496)

labor relations Dealing with employees when they are organized in a labor union. (p. 283)

large-batch technology The set of processes used when a product is made in assembly-line fashion by combining component parts into a finished product; also known as mass-production technology. (p. 244)

leader The role that a manager plays when hiring employees, motivating them, or dealing with behavioral processes. (p. 18)

leader-member relations Relationship between the leader and the members of a group. (p. 335)

leadership An influence process directed at shaping the behavior of others. (p. 326)

leadership behaviors Actions that set apart effective leaders and ineffective leaders. (p. 331)

leadership traits Stable and enduring characteristics that set leaders apart from nonleaders. (p. 331)

leading Guiding and directing employees toward goal attainment by motivating employees, managing group processes, and dealing with conflict and change. (p. 16)

legitimate power Power created and conveyed by the organization; the same as authority. (p. 328)

levels of strategy Corporate strategy, business strategy, and functional strategies. (p. 153)

liabilities Debts and other financial obligations that the firm must repay. (p. 473)

liaison The role a manager plays when dealing with people outside the organization on a regular basis; usually involves the establishment of a good working relationship. (p. 18)

licensing strategy The use of a contractual relationship that allows another firm to produce goods or services to the contracting company's specifications and perhaps under its name as well. (p. 582)

life stages Spans of years of human life, commonly labeled by chronological age as infancy and childhood, adolescence, young adulthood, adulthood, and senescence or old age. (p.622)

line positions Positions that are in the direct chain of command with specific responsibility for accomplishing the goals of the organization. (p. 227)

linear programming A method to determine the best combinations of resources and activities for certain types of problems. (p. 142)

liquidity ratios Ratios that reflect the ability of a company to cover its short-term debts with its current assets. (p. 474)

lobbyist Someone who works on a seat of government specifically to influence the legislators. (p. 84)

locational departmentalization Grouping together the jobs that are in the same place or in nearby locations. (p. 218)

long-range planning Planning for a period that can be as short as several years to as long as several decades. Top managers are responsible for these plans which are primarily associated with activities such as major expansions of products or facilities, developing top managers, issuing new stock or bonds, or the installation of new systems. (p. 132)

LPC model *L*east *p*referred *c*oworker model; a contingency model of leadership that suggests that appropriate forms of leadership style vary as a function of the favorableness of the situation. (p. 335)

m

mainframe computers Very large, very expensive computers that process enormous amounts of information in fractions of a second and may occupy entire rooms and cost millions of dollars. (p. 482)

maintenance stage The third career stage, during which time individuals examine their career goals and make necessary changes. (p. 623)

management A set of activities directed at the efficient and effective utilization of resources in the pursuit of one or more goals. (p. 8)

management by objectives (MBO) A technique specifically developed to facilitate the goal-setting process in organizations. (pp. 115, 279)

management excellence The practicing of eight basic management techniques that Peters and Waterman found to be characteristic of successfully managed corporations in the mid-1980s. (p. 55)

management information systems (MIS) 1) The branch of the quantitative school of management thought that involves the use of a system created specifically to store and provide information to managers. 2) An integrated and organized data bank that is accessible to appropriate employees and that provides relevant and timely information needed to make decisions. (pp. 49, 302)

management science The branch of the quantitative school of management thought that is concerned with the development of sophisticated mathematical and statistical tools and techniques that managers can use to enhance efficiency. (p. 48)

managerial ethics Ethics applied to management. (p. 68)

managerial grid A grid for assessing leadership style; uses axes representing concern for people and concern for production. (p. 560)

market factors Characteristics or conditions related to the buyers of the firm's products or services. (p. 580)

market share A company's sales (units or dollars) relative to total sales of all companies of a particular product or within a particular industry. (p. 481)

marketing Activities involved in getting consumers or other companies to want the goods and services provided by the organization. (p. 478)

marketing managers Individuals who are responsible for pricing, promoting, and distributing the products and services of the firm. (p. 13)

marketing ratios Ratios that are related to the marketing function, such as market share or profit margin on sales. (p. 481)

marketing strategy The functional strategy that relates to the promotion, pricing, and distribution of products and services by the organization. (p. 166)

mass-production technology The set of processes used when a product is made in assembly-line fashion by combining component parts into a finished product; also known as large-batch technology. (p. 244)

matrix design An organization design that allows a firm to combine the advantages of functional and product departmentalization. (p. 247)

mechanistic design An organization design that is based on limited communication systems, a relatively high level of specialization and standardization, and more independence than cooperation. (p. 247)

microcomputers Personal computers, or desktop machines, that cost from several hundred to a few thousand dollars and can usually handle all the information processing needs of a manager; may also serve as terminals tied to minicomputers or mainframes or may be linked to other micros in a network. (p. 482)

middle managers The largest group of managers extending from top management down to those immediately above first-line management. They implement the strategies and policies set by top management and coordinate the work of lower-level managers. (p. 11)

minicomputers Computers that are smaller than mainframes but larger than micros, costing from $25,000 to several hundred thousand dollars. (p. 482)

mission The way in which an organization attempts to fulfill its purpose. (p. 108)

monitor The role that a manager plays when actively watching the environment for information that may be relevant to the organization. (p. 18)

motivation The set of processes that determine behavioral choices—things that make people decide what to do. (p. 354)

MRP A *m*aterials *r*equirements *p*lanning technique that enables managers to organize complex delivery schedules. (p. 508)

multinational A company that operates in many different countries at the same time. (p. 572)

multiple constituencies Different people and groups with different interests. (p. 327)

multiple goals The concept that organizations must simultaneously pursue a variety of different goals. (p. 108)

n

need hierarchy A variety of needs classified into five specific groups and then arranged in a hierarchy of importance: physiological, security, belongingness, esteem, and self-actualization needs. (p. 356)

needs Drives or forces that initiate behavior—that cause people to do things. (p. 355)

negotiator The role that a manager plays when attempting to work out agreements and contracts that operate in the best interests of the organization. (p. 19)

networking Connecting independent computers directly together so that they can function in interrelated ways. (p. 311)

new venture units Also known as "skunkworks"; small, semi-autonomous, voluntary units used to develop new products or ventures for a firm. (p. 253)

noise Anything that disrupts the communication process. (p. 414)

nominal group technique (NGT) A structured process whereby group members individually suggest alternatives that are then discussed and ranked until everyone agrees. (p. 399)

nonmonetary budgets Budgets that express important variables in terms other than currency. (p. 471)

nonverbal communication Transmitting messages through body movements, facial expressions, and gestures. (p. 419)

norm A standard of behavior that the group develops for its members. (p. 391)

norming The third stage of group formation, characterized by the resolution of conflict and the development of roles. (p. 387)

not-for-profit organizations Organizations that do not have the making of a profit as one of their goals; e.g., religious, social service, and charitable organizations and foundations. (p. 619)

o

objective measures of performance appraisal Quantifiable indicators of how well an employee is doing in his or her job. (p. 278)

operating ratios Ratios obtained by comparing some item in the income statement to an asset; e.g., cost of goods sold divided by inventory, sales divided by assets, accounts receivable divided by average daily sales. (p. 476)

operational plans Narrow focused, short time frame plans supervised by middle managers and executed by supervisory managers; two kinds are standing and single-use plans. (p. 130)

operations budgets A detailed presentation in financial terms of the organization's operations for the coming period. (p. 471)

operations decisions Choices as to product or service line, capacity, planning system, organization of the operations function, human resources, technology, facilities, and controls. (p. 495)

operations management 1) The branch of the quantitative school of management thought that concerns the processes and systems an organization uses to transform resources into finished goods and services; similar to management science but focused more on application. 2) All the activities connected with an organization's production and operating system. (pp. 49, 492)

operations managers Individuals who are responsible for actually creating the goods and services of the organization; responsibilities also include production control, inventory control, and plant layout. (p. 13)

operations planning Day-to-day activities of operations management, such as forecasting demand, comparing projected demand with current capacity, and adjusting capacity to demand. (p. 497)

oral communication Transmitting messages by means of the spoken word. (p. 417)

organic design An organization design that is based on open communication systems, a low level of specialization and standardization, and cooperation. (p. 247)

organization change Alteration of the organization brought about by people, technology, communication, and competition. (p. 548)

organization chart Pictures or maps of organizations, comprised of a series of boxes connected by one or more lines to show positions and their relationship to one another. (p. 238)

organization design The overall configuration of positions and interrelationships among positions within an organization. (p. 238)

organization design strategy The functional strategy that is concerned with how the positions and divisions within the organization will be arranged. (p. 169)

organization development (OD) A planned, organization-wide effort to enhance organizational health and effectiveness through the systematic use of behavioral science techniques. (p. 559)

organization revitalization A planned effort to infuse new energy, vitality, and strength into an organization. (p. 561)

organizational conflict Disagreement within the context of an organizational setting between individual employees, groups, or whole departments. (p. 399)

organizational context Such situational factors as the way in which an organization deals with ethical situations and the behavior of leaders and peers. (p. 72)

organizational demographics The age, sex, education, race, ethnic background, country of national origin, and experience of the work force. (p. 608)

organizational dynamics The way in which organizations structure themselves and manage their employees. (p. 605)

organizational goals General goals for the entire organization. (p. 100)

organizational governance Rights and privileges of organizations and of the individuals within those organizations. (p. 601)

organizing Grouping activities and resources in a logical and appropriate way. (pp. 16, 210)

orientation A process wherein new employees are introduced to various types of information about their jobs and the organization. (p. 275)

output budget A nonmonetary budget that projects how many of each of the organization's products will be produced. (p. 471)

output devices Means used to make system information available to users. (p. 298)

overall cost leadership Trying to keep costs as low as possible so that the firm is able to charge low prices and increase sales volume and/or market share. (p. 166)

overcontrol Too much control; so much control that employees' independence and autonomy are limited. (p. 453)

overload The situation that occurs when the sender is transmitting too much information for the receiver to process adequately. (p. 423)

owners' equity Money invested in the business in return for ownership privileges. (p. 473)

P

participation Giving employees a voice in how things are done in organizations. (p. 365)

participation model A leadership model that addresses the question of how much subordinates should be allowed to participate in decision-making. (p. 340)

partners Two or more firms or people working together and sharing the risks and rewards of a particular project. (p. 105)

path-goal model A model of leadership that suggests

that the purpose of leadership in organizational settings is to clarify for subordinates the paths to desired goals. (p. 337)

payoff matrix A decision-making technique that involves the calculation of expected values for two or more alternatives, each of which is associated with a probability estimate. (p. 195)

people-focused change Changes related to the skills and performance of employees or to their attitudes, perceptions, behaviors, and expectations. (p. 558)

perceived role How the individual thinks he or she should behave in a group. (p. 388)

perception Processes by which we receive and interpret information from our environment. (p. 416)

performance appraisal 1) The organization's evaluation of an individual's level of performance. 2) A review of how well an employee is carrying out the tasks associated with his or her job. (pp. 278, 477)

performing The final stage of group formation, when the group moves toward accomplishing its goals. (p. 387)

personal ethics An employee's own values, predilections about right and wrong, and sense of justice and fairness. (p. 72)

PERT A *p*rogram *e*valuation and *r*eview *t*echnique that involves identifying the various activities necessary in a project, developing a diagram that specifies the interrelationships among those activities, determining how much time each activity will take, and refining and controlling the implementation of the project using the network. (p. 507)

physiological needs Things we need to survive—food, air, warmth, clothing. (p. 356)

plan Blueprint or framework used to describe how an organization expects to achieve its goals. (p. 126)

planned organizational change A systematic alteration of the organization upon sensing a need for a change ahead of time rather than waiting to be forced to respond. (p. 550)

planning Constructing a blueprint of goals, objectives, strategic plans, and tactical plans for managers to use in reaching the organization's objectives. (pp. 15, 126)

planning-control link The way in which planning and control are integrated within the business cycle. (p. 442)

planning horizon Time frame for planning. (p. 498)

planning system The means by which operations managers get the information they need and then provide information to other managers. (p. 496)

point system A job evaluation method that involves assigning or awarding points to each job according to the factors that characterize the job. (p. 281)

policies General guidelines that govern relatively important actions. (p. 131)

political action committee (PAC) Organizations that solicit money from a variety of organizations and then make contributions to several candidates for office in order to gain their favor. (p. 84)

political-legal dimension The dimension of the international environment that includes government stability, policies toward foreign trade, and investment incentives. (p. 575)

political-legal forces Forces of the general environment associated with the governmental and legal system within which the organization operates. (p. 102)

poor listening Not receiving accurate or complete communication because of failure to concentrate, letting attention wander, or daydreaming. (p. 422)

portfolio approach Views the corporation as a collection of different businesses, each of which can be increased, decreased, or even sold. (p. 158)

portfolio matrix A common approach to corporate strategy that views the activities of the corporation as a portfolio of businesses, each called a strategic business unit. (p. 160)

position power Power vested in the leader's position. (p. 336)

positive reinforcement A reward or desirable outcome that is given after a particular behavior. (p. 367)

postaction control Monitoring the quality and/or quantity of an organization's outputs. (p. 445)

power differences Inability of lower-level managers to communicate with higher-level managers. (p. 423)

power of buyers The extent to which customers can influence an organization. (p. 157)

power of suppliers The extent to which suppliers can influence an organization. (p. 155)

predispositions The tendency to perceive or act in a certain way because of previous experiences in one's background or environment. (p. 415)

probability The likelihood, expressed as a percentage, that an event will or will not occur. (p. 195)

problem solving Determining the one and only course of action that fits a situation. (p. 180)

process consultation Having an organization development expert observe the communication, decision making, and leadership processes in the organization and then suggest ways to improve them. (p. 561)

product departmentalization Grouping together the activities associated with individual products or closely related product groups. (p. 217)

product/service line The general products and/or services on which the organization will concentrate. (p. 495)

production factors Characteristics or conditions related to the manufacture of a firm's products. (p. 581)

production strategy The functional strategy that addresses questions concerning production quality, costs, techniques, location, efficiency, and compliance with governmental regulations. (p. 167)

productivity A measure of efficiency. (p. 518)

professionalism The status, methods, standards, or character of a particular field or activity. (p. 612)

profit budget An operations budget that summarizes the difference between projected revenues and projected expenses. (p. 471)

profit margin on sales Net income divided by sales. (p. 481)

profitability ratios Ratios that reflect how much a company made relative to what it took to earn that profit; calculated by dividing profit by sales, investment, or assets. (p. 476)

program Single-use plan for a large set of activities. (p. 131)

project Single-use plan similar to program but usually with a narrower focus. (p. 131)

prospecting A strategic business alternative that involves seeking new markets for a product or sevice. (p. 165)

protectionist techniques Attempts by a government to control international trade across its borders through such techniques as tariffs, export restraint agreements, and "buy national" laws. (p. 576)

punishment Reprimands, discipline, fines, etc. that are used to shape behavior by causing a reduction in unwanted behaviors. (p. 367)

pure domestic strategy A planned decision not to sell in another country. (p. 581)

purpose The reason for the existence of an organization. (p. 108)

q

quality The total set of features and characteristics of a product or service that bear on its ability to satisfy stated or implied needs. (p. 527)

quality assurance General label applied to an overall effort by an organization to enhance the quality of its products and/or services. (p. 531)

quality circles (QCs) Groups of employees that focus on how to improve the quality of products. (pp. 245, 396)

quality control Insuring that the inputs and outputs meet the desired levels of quality. (p. 502)

quantitative school School of management thought that emerged during World War II to apply mathematics and statistics to complex management problems. (p. 48)

question mark A product with a small share of a growing market, creating a question as to whether more resources should be invested in the hope of transforming the product into a star. (p. 161)

queuing model A quantitative decision-making technique that helps managers solve problems involving waiting lines to determine, for instance, the best number of operators to have on duty at various times of day. (p. 197)

r

ranking An approach to performance appraisal wherein the supervisor compares subordinates with one another and then places them in their relative positions in a continuum from high to low performance. (p. 278)

rating An approach to performance appraisal wherein the supervisor compares each subordinate with one or more absolute standards and then places that employee somewhere in relation to that standard. (p. 278)

ratio analysis Calculating and evaluating ratios of figures obtained from the balance sheet and income statement; may involve comparison of the organization's ratios from year to year or with an industry norm. (p. 473)

rational model An approach to decision-making that assumes the manager has complete and accurate information, has an exhaustive list of alternatives, is rational in choosing, and always has the best interests of the organization at heart. (p. 183)

raw materials inventory The supply of materials, parts, and supplies that the organization needs to do its work. (p. 501)

reactive change Change that occurs as a result of external (environmental) events rather than being planned. (p. 551)

receiver Person who receives a message from its sender. (p. 414)

recruiting The process of attracting a pool of qualified applicants who are interested in working for the company. (p. 271)

referent power Power based on personal identification, imitation, and charisma. (p. 329)

regulators Organizations or groups that actively attempt to influence the target organization; part of the task environment. (p. 104)

reinforcement Rewarding people's current behavior to motivate them to continue that behavior. (p. 366)

relative quality The level of quality interpreted in comparison to other alternatives. (p. 527)

reluctance Hesitancy or unwillingness to speak or act. (p. 422)

research and development limited partnerships (RDLPs) Consortia, usually among high technology firms, designed to do basic research. (p. 253)

research-and-development strategy The functional

strategy that relates to the invention and development of new products as well as the exploration of new and better ways to produce and distribute existing ones. (p. 168)

resistance The negative, uncooperative response of persons when their boss attempts to influence them. (p. 331)

resource allocator The role that a manager plays when determining how resources (e.g., dollars, personnel, space) will be divided up among different areas within the organization. (p. 19)

resource deployment The component of strategy that indicates how the organization intends to allocate resources. (p. 152)

responsibility A duty or obligation to carry out an assignment. (p. 219)

retrenchment strategy Cutting back of resources, as in worker layoffs and plant closings. (p. 158)

return on assets (ROA) A profitability ratio that shows how much a firm made relative to the amount it had invested in assets; determined by dividing net income by total assets. (p. 475)

return on equity (ROE) A profitability ratio that shows how much a company made relative to the amount of money invested; calculated by dividing net profit by total owners' equity. (p. 475)

revenue budget An operations budget that projects the sources and timing of incoming funds for the coming period. (p. 471)

reward Anything the organization provides in exchange for services. (p. 371)

reward power Power to grant and withhold various kinds of rewards. (p. 328)

risk Understanding the available options but lacking certainty as to the probabilities associated with each. (p. 181)

role Part a person plays in an organization. (p. 388)

role ambiguity Lack of clarity as to how an individual in a group is expected to behave. (p. 389)

role conflict Inconsistency or contradiction in the messages about a role that an individual is to play in a group. (p. 389)

role dynamics The process whereby a person's expected role is transformed to his or her enacted role. (p. 388)

rules and regulations Statements of how specific activities are to be performed. (p. 131)

S

---

safety and health guarantees Regulations designed to force companies to protect the safety and health of both employees and consumers. (p. 83)

salary A fixed compensation paid to an employee on a regular basis. (p. 280)

satisficing Selecting the first minimally acceptable alternative rather than making a more thorough search. (p. 185)

scheduling control Having the right things arrive and depart at the right time. (p. 503)

scientific management The subarea of classical management theory that focuses on the work of individuals, primarily defining the steps needed to complete a task and training employees to perform them efficiently while the manager assumes all planning and organizing responsibilities. (p. 40)

scope The component of strategy that specifies the position the firm wants to have in relation to its environment. (p. 152)

security needs The need to have a safe physical and emotional environment. (p. 357)

selection Choosing the best people for the job. (p. 273)

self-actualization needs The needs to grow, develop, and expand our capabilities. (p. 357)

semantics differences Misinterpretations that occur in communications when two persons assign different meanings to the same word. (p. 423)

semi-autonomous work groups Groups of workers who operate with no direct supervision to perform some specific task. (p. 245)

semivariable costs Costs that vary as a function of output but not necessarily in a direct fashion; e.g., equipment repairs, maintenance, and sometimes labor and advertising. (p. 471)

sender Person who transmits a message to a receiver. (p. 414)

sent role The role that others in the group communicate that they expect a given person to play. (p. 388)

short-range planning Planning for one year or less; focuses on day-to-day activities. (p. 133)

single-use plans Form of operational plan set up to handle events that happen only once. (p. 131)

small-batch technology The set of processes used when a product is made in small quantities, usually in response to customer orders; also known as unit technology. (p. 244)

smoothing Downplaying the importance of a problem. (p. 42)

social involvement Approach to social responsibility that involves not just fulfilling obligations and requests but also actively seeking other ways to help. (p. 80)

social obligation An approach that views social responsibility as an obligation mandated by societal norms and government regulation; thus the company meets its economic and legal responsibilities but does not go beyond them. (p. 78)

social reaction A social responsibility approach in which a firm not only meets its social obligations but also is willing to react to appropriate societal requests and demands. (p. 79)

social responsibility Obligations of the organization to protect and/or enhance the society in which it functions. (p. 74)

sociocultural dimension The dimension of the international environment that includes the human, cultural, and physical characteristics of a country. (p. 577)

sociocultural forces Forces of the general environment associated with the customs and values that characterize the society within which the organization is operating. (p. 103)

space budget A nonmonetary budget that details the allocation of plant or office space to different divisions or groups within the organization. (p. 471)

span of management The number of subordinates who report directly to a given manager. (p. 223)

spokesperson The role that a manager plays when acting as a company representative while presenting information of meaningful content and/or answering questions on the firm's behalf. (p. 18)

stability strategy A plan to maintain the status quo of an organization. (p. 158)

staffing Procuring and managing the human resources an organization needs to accomplish its goals. (p. 266)

staff positions Positions that are outside the direct chain of command; primarily advisory or supportive in nature. (p. 227)

standard operating procedures Specific guidelines for handling a series of recurring activities. (p. 131)

standards A measure or target against which performance will be compared. (p. 446)

standing plans Developed to handle recurring and relatively routine situations; types are policies, standard operating procedures, and rules and regulations. (p. 130)

star A business, within a portfolio matrix, whose products have a high share of a fast-growing market, thus generating large amounts of revenue. (p. 160)

statistical quality control A category of operational techniques that consists of a set of mathematical and/or statistical methods for measuring and adjusting quality levels. (p. 533)

status differences Inability of persons in low-status jobs and managers of higher status to communicate effectively with each other. (p. 423)

steering control Monitoring the quality and/or quantity of resources before they enter a company's system; also called preliminary control and feed-forward control. (p. 444)

storming The second stage of group formation, when members begin to pull apart as they disagree over what needs to be done and how best to do it. (p. 387)

strategic business unit (SBU) A division or related set of divisions (within a firm) that has its own competitors, a distinct mission, and a unique strategy. (p. 159)

strategic change A modification of an existing strategy or the adoption of a new one. (p. 555)

strategic planning Formulating the broad goals and plans developed by top managers to guide the general directions of the organization. (p. 129)

strategic plans Broad plans developed by top managers to guide the general directions of the organization. (pp. 129, 152)

strategy formulation The set of processes involved in creating or developing strategic plans. (p. 153)

strategy implementation The set of processes involved in executing strategic plans, or putting them into effect. (pp. 153, 170)

stress The condition that occurs when a person is subjected to unusual situations, difficult demands, or extreme pressures. (p. 605)

structural change Any organizational change directed at a part of the formal organizational system, such as its structural components, its overall organization design, or related systems such as the reward system. (p. 556)

subordinate's characteristics Personal traits of a subordinate, such as perceptions of ability, desire to participate in organizational activities, and willingness to accept direction and control. (p. 337)

subsystem interdependencies The dependence of subsystems within a parent system on one another, such that a change in one subsystem affects the other subsystems, or a need in one subsystem forces the development of a response in another subsystem. (p. 52)

subunit goals More specific goals for component parts of the organization. (p. 100)

suppliers Providers of resources to a firm; part of the task environment. (p. 105)

survey feedback Asking subordinates about their perceptions of their leader and then feeding back that information to the entire group. (p. 561)

symbolic leadership Leadership associated with establishing and maintaining a strong organizational culture. (p. 345)

synergy The extra results that occur when two people or units work together rather than individually. (pp. 52, 153)

system Interrelated parts or elements that function as a whole. (p. 296)

System 4 An organization design approach based on the premise that most organizations start out as bureaucracies and can be transformed to more appropriate models. (p. 241)

systems theory An approach to understanding how organizations function and operate by considering the process by which an organization receives inputs, transforms them into outputs, produces outcomes, and receives feedback. (p. 50)

T

---

tactical planning Focuses on people and action; concerned with how to implement strategic plans. (p. 130)

tall organization An organization that has several levels of management. (p. 224)

targeting Identifying and focusing on a clearly defined and often highly specialized market. (p. 166)

task environment The specific set of other organizations and groups with which the organization must interact, including customers, competitors, unions, regulators, and suppliers. (p. 104)

task force A temporary group within an organization created to accomplish a specific purpose (task) by integrating existing functional areas. (p. 394)

task group A group created by the organization to accomplish a limited number of goals within a stated or implied time. (p. 383)

task structure The degree to which a group's task is well defined and understood by everyone. (p. 336)

team building A series of activities and exercises designed to enhance the motivation and satisfaction of people in groups by fostering mutual understanding, acceptance, and group cohesion. (p. 558)

technical skills The skills a manager needs to perform specialized tasks within a particular type of organization, such as medical, financial, and engineering.

technological change Alterations related to technology, such as new equipment, new work processes or sequences, automation, and revised information processing systems. (p. 558)

technological dimension The dimension of the international environment that includes the availability of qualified workers as well as appropriate equipment. (p. 578)

technological forces Forces of the general environment associated with scientific and industrial progress. (p. 103)

technology The set of conversion processes used by an organization to transform inputs into outputs. (pp. 243, 497)

telecommunications Communication over some distance, usually by electronic means. (p. 311)

telecommuting Organizational members performing their work at home through the use of computers connected to the organization's computer. (p. 311)

teleconferencing Videoconferencing, which permits individuals in different locations to see and talk with one another. (p. 311)

test marketing Introducing a new product on a limited basis in order to assess consumer reaction on a small scale. (p. 479)

tests Examinations that are used to help managers select employees. (p. 273)

Theory X A pessimistic view of managers that assumes that workers dislike work and responsibility, thus requiring managers to control, direct, coerce, and threaten employees. (p. 47)

Theory Y An optimistic view of managers that assumes that workers enjoy work, seek responsibility, are bright and innovative, and are internally motivated. (p. 47)

Theory Z A theory proposed by William Ouchi to describe the use of a successful American management approach which capitalizes on the strengths of Japanese management models while remaining flexible enough to accommodate the American cultural differences. (p. 55)

third-party peace making An organization development (OD) effort concentrated on resolving conflict that has existed for a long time through the action of a consultant. (p. 561)

threat of new entrants The ease with which new competitors can enter a market. (p. 155)

threat of substitute products The extent to which a new product might supplant demand for an existing one. (p. 156)

time-series forecasting Plotting the subject of a forecast against time for a period of several years to determine the "best-fit" line for extending into the future. (p. 141)

top managers Those at the upper levels of the organization including the chief executive officer, president, and vice presidents. They set overall goals and determine strategy and policies. (p. 11)

total factor productivity Overall productivity; determined by dividing all outputs by all inputs. (p. 520)

traits Characteristics of a person. (p. 328)

transaction processing systems (TPS) Systems designed to handle routine and recurring transactions within the organization. (p. 301)

turnover Percentage of the organization's work force that leaves and must be replaced over a period of time. (p. 478)

two-factor view A way of describing employee needs, viewing satisfaction and dissatisfaction as being influenced by two independent sets of factors. (p. 357)

Type A people Individuals who tend to be very competitive and devoted to work, and they have a strong sense of urgency. (p. 606)

Type B people Individuals who are less competitive and less devoted to their work and have a weaker sense of urgency than do Type A people. (p. 607)

U

uncertainty Not being sure of the alternatives or their probabilities. (p. 182)

unions Labor organizations with which firms must frequently interact; part of the task environment. (p. 104)

unit productivity The amount produced or created by a single unit within the organization. (p. 519)

unit technology The set of processes used when a product is made in small quantities, usually in response to customer orders; also known as small-batch technology. (p. 244)

user friendly Easy to understand and use. (p. 310)

V

variable costs Costs that vary as a function of operations, e.g., raw materials, electricity to operate machines, and sales commissions. (p. 471)

variable interval schedule Providing reinforcement on a time-interval basis but the time intervals between reinforcement are not fixed. (p. 369)

variable ratio schedule Providing reinforcement on the basis of behaviors, but varying the number of behaviors an employee needs to display to get the reinforcement. (p. 370)

vertical communication Transmission of messages between bosses and their subordinates. (p. 420)

W

wage level A company's wages relative to the prevailing local or industrial wages. (p. 281)

wages Compensation (payment) to employees on an hourly, daily, or weekly basis, or by the piece. (p. 280)

wage structure The comparison of wages for different jobs within the company. (p. 281)

withdrawal A refusal to socialize with others. (p. 401)

work force composition ratio Percentage of work force that fall into certain demographic groups, such as black, Hispanic, female, or handicapped. (p. 478)

work-in-process inventory The parts and supplies that are currently being used to produce the final product, which is not yet complete. (p. 501)

work team Small, self-managing group of organizational members responsible for a set of tasks. (p. 395)

written communications Transmitting messages by means of memos, letters, reports, and notes. (p. 418)

Name and Company Index

ABC television network, 186, 405 (case)
Abercrombie & Fitch, 236 (case)
Academy of Management, 612
Adam, Everett E., 61, 201, 513
Adams, J. Stacey, 377
Adolph, Jonathan, 530
AEG, 163 (box)
Aetna Life and Casualty, 422
Afterthoughts, 125 (case)
Ahitov, N., 317
Airbus, 156, 181
Air India, 572
Air UK, 302 (box)
Ajinomoto, 596–597 (case)
Ajzen, I., 431
Akers, John, 343
Alcoa, 116, 140
Allaire, Yvan, 617
Allen Bradley, 383
American Airlines, 29–30 (case), 30 (illus.), 49, 70, 308, 422, 559, 561
American Airlines SABRE reservation system, 30
American Can Company, 73, 598
American Express (AmEx), 105, 119–121 (case), 120 (illus.), 166, 311
American Greetings, 440
American Information Technologies, 289 (case)
American Management Association, 74, 612
American Motors, 52
American Psychological Association, 74
AmEx (American Express), 105, 119–121 (case), 120 (illus.), 166, 311
AM International Incorporated, 629
Amit, Raphael, 487
Anderson, Henry R., 486
Anderson, Roger L., 232
Andrews, I. Robert, 261

Anheuser-Busch, 66
Ansberry, Clare, 88
Anthony, Robert N., 461
Anthony's, 174 (case)
Antonini, Joseph, 60 (case)
A. O. Smith Corporation, 380–381 (case), 381 (illus.), 382, 385, 395, 397, 404
Apple Computer, 11, 133, 254, 348–349 (case), 427, 428 (box), 432, 546 (case), 548
Applied Biotechnology, 599 (box)
Archibald, Nolan, 145–146 (case)
Arco Oil & Gas, 80 (illus.)
Argyle, Michael, 407
Armandi, Barry R., 31, 232, 233, 261, 319
Armstrong, C. Michael, 231 (case)
Arpin, J. C., 633
Arrow Shirts, 509
Arvida unit of Disney company, 6 (case)
Ashe, Mary Kay, 343
Asher, James J., 290
Ashland Oil, Inc., 87–88 (case)
Ashland Petroleum Company, 87 (case)
Ashmos, Donde P., 61
Astra, 60 (case)
Athey, T. H., 317
AT&T, 210, 213, 215, 289–290 (case), 470, 506, 574 (illus.), 588, 598, 601, 604 (box), 624
Austin, James E., 593
Austin Community College, 140
Automatic Data Processing, Inc., 306 (illus.)
Avia, 203, 438–439 (case)
Avis, 375 (illus.), 375–376 (case), 471
Avon, 224, 524

Babbage, Charles, 40
Backhard, Richard, 567

Baird, L. S., 201
Balkin, D. B., 91
Ball, Robert, 593
Baltimore Gas & Electric Company, 497 (illus.)
Baltimore Orioles, 485–486 (case)
Banana Republic, 104
Bank of America, 624
Barclay, Jim, 438 (case)
Barker, Jeffrey, 261
Barnard, Chester, 43
Barrett, Thomas M., 88
Barrett, William P., 465
Bart, Christopher K., 261
Bass, Bernard M., 349
Baughman, James P., 486
Bauman, Robert, 554 (box)
Bausch & Lomb, 161, 524
Bean, Leon Leonwood, 352 (case), 354
Beard, Donald W., 121
Beatrice, 375 (case)
Bechtel, 312
Bedeian, Arthur G., 233
Beecham Group PLC, 402, 554 (box)
Beech-Nut, 190, 191 (box), 421 (box)
Beer, Michael, 513, 566
Bell, Arthur H., 431
Bell, Cecil H., Jr., 567
Bell Atlantic, 289 (case)
Bell South, 289 (case)
Bendix, 585
Benetton, 126, 294–295 (case), 295 (illus.), 296, 298, 303, 313, 314–315
Benetton, Luciano, 294
Ben Franklin Stores, 59 (case)
Ben & Jerry's, 472 (illus.), 530 (box), 540
Benson, P. G., 633
Ben Taub Hospital, 383
Berlin, David, 442 (box)
Bethlehem Steel Corporation, 41, 213, 275, 511–512 (case), 512 (illus.)
Beutell, N. J., 634

B. F. Goodrich, 559
Bic, 166
Bikson, Tora, 318
Bilco Tools, 582 (box)
Bird, Barbara J., 541
Bird, Debbie, 8
Bisbett, R. E., 431
Black, Stewart J., 291
Black & Decker, 49, 116, 145–146 (case), 166, 628
Blake, Robert R., 560, 567
Bleven, Dennis P., 319
Blockbuster, 464–465 (case), 465 (illus.), 466, 467–468, 476, 484
Blomstrom, Robert L., 82, 89
Bloomingdale's, 29 (case)
Blue Cross Blue Shield, 311
Blumenthal, K., 633
Blumenthal, Michael, 546 (case), 547 (illus.), 564
Blumenthal, Robin G., 256
Boeing, 73, 103, 104, 105, 127, 156, 181, 221, 244, 253, 289 (case), 445, 572, 610
Bolles, R. N., 633
Bolton, A. A., 61
Bonaparte, Napoleon, 331
Boone, Louis E., 31
Borden, 173–174 (case), 259 (case), 580
Bowen, D. D., 634
Bowen, William, 539
Boyer, Edward, 121, 593
Bradspies, Robert W., 461
Brady, F. Neil, 88
Braniff, 70
Brice, H., 88
Bridgestone Tire Company, 169
Brigham, Eugene, 487
Bristow, Nigel J., 60
British Airways, 479 (box)
Brody, Michael, 633
Broedling, Laurie, 31
Brousseau, K. R., 633
Brown, Andrew C., 593
Bruno's Inc., 60 (case)
Brylane, 236 (case)
Buckner, Kathryn E., 291
Buena Vista Pictures, 6 (case)
Builders Square, 60 (case)
Burck, Charles G., 513

Bureau of Labor Statistics, 599
Burger King, 104, 120, 136, 156, 446–447
Burlington, 506
Burns, James M., 349
Burns, M. Anthony, 459–460 (case)
Burns, Tom, 261
Burroughs Corporation, 546–547 (case), 548, 550, 551, 562, 563
Byrne, John A., 625, 633

Cadbury, 151 (case), 159 (box), 172
Caldwell, Charles W., 261
Caldwell, James C., 486
Calvin Klein, 166.
Cammann, Cortlandt, 461
Campbell, 512 (case)
Campbell, Donald J., 232
Candela Laser Corp., 604 (box)
Canion, Rod, 200 (case)
Capital Communications, 186
Caplan, Frieda, 165 (illus.)
Carey, Susan, 302
Carlson, Eugene, 317
Carnegie, Andrew, 74
Carrell, Michael R., 290
Carroll, Archie B., 89, 487
Carroll, P. B., 232
Carroll, Stephen J., 61, 121, 291
Carson, Teresa, 625
Carter, Jimmy, 343
Cartwright, Dorwin, 406
Castro, Janice, 318
Caterpillar, 512 (case), 524, 565 (illus.), 565–566 (case), 601
Cavanaugh, Sharon P., 480 (illus.)
CBS Inc., 60 (case), 224, 405–406 (case), 444
C. C. Creations, 454 (box), 540
Celanese, 506
Cetus Corporation, 599 (box)
Chagai, 597 (case)
Chambourcy yogurt, 592 (case)
Champion, Jane, 633
Champion Spark Plug Company, 443
Champs, 125 (case), 125 (illus.)
Chaparral Steel Company, 362
Charan, Ram, 147, 179
Chase, Richard B., 61
Chase Manhattan Bank, 249

Chazen, Jerome, 167 (box)
Chemical Bank, 73
Chesapeake Corporation, 370 (illus.)
Chevrolet, 105
Chevron, 104, 493
Christie, Rick, 460
Chrysler, 37, 70, 107, 213, 327, 380 (case), 598
Chrysler minivan, 161
C. Itoh, 269 (box)
Citibank, 72, 607
Citicorp, 108, 421 (box), 590
Claiborne, Liz, 167 (box)
Clark, Susan G., 285
Clark, Will, 364
Clarke, Douglas A., 487
Clausing, Don, 539
Clean Harbors, Inc., 81 (box)
Cleveland, Jeanette N., 291
Clifford, Mark, 223
Coca-Cola Classic, 161
Coca-Cola Company, 10, 103, 139, 533 (illus.), 585
Cochran, Phillip L., 89
Cohen, Ben, 530 (box)
Cohen, Ira, 271 (illus.)
Coherent Inc., 604 (box)
Colby, Laura, 290
Cole, Diane, 633
Cole, Malcolm, 317, 318
Colgate-Palmolive, 90, 279, 471 (box)
Collingwood, Harris, 91
Compaq Computer, 108, 200 (illus.), 200–201 (case), 203, 546 (case), 572
Conbrough, J. A., 61
Condensed Milk Company, 592 (case)
Continental Airlines, 105, 167
Control Data Corporation, 403
Cooke, Morris, 43
Coons, A. E., 349
Cooper, Robin, 487
Coors, 457, 549
Corning Glass Works, 108, 516–517 (case), 517 (illus.), 518, 523, 528, 532, 536, 628
Courtney, R. S., 633
Covia Corporation, 302 (box)
Covin, Jeffrey G., 319
Cowan, A. L., 633
Coyle, William, 582 (box)

Crandall, Robert L., 29–30 (case), 30 (illus.)
Crest toothpaste, 161
Crittendon, Vicky L., 467
Crittendon, William F., 467
Crocker National Bank, 38 (box)
Cromie, Stanley, 433
Cuban American Foundation, 629
Cumming, Charles M., 291
Cummins, Robert, 431
Cummins Engine Company, 490–491 (case), 491 (illus.), 492–493, 498, 500–501, 509, 510
Cunningham, Harry, 59 (case), 180
Cypress Semiconductor Corporation, 115 (box), 615–616 (case)

Daewoo, 223 (box), 236 (case)
Daft, Richard L., 121, 233, 261, 513
D'Agostino, Carol, 603 (illus.)
Daiei, 60 (case)
Daimler-Benz, 162, 163 (box)
Dairy Queen, 532, 533 (box)
Dana Corporation, 525 (illus.)
Danforth, Douglas, 537 (case)
Daniels, John D., 593
Davenport, Carol, 121, 147
Davis, James H., 407
Davis, Keith, 82, 89, 431
Davis, Ralph, 224
Davis, Stanley M., 261
Day, Diana L., 174
Deal, Terrence, 253, 261
Deals, Vaughn, 526
Dean Witter Reynolds, Inc., 20, 66, 393 (box)
Dearborn, D. C., 431
Decker, Patrick, 513
De Geus, Arie P., 146
Delbecq, Andre L., 147, 201, 407
Del'Omo, Gregory, 291
Delta Air Lines, 49, 155–156, 255, 256
De Meuse, Kenneth P., 285
Dennis, David M., 467
Densmore, Greg, 89
DePree, D. J., 430 (case)
DePree, Max, 431 (case)
Derfler, Frank, 318
Dess, Gregory G., 121

Dewar, R., 541
Dial Corporation, 296
Dickson, William, 61
Diet Coke, 161
Dietrich Corporation, 159 (box)
Digital Equipment Corporation, 90, 256, 546 (case), 550, 562, 623
Disney, Roy, 6 (case)
Disney, Walt, 6 (case)
Disney Channel, cable TV, 6 (case)
Disney company, 6–7 (case), 7 (illus.), 8, 11–13, 17, 28, 133, 153, 166–167, 256, 465 (case), 548, 561
Disney Corporation, 100
Disney-MGM Studios Hollywood theme area, 7, 17
Ditka, Mike, 343
Dole, Elizabeth, 286 (illus.)
Domino's Pizza, 120
Donaldson, G., 201
Donovan, John J., 318
Dorr-Oliver, 582 (box)
Douglas, Paul, 286 (illus.)
Dow Chemical, 9, 19, 52, 108, 182, 373, 494 (box), 585
Dowling, William F., 261
Downs, Timothy M., 291
Dozier, Janelle B., 617, 633
Drake Beam Morin Inc., 269 (box)
Drexel Burnham Lambert, 66
Dreyfuss, Joel, 442, 517
Dr. Pepper, 133–134
Drucker, Peter F., 616
Dumaine, Brian, 31, 115, 121, 260, 372, 393, 428, 534, 539, 616
Duncan, W. Jack, 261
Dupin, Charles, 40
Du Pont, 76, 116, 372 (box), 526
Durcker, Peter F., 461
Duval, B. A., 633
Dvorak, John C., 541

Eason, Henry, 339
Eastern Airlines, 104, 167, 324 (case), 479 (box)
Eastman Kodak, 15, 17, 29 (case), 55, 90, 110, 152, 168, 578 (box), 609
Ebert, Ronald J., 61, 201, 513
Echlin Inc., 503 (illus.)

Eckley, Robert S., 566
Economic Development Administration, 629
Edison, Thomas, 516 (case)
Edmunds, Stahrl W., 89
Edwards, David, 421 (box)
E. F. Hutton, 66
Eichenwald, Kurt, 376
Eisner, Michael D., 6 (case), 7, 7 (illus.), 13, 16–17, 28, 133
E. J. Korvette, 59 (case)
Elbing, Alvar, 201
Ellesse, 438 (case)
Elliott, Stuart, 65
Emerson, Harrington, 43
Emery Air Freight, 440
Emhart Corporation, 146 (case)
Engle, Terry J., 467
Environmental Protection Agency, 84
Equal Employment Opportunity Commission, 84
Equal Opportunity Act, 629
Erickson, E. H., 633
Ernst, Harry, 487
Esmark, 375 (case)
Etzioni, Amitai, 201
EuroDisneyland, 133
Exxon, 18, 64–65 (case), 66, 76, 80, 86, 104, 120, 203, 210, 243

Fair Labor Standards Board, 84
Fantastic Sam's, 220 (box)
F. A. O. Schwartz, 502
Fargo, William, 119 (case)
Farley, Inc., 509
Farnham, Alan, 89
Fauber, Bernard, 59 (case)
Fayol, Henri, 43, 44 (table), 61
Fearon, Harold, 513
Federal Express, 85, 166, 316–317 (case), 524
Federal Trade Commission, 84
Federated Department Stores, 559
Feild, Hubert S., 291
Feldman, Daniel C., 407, 617
Ferrell, O. C., 487
Ferster, C. B., 377
Fiat, 135 (box)
Fiedler, Fred E., 335, 336, 349
Fields, Debbi, 128 (box)

Fireman, Paul B., 438–439 (case), 450
Firestone, 158, 422, 512 (case)
First City Bank Corporation, 105
First Nationwide Bank, of San Francisco, 60 (case)
Fishbein, Martin, 431
Fisher, Cynthia, 513
Fisher-Price toys, 16
Fitzgerald, Ella, 120 (illus.)
Flax, Steven, 617
Fleenor, C. Patrick, 31
Fleishman, Edwin A., 291
Florida Light and Power, 222 (illus.)
Flying Tigers, 316–317 (case)
Foard, Frederick C., 629
Follett, Mary Parker, 43, 45
Food and Drug Administration, 84
Foot Locker, 124–125 (case), 438–439 (case)
Ford, Robert C., 31, 232, 233, 261, 319
Ford Escort, 505 (box), 527–528
Ford Motor Company, 8–9, 76, 103, 107, 127, 135 (box), 139, 152, 157–158, 213, 254, 380 (case), 440, 470, 493, 502, 505 (box), 512 (case), 524, 525, 527, 623
Ford–West Germany, 603
Foust, Dean, 318
Fox, Mark S., 318
Fox, William M., 291
Franklin Mint, 557 (box)
Fredericksen, Sara, 140 (illus.)
French, John R. P., 349
French, Wendell L., 290, 487, 567
Friedman, Joshua, 617
Friedman, M. D., 617
Friedman, Milton, 76, 89
Frito-Lay, 130, 259 (case), 480
Fry, Louis W., 261
Fujii, Motoyuki, 597
Fujisawa, 596 (case)
Furr's Cafeterias, 60 (case)
Furst, Alan, 128
Futrell, David, 285
F. W. Woolworth Company, 59 (case), 124–125 (case), 125 (illus.), 126, 130, 135, 138

Gaber, Beverly, 353, 431
Galbraith, Jay, 407

Galileo, airline computer reservations system, 302 (box)
Gandhi, Mahatma, 331
Gannes, Stuart, 91, 167, 175, 201, 203, 439
Gannett, 559 (illus.), 629
Gantt, Henry, 42–43
The Gap, 237 (case)
Garrett, Thomas M., 69
Garvin, David A., 513, 528
Gasse, Y., 319
Gates, Bill, 599
Gault, Stanley, 98
Gemmons, Peter, 486
Geneen, Harold, 20
Genentech, 253
General Dynamics, 73
General Electric, 66, 81, 104, 127, 137, 138, 145 (case), 152, 159, 178–179 (case), 180, 194, 198–199, 221, 308, 445, 494 (box), 496, 500, 525, 534, 609, 624, 627
General Foods, 24, 96 (case), 116, 159, 215, 216 (illus.), 250–251, 373, 396, 444, 572, 624, 628
General Instruments, 582
General Mills, 24, 96 (case), 118
General Motors Acceptance Corporation (GMAC), 52
General Motors of Canada, 603
General Motors Corporation, 11, 49, 52, 107, 127, 135 (box), 158, 208 (case), 210, 224, 242, 243, 251, 252, 253, 266, 380 (case), 396, 432, 440, 448, 478, 600, 624, 628
Gent, Michael, 291
George, Claude S., Jr., 60, 317
Gerber, 191 (box)
Gerloff, Edwin, 431
Gersick, Connie J. G., 406
Gerson, Kathleen, 634
Gerster, D. K., 633
Gibson, Verna, 237 (illus.)
Gilbert, Nathaniel, 512
Gilbreth, Frank and Lillian, 40, 42
Gillen, Dennis J., 61
Gillette, 373
Gillick, Karen, 557
Gilman, H., 633
Ginsberg, Ari, 147

Gioia, 174 (case)
Glass, David, 429
Golden Valley Microwave, 202
Golden West Financial, 83
Goldstein, Joyce, 16 (illus.)
Goodyear Tire and Rubber Company, 84, 212
Gordon Food Service, 425 (illus.)
Gottlieb, Carrie, 31, 35
Gourmet Companies Inc., 625 (illus.)
Graicunas, A. V., 224, 233
Graves, Florence, 530
Gray, Dan, 358 (box)
Greenberg, Jerald, 377, 616
Greenberger, David B., 461
Greenfield, Jerry, 530 (box)
Greenhaus, Jeffrey H., 634
Greenwood, R. A., 61
Greenwood, R. G., 61
Greyhound, 610
Griffin, Ricky W., 61, 147, 201, 232, 261, 280, 281, 407, 513
Grindle, Howard, 261
Grove, Andrew S., 34–35 (case), 48, 57, 540, 541
Grush, Joseph E., 376
Gustafson, David H., 147, 407
Guzzardi, Walter, 174

Hage, J., 541
Hahm, Wendell, 318
Hall, Douglas T., 633
Hall, John R., 87–88 (case)
Hall, Rosalie J., 376
Hallmark Cards, 29 (case), 383, 440
Hambrick, Donald C., 147, 174, 175
Hannan, R. L., 633
Harley Davidson, 526, 526 (box)
Harris, Catherine L., 318
Harris, Roy J., Jr., 209
Hartford Insurance Group, 604
Hatfield, John D., 377
Hay Group Inc., 623
Heaton, Cherrill P., 31, 232, 233, 261, 319
Hector, Gary, 147, 539
Heinz, 191 (box)
Hellriegel, Don, 31
Helms, Jesse, 405 (case)
Hembree, Linda, 599

Hemond, Roland A., 485 (case)
Hemp, Paul, 51
Henderson, Monika, 407
Henderson, Richard I., 291
Henkoff, Ronald, 209, 513, 566
Henri Bendel, 236 (case)
Herald Square, 125 (case)
Hercules, 73, 90
Herman Miller Inc., 430–431 (case)
Herren, Laura M., 290
Hershey, Milton, 159 (box)
Hershey Foods Corporation, 151
   (case), 158, 159 (box), 172
Hertz, 375 (case)
Herzberg, Frederick, 232, 357, 376
Herzog, Frank, 300 (illus.)
Hewlett, William, 255 (illus.)
Hewlett-Packard, 20, 52, 55, 247,
   253, 254
Hickson, David J., 261
Hill, Charles W. L., 147, 174
Hill, Kenneth D., 31
Hill, Neil, 285
Hiram Walker, 107
Hisrich, R. D., 634
Hitachi, 571 (case), 591
Hitachi Consumer Products of Amer-
   ica, 339 (box)
Hitler, Adolph, 331
Hitt, Michael A., 61
Hoerr, J., 616
Hofer, Charles W., 146
Hoffman, Harry, 126
Hofstede, Geert, 593
Holder, Dennis, 353
Holley, William, Jr., 291
Hollywood Pictures, 6 (case)
Homans, George, 407
Honda Motor Company, 108, 140,
   366 (box), 502, 525, 526 (box),
   576
Honeywell, 241 (illus.), 506, 628
Hood, Robert H., 208 (case)
Horovitz, J. M., 461
Hoskins, Bob, 465 (illus.)
Houghton, James R., 516–517 (case),
   518, 532, 536
House, Robert J., 349
Houston Lighting & Power, 312 (il-
   lus.)
Hout, Thomas M., 539

Howard Savings Bank, 162 (illus.)
Huber, George P., 61, 201
Huey, John, 88, 146, 318, 411
Hughes, Donald T., 461
Huizenga, H. Wayne, 464–465 (case),
   465 (illus.)
Hunter, John E., 290
Huseman, Richard C., 377
Hutchins, Dexter, 617
Hymowitz, Carol, 634
Hyundai, 223 (box)
Hyundai Electronics, 582

Iacocca, Lee, 327
IBM (International Business Machines), 24, 30, 49, 80, 103, 105,
   152, 166, 168, 190, 200 (case),
   201, 213, 221, 224, 231–232
   (case), 253, 255, 256, 281, 311,
   348, 432, 448, 524, 546 (case),
   550, 562, 563, 578 (box), 598,
   602, 628
IBM personal computers, 160–161
Ichniowski, Casey, 291
ICI (Imperial Chemical Industries),
   252 (box)
IDQ (International Dairy Queen,
   Inc.), 533 (box)
IESE (Instituto de Estudios Superi-
   ores de la Emprese), 25 (box)
Illingworth, Monteith M., 51
IMEDE (International Management
   Development Institute), 25 (box)
IMI (International Management Insti-
   tute), 25 (box)
Imperial Chemical Industries (ICI),
   252 (box)
Indian Business Development Fund,
   629
Institute for Managing Diversity, 608
   (illus.)
Institut Européen d'Administration
   des Affaires, 25 (box)
Instituto de Estudios Superiores de la
   Emprese (IESE), 25 (box)
InsurUSA, 60 (case)
Intel Corporation, 34–35 (case), 35 (il-
   lus.), 43–44, 55–56, 57–58, 90,
   139, 247, 440, 540
Intel 80486 (or i486) chip, 43–44

Interjuice Trading Company, 191
   (box)
International Business Machines
   (IBM), 24, 30, 49, 80, 103, 105,
   152, 166, 168, 190, 200 (case),
   201, 213, 221, 224, 231–232
   (case), 253, 255, 256, 281, 311,
   348, 432, 448, 524, 546 (case),
   550, 562, 563, 578 (box), 598,
   628
International Business Machines
   (IBM) Japan Ltd., 602
International Dairy Queen, Inc.
   (IDQ), 533 (box)
International Harvester (Navistar),
   333, 563
International Management Institute
   (IMI), 25 (box)
International Management Develop-
   ment Institute (IMEDE), 25 (box)
Interplace/Transworld Recruit, 269
   (box)
Ireland, R. Duane, 61
Italtel, 289 (case)
ITT, 20, 559

Jackson, Jesse, 343
Jackson, S. E., 634
Jacobs, Eli S., 485–486 (case)
Jacobs, S. L., 633
Jago, Arthur G., 341, 349
Jaguar, 158
Janis, Irving L., 407
Jansen, Erik, 88
Jarrillo-Mossi, Jose Carlos, 91
J. C. Penney, 311
Jelinek, Mariann, 633
Jewell, Linda M., 406
JMB Realty Trust, 6 (case)
Jobs, Steven, 254, 348 (case), 599
John A. Frye, 438 (case)
John Hancock, 215
Johnson, George, 22 (illus.)
Johnson, James C., 31
Johnson, Ross, 539
Johnson & Johnson, 161, 256 (box),
   311
Johnson & Johnson disposable dia-
   pers, 256 (box)
Jones, E. F., 431

Jones, Gareth R., 147, 174
Jones, John L., 629
Jones, Reginald, 178 (case)
Jordan, Michael, 329 (illus.)
Junkins, Jerry, 570 (case)
Jupiter stores, 59 (case)

Kadlee, Daniel, 209
Kahn, Robert L., 407
Kaiser Aluminum, 266
Kanet, John, 513
Kanter, Rosabeth Moss, 31, 121
Kantrow, Alan M., 60
Kaplan, R. E., 201
Kast, Fremont, 61
Katz, David, 407
Katz, Robert L., 31
Kaufman, Steven B., 115, 616
Kellogg, 96–97 (case), 97 (illus.), 98, 105–106, 110–111, 118
Kellogg, Dr. J. H., 96 (case)
Kellogg, W. K., 96 (case)
Kendrick, John W., 539
Kennedy, Allen, 253, 261
Kennedy, Mike, 290
Kentucky Fried Chicken, 129, 130, 131, 259 (case)
Kerr, Steven, 31
Kerr, Susan, 318
Kidder, Robert, 307
Kidder Peabody, 183
Kids Locker, 125 (case)
Kiechel, Walter, III, 174, 376, 431, 461, 566, 633, 634
Kilby, Jack, 570 (case)
Kilman, Ralph H., 261
Kilonski, Richard J., 88
Kindel, Stephen, 260
King, Sharon R., 290
Kingsport Press, 302
Kinney Shoes, 124 (case), 125 (illus.)
Kirby, Robert, 537 (case)
Kirin Brewery Company, 596 (case)
Kirkland, Richard I., Jr., 252, 593
Kirkpatrick, David, 376, 494
KKR, 375 (case)
Klein, Janice A., 147
Klein, Katherine J., 376
KLM Royal Dutch Airlines, 302 (box)
Klonoski, Richard J., 69

K mart, 13, 52, 59–60 (case), 90, 111, 120, 124 (case), 154, 166, 180, 221, 308, 452, 478, 495, 500, 502, 519–520
Knight, Kenneth, 261
Knight-Ridder, 449–450
Kobe Steel, 571 (case), 591
Koloday, Harvey F., 261
Komatsu Ltd., 490–491 (case), 565–566 (case)
Kondrasuk, Jack N., 121
Koontz, Harold, 461
Korth, Christopher, 593
Kotter, John P., 567
Kozmetsky, George, 634
Kozmetsky, Ronya, 634
Kraar, Louis, 366, 396, 505, 513
Krainik, Ardis, 332 (illus.)
Kraus, William A., 567
Kreitner, Robert, 377
Kresge, Sebastian S., 59 (case)
Kresge Company, 59 (case), 124 (case)
Krisher, Bernard, 175
Kroger, 448
Kupfer, Andrew, 31, 290, 318
Kurtz, David L., 31
Kuzmits, Frank E., 290
Kyocera Corporation, 54 (illus.)
Kyowa Hakko Kogyo, 596 (case)

Labich, Kenneth, 290, 349, 406, 431, 479
LaBier, Douglas, 633
LaBonte, C. Joseph, 438–439 (case)
Lady Foot Locker, 125 (case), 125 (illus.)
L. A. Gear, 439 (case)
Lake Superior Paper Industries, 342 (illus.)
LaMothe, William E., 96 (case)
Landry, Tom, 343
Land's End, 81
Lane Bryant, 236–237 (case)
La Petite Boulangerie, 128 (box)
Larson, James R., Jr., 291
Laser Magnetic Storage International, 604 (box)
Lasers, 604 (box)
Latack, Janina C., 617, 633
Latham, Gary P., 291, 377

Lautenbach, T. L., 232
Lawler, Edward E., III, 233, 376, 377, 461
Lawrence, Calvin, 460
Lawrence, Paul R., 61, 261, 566
Leavitt, Harold J., 567
Lederer, Albert L., 317
Lee, S. M., 223
Lee Way Motor Freight, 259 (case)
Lehner, Urban C., 71
Lei, David, 147
Leonard-Barton, Dorothy, 567
Lerner, 236 (case)
Lever Brothers, 109–110, 586
Levinson, D. J., 633
Levi Strauss, 247, 345, 577
Levi Strauss International, 586
Lewis, Peter H., 291, 318
Lewyn, Mark, 290
LiCari, Jerome, 191 (box), 421 (box)
Lifecodes, 599 (box)
Likert, Rensis, 261, 349
Limited, 236–237 (case), 238, 247, 252, 254, 257–258
Limited Express, 236 (case)
Lincoln Electric, 47 (illus.)
Livnat, Joshua, 487
Liz Claiborne Inc., 167 (box)
L. L. Bean, 352–353 (case), 353 (illus.), 354, 360, 367, 374, 532
Lloyd's of London, 51 (box)
Locke, Edwin W., 121, 377
Lockheed, 157, 215 (illus.)
London Business School, 25 (box)
Loomis, Carol J., 290
Lorange, Peter, 146
Lorsch, Jay W., 201, 261, 486
Low, Murray B., 433
Lubin, Joann S., 265
Lucchino, Lawrence, 485 (case)
Lucky Goldstar, 223 (box)
Luthans, Fred, 31, 377

McBeth, John, 223
McCall, M. W., Jr., 201, 633
McCallum, Daniel, 40
McCaskey, Michael B., 431
McClam, John O., 513
McClelland, David, 376
McComas, Maggie, 513

McConkey, Dale, 233
MacCrimmon, Kenneth, 201
McDaniel, Reuben R., 201
McDonald, James P., 623
McDonald's, 79, 81, 104, 130, 156, 221, 478, 495, 533 (box), 556 (illus.)
McDonnell Douglas Corporation, 30, 73, 104, 156, 181, 208–209 (case), 209 (illus.), 210, 215, 222, 227, 229
McDonnell Douglas Corporation's DC-10 aircraft, 208 (case)
McGraw-Hill, 601
McGregor, Douglas, 47, 47 (table), 57, 61
McKim, Alan, 81 (box)
McLennan, Roy, 566
MacMillan, Ian C., 174, 175, 433
Macmillan Bloedel, 451 (illus.)
McQuade, Walter, 201
McQuaig, Bruce W., 461
McQuigg-Martinez, Beverly, 633
Magaziner, Ira, 223
Maggi chili powder, 592 (case)
Magnet, Myron, 88
Mahoney, Richard J., 192
Main, Jeremy, 25, 121, 318, 494, 557, 566, 571, 616
Makita, 145 (case)
Makosz, Paul G., 461
Makro Inc., 60 (case)
Mandela, Nelson, 344 (illus.)
Mandernack, Scott B., 291
Manning, Michael R., 616
Markland, Robert E., 61, 147, 201
Marriott, Bill, 324–325 (case), 325 (illus.), 326, 327, 334, 339, 346–347
Marriott, J. Willard, Jr., 324 (case)
Marriott Corporation, 105, 324 (case), 326
Mars, Forest, 150 (case)
Mars, Forest, Jr., 150 (case)
Mars, Frank, 150 (case)
Mars, John, 150 (case)
Mars Company, 150–151 (case), 151 (illus.), 152, 155, 159 (box), 170, 172
Martin, Janette, 295
Martin, Robert, 88

Martin Marietta, 313, 470
Marubeni, 269 (box)
Maslow, Abraham H., 47, 57, 61, 356–357, 373, 376
Mason, Donald F., Jr., 261
Mast Industries, 236 (case)
Matsushita Electric Industrial Co., 611
May, Bess Ritter, 487
Mayo, Elton, 61
Mayo Clinic, 20, 108
Maytag, 166, 213, 244
Mazda, 396 (box), 495, 505 (box), 580
MBB, 163 (box)
MCI Telecommunications, 232 (case), 289 (case)
Mehdenhall, Mark, 291
MEI Corporation, 259 (case)
Mellon Bank, 628
Memorex International, 485 (case)
Mercedes-Benz, 163 (box), 502
Mesloh, R. E., 88
Mettaloy, 442 (box)
Meyer, John W., 121
Miceli, Marcia P., 421, 616
Micracor Inc., 604 (box)
Midland Bank, 38
Miles, Edward W., 377
Miles, Raymond E., 175
Miles, Robert H., 232, 233
Miller, David W., 201
Miller, Edwin L., 618
Miller, Herman, 430 (case)
Miller, James P., 35
Miller, Lynn E., 376
Miller, M. W., 232
Miller, William H., 517
Miller brewery, 245, 549
Mills, Peter, 201
Milo malt-flavored beverages, 592 (case)
Minami, Kazumitsu, 338, 339 (box)
Mindell, Benjamin, 256
Minority Business Development Agency, 629
Mintzberg, Henry, 31, 232, 233, 261, 349, 406, 417, 431, 486
Mitchell, Terrence R., 349
Mitsubishi, 269 (box)
Mitsubishi Kasei, 596–597 (case)
Mitsui Petrochemical Industries, 596 (case)

Mitsui Toatsu Chemicals, 596 (case)
Mobil Corporation, 104, 578 (box)
Monsanto, 192, 249, 253, 457
Montana, Constanza, 634
Moomaw, Charles, 633
Moore, David, 22 (illus.)
Moore, Martha T., 60, 317
Moore, Thomas, 487
Moorhead, Gregory, 61, 261
Morgan, J. P., 74
Morita, Akio, 153 (illus.)
Morrison, A. M., 617, 633
Motel 6, 166
Motley, Michael T., 431
Motorola, 35 (case), 57, 114 (illus.), 276
Motowidlo, Stephan J., 616
Mouton, Jane S., 560, 567
Mowday, Richard T., 376
Mrs. Fields' Cookies, 128 (box)
MTU, 163 (box)
Mucayk, Jan P., 121
Munchus, George, 407
Munsterberg, Hugo, 45, 57, 61
Murdick, Robert G., 317
Murphy, Kevin R., 291
Mutual of Omaha Insurance, 629
Myers, Jane, 151

Nabisco, 96 (case)
Nader, Ralph, 78 (illus.)
Nadler, David A., 319, 461
Naisbett, John, 593
Nalachandra, R., 147
Napoleon, 331
Nash, Allan N., 291
National Broadcasting Company (NBC), 405 (case), 444
Navistar (International Harvester), 333, 563
NBC, 627
NBC (National Broadcasting Company), 405 (case), 444
NCR, 249, 253
Near, Janet P., 421, 616
NEC, 604 (box)
Needles, Belverd E., Jr., 486
Neiman-Marcus, 502
Nemetz, Patricia L., 261
Nescafé instant coffee, 592 (case)

Nestlé, 574, 580, 587, 589
Nestlé, Henri, 592 (case)
Nestlé Corporation, 25 (box), 103,
      172, 592–593 (case)
Neumann, S., 317
Newman, William H., 31, 461
New York Telephone Company, 622
Nike, 439 (case)
Nikko Securities, 269 (box)
Nippon Telegraph & Telephone, 71
      (box)
Nissan Motor Company, 103, 140,
      158, 244, 383, 490 (case), 574,
      576, 580
NOK, 442 (box)
North American Van Lines, 259
      (case)
Northwestern National Life In-
      surance, 422
Norton Simon, 375 (case)
Nossiter, Vivian, 233
Nulty, Peter, 65, 201, 616, 617
NWA, 302 (box)
Nynex, 289 (case)

Occupational Safety and Health Ad-
      ministration (OSHA), 83–84
O'Donnell, Cyril, 407
Ohlhausen, Peter, 51
Oncogene Science, 599 (box)
Oncor, 599 (box)
O'Reilly, Brian, 349, 523, 539, 571
O'Reilly, Charles A., 317
Osborn, A. F., 201
Osborne, Adam, 541
OSHA (Occupational Safety and
      Health Administration), 83–84
Ouchi, William G., 55, 61, 461
Outboard Marine Corporation
      (OMC), 100 (illus.)
Owen, Robert, 40
Owens, James, 261

Pacific Telesis Group, 289 (case)
Packard, John S., 616
Pacos, Roger L., 309
Page, Charles, 592 (case)
Page, George, 592 (case)
Paley, William, 405–406 (case)

Pan American Airlines (Pan Am), 479
      (box)
Paradyne Corporation, 289 (case)
Paramount Pictures, 6 (case)
Parasuraman, Saroj, 634
Park, Joe, 486
Pasewark, William R., 487
Patinkin, Mark, 223
Patten, Thomas H., Jr., 291
Pay Less Drug Stores, 60 (case)
Peat, Marwick, Mitchell & Co., 476,
      629
Pennzoil, 245
Pentech International Inc., 90
People Express Airlines, 54
Pepperidge Farm, 495
PepsiCo, 104, 129, 130, 131, 174
      (case), 259–260 (case), 303
Pepsi Cola, 129
Perot, H. Ross, 331
Peters, Thomas, 55, 56, 61
Petre, Peter, 179
Pfeffer, Jeffrey, 617
Pfizer, 585
Philip Morris, 79
Philips, 178 (case), 604 (box)
Physio-Control, Inc., 369 (illus.)
Pillsbury, 422
Pinder, Craig, 121, 376
Pipkin, Al, 461
Pitney Bowes, 622 (illus.)
Pizza Hut, 104, 129, 131, 259 (case),
      478, 493, 501, 533 (box), 556 (il-
      lus.)
Podems, Ruth, 557
Polaroid, 36, 169 (illus.), 396, 559
Porter, Lyman W., 376
Porter, Michael E., 147, 174, 539
Portis, Bernard, 285
Prentis, Eric L., 61
Pride, William M., 487
Prince, 174 (case)
Pringle, Charles D., 291
Probst, Gerald, 546–547 (case)
Procter & Gamble, 9, 13, 24, 55, 259
      (case), 300, 396, 444, 559, 580,
      629
Prudential Insurance, 213, 249, 303
PTL Ministry, 76
Pugh, Derek S., 261
Purolator Courier Corporation, 440

Quad/Graphics Inc., 282 (illus.)
Quadracci, Harry V., 282 (illus.)
Quaker Oats, 16, 96 (case)
Quality Croutons, 22 (illus.)
Quayle, Dan, 343
Quick, James C., 616
Quick, Jonathan D., 616
Quirt, John, 593

Radebaugh, Lee H., 593
Radio Corporation of America (RCA),
      116, 189
Radio Shack, 104, 200 (case), 502
Ragan, James W., 407
Raleigh, 104
Ralph Lauren, 166
Ralston Purina, 480
Rand, James, 291
Rapoport, Carla, 317
Rathke, Fran, 472 (illus.)
Raubitschek, Ruth S., 147
Raven, Bertram, 349
Rawl, Lawrence G., 64–65 (case), 65
      (illus.), 86
RCA (Radio Corporation of America),
      116, 189
Rea, Peter, 633
Read, Julie, 633
Reagan, Ronald, 343
Rebello, Kathy, 35
Rebstein, Larry, 634
Reck, Ross, 513
Recruit Company, 269 (box)
Recruit Company (Tokyo), 71 (box)
Recruit USA, 269 (box)
Redford, Robert, 64 (case)
Red Lobster, 104
Reebok, 91, 108, 166, 203, 438–439
      (case), 439 (illus.), 440, 446, 450
Reece, James, 486
Reed, Arthur, 302
Reed, John, 108
Reid, Peter C., 526
Reimann, Bernard C., 121
Reitz, M. Joseph, 406
Renshaw, Lisa, 627 (illus.)
Renter, Vincent, 513
Resnick, Stewart, 557 (box)
Retin-A, 256 (box)
Revlon, 161

R. H. Macy & Co., 236–237 (case), 258
Rhode, John G., 461
Richards, Max D., 121
Richman, Louis S., 539
Richman Brothers, 124 (case), 125 (illus.)
Ricks, David, 593
Right Guard deodorant, 161
Ringolsby, Tracy, 486
RJR, 107
Robbins, Stephen P., 407, 541
Roberts-Branch, Brenda, 625 (illus.)
Robinson, Frank, 486 (case), 486 (illus.)
Robinson, Michael A., 461
Rockart, J. F., 317
Rockefeller, John D., 74
Rockport, 203, 438–439 (case)
Rodgers, Thurman John, 615 (case)
Roethlishberger, Fritz, 61
Rogers, Glenn, 127 (illus.)
Rogers, T. J., 115 (case)
Rolex, 166, 502
Rolm, 232
Roosevelt, President Franklin D., 74
Rosemann, R. H., 617
Rosenzweig, James, 61
Ross, Joel E., 317
Ross, Sam M., 220 (box)
Rowan, Roy, 88, 421
Royal Dutch Shell, 587
Royer, Charles, 455 (illus.)
Rubbermaid, 98, 168
Ruch, William, 513
Ruffenach, Glenn, 317
Russell, Anne M., 634
Rux, Peter T., 290
Ryder System Inc., 459–460 (case), 460 (illus.)

Sabena, 302 (box)
Safeway, 9, 10, 13, 448, 601
Samsung, 223 (box), 525
Sandberg, William, 407
Sandholtz, Kurt, 618
Saporito, Bill, 91, 125, 151, 167, 174, 513
Sara Lee, 480
Sathe, Vijay, 91, 261, 461

Saturn automobile, 253
Saurage, J., 634
Saxton, Mary Jane, 261
Scarborough, Norman, 290
Schaefer, George, 565–566
Schaht, Henry B., 490 (case)
Schein, Edgar H., 633
Schendel, Dan, 146
Schering-Plough Research, 414 (illus.)
Schlesinger, Jacob M., 265
Schlesinger, Leonard A., 147, 567
Schmidt, Frank L., 290
Schmidt, Neal, 291
Schneider, Benjamin, 290
Schoenfeldt, Lyle, 513
Schuler, Randall S., 290
Schultz, Leslie, 533
Schweiger, David M., 407
Scott, W. Richard, 121
Sculley, John, 11, 348–349 (case)
Sears, 59 (case), 81, 104, 110, 166, 221, 224, 393 (box), 444, 502, 520, 601, 624
Sedgwick, John, 439
Seiko, 502
Seligman, Daniel, 461
Sellers, Patricia, 88, 97, 353
Serpa, Ray, 261
Sethi, S. Prakash, 89
Shaeffer, Ruth G., 290
Shamoon, Stella, 295
Shapero, A., 467
Shapiro & Cohen, Inc., 271 (illus.)
Sharplin, Arthur, 88
Shaw, James, 513
Shaw, Marvin E., 406, 407
Shell Oil Company, 105, 133 (illus.), 243, 574
Shepard, Rob, 47 (illus.)
Sherman, Stratford P., 179, 256
Shewmaker, Jack, 623
Shine, D. Bruce, 261
Siemens, 178 (case)
Sighand, Norman B., 431
Silk, L., 617
Simon, Herbert A., 201, 431
Simonds Rolling Machine Company, 41
Simplot, J. R., 612 (illus.)
Singapore Airlines, 302 (box)
Singer Sewing Machine Company, 247

Sinn, John W., 309
Siropolis, Nicholas C., 91
Sizes Unlimited, 236 (case)
Skil, 145 (case)
Skinner, B. F., 377
Slice, 129
Slocum, John, 31
Slutsker, Gary, 599
Smart, John R., 317
Smartfoods Inc., 259 (case)
Smith, Adam, 232
Smith, Frederick W., 316 (case)
Smith, Jaclyn, 59 (case)
Smith, Joel D., 208 (case)
Smith, N. R., 319
Smith, Page, 31, 89
Smith, Roger, 11
Smith, Sarah, 31
SmithKline, 554 (box)
SmithKline Beecham, 418 (illus.), 580, 628, 629
SMR Enterprises, 220 (box)
Snow, Charles C., 175
Sokol, L., 467
Solomon, Charlene, 634
Solomon, Jolie, 260
Sony, 495, 502, 525, 604 (box)
Southwest Airlines, 166
Southwestern Bell, 289 (case)
Sperry Corporation, 546–547 (case), 548, 550, 562, 563
Square One, 16 (illus.)
S. S. Kresge, 59 (case)
S. S. Kresge's Five and Ten Cent Stores, 59 (case)
Stair, Ralph M., 467
Stalk, George, Jr., 539
Stalker, G. M., 261
Standard Federal Bank, 60 (case)
Stanley Electronics, 394 (illus.)
Starbuck, William H., 617
Starr, Martin K., 201
Statewide Realty, 60 (case)
Staton, Tracy, 454
Stebbins, Michael W., 232
Steers, Richard M., 376, 618
Steinbrenner, George, 8, 20
Steiner, George A., 31, 146, 147
Stevenson, Howard H., 91
Stewart, Martha, 59 (case)
Stewart, Rosemary, 31, 146

Stewart, Thomas A., 31, 201, 349
Stith, Reverend Charles, 419 (illus.)
Stogdill, Ralph M., 349
Stokes, Bruce, 269
Stone, Andrea, 60
Stotka, Ann Marie, 61
Stouffer's frozen foods, 592 (case)
Strasser, Stephen, 461
Strickland, A. J., III, 174, 175
Strobel, Caroline D., 261
Studebaker, 52
Sturdivant, Frederick D., 89
Subaru, 104
Sullivan, Allanna, 65
Sullivan, Cornelius H., Jr., 317
Sumitomo, 269 (box)
Summers, E., 634
Summers, I., 201
Sun Company, 73, 90
Sundstrom, Eric, 285
Sunset Gardens, 202
Sutton, Edward E., 633
SWA, 302 (box)
Szwajkowski, Eugene, 88

Taco Bell, 129, 259 (case)
Taguchi, Genichi, 539
Takeda, 596 (case)
Takeshita, Noboru, 71 (box)
Tandem Computers, 432, 546 (case)
Tandy Corporation, 200 (case)
Tanzer, Andrew, 223
Target, 59 (case)
Taylor, Alex, III, 505, 634
Taylor, Benjamin J., 291
Taylor, Ford, 454 (box)
Taylor, Frederick W., 40–42, 61, 212, 232, 354
Taylor, Ronald, 201
TCBY Enterprises, 202
Team Viper, a group of Chrysler workers, 399 (illus.)
Teitelman, Robert, 260, 554
Telex Corporation, 485 (case)
Tenneco, 116, 127, 243
Terborg, James R., 232
Texaco, 50–51, 215, 524
Texas Air Corporation, 54, 104, 167
Texas Instruments, 13, 168, 200 (case), 215, 255, 257, 313, 373,

570–571 (case), 571 (illus.), 572, 583, 588, 589, 591, 610
Textron, 445 (illus.), 503 (illus.)
Thomas, H., 201
Thomas, Joseph, 513
Thomas, R. Roosevelt, 608 (illus.)
Thompson, Arthur A., 174, 175
Thompson, James D., 121, 407
Thompson S. A., 179 (case), 183
Thornton, G. C., III, 633
3M, 83, 90, 253
Tichy, Noel, 147, 179
Tiger International Inc., 316 (case)
Timex, 166, 502
Tisch, Laurence, 405–406 (case)
Tjosvold, Dean, 261, 377
Torbert, William R., 617
Toshiba, 178 (case), 345 (box)
Tosi, Henry L., 121, 487
Toto Ltd., 597 (case)
Touchstone Pictures, 6 (case)
Toyoda, Kiichiro, 264 (case)
Toyoda, Shoichiro, 264 (case)
Toyota, 103, 105, 140, 158, 208 (case), 253, 264–265 (case), 265 (illus.), 266, 274, 285, 600
Toys 'R' Us, 90, 202
Trans World Airlines (TWA), 29 (case), 479 (box), 601
Trautlein, Donald H., 512 (case)
Travelers Corporation, 303, 306
Triton Biosciences, 599 (box)
Trumpka, Richard, 286 (illus.)
Tuckman, B. W., 406
Tully, Shawn, 25
Turner, Ted, 405 (case)
Turner Broadcasting System, 81
Turner Construction, 275
Tushman, M., 319
TWA (Trans World Airlines), 29 (case), 479 (box), 601
Twomey, David P., 290

U-Haul, 460 (case)
Ulrich, David, 121
Unilever, 103, 572, 590
Union Carbide, 18, 52, 73, 103, 159, 188, 245, 524, 574, 586
Unisys, 376 (case), 546–547 (case), 548, 550, 556, 563–564

United Airlines, 29 (case), 302 (box), 479 (box)
United Parcel Service (UPS), 266
United Savings, 60 (case)
University National Bank & Trust Company, 529 (illus.)
University of Notre Dame, 383
Upjohn Company, 584 (illus.)
UPS (United Parcel Service), 266
Urwick, Lyndall, 43, 224
U. S. Department of the Interior, 629
Usery, W. J., 286 (illus.)
US Sprint, 289 (case)
U. S. Steel, 524, 563
US West, 289 (case)
USX, 524, 563
Uttal, Bro, 349, 567
Uyterhoeven, Hugo, 146

Vancl, Richard F., 146
Vanderbilt, Cornelius, 74
Van de Ven, Andrew H., 147, 407
Van Fleet, David D., 232, 233, 634
Van Fleet, E. M., 634
Vankatraman, N., 147
Van Velsor, E., 617
Varian Associates, 245 (illus.)
Venkatesian, Ravi, 491
Vent, Brian, 260 (illus.)
Ventres, Romeo, 173–174 (case)
Victoria's Secret, 236–237 (case)
Viviano, 174 (case)
Volkswagen, 580
Volvo, 166
Von Glinow, Mary Ann, 88
Vroom, Victor H., 341, 349, 376

Wade, Paula, 220
Walden Book Co., 52
Waldenbooks, 60 (case), 104, 126
Wallace, Wanda, 487
Wal-Mart, 23, 59 (case), 126, 158, 166, 254, 255, 410 (illus.), 410–411 (case), 411 (illus.), 412, 413, 425–426, 429, 520, 524, 623
Walsh, James P., 431
Walt Disney Pictures, 6 (case)
Walt Disney Productions, 55, 90
Walton, Sam, 254, 311, 410 (case), 413, 419, 425–426, 429, 599

Wang, An, 185 (illus.)
Wanous, John P., 407
Wartick, Steven L., 89
Waste Management Inc., 464 (case)
Waterman, Robert, 55, 56, 61
Watson, Hugh J., 487
Weber, Max, 43, 61, 261
Wegner, T., 88
Weiner, Steven R., 237
Weisshappel, Robert N., 114 (illus.)
Welch, Jack, 178–179 (case), 179 (illus.), 180, 183, 188–189, 194, 198–199
Wells, Henry, 119 (case)
Wells Fargo & Company, 37, 38, 38 (box), 119 (case), 422
Welsch, Glenn A., 487
Wendy's, 104, 156, 479–480
Wesray, 375 (case)
Western Electric, 45
Westinghouse, 49, 104, 107, 107 (box), 138, 253, 309 (box), 312, 376 (case), 500, 525, 537–538 (case), 548, 550 (illus.)
Westinghouse Electrical Systems Division, 309 (box)
Wexley, Kenneth N., 291
Wexner, Leslie H., 236 (case), 254
Weyerhaeuser, 440
Whirlpool, 74, 75

Whistler Corporation, 530
White, D. E., 201
White, R. P., 617
Whitely, William, 31
Wiersema, Margarethe F., 121
Wieters, David, 513
Wilkins, Alan L., 60
Williams, Edward Bennett, 485 (case)
Williams, Jerry O., 629
Williams, Richard E., 291
Williams, Walter F., 512 (case)
Willis, Rod, 526
Wilson Sporting Goods, 259 (case)
Winchell, William O., 539
Winger, Richard W., 295
Witney, Fred, 291
Wofford, Jerry, 431
Woodman, Richard, 31
Woodward, Joan, 261
Woolco, 59 (case), 124 (case)
Woolworth Express, 125 (case)
Wormley, Wayne M., 634
Worthy, Ford S., 31
Worthy, James C., 513
Wozniak, Steven, 348 (case)
Wrege, Charles D., 61
Wren, Daniel A., 60, 61, 261, 317
Wright, Peter, 291
Wright, Robert C., 627
Wriston, Walter, 108

W. T. Grant Co., 52, 59 (case)
Wulf, Steve, 486
Wyman, Thomas, 405–406 (case)

Xerox, 221, 266, 276 (illus.), 506, 598, 629

Yale University, 502
Yamaha, 104, 526 (box)
Yamanouci, 596 (case)
Yetton, Philip W., 349
Yontz, Margaret A., 407
Yoo, S., 223
Yoshikawa, Aki, 597
Yukl, Gary A., 343, 349
Yu Yu Industrial, 584 (illus.)

Zakon, Alan, 295
Zaleznik, Abraham, 349
Zander, Alvin, 406
Zapmail facsimile system, 317 (case)
Zax, Jeffrey S., 291
Zedeck, S., 634
Zimmerer, Thomas W., 290
Zimmerman, Richard, 159 (box)
Zmud, R. W., 317
Zoglin, Richard, 89
Zwicker, D. A., 81

Subject Index

Absenteeism, 478
Acceptance sampling, 533
Accountability, manager's creation of, 220
Accuracy, in organizational control, 450 (table), 451–452
Achievement, need for, 359–360
Adaptation model, 163–165, 164 (illus.)
Adjustment, in organizational control, 447 (illus.), 449
Administrative management, 14, 43–44, 44 (table)
Affiliation, need for, 359
Affirmative action, 630–631
Alcoholism in workplace, 609–610
Alternate ownership patterns, 253
Alternative(s)
  in decision making, 188–190, 189 (illus.)
  expected value of, in payoff matrix, 195
Analysis, environmental, 155–158, 156 (illus.), 157 (illus.)
Application blanks, 273
Artificial intelligence, 310 (illus.), 312–313
Assembly line, 42
Assessment centers, in selection of managerial employees, 273
Attitudes, as behavioral process, 415–416
Audits, 476–477
Authority, management of in organizing process, 219–222, 221 (illus.), 222 (illus.)
Automation, 509, 524

Balance sheet, in ratio analysis, 473–474, 474 (illus.)
Behavioral model of decision making, 184 (table), 184–185

Behavioral processes, and communication, 415–416, 416 (illus.)
Behavioral school of management theory, 45–48, 47 (illus.)
Behavioral science, 47–48
Belonging, need for, 357
Benefits, 282 (illus.), 282–283
  legal constraints on, 267–268, 268 (table)
Break-even analysis, 142, 143 (illus.)
Budget(s), 468–473, 469 (illus.), 472 (illus.), 472 (table)
  costs, 471–472
  financial, 470, 471 (table)
  nonmonetary, 471, 471 (table)
  operational, 471, 471 (table)
Budgeting process, 469 (illus.), 469–470
  management of, 472 (table), 472–473
Bureaucratic design, 240 (illus.), 240–241
Business
  and employee, 69–70
  and environment, 70–71
  strategy, 154, 163–166, 164 (illus.), 165 (illus.)
Business schools, in Europe, 24
Buyers, power of, 157

Capacity, and operations decisions, 495–496
Career(s)
  choice of, 619–622, 621 (illus.)
  counseling, 625
  defined, 619
  dual, 630
  information systems, 627
  issues, 607–608, 630–631, 631 (illus.)
  management, 624–625
  military, 619

  and minorities, 627, 629 (table), 629–630
  overseas, 620, 620 (illus.)
  pathing, 625 (table), 625–626
  planning, 624, 631 (illus.)
  resources planning, 626 (illus.), 627
  stages of, 622 (illus.), 622–624, 623 (illus.)
  and women, 627 (illus.), 627–629, 628 (illus.)
Cash cows, in portfolio matrix, 161
Centralization, 222
  of information system, 303
Certainty, as a decision-making condition, 181
Chain of command, 227–228, 228 (illus.)
Change
  environmental, 246
  organizational, 500
  resistance to, and planning process, 137–138
  strategic, 555 (table), 555–556
  structural, 555 (table), 556–557
  technological, 555 (table), 558
  see also Organizational change
Charisma, 343–344, 344 (illus.)
Chief information officer (CIO), 422
CIM (Computer-integrated manufacturing theory, 505
Classical school of management theory, 40–45
Coalitions, and decision making, 186
Codes of conduct, 73–74, 75 (illus.)
Coercion, 329
  and power, 328
Cohesiveness, group, 390, 391 (illus.), 392 (illus.)
Collective bargaining, 285–287, 286 (illus.)
  grievance procedure, 287
Commitment
  escalation of, 185–186
  as outcome of power, 331

Committee(s), management of, 393, 394–395
Communication
 barriers to, 422 (illus.), 422–423
 behavioral processes and, 415–416, 416 (illus.)
 defined, 412
 formal network, 420 (illus.), 420–422
 of goals, 113 (table), 114
 grapevine, 426–427, 427 (illus.)
 horizontal, 420 (illus.), 421
 improving, 424 (illus.), 424–426, 425 (illus.)
 information systems and, 421–422
 and international business, 587–588
 model, 414–415, 415 (illus.)
 nonverbal, 419, 419 (illus.)
 oral, 417 (table), 417–418
 pervasiveness of, 412–413, 413 (table)
 in planning, 139
 process of, 413–416, 414 (illus.), 415 (illus.), 416 (illus.)
 vertical, 420 (illus.), 420–421
 written, 418 (illus.), 418–419
Company productivity, 519–520
Compensation, legal constraints on, 267–268, 268 (table)
 see also Benefits
Competition, and quality, 529–530
Competitive advantage, 152
Competitive strategies, 165 (illus.), 165–166
Competitors, in task environment, 104, 105 (illus.)
Complexity
 environmental, 246
 of management, 9
 and organizational control, 440
Compliance, as outcome of power, 331
Compounding, and organizational control, 440
Computer-integrated manufacturing systems (CIM), 505
Computers
 and control, 482–483
 in the future, 604
 software, 310 (illus.), 311
 use in planning, 143

Conceptual skills, 20–21, 21 (illus.)
Concurrent control, 444 (illus.), 444–445
Conduct, codes of, 73–74, 75 (illus.)
Conflict, group, 399–403, 400 (illus.)
Contingency events, identification of, 136–137
Contingency planning, 134–137, 136 (illus.), 140
Contingency theory
 of control, 54
 of management, 53–54, 54 (illus.)
Continuous process technology, 245
Continuous reinforcement schedule, 369
Control
 concurrent, 444 (illus.), 444–445
 contingency theory of, 54
 cost, 505–506
 in international business, 589–590
 multiple, 445–446
 of operations, 497
 and organizational complexity, 440
 organizational. See Organizational control
 postaction, 444
 quality, 502–503
 steering, 445
Controller, 456 (illus.), 457
Controlling, 17
Control techniques
 budgets, 468–473, 469 (illus.), 471 (table), 472 (illus.), 472 (table)
 and computers, 482–483
 financial analysis, 473–477, 474 (illus.), 475 (illus.)
 for human resources, 477–478
 importance of, 466
 marketing, 478–481, 480 (illus.), 481 (illus.)
 strengths and weaknesses of, 468–469
Corporate culture
 components of, 254 (illus.), 254–255
 consequences of, 254 (illus.), 255–257
 defined, 253
 determinants of, 254, 254 (illus.)
Corporate strategy, 154, 158–162, 160 (illus.), 161 (illus.), 162 (illus.)
Cost
 control, 505–506
 and quality, 530

Country productivity, 520
Customer(s)
 departmentalization by, 218–219
 in task environment, 104, 105 (illus.)

Debt ratios, 475
Decentralization, 221–222, 222 (illus.)
 see also Delegation
Decisional roles, 18–20, 19 (illus.)
Decision making, 15–16, 185 (illus.)
 alternatives in, 188–190, 189 (illus.)
 approaches to, 183–186, 184 (table)
 behavioral model of, 184 (table), 184–185
 coalitions and, 186
 conditions, 181–183, 182 (illus.)
 definition of problem in, 187–188
 evaluation, 191–192, 192 (table)
 by groups, 397–399, 398 (table), 399 (illus.)
 innovation process and, 193 (illus.), 193–194, 194 (illus.)
 and political behavior, 186
 problem solving, compared with, 180–181, 181 (illus.)
 process, 187 (illus.), 187–192, 189 (illus.), 192 (table)
 techniques, 194–198, 196 (illus.), 197 (illus.)
Decision support system, 301 (table), 302–303
Decision trees, 196–197, 197 (illus.)
Decline stage, of career, 623 (illus.), 624
Delegation, 219–220, 221 (illus.)
 barriers to, 220–221
 as organizational concept, 211
Delphi forecasting, 141
Demographics, 608, 608 (illus.)
Departmentalization, 215–219, 216 (illus.), 217 (table)
Development, see Organization development
Diagnostic skills, 21 (illus.), 21–22, 22 (illus.)
Differentiation, competitive strategy, 165 (illus.), 165–166
Direct investment strategy, 583–584

Discipline, in collective bargaining agreements, 286
Disseminator, as management role, 18, 19 (illus.)
Distributed information system, 303
Distribution models, 197, 198
Disturbance handler, as management rule, 19, 19 (illus.)
Divisional organization design, 250–252, 251 (illus.)
international, 585, 585 (illus.)
Dogs, in portfolio matrix, 162
Drugs, in workplace, 609
Dual incomes and dual careers, 630
Dynamics, organizational, 605

Economic environment, 576–577
Economic forces of organization, 102 (illus.), 102–103
Economic sector, 619
Education, in successful management, 23–24, 24 (illus.)
Effectiveness
group, factors influencing, 224–227, 226 (illus.)
in successful management, 23
Efficiency, in successful management, 22–23
Employee
participation of, as motivating factor, 365–366
relationship with business, 69–70
selection, legal constraints on, 267–268, 268 (table)
Employee stock ownership plans (ESOPs), 253
Enacted role, 388–389
Entrepreneur, as management role, 19, 19 (illus.)
defined, 90
Entrepreneurial leadership, 344
Entropy, 52
Environment
and business, 70–71
and effective planning, 137
general, 101–103, 102 (illus.)
interaction with, in systems theory, 52
international, 575–580
and organizational control, 440

and organizational goals, 106 (illus.), 106–107
socio-cultural, 577
in strategic planning, 155–158, 156 (illus.), 157 (illus.)
task, 104–105, 105 (illus.), 580
technological, 578–579
uncertainty in, 246
Environmental forces, 155–157, 156 (illus.)
Equifinality, 52
Equity theory of motivation, 364 (illus.), 364–365
Establishment stage of career, 623, 623 (illus.)
Esteem needs, 357
Ethics
codes of conduct, 73–74, 75 (illus.)
defined, 66–67
formation, 67 (illus.), 67–68
and management, 65 (illus.), 68–73, 69 (table), 72 (illus.)
top-management support for, 73
see also Social responsibility
Europe, business schools in, 24
Evaluation
in organizational control, 447 (illus.), 449
of results, in decision making, 191–192, 192 (table)
of training and development, 277
Expectancy model of human motivation, 361 (illus.), 361–362
Expected role, 388
Expected value of alternative, in payoff matrix, 195
Expense, and planning process, 138
Experience, in successful management, 24, 24 (illus.)
Expert power, 328–329
Exploration stage, of career, 622, 622 (illus.), 623 (illus.)
External audits, 476

Facilities
and operations decisions, 496
and productivity, 524
Feedback
facilitated by oral communication, 417
in performance appraisal, 280

Figurehead, as management role, 18, 19 (illus.)
Finance managers, 13
Financial analysis
audits, 476–477
ratio analysis, 473–476, 474 (illus.), 475 (illus.)
see also Budgets
Financial resources, in organizational control, 441 (illus.), 441–442
Financial strategy, 166–167, 168 (table)
First-line managers, 11, 12 (table), 21 (illus.)
Fixed interval schedule of reinforcement, 369
Fixed ratio schedule of reinforcement, 369–370
Flat organization, 224, 225 (illus.)
Flexibility, 535
in organizational control, 450 (table), 452
and productivity, 524
Forced mobility, 607
Force-field analysis, 554–555
Forecasting, 140 (illus.), 140–141, 141 (illus.)
supply and demand, in human resource planning, 269–270, 270 (illus.), 271 (illus.)
technological, 140
Formal information systems, 301, 301 (table)
Function(s)
departmentalization by, 216 (illus.), 216–217, 217 (table)
of management, 15 (illus.), 15–17, 16 (illus.)
Functional groups, management of, 392–393
Functional strategy, 154

General environment of organization, 101–103, 102 (illus.)
Global interdependence, 601–603
Goals
communication of, 113 (table), 14
defined, 9
inappropriate, 111, 111 (table)
multiple, 108–111, 109 (illus.), 110 (illus.)

Goals (cont'd)
  optimization of, 110
  organizational, *see* Organizational
    goals
Goal setting
  contingency theory of, 54
  effectiveness of, 111 (table),
    111–114, 113 (table), 114 (illus.)
  management by objectives (MBO),
    115–117, 117 (illus.)
  organizational environments and,
    101–106, 102 (illus.)
  and planning process, 138
  process, 98–100, 99 (illus.), 100 (il-
    lus.)
  theory of motivation, 365
Governance, *see* Organizational gover-
    nance
Government
  influence of business on, 84 (table),
    84–85
  regulation, 83–84, 84 (table)
  and social responsibility, 83–85
Grand strategy, 158
Grapevine, 426–427, 427 (illus.)
Grievance procedure, in collective
    bargaining agreements, 287
Group(s)
  cohesiveness of, 390, 391 (illus.),
    392 (illus.)
  conflicts, 399–403, 400 (illus.)
  decision making by, 397–399, 398
    (table), 399 (illus.)
  defined, 383
  developmental stages of, 386 (illus.),
    386–387, 387 (illus.)
  effectiveness, factors influencing,
    224–227, 226 (illus.)
  and informal organizations, 388
  kinds of, 383–384, 384 (illus.)
  management of, in organizations,
    392–397, 394 (illus.)
  norms, 391–392, 392 (illus.)
  reasons for joining, 385 (table),
    385–386
  role dynamics of, 388–390
Growth strategy, 158

Hawthorne studies, 45–46
Height of organization, 224, 225 (il-
    lus.)

Horizontal communication, 420 (il-
    lus.), 421
Human motivation, *see* Motivation
Human needs, *see* Needs
Human relations movement, 46 (il-
    lus.), 46–47, 47 (table)
Human resources
  benefits, 282 (illus.), 282–283
  control techniques, 477–478
  labor relations, 283–287
  managers, 13–14
  and operations decisions, 496
  in organizational control, 441, 441
    (illus.)
  performance appraisal, 278–280,
    279 (illus.)
  planning for, 268–271, 270 (illus.),
    271 (illus.)
  ratios, 478
  selection of, 271–275, 274–275 (il-
    lus.)
  strategy, 168 (table), 169
  training and development of, 276
    (illus.), 276–277, 277 (table)
  wages and salaries, 280 (table),
    280–282, 281 (table)
Hybrid organization designs, 253

Implementation
  of alternative, in decision making,
    190–191
  of strategy, 152, 170, 171 (illus.)
Importing/exporting strategy, 581–582
Inappropriate goals, 111, 111 (table)
Income statement, in ratio analysis,
    473–474, 474 (illus.)
Individual productivity, 518–519
Individual wage decisions, 282
Industry productivity, 520
Informal information system, 301, 301
    (table)
Informal organizations, 388
Information, effective, 298
Informational roles, 18, 19 (illus.)
Information resources, in organiza-
    tional control, 441, 441 (illus.)
Information systems
  artificial intelligence, 310 (illus.),
    312–313
  centralized versus distributed, 303
  components of, 298–299, 299 (illus.)

computer software, 310 (illus.), 311
  definitions, 296, 297 (illus.)
  effective information, 298
  effects on organizations, 307–309,
    308 (table)
  formal, 301, 301 (table)
  hypertext, 310 (illus.), 313
  informal, 301, 301 (table)
  integration of, 305 (illus.), 305–306
  international business, management
    and, 587–588
  kinds of, 301 (table), 301–303
  limitations of, 309–310
  in managerial communication,
    421–422
  and manager's job, 297
  needs of organization for, 299–300,
    303, 304 (illus.)
  telecommunications, 310 (illus.),
    311–312
  using, 306 (illus.), 306–307
Innovation, in decision making, 193
    (illus.), 193–194, 194 (illus.)
In-process sampling, 533
Integration
  in effective planning, 139–140
  in organizational control, 449–450,
    450 (table)
Intermediate planning, 133
Internal audits, 476–477
International business
  communication, 587–588
  control in, 589–590
  defined, 572
  divisional design, 585, 585 (illus.)
  growth of, 573 (illus.), 573–574,
    574 (illus.)
  information systems and, 587–588
  leading in, 588–589
  managers, 14
  organization design of, 584–587,
    585 (illus.), 586 (illus.)
  planning for, 580–584, 581 (table),
    583 (illus.), 584 (illus.)
  staffing, 587
  strategies, 581 (table), 581–584, 583
    (illus.), 584 (illus.)
International environment
  general, 575–579, 576 (illus.), 579
    (illus.)
  task, 580

International forces of organization, 102 (illus.), 103
International matrix, 586 (illus.), 586–587
Interpersonal communication, *see* Communication
Interpersonal roles, of managers, 18, 19 (illus.)
Interpersonal skills, 20, 21 (illus.), 24 (illus.)
Interviews, of job applicants, 273
Inventory
    control, 501–502, 502 (illus.)
    models, 197

Job
    alternatives to specialization, 213–215, 214 (illus.)
    analysis, 268–269
    creation and design, 211–212, 215 (illus.)
    design, contingency theory of, 54
    enlargement, 213–214
    enrichment, 214
    evaluation, point system, 280 (table), 281, 281 (table)
    grouping, 211, 215–219, 216 (illus.), 217 (table)
    rotation, 213
    specialization, 40–43, 41 (illus.), 42 (illus.), 212 (illus.), 212–213
Jockeying among contestants as an environmental force, 156
Joint ventures, 583
Judgmental methods of performance appraisal, 278
Just-in-time (JIT) scheduling, 504, 504 (illus.)

Labor relations, 283–287
    legal constraints on, 267–268, 268 (table)
Large-batch technology, 244
Leader, as management role, 18, 19 (illus.)
Leadership
    behaviors, 331–334, 333 (illus.)
    challenges of, 327
    and charisma, 343–344, 344 (illus.)

contingency theory of, 54
entrepreneurial, 344
integrative framework for major factors of 342–343, 343 (illus.)
LPC model of, 335–337, 336 (illus.)
management, compared with, 326, 327 (illus.)
participation model of, 340–342, 341 (illus.), 342 (illus.)
path-goal model of, 337–339, 338 (illus.)
and power, 328–331, 329 (illus.), 330 (table)
situational approaches to, 334 (illus.), 334–343
symbolic, 345
traits of, 331
Leading, 16–17, 18, 19 (illus.)
    in international business, 588–589
Legitimate power, 328
Levels of management, *see* Management
Liaison, as management role, 18, 19 (illus.)
Licensing strategy, 582–583
Linear programming, 142
Line manager, responsibility for organizational control, 456, 456 (illus.)
Line positions, 227–228, 228 (illus.)
Liquidity ratios, 474–475
Location, departmentalization by, 217 (table), 218
Long-range planning, 132 (illus.), 132–133
LPS model of leadership, 335–337, 336 (illus.)

Maintenance stage, of career, 623 (illus.), 623–624
Management
    activity in, 8, 9
    administrative, 14, 43–44, 44 (table)
    areas of, 13–14
    changes in, 598–601, 600 (illus.)
    of committees, 393–395
    complexity of, 9
    defined, 8–9
    and ethics, 65 (illus.), 68–73, 69 (table), 72 (illus.)

excellence, 55–56, 56 (table)
of functional groups, 392–393
functions of, 15 (illus.), 15–17, 16 (illus.)
in the future, 598–613
information systems, 49, 301 (table), 302
leadership, compared with, 326, 327 (illus.)
levels of, 11, 12 (table), 21 (illus.)
by objectives (MBO), 115–117, 117 (illus.), 279
pervasiveness of, 10, 10 (table)
problems, in adaptation model, 164, 164 (illus.)
productivity enhancement through, 524
roles, 17–20, 19 (illus.)
skills, 20–22, 21 (illus.), 22 (illus.)
span of, 223–227, 225 (illus.), 226 (illus.)
of task forces, 393–394
Management information systems, 49, 301 (table), 302
Management science, 48–49
Management theory
    behavioral school, 45–48, 47 (illus.)
    classical school, 40–45
    contingency theory, 53–54, 54 (illus.)
    importance of, 37 (illus.), 37–38
    and management excellence, 55–56, 56 (table)
    origins of, 37–40, 39 (illus.)
    quantitative school, 48–50
    systems theory, 50–52, 52 (illus.)
    Theory Z, 55
Managerial grid, 560 (illus.), 560–561
Managers
    administrative, 14
    authority of, 219–222, 221 (illus.), 222 (illus.)
    and communication, 420 (illus.), 420–426, 423 (illus.), 424 (illus.), 425 (illus.)
    differentiation of, 11–14, 12 (table), 21 (illus.)
    first-line, 11, 12 (table), 21 (illus.)
    functions of, 15 (illus.), 15–17, 16 (illus.)
    and information systems, 297

Managers (cont'd)
  line and staff positions of, 227–228, 228 (illus.)
  middle, 11, 12 (table), 21 (illus.)
  roles, 17–20, 19 (illus.)
  selection of, 273
  skills of, 20–22, 21 (illus.), 22 (illus.)
  top, 11, 12 (table), 21 (illus.)
Marketing
  control, 478–481, 480 (illus.), 481 (illus.)
  managers, 13
  ratios, 481
  strategy, 166, 168 (table), 169 (illus.)
Maslow's need hierarchy, 356 (illus.), 356–357
Mass production technology, 244
Material Requirements Planning (MRP), 503 (table), 508–509
Matrix organization design, 247–250, 249 (illus.)
  international, 586 (illus.), 586–587
Michigan studies of leadership behaviors, 332
Middle managers, 11, 12 (table), 21 (illus.)
Minorities, 627, 629 (table), 629–630
Mobility, forced, 607
Monitor, as management role, 18, 19 (illus.)
Motivation
  contingency theory of, 54
  and employee participation, 365–366
  and equity in workplace, 364 (illus.), 364–365
  expectancy model of, 361 (illus.), 361–362
  goal-setting theory of, 365
  history of, 354–355
  performance and satisfaction, relationship between, 363 (illus.), 363–364
  process of, 355 (illus.), 355–356
  and productivity, 525–526
  and reinforcement, 366–370, 368 (illus.), 369 (illus.)
  and reward systems, 370 (illus.), 370–373, 371 (table)
  see also Needs

MRP (Material Requirements Planning), 503 (table), 508–509
Multiple constituencies, 327
Multiple controls, 445–446
Multiple organizational goals, 108–111, 109 (illus.), 110 (illus.)

Needs
  achievement, 359–360
  affiliation, 359
  assessment, training and development, 276
  belonging, 357
  esteem, 357
  Maslow's hierarchy of, 356 (illus.), 356–357
  physiological, 356–357
  security, 357
  self-actualization, 357
  two-factor view of (Frederick Herzberg), 357–359, 359 (illus.)
Needs assessment, training and development, 276
Negotiator, as management role, 19, 19 (illus.)
New entrants, threat of, 155
New venture units (skunkworks), 253
Nonmonetary budgets, 471, 471 (table)
Nonverbal communication, 419, 419 (illus.)
Not-for-profit organizations, 619–620

Objective measures of performance appraisal, 278
Objectivity, in organizational control, 450 (table), 450–451
Ohio State studies, of leadership behaviors, 333–334
Operating ratios, 476
Operational budgets, 471, 471 (table)
Operational planning, 130–131, 131 (table)
Operations
  decisions, 495–497
  enhancement of productivity through, 524, 534–535
  flexibility of, 535
  management. *See* operations management

  managers, 13
  planning, 497 (illus.), 497–498
  and quality improvements, 532–533
  speed of, 534 (table), 534–535
Operations control
  of cost, 505–506
  of inventory, 501–502, 502 (illus.)
  of quality, 502–503
  of scheduling, 503 (illus.), 503–505, 504 (illus.)
  techniques, 506 (illus.), 506–509, 507 (illus.), 508 (table), 532–533
Operations management, 49, 498–501, 499 (illus.)
  defined, 492, 493 (illus.)
  importance of, 492–494
  trends in, 509
Oral communication, 417 (table), 417–418
Organic organization design, 247, 248 (table)
Organization(s)
  development, *see* Organization development
  -environment interface, in strategic planning, 157 (illus.), 157–158
  height of, 224, 225 (illus.)
  informal, 388
  of operations function, 496
Organizational change, 500
  people-focused, 555 (table), 558
  planned, 550–552, 551 (illus.)
  reasons for, 548–549, 549 (illus.), 550 (illus.)
  resistance to, 553 (table), 553–555
  structural, 555 (table), 556–557
  technological, 555 (table), 558
Organizational control
  approaches to, 443–446, 444 (illus.), 445 (illus.)
  areas of, 441 (illus.), 441–442
  effective, 449–452, 450 (table), 451 (illus.)
  multiple, 445–446
  and organizational complexity, 440
  planning-control link, 442–443, 443 (illus.)
  reasons for, 440–441
  resistance to, 452–455, 453 (table), 455 (illus.)

responsibility for, 456 (illus.), 456–457
steps in, 446–449, 447 (illus.)
Organizational culture, *see* Corporate culture
Organizational demographics, 608, 608 (illus.)
Organizational dynamics, 605
Organizational goals
  defined, 98
  environment and, 106 (illus.), 106–107
  multiple, 108–111, 109 (illus.), 110 (illus.)
  setting, *see* Goal setting
Organizational governance, 601
Organization chart, 238 (illus.), 238–240
Organization design
  alternate ownership patterns, 253
  contingency factors, 243–247, 244 (illus.), 245 (illus.), 246 (illus.)
  contingency theory of, 54
  defined, 238
  divisional, 250–252, 251 (illus.)
  history of, 240 (table), 240–242, 241 (illus.), 242 (illus.)
  hybrid, 253
  international, 584–587, 585 (illus.), 586 (illus.)
  matrix, 247–250, 249 (illus.)
  new venture units (skunkworks), 253
  organic, 247, 248 (table)
  organization charts, 238 (illus.), 238–240
  strategy, 168 (table), 169–170
  see also Corporate culture
Organization development
  defined, 559
  techniques, 560 (illus.), 560–561
Organization revitalization, *see* Revitalization
Organizing, 16
  authority and responsibility, 219–222, 221 (illus.), 222 (illus.)
  components and concepts of, 211
  line and staff positions, 227–228, 228 (illus.)
  for operations, 499 (illus.), 499–500
  ownership patterns in, 253

process, 210–211
span of management, 223–227, 225 (illus.), 226 (illus.)
Orientation, of new employees, 275
Overall cost leadership, 166

Participation
  in effective planning, 139
  model of leadership, 340–342, 341 (illus.), 342 (illus.)
  and productivity, 525 (illus.), 525–526
Partners, in task environment, 105, 105 (illus.)
Path-goal model of leadership, 337–339, 338 (illus.)
Payoff matrix, 195, 196 (illus.)
People-focused change, 555 (table), 558
Perceived role, 388–389
Perception, as behavioral process, 416
Performance and satisfaction, relationship between, 363 (illus.), 363–364
Performance appraisal, 278–280, 279 (illus.), 477–478
Performance assessment, in organizational control, 447 (illus.), 448
PERT (program evaluation and review technique), 506 (illus.), 507 (illus.), 507–508
Physical resources, in organizational control, 441, 441 (illus.)
Physiological needs, 356–357
Planning, 15–16
  contingency, 134–137, 136 (illus.)
  contingency theory of, 54
  -control link, 442–443, 443 (illus.)
  defined, 126
  effectiveness improvement, 139 (table), 139–140
  horizon, 498
  intermediate, 132
  kinds of activities, 128–131, 129 (illus.), 131 (table)
  long-range, 132 (illus.), 132–133
  operational, 130–131, 131 (table)
  responsibilities for, 126–128, 127 (illus.)
  roadblocks to 137 (table), 137–138
  short-range, 133

system, and operations decisions, 496
tactical, 130
time frames for, 132–134, 134 (illus.)
tools and techniques for, 140–143, 141 (illus.), 143 (illus.)
  see also Strategic planning
Point system, in job evaluation, 280 (table), 281, 281 (table)
Political behavior, and decision making, 186
Political-legal environment, 575–576, 576 (illus.)
Political-legal forces of organization, 102, 102 (illus.)
Portfolio, matrix, 160–162, 161 (illus.)
Postaction control, 444 (illus.), 445
Power
  coercive, 328
  and decision making, 186
  and leadership, 328–331, 329 (illus.), 330 (table)
  limits of, 330
  outcomes of, 330 (table), 330–331
  types of, 328–329, 329 (illus.)
  uses of, 329–330
  see also Authority
Probability, in payoff matrix, 195
Problems, management, in adaptation model, 164, 164 (illus.)
Process consultation, 561
Product, departmentalization by, 217 (table), 217–218
Production strategy, 167–168, 168 (table)
Productivity
  defined, 518
  facilities and, 524
  forms of, 520
  importance of, 520
  improving, 523–527, 524 (table), 525 (illus.), 534–535
  levels of, 518–520, 519 (illus.)
  and quality, 526–527, 529
  training and development and, 525
  trends in, 521 (illus.), 521–523, 523 (illus.)
Product/service line, and operations decision, 495
Profitability ratios, 476

Program evaluation and review technique (PERT), 506 (illus.), 507 (illus.), 507–508
Public relations managers, 14
Pure domestic strategy, 581

Qualitative goals, 111 (table), 112
Quality
  assurance, 531 (illus.), 531–532
  characteristics of, 527–528, 528 (table)
  competition and, 529–530
  defined, 527
  importance of, 529 (illus.), 529–530
  improving, 531 (illus.), 531–535
  operational techniques for improving, 532–533
  and productivity, 526–527, 529
Quality circles
  management of, 396–397
  in System 4 organization, 245
Quality control, 502–503
  statistical, 533
Quantitative goals, 111 (table), 112
Quantitative school of management theory, 48–50
Question marks, in portfolio matrix, 161
Queuing models, 197–198

Ranking, in performance appraisal, 278
Rating, in performance appraisal, 278
Ratio analysis, 473–476, 474 (illus.), 475 (illus.)
Rational model of decision making, 183–184, 184 (table)
Recruiting, 271–273
Referent power, 329, 329 (illus.)
Regulators, in task environment, 104, 105 (illus.)
Reinforcement
  kinds of, 367–368, 368 (illus.)
  processes of, 366–367
  schedules of, 368–370
Research and development
  limited partnerships (RDLPs), 253

managers, 14
strategy, 168–169
Resistance
  to change, 137–138
  as outcome of power, 331
Resource(s)
  allocator, as management role, 19, 19 (illus.)
  deployment, 152
  use of, 8–9
Responsibility, management of in organizing process, 219–222, 221 (illus.), 222 (illus.)
Retrenchment strategy, 158
Return on assets (ROA), 475
Revenue forecasting, 140
Revitalization
  of company through management, 6–7
  defined, 561
  reasons for, 561
  stages in, 562 (illus.), 562–563
Reward
  power, 328
  systems, 370 (illus.), 370–373, 371 (table)
Risk, as a decision making condition, 181–182
Robotics, 42 (illus.), 524
Role
  ambiguity, 389
  conflict, 389–390
  dynamics of groups, 388–390

Safety and health, legal constraints on, 267–268, 268 (table)
Salary, 280 (table), 280–282, 281 (table)
Satisficing, 185
SBU (Strategic business unit), 159–160, 160 (illus.), 163, 251
Scheduling control, 503 (illus.), 503–505, 504 (illus.)
Scientific management, 40–43, 41 (illus.), 42 (illus.)
Security needs, 357
Self-actualization needs, 357
Semi-autonomous work groups, in System 4 organization, 245

Sent role, 388
Sequence, departmentalization by, 219
Service line, 495
Setting standards, in organizational control, 446–448, 447 (illus.)
Short-range planning, 133
Single-use plans, 131, 131 (table)
Situational constraints, and planning process, 138
Size of organization, contingency factor in organization design, 243, 244 (illus.)
Skunkworks, 253
Small-batch technology, 244
Smoking, in workplace, 609–610
Social involvement, approach to social responsibility, 79 (illus.), 80 (illus.), 80–81
Social obligation, approach to social responsibility, 78–79, 79 (illus.)
Social reaction, approach to social responsibility 79 (illus.), 79–80
Social responsibility
  approaches to, 78–81, 79 (illus.), 80 (illus.)
  areas of, 82 (table), 82–83
  arguments regarding, 76–78, 77 (table), 78 (illus.)
  and government, 83–85, 84 (table)
  history of, 74–75
Sociocultural environment, 577
Sociocultural forces of organization, 102 (illus.), 103
Span of management, 223–227, 225 (illus.), 226 (illus.)
Speed of operations, 534 (table), 534–535. *See also* Time
Spokesperson, as management role, 18, 19 (illus.)
Stability strategy, 158
Staffing
  human resource planning, 268–271, 270 (illus.), 271 (illus.)
  international business, 587
  legal constraints on, 267–268, 268 (table)
  orientation, 275
  process of, 266–267, 267 (illus.)
  recruiting, 271–273
  selection, 273

Staff positions, 227–228, 228 (illus.)
Standing plans, 130–131, 131 (table)
Stars, in portfolio matrix, 160–161
Statistical quality control, 533
Steering control, 444, 444 (illus.)
Strategic business unit (SBU), 159–160, 160 (illus.), 163, 251
Strategic change, 555 (table), 555–556
Strategic planning, 129 (illus.), 129–130, 130
  business strategy, 163–166, 164 (illus.), 165 (illus.)
  environmental analysis, 155–158, 156 (illus.), 157 (illus.)
  functional strategies, 166–170, 168 (table), 169 (illus.)
  grand strategy, 158
  international, 580–584, 581 (table), 583 (illus.), 584 (illus.)
  portfolio approach, 158–162, 160 (illus.), 161 (illus.), 162 (illus.)
  strategy implementation, 170, 171 (illus.)
Strategy
  business, 154, 163–166, 164 (illus.), 165 (illus.)
  components of, 152–153
  corporate, 154, 158–162, 160 (illus.), 161 (illus.), 162 (illus.)
  formulation and implementation, differentiated, 152
  implementation, 170, 171 (illus.)
  levels of, 153–155, 154 (illus.)
  and quality assurance, 531
Stress, 605–607, 606 (illus.)
Structural change, 555 (table), 556–557
Substitute products, threat of, 156–157
Subsystem interdependencies, 52
Successful management
  defined, 22
  education, as element of, 23–24, 24 (illus.)
  effectiveness, 23
  efficiency, 22–23
  experience, as element of, 24, 24 (illus.)
Suppliers
  power of, 155–156

in task environment, 105, 105 (illus.)
Supply and demand, in human resource planning, 269–271, 270 (illus.), 271 (illus.)
Survey feedback, 561
Symbolic leadership, 345
Synergy, 52, 153
System 4 design, 241 (illus.), 241–242, 242 (table)
Systems theory of management, 50–52, 52 (illus.)

Tactical planning, 130
Tall organization, 224, 225 (illus.)
Targeting, 166
Task environment, 104–105, 105 (illus.), 580
Task forces, management of, 393–394
Team building, 561
Technical skills, 20, 21 (illus.), 22 (illus.)
Technological change, 555 (table), 558
Technological environment, 578–579
Technological forces of organization, 102 (illus.), 103
Technological forecasting, 140
Technology
  continuous process, 245
  environment, 245–247, 246 (illus.)
  in the future, 603 (illus.), 603–605
  large-batch, 244
  mass-production, 244
  and operations decisions, 496
  in organization design, 243–245, 245 (illus.)
  and productivity, 524
  and quality assurance, 532
  small batch, 244
  see also Information systems
Telecommunications, 310 (illus.), 311–312
Test marketing, 479–480, 480 (illus.), 481 (illus.)
Tests for job applicants, 273
Theory X, 47, 47 (table)
Theory Y, 47, 47 (table)
Theory Z, 55
Third-party peace making, 561

Time
  departmentalization by, 219
  and planning process, 138
Timeliness, in organizational control, 450 (table), 452
Time-series forecasting, 141, 141 (illus.)
Top managers, 11, 12 (table), 21 (illus.)
  ethical behavior, support of, 73–74
  role in planning, 139
Total factor productivity, 520
Training and development
  evaluation of, 277
  needs assessment, 276
  and productivity, 525
  techniques, 276, 277 (table)
Transaction-processing system, 301 (table), 301–302
Turnover, 478
Two-factor view of human needs (Frederick Herzberg), 357–359, 359 (illus.)

Unattainable goals, 111 (table), 112
Uncertainty
  as a decision-making condition, 182
  environmental, 246
Unions
  collective bargaining, 285–287, 286 (illus.)
  formation of, 283–284, 284 (illus.)
  in task environment, 104, 105 (illus.)
Unit productivity, 519
Unit technology, 244
Unpopular decisions, 327–328
User-friendly information systems, 306

Variable interval schedule of reinforcement, 369
Variable ratio schedule of reinforcement, 370
Vertical communication, 420 (illus.), 420–421

Wage-level decision, 281–282
Wages, 280 (table), 280–282, 281
    (table)
Wage structure decision, 281
Women, and career(s), 627 (illus.),
    627–629, 628 (illus.)

Work force composition ratios, 478
Work groups, semi-autonomous,
    245
Working conditions, legal constraints
    on safety and health, 267–268,
    268 (table)

Work teams, management of, 394 (il-
    lus.), 395
Written communication, 418 (illus.),
    418–419